THE

PUBLICATIONS

OF THE

PIPE ROLL SOCIETY

VOLUME CII

NEW SERIES – VOLUME LXIV

THE

GREAT ROLL OF THE PIPE

FOR THE

TENTH YEAR OF THE REIGN

OF

KING HENRY III

MICHAELMAS 1226

(Pipe Roll 70)

NOW FIRST PRINTED FROM THE ORIGINAL
IN THE NATIONAL ARCHIVES

BY
ERIC GALLAGHER
AND
† LESLEY BOATWRIGHT

PRINTED FOR THE PIPE ROLL SOCIETY BY
THE BOYDELL PRESS
2022

First published 2022

A Pipe Roll Society publication
published by The Boydell Press
an imprint of Boydell & Brewer Ltd
PO Box 9, Woodbridge, Suffolk IP12 3DF, UK
and of Boydell & Brewer Inc.
668 Mt Hope Avenue, Rochester, NY 14620–2731, USA

website: www.boydellandbrewer.com

ISBN 978-0-901134-82-0

A CIP catalogue record for this book is available from the British Library

This publication is printed on acid-free paper

MIX
Paper from responsible sources
FSC® C013056

Printed and bound in Great Britain by
TJ Books Limited, Padstow, Cornwall

CONTENTS

PREFACE BY THE GENERAL EDITORS

With this volume, the Pipe Roll Society returns to its original scholarly purpose by resuming the publication of the records of the English royal exchequer in the Middle Ages. This volume contains the first published edition of the Pipe Roll for 10 Henry III (Michaelmas 1226), edited by Dr Eric Gallagher and the late Dr Lesley Boatwright. We would like to to dedicate this volume to Lesley's memory. She was a Trustee of the Friends of the National Archives, a brilliant Latinist and an excellent scholar of medieval records, who readily and generously offered advice to her peers and younger scholars. The Society would also like to express its thanks, once again, to the Stenton Fund of the British Academy for a grant in aid of publication, and to Caroline Palmer and the staff at Boydell and Brewer for seeing another volume through to publication.

Paul Dryburgh, The National Archives, UK
Louise J. Wilkinson, The University of Lincoln, UK

PREFACE BY THE VOLUME EDITORS

I would like to thank my fellow editor Lesley Boatwright for her patience with my Latin and for her suggestions on some difficult abbreviations. Unfortunately, Lesley did not live to see the fruit of her labours as she died in 2012. I would also like to thank the General Editors, Paul Dryburgh and Louise Wilkinson, and the Society for the opportunity of co-editing one of these Pipe Rolls with Lesley and for providing the money for the CD copies to be made at The National Archives for our use in transcribing the roll.

Eric Gallagher
(on behalf of Lesley Boatwright and Eric Gallagher)

INTRODUCTION

The Roll

This roll is the ninth of the reign of Henry III and covers the tenth Exchequer year, extending from the accounting period Michaelmas 1225 to Michaelmas 1226. It also includes a series of accounts from the following:

- Walter Foliot for a quarter part of the tenth year of Henry III,[1]
- Bamburgh in Northumberland for the years nine and ten,
- Windsor from Michaelmas in the eighth year to Michaelmas in the tenth year,
- Works at the castle of Dover from 12 May of the tenth year until 12 March of the eleventh year,
- Peter son of Herbert for receipts of the farms of Yorkshire in the eighth year,
- Manor of Bloxham, Oxfordshire, for three quarters of the tenth year,
- Thomas of Cirencester for the tenth year,
- Thomas of Cirencester for lands of the earl of Devon, for the tenth year,
- Thomas of Cirencester for profits from five manors,
- Thomas of Cirencester for chattels of fugitives from the lands of the earl of Devon,
- Thomas of Cirencester for manors of the king in Devon and
- Account of W. bishop of Carlisle.

The above are all included on the final rotulet of this Pipe Roll.

The roll was written between the beginning of October 1226 and the beginning of September 1227. There are frequent references to previous rolls, especially to *rotulo precedenti* or *rotulo ix* (that is 9 Henry III), and there are frequent references to *rotulo sequenti*, the roll of the eleventh Exchequer year of the reign. The views of the *rotulo sequenti* were being taken at the Exchequer in the spring of 1227. There are references to later rolls, for example *rotulo xvj*, or 16 Henry III, although it is suspected that this refers to the roll of 16 John. There is a reference to *rotulo xviijo R.E.* in the Gloucestershire roll, which would be the eighteenth year of Edward II as the hand is approximately 100 years later.

The roll is mostly in good condition but there have been a number of strengthening tapes which have obscured parts of the left or right areas of the roll. Most rotulets within the roll have two membranes of parchment stitched together, which on occasion have obscured the text on the last line of the top membrane or the first line of the bottom membrane.

[1] The tenth year of Henry III's reign was from 28 October 1225 to 27 October 1226.

Chronology of Accounts in the Roll

The views of account for the counties in year 10 of the reign of Henry III that are recorded in the memoranda rolls were taken in the late spring of 1226 during the Easter and Trinity terms. These items are from the King's Remembrancer's Roll E 159/8 and the Lord Treasurer's Remembrancer's Roll E 368/8. Where there are gaps in the table below for either roll it indicates that no date could be found for a view or account.

Table 1: Dates of Views on Memoranda Roll

Date	Counties	KR Mem Roll 11 Henry III E 159/8	LTR Mem Roll 10 Henry III E 368/8
1226			
No date[2]	London		18d.
6 May	Gloucestershire	3d.	14d.
11 May	Dorset	3	12d.
14 May	Devon	3d.	12d.
15 May	Shropshire	3	12d.
19 May	Nottinghamshire and Derbyshire	1	
19 May	Herefordshire	1	
20 May	Somerset	2	11
20 May	Lancaster	3d.	11
24 May	Northumberland		11
25 May	Buckinghamshire and Bedfordshire	2	11
23 June[3]	Surrey	1	11d.
25 June	Cambridgeshire and Huntingdonshire	4	11d.[4]
5 July	Kent	1[5]	11d.
5 July	Norfolk and Suffolk	4d.	11d.
7 July	Sussex	4d.	11d.

[2] There is a mention of a view for London in the Lord Treasurer's Remembrancer's Roll E 368/8 but no date provided. There is no mention of a view in the King's Remembrancer's Roll.

[3] … *die lune ante feste* [*sic*] *S* is what King's Remembrancer's Roll E 159/8 has but the saint's name is unfinished.

[4] This membrane has *die veneris prox' post Nat' Sancti Johannis* or 26 June 1226. This is a day later than the King's Remembrancer's Roll which has *in crastino festi sancti Johannis* which makes it 25 June 1226.

[5] There is a reference to a view of Kent in the King's Remembrancer's Roll E 159/8 on this membrane but the date is not decipherable. The date comes from E 368/8.

13 July	Berkshire	2d.	10d.
14 July	Northamptonshire	2d.	10
15 July	Yorkshire	2d.	17d.

The memoranda rolls also record the dates the accounts were taken between 1 October 1226 and 3 September 1227 beginning with Surrey. The membranes shown below were taken mostly from the Lord Treasurer's Remembrancer's Roll E 368/10 as the equivalent King's Remembrancer's Roll E 159/9 contains mostly accounts for year 11 Henry III.

Table 2: Dates of Accounts on Memoranda Rolls

Date	**Counties**	**KR Mem Roll** 12 Henry III E 159/9[6]	**LTR Mem Roll** 11 Henry III E 368/10[7]
1226			
1 October	Surrey		14
3 October	London and Middlesex		14d.
5 October	Cumberland		14
6 October	Northamptonshire		14
14 October	Cambridgeshire		14d.
27 October	Northumberland		15
27 October	Lancaster		15d.
29 October	Devon		15
29 October	Hampshire		15d.
12 November	Lincolnshire		13
1 December	Buckinghamshire and Bedfordshire		13d.

6 This roll should normally be expected to contain the account details of 10 Henry III but it contains mostly account details for 11 Henry III apart from the two items at the end of this table.

7 There is something odd about the entries in the roll and that is that all the later accounts are in the early part of the roll and all the early accounts, that is those after Michaelmas in 1226, appear later in the Memoranda Roll.

Date	Counties	KR Mem Roll 12 Henry III E 159/9[8]	LTR Mem Roll 11 Henry III E 368/10[9]
1227			
14 January[10]	Norfolk and Suffolk		13
14 January	Wiltshire		12
20 January	Essex		12d.
31 January	Shropshire		11
4 February	Staffordshire		11
6 February	Nottinghamshire and Derbyshire		11
14 February	Cornwall		11
19 or 26 February?[11]	Berkshire		11d.
28 February	Worcestershire		11d.
18 March	Kent		10
26 April	Gloucestershire		10d.
6 May	Herefordshire		10d.
10 May	Oxford		9
16 May	Yorkshire		9[12]
14 June	Dorset		9[13]
17 June	Somerset		9d.[14]

8 This roll should normally be expected to contain the account details of 10 Henry III but it contains mostly account details for 11 Henry III apart from the two items at the end of this table.

9 There is something odd about the entries in the roll and that is that all the later accounts are in the early part of the roll and all the early accounts, that is those after Michaelmas in 1226, appear later in Memoranda Roll.

10 The Latin for the date is a bit indistinct. I have *in crastino sancti Eil'ria*. I assume this could be St. Hilary whose feast day was 13 January unless it is for St. Hilarion in which case the feast day was 21 October. However, all the other counties being accounted for around this time all refer to St. Hilary in January. I have assumed the same for these counties.

11 In the roll it is definitely *veneris* so this date could be Friday 19 February or Friday 26 February. The rest of the date is not possible to decipher but indicates that it might be connected with Shrove Tuesday or the first day of Lent as the text shows … *die veneris ante cin'er* or *cin'es* or *an'er* or *av'er* or *av'es*. However, there is not enough to be sure.

12 This account also appears in the Memoranda Roll E 368/9 on rotulet 7.

13 This account also appears in the Memoranda Roll E 368/9 on rotulet 7.

14 This account also appears in the Memoranda Roll E 368/9 on rotulet 7d.

14 July	Account of Thomas of Cirencester		9d.[15]
29 August	Sussex		10
3 September	Warwickshire and Leicestershire		10
1228[16]			
10 April	Essex	10d.	
25 June	Rutland	7d.	

Sheriffs and Accounts

Accounts for twenty-nine shrievalties appear in the roll with only Rutland and Westmorland not appearing here. There are a number of sheriff changes during the year who eventually accounted for their county as shown in the Memoranda Roll. Gloucestershire received a new sheriff William de Putot on 27 December 1225.[17] He took over from Ralph Musard who had been sheriff from 3 December 1220.[18]

Oxfordshire also received a new sheriff, Godfrey of Crowcombe, who took over from Walter Foliot on 31 December 1225.[19] Oxfordshire was subject to a few changes of sheriff over a relatively short time. Fawkes de Bréauté had held the shrievalty of Oxford until the king's resumption of castles and shrievalties at Christmas 1223. He was followed by Richard de Ripariis as part of this settlement in December 1223.[20] Richard was then followed by Walter Foliot on 29 April 1225.[21]

Wiltshire received its new sheriff, Simon de Hal, on 23 March 1226 and Ela the countess of Salisbury was also ordered to hand over the castle of Salisbury to Simon as part of his shrievalty.[22]

On 22 June 1226, William the son of Henry was appointed sheriff of Somerset and Dorset from John Russell the previous sheriff of Somerset and from Ralph Gernun the previous sheriff of Dorset.[23] William did not account for either county in the Exchequer; this was done by Gilbert of Stalbridge for Dorset and William de Sorwell for Somerset.[24]

15 This account also appears in the Memoranda Roll E 368/9 on rotulet 6.

16 The two entries below are very odd: Rutland because it does not appear in the Pipe Roll at all and Essex because this is the second time year 10 Henry III has been accounted for. I can only assume that either the Exchequer was not satisfied with the Essex account or the clerk for this Memoranda Roll has made a mistake.

17 *Patent Rolls, 1225–32*, 8.

18 *Patent Rolls, 1216–25*, 273–4.

19 *Patent Rolls, 1225–32*, 9.

20 *Patent Rolls, 1216–25*, 418.

21 *Patent Rolls, 1216–25*, 524. Richard was ordered to hand over the county and castle of Oxford and county farm to Simon.

22 *Patent Rolls, 1225–32*, 25.

23 See *Patent Rolls, 1225–32*, 45 for the appointment of William son of Henry; *Patent Rolls, 1216–25*, 419 for the appointment of John Russell; and *Patent Rolls, 1216–25*, 364 for the appointment of Ralph Gernun.

24 See Memoranda Roll E 368/10 rotulets 9 and 9d respectively.

Some sheriffs were appointed after the end of the 10th year of the reign of Henry III but accounted for the money at the Exchequer. Ralph son of Reginald was appointed sheriff of Lincolnshire on 18 November 1226 and he had already accounted for the money on 10 November 1226. He was also indicated in this Pipe Roll as being responsible for the king's farm of the county as well as acting for Hugh the bishop of Lincoln.[25] William de Stuteville was appointed sheriff of Warwickshire and Leicestershire on 1 May 1227 and it is noted in the Patent Rolls[26] that he was to take over from the previous sheriff Robert Lupus, who had been noted in this Pipe Roll as being responsible for the king's farms in these counties.[27] Even so a totally different person accounted for the money in the Exchequer – Herbert the clerk,[28] who had also accounted for these counties in the ninth year of Henry III.[29]

Taxation

No new scutages were levied in this accounting year, but arrears were still coming in from previous scutages, especially those of Montgomery and Bedford, imposed in October 1223 and June 1224 respectively.

The most detailed scutage returns appear to be for honours within a county, such as those for the honour of Boulogne in Essex/Herts (mm. 2–2d) and the honour of Wallingford in Berkshire (m. 6). The return for Cambs/Hunts has a list of knights of the honour of Richmond holding from the Count of Brittany and owing the scutage of Montgomery in these counties *quia comes nec aliquis pro eo fuit in exercitu* (m. 12). Of the 29 counties and pairs of counties accounting this year, 15 did not find it necessary to list scutage details under individual headings.[30] The accounts for Worcestershire do not so much as mention the word 'scutage'. Where there are individual headings for scutages, the lists are often short: in Devon, for example, there are five names listed for the scutage of Montgomery and four, three of which also appear in the Montgomery list, for the scutage of Bedford. Gloucestershire has just two names listed for the scutage of Bedford, though a third debtor, Hugh Giffard, is listed separately later as owing 5 marks for the scutage of Montgomery and 5 marks for the scutage of Bedford.

An individual's scutage debts may be listed together with his other debts, as for Geoffrey, son of Geoffrey de Neovill, in Lincolnshire; grouped together as scutage, as with Stephen Flandr' in Devon (who owed for the scutage of Bytham as well as Montgomery and Bedford), or scattered throughout the listings, as with Richard de Kahaigne in Sussex.

The headed lists from Lancashire, and from Notts/Derbs, showed debts or payments of small sums of 2 or 4 marks, representing payments for one or two knights' fees. Other county collectors had to deal with debts

25 See below under Lincolnshire, p. 60.

26 See *Patent Rolls, 1225–32*, 121.

27 See Warwickshire and Leicestershire p. 111.

28 See Lord Treasurer's Remembrancer Roll E 368/10 rotulet 10.

29 See Lord Treasurer's Remembrancer Roll E 368/9 rotulet 19.

30 Four of these 15 (Kent, Oxon, Sussex, and Yorks) had a heading for the Prest of Poitou.

differing widely in scale: in Somerset, three men each owed 2 marks or less for the scutage of Bedford, but five other people had liabilities ranging from 25s. to £55 and so had either not passed down the obligation to their tenants, or were collecting it from them.

It is noticeable that some scutage debts are for fees which the holder *non cognoscit*, does not acknowledge. Nearly all are clerical: the bishop of Ely owes 24½ marks for the first scutage of the king for fees which he does not recognise in Cambs/Hunts; the see of Exeter owes 31 marks for fees recognised and 35 marks for fees not recognised (scutage of Montgomery); the abbess of St. Edward paid 70s. for the scutage of Bytham, but owed a total of £14 10s. for fees she did not recognise *pro pluribus scutagiis*.

The trend noticed by Emilie Amt[31] appears to hold good: debtors paid their debts for earlier scutages first – or perhaps that is how the clerks assigned the money produced. Some earlier debts are noted: the 'first scutage of the king' is still being sought (and sometimes paid) in ten counties or groups of counties, including Beds/Bucks, Herefordshire, and Lincolnshire, who list this scutage under its own heading. William Crassus senior in Gloucestershire owes 100 marks for it; in Surrey Matthew de Thorinton (who is paying off his debts at the rate of £10 p.a.) owes £27 for it. These entries are mainly for magnates, such as Hubert de Burgh (Notts/Derbs), William de Brewer junior (Surrey), and William, late earl of Salisbury (Wilts).

Money was still owed by about 20 people specifically for the scutage of Bytham (1221) and by at least 35 for the scutage of Poitou (1214), though the true figure is obscured by listings such as *pro pluribus scutagiis*.

The overall impression is that scutage payments were eventually cleared by debtors, even if this happened years after they were first levied. The system of consolidating varied debts into one overall sum and arranging for annual instalments to be paid went some way towards this.

The uprising of Falkes de Bréauté not only generated the scutage of Bedford, but also prompted the church to grant a carucage in 1224 of 6s. 8d. per plough on its demesne lands, and 2s. per plough on its tenants' lands. This was the last carucage to be levied (the previous one, the last lay carucage, had been in 1220). It is not clear whether the arrears of carucage listed in this roll are for the 1220 or 1224 imposts, but, as many of them are described as for a county, they are probably for the 1220 one.

The conquest of Poitou by Louis VIII of France in 1224 necessitated the raising of a substantial sum of money. A special tax of a fifteenth on moveable property was proposed by the Justiciar, Hubert de Burgh, and agreed at a Great Council at Westminster on 2 February 1225 in return for a reissue of the Charters. It was to be collected in two instalments, at Trinity and Michaelmas 1225. Half was to go to Winchester in the custody of the bishop of Salisbury, and the other half, eventually, to the Tower of London. The rolls for Cornwall, Hampshire, Shropshire, Notts/Derbs, Sussex, and Dorset have accounts for collecting and moving the money raised, and the roll for Surrey deals in detail with the archbishop of Canterbury's arrangements concerning this impost. The final entry on m. 15d (whose legibility is impaired by a mending strip over the right hand edge of the membrane)

31 *NS 54*, p. ix.

is the bishop of Carlisle's account (on behalf of the archbishop of York, himself, and Philip de Aubineio) of moneys received from various sources for this fifteenth, and how it was spent on hiring ships and in repaying a loan of 50 marks to the count of Brittany.

Finally, a few individual taxes appear. The sheriff of Cumberland accounts for £80 10s. 8d. for nutgeld; the men of Kingston-on-Thames are liable for 20s. for the year (and 79s. for previous years) for not collecting revenue for the Queen's Wool; the sheriffs who held the county of Kent for the past 49 years owe £49 for the lestage of Sandwich; and the citizens of London still owe 2,000 marks' tallage for the relaxing of the interdict.

Consolidated and Attermined Debts

The Exchequer's attempts to recover debts by a policy of consolidation and attermination continued – that is, by aggregating debts into one overall sum and arranging for regular instalments to be paid. In many instances, the policy seems a practical way of ensuring payment. For example, in Northamptonshire, Robert de Pinkeinny owed £227 4s. 2d., which he was paying off at a rate of £40 a year: this would take him just over five years. Warin de Munchansi, in Kent, owed £478 3s. 4d., and was paying £80 a year, and so would be clear of the debt in six years. On the other hand, also in Northamptonshire, Eustace de Watford owed the vast sum of 2023 marks (£1348 6s. 8d.) but was paying a mere 5 marks (£3 6s. 8d.) a year: the debt would be paid off in just over 400 years' time. In Lincolnshire, John son of Geoffrey de Nevill owed £991 5s. 4d., and his instalments were set at £5 a year, which would mean his descendants would be clear of the debt almost two hundred years later, in about 1424. The longest time of all was the 945 years it would have taken Roger de Limes to pay off his debt of £314 15s. at the set rate of half a mark (6s. 8d.) a year; indeed, it would have taken his descendants well into the twenty-second century.

There are many examples of extended time in which to pay off a debt, but few indications about the reasons for the arrangement. In just one instance, we are told that Richard de Boresworðe was paying off his debt of £136 17s. 11d. by instalments of £3 a year *quia pauper est*, because he is poor. Perhaps the Exchequer regarded small but regular payments as preferable to larger haphazard ones. A few instalments are noted as *per breve Regis*, by the king's writ.

It cannot always have been envisaged that these rates would remain constant in every case throughout the period of indebtedness. William de Estr' of Somerset had a debt of £283 13s. 4d., which he was repaying at a rate of £4 a year *quamdiu Regi placuerit*, as long as it pleases the king. Another such debtor was John de Thorp, paying 10s. a year *quamdiu Regi placuerit* on his debt of £48 16s. 8d. incurred in the reign of King John. We also find that Reginald de Cornhill, who owed £2432 9s. 2d., paid £40 this year,[32] to reduce his debt to £2392 9s. 2d., but in future his annual instalments would be less, at 20 marks, or £13 6s. 8d.

[32] He had paid £40 a year for at least two previous years, 1223 and 1224 (*NS 56*, p. 95; *NS 54*, p. 145).

In all, for this accounting year, 277 debts were being paid by instalments, of which 80 (29%) were for sums over £100. On analysis, however, it can be seen that not all of these debts were the result of consolidation of various smaller debts into one lump sum.

At the lower end of the scale, the sudden imposition of an obligation to pay a sum of money might stretch a person's finances beyond the possible. There are instances of judicial amercements being payable by specified instalments: Robertus *cuvarius* was amerced 18s. 8d., to be paid off at a rate of 4s. a year; and, in Yorkshire, two men surnamed Spaldington were amerced £9 18s. 8d. and £9 15s. respectively, and paid it by annual instalments of 3s. 4d. and 6s. 8d. respectively, sums which may perhaps indicate how much money each man had available. A debt might be inherited and instalments arranged: Sampson son of Laurence de Tiebrig arranged to pay his father's £50 2s. debt for trespass at a rate of £1 a year. Alan bursarius accounted for 157 marks for his father's amercement, and was paying it off at 1 mark a year. Beatrice, daughter of Stephen de Turneham, paid off her father's debt of £27 15s. 6d. at £5 a year. Sometimes it appears that the debtor has entered into a transaction with the king, and that agreed instalments might be part of the transaction: Richard, son of Hugh, and Matilda his wife, accounted for a debt of 187½ marks – and a palfrey – to have seisin, and paid 5 marks a year for it. Ralph de Bray owed £125 to have the king's grace, and was paying £50 a year.

Financial constraint cannot always have been the reason for paying in instalments. Both the archbishop of Canterbury and the archbishop of York pay by instalments, as do the Templars, whose debt of £57 5s. for Margaret de Percy dated back to the reign of Richard I and was being paid off at the rate of £2 10s. a year.

Sometimes these debts are civic rather than personal. The citizens of Lincoln had a debt of £753 6s. 2d., which they were paying off at £66 13s. 4d. a year; the people of Basingstoke likewise owed £196 4s., and were paying £20 a year, and Simon de Sancto Laurencio owed £19 7s. 2d. from the farm of Southampton while he was bailiff. He paid £1 a year towards this debt.

Turning to some particular individuals noted by previous editors, one of the people whose debts (or, rather, whose husband's debts) had been organised in 1224 for payment was Margaret de Ripariis, by now the widow of Falkes de Bréauté. Then, she had owed £799 1s. 3d. plus £100 from a loan, and 8 marks (£5 6s. 8d.) received as scutage.[33] In this roll, she owes £602 11s. 5d. (and two casks of Anjou wine), and pays £200, reducing the debt to £402 11s. 5d. (and the wine). Her future annual instalments are also to be £200. Thomas de Moulton[34] was now paying £100 a year, and his debt had decreased to £442 2s. 8d. William de Albini continued to pay the £10 a year arranged in 1224,[35] and after 1226 owed £3338 1s. 0½d. and a palfrey. Nigel de Mowbray was paying the slightly more realistic sum

33 *NS 54*, p. xii.
34 *NS 56*, p. xi.
35 *NS 54*, p. xiii.

of £80 a year on his debt of £1836 18s. 2d.,[36] but had incurred the further obligation to pay £87 1s. 3d. for the scutage of Montgomery. Neither John de Gray nor Pandulf Masca, bishops of Norwich, now appear to owe large sums of money to the Exchequer.

Finally, some individual cases shed some light on the instalment process. Simon de Yffeld accounted for 100 marks (£66 13s. 4d.) for the king's grace, paid in £13 7s., and owed £53 6s. 4d., to be paid off in yearly instalments of 10 marks (£6 13s. 4d.). For this, he had to find sureties, and produced no fewer than 29, some guaranteeing as little as 2 marks (£1 6s. 8d.). Alexander of Sawbridgeworth, a cleric, accounted for £10 10s. 11d. from money he had in his custody at the siege of Bytham Castle. He paid back 10 marks (£6 13s. 4d.) and would pay the rest back in instalments of 5 marks (£3 6s. 8d.). Henry de Hasting accounted for 50 marks to have seisin of his father's lands, and arranged to pay 12½ marks at Easter and Michaelmas year 10 and Easter and Michaelmas year 11, thus clearing the debt in two years. Likewise, in Kent the archbishop of Canterbury accounted for a debt of £311 2s. 3d., which was to be settled by instalments of £33 6s. 8d. twice a year, but after four such instalments then the payments were to be increased to £100 a year. The first payment was to be at Michaelmas year 11. Similar arrangements were made by William de Sancto Johanne in Sussex.

Castles

In this Pipe Roll castles are mentioned on many occasions, often just to indicate the person responsible for custody of the castle for the king for which he received payment. Perhaps of more interest are the payments made for persons who work in the castle or are assigned to the castle for its protection. Sometimes these can be quite detailed, of which more below. There are also quite a number of instances where money is shown for works on or within a castle and for repairs to parts of a castle, for example to turret walls or roofs. Sometimes you get all three types of payments coming together at one castle.

Thirty-nine payments are made to custodians of a castle in the Pipe Roll. Sometimes it is obvious that the sheriff of the county is the custodian of the castle as the roll is specific that it is the sheriff who is being paid. The sheriff of Shropshire (Hugh Despenser) is paid sixty marks for custody of the castles of Shrewsbury and Bridgnorth and for custody of the county[37] or the sheriff of Northamptonshire is paid £15 for custody of the castle at Northampton (Ralph de Trublevill).[38] At other times the name of the person is specified as being in custody of the castle. The name of the person given custody of the castle of Hertford was Richard de Argentoem for £20[39] and of Bridgnorth in Shropshire was Thomas Maudoit for £33 11s.

[36] *NS 54*, p. xiii.

[37] See Shropshire below p. 146 and *Patent Rolls, 1216–25*, 417.

[38] See Northamptonshire below p. 44 and *Patent Rolls, 1216–25*, 418.

[39] See Hertfordshire below p. 20 and *Patent Rolls, 1216–25*, 421 for his appointment on 18 January 1224. He was also appointed to Cambridge, Huntingdon, and Essex at the same time.

4d.[40] For a complete list of all payments for custody of castles see Table 1 at the end of this section.

There are a number of instances in the roll where there is some breakdown of personnel serving in a castle and some of their rates of pay are shown in the roll. Roger and Boniface de Quatuor maris are two mounted crossbowmen who are paid 7½d. a day whereas Roger de Bosco is a foot crossbowman who is only paid 3d. a day.[41] Crossbowmen were obviously on a variable rate of pay as in the castle of Windsor there were 6 foot crossbowmen paid at a rate of 3½d. per day.[42] The total paid out to John Wascelin, the custodian and constable of Bamburgh, for the crossbowmen is £27 7s. 6d. and is paid in differing amounts in three unequal periods. The highest payout was for 73 knights' service at Windsor Castle each getting 20 shillings a year for the years 9 and 10 Henry III.[43] This would mean that the custodian would get £146 for the two years' service of the knights. There are other categories of service within a castle which are shown in the text. As well as knights and crossbowmen there are watchmen (up to 2d. per day), oxherds, porters (up to 4d. per day with groom), parkers (2d. per day), and grooms are mentioned as being part of a castle's staff – see Table 2 below for a complete list and for their rates of pay where provided in the text.

Many castles are shown in the text as having works on or repairs to a castle, or part of a castle, or having provisions for a castle and these are shown in Table 3 below. These can range from replacement of gutter tiles, repair of homes within the castle, repair of castle towers, or roofs. Some of these repairs may be a hangover from the revolt of Fawkes de Bréauté and his brother William in 1224, which is mentioned in the text in a number of instances as resulting from the siege of Bedford.[44] There is no mention in the text of any repairs or works at Bedford Castle or Plympton which also suffered siege during the revolt of Falkes and his brother.

There are some interesting repairs done in Marlborough Castle to the queen's accommodation, presumably to make a future consort more comfortable while she stayed there, as well as more secure. There is a mention of a palisade around her treasury at the castle as well as work on her chamber, including the windows.[45]

As well as rates of pay or repairs there are in the text, especially in *rotulet 15*, lists of food and clothing for certain people in the castle of

[40] See Shropshire below p. 146 and *Patent Rolls, 1225–32*, 126 where Thomas is confirmed as being custodian of Bridgnorth on 3 June 1227. This is after the end of the accounting period of this Pipe Roll, so the clerk is either giving us some advance information or this entry was put in after the appointment, or the Patent Rolls are in error.

[41] See Northumberland below p. 53.

[42] See Account of Walter and Others below p. 262 and *Calendar of Liberate Rolls, 1226–40*, 10 for items 19–26 in Table 2 below.

[43] See Account of Walter and Others below p. 267. However, it may be that the knights owed 20 shillings per annum service to the king for these years. I think this is more likely.

[44] For the best current account of the siege and its aftermath see D. A. Carpenter, *The Minority of Henry III* (London, 1990), pp. 351–70.

[45] See Wiltshire below p. 248.

Berkhamstead and Hemel Hempstead, for example of harrowmen and ploughmen at the time of the harvest. It also indicates the numbers of draught animals and cart horses required. It provides the amount of food required but not the cost.[46] There are similar amounts of food etc., some with costs for the service of some other manors.[47]

The works at Dover Castle mentioned below were probably part of the extensive works done on the castle after the siege by Louis of France in 1217.

The appendices to the introduction below are an indication of those responsible for castles, those working within a castle and work being performed within a castle that is contained within this Pipe Roll. Where possible cross references have been made with other rolls for the items within the table unless the item is mentioned within the text above, in which event it is cross referenced at that point.

Miscellaneous Matters

The most surprising entry in this roll comes in the Gloucestershire account (m. 7), where it is recorded that the people of Gloucester owe 100s. blanched from the old increment of the borough (*de veteri cremento burgi*), and a line was interpolated a hundred years later to say they answered for it in roll 18 of Edward II.[48]

The roll, particularly in the Hampshire section, contains details of both money and equipment transported to Portsmouth and Portchester to be taken to Gascony for the use of Richard, the king's brother, who had just been created count of Poitou at the age of 16 (in early 1225) and sent with the earl of Salisbury and others to defend Gascony from the onslaught of Louis VIII. For example, 10,000 crossbow bolts were sent from Dorset to Portsmouth at a cost of 11s. 6d. (m. 14). Hurdles (*cleia*), some *cooperta*, 'covered', and 'bridges' (*pontes*, planking, duckboards, etc.) were made in Sumburne, Andover, the New Forest, and elsewhere and transported to Portchester and Southampton, presumably as prefabricated fortifications for the barracks. 500 marks were sent to Yarmouth in the Isle of Wight to pay the troops about to embark on this expedition (Hants). A further sum of 3,000 marks arising from the clerical fifteenth was sent to the Tower of London for Richard's use. £1,000 given to Richard by the king of Scots cost £4 3s. 8d. to transport from York to Nottingham (Yorkshire), but the Nottinghamshire accounts only show 38s. 2d. for the carriage of proceeds of the fifteenth from Nottingham to Winchester (Notts).

Much information is given in the Hampshire account on the transporting of wine to various places, especially royal residences, showing the importance of Southampton as an entry port for this trade. Preparations for the king's Christmas festivities appear: two casks of wine are to go to

46 See Account of Walter and Others below p. 275.

47 See Account of Walter and Others below pp. 275–80.

48 On the strenuous attempts in the reign of Edward II to levy outstanding debts as far back as a century or more, see M. C. Buck, 'Reform of the Exchequer 1316–26', *EHR*, ccclxxxvii (April 1983), pp. 241–60.

Winchester, and two tuns to Clarendon for Christmas; the Gloucestershire authorities paid £6 4s. 10½d. for 24 good fresh salmon to go to Winchester (and £8 4s. 3d. for 40 fresh and salted salmon and 24 lampreys to go to London for the king for Ash Wednesday); and, indeed, the London accounts show 4s. paid to convey the king's clothes to Winchester for Christmas.

Large sums were due from the farm of Cornish tin (Cornwall, Devon) and other mining areas (Northumberland). John son of Richard and Stephen de Croy were the main farmers of Cornish tin. The exact sums involved are obscured by the details of each man's instalments, but John son of Richard owed a total of £824 in arrears. William son of Erkenbauð owed over £2,000 for the farm of the mining rights at Carlisle, though the period which this sum covered is not specified.

Several counties record proceedings from the forest eyre of Hugh de Nevill in 1224–5 (Northants, Notts/Derbs, Worcs, Dorset).[49]

Building work was proceeding at the Tower of London, under the direction of Thomas de Blunville: £20 4s. 7d. was paid for 20 cartloads of lead to roof a *nova turella* being made there.

Traces of the civil war are still to be seen. The burgesses of Bedford were pardoned 60s. because of damage caused to their land by the siege of Bedford Castle (m. 5). In Gloucestershire (m. 7) 12d. was paid to the widow of a royal miner ([*vidua*] ... *minatoris regis*) who died in the service of the king at Bedford, presumably as a sapper. Philip Marc owed the profit of the counties of Nottinghamshire and Derbyshire for 1223–4, but was pardoned these for his expenses in the siege of Bedford Castle and the custody of Nottingham Castle.

Other individuals whose troubles impinged on the record of royal finances include William le Gersere, who was pardoned ½ mark for a pledge because he was both a poor man and *cruce signatus*, had taken the cross (Berks); Agnes, widow of Matthew Malpalu, who though pregnant had taken the habit of religion at the hospital of St. Leonard in York – and two men owed 10 marks to have a writ to inquire if she had done this willingly or been forced into it (Yorkshire); and a *pauper vidua*, poor widow, who had received 1 mark from William, late earl of Devon, for life, was in fact the mother of the abbot of Quarr (Hants).

Five entries record the appearance of individuals before the barons of the Exchequer to make grants, etc., and have them enrolled here in the Pipe Roll (m. 1, m. 2, m. 13, m. 14).[50]

[49] *NS 54*, p. xiii.
[50] *NS 56*, p. xii.

APPENDICES TO THE INTRODUCTION

Appendix I

List of Castles in Text with Custodians

No	Rotulet	Castle	County	Custodian	Amount
1	1	Scarborough	Yorkshire	Geoffrey de Nevill,[51] Richard de Alencun	£200 for Geoffrey, £90 for Richard
2	1	Pickering	Yorkshire	Geoffrey de Nevill, Richard de Alencun	The above amounts are for both castles in 1 & 2
3	2	Colchester	Essex	E[ustace de Fauconberg], bishop of London[52]	£12
4	2	Hertford	Herts	Richard de Argentoem	£10
5	3	Carlisle	Cumb	W[alter] bishop of Carlisle – Yr 10[53]	£42 12s.
6	3	Carlisle	Cumb	W[alter] bishop of Carlisle – Yr 9	£40
7	3	Carlisle	Cumb	W[alter] bishop of Carlisle – Yr 8 – 3 parts of year	£30
8	3	Carlisle	Cumb	W[alter] bishop of Carlisle	£62 6s. 5d.
9	3	Northampton	Northants	Sheriff (Ralph de Trublevill)	£15
10	3	Bamburgh	Northumb	John Wascel'	120 marks
11	4	Plympton	Devon	John de Baiocis – 3 parts of year[54]	No amount shown
12	4	Tamworth	Staffs	Robert Marmiun senior	£171 13s. 4d.
13	5	Portchester	Hants	Bishop of Salisbury[55]	£10
14	5	Winchester	Hants	Bishop of Salisbury	£44 15s. 1d.

51 *Patent Rolls, 1216–25*, 145. This indicates that Geoffrey had been sheriff of Yorkshire since 30 March 1218.
52 *Patent Rolls, 1216–25*, 417.
53 *Patent Rolls, 1216–25*, 326.
54 *Patent Rolls, 1216–25*, 468.
55 *Patent Rolls, 1216–25*, 420.

15	7	Gloucester	Gloucs	Sheriff (William de Putot)[56]	50 marks
16	7	Carisbrooke	Hants	Walerand[57]	£20 [per year][58]
17	7	Christchurch	Hants	Walerand – Yr 10	£3 0s. 10d.[59]
18	7	Christchurch	Hants	Walerand – Yr 9 & part of Yr 8	£5 6s. 5d.
19	8	Salisbury	Wilts	Walter son of Walter of Dunstanvill	£4 15s.
20	8	Worth	Wilts	Robert de Turevill'	£5 bl.
21	8	Mere	Wilts	Luke de Drumar'	£18 bl.
22	8	Chelworth	Wilts	Hugh de Stamford	£4 bl.
23	8	Marlborough	Wilts	Hugh de Stamford[60]	£16 bl.
24	8	Corsham	Wilts	Hugh de Stamford	See 25 below
25	8	Gastard	Wilts	Hugh de Stamford	£10 bl. for 24 and 25
26	8	Bridgnorth	Salop	Thomas Maudoit[61]	£33 11s. 4d.
27	8	Shrewsbury	Salop	Sheriff (Hugh Despenser)	60 marks
28	9	Lancaster	Lancs	William de Ferrers, earl of Derby[62]	See 29 below
29	9	West Derby	Lancs	William de Ferrers, earl of Derby	100 marks for 28 and 29
30	9	Canterbury	Kent	William de Hardres	20 marks
31	9	Canterbury	Kent	William de Hardres – for 140 days of Yr 9	£6 6s.
32	9	Hereford	Herefs	Sheriff – custodian of castle in county (Ralph son of Nicholas).[63]	£125 15s.[64]
33	10	Orford	Suffolk	Richard Agoillun[65]	30 marks

56 *Patent Rolls, 1225–32*, 8.
57 *Patent Rolls, 1216–25*, 427.
58 *Calendar of Liberate Rolls, 1226–40*, 15.
59 *Calendar of Liberate Rolls, 1226–40*, 15–16.
60 *Patent Rolls, 1216–25*, 428 has Robert de Meisy as the custodian of this castle and Corsham in item 24.
61 *Patent Rolls, 1225–32*, 126 where Thomas is to hand over custody of Bridgnorth Castle but no indication in the rolls as to when he was given custody.
62 *Patent Rolls, 1216–25*, 418.
63 *Patent Rolls, 1216–25*, 414.
64 *Calendar of Liberate Rolls, 1226–40*, 36 has the value of 300 marks for this castle.
65 *Patent Rolls, 1216–25*, 492.

List of Castles in Text with Custodians (continued)

No	Rotulet	Castle	County	Custodian	Amount
34	10	Framlingham	Suffolk	Hubert de Burgh for Roger Bigod until he is of age[66]	£20 per year
35	11	Nottingham	Notts	Ralph son of Nicholas[67]	£100[68]
36	11	Bolsover	Derbs	Robert de Tatteshall[69]	£30 per year
37	12	Oxford	Oxon	Walter Foliot[70] & Godfrey of Crowcombe[71]	
38	12	Woodstock	Oxon	Walter Foliot	£28 0s. 6½d. for 37 and 38
39	13	Newcastle upon Tyne	Northumb	William Brewer Junior[72]	£30
40	13	Marlborough	Wilts	Robert Lupus	40 marks a year?
41	15	Windsor	Berks	William Maudoit (Osbert Giffard?)	£18 5s. per quarter part of year 10 plus 15 days
42	15	Odiham	Hants	Adam de Bendeng'[73]	10 marks
43	15	York	Yorks	Peter son of Herbert[74]	
44	15	Pickering	Yorks	Peter son of Herbert	
45	15	Pontefract	Yorks	Peter son of Herbert	£415 15s. 11d. for custody of 43, 44 & 45 for King John in civil war

66 *Patent Rolls, 1225–32*, 66. Hubert was given custody on 2 May 1226.

67 *Patent Rolls, 1216–25*, 500.

68 *Calendar of Liberate Rolls, 1226–40*, 36 has the same amount.

69 *Patent Rolls, 1225–32*, 28.

70 *Patent Rolls, 1216–25*, 524. This also covers his appointment to the king's houses at Woodstock.

71 *Patent Rolls, 1225–32*, 9. Godfrey was appointed on 31 December 1225. The amount owed to Godfrey is not known as it is combined with repairs to the castle, etc. – see Table 3 no 56 below.

72 *Patent Rolls, 1216–25*, 365.

73 In the index of *Patent Rolls, 1216–25*, 639 Osbert Giffard is shown as the constable of Windsor and Odiham Castles but there is no obvious indication of his appointment. However, *Calendar of Liberate Rolls, 1226–40*, 16 shows Adam de Bendeng' has custody of the castle of Odiham.

74 *Patent Rolls, 1225–32*, 38 indicates Robert de Cokefeld was made sheriff of Yorkshire on 25 May 1226.

Appendix II

Payments to Individuals in Castles in Text

No	Rotulet	Castle	County	Service	Rate of Pay	Amount
1	3	Bamburgh	Northumb	mounted crossbowmen	7½d. per day	See 2 below
2	3	Bamburgh	Northumb	foot crossbowmen	3d. per day	£27 7s. 6d. for one year for nos 1 & 2
3	7	Bristol	Gloucs	10 foot sergeants	3½d. per day each	See 4 below
4	7	Bristol	Gloucs	10 foot sergeants	3d. per day each	1. £16 15s. 10d. from day of Epiphany [6 January 1226] until nearest Sunday prior to feast of St. Gregory [8 March 1226] [62 days] 2. £1 1s. 8d. until feast of St. Gregory [Thursday 12 March 1226]
5	7	Bristol	Gloucs	10 foot sergeants	3½d. per day each	See 6 below
6	7	Bristol	Gloucs	10 foot sergeants	3d. per day each	1. £12 3s. 9d. from feast of St. Gregory [Thursday 12 March 1226] to close of Easter [Sunday 19 April 1226][75] [38 days] 2. £15 8s. 9d. from nearest Thursday before feast of St. Margaret [16 July 1226] to morrow of Nativity of St. Mary [Wednesday 9 September 1226] [57 days][76]

[75] This might be until Wednesday 20 April 1226 according to C. R. Cheney, *Handbook of Dates* (Cambridge: Cambridge University Press, 1995), p. 65. I make this total as £10 5s. 10d. not as shown in the text. There is very heavy rubbing on the right-hand side of the membrane which u/v was not able to provide an answer as to when around the feast of St. Gregory we start to calculate from; that is the 38 days may be incorrect.

[76] This is what is shown in the text, see Gloucestershire, p. 127. But, I calculate it as 56 days.

No	Rotulet	Castle	County	Service	Rate of Pay	Amount
7	7	Bristol	Gloucs	35 men and 20 horses		For 1 year and 29 weeks for Eleanor sister of King and her household – £265 9s. 4½d.
8	7	Christchurch	Hants	2 men and horses, 1 forester on horseback by the keep		20 shillings for the men and horses and 13s. 4d. for the forester on horseback
9	7	Christchurch	Hants	4 servants – 2 within keep and 2 outside	10s. a year each	£2
10	7	Christchurch	Hants	2 foot foresters	5s. a year each	10s.
11	9	Hereford	Herefs	Fletcher	3d. a day	£1 6s. 0d. for 104 days in 10 Henry III
12	9	Hereford	Herefs	Fletcher[77]	4d. a day	£4 10s. 4d. for 271 days
13	9	Hereford	Herefs	Smith and brother for making crossbow bolts	9d. per day for both – 100 crossbow bolts a day	£13 13s. 9d. for one year from feast of St. Michael in year 10 to the same in year 11
14	13	Plympton	Devon	Knights and sergeants		£76 13s. 4d. to Bishop of Exeter for his knights etc. for siege of Plympton
15	13	Ludgershall	Wilts	4 ploughmen and 1 carter for 2 years and 4 parts of year		£2 14s. 9½d.
16	14	Bristol	Gloucs	10 sergeants	3d. per day each	See 17 below for inclusive total
17	14	Bristol	Gloucs	10 sergeants	3½d. per day each	£10 16s. 8d. for 40 days
18	15	Bamburgh	Northumb	6 oxherds and 1 carter		50s. 3d for one year
19	15	Windsor	Berks	constable	2s. per day	£63 17s. 6d. for year 9 and 3 parts of year 10 Henry III
20	15	Windsor	Berks	2 knights	12d. per day each	£63 17s. 6d. for same period as 12 above

77 Same person as 11 above but different rate per day.

21	15	Windsor	Berks	2 mounted sergeants	6d. per day each	£31 18s. 9d. for same period as 12
22	15	Windsor	Berks	1 porter with groom	4d. per day	£10 12s. 11d. for same period as 12
23	15	Windsor	Berks	6 foot crossbowmen	3½d. per day each	£55 17s. 9½d. for same period as 12
24	15	Windsor	Berks	4 watchmen	1½d. per day each	£15 19s. 4½d. for same period as 12
25	15	Windsor	Berks	1 clerk	12d. per day	£31 18s. 9d. for same period as 12
26	15	Windsor	Berks	73 knights for watch and ward	20s. per annum each	£146 for years 9 and 10 Henry III
27	15	Odiham	Hants	constable	18d. per day[78]	£27 7s. 6d. for year 9 Henry III
28	15	Odiham	Hants	2 mounted sergeants	6d. per day each	£18 5s. 0d. for same period as 27 above
29	15	Odiham	Hants	1 watchman, 1 porter and 1 parker	2d. per day each	£9 2s. 6d. for same period as 27
30	15	Berkhamstead	Herts	7 ploughmen, 1 doorkeeper, 1 carter, 1 handmaid, in castle		£1 1s. 6d.
31	15	Berkhamstead	Herts	payments to 1 forest beadle, 1 reeve		11s. 10d.
32	15	Berkhamstead	Herts	Payments to 2 watchmen		13s. 4d.
33	15	Hemel Hempstead	Herts	victuals and payments to constable, squires, 4 grooms, 1 chaplain, clerks, 1 reeve, 1 sergeant, 1 treasurer, 1 cook, 1 forester with groom, 1 doorkeeper, 1 carter		£28 14s. 5½d.
34	15	Hemel Hempstead	Herts	Livery of constable, clerk, under constable, seneschal, doorkeeper, and forester		£5

78 *Calendar of Liberate Rolls, 1226–40*, 10 for this item and also items 28 and 29.

Appendix III

Payments for Repairs to, Builds in, and Work on Castles in Text

No	Rotulet	Castle	County	Repair/Build/Works at	Amount
1	1	Scarborough	Yorks	Repair	See 2 below
2	1	Pickering	Yorks	Repair	£40 for 1 & 2
3	1	Scarborough	Yorks	Works at	100 marks
4	1	Knaresborough	Yorks	Repair of houses in	£10
5	2	Hertford	Herts	Repair of gate in	£10
6	2	Hertford	Herts	Works at	20 marks
7	2	Hertford	Herts	Build houses in	£18 4s. 1d.
8	2	Colchester	Essex	Works at	£20
9	2	Colchester	Essex	Provisioning of	£20
10	2	Hertford	Herts	Works at	£10
11	3	Carlisle	Cumbs	Work on a gaol	£6 13s. 4d. (10 marks)
12	3	Northampton	Northants	Repair	£5
13	3	Garnsey[79]	Northants	Works at	£66 19s. 1d.
14	3	Bamburgh	Northumb	Work at	£4
15	3	Newcastle	Northumb	Watch and ward	£32 4s. 5d. – expressed as 48 marks 4s. 5d.
16	3	Bamburgh	Northumb	Watch and ward	£3 6s. 8d. (5 marks)

79 According to *Calendar of Liberate Rolls, 1226–40*, 7 this might be Jersey or Guernsey.

17	4	Lincoln	Lincs	Works at	£5 (100s.)
18	5	Rockingham	Northants	Works at	£13 6s. 8d. (20 marks)
19	6	Wallingford	Berks	Works on wall near to bridge in castle	£5 7s. 5½d.[80]
20	6	Wallingford	Berks	Improvements to houses in castle	£5
21	7	Gloucester	Gloucs	Repair of house in	£10 5s. 1d.
22	7	Gloucester	Gloucs	Repair of palisade round castle of	£5 0s. 7d.
23	7	Gloucester	Gloucs	Repair of king's chamber in	£4 16s. 0½d.
24	7	Bristol	Gloucs	Robes for 7 watchmen in castle	£5 6s.
25	7	Bristol	Gloucs	Repair of houses in castle of	£21 9s. 11d.
25	7	Bristol	Gloucs	4 casks of wine purchased	£5 8s.
26	7	Bristol	Gloucs	162 sheep purchased of which 44 dead and 15 skins of sheep	£8 1s.
27	7	Bristol	Gloucs	29 skins of sheep	
28	7	Bristol	Gloucs	125 quarters of corn	£31 5s.
29	7	Bristol	Gloucs	2 casks of wine to remain in castle	
30	7	Bristol	Gloucs	Meat of 31 oxen to remain in castle	£4 13s.
31	7	Bristol	Gloucs	24 bacons to remain in castle	£1 10s.
32	7	Bristol	Gloucs	148 cheeses to remain in castle	£1 10s. 10d.
33	7	Carisbrooke	Hants (IOW)	Repair of houses and a grange outside the keep	£1 2s.
34	8	Salisbury	Wilts	Repairs of houses	£2 10s.

80 See *Calendar of Liberate Rolls, 1226–40*, 19 where the debt is still outstanding in 1227 and the account is being asked to be settled.

No	Rotulet	Castle	County	Repair/Build/Works at	Amount
35	8	Marlborough	Wilts	Works at	£10
36	8	Devizes	Wilts	Works at	£24 13s. 5d.
37	8	Bridgnorth	Salop	Repair of towers of outer wall and old great chimney in King's chamber	£13 16s. 9d.
38	8	Bridgnorth	Salop	Repair of houses and castle of	See 39 below
39	8	Shrewsbury	Salop	Repair of houses and castle of	£10
40	9	Lancaster	Lancs	Repair	£17 10s.
41	9	Rochester	Kent	Works on towers of	£20 1s.[81]
42	9	Rochester	Kent	Improvements to storehouse and repair to Buttery	£8 19s. 6d.
43	9	Rochester	Kent	For work on horseshoes for a military engine in	£2
44	9	Rochester	Kent	Works on towers in	£150
45	9	Rochester	Kent	Repair of houses in	£1 11s.
46	9	Canterbury	Kent	Repair of houses in	£2
47	9	Hereford	Herefs	6 casks of wine from Bristol to Hereford for works of the king	£1 0s. 7d.
48	9	Hereford	Herefs	10 casks of wine from Bristol to Hereford for works of the king	£1 14s. 11d.
49	9	Hereford	Herefs	Purchase of iron, steel, wood, charcoal, and casks for making crossbow bolts and inserting the feathers on the bolts.	£10 2s. 3½d. – see 13 Table 2

[81] See *Calendar of Liberate Rolls, 1226–40*, 22 where the debt is still outstanding in 1227 and the account has been paid and is being asked to be settled.

50	9	Hereford	Herefs	Repair of houses in	£5
51	10	Orford	Suffolk	Works at	30 marks
52	10	Devizes	Wilts	Provisioning of in time of K. J.	Quit by writ of king
53	11	Nottingham	Notts	Carriage of 10 casks of wine from Lincoln to Nottingham	£2 2s. 8d.
54	11	Nottingham	Notts	Repair of castle and houses in	£5 17s. 10d.
55	12	Oxford	Oxon	Repair of houses, hall, chamber, and chapel of the king	£4 6s. 7d.
56	12	Oxford	Oxon	Repair of King's chapel, works on a buttery and storeroom, works on fireplace in King's wardrobe and chamber, leading of roofs of these rooms and towers and repair of houses	See 57 below
57	12	Woodstock	Oxon	Repair of broken barbican and repair of houses	£164 0s. 4d. for 56 and 57 and 37 in Table 1 above for Godfrey of Crowcombe
58	12	Oxford	Oxon	Repair of houses, hall chamber, and chapel of king	£4 6s. 7d.
59	13	Dover	Kent	Purchase of 20 carts of lead for work at castle	£41 7s.
60	13	Tower of London	London	Purchase of charcoal for works at	£2 2s.
61	13	Tower of London	London	6 carts of lead bought and paid for by Thomas de Blunvill' for new tower roofing	£12 3s.
62	13	Tower of London	London	4 carts of lead for the same tower roof	£8 1s. 7d.
63	13	Tower of London	London	2 pairs of curtain walls for king's chapel	12s. 3½d.

No	Rotulet	Castle	County	Repair/Build/Works at	Amount
64	13	Tower of London	London	Charcoal for works of Thomas de Blunvill'	3s. 11d.
65	13	Newcastle upon Tyne	Northumb	Watch and ward for 2 years previously	£64 8s. 10d. – expressed as 96 marks 8s. 10d.
66	13	Marlborough[82]	Wilts	Works at	£55 6s. 8d.
67	13	Marlborough	Wilts	Making sluice gates and locks around the castle to retain water	£4 18s. 7½d.
68	13	Marlborough	Wilts	Works on a new kitchen, roof for furnace, stone roofing for kitchen	£11 15s. 4½d.
69	13	Marlborough	Wilts	Works on small chamber with stone roofing	£3 15s. 9½d.
70	13	Marlborough	Wilts	Repair of steps in front of treasury and repair of stone roof	£1 11s. 7½d.
71	13	Marlborough	Wilts	Repair of passage below the hall and steps	12s. 7d.
72	13	Marlborough	Wilts	Work on palisade of Queen's treasury	£2 1s. 6d.
73	13	Marlborough	Wilts	Repair of Queen's chamber with lead and moulding, gable wall raised with tints and lead, other repairs to the same room and repairs to iron windows	£7 15s. 5d.
74	13	Marlborough	Wilts	Purchase of stone for one turret, behind the leaded chamber, containing two floors and carriage of the stone and sand	£17 7s. 5½d.
75	13	Marlborough	Wilts	Works and carriage of one beacon	£5 18s. 11d.

82 See *Calendar of Liberate Rolls, 1226–40*, 18 where some of this work at Marlborough Castle in items 66–75 has still not been paid and is being asked to be settled.

76	13	Marlborough	Wilts	Covering of one roof and kitchen next to the door with stone and repair of storeroom, hall and other houses in castle	£37 11s. 8½d. for three years
77	13	Ludgershall	Wilts	Works on one turret near to the door, glass windows bought for the chapel and ?[83] for houses	£6 14s. 6d.
78	13	Ludgershall	Wilts	Purchase of iron and steel for four plough-teams and for work on the plough-teams	£4 8s. 9½d.
79	14	Sherborne	Dorset	Repairs to castle of	£5
80	15	Nottingham	Notts	Purchase of gutter tiles and carriage	£1 8s.
81	15	Peak	Derbs	Repair of houses	£4 12s.
82	15	Bolsover	Derbs	Repair of houses	£2 5s.
83	15	Bolsover	Derbs	Works on a kitchen	£4 15s.
84	15	Bamburgh	Northumb	Repair of towers and houses in castle of	£9 12s. 10½d.
85	15	Bamburgh	Northumb	Payments of 6 oxherds and 1 carter and boonwork for ploughing and cart service	£2 10s. 3d.
86	15	Bamburgh	Northumb	Work on tower floors and lead roofs with the turret near king's chamber	£44 1s. 1d.
87	15	Bamburgh	Northumb	Purchase of 4 casks of wine to provision the castle	£5 12s. or 28s. each cask
88	15	Bamburgh	Northumb	Carriage of wine in 86 above from Berwick to Bamburgh	7s.
89	15	Bamburgh	Northumb	Purchase of 20 oxen for ploughing	£8 6s. 8d.

83 It is not possible to determine at this time what was bought for the houses.

No	Rotulet	Castle	County	Repair/Build/Works at	Amount
90	15	Bamburgh	Northumb	Payments of 6 oxherds and 1 carter for boonwork and for ploughing and cart service	£2 9s. 7d. for all the year
91	15	Windsor	Berks	Works on castle – payment to Amalric de Parco	£5 4s.
92	15	Odiham	Hants	Repair of palisade around towers of castle of Odiham, repair of chimney in towers	£7 5s. 0½d.
93	15	Odiham	Hants	Repair of roofs with new or repaired leading	£4 3s.
94	15	Odiham	Hants	Repair of houses and barns	£1 6s. 8d.
95	15	Dover	Kent	Works on new tower in the moat near to the gateway including purchase of timber and lead and carriage of sand and water, stone and other necessary items	£466 13s. 0½d. – expressed as 699 marks 13s. 0½d.
96	15	Berkhamstead	Herts	Works on great bridge of the castle and repair of the barn	£6 3s. 10½d.
97	15	Hemel Hempstead	Herts	Iron work on 2 carts and horseshoes, 12 draught animals and two cart horses, repair of houses, a hedge and other small expenses for the autumn boonwork and wheat reaped and gathered, hay mown and gathered, wheat threshed and payments for 4 ploughmen, forest reeve and a handmaiden	£7 0s. 11½d.

EDITORIAL CONVENTIONS

In editing this edition of the Pipe Roll, we (the volume editors) have mainly followed the abbreviations and other textual rules laid down by Lady Stenton in the first volume of the New Series of the Pipe Roll Society publications in 1925 for 2 Richard I. These were:

R. for *Rex* and its cases;

Vic. for *Vicecomes* and its cases;

r.c. for *reddit compotum* and *reddunt compotum*;

In thes. for *In thesauro*;

lib. for *liberavit* or *liberaverunt*;

li., s., d. for *libra*, *solidus,* and *denarius*, and their cases;

dim. m. for *dimidia marca* and its cases;

Et Q.E. for *Et Quietus* (or *Quieta*) *Est*; and Et Q.S. for *Et Quieti Sunt*;

f. for *filius* and its cases (but *filia* is extended in full);

bl. for *blancorum*

num. for *numero*

Lady Stenton also made decisions about how to extend a few words: *pro def'* was always extended as *pro defalta*, not as (the equally possible) *pro defectu*; and *wap'* was extended as *wapentacum*, because she rejected the form *wapentagium* as unjustified. *Francpl'* was regarded as a singular noun unless there was evidence to the contrary. Subsequent editors have all followed these conventions.

One or two more such conventions have developed. A large decorated capital R in the text may stand for *rotulus* as well as *Rex*, and is transcribed as *rotulus*. And *R. J.*, which stands for *Rex Johannes*, and its cases, remains simply as *R. J.*, whatever the case (usually genitive, as in *in R.vij*° *R. J.*, 'in the seventh rotulet of King John').

There is also the problem of extending abbreviated words. Lady Stenton did not extend place-names, and only extended personal names when there was absolutely no doubt about the correct extension. She also left words in the text suspended if she felt there was any doubt about the correct extension. This approach has become somewhat modified over the years.

For place-names, *-ha'* is now printed as *-ham* by most editors.

For personal first names a tendency seems to have developed by previous editors to assume masculinity: *Philip'* becomes *Philippus* rather than remain suspended to indicate it might stand for *Philippa*.

A similar convention has developed of extending some words which relate to number. For example *pro debit'* invariably becomes *pro debito* – singular when it could equally stand for *pro debitis* – plural. We have only extended this in the plural if there are strong indications that it should be plural – for example the actual number is shown as in *pro duobus debitis*.

Similar examples are: *v.v.* for *vino vendito*, not *vinis venditis* and *transgress'* as *transgressione*, not *transgressionibus* etc.

On the other hand, the expression *de debit' Judeorum*, 'concerning the debt(s) of the Jews', is probably a plural, and we have treated it as such. And 'alms' and 'arrears' feel naturally plural, so we have extended *in elem const'* to *in elemosinis constitutis*, and *arrerag'* to *arreragia*.

Some descriptive expressions may be finished by either a noun in the genitive or an adjective: *de prestito Pict'* (*Pictavie* or *Pictavensi*?), *de censu forest'* (*foreste* or *forestario*?). It seems to have become the rule to prefer the genitive noun in such expressions – but to leave (e.g.) *episcopus Sar'* abbreviated, rather than choose between *Saresberie* and *Saresberiensis*.

'For a false claim', is invariably *pro fl' cl'* or *pro flo clam'*, never written in full. The *f'* or *flo* may obviously be extended to *falso*, but there is absolutely no indication throughout this document whether the clerk is using the form *clameo* or *clamore*. We have used the latter form rather than retain the suspension.

The abbreviation *resp'* now seems to be thought of as standing for part of the verb *respondere*, 'to answer', and in many instances this is manifestly correct; but there are places where *respice*, 'look', could equally be correct; *set resp' in dorso* 'but look on the dorse' is as good sense as 'but he answers on the dorse'. *Resp'* could also stand for other tenses: *respondebit*/*respondebunt*, or *respondit*/*responderunt*. Indeed, on rot. 8 dorse, under Staffordshire, we read that Henry de Tracy *finivit in Devon'* when standing surety for the heir of Thomas de Erdinton', which proves that the clerks sometimes annotated these entries in the past tense.

Grammar

It soon became clear from a number of examples written in full that the clerks preferred to use the gerundive rather than the gerund followed by a direct object: *pro h*[*abe*]*nd' terra* must stand for *pro habenda terra*, and *pro justic' Willelmo* must stand for *pro justiciando Willelmo*. On rot. 3d, the phrases *pro essarto suo in Salceto in pace h*[*abe*]*ndo* and *pro bosco suo de Bruskhawe claudendo* are good, clear examples of this usage, and we have thus extended all such phrases as gerundives.

That *remanens*, 'remainder, rest of', which is a participle in origin, is used as a noun is shown repeatedly by its use with the genitive: *de remanenti compoti sui, de remanenti eiusdem crementi*.

Annotations

Annotations in the text have not been expanded. These are usually found in the margin of the membrane. They have been italicised. These are: *f'*, normally standing for items currently in the farm of the king, or *p*, standing for *pars*, which indicates that less than half what is owed has been paid into the Treasury and *t*, standing for *totum* which means that all the outstanding debt has been paid into the treasury.

General

Capitals in the manuscript have not been followed. They are only used at the beginning of sentences, for names of persons, places and the great offices of state, Justiciar, Chancellor, and Treasurer.

The Latin words in the text have not been extended if there are any doubts of the correct extension.

Interlineations by the clerks in the text have been marked in this edition by use of round brackets around the word or phrases that are interlined and with a superscript *i*. Cancellations by the clerk, usually shown with the word or words underlined, are shown with round brackets with a superscript *c*. Where the words in the text have been erased but can still be read they are also put within round brackets but with a superscript *d*. Where there is text that has been erased but is illegible any substitutions are shown within square brackets and footnoted to indicate where the substitution has been obtained. If the illegible words can be restored with certainty but without any authority they are placed within square brackets and with a superscript *s*.

If it is obvious that some text was written at a different time from the majority of the text this is shown in italics. These would often be obvious because they were written in a different ink or by a different hand.

Any ruled lines left blank of text by the clerk are shown as follows: [*One line blank*], [*Two lines blank*], etc.

The roll is mainly written in a legible hand but certain letters are not easily distinguishable. For example, *u* and *v*, *c* and *t*, and occasionally *c* and *e*.

Footnotes

In keeping with earlier editions of Pipe Rolls that have been published by the Society, references to published Pipe Rolls appear in the footnotes to this volume as *NS* for New Series, with their volume number. For example, *The Great Roll of the Pipe for the Seventh Year of the Reign of King Henry III, Michaelmas 1223*, ed. Adrian Jobson & C. F. Slade, The Pipe Roll Society, new series 56 (London, 2008), is referred to as *NS 56*.

THE GREAT ROLL OF THE PIPE

for the

TENTH YEAR OF THE REIGN OF

KING HENRY III

Michaelmas 1226

(Pipe Roll 70)

[*Rot.* I *Mem.* I]

EBORAC[1]

ANNUS DECIMUS REGIS HENRICI TERCII

EVERWIKESIR'

Eustachius de Luddham ut custos pro se et Roberto de Cokefeld' reddit compotum de CCCC et xl li. et vij s. et iij d. bl. de firma comitatus. In thes. nichil.

Et in elemosinis constitutis militibus de Templo j m. Et in decimis constitutis canonicis de Sancto Oswaldo xviij li. et v s. Et in terris datis monialibus de Molseby xxx s. in soca de Esingewald'. Et canonicis de Martone xl s. [in][2] Hoby. Et in quietancia terre de Brigham quam Henricus R. primus dedit Waltero f. Osberti f. Algrim de Frisemareis xxiiij s. de quibus homines de Driffeld' respondent infra. Et archiepiscopo Rothom' xl li. bl. in Killum. Et in Walesgrave x li. bl. de quibus homines de Scardeburg' respondent infra. Et in Driffeld' lxv li. et ij s. et iij d. et ob. bl. de quibus homines ville respondent infra. Et in Scalleby C et xvj s. bl. de quibus homines ville respondent infra. E[t][3] in Pikering' xxiiij li. et xv s. bl. de quibus Vic. respondet infra. Et in wapentak' de Pikering' C et xij s. et viij d. de quibus iiij li. sunt bl. de quibus Vic. respondet infra. Et in Poclinton' xxviij li. bl. de quibus Vic. respondet infra. Et Petro de Brus x m. bl. in wapentak' de Langeberg' de quibus respondet infra. Et in civitate

1 This word for York is in the area of the membrane above the string which holds the roll together.

2 The edge of the membrane is worn at this point. Wording is from E 372/68, rot. 13, m. I.

3 The edge of the membrane is worn at this point.

Eborac' C li. bl. de quibus cives respondent infra. Et Rade cum herede Alani Wastehoese x li. in Sneid'. Et in soca de Walesgrave xxj li. et xvij s. et j d. de quibus Vic. respondet infra. Et Johanni constabulario Cestr' xx li. in Sneid'. Et in (*Burgo* et in[i]) Cnarreburc xxij li. bl. de quibus archiepiscopus Ebor' respondet infra in compoto suo.

[*One line blank*]

Et Roberto de Cokefeld' xl li. ad reparationem castrorum de Scardeburg' et de Pikering' per breve R. (de quibus respondet infra[i]). Et Galfrido de Nevill' ad custodiam predictorum castrorum de anno ix^{o} R. CC li. per breve R. Et Ricardo de Alencun quater xx et x li. ad opus ipsius Galfridi ad predictam custodiam a festo Sancti Michaelis anno ix^{o}[1] usque ad Dominicam proximam post annunciationem beate Marie anno x^{mo} que tunc fuit tres septimane ante Pasch'[2] per breve R. quod attulit de allocandis C li. de dim. anno. Et pro j palefrido quem Eustachius de Ludham emit ad opus R. et quem R. recepit apud Westm' iiij^{or} li. et x s. per breve R. Et in expensis duorum gaiolariorum ad custodiam gaiole de Ebor' a festo Sancti Edmundi R. ix^{o}[3] per annum integrum lx s. per idem breve. Et in custo quod idem Eustachius posuit ad custodiendum vivarium R. in Ebor' per eundem annum integrum j m. per idem breve. Et in custo quem idem Eustachius posuit in custodia predicte Gaiole de Ebor' per dimidium annum R. x^{m} xv s. per idem breve. Et in conductu M. librarum quas R. Scot' dedit Ricardo fratri R. ab Ebor' usque Noting' iiij li. et iij s. et viij d. per breve R. Et in custo quem idem Eustachius posuit in Willelmo vinitore et sociis suis assignatis ad insidiandum et capiendum Robertum de Werreby malefactorem xxviij s. per breve R. Et habet (Eustachius[i]) de superplus CC et lxvj [li.] [et] ix s. et x d. et ob. bl. de quibus ix li. [et] vij s. et vij d. bl. locantur ei infra in firma de Pkering'.[4] Et restant ei locande CC et lvij li. et ij s. et iij d. et ob. bl. qui sunt ei extensi ad CC et lxx li. et xij s. et ij d. et ob. num. de quibus xxj li. et v s. et x d. locantur ei infra in pluribus firmis. Et restant ei locande CC et xlix li. et vj s. et iiij d. et ob. quod totum locatur ei infra in proficuo.

[*One line blank*]

f' Idem Vic. r.c. de CCC et quater xx et vij li. et viij s. et iiij d. de proficuo Comitatus de anno preterito et hoc dim. anno. In thes. nichil. Et in expensis predicti Eustachii pro custodia Comitatus per predictum tempus quater xx et vij li. et viij s. et iiij d. Et in superplus quod habet supra CC et xlix li. et vj s. et iiij d. et ob. Et debet l li. et xiij s. et vij d. et ob.

f' Robertus de Cokefeld' Vic. [*blank*] quater xx li. de proficuo Comitatus de tempore suo de hoc anno. *Scilicet* (*de*[i]) *alio dimidio anno*.[5]

f' Cives Eborac' r.c. de C et lx li. num.[6] de firma Civitatis sue. In thes. C et vj li. et viij s. et xj d. num. Et in defalta monetariorum viij m. Et in

1 Monday 29 September 1225.

2 Sunday 29 March 1226.

3 St. Edmund has two feast days. This is probably 29 April 1225. The other possibility is 20 November 1224.

4 This is what the clerk has written for Pickering located in the North Riding.

5 *Scilicet de alio dimidio anno* over an erasure.

6 *C et lx li. num.* written over an erasure.

elemosinis constitutis militibus de Templo j m. Et in liberatione constituta David f. Thome lardinar' vij li. et xij s. et j d. Et ipsis civibus in relaxatione firme sue xl li. quamdiu R. placuerit. Et Q.S.

[*Two lines blank*]

f' Idem cives [*blank*] lxxix s. et ix d. de firma propresturarum. In thes. [*blank*] Et in defalta pro vasto ix s. Et hospitali Sancti Leonardi ix s.

Idem cives [*blank*] xiij li. et v s. de eadem firma de pluribus annis preteritis.

f' Idem cives r.c. de xxxij d. de firma domus Martini le Vaillant. Et de x s. de firma domus Stephani (f.[i]) Alexandri quam tenuit de Áàron Judeo. In thes. lib. Et Q.S.

f' Telarii Ebor' r.c. de x li. pro gilda sua. In thes. C s. Et debent C s.

Idem telarii debent C et x^{m} li de pluribus annis preteritis de tempore R. J. et R. huius sicut continetur in rotulo precedenti.

f' Hugo de Seleby r.c. de xij d. de firma domus quam tenuit de Áàron. In thes. lib. Et Q.E.

f' Petrus de Brus r.c. de x m. (bl.[i]) de firma de Langeberge wapent'. In thes. vj li. et viij s. et vij d. bl. Et debet iiij [s.] et ix d. bl. Idem r.c. de eodem debito. In thes. lib. Et Q.E.

f' Idem P. r.c. de xx li. num. de cremento eiusdem wapent'. In thes. lib. Et Q.E.

f' Homines de Scardeburg' r.c. de x li. bl. de firma de Walesgrave. In thes. ix li. et xv d. bl. Et debent xviij s. et ix d. bl. qui sunt eis extensi ad xix s. et iij d. num. et respondent infra. (Et debet v s. et xj d. set respondet...[i]).[1]

f' Idem homines r.c. de xxxiij li. de antiqua firma de Scardeburg. Et de xxxiij li. num. de novo cremento eiusdem ville. Et de xix s. et iij d. sicut supra continetur. In thes. nichil. Et Roberto de Cokef' ad operationes castri (de Scardeburg' de quibus respondet in[fra][i]) C m. per breve R.

f' Homines de Pokelinton' r.c. de xl li. bl. de firma ville sue. Et de v m. pro j palefrido de antiqua firma per breve R. quamdiu R. placuerit. In thes. xxv li. et xij s. et iiij d. bl. Et debent xiiij li. et vij s. et vii[j][2] d. bl. Et v m. num. Idem r.c. de eodem debito. In thes. xvj s. et vj d. bl. Et debent xiij li. et xj. s. et vij d. bl.[3] et v. m. num.

f' Idem homines r.c. de xl s. de novo cremento ville sue per predictum breve. In thes. lib. Et Q.S.

Idem homines r.c. de v m. pro j palefrido pro habendo sic villam suam ad firmam sicut continetur in eodem brevi. In thes. lib. Et Q.S.

f' Homines de Scalleby et de Clopton' r.c. de xxx li. num. (pro[4] xxiiij li. bl.[i]) de firma ville sue per breve R. quamdiu R. placuerit. In thes. xxiiij li. Et debent vj li.

1 *Infra* or (less likely) *supra* here. This insertion is the ending of the item below.

2 A strip of paper or parchment has been stuck over the edge of the membrane to strengthen it. This has obscured the final 'j' of *viij* d. The arithmetic confirms that this is in fact eight pence.

3 16s. 6d. from £14 7s. 8d. is £13 11s. 2d. not £13 11s. 7d.

4 In previous years this has normally been *xxiiij bl.* from the farm. See *NS 56*, p. 148. This indicates the rate of exchange between blanched and unblanched money.

f' Abbas de Kirkestall' [*blank*] quater xx et x li. de firma de Colingeh' et Bardes'. Et CC et lxx li. de eadem firma de tribus annis preteritis.

Robertus de Cokefeld' [*blank*] xl li. quas recepit de Eustachio de Ludham sicut supra continetur. Et [*blank*] C m. quas recepit de hominibus de Scardeburg' sicut continetur ibidem.

f' Idem Vic. r.c. de iiij m. de remanenti (firme[c])[1] terre Roberti de Wattevill' in Torp Sancti Andree. Et de iij s. de firma de Turgramesby. Et de xij d. de ij bovatis terre in Swillinton'. In thes. lib. Et Q.E.

f' Idem Vic. r.c. de j m. de firma terre Ricardi de Sproxton'. In thes. dim. m. Et debet dim. m.

f' Idem Vic. (debet[c]) (r.c. de[i]) ij s. de redditu forgie in bosco de Leveseham. In thes. per (Vic.[c]) (Radulfum[i]) de Bolebecc' lib.

f' Homines de Driffeld' r.c. de lxxij li. bl. de firma ville sue. Et de vj li. bl. de remanenti eiusdem firme de anno preterito. In thes. lxxv li. et xiiij s. et vj d. bl. Et debent xlv s. et vj d. Idem reddunt compotum de eodem debito. In thes. lib. Et Q.S.

f' Rogerus de Hal r.c. de ij m. et dim. de firma terre que fuit Osberti de Brigham per breve R.

Idem Vic. [*blank*] xxxij s. de firma eiusdem terre de anno preterito.

f' Alanus de Kinthorp et Walterus Boye r.c. de xl s. de firma foreste de Pikering'. Et de xx s. de remanenti eiusdem firme de anno preterito. In thes. lib. Et Q.S.

f' Radulfus de Bolebecc' r.c. de[2] iiij m. de censu foreste de Scardeburg'. Et de iiij m. de eodem censu de anno preterito. Et de ij m. de remanenti eiusdem census de anno viij[o]. In thes. vj m. Et debet iiij m.

f' Idem Vic. debet vj s. de firma ij[arum] bovatarum terre de Kirkeby in Crendal'. Et lxxij s. de eadem firma de pluribus annis preteritis. Set ut Vic. dicit terra vasta est.

Radulfus de Bolebecc' debet xiiij s. de redditu forgie (in bosco[i]) de Leveseham de pluribus annis preteritis sicut continetur in rotulo vj[o].

f' Idem Vic. r.c. de xxiiij li. et xv s. bl. de firma de Pikering'. Et de iiij li. bl. de wapent' de Pikering'. Et de xv li. et v s. bl. de veteri cremento de Pikering'. In thes. xxj li. et vij s. et ij d. bl. per Robertum. Et xij li. et x[ij][3] s. et v d. bl. per Eustachium. Et in superplus quod (idem Eustachius habet)[i] (habent[c]) supra ix li. et vij s. et vij d. bl. Et debet Robertus xij s. et x d. bl.

f' Idem Vic. r.c. de xxxij s. et viij d. num. de wapent' de Pikering'. In thes. xvj s. et iiij d. per Robertum. Et in superplus quod Eustachius habet supra post corpus Comitatus xvj s. et iiij d. Et Q.E.

f' Idem Vic. r.c. de xix li. et xxij d. et iij[bus] quadrantibus num. de novo cremento de Pikering'. In thes. ix li. et x s. et xj d. et ob. per Robertum. Et in predicto superplus ix li. x s. et xj d. et ob. Et Q.E.

Idem Vic. r.c. de xlvj s. de remanenti eiusdem crementi de anno preterito. In thes. lib. Et Q.E.

f' Idem Vic. r.c. de xxj li. et xvij s. et j d. num. de firma Soke de Walesgrave.

1 This is crossed out by the clerk but it is required as shown in the item below.

2 The word *de* is repeated.

3 If the arithmetic is correct this should be twelve shillings but the strengthening tape at the right hand side of the membrane is obscuring the *xii*.

In thes. x li. et xviij s. et vj d. et ob. per Robertum. Et in predicto superplus x ([e]) li. et xviij s. et vj d. et ob. Et Q.E.

Homines de Scardeburg' r.c. de v s. et xj d. de remanenti firme ville sue sicut supra continetur. In thes. lib. Et Q.S.

W. archiepiscopus Ebor' r.c. de DCCCC m. de pluribus debitis contentis in Oxon' in rotulo viij^{o} qui requirebatur ibidem. per annum CC m.

Nigellus de Molbray r.c. de M et DCCC et xxxvj li. xviij s. (et ij d.[i]) de pluribus[1] debitis contentis in rotulo viij^{o}. In thes. quater xx li. Et debet M et DCC[2] et lvj li. xviij s. et ij d. Et quater xx (et vij li. et xv d.[i]) li.[3] de scutagio (de Mungumeri[i]).[4] per annum quater xx li.

Heres Galfridi Luterell' r.c. de CC et j li. et xiij s. et v d. de pluribus debitis contentis ibidem. In thes. x li. Et debet C et quater xx et xj li. (et xiij s.[i]) et v d. de quibus Philippus Marc debet respondere.
per annum x li.

Petrus f. Herberti [*blank*] iiij li. vij s. et v d. de remanenti firme de Chaugrave. Et vj m. de scutagio Pictavie. Et iiij m. de primo scutagio R. Et liij m. de prestito Pict'. Et ij bonos falcones altanos.[5] E[t] vj li. de scutagio Pict' de feodis archiepiscopatus Ebor' dum habuit custodiam sicut continetur in rotulo viij^{o}.

Prior de Giseburn' r.c. de x li. et xiiij s. de debitis Áàron pro Ricardo Blundo. In thes. C s. Et debet C et xiiij s. per annum C s.

Ysabella de Brus r.c. xiij li. et iiij s. sicut continetur in rotulo ix^{o} R. J. In thes.

Johannes f. Hugonis de Steinton'[6] r.c. de xiiij et xv s. et viij d. pro habenda gratia R. J. In thes. xl s. Et debet xij li. et xv s. et viij d.
per annum xl s.

Albertus de Scardeburg' debet xv li. et x d. de misericordia.

Radulfus de Bolebecc' r.c. de CC et iiij li. et v d. de pluribus debitis contentis in rotulo ij^{o}. In thes. xv li. Et debet C et quater xx et ix li. et v d.
per annum xv li.

(Willelmus[i]) Eustachius[7] de Vesci r.c. de xx m. pro habendo judicio. Et de v m. pro habendo precipe. Et de x li. pro habenda parte de Brumton'.

1 The written amount and content within the brackets have been considerably rubbed and there are probably some erasures.

2 From this point the entry is written over an erasure.

3 The clerk did not cross out the superfluous '*li.*'.

4 The written amounts and contents within the brackets have been considerably rubbed and there may have been erasures. The clerk was also trying to squeeze a lot of writing in a small space.

5 The 'n' in *altanos* has been rubbed and is almost illegible.

6 It looks as though the debt has passed to the son as in *NS 54*, p. 209 where there is a reference to the debt by Hugh for the same amount and for the same reason.

7 *Eustachius* is underlined in the manuscript. Is it to emphasise that the clerk meant to write *Eustachius* instead of *Willelmus*? The clerk did not cross out *Willelmus*. In *NS 54*, p. 209 the clerk indicates that it was the 'heirs of Eustace de Vesci' not just 'Eustace de Vesci' as we have here. Previous Pipe Rolls also indicate 'Heirs of Eustace de Vesci'. Perhaps William is the heir of Eustace de Vesci? One other possibility is that the clerk intended to write *Willelmus comes Saresberie* who in *NS 48*, p. 12 is shown as being responsible for the fees of Eustace de Vesci.

Et de xliij li. et dim. m. de scutagio Willelmi de Molbrai. Et de x m. pro Willelmo Cons[...][1] de eodem. Et de xlviij li. et j m. de scutagio Pict'. Et de xlviij m. et viij s. et xj d. de primo scutagio R. Et de xx s. de scutagio Pict' pro dim. feodo in Cnarreburc. Summa C et lviij li. xv s. et vij d. In thes. xl l[i.][2] Et debet C et xviij li. xv s. et vij d. per[3] annum xl li.

Idem W.[4] debet C m. et j palefridum pro habendo portu.

+ Ricardus f. Hervic' debet v m. de v° scutagio. + Willelmus diaconus debet C s.[5] de misericordia. Willelmus de Corneburc debet M m. pro habenda gratia R. (Set Engelramus f. Engelrami respondet infra.ⁱ) Gerardus de Stockel' debet quater xx et ij m. et x s. de misericordia. Pet[rus de][6] Brus debet ij optimos berseretos sicut continetur in rotulo xiij° R. J. Nicholaus de Stutevill' debet vj millia et DC et lxv li. et j m. pro habenda hereditate sua. + Tom' de Kellinton' debet lxvj s. de misericordia for[este].[7]

[*Rot.* I *Mem.* 2]

[*One line blank*][8]

Petrus Ward r.c. de xiiij s. et xj d. de misericordia. In thes. iij s. Et debet xj s. et xj d.

Thomas Bradax r.c. de xij li. et v s. et iiij d. de misericordia patris sui. In thes. v s. Et debet xij li. et iiij d.

Ricardus Dagun r.c. de xiij li. et j m. de ij debitis. In thes. x s. per Willelmum de Ebor'. Et debet xiij li. et xl d. per annum x s.

Osbertus de Spaldinton' r.c. de ix li. et xviij s. et viij d. de misericordia. In thes. xl d. Et iterum xl d. Et de[bet][9] ix li. et xij s. per annum xl d.

Jacobus de Spaldinton' r.c. de ix li. et xv s. de eodem. In thes. dim. m. Et debet (ix li.ⁱ) viij s. et iiij d. per annum dim. m.

Nicholaus de Stuetevill' [*blank*] MMM et C et lvij li. et xiiij s. et ij d. et vj palefridos et x equas de pluribus debitis patris sui et suis propriis, sicut continetur in rotulo precedenti.

Engelramus f. Engelrami de Corneburc r.c. de M marcis pro Willelmo de Corneburc sicut supra continetur. In thes. nichil. Et in perdona ipsi

---

It could also be that there is now a *Willelmus de Vesci* and that the clerk crossed out *Eustachius*.

1 The membrane has worn away at the extreme right hand edge and the last letters are missing.

2 The membrane has worn away at the extreme right hand edge and the last letter is missing.

3 There is a stain and possibly an erasure under the 'p' of *Per*.

4 This has to be the same William who was interlined at the start of the Eustace de Vesci items.

5 Heavy rubbing here. It has not been possible to see what was erased.

6 The remainder of the first name is missing as it is on the right hand edge of the membrane and it has worn away.

7 The right hand edge has been worn away.

8 The membrane is stitched completely across the membrane. It is also creased. Nothing is under the stitching.

9 The clerk put *de.* but the sum he owes is correct if he pays two payments of 40d.

Engelramo M m. per breve R. (J.[i]) in quo continetur quod R. eas perdonavit quia predictus Willelmus obiit[1] (in prisona R. J. patris R. Et Q.E.[i])[2]

Robertus de Lelay r.c. de lxxix li. et xvj s. et viij d. sicut continetur in rotulo iiij°. In thes. C s. Et debet lxxiiij li. et xvj s. et viij d. per annum C s.

Milites episcopatus Donolm' r.c. de xxx m. de fine suo de loquela Gilleberti Hansard'. In thes. lib. Et Q.S.

Robertus le Wáássur r.c. de quater xx et ij li. et x d. de pluribus debitis contentis in rotulo ij°. In thes. xxj li. et dim. m. Et debet lx li. et xiiij s. et ij d. Idem r.c. de eodem debito. In thes. vij li. Et debet liij li. et xiiij s. [et ij d].[3]

Alanus de Kinthorp' r.c. de viij li. et xviij s. et iiij d. de misericordia foreste. In thes. ij m. Et debet vij li. et xj s. et viij d. per annum ij m.

Willelmus le Váássur r.c. de xlj li. et x s. et j d. de pluribus debitis contentis in rotulo ij°. In thes.

Alexander Burdun r.c. de vij li. pro vasto. In thes. ij m. Et debet C s. et j m. per annum ij m.

Abbas Ebor' r.c. de x li. et xl d. et j bono palefrido pro deliberatione Johannis de camera. In thes. C s. Et debet C s. et xl d. et j bonum palefridum.[4]

Adam f. Rogeri de Hilton' r.c. de vij li. et viij s. de debitis Judeorum. In thes. ij m. Et debet vj li. et xvj d. per annum ij m.

Elyas de Okelestorp' r.c. de xix li. et x s. et iiij d. de iij debitis contentis in rotulo ij°. In thes. xx s. Et debet xviij li. et x s. et iiij d. per annum xx s.

Comitatus Ebor' r.c. de C et xj li. et xvij s. et iiij d. de ij[bus] misericordiis contentis in rotulo vij°. In thes. (per Eustachium de Ludham[i]) xx li. et iiij s. et viij d. Et debet quater xx et xj li. xij s. et viij d.

Willelmus de Maullay debet xv m. de scutagio Wallie de feodis Willelmi Bastard'. Robertus de Neovill' clericus (*set respondet in Norwic' in rotulo sequenti*[i])[5] debet C et j li. de pluribus debitis contentis in rotulo vj°. + *Rogerus de Basingeh' debet xx m. pro habenda pace.*

Ricardus de Schelton' r.c. de xl m. pro habenda terra. In thes. xl m per j talliam ante guerram allocatam precepto Hugonis de Burgo justiciarii coram R. Cycestr' episcopo Regis Cancellario et aliis baronibus de scaccario. Et Q.E.

Robertus Blaclif' r.c. de xxv li. et v s. quia fuit convictus. In thes. xij d. Et debet xxv li. et iiij s.

1 There should be an insertion point here which relates to the insertion which is on the line above.
2 This interlineation was on the end of the item above.
3 Calculated value from the arithmetic shown in the text.
4 There is possibly something rubbed out at the end of the line.
5 The interlineation is actually above the *de Neovill'* and it is not certain if it pertains to this entry. There is no sign indicating an interlinear entry either on this entry or the one above. This and the last sentence in this paragraph were written at different times and possibly by a different hand.

Robertus f. Serlonis r.c. de xix li. et x. s. et j d. pro eodem. In thes. xij d. Et debet xix li. et ix s. et j d.

Adam de Novo Mercato r.c. de xij li et iij palefridis de iij^{bus} debitis sicut continetur in rotulo precedenti. In thes. xx m. Et debet xiij m. de palefridis de quibus M. de Pateshill' debet eum adquietare sicut recognovit.

Idem Vic. debet xiiij li. et iij s. et xj d. de minutis particulis foreste. Ricardus de Mariscis debet lxj li et xiij s. et vj d. de tribus debitis contentis in rotulo precedenti. Mabilia de Warberton' (set respondet infra^{i})[1] debet terciam partem de lx m. pro justiciando Aluredo de Plasset.

Ysabella que fuit uxor Hugonis f. Simonis r.c. de ij m. et dim. pro viro suo sicut continetur in rotulo xiiij^{o} R. J. In thes. lib. Et Q.E.

f' Hugo de Neovill' [*blank*] C s. de firma de Galtris. Et [*blank*] C s. de eadem firma de anno preterito.

Mabilia de Warberton' debet xx m. pro justiciando Aluredo de Plesset' quod reddat ei lx m. sicut supra continetur, set non debet summoneri quia non habuit nec habere potuit pro quo promisit.

AMERCIAMENTA PRO DUELLO

Hugo de Maunneby r.c. de vij li. et dim. m. pro eodem. In thes. l s. Et debet iiij li. et xvj s. et viij d.

Ricardus de Wivelestorp r.c. de xj m. de eodem. In thes.

Willelmus Tuschet r.c. de v m. pro eodem. In thes. dim. m. Et debet iiij m. et dim.

\+ Ricardus de Glentham debet xxx m. de fine suo. + Johannes f. Rogeri debet j palefridum pro habendo brevi de recto versus Galfridum Picot.

Wapent' de Ainesti r.c. de xxxv li. et ij s. de misericordia foreste. In thes. dim. m. per Radulfum de Normann'vill'. Et debet Wapent' xxxiiij li. et xv s. et iiij d. de quibus Simon de Hauton' et Sarra uxor eius debent x m. et respondent infra et Radulfus de Normanvill' de ix m. et dim. et respondet ibidem. Et debet Wap' xxj li. et xv s. et iiij d.

Simon de Hauton' et Sarra uxor eius r.c. de x m. de misericordia Wap' de Anesti sicut supra continetur per breve R.

Radulfus de Normann'vill' [*blank*] ix m. et dim. de eodem.

Walterus Boye r.c. de xlij li. et xvij s. et iiij d. pro habenda gratia R. J. In thes. xl s. Et debet xl li. et xvij s. et iiij d. per annum xl s.

Johannes de Beverlac' r.c. de xxxij li et xviij s. et ij d. pro Thoma de Hothum sicut continetur in rotulo vj^{o}. In thes. xx m. Et debet xix li. et xj s. et vj d. Idem r.c. de eodem debito. In thes. xix li. et xj s. et vj d. per j talliam ante guerram continentem xxv li. et allocatam precepto Huberti de Burg' justiciarii coram R. Cycestr' episcopo Regis Cancellario et aliis baronibus de scaccario. Et Q.E.

[1] The interlinear item is above the line, there is no mark to indicate which line has the insertion. Mabel has in previous Pipe Rolls put off answering for the debt. See *NS 48*, p. 110 for Sussex and *NS 54*, p. 167 for Sussex, which also indicates that she will answer under Yorkshire.

COMPOTUS DE CNARREBURG' ET PONTE BURGI CUM PERTINENCIIS

f' Walterus archiepiscopus Ebor', Adam de Stavel' clericus pro eo r.c. de CC li. de firma de Cnarreburg' cum pertinenciis, quam firmam R. ei concessit quamdiu sibi placuerit per breve suum sicut continetur in eodem brevi. In thes. C li.

Et ipsi R. in garderoba sua quater xx et v li. per breve eiusdem quod est in forulo marescalli in Oxon'. Et in reparatione domorum R. in castro de Cnarresburg' x li. per breve eiusdem. Et debet C s.

[*One line blank*]

Idem W. [*blank*] xij li. iij s. et vj d. de remanenti compoti sui contenti in rotulo precedenti post Devon', scilicet pro blado pro tanto appreciato.

Idem W. debet respondere de toto blado anni ix^{ni} sicut continetur ibidem.

Idem W. [*blank*] xxvij li. et v s. de remanenti predicti compoti de blado pro tanto appreciato.

[*One line blank*]

Idem W. r.c. de liiij s. de ix bobus Falkesii de Breautéé apud Harewode inventis et venditis. Et de xlv[1] s. de xxij boviculis ibidem inventis et venditis. Et de vj li. et xv s. de xxx quarteriis frumenti eiusdem ibidem venditis. Et de viij li. et ij s. et vj d. de C et l quarteriis avene eiusdem ibidem venditis. Et de xliiij s. et v d. de xiij quarteriis siliginis eiusdem ibidem venditis. Summa xxij li.[2] et xj d. In thes. lib. Et Q.E.

Thomas de Birkin r.c. de xix li. et xiiij d. et ob. pro Thoma de Hothum. In thes. C s. Et debet xiiij li. et xiiij d. et ob. per annum C s.

Johannes de Bellovere r.c. de lxiiij s. et vj d. et ob. pro eodem Thoma. In thes. iiij m. Et debet xj s. et ij d. et ob.

Willelmus de Valoinnes debet lvij li. et xvj s. et viij d. pro falso clamore et dissaisina. Brianus f. Alani debet j m. pro habendo pone contra Ranulfum f. Henrici. Johannes Flambard' debet lx s. de ij^{bus} debitis contentis in rotulo viij^{o}.

Robertus de Ros r.c. de CC et xxxij li. et xvj s. et xj d. de pluribus debitis contentis in rotulo precedenti. In thes. l m. per templarios. Et debet C et quater xx et xix li. et x s. et iij d. per annum l m.

Walterus f. Jacobi r.c. de liiij s. et viij d. pro deliberatione sua. In thes. dim. m. Et debet xlviij s.

[*One line blank*]

DE PRESTITO PICTAVIE

Thomas de Colevill' et Andreas de Falcoberg' debent xij m. de eodem super honorem de Alba mar'. Robertus de Frisebois et Hugo le Váássur debent xj m. de eodem super eundem honorem. Thomas miles et Henricus de Estléé debent v m. de eodem. Hugo Painel debet xxxj m. de eodem.

1 There is a smudge here and possibly some erasure.

2 *Summa xxij li.* written over an erasure.

Johannes Daivill' r.c. de C et v s. et xj d. de pluribus debitis contentis in rotulo viij^{o}. In thes. lib. Et Q.E.

Willelmus f. Radulfi et Radulfus de Neovill' r.c. de xlvj s. et x d. de remanenti compoti sui de escaetis in Everwikesir'. In thes. xxiij s. et iij d. per Radulfum f. Willelmi. Et debent xxiij s. et vij d.

Ricardus de Percy (r.c. de^{c}) (debet^{i}) xiiij li. et j m. de catallis Comitisse de Warew'. Roaldus Constabularius Richem' debet vj loricas et vj paria cóópertoriorum ferreorum et vj paria caligarum ferrearum et vj galeas sicut continetur in rotulo iiij^{o}.

Ricardus de Percy r.c. de C et xlvij li de pluribus debitis contentis in rotulo vj^{o}. In thes. xx m. Et debet C et xxxiij li et j m. per annum xx m.

Johannes Constabularius Cestr' debet C et lxvj li. et x s. et viij d.[1] de pluribus debitis contentis in rotulo viij^{o}, set respondet in dorso per partes.[2]

Hugo Painel r.c. de xj li et xij s. et iij d. de pluribus debitis contentis ibidem. In thes. v m. Et debet viij li v s. et vij d. per annum v m.

Thomas Pict' r.c. de xlij m. et dim. de ij^{bus} debitis contentis in rotulo vj^{o}. In thes. xl s. Et debet xxvj li. et dim m. per annum xl s.

Roaldus Constabularius Richem' r.c. de C et lxiiij li et xj s. et viij d. de pluribus debitis contentis in rotulo vj^{o}. In thes. xx li. Et debet C et xliiij li xj s. et viij d. per annum xx [li.][3]

Henricus Walensis r.c. de C et vj li et xix s. et viij d. de fine patris sui. In thes. xl m. Et debet quater xx li et vj s. et iiij d. per annum x[x m.]

Idem Vic. r.c. de ij m. de herede Ade de Stavel'. Et de dim. m. de Rogero de Rodes. Et de xx d. de Eborardo f. Alexandri. Et de xx d. de Willelmo f. Herberti. In thes. lib. Et Q.[S.]

Amabilia de Gateles debet dim. m. pro iniusta detentione. Johannes de Stavel'[4] debet dim. m. pro eodem. Henricus de Bolon' debet x m. pro habendo brevi.

Adam de Walton' debet x s. ut tradatur in ballio. + Stephanus f. Hugonis debet dim. m. pro iniusta detentione. + Galfridus de Rodes debet dim. m pro eodem. Robertus de Limberg' debet[5] xxj li. et xij s. et v d. et ob. pro habendo [...].[6]

W. archiepiscopus Ebor' debet xlvij m de primo scutagio de feodis que non recognoscit. + Robertus de Stappelton' debet terciam partem de xj m. sicut continetur in rotulo iiij^{o}.

1 The clerk has tried to rub out the 'e' of *de* so as to indicate the *d. of denarios*.

2 At the right hand edge of the membrane there has been a tear which TNA has repaired at some time in the past. The right hand edge of this tear has some writing on it most of which is indecipherable. It is possible that TNA has missed lining up the torn part by one line of text. What can be deciphered at the right hand edge of each line will be included.

3 The *li.* is missing because of the tear and it cannot be read on the right hand side of the tear.

4 The clerk has written *Stavel'* here but in *NS 54*, p. 214 he is shown as *Johannes de Stanleg'* as he is also described in the previous three Pipe Roll editions by the Pipe Roll Society. John of Stanley is assumed to be the correct name in the index but cross-referenced.

5 The word *debet* is repeated.

6 The rest of the item is missing because of the tear at the right hand edge. It is suspected the missing word was '*brevi*'.

W. comes Albemar' [*blank*] xx m. pro Petro de Faucoberg' de relevio. Et xij li. et x s. pro Simone de Cambrinton'. Et de xl m. de primo scutagio. Et v m. pro j palefrido. Et xvij s. de catallis cuiusdam [...].[1]

Summa lvj li. et xiij s. et viij d.[2]

Idem W. debet xl m. quas recepit de tallagio de Driffeld'. Et xxvj m. de scutagio Pict' de feodis de Rumiliac'. Et x li. de scutagio de Byham. Et vj li. et x s. de eodem de feodis de Rumiliac'. Et xxvj m. de primo [scutagio] [...] de Rumiliac'. Et iiij m. de scutagio Scot' qui requirebatur in Norf' in rotulo precedenti. Thomas de Mohaut debet viij s. de misericordia. + Walterus f. Rankill' debet xl d. de misericordia. + Godefridus cisor debet xl d. pro plegio.

Willelmus de Heselinton', Goda uxor eius pro eo r.c. de xxv s. et vj d. pro transgressione. In thes. nichil. Et in perdona ipsi Gode xxv s. et vj d. per breve R. Et Q.[E.]

Robertus f. Ricardi r.c. de j m. pro licencia concordandi. In thes. ij s. Et debet xj s. et iiij d.

Willelmus f. Hugonis r.c. de v s. et viij d. quia non est prosecutus. In thes. iiij s. Et debet xx d.

f' + Osbertus f. Radulfi debet xx d. quia non habuit. + Stephanus f. Serlonis debet xl d. de misericordia. + Joseph f. Radulfi debet iiij s. et viij d. quia non est prosecutus. + Thomas f. Thome debet dim. m. pro iniusto impedimento. + Alanus de Stibeton' debet dim. m. .... + Adam f. Agnetis debet j m. pro dissaisina. + Willelmus Juvenis debet dim. m. quia non habuit. + Henricus f. Galfridi debet dim. m. quia non habuit. + Adam f. Siward' debet dim. m. pro plegio. + Willelmus vinitor debet dim m. pro vino vendito. + ...[3] debet j m. quia non est prosecutus. + Hugo f. Hugonis de Bovinton' debet dim. m. pro plegio. + Simon le Furnier debet dim. m. pro iniusta detentione. + Andreas de Catton' debet ij m. quia non est prosecutus. + Hugo de Poclinton' debet dim m. [pro eodem]. + Ricardus f. Lefwini debet dim. [m.] pro dissaisina. + Adam f. Matillid' debet j m. pro falso clamore. + Alexander nepos Alexandri de Dorset' debet dim. m. pro dissaisina. + Ricardus nepos Roberti prepositi debet dim. m. pro defalta. + Willelmus crassus de Beverlaco [debet dim.] m. pro vino vendito. + Johannes f. Sampsonis debet dim. m. pro plegio. + Nicholaus f. Bernolfi debet dim. m. pro falso appello. + Henricus Brunus debet dim. m. pro vino vendito. + Nicholaus f. Reginaldi de Langeton' debet dim. m. pro [dissaisina. + Robertus] Luvel debet dim. m. pro eodem. + Robertus le Oste debet dim. m. quia non habuit. + Johannes de Giseburn' debet dim. (m.[i]) pro eodem. + Mabilia f. Ricardi debet dim. m. pro eodem. + Nicholaus de Schapecot' debet dim. m. pro [eodem. + Willelmus de] Bretegat' debet dim. m. pro dissaisina. + Willelmus f. Willelmi debet dim m. pro eodem. + Thomas f. Radulfi debet dim. m. de catallis plurium.

1 The rest is missing.

2 The individual amount for the Earl of Aumale in total comes to £49 7s. not £56 13s. 8d. It is just possible that there is some missing text on the right margin.

3 The name is too indistinct to make out because the membrane is very rubbed here and is affected by the right hand tear. It is probably *Robertus persona de Stratton'*. See *NS 54*, p. 215.

+ Willelmus f. Ade debet dim. m. pro defalta. + Willelmus f. Siward' debet dim. m. quia non habuit. [+ Willelmus de][1] Welles debet iij m. pro dissaisina. + Hugo de Manneby debet xx s.[2] pro habenda jurata. + Jeronimus de Haldaneby debet dim. m. quia non habuit. + Mauricius de Stainwigges debet dim. m. pro dissaisina. + Johannes de Hardeclive [debet dim. m. pro eodem.] + Walterus f. Johannis debet dim. m. pro plegio. + Gillebertus Hansard' debet j m. pro eodem. + Rogerus f. Arnoldi debet dim. m. pro falso clamore. + Stephanus f. Radulfi debet xl d. pro eodem. Elyas de Menningthorp debet dim. m. [quia non habuit.][3]

RESPICE IN TERGUM

[*Rot.* 1d, *Mem.* 1]

Hugo de Fossham r.c. de ij s. et viij d. quia retraxit se. In thes. lib. Et Q.E.

Thomas de Scotton' r.c. de xx d. pro concelamento. In thes. lib. Et Q.E.

Simon de Horewigge debet xl d. pro vino vendito. + Arnoldus f. Ernisii debet dim. m. pro plegio. + Ivo f. Rogeri[4] debet dim. m. pro plegio. + Helena f. Simonis debet xl d. quia non est prosecuta. + Radulfus de Sandal' debet dim. m. pro defalta. + Walterus de Neubigging' debet dim. m. quia non habuit. + Adam f. Ogeri debet dim. m. pro eodem. + Johannes de Ipro[5] debet medietatem de xxij li. et dim. m. pro distringendis Galfrido et aliis ann[otatis][6] in rotulo iiij.

Petrus de Maullay r.c. de CCC et xxiij li. et vj s. et iiij d. de pluribus debitis contentis in rotulo precedenti. Et de x m. pro dissaisina (unde amerciatus fuit coram R.^{i}) in Dorset in itinere M. de Pateshill' in anno ix^{o}.[7] Et de xl s. et ix d. de catallis Walteri Buc qui [in]quirebantur in eodem itinere ibidem. Et de xx s. quos recepit de Tedderinga de Mappothie pro fuga ipsius Walteri qui requirebatur ibidem. Et de lvj s. et viij d. de catallis Ricardi de Wrotham qui abiuravit regnum qui requirebatur ibidem.

Willelmus f. Willelmi f. Sirich' r.c. de xv li. et xiiij d. de parte sua de fine pro cambio. In thes. C s. Et debet x li. et xiiij d. per annum C s.

1 Supplied from *NS 54*, p. 215. It is the same as in *NS 56*, p. 157.
2 '*s*' partly erased.
3 All the items in square brackets have been deduced from *NS 54*, p. 215 because the right hand edge has been heavily rubbed over the years which has made it impossible to read in parts. There is also a tear on this edge.
4 In *NS 54*, p. 216 Roger is shown as coming from Warter in the East Riding of Yorkshire.
5 In *NS 54*, p. 216 John is shown as *Johannes Rufus de Ypro*.
6 In *NS 54*, p. 216 and in *NS 56*, p. 158 the clerk in the Exchequer uses the word *continetur*. It is possible that the clerk meant to write the word *annotatus* meaning 'noted' in *rot. iiij*. In *NS 54*, p. 216 it is shown as *rotulo iii*.
7 There was no eyre in Dorset in 1225 but there might have been an assize of *novel disseisin*. From the next item it seems there might have been a gaol delivery at the same time.

Adam de Warum r.c. de xxij li. et vj s. et v d. de parte sua de eodem. In thes. xiij m. Et debet xix li. xiij s. et j d. per annum iiij m.

Willelmus Turkill' r.c. de xxviij li. et iij s. de parte sua de eodem. In thes. xl s. Et debet xxvj li. et iij s. per annum xl s.

Hugo f. Lefwini r.c. de xix li. et v s. et j d. de parte sua de eodem. In thes. v m. Et debet xv li. et xviij s. et v d. per annum v m.

Eborardus Bradax r.c. de xxxiiij li. et ij d. de eodem de parte sua. In thes. xv s. et vj d. Et debet xxxiij li. iiij s. et viij d. per annum[1]

Alicia que fuit uxor Roberti de Hugat' r.c. de j m. pro justiciando Decano. In thes. lib. Et Q.E.

Juliana que fuit uxor Thome f. Hugonis r.c. de vj li. et xiiij s. pro summonendis debitoribus suis. In thes. x s. Et debet vj li. et iiij s. per annum x s.

Simon de Emeteshell' debet xl d. pro plegio. + Thomas de Etton' debet j m. pro summonendo Ingelramo sicut continetur in rotulo iiij^{o}. + Walterus Bade debet j m. ut tradatur in ballio. + Rannulfus de Emetewell' debet dim. m. pro plegio.

Homines de Esingewald' [*blank*] ij m. et dim. pro habendo mercato.

Willelmus de Tikehill' et socii sui debet [*sic*] dim. m. pro habendo brevi sicut continetur in rotulo iiij^{o}. Comitatus Ebor' debet C m. pro habendo respectu. + Willelmus de Norewic' debet j m. pro vino vendito.

Rogerus de Monte begon' [*blank*] xxij m. et dim.

Robertus de Percy r.c. de lvij li. et viij s. et vj d. et ob. de pluribus debitis contentis in rotulo iiij^{o}. In thes. x m. per Eustachium. Et item x m. per R. de Bass'.[2] Et debet xliiij li. et xxij d. et ob. per annum xx m.

Robertus de Ros junior debet v m. quia interfuit cum patre suo ad feras capiendas in Galtris (set respondet in Norhumberland' in rotulo sequenti^{i}).[3] + Willelmus de Neovill' debet xl s. pro eodem. Willelmus de Boeles debet viij m. de ij debitis contentis in rotulo vij^{o}. *Set respondet infra.*

Willelmus Burdet r.c. de xl s. pro feris captis in Galtris. In thes. lib. Et Q.E.

Willelmus Hairun r.c. de v m. pro eodem. In thes. iiij m. Et debet j m.

Adam de Stavele r.c. de l s. de scutagio Pict' de honore de Cnarresburg'. In thes. lib. Et. Q.E.

Nicholaus persona de Trailli persona de Tichemers debet xx m pro leporariis habitis contra assisam. + Thomas de Etton' debet dim. m. pro licencia concordandi cum J. de Surdeval. + Petrus de Centumputeis debet v m. pro defalta sicut continetur in rotulo vij^{o}.

Abbas de Seleby r.c. de x m. pro habenda custodia abbatie sue. In thes. lib. Et Q.E.

Petrus de Brus r.c. de lxxiiij li. et xvj s. In thes. xl m. Et debet xlviij li. et ij s. et viij d. per annum xl m.

1 The amount is missing.

2 The writing is smudged at this point but it looks as though the clerk has written either *Bass'* or *Basf'*.

3 This interlineation possibly belongs to this item but there is no obvious point to indicate where it should go with a '^' in the text.

DE PLACITIS FORESTE

Willata de Hoby debet j m. de misericordia.

Johannes de Aivill' debet v m. pro contemptu. Henricus de Neovill' de Burreðe debet xl m. pro eodem. Malveisin de Hersin debet v m. pro eodem. Willelmus de Molbray debet v m. pro eodem. Walterus de Soureby debet l m. pro eodem. Yllaria Trussebut debet x m. pro veteri vasto (set respondet infra[i]).[1] Nicholaus de Anesty r.c. (de[i])[2] v m. pro eodem. In thes. lib.

Et Q.E.[3]

Fulco f. Warini r.c. de v m. pro contemptu. In thes. nichil. Et in perdona ipsi Fulconi v m. per breve R. Et Q.E.

Gillebertus de Aquila r.c. de v m. pro eodem. In thes. lib. Et Q.E.

Idem Vic. r.c. de xxx li. de villata de Scardeburg de tallagio. Et de ix m. de villata de Driffeld' de eodem. Et de x m. de Burgensibus de Hedon'. In thes. lib. Et Q.E.

Ricardus de Percy debet j m. pro habendo brevi de attingendis xij sicut continetur in rotulo viij.

Willelmus de Givedal' r.c. de x m. pro habenda saisina. In thes. lib.

Et Q.E.

Robertus Ingelram et Johanna uxor eius r.c. de v m. pro summonendo Ricardo de Percy. In thes. iiij m. Et debet j m.

Willelmus de Boeles r.c. de viij m. sicut supra continetur. In thes. nichil. Et in perdona ipsi Willelmo viij m. per breve R. quod est in forulo marescalli in Notingehamsir'. Et Q.E.

DE AMERCIAMENTIS ET IMBLADIAMENTIS PER B. DE INSUL'

Idem Vic r.c. de viij s. et ix d. de maiore Huntinton'. Et de viij s. et iiij d. de villata de Esingwald'. In thes. lib. Et Q.E.

Ricardus f. Swani r.c. de xx s. de fine. In thes. dim. m. Et debet j m. Set Simon de Hal respondet infra pro eo.

Prior Sancte Trinitatis r.c. de xij s. pro bosco. In thes. (xij[e]) vj s. Et debet vj s.

Willata de Holteby debet dim. m. pro nova frussura. Villata de Flexton' debet v s. et vj d. et ob. pro vj acris. Villata de Cotingwid' debet viij s. et iiij d. pro vasto. Thomas de Fuleford' debet v m. pro transgressione. Prior de Giseburn' debet[4] x m. pro domibus et fossatis. Villata de Grimeston' debet x s. pro novo essarto. Canonici de Wartr' debent vj s. et vj d. pro xiij acris.

Simon de Hal r.c. de j m. de Ricardo f. Swani sicut supra continetur. Et de v m. de magistro de Wicham. Et de j m. de Hugone Ami. Et de v s. de Hugone pincerna. Et de l m. sicut infra continetur. In thes. nichil. Et in perdona ipsi S. xxxviij li et v s. pro brevi[5] R. pro pluribus

1 Again there is no indication as to where this interlinear item goes.

2 *r.c.* is written over an erasure.

3 *Et Quietus Est* written for *Et Quieti Sunt*.

4 *debet* is repeated in error.

5 *pro brevi Regis* written for *per breve Regis*.

expensis suis ann[otatis] in eodem brevi quod est in forulo marescalli in anno sequenti.

Et Q.E.

Idem Vic. r.c. de dim. m. de Ricardo de Sproxton' de Mungumeri. Et de dim. m. de eodem R. de scutagio de Bedeford'. Et de ij m. de Johanne Malebiss' de scutagio de Bedef'. Et de v m. et xx d. de Henrico de Neovill' de Burreðe de scutagio de Mungumeri. In thes. lib. Et Q.E.

Yllaria Trussebut r.c. de vj li. et j m. de scutagio Pict' de feodis de Trussebut. Et de lvij s. et x d. et ob. de eodem scutagio de feodis de Wartr'. Et de vj m. et viij s. et xj d. de primo scutagio de feodis Trussebut. Et de xxxix s. et iij d. de eodem feodis de Wartr'. Et de vj m. et viij s. et xj d. de scutagio de Mungumeri de feodis Trussebut. Et de xxxix s. et iij d. de feodis de Wartr'. In thes. in rotulo v^{o} in Everwikesir' vj m. et viij s. et xj d. Et iterum in thesauro in rotulo ix^{o} in Lincoll' v m. Et in perdona ipsi Hillarie in rotulo viij^{o} in Linoll' [*sic*] ij m. per breve R. Et debet xiij li. et v s. et iij d. et ob. Eadem r.c. de eodem debito. In thes. lvj s. et viij d. et ob. Et debet x li. et viij s. et vij d. Set respondet in Linoll'sir'.

[*One line blank*]

DE OBLATIS

Idem Vic. r.c. de dim. [m.] de Willelmo de Lascell' pro habendo pone. (Et de x m. de hominibus de Clopton' pro pastura exolenda,[1] sicut continetur in rotulo precedenti[c]) (quia infra[i]). Et de ij m. de Thoma Hay pro habendo brevi. Et de dim. m. de Willelmo de Lainethorp. Et de j m. de Willelmo de Sothill'. Et de dim. m. pro Roberto de Wauton'. In thes. lib.

Et Q.E.

Homines de Clopton' r.c. de xx s. de firma pasture de Brakinthweit et Sores, sicut continetur in rotulo precedenti, in linea cancellata. In thes. lib.

Et Q.S.

Robertus de Bereford' debet xx s. pro iniusta detentione versus Sigritham que fuit uxor Ricardi f. eiusdem Roberti.

Ricardus Mansellus r.c. de vj li. et ix s. et iiij d. de debitis Judeorum. In thes. j m. Et debet C et xvj s. per annum j m.

Nicholaus de Stutevill' debet xlv li. de pluribus debitis contentis in rotulo precedenti.

Idem N[icholaus] r.c. de lxxj li. de debitis Judeorum. In thes.

Simon de Hal r.c. de C m. de pluribus debitis contentis in rotulo precedenti. In thes. xxv m. Et debet lx(x[i])v m. Idem r.c. de eodem debito. In thes. nichil. Et in perdona ipsi S[imoni] xxv m. per breve R. Et debet l m. (*Set respondet supra*[i])[2]

Homines de Scalleby r.c. de x m. pro habenda pastura in haya de Scalleby quamdiu R. placuerit reddendo inde annuatim xx s. In thes. v m. Et debent v m.

Robertus de Veteri ponte debet M et DCCCC et quater xx et xvij li. et

[1] Recte *excolenda*.

[2] This is written very faintly above the end of the main text.

xj s. et vj d. et v dextrarios de precio pro v doliis vini, sicut continetur in rotulo compotorum in anno precedenti.

Brianus de Insula [*blank*] lxxvij li et xix s. et iij d. de pluribus debitis contentis in rotulo precedenti.

Homines de Clopton' r.c. de x m. pro pastura excolenda, sicut supra continetur.

NOVA OBLATA

Willelmus f. Olive debet j m. pro habendo brevi de attingendis xij juratoribus assise nove dissaisine capte apud Ebor' coram justiciariis assignatis contra Henricum de Huperun et Ricardum Thom' de communa pasture in Soureby.

Thomas de Blumvill' debet C m. pro habenda custodia et maritagio filie et heredis Radulfi de Killingthorp (set respondet in Norf' in rotulo sequenti[i]),[1] qui de R. tenet in capite in Killingthorp si escaetor[2] possit ei liberare terram quam predictus Radulfus tenuit de Petro de Malo lacu, et si non possit dabit R. xl m. pro predicta custodia et maritagio. Hugo Pudding' de Ebor' et Willelmus de Camera de Beverlac' debent x m. pro habendo brevi ad inquirendum utrum Agnes que fuit uxor Mathei Malpalu invita et pregnans vi susceperit habitum relligionis hospitalis Sancti Leonardi Ebor' et vi detineatur in eodem hospitali, an ea gratis in dictum hospitale sororem se reddiderit. Petrus de Touleston' debet xx s. pro habendo brevi de attingendis xij juratoribus de tenemento in Eketon'. Stephanus de Crancewic debet dim. m. pro summonendo Thoma de Crancewic ad tenendum conventionem de terra in Crancewic'.

Willelmus Haget r.c. de xl s. pro falso clamore versus moniales de Molseby per plegium Gilleberti Fluri de Comitatu Linc'. In thes. xx s. Et debet xx s.

Nicholaus de Yeland' debet dim. m. pro licencia concordandi cum Johanne de Torenton'. Willelmus Malesoeures debet j m. pro eodem cum Stephano de Mesnill'. Ranulfus f. Henrici debet dim. m. pro eodem cum Alexandro le Brett.

Idem Vic. r.c. de dim. m. de Simone de Mohaut pro licencia concordandi. Et de dim. m. de Willelmo de Mohaut pro eodem. Et de xx s. de abbate de Melsa pro eodem. Et de dim. m. de Ricardo de Beverlac' pro eodem. Et de dim. m. de Alexandro le Bret pro eodem. Et de dim. m. de Widone Basset pro eodem. In thes. lib. Et Q.E.

W. comes Albe mar' debet l m. pro iniusta detentione versus Willelmum f. Eustachii (in itinere Thome de Haiden'[i]).[3] Ricardus de Percy debet xx m. pro dissaisina in itinere Roberti de Laxinton'. Petrus de Maullay debet xl

1 Again there is no insertion indicator.

2 This is an uncertain reading.

3 There is no indication of Thomas Heyden ever leading an eyre in Yorkshire, or anywhere else. The last eyre in Yorkshire for this Pipe Roll was in 1218–9. See D. Crook, *Records of the General Eyre* (London, 1982), pp. 75–6. There was an eyre started in October 1226 for Yorkshire but he was not present for that county: ibid., pp. 78–9. It is possible that he was appointed to lead an assize in Yorkshire between the eyre of 1218–9 and this Pipe Roll. There is no mention of it in the Patent Rolls.

m. pro eodem in eodem itinere. Willelmus de Percy debet x m. pro falso clamore in eodem itinere.

Homines de Scalleby r.c. de xx s. de firma pasture in haya de Scalleby sicut supra continetur. In thes. lib. Et Q.S.

AMERCIAMENTA PER ROBERTUM DE LAXINTON' ET SOCIOS SUOS[1]

Idem Vic. r.c. de CCCC et quater xx et v m. et vij s. et viij d. de misericordiis hominum et catallis fugitivorum et suspensorum quorum nominibus preponitur littera *T*[2] in rotulo, quem predicti [justiciarii] liberaverunt in thesauro. In thes. lib. Et Q.E.

[3]Walterus de Schelton' r.c. de dim. m. pro defalta. In thes. xl d. Et debet xl d.

[*Rot.* 1d *Mem.* 2]

[4]Willata de Catteby r.c. de j m. pro eodem. In thes. x s. Et debet xl d.

Odardus f. Henrici r.c. de x m. quia retraxit se. In thes. v m. Et debet v m.

Jacobus f. Gilleberti r.c. de xx s. ut sit sub plegio. In thes. j m. Et debet dim. m.

Robertus de Neuby r.c. de dim. m. pro defalta. In thes. ij s. Et debet iiij s. et viij d.

Willata de Notton' r.c. de iij s. et vj d. de catallis deine. In thes. iij s. Et debet vj d.

Idem Vic. r.c. de xl s. et iiij d. de catallis Thome f. Hugonis. In thes. ij m. et (dim.[i]) Et debet dim. m. set respondet infra.

Galfridus f. Willelmi servientis r.c. de j m. pro dissaisina. In thes. dim. m. Et debet dim. m.

Jordanus Foliot r.c. de xx s. pro eodem. In thes. x s. Et debet x s.

There is a mention in a heading of 'Thomas Heyden and his associates' in *NS* 54, p. 96 for Essex.

1 This cannot be the eyre in Yorkshire in 1226–7 as Robert de Lexinton was not part of the judicial team for this county. Also according to Crook it took place after this accounting period. See Crook, *Records of the General Eyre*, pp. 78–9. He was not involved in the 1218 eyre in Yorkshire either.

2 This means that those persons that have fully paid their debt via the sheriff are marked with a letter 't' for *totales* on the Pipe Roll. See *Receipt Rolls – NS* 55, p. xxxiv for Nicholas Barratt's explanation of the system of marginal letters on the Pipe Roll. Those debts marked with a 't' in the previous Pipe Roll have now been settled in this Pipe Roll as a bulk payment by the sheriff. Those debts marked with a 't' in this Pipe Roll will be cleared in 11 Henry III Pipe Roll etc. Unfortunately, for the Yorkshire membrane there are no letter marginations down the left hand side of the membrane because they are either hidden by the strengthening material or they have worn away. Where there are two items of debt shown on the same line the marginated letter is shown on the right hand entry only.

3 The following items are written on the left hand side of the membrane only.

4 There is stitching right across the membrane at this point. There is some overlapping of the stitched membranes, which has obscured some of the text.

[1]*d* Galfridus de Mikelefeld' r.c. de dim. m. quia non habuit. In thes xl d. Et debet xl d.
[2]+ Johannes f. Hugonis r.c. de dim. m. pro eodem. In thes. xl d. Et debet xl d.
d Willelmus de Birkethwett r.c. de dim. m. pro eodem. In thes. ij s. Et debet iiij s. et viij d.
d Robertus Maresc' r.c. de dim m. pro eodem. In thes. xl d. Et debet xl d.
t Villata de Scallebroc r.c. de xvij s. iiij d. ob. de catallis. In thes. xiij s. vj d. Et debet iij s. x d. ob.
p Idem Vic. (Eustachius[i]) r.c. de viij s. de catallis Wadin. In thes. viij d. Et debet vij s. et iiij d. fin'.[3]
(*p*[i]) Thomas le furbur r.c. de ij m. ut sit sub plegio. In thes. j m. Et debet j m.
t Robertus de Alkesia r.c. de dim. m. quia non habuit. In thes. xl d. Et debet xl d.
t Robertus pistor r.c. de dim. m. pro dissaisina. In thes. xl d. et debet xl d.

[4]Thomas Turpin r.c. de dim. m. quia non habuit quem plegiavit. In thes. lib. Et Q.E.

Idem Vic. r.c. de dim. m. de catallis Thome f. Hugonis sicut supra continetur. Et de dim. m. de Rannulfo f. Hugonis de Merkinton' quia non habuit quem plegiavit. Et de dim. m. de Radulfo f. Ricardi de Hille de Haukewell' pro eodem. Et de dim. m. de Gilleberto del Wro pro dissaisina. Et de dim. m. de Patricio de Westdal' pro falso clamore. Et de iij s. de villata de Stubbhus de catallis Alexandri plumbarii de Notton' fugitivi. Et de xx s. de villata de Bifford' de catallis Rogeri Bacu[n] fugitivi. In thes nichil. Et fratribus militie templi lvj s. et iiij d. per libertatem carte R. Et Q.E.

Idem Vic. r.c. de j m. de Gregorio de Hugat' quia non habuit. Et de dim. m. de Adam Bataill' pro falso clamore. Et de dim. m. de Willelmo de Hugat' quia non habuit. Et de xl s. de priore de Malton' quia non est prosecutus. Et de dim. m. de priore de Elreton' pro eodem. Et de dim. m. de Adam Bataille quia non habuit. Et de dim. m. de Willelmo de sancto Jacobo quia non habuit. In thes. nichil. Et monialibus de Simplingeh' ij m. et dim. per libertatem carte R. Et Q.E.

Simon de Staingrive r.c. de C m. de fine quem fecit coram predictis justiciariis pro morte Johannis Witspere unde rettatus fuit. In thes nichil. Et in perdona ipsi Simoni C m. ad se sustentandum in servicio R. per breve R. Et Q.E.

Abbas de Beyland' r.c. de xl s. pro falso clamore. In thes. nichil.

Rogerus f. Stephani debet dim. m. quia non habuit. (*d*[i])[5] Alanus f. Michaelis de Westingeby debet dim. m. pro defalta. (*d*[i]) Rogerus forestarius

1 The following items are written on the right hand side of the membrane only.

2 This item is totally obscured by the overlapping flap caused by the stitching over the two membranes together.

3 A different clerk has written this word. It could be either *finis* or *finem*.

4 The following entries are written across the whole membrane.

5 The clerk has inserted the prefixing letter above the line of the item, noting what is to happen to the debt. See *Receipt Rolls – NS* 55, p. xxxiv. There should probably be one for the first item but it is missing because the left hand edge has worn away.

debet dim. m. pro eodem. (*t*[i]) Johannes pictor debet dim. m. pro eodem. (*d*[i]) Willelmus frater Roberti de Pikehal' debet dim. m. quia non habuit. (*t*[i]) Willelmus f. Warini de Asquith' debet x s. quia retraxit se, per plegium Simonis de Cykeshou et Alexandri de Torenton'. (*d*[i]) Rogerus f. Roberti de Frestun' de valle de Pikering' debet dim. m. quia non habuit. (*d*[i]) Nicholaus f. Helewis' debet dim. m. quia non est prosecutus per plegium Galfridi mercerii et Willelmi f. Rogeri. (*d*[i]) Marsil' de Engelby debet dim. m. quia non habuit. (*d*[i]) Johannes f. Hugonis de Tresc debet dim. m. quia non est prosecutus. (*d*[i]) Hugo f. Hugonis de Tresc debet dim. m. pro eodem. (*d*[i]) Herbertus de Mildeby debet dim. m. quia non habuit. (*t*[i]) Silvester de Hamerton' debet dim. m. pro eodem. (*d*[i]) Adam persona de Melingfliet debet xl s. pro dissaisina. (*d*[i]) Idem Vic. debet iij s. de catallis Alani de Besacr' fugitivi. Et x s. et ix d. de catallis Malgeri de Stokbrige fugitivi. Et ij s. de catallis Ricardi de Benetile fugitivi. (*t*[i]) Villata de Friston' debet iiij s. et vj d. de catallis Ranulfi Scalle fugitivi. (*t*[i]) Villata de Norton' debet iij s. de catallis Willelmi Schortred. (*d*[i, c]) Villata de Barneslay debet xv d. de catallis Ricardi f. Ivonis. (*d*[i]) Idem Vic. debet ix s. de catallis Hugonis molendinarii fugitivi. (*d*[i]) Rogerus de Bulrum debet dim. m. ut sit pro plegio per plegium Joscei de Bulrum et Hugonis fratris eius. (*t*[i]) Johannes le Mascun de Doddeworde' debet dim. m. quia non habuit. (*d*[i]) Johannes f. Walding' debet dim. m. quia non est prosecutus per plegium Sampsonis de Pumeray et Johannis clerici de Clyve. (*d*[i]) Henricus de Merkinton' debet dim. m. quia non est prosecutus. (*t*[i]) Philippus de Colevill' debet dim. m. pro eodem. (*d*[i, c]) Jordanus de Scholand' debet dim. m. ut sit sub plegio per plegium Rannulfi f. Henrici. (*p*[i]) Willelmus Slecht debet dim. m. pro eodem per plegium Alexandri de Witun' et Roberti f. Alani de Sutton'. (*p*) Bartholomeus de Oterinton' debet viij m. quia non habuit. (*t*[i]) Ricardus prepositus de Sandal' debet dim. m. pro eodem. (*d*[i]) Johannes serviens de Sandal' debet dim. m. pro eodem.

Villata de magna Wirkeshal' debet dim. m. pro defalta. Rogerus f. Liolf' debet dim. m. pro eodem. Ricardus Metcorn' debet dim. m. pro eodem. Gillebertus de turribus debet dim. m. pro eodem. Radulfus de Longaker debet dim. m. pro eodem. Villata de Leke debet dim. m. pro eodem. Robertus de Hulmo debet dim. m. pro falso clamore. Walterus f. Herberti de Spaldinton' debet dim. m. quia non habuit. Michael de Screingeha' debet dim. m. pro eodem.

[I]dem Vic. debet xxxij s. et vj d. de catallis Roberti Hod fugitivi. Villata de Marton' debet xxx s. et vj d. de catallis Ivonis de Marton' fugitivi.

Villata de Oteringeham debet ij m. de catallis Willelmi Warin' fugitivi.

[J]ohannes constabularius Cestr' r.c. de quater xx et ix li. et x s. de scutagio Pict' de feodis suis propriis. Et de xl li. de eodem scutagio de feodis Guidoni de Laval. In thes. nichil. Et in perdona ipsi Johanni C et xxix li. et x s. per breve R. Et Q.E.

[I]dem J[ohannes] debet vij li. et dim. m. de primo scutagio R. de feodis de Lascy. Et xl m. de eodem de feodis de Laval'. Et ij m. de eodem de j feodo in Sneid'. Et xxxiij s. et viij d. de catallis plurium utlagatorum contentis in rotulo anni vj.

[Y]llaria Trussebut r.c. de x m. pro veteri vasto sicut supra continetur. In thes. v m. Et debet v m.

[*One line blank*]

[1]*[K]arolus f. Willelmi et Margareta uxor eius debent dim. m. ut scribatur in magno rotulo quod Robertus f. Johannis de Ry venit coram baronibus de scaccario et ibi remisit et quietum clamavit predicto Karolo et Margarete uxori sue et heredibus suis totum jus et clamium quod habuit vel habere potuit in omnibus terris illis quas predictus Karolus et Margareta uxor eius tenent in Brigenhal' et in Clif cum omnibus pertinenciis suis et in terra de Grethingeham cum medietate advocationis ecclesie eiusdem ville, quam idem Carolus tenet cum (aliis*[i]*) pertinenciis suis sine aliquo impedimento in quibus idem Robertus aliquando putabat se ius habere habendas et tenendas imperpetuum eidem Karolo et Margarete uxori sue et heredibus suis libere quiete pacifice, sine omni molestia et clamio et exactione de predicto Roberto et heredibus suis. Et quod hanc remissionem et quietam clamanciam fecit predictus Robertus predicto Karolo et Margarete uxori sue et heredibus suis coram Martino de Pateshill' et aliis justiciariis de banco apud Westm'. Et pro hac remissione et quieta clamatione predicti Karolus et Margareta dederunt eidem Roberto xl m. argenti.*

[*Rot.* 2 *Mem.* 1]

ESSEX' ET HERTFORD'

Willelmus de Culeworðe' ut custos r.c. de DC et xlv li. et ij s. et iiij d. bl. de firma Comitatuum. In thes. quater xx et xviij li. et xvij s. et v d. bl.

Et in elemosinis constitutis militibus de Templo iiij m. Et infirmis de Sancto Albano xxx s. et v d. Et in liberatione constituta Matill' de Herlaue nutrici R. J. vj li. et xx d. Et Godefrido Spigornell' xlv s. et vij d. et ob. Et Roberto de Alemann' lx s. et x d. Et Walwano nuncio lx s. et x d. Et Roberto scutellario lx s. et x d. Et Willelmo de Stiviton' xxx s. et v d. Et Arnaldo caretario xlv s. et vij d. et ob. Et Eve nutrici fratris R. xxx s. et v d. Et Waltero capellano ministranti in capella Sancti Stephani Westm' l s. Et Ricardo Turnevielle xxx s. et v d. Et Gilleberto Fael xxx s. et v d. Et infirmis de Meaudon' xxx s. et v d. Et E. episcopo Lond' x li. et xvij d. in Meaudon'. Et Willelmo de Landa x li. et xvij d. in eadem villa. Et Roberto Mantel vij s. et v d. in eadem villa. Et in quietantia redditus abbatisse de Berking' in hundredo de Beghentr' lx s. Et E. episcopo Lond' xij li. in hundredo de Tendring ad custodiam castri Colecestr'. Et priori de Hadfeld' quater xx et x li. (*set respondet infra*[i]) in Hadfeld' (*de quibus respondet infra*[i]).[2] Et in Havering' C et x li. bl. de quibus homines ville respondent infra. Et in villa de Writel' C et xx li. bl. de quibus compotus redditur per se. Et in villa de Neuport xl li. bl. de quibus compotus redditur per se. Et in Esenden' et Beiford' xx li. de quibus Ricardus de Argentoem (pro custodia

[1] This is a fine written in a different hand and probably later than the original. It has not been possible to locate the fine in any of the three volumes of *Calendar of Fine Rolls* printed for the reign of Henry III.

[2] It looks as though a clerk has indicated the same thing in two separate places. It looks as if they are different clerks from the handwriting.

castri de Hertford'c) respondet infra. Et eidem xj li. in molendino de Hertford' de quibus respondet infra. Et in villa de Hertford' xx li. de quibus homines ville respondent infra. Et G. de Clara comiti Hertford' xxxiij li. et xx d. de tercio denario Comitatus. Et Ricardo de Ripariis C s. in hundredo de Angre. Et priori de Hadfeld' quater xx et x li. in Hadfeld' de quibus respondet infra, set amodo non debet allocari in corpore Comitatus nisi quater xx li. tantum quia sic allocatum fuit B. de Lucy tempore R. H. avi R. et postea extensum ad C s. ultra tercio anno R. J. quando datum fuit Pagano de Rocheford'[1] tempore R. huius ad alios C s. pro decimis eiusdem manerii sicut continetur in rotulo anni tercii R. huius.

Et Ricardo de Argentoem constabulario de Hertford' x li. ad portam castri de Hertford' reparandam per breve R. Et eidem Ricardo xx m. ad operationem castri eiusdem per breve eiusdem. Et in carriagio domus marescalcie de parva Berchamsted' usque ad Hertfeld' et in custo posito ad eam erigendam infra predictum castrum xviij li. iiij s. et j d. per breve eiusdem. Et debet xj s. et ij d. bl. Idem r.c. de eodem debito. In thes. lib. Et Q.E.

f' [*One line blank*]

Idem Vic. r.c. de x s. de firma propresture de Dinesle quam Willelmus Pollard' tenuit. In thes. nichil. Et priori (hospitalis[i]) Sancte Marie de Wimundele x s. per breve R. quamdiu R. placuerit. Et Q.E.

f' Idem Vic. r.c. de xxxix li. et ix s. de proficuo Comitatus hoc anno. In thes. ix li. et ix s. Et ipsi Vic. ad expensas suas adquietandas xxx li. Et Q.E.

[*One line blank*]

f' Abbas de Wautham r.c. de lx li. de firma de Wautham. In thes. lvij li. x s. et viij d. Et in terra quam Ricardus f. Alcherii tenet xlix s. et iiij d. Et Q.E.

f' Prior Sancte Trinitatis Lond' r.c. de iiij s. de firma de Cornéé. In thes. lib. Et Q.E.

f' Idem Vic. r.c. de v s. de firma de Birchhangr'. In thes. lib. Et Q.E.

f' Robertus la Waite r.c. de xiij d. de firma j virgate terre sicut continetur in rotulo viij R. J. qui debent dari in elemosinam per manum thesaurarii. Lib. thesaurario. Et Q.E.

f' Abbas de Strafford' r.c. de xxxj li. et xij d. de firma de Subir' et de Hamme. In thes. lib. Et Q.E.

Willelmus f. Rogeri (Galfr'[i])[2] Bataill' r.c. xvj li. (et j m.[i]) de misericordia patris sui. In thes. dim. m. Et debet xvj li. et dim. m.

Hawisia de Lanval' r.c. de C et lxij li. et xviij s. de ij^{bus} debitis contentis in rotulo xvj^{o} R. J. In thes. l s. Et debet C et lx li. et viij s.

S. Cant' archiepiscopus r.c. de CC et xix li. et iij s. et iiij d. de ij^{bus} debitis contentis in rotulo precedenti. In thes. xx m. Et debet CC et v li. et xvj s. et viij d. Set respondet infra.

Radulfus de Bello campo *debet* C et xvij li. et iij s. et iiij d. sicut

[1] Something is crossed out after this name.

[2] It is unclear why the clerk inserted this interlinear name as in previous volumes William is only shown as the son of Roger Bataill'. It might be possible that Geoffrey Bataill' is also rendering account along with William.

continetur in rotulo vij^{o}. *Set Nicholaus filius suus respondet pro eo in Cantebrig'sir*.

Ricardus Furmin (*Abbas de Oseneie pro eo*[1]) r.c. de xxj m. pro habenda uxore sicut continetur in rotulo x^{o} R. J. *In thes. per eundem abbatem lib. Et Q.E.*[1]

Hugo de Bosco debet xxx li. et x s. sicut continetur in rotulo ix^{o} R. J. Abbas de Sancto Albano debet CCC m. de misericordia foreste in Everwikesir'. Thomas de Neovill' clericus debet xij li. de scutagio Pict' sicut continetur in rotulo vj^{o}.

Radulfus Gernun r.c. de quater xx et v li. et iij s. et iiij d. de iij^{bus} debitis contentis in rotulo viij^{o}. In thes. x m. Et debet lxxviij li. et x s. *Set respondet in dorso*. per annum x m.[2]

Thomas de Danmartin [*blank*] xiiij s. et v d. et ob. de pluribus debitis contentis in rotulo vij^{o}.

Radulfus le Moinne r.c. de xxxv s. et viij d. de pluribus debitis contentis in rotulo viij^{o}. In thes. j m. Et debet xxij s. et iiij d.

Ricardus de Munfichet de Wendlington' r.c. de xiij li. iiij s. et v d. pro dissaisina. In thes. ij m. Et debet xj li. et xvij s. et ix d.

Vitalis Engainne r.c. de vj m. et dim.[3] pro Roberto de Curten' pro essarto facto sine Licencia. In thes. xl s. Et debet xlvj s. et viij d.

Mauricius de Borham et Odo Burnard' heredes Alexandri f. Geroldi debent xlij s. et iiij d. de debitis Ááron pro eodem Alexandro. Set respondent in Buking'.

Willelmus de Alegat' r.c. de quater xx et ix m. et vij s. et viij d. de misericordia patris sui. In thes. xx s. Et debet lviij li. xiiij s. et iiij d. Idem r.c. de eodem debito. In thes. dim. m. et debet lviij li. (et vij s. et viij[4] d.[1]) [5]

Sampson f. Laurencii de Tiebrig' r.c. de l li. et ij s. pro transgressione patris sui. In thes. xx s. Et debet xlix li. et ij s. per annum xx s.

Helto Faucillun r.c. de xxj li. et xj s. et viij d. de pluribus debitis contentis in rotulo precedenti. In thes. ij m. et dim. Et debet xix li. et xviij s. et iiij d. Set respondet infra.

Robertus Mantel r.c. de CCCC et xlij li. et xviij s. et vij d. et ob. de pluribus debitis contentis in rotulo viij^{o}. In thes. xx m. per Abbatem de Meaudon'. Et debet CCCC et xxix li. et xj s. et xj d. et ob. per annum xx m.

Philippus f. Hugonis r.c. de xvj li. et ij s. et viij d. pro patre suo ut deliberetur á prisona. In thes. x s. Et debet xv li. et xij s. et viij d.

Rogerus de Merkeshal' r.c. de xj s. et viij de relevio suo. In thes. dim. m. Et debet v s. Idem r.c. de eodem debito. In thes. lib. Et Q.E.

Willelmus f. Hugonis de Berchamsted' debet xx s. ut possit venire ad pacem. Willelmus Cokainne debet C m. ut deliberetur á prisona.

1 The items in italics were written in a different hand from the main text.

2 There is a line under this phrase as though it has been crossed out by the clerk but the line may also have been partially rubbed out as it is very faint.

3 From 'r.c.' to this footnote in the text there is smudging on the membrane.

4 Inserted over an erasure.

5 There is no obvious insertion sign here but the remainder of the sum owing is shown at the extreme right hand side of the membrane on the line above.

Radulfus f. Rogeri de Ging' r.c. de iiij li. et ij d. pro festinando judicio. In thes. xl s. Et debet xl s. et ij d.

Johannes de Hadfeld' [*blank*] ij m. ut tradatur in custodia sicut continetur in rotulo xiij^{o}. Ricardus f. Hugonis et Matill' uxor eius r.c. de C et quater xx et vij m. et dim. et ij palefridis pro habenda saisina. In thes. v m. Et debet C et quater xx et ij m. et dim. et ij palefridos. per annum v m. + Stephanus f. Reginaldi debet dim. m. pro falso clamore. + Willelmus le Prouz debet dim. m. pro dissaisina. + Galfridus f. David et Robertus f. Roberti debent xx s. ut sint extra prisonam. + Willelmus Hosatus et Edricus telarius debent xx s. quia non habuerunt quem plegiaverunt. + Adam f. Sigar debet dim. m. pro habenda inquisitione. Robertus de Cornevill' debet iij m. pro defalta (*set respondet infra*^{i}).[1] Radulfus f. Roberti de Hockel' debet viij s. et iiij d. pro resummonenda assisa (*set respondet infra*^{i}).[2] Villata de Chingeford' debet dim. m. pro defalta foreste (*set respondet infra*^{i}).[3] Robertus de Mara debet xx s. pro habendo precipe. Robertus Mantel debet C et xij s. pro Matheo fratre suo de minutis particulis foreste dum idem M[atheus] fuit Vic. sicut continetur in rotulo xvj^{o}.

Laurencius de Boueries r.c. de dim. [m.] quia non est prosecutus. In thes. lib. Et Q.E.

Saherius Bataill' r.c. de xxxvj li. et j m. de pluribus debitis contentis in rotulo ij^{o}. In thes. iiij m. Et debet xxxiiij li per annum iiij m.

Heres Henrici Pelerin r.c. de xx li. et iiij s. et viij d. de ij^{bus} debitis contentis in rotulo (prec^{c}) viij. In thes. ix s. Et debet xix li et xv s. et viij d.

Ricardus f. Hugonis r.c. de xix m. (de^{c}) pro plegio Bertram de Aubineio. In thes. j m. Et debet xviij m. per annum j m.

Idem Vic. r.c. de xl s. de Roberto de Cornevill' pro defalta foreste sicut supra continetur. Et de dim. m. de Herberto capellano, G. de Bocl[and] pro eodem sicut infra continetur. In thes. nichil. Et in perdonis predictis R. et H. iij m. et dim. per breve R. Et Q.E.

DE PRESTITO PICTAVIE

Radulfus f. Roberti de Hockel' r.c. de viij s. et iiij d. sicut supra continetur. In thes. iiij s. Et debet iiij s. et iiij d.[4]

Willelmus de Stok' debet xiiij m. et dim. de eodem. Robertus de Mar' debet xj m. de eodem. Henricus de Gray debet xliiij m. de eodem. Willelmus de Lanval' debet xxxvij m. de eodem. Rogerus de Neovill' debet viij m. de eodem pro milite suo. Willelmus Tresgoz debet vij m. de eodem pro milite suo. Willelmus de Haya debet v m. (et dim.^{i}) de eodem. Johannes de Rochef' debet vij m. de eodem. Ricardus f. Willelmi debet vij m. de eodem pro milite suo. Fulco de Cant'lupo debet xij m. de eodem

1 This is very faint and looks to be in a different hand.

2 There is some rubbing of the word '*set*' and also some smudging of the name prior to the interlinear words.

3 The interlinear words are in a different hand.

4 The following passage is on the same line as the heading, presumably added later. It is in the same hand as the rest of the document.

pro milite suo. Radulfus Chednedoit debet ij m. de eodem. Willelmus de Curton' debet xij m. de eodem.

Ricardus de Ripariis r.c. de D et xvj li. et x s. et ij d. de pluribus debitis contentis in rotulo viij. In thes. x li. Et debet D et vj li. et x s. et ij d.

per annum x li.

Radulfus Gernun debet viij li. et xiij s. et viij d. et ob. (*set respondet in dorso*[i]) de ij firmis contentis in rotulo viij^{o}. Et xx s. (de catallis[i]) Walteri le Cunte (*set respondet ibidem*[i]) fugitivi qui requirebatur in Wiltes'[1] in itinere M. de Pateshill'. Et iiij m. et x s.[2] (*set respondet ibidem*[i])[3] de ij^{bus} scutagiis contentis in rotulo precedenti.

Vitalis Engainne [*blank*] lj li. et xij s. et vj d. de iij^{bus} debitis contentis in rotulo precedenti.

Godefridus de Lovain debet xx li. de scutagio Pict' de feodis de Eistan'. Et xiiij m. et dim. de primo scutagio R. Et lxx s. de scutagio de Byham.

Helto Faucillun r.c. de xix li. et xviij s. et iiij d. de pluribus debitis contentis in rotulo precedenti. In thes. ij m. et dim. Et debet xviij li. et v s. Et iiij li. de debitis Judeorum qui requirebatur in Judaismo.

per annum v m.

Andreas de Helyun debet iij m de scutagio Pict' de dominico suo (set respondet infra[i]). Johannes f. Petri de Stanford' debet xx s. pro habendo precipe (set respondet in Kent[i]). Willelmus Rufus de Dilce debet dim. m. pro iniusta detentione (set respondet in Kent[i]). + Galfridus Bacun debet dim. m. pro falso clamore sicut continetur in rotulo vij^{o}.

Johannes camerarius r.c. de xxij s. et xj d. de ij^{bus} debitis contentis in rotulo precedenti. In thes. lib. Et Q.E.

+ Radulfus f. Alicie de Reindon' debet dim. m. pro habenda assisa sicut continetur in rotulo primo. Baldewinus constabularius Bolon' debet xv li. pro habenda saisina de Sopiland' sicut continetur in rotulo ij^{o}. + Willelmus de Taiden' debet dim. m. pro licencia concordandi.

Robertus f. Philippi debet quater xx et v m. pro habenda gratia R. J. Ricardus de Ripariis debet xxviij s. et v d. de remanenti compoti sui de Eston' Falkesii de Breaut'. Et xxiij s. et vj d. de compoto de Neweton' eiusdem (qui requirebatur in R. compotorum[i]).[4]

Ricardus de Borham et Richard de Stapelford' [*blank*] x m. pro Eborardo de la Boveriere pro habenda custodia sicut continetur in rotulo primo.

Henricus Buckesfot r.c. de dim. m. pro habendo brevi. In thes. lib.

Et Q.E.

1 There is no mention in Crook, *Records of the General Eyre* for this county during the eyre of 1218–22. It is possible that Pattishall visited it as an assize justice. It has not been possible to find a reference in the Patent or Close Rolls of his appointment. There is a further mention of Walter and Ralph Gernun in Wiltshire below.

2 There is possibly a faint insertion mark between the '*x*' and '*s.*'. However, it should be after the '*s.*'.

3 The items in italics, although they appear to be in the same hand, may have been added later as they are written in a lighter ink.

4 This insertion is on the line below with an insertion sign at the end of the line after *eiusdem*. The insertion also has a line from the end of the insertion to the end of the line above.

Gillebertus camerarius [*blank*] dim. m. pro habendo appello apud Westm' per plegium Radulfi Gernun.

Ricardus de Munfichet r.c. de lvj li. de pluribus scutagiis contentis in rotulo viij^{o}. In thes. xx m. Et debet xlij li. et j m. per annum xx m.

Robertus de Mara debet ij m.[1] de primo scutagio R. Ricardus de Bromfeld' debet xv s. et viij d. de iij^{bus} debitis contentis in rotulo ij^{o}.

S. archiepiscopus Cant' r.c. de CC et v li. et xvj s. et viij d. de ij^{bus} debitis sicut supra continetur. In thes. xl li. Et debet C et lxv li. et xvj s. et viij d. de quibus Stephanus nepos eius debet amodo respondere.

per annum xl (j^{d}) m.[2]

[*Rot.* 2 *Mem.* 2]

[*One line blank*]

Thomas Bainnard' r.c. de iiij li. et iiij s. et vj d. et ob. de pluribus scutagiis contentis in rotulo vij^{o}. In thes. xl s. Et debet xliiij s. et vj d. et ob. per annum xl s.

Willelmus Pinel r.c. de iiij s. pro dissaisina. In thes. ij s. Et debet ij s.

Philippus de Hertford' r.c. de xxiij s. et iiij d. pro summonendo comite Gloec'. In thes. xx s. Et debet iij s. et iiij d.

Thomas de Stansted' r.c. de xvj d. pro transgressione. In thes. lib.

Et Q.E.

Hugo et Walterus de Gellham debent dim. m. pro falso clamore. + Johannes nepos Willelmi de Gellham debet x s. pro eodem. + Simon de Cramfeld' debet dim. m. pro iniusta detentione. (+^{i}) Robertus Bridd debet dim. m. quia non est prosecutus. + Willelmus Diaconus debet dim. m. pro vino vendito. + Godefridus clericus et Elicia uxor eius debent dim. m. quia non est [*sic*] prosec[uti] + Ricardus parmentarius et Willelmus Godefr' debent dim. m. pro plegio. + Ricardus f. Friede debet dim. m. pro dissaisina. + Hugo et Willelmus potarius debent dim. m. pro plegio. Johannes de Essartis debet dim. m. pro plegio. + Johannes f. Walteri debet dim. m. pro licencia concordandi. + Alina de Bernar' debet dim. m. pro falso clamore. Decena Roberti Plot debet dim. m. pro plegio. + Ricardus f. Dier' debet j m. pro transgressione. + Galfridus de Martiwas debet dim. m. pro plegio. + Hundredum Dacorum debet xxj s. pro murdro. Hundredum de Rocheford' debet xl s. pro eodem. Walterus de Bures [debet] dim. m. pro plegio. Willelmus de Tichenho debet xl d. de fine.

Rogerus Bagod et Ricardus de Pelham r.c. de dim. m. pro licencia concordandi. In thes. lib. Et Q.S.

Guido de Chasteillun comes de Sancto Paulo debet C. li. pro relevio suo. (Willelmus de Moncell'^{c}) (Robertus de Cerne^{i})[3] debet xliiij s. et v d. pro habenda feria sicut continetur in rotulo iij^{o}. + Robertus caretarius

[1] There is smudging from the beginning of this line to this footnote in the text.

[2] There is an indication of something rubbed out. It is '*j*'. There is an indication by u/v at TNA of something else rubbed out which is '*m*'. In *NS 54*, p. 100 it indicates that payment is 40 marks a year.

[3] In *NS 54*, p. 105 Robert is shown as having paid in some money, not that he is partially responsible for the debt.

et Alicia uxor eius debent dim. m. pro habendo pone sicut continetur in rotulo vj^{o}.

Ysabella comitissa Oxon' r.c. de MM et C et xxxij li. et xj d. de pluribus debitis contentis in rotulo vj^{o}. In thes. CCCC li. Et debet M et DCC et xxxij li et xj d. per annum CCCC li.

Eadem Y. debet xxvij li. et vj s. et vij d. et ob. pro comite Albric' de minutis particulis foreste dum fuit Vic. Et vj li. et x s. de ij^{bus} scutagiis contentis in rotulo precedenti de honore Bolon'.

Willelmus f. Cristine debet dim. m. pro plegio. + Gillebertus de Soppa debet dim. m. pro eodem. + Alienor' filia Roberti debet quartam partem de xx m. pro summonenda Matillide sicut continetur ibidem. + Hugo de Luiton' debet ij m. pro summonendo Roberto sicut continetur ibidem. + Willelmus f. Turstani debet iiij m. pro habendo pone sicut continetur ibidem. (+[i]) Simon de Esenden' debet dim. m. pro plegio. Galfridus clericus de Bisseie[1] debet dim. m. pro falso clamore.

[R]adulfus[2] le Brett r.c. de lxij s. et iiij d. de pluribus scutagiis contentis in rotulo vj^{o}. In thes. x s. Et debet lij s. et iiij d. per annum x s.

[A]lina de Ardern' [*blank*] xxj s. et x d. de eisdem scutagiis.

[N]icholaus f. Wigani Bruton' r.c. de xxiiij li. et viij s. de fine pro patre suo sicut continetur in rotulo vij^{o}. In thes. dim. m. Et debet xxiiij li et xx d. per annum dim. m.

[R]obertus de Pinkeinni r.c. de lvij s. et ix d. pro relevio suo sicut continetur in rotulo viij. In thes. xl s. Et debet xvij s. et ix d.

[G]alfridus de Ardern' [*blank*] C s. de ij^{bus} debitis contentis in rotulo precedenti. (Et deb'[d])

Hugo de Balleol' r.c. de CC et xlviij li. de pluribus debitis contentis in rotulo vij. Et xj li. et dim. m. de iij(*bus scutagiis honoris Bolon'*[i]) contentis in rotulo precedenti. *Set respondet in Norhumberland' in rotulo sequenti.*[3]

[H.] de Neovill' debet v milia marcarum pro habenda benevolentia R. Et lxxvij li. de cremento de Gillingeh' de pluribus annis preteritis. Set non debet summoneri donec R. preceperit.

G. comes de Clar'[4] r.c. de CC et lxiiij li. et xix s. et iij d. de scutagio Pict' de feodis de Clar'. Et de CC et xiiij m. et xij s. et viij d. de eisdem feodis de primo scutagio R. Et de CCC et xlviij li. et j m. de pri[mo][5] scutagio R. de honore Glovernie. Et de xlvj li. de scutagio Pict' de medietate honoris comitis Giffard'. Et de quater xx et vj m. de primo scutagio R. de medietate eiusdem honoris. Et de xiij li. de scutagio Pict' de maritagio matris sue. Summa DCCC et lxxiij li. et v s. et iij d. In thes. nichil. Et in superplus quod idem comes habet in rotulo vj anni R. post Norhumberland' C et quater xx et iiij li. et xiij s. et iij ob. Et in firma de la Berton' extra B[...] á crastino sancti Clementis[6] anno vij^{o} R. usque ad

1 In *NS 54*, p. 106 he is shown as Geoffrey the clerk of *Busseie* (or *Bussey*).
2 The left edge of the membrane has been torn, losing the initial capital in this and following entries.
3 This is written in a different hand and is fainter than the rest of the passage.
4 See *NS 54*, p. 107 for the same passage.
5 The very right edge of the membrane has been lost at this point.
6 Tuesday 24 November 1222.

festum sancti Michaelis anno eiusdem x^{o}[1] scilicet per iij annos C et xxij li. et xviij s. et iiij d. et ob. scilicet quolibet anno xl li. xix s. et v d. et ob. Et debet Dlxv li. xiij s. et ix [d.]

Radulfus de Tóóni debet xiiij li. et j m. de iiij debitis contentis in rotulo precedenti (*set respondet ex alia parte rotuli*[i]). Et (*de*[i]) C li. pro habenda custodia terre et heredis Hugonis Poinz qui requirebatur in Kent in rotulo precedenti. Et iij m. de ij^{bus} debitis contentis in Gloec' in rotulo precedenti.

Herbertus capellanus G. de Bocland' debet dim. m. pro defalta in foresta. (*Set respondet supra.*) + Reginaldus de la Ruede debet xx s. quia fuit contra vadium et plegium. Johannes episcopus Elyensis debet iij m. pro habenda inquisitione. + Hubertus porcarius[2] de Horkeleg' debet dim. m. pro novo essarto et proprestura. + Thomas capellanus debet j m. pro novo essarto. G. comes Glovern' debet xxxiij li. et xv s. de carrucagio assiso ad ij s. in Gloec'sir'. Et xxvij li. et xiiij s. de eodem in Surr' sicut in rotulo de eo[dem].[3]

Idem Vic. r.c. de xlviij s. et xj d. et ob. de minutis particulis foreste. In thes. vij d. et ob. Et abbati Colecestr' ij s. et vj d. per libertatem carte R. Et debet xlv s. et x d.

Gervasius de Aldermannebir' r.c. de iiij li. pro summonendo Thoma de Bavelingeh'. In thes. xx s. Et debet lx s.

Ricardus f. Radulfi et Johannes frater eius [*blank*] iij s. et viij d. pro transgressione.

Johannes de Ginges r.c. de x m. de prestito ei facto sicut continetur in rotulo viij^{o}. In thes. xxiij s. et iiij d. Et debet C et x s.

Osmundus capellanus debet dim. m. pro habendo pone sicut continetur in rotulo vij^{o}. (Alicia de Brette'[c]) + Bartholomeus de Wokindon' debet dim. m. pro defalta. Robertus faber de Colecestr' debet dim. m. pro concordia facta sine licencia.

Alicia de Brettewell' r.c. de dim. m. pro defalta. In thes. lib. Et Q.E.

Ricardus f. Alexandri et Ricardus de Wudewic' r.c. de dim. m. ut sint quieti de plegio. In thes. lib. Et Q.E.[4]

Johannes de Cornere[5] debet dim. m. pro habendo brevi contra Willelmum Faucillun (*sed respondet in Norf' in rotulo sequenti.*[i]).[6] + Hugo de Cant'lup' debet j m. pro habendo recordo. Sibilla de Francheterre debet j m. pro summonendo Henrico [de Bures][7] sicut continetur in rotulo viij^{o}.

Villata de Neweport r.c. de xx s. et viij d. de tallagio ultimo assiso. In thes. dim. m. Et debet xiij s. et viij d.

Ricardus Brunus de Colecestr' debet dim. m. pro licencia concordandi. + Ricardus f. Walteri debet dim. m. pro licencia concordandi. + Ricardus

1 Tuesday 29 September 1226.
2 *parcarius* in *NS 54*, p. 107.
3 The strengthening tape has masked the rest of the word.
4 *Et Quietus Est* written for *Et Quieti Sunt*.
5 In *NS 54*, p. 109 he is shown as John de Coidmeres.
6 This is written in a different hand and is fainter than the rest of the passage.
7 Supplied from *NS 54*, p. 109.

f. Ailrich' debet j m. pro eodem. Gillebertus de Oddewell' debet dim. m. pro habendo pone.

Robertus de Turevill' [*blank*] lxj s. pro habenda saisina sicut continetur in rotulo viij^{o}. Et x s. pro Nicholao f. Henrici f. Fulcherii quem habet in custodia reddendo infra annum undecimum per breve R.

Amicia que fuit uxor Rogeri de Mescing' r.c. de v m. ut possit se maritare. In thes. j m. Et debet iiij m.

Adam Wille r.c. de xl d. pro dissaisina. In thes. lib. Et Q.E.

Villata de Chingeford' de parte canonicorum Sancti Pauli Lond' r.c. de dim. m. pro defalta sicut supra continetur. In thes. nichil. Et ipsis canonicis dim. m. per libertatem carte R. Et Q.E.

Villata de Colecestr' [*blank*] xj li. de ultimo tallagio.

Villata de Hertford' r.c. de j m. de eodem. In thes. nichil. Et priori hospitali Jerl'm j m. de Clemente de Hertford' hospite eorum per libertatem carte R. Et Q.E.

Hugo de Neovill' r.c. de xxxviij li. et j m. pro habenda medietate manerii de Stokescurci. In thes. xx m. Et debet xxv li. et dim. m.

Andreas de Helyun r.c. de iij m. de scutagio Pict' sicut supra continetur. In thes. lib. per ij taleas de ante guerram allocatas per H. de Burgo justiciarium coram R. Cycestr' cancellario R. et J. Bathon' episcopo. Et Q.E.

DE SCUTAGIO MILITUM HONORIS BOLON'

Baldewinus de Ripar' r.c. de xvj li. et j m. de iij^{bus} scutagiis contentis in rotulo precedenti. In thes. nichil. Et in perdona ipsi Baldewino x m. de scutagio Bedef' per breve R. Et debet x li.

Robertus de Pinkeinni r.c. de quattuor m. de scutagio Pict'. In thes. x s. Et[1] debet xliij s. et iiij d.

Milo de Sumeri r.c. de xxij s. et ij d. et ob. de ij scutagiis contentis ibidem. In thes. j m. Et[2] debet viij s. et x d. et ob.

Beatricia de Lucy [*blank*] xxj s. et j d. de iiij^{or} scutagiis contentis ibidem.

Henricus de Merc r.c. de ix li. de iij scutagiis contentis ibidem. In thes. ij m. et dim. Et debet vij li. et dim. m.

Willelmus de Criketot r.c. de iiij m. de eisdem scutagiis sicut continetur ibidem. In thes. xx s. Et debet ij m. et dim.

Ricardus de Witsand' r.c. de xx s. de ij scutagiis contentis ibidem. In thes. dim. m. Et debet j m.

Maria Malegreffe r.c. de iij m de predictis scutagiis. In thes. lib. Et Q.E.

Alulphus de Bouton' [*blank*] xl s. de scutagio Pict'.

Johannes f. Bernard' r.c. de lvj s. et viij d. de predictis scutagiis. In thes. dim. m. Et debet l s.

Warinus de Bassingeburn' r.c. de xx s. de eisdem scutagiis. In thes. lib. Et Q.E.

Comes de Gisnes debet lix li. et x s. de iiij^{or} scutagiis contentis in rotulo

1 Smudged.
2 Smudged.

precedenti. Hugo de Cant'lup' debet viij li. et xx d. de eisdem scutagiis. Margareta de Creissi debet xlv li. et x s. de eisdem scutagiis.

Sibilla de Fiednes r.c. de xxxv li. et dim. m. de eisdem scutagiis. In thes. xx s. per Guidonem de Hathfeld' et Willelmum de Marci. Et xxvj s. per Gillebertum de Breautéé. Et debet S[ummam] xxxiij li. et viij d. Set respondet in Surr'.

Ingelramus de Merc r.c. de ix li. et xvj s. et viij d. de predictis scutagiis. In thes. j m. Et debet ix li. et iij s. et iiij d.

Johannes de Blendec r.c. de lxxviij s. et iiij d. de eisdem scutagiis. In thes. j m. Et debet lxv s.

Thomas de Dammartin[1] r.c. de lix s. et viij d. de eisdem scutagiis. In thes. dim. m. per ipsum T[homam]. Et x s. per Gillebertum de Sancto Claro. Et debet T. xliij s.

[A]lexander[2] de Brichtlinges' debet xlviij s. et x d. de eisdem scutagiis de feodis Triket. Baldewinus de Oistewic debet xxj li. et v s. de eisdem scutagiis contentis ibidem. Set Johannes de Vallibus tenet terram ipsius B. de Ballio R. quamdiu (R. placuerit et non debet summoneri donec R. aliud preceperit.[i])[3]

[W]illelmus Rufus r.c. de xlj s. et viij d. de eisdem scutagiis. In thes. x s. Et debet xxxj s. et viij d. (*Set respondet in dorso rotuli.*[i])

[R]obertus de Tresgoz debet xx li. et j m. de eisdem scutagiis (set respondet in Heref' in Wallia.[i]) Johannes de Merc debet x li. et dim. m. de eisdem scutagiis. (Et xx s. de scutagio de Biham.[i]) Canonici Sancte Trinitatis Lond' debent iij m. et dim. de eisdem scutagiis.

[P]rior Sancti Botulph' Colecestr' r.c. de xl s. de scutagio Pict'. In thes. lib. Et Q.E.

[E]gidius de Merc r.c. de C et viij s. de pluribus scutagiis contentis ibidem. In thes. (xx s.[e]) ij m. Et debet iiij li. et xvj d. Idem r.c. de eodem debito. In thes. ij m. per Radulfum de Carevill'. Et debet liiij s. et viij d. (set respondet in dorso rotuli.[i])

[R]adulfus de Rouecestr' r.c. de xiiij li. et dim. m. de eisdem scutagiis. In thes. C s. (Et debet[i]) ix li. et dim. m.

[Her]es Comitis H. le Bigod' debet xiij li. et dim. m. de ij scutagiis contentis in rotulo precedenti. Johannes de Borham debet xl s. de scutagio Pict'.

Ricardus de Ripariis [*blank*] x li. de ij scutagiis contentis ibidem.

Executores testamenti Nicholai de Anesti r.c. de iiij li. et dim. m. de pluribus scutagiis contentis ibidem. In thes. nichil. Et in perdonis ipsis executoribus iiij li. et dim. m. per breve R. in quo continetur quod Willelmus de Musterell' et Engelram f. eius concesserunt per cartam suam quam predicti executores protulerunt coram baronibus Huberto armigero avo predicti Nicholai maneria de Radewell' et Gellham per xv li. per annum, ita quod si aliquod scutagium exigatur de predictis maneriis computabitur in predicta firma xv li. Et Q.S.

1 There is a smudge over the second *a* in '*Dammartin*'.
2 The left edge of the membrane is damaged from this point; initial capitals have been lost in a number of cases.
3 This is on the line below as an insertion at the end of that item.

[G]alfridus de Fercles r.c. de vij li. et dim. m. de eisdem contentis ibidem. In thes. xxvj s. Et debet vj li. et viij d.

[Wi]llelmus de Haya [*blank*] vj li. et j m. de ij^bus scutagiis contentis ibidem.

Hugo de Neovill' et Rollandus de Axsted' [*blank*] x li. de scutagio Pict', scilicet Hugo iiij li et Rollandus vj li, (*set respondet in Surr'*^i) sicut recognoverunt coram baronibus scaccarii.

[Idem] H. [*blank*] vij m. de ij scutagiis contentis ibidem.

[Ro]bertus f. Walteri debet xl s. de scutagio Pict'.

[H]ugo f. Ascelini r.c. de xj s. et iiij d. de pluribus scutagiis contentis ibidem. In thes. iij s. et iiij d. Et debet viij s.

RESPICE IN TERGUM

[*Rot.* 2d *Mem.* 1]

W. de Mandevill' comes Essex' debet x s. de scutagio Pict'. Willelmus de Kayheu debet xx s. de eodem. Milo de Sumeri et Emma de Marcy et Robertus de Pinkeinny debent j m. de primo scutagio.

Philippus f. Ascelin' r.c. de v m. de pluribus scutagiis contentis in rotulo precedenti. In thes. j m. Et debet iiij m. Idem r.c. de eodem debito. In thes. nichil. Et in perdona ipsi Philippo ij m. de scutagio de Bedef' per breve R. Et debet ij [m.][1]

Henricus f. Alcherii r.c. de xix s. et ij d. de iij^bus scutagiis contentis ibidem. In thes. x s. Et debet ix s. et ij d.

Hamo de Crievequer debet iiij li. et j m. de ij scutagiis contentis ibidem. Set non debet summoneri propter causam ex alia parte rotuli annotatam super executores testamenti Nicholai de Anesti. Et W. episcopus Lond' episcopus [*sic*] quietus est de lxx s. de scutagio primo R. per eandem causam de eodem feodo. Fratres militie Templi debent iij m. de primo scutagio. Radulfus Gernun debet x m. pro claudendo bosco deleit, sicut continetur in originali de anno ix.

f' Hamo de Crievequer r.c. de x li. de firma de Claret' de eodem honore de termino Sancti Andree et Sancti Johannis. In thes. lib. Et Q.E.

f' Walterus de Langeton' qui habet in uxorem filiam et heredem Nicholai de Anesti [*blank*] xv li. de firma Radewell' eiusdem honoris.

f' Ysabella comitissa Oxon' r.c. de x li. de firma de Gelham eiusdem honoris. Et de C s. de remanenti eiusdem firme de anno preterito. (*de termino Sancti Andree et Sancti Johannis.*^e) In thes. x li. Et debet C s. (*In thes. lib. Et Q.E.*^e)

f' Willelmus Britto de Chiggewell' r.c. de iiij d. de firma cuiusdam terre in Iclinton' eiusdem honoris. In thes. lib. Et Q.E.

Idem Vic. r.c. de lx s. de perquisitis eiusdem honoris de toto anno. In thes. lib. Et Q.E.

Egidius de Merc r.c. de liiij s. et viij d. de pluribus scutagiis[2] contentis

[1] Membrane damaged at this point.

[2] There is something rubbed out between *scutagiis* and *contentis*. It is not possible

ex alia parte rotuli. In thes. xxviij s. per Radulfum de Carevill'. Et debet ij m.

DE SCUTAGIO DE MUNGUMERI DE FEODIS MILITUM DE COMITATU

Thomas Bainnard' debet v m. de ij scutagiis contentis in rotulo precedenti. Galfridus de Saukevill' debet ij m. de scutagio de (Mungumeri[c]) Bedeford' de j feodo Peverell' qui requirebatur in Noting' in rotulo precedenti. (Set habuit quietantiam per breve R. in Oxon'[i])

Johannes camerarius r.c. de j m. de scutagio de Mungumeri. In thes. lib. Et Q.E.

Willelmus de Reimes debet xvj m. de eodem. Adam de Herdeberg' debet xx s. de ij[bus] scutagiis contentis ibidem. Andreas de Helyun debet j m. de scutagio de Mungumeri. Set postea habuit quietantiam per breve R.

Robertus de Mara r.c. de ij m. de eodem. In thes. dim. m. Et debet xx s.

Willelmus de Pesemere r.c. de dim. m. pro iniusta captione. In thes. xl d. Et debet xl d.

Abbatissa de Berking' r.c. de dim. m. pro licencia concordandi. In thes. lib. Et Q.E.

Radulfus de Tóóni r.c. de xiiij li. et j m. sicut continetur ex alia parte rotuli. In thes. nichil. Et ipsi Radulfo xiiij li. et j m. in parte solutionis C m. quas percipit per annum ad se sustentandum in servicio R. per breve R. Et Q.E.

DE OBLATIS

f' Prior de Hadfeld' r.c. de C li. de firma manerii de Hadfeld' sicut continetur in rotulo precedenti. In thes. lib. Et Q.E.

Idem prior r.c. de quater xx m. pro habendo predicto manerio ad talem firmam. In thes x m. (… s[e])[I] Et debet lxx m.

Idem prior debet xxxvj li. de (venditione[c]) (precio[i]) bladi et affrorum et bovum inventorum in eodem manerio sicut continetur in rotulo precedenti.

Radulfus f. Nicholai [*blank*] xliiij (s.[i]) de precio viij bovum et iiij affrorum Hugonis de Cant'lupo apud Smetheton' inventorum, scilicet quilibet bos iiij s. et quilibet affrus iij s. sic appreciatorum per breve R.

Idem Vic. r.c. de dim. m. de Johanne de Bernieres. Et de dim. m. de Sampsone f. Fulconis. Et de xx s. de Abbatissa de Berking'. In thes. lib. Et Q.E.

Rogerus de Wenaveston' r.c. de x m. pro habenda in uxore filia Briani le Ewier. In thes. v m. Et debet v m.

Willelmus Rufus r.c. de xxxj s. et viij d. de pluribus scutagiis contentis ex alia parte rotuli. In thes. nichil. Et in perdona ipsi Willelmo j m. de dim. feodo de scutagio Bedef' per breve R. Et debet xviij s. et iiij d.

---

to say what it is.

I The amount of shillings rubbed out has not been possible to determine.

NOVA OBLATA

f' Prior hospitalis Sancte Marie de Wimundele r.c. de x s. de firma terre quam Willelmus Pollard' aliquando tenuit in Dineslé quam R. ei concessit per talem firmam quamdiu sibi placuerit. In thes. lib. Et Q.E.

Matheus de Lovain [*blank*] l li. pro relevio suo de feodis x militum que Godefridus pater suus tenuit de R. in capite et que ipsum hereditarie contingunt et de quibus R. cepit homagium suum per plegium Henrici de Crammovill', Willelmi de Arden', Roberti de Wauton', Willelmi de Herlaue, Willelmi de Blancmustier, Willelmi de Wauton', Warini f. Gilleberti, Willelmi de Hispania.

Robertus de Pinkeinni et Milo de Sumeri [*blank*] x m. pro relevio suo de terra que fuit Biatricie de Lucy amite ipsorum Roberti et Milonis unde R. cepit homagia ipsorum.

Idem Vic. r.c. de dim. m. de Hugone fabro de Fering' pro licencia concordandi cum Rogero f. Willelmi. Et de dim. m. pro eodem cum Matillide. Et de dim. m. de Gilleberto de Lond' de Clarette pro eodem cum Radulfo dispensario. Et de dim. m. de Simone de Pirhou pro eodem cum Johanna de Waleden'. Et de (xx s.^{c}) (j m.^{i}) de Willelmo de Mulesham pro eodem cum Willelmo de vij^{tem} fontibus. In thes. lib. Et Q.E.

Thomas f. Stephani debet dim. m. pro habenda inquisitione per plegium Roberti de Basing'. Robertus Archerius de Tappelaw' debet xx s. pro eodem per plegium Ricardi Reinger maioris Lond'. Radulfus Gernun debet j m. pro eodem (set respondet infra^{i}) cum Ricardo de Munfichet.

Warinus de Rumford' r.c. de j m. pro transgressione per plegium Willelmi de Markedich'. In thes. dim. m. Et debet dim. m.

Ricardus de Munfichet debet j m. pro licencia concordandi cum Radulfo Gernun. Simon Blundus de Lond' debet dim. m. pro ij^{bus} acris de pastura sua in Ginges claudendis.

Robertus Bainnard' debet dim. m. (set respondet in Norf' in rotulo sequenti^{i}) pro eodem cum Johanne f. Walteri. Nicholaus (de Turevill' debet^{c})[1] (f. Henrici f. Fulcherii^{i}) x s. pro eodem cum David de Sandervill'. Set respondet supra.

Idem Vic. r.c. de x s. de David de Sandervill' pro eodem cum Nicholao f. Henrici. Et de dim. m. de Luca le Moinne pro eodem cum Gilleberto le Moinne. Et de x s. de Ricardo f. Ricardi de Lesceuechirche pro eodem cum Bernero de Rothom'. Et de x s. de eodem Bernero pro eodem. In thes. lib. Et Q.E.

Radulfus Gernun [*blank*] lxxviij li. et x s. de iij^{bus} debitis de quibus finem fecerat sicut continetur ex alia parte rotuli. Et viij li. et xiij s. et viij d. et ob. de ij^{bus} firmis sicut continetur ibidem. Et xx s. de itinere M. de Pateshill' sicut continetur ibidem (set respondet in Wiltes' in rotulo sequenti^{i}.) Et dim. m. pro Gilleberto camarario sicut continetur ibidem (set respondet in rotulo sequenti^{i}.) Et x m. pro leporariis captis. Et iiij m. et x s. de ij^{bus} scutagiis de honore Bolon' sicut continetur (ibidem^{i}.) Et j m. pro licencia concordandi sicut supra continetur. per annum x li.

Idem R. r.c. de iiij palefridis pro habenda saisina terre Willelmi de

[1] This has wrongly been underlined for deletion.

Suðechirche. Et de xx (s.ⁱ) pro quodam essarto faciendo in Taiden'. In thes. nichil. Et in perdonis ipsi Radulfo iiij palefridis et xx s. per breve R. in quo continetur quod protestatum est coram R. quod nec saisina terre illius habuit nec essartum illud fecit. Et Q.E.

Hugo de Marines r.c. de xvij li. de debitis Judeorum. In thes. C s. Et debet xij li.[1] per annum C s.

Galfridus de Matham r.c. de xvj li. et x s. et ij d. de eodem. In thes. xxxv s. Et debet xiiij li et xv s. et ij d.

Radulfus de Bosay r.c. de xxxvj li. et xvj s. et viij d. de eodem. In thes. dim. m. Et debet[2] xxxvj li. et x s.

Thomas Picot r.c. de (xxᵈ) xxiij li. et xvij s. et viij d. de eodem. In thes. x s. Et debet (xᵈ) xxiij li. xvij s. et viij d.[3] Idem r.c. de eodem debito. In thes. x s. Et debet xxij li. et xvij s. et viij d. per annum xx s.

Gillebertus Anglicus r.c. de l li. et iij s. de eodem. In thes. xl s. Et debet xlviij li et iij s.

Johannes de Bassingeburn' r.c. de ij m. de eodem. In thes. lib. Et Q.E.

Warinus Quentin r.c. de viij li. et j m. de eodem. In thes. ij m. Et debet vij li. et dim. m.

W. de Mandevill' comes Essex' [*blank*] MMM et DCC et quater xx et viij li. et xvij s. et iij d. de pluribus debitis contentis in rotulo precedenti.

Radulfus Gernun tunc Vic. Dorset' debet viij s. de catallis Johannis parmentarii et sociorum suorum fugitivorum qui requirebatur in Dorset' in itinere M. de Pateshill'[4] et sociorum suorum.

Ricardus de Argentoem r.c. de vj li. de remanenti compoti sui de villa de Hertford' et aliorum contentorum in rotulo precedenti. In thes. nichil. Et in donis ipsi Ricardo vj li. ad se sustentandum in servicio R. per breve eiusdem. Et Q.E.

f' J. de Ric' [*blank*] xx (ijᵈ) li. de firma de Esenden' et de Beiford'. Et [*blank*] xj li. de firma molendini de Hertford'.

E. Lond' episcopus r.c. de xx li. quas recepit de W. quondam Lond' episcopo qui illas receperat ad garnisturam castri de Colec'. In thes. nichil. Et in operatione predicti castri xx li. per breve R. et per visum Radulfi clerici et Galteri Ursi. Et Q.E.

f' Burgenses de Hertford' r.c. de xx li. de firma ville sue. In thes. nichil. Et Ricardo de Argentoem constabulario castri Hertford' x li. ad operationem eiusdem castri de dim. anno per breve R. Et eidem Ricardo x li. de alio dim. anno ad custodiam eiusdem castri et amodo totum donec (Rexⁱ) aliud preceperit per breve eiusdem. Et Q.S.

1 There looks like some rubbing of the 'x' and the 'l' in this amount.

2 There has been some rubbing out here.

3 This is a repeat of the original debt amount. There has been much rubbing on the membrane here.

4 This might relate to the eyre of 1218–22, but according to Crook, *Records of General Eyre*, p. 73 Pattishall did not take the eyre in Dorset in 1218 nor did he take it in 1227, the next eyre. This was taken by Thomas of Moulton. Pattishall was perhaps intended to take the circuit in which Dorset appears in the eyre of 1226–9 but was replaced by Moulton. One other possibility is that a gaol delivery was undertaken by Pattishall when Ralph Gernun was sheriff of Dorset. It has not been possible to find a reference to Pattishall being in Dorset prior to Michaelmas 1225.

f' Homines de Colecestr' r.c. de xl (li.^{i}) bl. de firma ville sue. In thes. xxxj li. viij s. iiij d. (bl.^{i}). Et in elemosinis constitutis monachis de Colecestr' xx s. Et in defalta iiij^{or} monetariorum iiij li. Et in defalta bosci de Kingeswode xl s. Et anachorite Sancti Jacobi xv s. et ij d. et ob. Et debent xxiiij s. et ij d. (v^{d}) et ob. bl. Idem r.c. de eodem debito. In thes. lib. Et Q.S.

[*One line blank*]

Idem homines [*blank*] C et lxviij li. et xvj d. de veteri tallagio. Et [*blank*] vij li. de novo tallagio.

Nicholaus f. Walteri r.c. de l s. et iiij d. de misericordia. In thes. xx s. Et debet xxx s. et iiij d.

Henricus f. Gode debet dim. m. pro vino vendito. Palmerius debet x s. de eodem. Manasserus debet dim. m. pro eodem. Johannes de Leircestr' debet dim. m. pro eodem.

f' Homines de Havering' r.c. de C et x li. bl. de firma ville de Haveringe sicut continetur in rotulo precedenti. In thes. lxxvij s. et vj d. bl. Et in elemosinis constitutis canonicis de Sancto Bernardo xxv li. Et Hospitali de Gravesand' j m. in terra que vocatur Leghe. Et Henrico de Taiden' xx s. pro excambio bosci de Taiden'. Et Johanni de Cantuar' xxx s. et v d. (Et Johanni de Cantuar' xxx s. et v d.^{c}) Et in cremento parci de Havering' ij m. et dim. Et Johanni capellano ministranti in capella R. de Havering' l s. Et Willelmo parcario xlv s. et vij d. et ob. ad custodiam domorum R. de Havering'. Et fratribus Hospit' Jerl'm' lxxv li. et iiij s. et viij d. per breve R. in parte solutionis arreragiorum denariorum eis debitorum de CCC m. quas Regi commodaverunt apud Bedeford'. Et Henrico f. Alcherii ij m. per breve (R.^{i}) ad emendationem domorum R. de Havering'. Et debent ix s. et viij d. et ob. bl. Idem r.c. de eodem debito. In thes. lib. Et Q.S.

H. de Neovill' [*blank*] quater xx et iij li. et xvj s. et vj d. et ob. de pluribus debitis contentis in rotulo precedenti post Roteland'.

AMERCIAMENTA DE ITINERE SIMONIS DE HAL[1] ET SOCIORUM EIUS

[*One line blank*]

Prior Hospit' Jerl'm' [*blank*] xx m. pro dissaisina.

Ricardus de Chileham debet xx m. pro eadem (set respondet in Kent in rotulo sequenti.^{i})[2] Didonius de Estwude debet dim. m. quia non est prosecutus. Heres Gilleberti Grossi debet xx s. pro patre suo quia non habuit.

Idem Vic. r.c. de lxxvij m. et x s. et x d. de eodem itinere in Essex. Et de xxxiiij m. et viij s. et viij d. de eodem itinere in Hertfordschir' de misericordiis hominum decenarum villarum et de catallis fugitivorum quorum nominibus preponitur littera *t* et quorum debita et cause debitorum

[1] This must relate to a separate visit to the county for the purpose of holding an assize and gaol delivery as it is too early for the eyre in Essex and Hertfordshire from October–December 1227. There is no evidence in Crook that he took part in the earlier eyre of 1218–22. See Crook, *Records of General Eyre,* pp. 71–86 for both eyres. We can find a reference to this assize being set up on 30 August 1225. See *Patent Rolls 1216–1225,* 599.

[2] This is written in different ink and possibly by a different clerk.

annotantur in rotulo quem predicti liberaverunt in thesauro. In thes. lib. In CC et j talea. Et Q.E.

d [1]Henricus Gurnin r.c. de dim. m. pro defalta. In thes. xl d. Et debet xl d.

[*One line blank*]

[*Rot.* 2d *Mem.* 2]

d Warinus de Rumford' r.c. de dim. m. quia non est prosecutus. In thes. v s. Et debet xx d.

p Willelmus f. Huberti r.c. de dim. m. pro defalta. In thes. xl d. et debet xl d.

t Willelmus de Gelham r.c. de dim. m. quia non est prosecutus. In thes. xl d. Et debet xl d.

t Matill' relicta Walteri r.c. de dim. m. pro eodem. In thes. xl d. Et debet xl d.

t Robertus Maresc' r.c. de dim. m. pro eodem. In thes. xl d. Et debet xl d.

t Godefridus f. Bricii r.c. de dim. m. pro eodem. In thes. xl d. Et debet xl d.

t Johannes parvus r.c. de dim. m. pro dissaisina. In thes. xl d. Et debet xl d.

d Johannes Wigge r.c. de dim. m. pro plegio. In thes. xl d. Et debet xl d.

(Galfridus de Westbir' r.c. de dim. m. pro eodem. In thes.[c]) quia inter totale. Et debet [*blank*]

d Hamo dispensator r.c. de dim. m. pro defalta. In thes. xx d. Et debet v s.

Gervasius de Aldermannebir' r.c. de xl s. pro eadem. In thes. dim. m. Et debet ij m. et dim. (set respondet post Warewic').

p Nicholaus de Uting' r.c. de dim. m. pro eadem. In thes. ij s. Et debet iiij s. et viij d.

t Helto Faucillun r.c. de dim. m. pro dissaisina. In thes. iiij s. iiij d. Et debet ij s. et iiij d.

t Johannes f. Willelmi r.c. de j m. pro eodem. In thes. dim. m. Et debet dim. m.

t Prior de Colum r.c. de C s. pro pluribus dissaisinis. In thes. lxxv s. Et debet xxv s.

t Ricardus Panel r.c. de dim. m. pro plegio. In thes. iij s. Et debet iij s. et viij d.

t Walterus f. Swani r.c. de dim. m. pro eodem. In thes. iij s. Et debet iij s. et viij d.

p Radulfus Anglicus r.c. de j m. pro falso clamore. In thes. dim. m. Et debet dim. m.

t Willelmus f. Petri r.c. de j m. pro dissaisina. In thes. iiij s. Et debet ij s. et viij d.

t Hugo f. Mathei r.c. de dim. m. pro defalta. In thes. xl d. Et debet xl d.

p Willelmus de Wrestling'worðe r.c. de dim. m. pro eodem. In thes. [*blank*] Et debet [*blank*].

[*Rot.* 2d *Mem.* 1]

1 The following entries are written on the left hand side of the membrane only.

[1]*t* Algarus et Ricardus potarii r.c. de j m. ut sint sub plegio. In thes. dim. m. Et debet dim. m.
[*One line blank*]

[*Rot.* 2d *Mem.* 2]

p Thomas Golding' r.c. de lx (s.[i]) et j d. pro recreantis'. In thes. xx s. Et debet xl s. et j d.
t Decena Alexandri Rufi r.c. de dim. m. pro fuga. In thes. ij s. Et debet iiij s. et viij d.
t Decena Germani de Reindon' r.c. de dim. m. pro eodem. In thes. vj s. Et debet viij d.
Galfridus f. Simonis (r.c. de [c]) v m. ut habeat veredictum. In thes. [*blank*] Et debet [*blank*] Set respondet infra.
p Rogerus f. Roberti r.c. de xl s. pro transgressione. In thes. xx s. Et debet xx s.
t Hundredum de Dunmaw' r.c. de j m. pro eodem. In thes. viij s. viij d. Et debet iiij s. et viij d.
p Andreas et Willelmus de Bocland' r.c. de xl s. ut sint sub plegio. In thes. j m. Et debent ij m.
p Decena Willelmi Sco r.c. de dim. m. pro fuga. In thes. xl d. Et debet xl d.
p Decena Ysáác de Fairsted' r.c. de dim. m. pro eodem. In thes. xl d. Et debet xl d.
p Petrus f. Arn' molend' r.c. de ij m. de fine. In thes. j m. Et debet j m.
t Villata de Terling' r.c. de j (m.[i]) pro receptamento. In thes. viij s. Et debet v s. et iiij d.
Simon de Yffeld' r.c. de C m. ut sit in ballio. In thes. [*blank*] Et debet [*blank*]. Set respondet infra.
t Tom' de Lokeley r.c. de dim. m. pro defalta. In thes. ij s. Et debet iiij s. et viij d.
p Sampson Juvenis r.c. de C s. pro dissaisina. In thes. xx s. Et debet iiij li.
p Stephanus Ailmeri r.c. de dim. m. pro eodem. In thes. [*blank*] Et debet [*blank*]
d Galfridus Brito r.c. de dim. m. pro plegio. In thes. xl d. Et debet xl d.
t Willelmus de Erdel' r.c. de dim. m. pro eodem. In thes. xl d. Et debet xl d.
t Willelmus de Kanvill' r.c. de dim. m. pro defalta. In thes. xl d. Et debet xl d.
d (Henricus[c]) (Hundredum[i]) Dacus[2] r.c. de j m. pro falsa presentatione. In thes. ix s. et viij d. Et debet iiij s.
p Eudo de Honile r.c. de v m. pro habenda inquisitione. In thes. j m. Et debet iiij m.
d Decena Ricardi f. Hugonis r.c. de dim. m. pro fuga. In thes. iij s. Et debet iij s. et viij d.

[1] The following entries are written on the right hand side of the membrane only.
[2] The clerk has crossed out *Henr'*, interlined *hundr'*, and had already written *Dac9* for Dacus when he crossed out *Henr'* as the hundred is Dacorum in Hertfordshire. He would have written a different abbreviation if he had realised what should have been written from the start, e.g. *Dacor'*.

[1]*d* Stephanus decanus de Herlaue debet dim. m. pro dissaisina. (*t*) Ricardus de Persted' debet dim. m. pro defalta. (*t*ⁱ) Radulfus clericus de Ging' debet dim. m. pro eodem per plegium Willelmi f. Ricardi de Taxsted'. (*t*ⁱ) Leffwinus de Chissebroc debet dim. m. per plegium[2] Nicholai le grant. (*d*ⁱ) Johannes f. Michaelis de Havering' debet dim. m. quia non est prosecutus. (*p*ⁱ) Decena Nicholai f. Matillidis debet dim. m. pro fuga ipsius Nicholai. (*p*ⁱ) Radulfus de Ry debet dim. m. pro plegio eiusdem decene. (*d*ⁱ) Ricardus f. Alani de Bercholt debet dim. m. pro defalta. (*d*ⁱ) Simon Haver de Burgested' debet dim. m. (proⁱ) plegio Ade f. Johannis. (*d*ⁱ)[3] Willelmus de fonte de Botulph' piri debet dim. m. pro eodem. (*d*ⁱ) Albricus persona de Perendon' debet dim. m. pro dissaisina. (*d*ⁱ) Hugo capellanus de Auvilers debet dim. m. pro eodem. (*p*ⁱ) Walterus de Nutel' debet dim. m. pro eodem. (*p*) Alexander de Kelmeshou debet dim. m. quia retraxit se. (*d*ⁱ) Robertus gut de Cristeshal' debet dim. m. pro defalta. (*d*ⁱ) Willelmus de Hoyland' debet dim. m. pro defalta. (*b*ⁱ) Johannes capellanus de Terling' debet dim. m. quia non est prosecutus. (*d*ⁱ) Walkelinus de Quenhagh' debet (dim. m.ⁱ) pro plegio Johannis de Haddham. (*d*ⁱ) Ricardus cementarius de Coggeshal' debet dim. m. pro defalta. (Walterus de Cadamo de Cestreford' debet dim. m. pro eodemᶜ) (quia quietus est inter totalia. Episcopus Lond'ⁱ)[4] Decena Spict de parva Burghested' debet dim. m. pro fuga ipsius Spicht. (*d*ⁱ) Decena Stephani le Malle fugitivi de Hadleg' debet dim. m. (*t*ⁱ) Decena Ricardi Friðesand' debet dim. m. pro fuga. *Col'*[5] *d* Decena Andree Caretarii debet dim. m. pro fuga. (*d*ⁱ) Decena (coletⁱ)[6] Galfridi Taseler fugitivi debet x s. pro fuga. (*d*ⁱ) Decena Radulfi Grim' fugitivi debet x s. pro fuga. (*t*ⁱ) Decena Petri (filiiⁱ) Guelot' debet dim. m. pro fuga. (*d*ⁱ) Walterus de Horningedon debet dim. m. pro plegio Radulfi clerici de Magna Burgested'. (*p*ⁱ) Decena Eborardi de Butenay debet dim. m. pro fuga. (*d*ⁱ) Walterus de Cant'lupo (debetᶜ) persona ecclesie de Henxsteworðe debet ij m. pro dissaisina. Willelmus[7] f. Johannis de Hamelehamsted' debet j m. pro dissaisina (set respondet in hac lineaⁱ) per plegium Rogeri de Denham. Johannes f. (Walthamⁱ)[8] Ricardi de Brikedon' debet dim. m. pro falso clamore. (Willelmus f. Johannis r.c. de j m. sicut continetur in hac linea. In thes. lib. Et Q.E.ⁱ)

1 From now onwards the following entries are written across the membrane.

2 *per plegium* is repeated in error.

3 '*d*' written over a '*t*' here.

4 The bishop of London is written above the beginning of this next sentence. It looks as though *episcopus Lond'* 't' is written above this bit. One a little further down has Colet written above it in much the same way. Why the bishop is involved it is difficult to say.

5 This is is very faint on the membrane.

6 This is immediately above *Decena*. It is also possible that the word should be part of the line above.

7 It looks as though the clerk started to write *Walterus* then changed his mind and rubbed out part of the 'a' and the 't' in Walter and inserted *Willelmus* instead. See below for the insertion where the clerk has clearly written *Willelmus filius Johannis*.

8 This place-name is interlined above 'John the son of Richard' but there is no crossing out of this place, or Brickendon or any other obvious place.

Idem Vic. r.c. de xxxv s. et vj d. de catallis Willelmi Puttoc suspensi. In thes. nichil. Et Johanni Maresc' xxxv s. et vj d. de dono R. per breve eiusdem. Et Q.E.

d Johannes f. Walteri [*blank*] xl s. ut habeat iiij^or^ milites in augmentum jurate sue versus Robertum Bainnard' per plegium Johannis parvi de Teie et Roberti del Broc et Henrici f. Willelmi.

d Petrus clericus serviens de Wiham [*blank*] xx s. de fine per plegium Galfridi de Samundeshey, Willelmi Maudoit, Hugonis de Illeg' et Nicholai de Ulting'.

d Galfridus f. Simonis r.c. de v m. ut habeat veredictum sicut supra continetur per plegium Willelmi de Hobrig' de j m., Roberti de Welles de j m., Hugonis de Bibleworðe de j m., Willelmi Luvel de j m. et Johannis de Westewic' de j m. In thes. ij m. per Willelmum de Hobrig' et per Hugonem de Biblesworðe. Et dim. m. per Robertum de Welles. Et debet ij m. et dim.

Simon de Yffeld' r.c. de C m. ut sit in ballio ad eundum ad R. ad gratiam suam impetrandam de quodam retto unde rettatus fuit. Ita tamen quod si gratiam non possit invenire habeat iudicium suum et de predictis C m. sunt plegii Robertus de Sutton' de x m., Hasculfus Gernet de ij m., Hugo de Lazande de ij m., Thomas Beivin de ij m., Rogerus de Stistede de ij m., Willelmus de Schaldeford' de iiij m., Henricus de Merc de iiij m., Ricardus f. Simonis de vj m., Simon de Oddewell' de iij m., Willelmus de Toppefeld' de iij m., Ricardus Bataille de iiij m., Radulfus de Beclande de iij m., Ricardus de Bridebroc de ij m., Robertus de Welles de v m., Johannes de Stebbing' de ij m., Johannes de Westewic de ij m., Radulfus f. Willelmi de v m., Willelmus de Culeworðe de ij m., Guido de Hadfeld' de ij m., Johannes de Hida de ij m., Nicholaus Pechie de ij m., Thomas de Foll(-eug'^d^)[1] de iij m., Galfridus de Heirun de ij m., Ricardus de Westorp' de ij m., Abbas de Coggeshal' de v m., Simon de Cant'lupo de v m., Adam f. Willelmi f. Fulconis de v m., Willelmus de Hyspania de Finchingefeld' de v m., Ricardus Maudoit de v m. In thes. xiij li. et vij s. Et debet liij li. et vj s. et iiij d. per annum x m.

Dimidium[2] hundredum de Wautham r.c. de j m. pro transgressione. In thes. xxvj d. Et Decano et Capitulo ecclesie sancti Pauli Lond' xiiij d. per libertatem carte R. Et Abbati de Wautham x s. per libertatem carte R. Et Q.E.

Idem Vic. r.c. de dim. m. de Benedicto de pute de Wautham pro dissaisina. Et de dim. m. de Benedicto Marescall' de Wautham pro eodem. Et de dim. m. de (Benedicto^c^) (Baldewino^i^) le Cornur pro eodem. Et de dim. m. de Mauricio de Langerig' pro defalta. Et de xxxiiij s. de catallis Johannis de Epping' suspensi. Et de dim. [m.] de decena Galfridi clerici de Epping' et Rogeri parcarii pro fuga eorum. Et de dim. m. de decena Rogeri f. Warini fugitivi. (Et de iiij s. de catallis Bartholomei.^c^) Et de v

[1] There has been considerable rubbing out here, which is also on the right hand edge of the membrane. There is something written but it is virtually unreadable.

[2] There is something written in different ink round the D of *Dimidium*. It appears to be *S[ancti] P[auli] Lond' Ab[bati] Wau[tham]*.

s. de catallis Willelmus [*sic*] Gedott fugitivi. In thes. nichil. Et Abbati de Wautham lxxix s. per libertatem carte R. Et Q.E.

Idem Vic. r.c. de xxv s. et viij d. de catallis Michaelis de Bocherst suspensi. In thes. nichil. Et predicto Abbati xxv s. et viij d. per libertatem carte R. Et Q.E.

Idem Vic. r.c. de dim. m. de Reginaldo de Lagare pro defalta. Et de dim. m. de Godebold' de Horningedon' pro eodem. Et de dim. m. de Philippo forestario pro eodem. Et de dim. m. de Roberto de Turroc pro dissaisina. Et de dim. m. de Ricardo Travers pro eodem. Et de dim. m. de Johanne de Bouton' pro plegio. Et de dim. m. de Willelmo de Fonte pro dissaisina. Et de dim. m. de Elya Scoto de Peltindon' pro eodem. Et de dim. m. de Ricardo de Hobrig' pro eodem. (Et de j m. de Willelmo draperio pro eodem (quia in Lond'[i])[c]). Et de dim. m. de Roberto Norman pro defalta. Et de dim. m. de Sewal' de Crunden' pro eodem. Et de dim. m. de Ricardo de Linor pro dissaisina. Et [de] dim. m. de Johanne Triket pro defalta. Et de dim. m. de decena Simonis f. Willelmi de Copford' et Johannis f. Radulfi de Bramlé, fugitivorum. Et de xxxj s. et vj d. de catallis Hamonis f. Torald' et Elye de Herst suspensorum. Et de dim. m. de villata Bosci arsi pro receptamento Nicholai Koke fugitivi qui non fuit in decena. Et de dim. m. de decena Galfridi f. Ailwine de Chiche fugitivi. In thes. nichil. Et episcopo Lond' vj li. et (xij[e]) (xviij[i]) s. et (vj[c]) (ij[i]) d. per libertatem carte R. Et Q.E.

(*Decano Sancti Pauli London'*)[1] Idem Vic. r.c. de dim. m. de decena Rogeri de Goldingeton' et Reginaldi fratris eius fugitivorum. Et de x m. de Willelmo de Burneham pro transgressione. Et de j m. de villata de Kirkeby pro receptamento Roberti Drauelere qui non fuit in decena. In thes. nichil. Et decano et capitulo sancti Pauli Lond' vij li. et j m. Et Q.E.

Idem Vic. r.c. de dim. m. de Johanne de Litlebir' quia non est prosecutus. Et de dim. m. de Willelmo f. Aitrop' pro plegio. Et de dim. m. de Willelmo del Broc et de[2] Rotendon' pro defalta. Et de dim. m. de Ricardo del Broc pro eodem. Et de dim. m. de Willelmo Francolano pro eodem. Et de dim. m. de Willelmo de Ludewic pro eodem. Et de dim. m. de Willelmo de Waterschipewude de Hadfeld' (pro eodem.[i]) Et de dim. m. de Hugone f. Gregorii pro dissaisina. Et de dim. m. de Waltero Fughel de Keleshell' pro defalta. Et de dim. m. de Warino f. Alexandri pro plegio. Et de dim. m. de Warino f. Willelmi pro eodem. In thes. nichil. Et episcopo Elyensi v m. et dim. per libertatem carte R. Et Q.E.

Idem Vic. r.c. de dim. m. de Radulfo f. Thome de Kelleveden' pro falso clamore. In thes. nichil. Et archiepiscopo Cant' dim. m. per libertatem carte R. Et Q.E.

Idem Vic. r.c. de xliiij s. de catallis Petri de la Burne suspensi. In thes. nichil. Et abbati Sancti Edmundi xliiij s. per libertatem carte R. Et Q.E.

Idem Vic. r.c. de j m. de villata de Raudac pro transgressione. In thes. nichil. Et fratribus militie Templi j. m. per libertatem carte R. Et Q.E.

Idem Vic. r.c. de dim. m. de Roberto de la Felde pro defalta. In thes.

1 This is written in the margin in a different ink and script. Possibly it is to highlight that the dean of St. Paul's is to get the money.

2 The *et* and *de* are written almost together as though one word. The *et* is superfluous.

nichil. Et fratribus Hospitalis Jer'lm dim. m. per libertatem carte R.

Et Q.E.

Willelmus de Stanford' de Estorp' r.c. de dim. m. pro defalta. In thes. xl d. Et debet xl d.

Idem Vic. r.c. de dim m. de catallis Ricardi f. Galfridi. In thes. xl d. Et debet xl d.

Idem Vic. r.c. de iiij s. et iij d. de catallis Bartholomei de Gingeford'. In thes. lib. Et Q.E.

Idem Vic. r.c. de xx s. de Petro clerico de Witham pro stultiloquio. In thes. nichil. Et fratribus militie Templi xx s. per libertatem carte R.

Et Q.E.

[1]Adam de Walden' [*blank*] dim. m. ut scribatur in magno rotulo quod Willelmus de Neovill' venit coram baronibus de Scac[c]ario et coram eis recognovit quod tradidit Ade predicto ad firmam totam terram suam de Walden' cum hominibus, homagiis, serviciis, domibus, gardinis, boscis et omnibus aliis pertinenciis tenendam dicto Ade vel attornatis suis per terminum xxxij annorum completorum termino suo incipiente anno dominice incarnationis M^{o} CC^{o} xx^{o}ix^{o} quolibet anno pro j m. argenti et quod dictus Adam anno domini M^{o} CC^{o} xx^{o}v^{o} ante natalem incipiet recipere redditus et servicia hominum ad dictam terram pertinentium scilicet iiij^{or} annis ante inceptionem termini predicti et adquietabit totam predictam terram de serviciis debitis tam Regi quam capitalibus dominis et quod[2] [do]mos et alia pertinencia sustinebit integra et illesa et sine deterioratione. Et si meliorationem imposuerit usque ad estimationem C s. vel minus in fine dicti termini dictus W. vel heredes sui totum custum dicto A[de] vel eius assignatis plenarie solvent si s…,[3] prius solutum non fuit. Et nisi fecerint dictus A[dam] vel eius assignati totam predictam terram cum pertinenciis tenebunt per annum de anno in annum donec custum suum per visum legalium hominum perceperint. Et si W[illelmus] vivente uxore sua in fata decesserit et ipsa recuperaverit do[tem] suam dictus A[dam] vel eius assignati post predictum terminum computabit annos a recuperatione et iacturam firme sue per amissionem tercie partis et tenebit post terminum predictum ij^{as} partes terre cum pertinenciis ad tot annos quot sufficiant ad satisfactionem predicte iacture comput[abit] firma terre totius pro j m. per annum et ij^{bus} partibus pro ij^{bus} partibus marce et amissionem tercie partis pro tercia parte marce. Et dictus A[dam] dedit dicto W[illelmo] premanibus totam firmam, scilicet xxxij m. Et Mab' uxor dicti W[illelmi] ij m. Et in fine dictorum annorum per r…[4] tenuerint secundum quod supra continetur terra predicta cum pertinenciis liberabitur dicto W[illelmo] vel

1 See Introduction, pp. 12–13 where William de Neovill' would have appeared at the Exchequer on 20 January 1227 or 10 April 1228.

2 The membrane is damaged at the right hand edge here and for the next three lines. It is possible that there are some words or part of words missing here.

3 The sense is that William or his heirs will recompense Adam for improvements made costing 100s. or less – probably this should be more but the clerk made a mistake and put in *minus* instead of *maius*.

4 The word missing is at the extreme right hand side of the membrane and is extremely rubbed, and the membrane is also torn at this point.

heredibus suis absoluta. Et quod hanc conventionem firmiter observandam uterque pro se et heredibus suis iuravit sine fraude tenendam. Et quod dictus W[illelmus] et heredes sue dicto A[de] vel eius assignatis predictam conventionem warantizabunt contra omnes homines iudeos et Christianos.
[*Nine lines blank*]
[*Endorsed*] ESSEXIA (emendatus[i]) ET HERTFORDSCHIR'[1] (emendatus et item emendatus totum[i])[2]

[*Rot.* 3 *Mem.* 1][3]

CUMBERLAND'

Walterus episcopus Carleolensis Robertus f. Willelmi de Hampton' ut custos pro eo r.c. de C et xiiij li. et iiij d. num. de firma de Cumberland'. In thes. xl li. et xiij s. et xij d.

Et in elemosinis constitutis militibus de Templo j m. Et in superplus quod habuit in anno preterito xiiij d. Et debet lxxij li. et xij s. et ij d. Idem r.c. de eodem debito. In thes. nichil. Et in operatione cuiusdam gaiole in castro Carleol' x m. per breve R. Et debet lxv li. et xviij s. et x d.
[*One line blank*]
f' Idem Vic. r.c. de quater xx et ij li. et xij s. de proficuo Comitatus de hoc anno. In thes. xl li. Et debet xlij li. et xij s. *Set respondet infra cum proficuo anni preteriti.*
f' Idem Vic. r.c. de viij li. de cremento ville de Cardoil facto per homines Civitatis. Et de xij d. de Willelmo de Jouneby de quadam turbaria. In thes. lib. Et Q.E.
f' Idem Vic. r.c. de quater xx li. et x s. et viij d. de nutegeldo. In thes. lviij li. et xij s. et iiij d. Et canonicis de Carleol' xxxvij s. et iiij d. Et Roberto de Vallibus xviij li. et xiij s. et j d. Et Henrico f. Fulcherii nepoti et heredi Ade salsarii xxvij s. et xj d. Et Q.E.
f' Idem Vic. r.c. de ij s. de firma molendini de Racton'. Et de v s. de firma de Racton'. Et de dim. m. de firma de Schelton'. Et de xx s. de molendino tanerez. Et de ij s. de firma Lande de Grenewra. Et de vj s. de monachis de Holcoltram (et de firma de Hochthweit[i]). Et de xx s. de firma de Holweri. Et de xij d. de firma cuiusdam placéé in Cardoil. Et de xij d. de Thoma de Racton' de quadam placea. In thes. lib. Et Q.E.
f' Idem Vic. r.c. de x m. de censu foreste de Cardoil. Et de ij s. de firma terre de Brunrig'. Et de vj d. de Alano de Caldebecc'. Et de vj d. de Gilleberto molendinario de molendino fulerez. Et de xl d. de Henrico de Racton'. Et de vj d. de firma cuiusdam domus in Cardoil. Et de vj d. de Gilleberto molendinario pro essarto. Et de vj d. de eodem Gilleberto pro molendino tanerez. Et de ij d. de firma iiij pedum terre in Cardoil. Et de ij s. de Arnaldo de firma viij acrarum terre de eodem tempore. Et de x m.

1 There are three vertical dots after *Essexia*, *et* and *Hertfordschir'*.
2 The docket is written upside down at the foot of the membrane.
3 There is a diagonal tear running down the membrane, stitched together before it was written on: the text carefully avoids the line of stitching.

de firma minarie de Cardoil. Et de ij s. et vj d. de Henrico f. Rogeri de (quadam^i) terra in Racton'.[1] In thes. lib. Et Q. E.

f' Idem Vic. r.c. de ij s. et vj d. de Stephano de Racton' de quadam terra in Racton'. Et de dim. m. de Galfrido de Seburgeham de quadam terra in Seburgeham. Et de ij s. de Hugone de Tibay pro iiij acris terre in campis de Carleol'. Et de ij d. de Jordano portario de quadam placea in Carleol'. Et de ij s. et vj d. de Ivone de Racton' de quadam terra in Brankethweit. In thes. lib. Et Q.E.

f' Robertus f. Alani de Caudebecc' r.c. de ij m. pro assarto. In thes. lib. Et Q.E.

f' Adam salsarius r.c. de j libra piperis. In thes. lib. Et Q.E.

f' Thomas de Crofton' r.c. de iij s. de j carrucata terre in Morton'. In thes. lib. Et Q.E.

f' Abbas de Holcoltram r.c. de dim. m. de firma x acrarum terre in Caldebec quamdiu R. placuerit. Et de dim. m. de eadem firma de anno preterito. In thes. lib. Et Q.E.

f' Idem Vic. r.c. de xiiij s. de furno de Penreðe. In thes. lib. Et Q.E.

f' Idem Vic. r.c. de xlij li. et j m. de firma propresturarum. In thes. nichil. Et Willelmo de Yreby xiiij li. et xj s. et iij d. in Gameleby et Glassoneby. Et Henrico f. Fulcherii nepoti et heredi Ade salsarii iiij li. et xvj s. Et Roberto de Ros xxiij li. et vj s. et j d. in Karlaton' et Soureby et Holbrichteby. Et Q.E.

Prior de Carleol' [*blank*] xx li. quas debuit H. Dubliniensi episcopo.[2]

Ricardus de Mariscis debet x m. pro Roberto de Vallibus. Walterus f. Bernard' debet ij m. de j palefrido. (*Set respondet infra.*^i) Walterus Maresc' debet dim. m. pro Waltero f. Bernard'. Robertus de Ros debet xl s. pro Roberto de Wilton' sicut continetur in rotulo viij.

Nicholaus de Neovill' clericus debet iiij m. pro Roberto filio Willelmi sicut continetur in rotulo xiiij^o. Rogerus de Bello campo debet terciam partem de xxv m. pro justiciando Willelmo filio Ade.

Robertus de Waðepol r.c. de xj m. et x s. pro Ricardo Truite. In thes. x m. Et debet ix m. et x s.[3] per annum ij m.

Comes Albe mar' r.c. de x m. pro x equabus pro Alicia de Rumeilli sicut continetur in rotulo xj. In thes. v m. Et debet v m.

Robertus de Vallibus debet x m. de prestito Pict'. Ricardus Gernun debet v m. de eodem pro Ricardo de Brumford'. Fulco de Sules debet C li. et iij palefridos pro habenda terra que fuit Ranulfi de Sules. Biatricia filia Alexandri debet dim. m. ut tradatur in ballio de qua Robertus de Veteri ponte debet respondere (*Set respondet in* (*Buke*)^i.) quia Thomas f. Johannis ballius suus illam recepit sicut recognovit. (*Set Wakes'*[4] *in rotulo precedenti.*^i) Robertus de Castro Cairoc debet xx s. pro habendo brevi. Walterus episcopus Carleol' debet xxxiiij s. et x d. et ob. de cremento Comitatus Linc'. Robertus de Castro Cairoc debet x m. pro habendo precipe contra Adam de Tindal' et alios.

[1] Not enough space was left for the name *Racton'*, which is squashed in.
[2] *episcopo* written for a*rchiepiscopo*.
[3] Figures checked; the arithmetic is wrong.
[4] Uncertain reading.

Robertus de Vallibus r.c. de xx s. de primo scutagio. In thes. lib. Et Q.E.

Walterus f. Bernard' r.c. de ij m. sicut supra continetur. In thes. lib. Et Q.E.

DE OBLATIS

Robertus de Waðepol et Margareta uxor eius [*blank*] ij m. pro relevio suo sicut continetur in rotulo precedenti.

Robertus de Vallibus r.c.[1] de x m. pro plegio Henrici f. comitis. In thes. lib. Et Q.E.

Idem Robertus habet quietantiam de scutagio de Mungumeri per breve R. Et similiter de scutagio Bedeford'.

Robertus de Brus r.c. de j m. de scutagio de Bedeford. In thes. lib. Et Q.E.

[*One line blank*]

NOVA OBLATA

Odardus f. Ade de Wigorn' [*blank*] x m. pro relevio suo de terra quam idem Adam de R. tenuit in capite. Et xx m. de misericordia patris sui.

[*One line blank*]

DE AMERCIAMENTIS PER ROBERTUM DE LAXITON' ET SOCIOS SUOS

Idem Vic. r.c. de lj li. et dim. m. de misericordiis hominum et catallis fugitivorum quorum nominibus preponitur littera *t* in rotulo quem predicti liberaverunt in thesauro. In thes. lib. Et Q.E.

Simon de Orreton' debet xx s. quia noluit facere preceptum Justic'.

Idem Vic. r.c. de iiij li. et v s. et viij d. de catallis Simonis de Holegat'. Et de xv s. et iiij d. de catallis Ketell' de Hale. In thes. nichil. Et fratribus hospitalis Jerl'm C et j s. per libertatem carte R. Et Q.E.

Idem Vic. r.c. de C et v li. et vij s. et v d. de proficuo Comitatus de tribus partibus anni viij et de toto anno ix^{o}. Et de xlij li. et xij s. de remanenti proficui huius anni sicut supra continetur. In thes. nichil. Et W. episcopo Carleol' xlij li. et xij s. pro custodia castri Carl' de anno x^{mo} per breve R. Et eidem pro eadem custodia anno ix^{no} xl li. per idem breve. Et eidem pro eadem custodia de tribus partibus anni viij videlicet a die Natalis Domini usque ad festum Sancti Michaelis (xxx^{i})[2] li. per idem breve. Et debet xxxv li. et vij s. et v d.

Robertus de Ros debet lxxix li. et x s. pro Thoma de Muleton' quos Alanus de Caudebecc ballivus eiusdem recepit de fine Ade de Morevill' dum fuit Vic. de Cumberland' sicut recognovit sicut continetur in Linc'sir.

[*One line blank*]

1 *r.c.* written over an alteration.

2 This sum is interlined above a sum which is now illegible.

W. episcopus Carleol' r.c. de lxij li. et vj s. et v d. de remanenti compoti sui contenti in rotulo compotorum. *In thes. nichil. Et ipsi episcopo ad custodiam Castri Carleol' lxij li. vj s. et v d. per breve R.*[1] *Et Q.E.*
[*Three lines blank*]

NORHANTESIR'

Radulfus de Trublevill' Radulfus de Wassingeburg pro eo ut custos r.c. de CC et xxx li. et vij s. et iiij d. bl. de firma Comitatus. In thes. nichil.

Et in elemosinis constitutis militibus de Templo j m. Et in terris datis. Et Willelmo Lungespee et Idonéé de Kanvill' uxori sue xxx li. bl. in Sutton' per breve R. Et eisdem C s. in Suttonehundred et Abbodestanehundr' per idem breve. Et in Clive xij li. bl. de quibus compotus redditur per se. Et Waltero de Preston' xx li. bl. in Gretton' de quibus respondet infra. Et Henrico de Braibroc viij li. bl. in Corby de quibus respondet infra. Et in Thorp' xv li. bl. de quibus Vic. respondet infra. Et in Tingden' xxiiij li. bl. de quibus Vic. respondet infra. Et in Brikestok' x li. bl. de quibus compotus redditur per se. Et in Falewelé x li. bl. de quibus compotus redditur per se. Et Willelmo Maresc' xiiij li. bl. in Norton'. Et eidem iiij li. bl. in Norton' de quibus respondet infra. Et Johanni de Cancell' cum filia et herede Roberti f. Hugonis xiiij li. bl. in Upton'. Et Willelmo de Albineio xl s. in Stokes. Et Nicholae de Haya xv li. in Dudinton' quamdiu R. placuerit. Et in Abbethorp xiiij li. bl. de quibus Vic. respondet infra. Et R. comiti Cestr' xxx li. bl. in Nessinton' cum herede comitis David usque ad etatem ipsius heredis. Et in capellano ministranti in capella de Selveston' l s. de liberatione sua.
[*One line blank*]

Et in reparatione domorum Regis de Selveston' xiij li. et x d. per breve R. et per visum Ernold' de Selveston' et Henrici de Branteston'. Et in reparatione domorum Regis de Brikestok' x m. per breve eiusdem et per visum Alexandri de Aclé et Willelmi Pohier. Et in obstructione Brecke vivarii R. ibidem xxxiiij li. et x s. et ix d. per idem breve et per visum predictorum. Et in carriagio xxij doliorum vini que Vic. recepit per Thomam de Muleton et Willelmum de Haverhill' missorum per diversa loca lxix s. et x d. et ob. per breve R. Et in carriagio venationis quam Walterus de Preston' cepit in Saliceta misse apud Lond' et liberate Odoni aurifabro ad opus Regis vj s. per breve eiusdem. Et in emendatione castri de Norhanton' C s. Et in liberatione Thome de Weston' qui moram fecit apud Geitinton' cum j garcione iij leporariis et iiij^{or} girefalconibus qui ceperunt per diem vij d. a crastino Sancti Michaelis anni ix^{ni} usque ad diem mercurii proxime post festum apostolorum Simonis et Jude[2] utraque die computata xvij s. et vj d. per breve R. Et in conductu Ricardi f. Nigelli usque Lond' xv s. et vj d. per breve eiusdem. Et habet de superplus lix li. et xix s. et xj d. et ob. bl. extensos ab lxij li. et xix s. et xj d. et ob. num. quod totum locatur ei infra.[3]

1 These two sentences are written in paler ink.
2 Wednesday 29 October 1225.
3 Last four words written to the right of the entry on the line below.

f' Idem Vic. r.c. de xl li. et xv s. et ix d. de proficuo Comitatus hoc anno. In thes. nichil. Et in superplus quod habet supra xl li. xv s. et ix d. Et Q.E.

f' Hugo Rufus r.c. de C s. de cremento hundredi de Falewelé. Et de l s. de remanenti eiusdem crementi de anno preterito. In thes. lib. Et Q.E.

Idem Hugo r.c. de xxv li. de arreragiis eiusdem crementi de pluribus annis preteritis. In thes. x li. Et debet xv li. per annum x li.

f' Burgenses Norhant' r.c. de C et xx li. de firma ville sue. In thes. C et xvj li. et xvj s. et viij d. Et in elemosinis constitutis militibus de Templo j m. Et monachis eiusdem ville xx s. Et in defalta redditus ville super domos vastas x s. Et Johanni de Cancell' cum filia et herede Roberti de Bella aqua xx s. Et Q.E.

[*One line blank*]

f' Idem Burgenses (r.c. de[c]) (debet[i]) iiij s. de firma propresturarum. Et de ij s. de firma terre Ricardi Gubiun.

f' W. Marescallus r.c. de iiij li. bl. de firma de Norton'. In thes. xlviij s. et vj d. ob. (bl.[i]). Et monachis de Luffeld' xxx s. Et debet ij s. et xj d. et ob. bl. Idem r.c. de eodem debito. In thes. lib. Et Q.E.

f' Idem Vic. r.c. de ij s. de firma lande de Bustardeleg'. Et de xij d. de firma de Hou. Et de xij d. de firma Willelmi f. Rannulfi de Blarewic. Et de xv d. de firma Rogeri de Eston'. Et de ix d. de firma Willelmi de Horton'. Et de ij s. de firma Willelmi de Carevill'. In thes. lib. Et Q.E.

f' Henricus de Braibroc r.c. de xl s. de firma Parve Weledon'. (In thes. vij li. et xiiij s. et viij d. bl. Et xl s. num. Et debet v s. et iiij d. bl.[c]) (*quia infra*[i]). In thes. lib. Et Q.E.

f' Idem H[enricus] r.c. de viij li. bl. de firma de Corby. Et de xl s. num. de cremento eiusdem. In thes. vij li. xiiij s. et viij d. Et xl s. num. Et debet v s. et iiij d. bl. Idem r.c. de eodem debito. In thes. lib. Et Q.E.

f' Walterus de Preston' r.c. de xxv li. de firma de Gretton' quam firmam debet reddere semper ad festum Sancti Michaelis per breve R. In thes. lib. Et Q.E.

f' Homines de Clive r.c. de xl li. de firma ville sue. In thes. lib. Et Q.S.

f' Henricus de Hauvill' [*blank*] xviij li. de firma de Brikestok'.

f' Homines de Tingden' r.c. de xliij li. de firma ville sue. In thes. xxxiiij li. et x s. Et Reginaldo de Welleford' lxx s. pro excambio bosci sui. Et in elemosinis constitutis canonicis de Croxton' C s. pro anima R. J. Et Q.S.

f' Homines Norhant' debent lx s. de exitu fabrice monetarie Norhant'. Et xxiiij li. de eodem exitu de pluribus annis preteritis

f' Idem Vic. r.c. de xlvij li. et xvij s. de firma de Thorp. In thes. xxxij li. et xvij s. Et ad custodiam castri Norhant' xv li. Et Q.E.

f' Idem Vic. r.c. de xv li. de firma de Falewele. In thes. lib. Et Q.E.

f' Idem Vic. r.c. de xij li. de firma de Selveston'. In thes. lib. Et Q.E.

[*Rot.* 3 *Mem.* 2]

f' Idem Vic. r.c. de xxx li. de firma de Geitinton'. In thes. xix li. et xv s. et ix d. Et in superplus quod habet supra x li. et iiij s. et iij d. Et Q.E.

f' Idem Vic. r.c. de xxiiij li. de firma de Abbethorpe. In thes. xij li. et ob. Et in predicto superplus xj li. et xix s. et xj d. et ob. Et Q.E.

Walterus de Preston' r.c. de CC li. et quater xx et xvj li. et xvij s. et x d. de pluribus debitis contentis in rotulo ij°. In thes. x li. Et debet CC et quater et xx xvj li. et xvij s. et x d. per annum (ad festum Sancti Michaelis[i]) x li.

Abbas de Burgo r.c. de C et x li. et xviij s. et viij d. de pluribus debitis contentis in rotulo v°. In thes. l m. Et debet lxxvij li. et xij s. per annum l m.

Burgenses de Norhant' [*blank*] C et quater xx et xj li. et xv s. et viij d. de pluribus debitis contentis in rotulo iiij°.

\+ Rogerus decanus de Patheshill' debet xxx m. pro viridi. Heres Willelmi filii Radulfi de Kahaign' debet xviij li. et j m. sicut continetur in rotulo viij R. J. (*Set respondet infra cum aliis debitis.*[i]) Baro clericus debet xl s. pro habenda inquisitione.

Petrus de Weston' r.c. de quater xx et[1] xvj li. et xvj s. et viij d. de ij^{bus} debitis contentis ibidem. In thes. C s. Et debet quater xx et xj li. et xvj s. et viij d. per annum C s.

Galfridus de Toft r.c. de viij li. et xix s. pro patre suo de recto foreste. In thes. x s. Et debet viij li. et ix s.

Hugo Revel r.c. de xvij s. pro eodem. In thes. lib. Et Q.E.

Guido de Waittervill' r.c. de C et xviij s. et viij d. de iij^{bus} debitis contentis in rotulo ij°. In thes. lib. Et Q.E.

Magister Michael Belet [*blank*] iiij li. pro Henrico de Braibroc sicut continetur in rotulo vij°.

Comes David debet CCC et xxvj li. et vij s. de pluribus debitis contentis in rotulo xiiij° R. J. Philippus Malebranche debet terciam partem de x li. et iij s. et vj d. pro justiciando Rannulfo Garri. Adam Brunus debet j m. pro habendo pone contra Ricardum de Brackel'.

Galfridus de Lucy r.c. de M et xxviij li. et xv s. et ix d. et ob. de iij^{bus} debitis contentis in rotulo iij°. In thes. xx m. Et debet M et xv li. et ix s. et iij ob. (*Set respondet in dorso.*[i]) per annum xx m.

Radulfus Basset de Welledon' r.c. de C et lij li. et xvj d. et ob. de pluribus debitis contentis in rotulo ij°. In thes. xxiij li. et xx d. Et iterum lxxj s. et viij d. Et debet C et xxv li. et viij s. et ob. per annum xx m.

Robertus de Chaucumb' r.c. de CC et xliij li. et viij s. et iiij d. de ij^{bus} debitis contentis in rotulo vij°. In thes. x li. Et debet CC et xxxiij li. et viij s. et iiij d. per annum x li.

Robertus Blundus r.c. de lx li. et dim. m. de ij^{bus} debitis contentis in rotulo v°. In thes. xl s. Et debet lviij li. et dim. m. per annum xl s.

Robertus f. Henrici r.c. de xlviij li. et x s. et j palefrido pro licencia concordandi sicut continetur in rotulo xiiij. In thes. xl s. Et debet xlvj li. et x s. et j palefridum. per annum xl s.

Robertus filius Ricardi de Leicr' r.c. de xxij li. et xvj s. et xj d. et j palefrido de ij^{bus} debitis contentis in rotulo v°. In thes. x m. Et debet xvj li. et iij s. et vij d. et j palefridum. per annum x m.

[1] *et* repeated in error.

Eustachius de Watford' r.c. de MM et xxiij m. de ij^{bus} debitis contentis ibidem. In thes. v m. Et debet MM et xviij m.[1] per annum v m.

Radulfus messor debet dim. m. pro dissaisina. Ricardus f. Edithe debet dim. m. pro eodem. Godwinus Oldcorn' debet ij s. et viij d. quia non habuit. Johannes de Witeringe debet dim. m. pro falso clamore per plegium Hugonis filii Roberti de Sculethorp.

Thomas f. Roberti r.c. de x d. pro[2] eodem. In thes. lib. Et Q.E.

Vitalis Engainne debet xl s. de prestito Pict' pro militibus suis. Robertus de Ferrariis debet xlij m. de eodem. Johannes Malesoeures debet iij m. de eodem. Robertus de Salicet' debet xix m. de eodem.

Robertus de Pauilly r.c. de xx s. de scutagio Pict' de honore Peverell'. In thes. lib. Et Q.E.

Radulfus Passelewe debet terciam partem de C s. pro justiciando Radulfo f. Ade. Sampson f. Matillidis debet terciam partem de vj m. pro justiciando Johanne Fauvel. Hugo de Hauvill' debet iiij m. de remanenti firme de Geitinton. Hubertus de Burgo debet j unciam auri ut scribatur. Thomas Picot debet dim. m. pro licencia concordandi.

Willelmus Cardun r.c. de xvj li. et xvj s. et viij d. pro habendo brevi sicut continetur in rotulo primo. In thes. xxx s. Et debet xv li. et vj s. et viij d. Idem r.c. de eodem debito. In thes. xxx s. Et debet xiij[3] li. xvj s. viij d. per annum lx s.

Rogerus f. Theobaldi [*blank*] ix li. et ij s. pro Abraham f. Muriell' sicut continetur in rotulo precedenti.

f' Hugo de Neovill' [*blank*] xx li. de firma foreste de Norhamt'. In thes. Et in decimis constitutis canonicis Linc' xl s.

Idem H. [*blank*] xviij li. de eadem firma de anno preterito. Et [*blank*] xxiiij li. et j m. de remanenti eiusdem firme de anno vij et viij^{o}. per annum xl li.

Robertus de Pinkeinny r.c. de CC et xxvij li. et iiij s. et ij d. de pluribus debitis contentis in rotulo iij^{o}. In thes. xx li. Et debet CC et vij li. et iiij s. et ij d. Idem r.c. de eodem debito. In thes. xviij li. et vj d. Et debet C et quater xx et ix li. et iij s. et viij d.[4]

Hugo Rufus r.c. de xj li. et xj s. et j d. pro habenda benevolentia R. In thes. xj m. Et debet iiij li. et iiij s. et v d.

Walterus f. Simonis f. Walteri r.c. de C et v li. et dim. m. et j dextrario et j palefrido de pluribus debitis contentis in rotulo viij^{o}. In thes. C s. Et debet C li. et dim. m. et j dextrarium et j palefridum. Idem r.c. de eodem deb. In thes.[5] C s. Et debet quater xx et xv li. et dim. m. et j dextrarium et j palefridum. per annum x li.

Simon feutrarius [*blank*] iij s. de misericordia.

Abbatia de Burgo [*blank*] x li. et xij s. et iij d. de scutagio Pict'.

+ Hugo Flandr' debet xxxij s. de misericordia. + Willelmus Longus de

[1] At the rate of five marks a year, it would take him just over 400 years to pay off this debt.

[2] For *pro* the clerk first wrote *d*, then changed it to *p*.

[3] This sum has been amended and is written over an erasure.

[4] *et ix li. et iij s. et viij d.* written on the line above.

[5] The rest of this entry is written at the end of the next line.

Tingden' debet dim. m. quia non habuit. + Robertus frater Ricardi de Hechham debet dim. m. pro defalta. + Elyas f. Willelmi debet dim. m. quia non est prosecutus. + Walterus f. Winemeri debet dim. m. pro eodem.[1]

Vincencius de Norhant' et Ysabella uxor eius r.c. de v s. et viij d. de eodem. In thes. ij s. Et debent iij s. et viij d.

Matheus f. Herberti debet dim. m. quia non habuit. + Hugo f. Edeline debet dim. m. ut replegietur. + Simon f. Ricardi de Colebois debet dim. m. pro falso clamore. + Galfridus f. Fulconis de Nessoburgi[2] debet dim. m. ut replegietur. + Adam f. Walteri et Felicia filia Walteri debent dim. m. pro licencia concordandi. + Gillebertus f. Theobaldi debet dim. m. pro falso clamore. + Walterus nuncius debet xj s. et iiij d. pro vino vendito. + Willelmus f. Roberti de Leircr' debet iiij s. et viij d. pro eodem. Galfridus de Greneburg' debet dim. m. pro falso clamore. Reginaldus de Pelevill' debet dim. m. pro vino vendito. + Ricardus Scherewind debet j m. pro justiciando priore sicut continetur in rotulo v°. + Henricus decanus de Undel' debet v m. pro stultiloquio.

Willelmus de Suburg' r.c. de xliiij s. et v d. scilicet tercia parte de x m. pro justiciando Berengario sicut continetur in rotulo v°. In thes. dim. m. Et debet xxxvij s. et ix d. per annum dim. m.

Heres Willelmi de Curten' debet xxxij li. et xv s. et x d. de medietate debiti eiusdem Willelmi sicut continetur in rotulo precedenti. Ricardus de Brackel' tunc Vic. Oxon' debet xxix s. et iiij d. de catallis Willelmi Iep qui abjuravit regnum.

Willelmus de Leicr' r.c. de xiiij s. et viij d. de misericordia. In thes. iiij s. Et debet x s. et xviij d.

Galfridus de Stokes de Bosiat' r.c. de ij m. et dim. pro novo essarto. In thes. lib. Et Q.E.

Idem Vic. r.c. de vj li. et xxij d. de minutis particulis foreste. In thes. nichil. Et in perdona Willelmo Briewerr' de amerciamento iiij hominum suorum de Bliseworðe xxxiiij s. et v d. (per breve R.ⁱ). Et debet iiij li. et vij s. et v d.

[*One line blank*]

Radulfus Officialis Oxon' debet v m. pro defalta. Ricardus de Midelinton' debet dim. m. pro defalta. Parsona de Lilleford' debet dim. m. pro leporariis habitis contra assisam. Magister Thomas de Haregrave debet dim. m. pro falso clamore.

Idem Vic. r.c. de dim. m. de Thoma f. Rogeri de Cotstoke. Et de xvj s. de Josceo f. Samuelis. Et de vj li. et iij s. et iiij d. de Berengar' le Moine. In thes. lib. Et Q.E.

Ricardus de Mucegros [*blank*] xxv li. et x s. de pluribus debitis et scutagiis sicut continetur in rotulo viij°.

Saherius de Sancto Andrea r.c. de xix li. de eisdem sicut continetur ibidem. In thes. vj li. Et debet xiij li. per annum vj li.

1 *m. pro eodem* written on the line above.

2 This might refer to the Nassaborough hundred or the ness of Nassaborough which eventually formed the soke of Peterborough. See *Cambridge Dictionary of English Place Names* (Cambridge, 204), p. 429.

Simon de Mucegros r.c. de xvij li. et x s. sicut continetur ibidem. In thes. vj li. Et debet xj li. et x s. per annum vj li.

Robertus de Haldaneby r.c. de lxx s. et ix d. de eodem sicut continetur ibidem. In thes. ij m. Et debet xliiij s. et j d. per annum ij m.

Simon de Turevill' qui habet unam heredum Willelmi de Turevill' r.c. de xvj li. de pluribus debitis et scutagiis ipsius Willelmi. In thes. ij m. Et debet xiiij li. et j m.

Rogerus de Crest qui habet aliam heredum ipsius Willelmi [*blank*] xvj li. de eisdem.

Heres Willelmi de Kahaign' debet xviij li. et j m. sicut supra continetur. Et xj li. et ix s. et ij d. de pluribus debitis et scutagiis sicut continetur in rotulo viij°. Et xv li. et ix s. et ij d. de iij^bus^ scutagiis contentis in rotulo precedenti.

Ricardus de Gray r.c. de xiiij li. pro Johanne de Humez de eodem. In thes. lxx s. Et debet x li. et x s. per annum vij li.

Idem Vic. r.c. de lx s. de Merston' de feod' de Wivill'. Et de l li. de Simone de Briclesworðe. Et de j m. de Baldewino de Beton'. In thes. lib. Et Q.E.

Petrus Passelew' [*blank*] ij s. et viij d. pro plegio.

Radulfus Passelew' debet dim. m. pro dissaisina. Galfridus de Norton' debet iij m. de vj° scutagio R. J. sicut continetur in rotulo viij°. + Robertus de Bakepoiz de Sutton' debet j m. pro dissaisina sicut continetur ibidem. Willelmus de iiij maris debet xl d. pro habendo pone.

Idem Vic. r.c. de v m. de scutagio de Mungumeri de honore de Chokes. In thes. iij m. Et debet ij m.

Idem Vic. r.c. de vj m. de scutagio de Bedeford' de eodem honore. In thes. nichil. Et W. de Insul' iij m. in (Henewik' et^c^) Wenegrave per breve R. allocatum in Buk'. Et debet iij m.

Idem Vic. r.c. de j m. de Vitale Engainne de scutagio de Bedef'. Et de j m. de Hugone f. Ricardi de Wudecroft. In thes. lib. Et Q.E.

Comes de Ferrariis debet j m. de primo scutagio Regis pro Willelmo de Vernone quam Radulfus f. Nicholai tunc senescallus eius recepit qui requirebatur in Buk'.

DE OBLATIS

Abbas de Bittlesden' r.c. de x m. pro licencia essartandi sicut continetur in rotulo precedenti. In thes. lib. Et Q.E.

Robertus de Leicr', Burgensis Norhant' [*blank*] xxxiiij li. pro blado de Bricleswordðe sicut continetur ibidem.

Henricus de Basevill' debet dim. m. pro licencia concordandi sicut continetur in rotulo precedenti.

Philippus de Albineio debet respondere de xx s. de singulis feodis militaribus tenentium de honore comitis Leicr'[1] sicut continetur in rotulo precedenti.

Henricus de Braibroc r.c. de quater xx et x li. et viij s. et iiij d. de

1 Simon de Montfort, 5th earl of Leicester, died in 1218. His son and heir Amauri de Montfort styled himself earl of Leicester but was not recognised, and surrendered

pluribus debitis contentis in rotulo precedenti. In thes. xxx li. Et debet lx li. et viij s. et iiij d. Idem r.c. de eodem debito. In thes. ante guerram iiij li. pro[1] Greseleg' sicut continetur in rotulo de receptis de dim. anno xvij, que allocantur ei per Justiciarios. Et debet lvj li. viij s. et iiij d.

per annum [*illegible*].

NOVA OBLATA

Abbas de Burgo r.c. de ij palefridis pro habendis in manu et custodia sua usque ad etatem Rogeri f. et heredis Rogeri de Torpel terris cum pertinenciis que fuerunt ipsius Rogeri, quas tenuit de eodem Abbate si attachiatus fuerit per [*illegible*][2] quam Regis fieri precepit de terra quam idem Rogerus de R. tenuit in capite quod ipsam de R. tenuerit per servicium militare. In thes. x m. pro palefridis. Et Q.E.

Idem Abbas r.c. de xl li. de firma predictarum terrarum ipsius Rogeri quam firmam idem Abbas reddet annuatim ad scaccarium ad ij^{os} terminos anni scilicet medietatem ad pasch' et medietatem ad festum Sancti Michaelis quod terre fuerunt in manu et custodia ipsius Abbatis.

[*One line blank*]

RESPICE IN TERGUM

[*Rot.* 3d *Mem.* 1]

DE BANCO

Idem Vic. r.c. de xlvj [s.] de catallis Walkelini et Thome f. Goldmere suspensorum. Et de dim. m. de Abbate de Sancto Ebrulf' pro licencia concordandi. Et de j m. de Johanne clerico de Cottesgrave. In thes. lib.

Et Q.E.

Ricardus de Chokes r.c. de xl s. pro iniusto impedimento per plegium Willelmi de Cattesbroke et Walteri de Langeport. In thes. xx s. Et debet xx s.

Idem Vic. r.c. [de] x m. de hominibus Comitatus de Norhant' pro auxilio habendo. Et de xl s. de Priore Sancti Andree Norhant' pro bosco suo de Kingesbir' claudendo. Et de j m. de Willelmo de Horton' pro essarto suo in Salceto in pace habendo. Et de xl s. de Egelino de Dummart pro pastura bosci de Raggel' habenda. Et de ij m. pro Amabilia de Bello campo pro viij acris essarti in Bosco de Wotun'.[3] In thes. lib. Et Q.E.

Willelmus filius Hamonis debet j m. pro bosco suo de Bruskhawe claudendo.[4]

[*One line blank*]

---

his claims to his younger brother Simon, perhaps in 1229 (*Handbook of British Chronology*, p. 435).

[1] Entry from this point completed on the line below.

[2] Perhaps a word like *conventionem*, covenant, stipulation.

[3] There is an identical entry in the Norfolk and Suffolk account: see p. 187.

[4] A vertical mending strip to cover the stitching-up of the tear begins here, occasionally obscuring part of a word.

AMERCIAMENTA DE ITINERE M. DE PATES[HIL]L' ET SOCIORUM SUORUM

Idem Vic. r.c. de C et x m. de misericordiis hominum, villarum et decenarum quorum nominibus preponitur littera [T] in rotulo quem predicti liberaverunt in thesauro. In thes. lib. in C et quater xx^{ti} et j talea. Et Q.E.

Idem Vic. r.c. de xxiiij s. de catallis Willelmi filii Walteri suspensi. In thes. xviij s. Et debet vj s. T. de Cyrecestr' r.c. de eodem debito. In thes. lib. Et Q.E.

f' Decena Roberti de Herdewic' in Welleford' [*blank*] dim. m. pro fuga Johannis Gos.

Walterus de Godarðvilla [*blank*] xxix s. de catallis Willelmi de Keilmers et Willelmi Bonhumme.

Idem Vic. debet xx s. de catallis Willelmi filii Rogeri. Et iij s. de catallis Galfridi filii capellani extra francoplegium qui abiuravit regnum. Terra templariorum in Winewic debet dim. m. pro receptamento eiusdem Galfridi.

Ingaldus de Ardern' debet dim. m. pro falso clamore.

Idem Vic. debet dim. m. de catallis Roberti le Taillur in Dingel' pro fuga ipsius Roberti. (*Set T. de Cyrecestr' respondet infra.*[i]) Falco de Breautéé debet xxvj s. de catallis Radulfi Wischard' fugitivi. (*Set resp' in Oxon' in rotulo precedenti.*[i]) Decena Simonis le Stodherde de Erningewurðe debet dim. m. pro fuga Radulfi Bil. Rogerus Alwin' debet dim. m. quia non fecit sectam post Robertum Wine cum Thoma Wine de magna Acle. Willelmus de Walmeford' clericus debet dim. m. ut possit esse sub plegio.

Galfridus de Lucy r.c. de M et xv li. et ix s. et iij ob. de pluribus debitis sicut continetur ex alia parte rotuli. In thes. nichil. Et in operatione castri de Gernesia lxvj li. et xix s. et j d. per breve R. in quo continetur quod R. concessit eidem Galfrido quod singulis annis allocentur ei de hac summa in predicto debito xx m. donec predicte lxvj li. et xix s. et j d. ei perallocentur et quod de residuo debito quod debebit R. postquam ei allocate fuerint predicte lxvj li. et xix s. et j d. reddat R. singulis annis xx m. donec predictum debitum persolvatur. Incipiet autem hec allocatio ad pasch' anni xj.

DE ITINERE H. DE NEOVILL' DE PLACITIS FORESTE

[1]Hugo de Sancto Martino r.c. de j m. pro iij acris de riffleto suo proprio essartandis et excolendis apud Lillingesta[n] In thes. lib. Et Q.E.

Henricus f. Wilekin' et Willelmus de Hatton' debent xx s. pro essarto de Barewe [*f'*][2] continente v acras in parrochia de Passeh' vastato in guerra et distante longe a cóóperto et dabunt ij s. per annum. Abbas de Grestein debet j m. pro ij acris pasture sue de Grafton' frussandis et ex[c]olendis. Homines R. de Abbethorp debent iij m. pro [*f'*] j placea vasta in Abethorp

[1] This entry runs for six continuous lines, but each line except the first is preceded by a marginal *f'*, shown here as [*f'*].

[2] The beginning of this entry is written on the line above.

excolenda continente v acras xv d. per annum pro quietantia regardi. Werreis de Suwic debet dim. m. pro j acra de pastura de dominico R. de Abethorp ex[c]olenda juxta Sumereslað per annum iiij d. Robertus de Pilketon' debet dim. m. pro [*f'*] ij acris de pastura de Pilketon' excolendis de terra propria. Nicholaus de Bassingeburn' debet xx s. pro j acra parci de riffleter et parci de frisco per annum iiij d. Willelmus de Hatton' debet dim. m. pro iij acris per annum ix d. Henricus Gubiun debet ij m. pro [*f'*] j angulo (riffleti[s]) de terra sua propria continente ij acras. Willelmus de Pirie debet j m. pro iij acris xij d. per annum. Prior de [L]uffeld' debet xx s. pro quadam (pastura[c]) placea bosci vastata in guerra excolenda de Bosco de Norton'. [T.] de Cyrecestr' r.c. de dim. m. de catallis Roberti cisoris. In thes. lib. Et Q.E.

NORTHUMBERLAND'

Johannes f. Roberti Guido de Clavering' ut custos r.c. de CC et xl li. et xviij s. et iiij d. num. de firma Norhumberland'. In thes. xxxiij li.

Et in elemosinis constitutis militibus de Templo j m. Et in liberatione constituta Roberto portario de Baemburc lx s. et x d. Et in terris datis Regi Scotie x li. in Tindal. Et Johanni f. Roberti f. Rogeri xxxij li. et ij s. in Werkeworðe cum pertinenciis. Et eidem xxx li. in Neweburn'. Et eidem xxx li. in Corbrige de quibus respondet infra. Et eidem xx li. in Robir'. Et episcopatui Donolm' xxiij li. et xiiij s. et iij d. in wapentaco de Seberg'. Et in villa de novo castro l li. de quibus homines ville respondent infra. Et in quietantia terrarum quas Elyzabeth que fuit uxor Willelmi Bardulf habet in Heppedal'[1] l s. Et in quietantia terre Michaelis f. Michaelis et participum suorum heredum Rogeri de Flammavill' in Witingeham xl s. Et in superplus quod habet in anno preterito iiij li. et iij s. et ix d.

[*One line blank*]

Et pro ferramentis prison' iij s. et vij d. Et Johanni carpentario moram facienti in castro de Baemburg' iiij li. de liberatione sua quamdiu R. placuerit. Et habet de superplus iiij li. et ix s. et v d. de quibus iij m. et dim. locantur ei infra in tribus debitis. Et restant ei locandi xlij s. et ix d. de quibus xlij s. locantur ei infra in propresturis. *Et restant ei locandi ix d.*

f' Idem Vic. [*blank*]. Et de anno preterito.

f' Idem Vic. r.c. de vj d. de firma domus Walteri tinctoris. Et de ij domus[2] Willelmi f. Hugonis. In thes. lib. Et Q.E.

f' Idem Vic. r.c. de j m. de firma cuiusdam domus que fuit Willelmi f. Erkembald' quam Thomas f. Alani tenet. Et in thes. lib. Et Q.E.

f' Idem Vic. r.c. de ij m. de firma cuiusdam alterius domus que fuit eiusdem Willelmi quam Willelmus sellarius tenet. In thes. lib. Et Q.E.

f' Idem Vic. [*blank*] xlviij m. et iiij s. et v d. de warda debita novo castro de hoc anno. Et [*blank*] xlviij m. et iiij s. et v d. de eadem warda de anno preterito.

[1] This is what is written but in *NS 48*, p. 9, *NS 56*, p. 16, and *NS 54*, p. 66 this is written *Heppehal'*, which is probably correct as no place called *Heppedal'* can be located.

[2] Written for *ij s.* [or *ij d.*] *de firma domus*?

[*One line blank*]

f' Johannes f. Roberti r.c. (de xxx li.[i]) de firma de Corbrig'. Et de x li. de cremento eiusdem ville. In thes. lib. Et Q.E.

f' Idem Vic. r.c. de xlvij li. et ij s. et vij d. de firma propresturarum sicut continetur in anno xxxiij R. Henrici secundi. In thes. l s. Et in terris datis heredi Eustachii de Vescy vj li. et xviij s. et v d. in Spindlesham.[1] Et in terris quas Kempe balistarius tenuit quas Burgenses de novo castro modo tenent C et x s. et vj d. Et in quietantia quam episcopus Donolm' habet in wapentaco de Seberg' dim. m. Et heredibus Philippi de Ulecot' xxix li. et xv s. in Nafferton' et Matefen. Et in superplus quod habet supra xlij s. Et Q.E.

f' Idem Vic. r.c. de v m. de warda debita novo castro de Baemburc. In thes. nichil. Et Johanni Wascel' constabulario de Bamberc v m. quamdiu R. placuerit sicut continetur in rotulo precedenti. Et Q.E.

f' Idem Vic. r.c. de xxiiij s. de firma de Yatlinton'. Et de viij d. de terra Torphini. Et de vj d. de quodam mes[u]agio in Baemberc. Et de iij d. de placea Gilleberti Maresc'. In thes. lib. Et Q.E.

f' Idem Vic. r.c. de xx li. de cornagio. In thes. xvij li. et ij s. et viij d. Et Priori de Tinemue xxiiij s. Et super terras Regis Scotie ij m. et dim. Et Q.E.

f' Michael f. Michaelis r.c. de j spervario mutario de firma terre que fuit Uchtred' f. Gamell'. In thes. (nichil[i]). Et ipsi R. j spervarium mutarium. Et Q.E.

f' Homines de novo castro r.c. de C li. de firma ville sue. In thes xij s. et vj d. Et Johanni Wascel' constabulario de Baemburg' lx m. per breve R. in parte solutionis C m. quas percipit per annum ad custodiam predicti. Et item eidem Johanni xxxij li. per breve eiusdem quod predicti burgenses attulerunt de liberandis eidem Johanni lx m. in parte solutionis C et xx m. quas percipit per annum ad custodiam predicti castri. Et Rogero et Bonefacio de iiij[or] maris balistariis equitibus moram facientibus in castro de Baemburc quorum uterque habet per diem vij d. et ob. de liberatione sua a crastino Sancti Michaelis usque ad purificationem beate Marie.[2] Et Rogero de Bosco pediti moram facienti ibidem qui habet per diem iij d. de eodem tempore ix li. et ix s. per breve R. Et eisdem B. et R. balestariis de liberatione sua a crastino purificationis beate Marie prescripto usque ad octabas Sancte Trinitatis et Rogero de Bosco predicto de liberatione sua per idem tempus x li. et viij s. et vj d. per breve eiusdem. Et eisdem R. et B. et R. de liberatione sua a predictis octabis Sancte Trinitatis usque ad festum Sancti Michaelis vij li. et x s. per breve eiusdem. Et Q.S.

Johannes f. Roberti [*blank*] j bonum chaszur'.[3]

[1] In *NS 54*, p. 67 the place is shown as *Spindesham*. The editor and some previous editors of earlier volumes have a similar name. They have indexed it as Spindle in Northumberland but there is no place in Northumberland with this name. It may be Spindlestone.

[2] Monday 2 February 1226.

[3] From now on, a mending strip down the left hand side obscures any use of the annotation *f'*.

Adam de Hareden' debet xxx li. et x s. de fine facto tempore H. Donolm' episcopi.

Willelmus de Latton' r.c. de xxvj li. ut duellum procedat. In thes. xxv s. Et debet xxiiij li. et x s. Idem r.c. de eodem debito. In thes. x li. Et debet xiiij li. et x s. (*per annum x li.*)[1]

Johannes de Thorp r.c. de xlviij li. et xvj s. et viij d. quia cepit finem sicut continetur in rotulo primo R. J. In thes. x s. Et debet xlviij li. et vj s. et viij d. per annum xx s. quamdiu R. placuerit.

Ricardus Bertram r.c. de[2] xxiiij li. et xiiij s. et iij d. et j palefrido pro Mabilia de Clere sicut continetur in rotulo ij°. In thes. xix li. et iiij s. Et debet C et x s. et iij d. et j palefridum.

Jacobus de Chauz debet xij m. et dim. de prestito Pict'. Johannes de Chauz debet xij m. et dim. de eodem. Hugo de Balleol' debet xxxvj m. de eodem. + Walterus Tuillet debet ij s. et viij d. pro dissaisina.

Elizabeth Taillebois r.c. de xxxviij li. et x s. et xj d. et ij palefridis sicut continetur in rotulo precedenti. In thes. x m. Et debet xxxj li. et xvij s. et vij d. et ij palefridos. per annum x m.

Petrus de Vallibus r.c. de lx li. et xij d. et v palefridis contentis in rotulo xv in Cumberland. In thes. iiij m. Et debet lvij li. et vij s. et viij d. et v palefridos. per annum iiij m.

Walterus faber de Roffa debet dim m. pro defalta. Stephanus de Sancto Albino debet ij palefridos pro habendo precipe sicut continetur in rotulo iiij°. Simon de Rofa et Waldelf' belle[3] debent ij m. et dim. pro habenda loquela sicut continetur in rotulo precedenti.

Sampson de Cornubia r.c. de v m. scilicet tercia parte xv m. pro justiciando Rogero sicut continetur in rotulo iiij°. In thes. dim. m. Et debet iiij m. et dim.

Elysabeth Taillebois r.c. de l s. de ij^{bus} scutagiis contentis in rotulo v. In thes. ij m. Et debet xxiij s. et iiij d. Eadem r.c. de eodem debito. In thes. j m. Et debet x s.

Daniel f. Nicholai et participes sui r.c. de viij m. pro Philippo de Ulecot'. In thes. lib. Et Q.E.

Henricus de Rudune r.c. de xx s. de tallagio. In thes. lib. Et Q.E.

Rogerus de Hodesac debet iiij m. quas recepit sicut continetur in rotulo[4] viij. Set non debet summoneri quia idem Rogerus debet inde respondere super compotum suum per breve R. Willelmus de Lumeléé debet C s. pro habenda terra sicut continetur in rotulo viij. (*Set respondet infra.*[1])

Hugo de Balleol' r.c. de lx m. de scutagio de Mungumeri. Et de xlviij m. de scutagio de Bedeford'.

Willelmus f. Erkenbauð [*blank*] MM et C liiij li. de firma minarie de Cardoil de tempore quo tenuit minariam.

[*One line blank*]

Gillebertus de Laval r.c. de ij m. de scutagio de Bedef'. In thes. xx s.

1 These words are very faint.
2 A horizontal line is drawn between this word and the next.
3 Perhaps *Waldelf' f. belle*, with one *f.* omitted?
4 *rotulo* repeated.

Et debet dim. m. Idem r.c. de eodem debito. In thes nichil. Et in superplus quod Vic. habet supra dim. m. Et Q.E.

Henricus Bec debet v m. pro habendo maritagio sicut continetur in rotulo viij. Galfridus de Coismeres (*Set respondet infra.*[i]) debet ij palefridos pro habenda saisina. Radulfus de Staverford debet ij bonos palefridos ut deliberetur a prisona.

Willelmus de Lumeley r.c. de C s. pro habenda terra sicut supra continetur. In thes. lib. Et Q.E.

DE OBLATIS

Rogerus Bertram r.c. de v m. pro feria sua de Mudford' sicut continetur in rotulo precedenti. In thes. xl s. Et debet ij m. Idem r.c. de eodem debito. In thes. lib. Et Q.E.

Willelmus de Hawelton' r.c. de v m. et dim. pro habenda jurata sicut continetur ibidem. In thes. xl s. Et debet ij m. et dim. Idem r.c. de eodem debito. In thes. nichil. Et in superplus quod Vic. habet supra ij m. et dim. Et Q.E.

Adam Bertram r.c. de xl s. pro licencia concordandi. In thes. lib. Et Q.E.

Galfridus de Coismeres r.c. de x m. pro ij[bus] palefridis sicut supra continetur. In thes. lib. Et Q.E.

NOVA OBLATA

Robertus de Albeinn' (debet[d]) (r.c. de[i]) iij m. pro habendo pone contra Johannem de Normann'vill' de terra in Fenwic' et Matefen. In thes. lib. Et Q.E.

[P]rior de Tinemue r.c. de xx s. pro habenda jurata apud Westm'. In thes. x s. Et debet x s. Idem r.c. de eodem debito. In thes. lib. Et Q.E.

[*One line blank*]

AMERCIAMENTA PER ROBERTUM DE LAXINTON ET SOCIOS SUOS

[Idem] Vic. r.c. de xxv m. et xxij d. et ob. de misericordiis hominum et villarum quorum nominibus preponitur littera *t* in rotulo quem predicti liberaverunt in thesauro. In thes. lib. in xxxviij taleis. Et Q.E.

[J]ohannes f. Waldelf' r.c. de j m. pro dissaisina. In thes. dim. m. Et debet dim. m. De quibus[1] Vic. debet eum adquietare sicut recognoscit et respondet infra.

[Ro]bertus f. Stephani de Prestefen r.c. de xl s. pro eadem. In thes. xx s. Et debet xx s. De quibus Vic. debet eum adquietare sicut recognoscit et respondet infra.

[1] In this and subsequent repetitions of this clause, the clerk uses *quibus* whether appropriate or not (in this instance, it should be *qua*, agreeing with *marca*); similarly, when a vill is to be acquitted, the word used is still *eum*, not *eam*.

. . .'[1] de Jesemue r.c. de j m. pro eodem. In thes. dim. m. Et debet dim. m. De quibus Vic. debet eum adquietare sicut recognoscit et respondet infra.

[*Rot.* 3d *Mem.* 2]

Willelmus de Rock r.c. de v m. pro eodem. In thes. ij m. Et debet iij m. De quibus Vic. debet eum adquietare sicut recognoscit et respondet infra.

Thomas de Welpinton' r.c. de xl s. quia non est prosecutus. In thes. xx s. Et debet xx s. De quibus Vic. debet eum adquietare sicut recognoscit et respondet infra.

Hugo de Lakeneby r.c. de xxx s. pro eodem. In thes. x s. Et debet xx s. De quibus Vic. debet eum adquietare sicut recognoscit et respondet infra.

Hugo f. Rogeri de Heiesande r.c. de j m. pro falso clamore. In thes. dim. m. Et debet dim. m. De quibus Vic. debet eum adquietare sicut recognoscit et respondet infra.

Rannulfus de Calverdon' r.c. de x li. ut sit sub plegio. In thes. x m. Et debet v m. De quibus Vic. debet eum adquietare sicut recognoscit et respondet infra.

Villate de Wudehorn' et de Setton' et de Herst et de Heiden' et de Elleington' r.c. de xl m. pro dissaisina. In thes. xx m. Et debent xx m. Eadem r.c. de eodem debito. In thes. vj li. et xix s. et viij d. Et debent vj li. et vij s.

Petrus de Insul' r.c. de iij m. pro eodem. In thes. xx s. Et debet xx s. De quibus Vic. debet eum adquietare sicut recognoscit et respondet infra.

Magister Hospit' de novo castro de Westgat' r.c. de j m. pro habendo brevi de attingendis xij. In thes. dim. m. Et debet dim. m. De quibus Vic. debet eum adquietare sicut recognoscit et respondet infra.

Elyas de Twisel' r.c. de lx s. pro falso appello. In thes. xx s. Et debet xl s. De quibus Vic. debet eum adquietare sicut recognoscit et respondet infra.

Johannes f. Roberti r.c. de C s. pro transgressione. In thes. vij m. Et debet dim. m. De qua respondet infra.

Rannulfus Rufus de novo castro r.c. de j m. ut sit sub plegio. In thes. dim. m. Et debet dim. m. De quibus Vic. debet eum adquietare sicut recognoscit et respondet infra.

Bertramus faber de Eland' r.c. de xij s. pro plegio. In thes. dim m. Et debet v s. et iiij d. De quibus Vic. debet eum adquietare sicut recognoscit et respondet infra.

Villata de Schotton' r.c. de xvj s. de catallis Ade le Cyr et Edmundi fleccarii fugitivorum. In thes. x s. Et debet vj s. De quibus Vic. debet eum adquietare sicut recognoscit et respondet infra.

Villata de Langeton' r.c. de viij s. de catallis Roberti bercarii et Reginaldi f. sui et Petri messoris fugitivorum. In thes. dim. m. Et debet xvj d. De quibus Vic. debet eum adquietare sicut recognoscit et respondet infra.

Robertus de Wittecestr' (r.c.[c]) r.c. de xxiiij s. et ij d. de catallis Roberti f. Edmundi de Belesho. In thes. xvj s. ix d. et ob. Et debet vij s. iiij d. et ob. De quibus Vic. debet eum adquietare sicut recognoscit et respondet infra.

[1] The foot of the membrane has been torn away at this point.

Villata de Hotthal' r.c. de xiij s. de catallis Radulfi f. Uchtred' fugitivi. In thes. x s. Et debet iij s. De quibus Vic. debet eum adquietare sicut recognoscit et respondet infra.

Villata de parva Swiburn' r.c. de xxviij s. de catallis Rogeri f. Essot. In thes. xiiij s. Et debet xiiij s. De quibus Vic. debet eum adquietare sicut recognoscit et respondet infra.

Villata de Gosefeld' r.c. de xx s. de catallis Rannulfi fugitivi. In thes. x s. Et debet x s. De quibus Vic. debet eum adquietare sicut recognoscit et respondet infra.

Idem Vic. r.c. de xxiij m. et vij s. et ob. quos recepit de suprascriptis hominibus sicut supra continetur. In thes. nichil. Et in suprascripto superplus dim. m. Et debet xxiij m. et iiij d. et ob.

[*One line blank*]

Idem Vic. [*blank*] j m. de Radulfo de Witelé pro falso clamore. Et (de[i]) dim. m. de Fulcone Baignard' quia non est prosecutus. Et de dim. m. de Elya forestario pro dissaisina. Et de dim. m. de Rogero f. Alivue ut sit sub plegio. Et de dim. m. de Henrico f. Olkill' pro eodem. Et de dim. m. de Roberto f. Goscelini pro eodem. Et de vj s. et v d. de villata de Erdeston' de catallis Rollandi de Tindal' fugitivi. Et de xiiij s. de villata de Benleg' de catallis Philippi de Crawel' fugitivi. Et de vj s. de villata de Schotton' de catallis Roberti Gray fugitivi que omnia debita idem Vic. recepit sicut recognovit. *Summa lxxiij s. et j d.*

[*One line blank*]

[A]dam de Trewic debet dim. m. quia non est prosecutus. Villata de Crenlaw' debet xv s. de catallis Philippi de Crawelawe fugitivi. Villata de Hothal' debet v s. de catallis Uchtred' de Ringwud' fugitivi.

[*One line blank*]

CORNUBIA[I]

Debita Comitatus Cornubie pertinentia ad R. et non fit hic mentio de corpore Comitatus quia Comes Ricardus frater R. habet Comitatum de dono R. quamdiu R. placuerit.

Henricus filius Willelmi r.c. de xxxvj li. (d.[d]) et iij s. et iiij d. ut possit concordare sicut continetur in rotulo xvj^{o} R. J. In thes. x m. Et debet xxix li. et x s. per annum x m.

Episcopus Exon' debet x m. pro bosco suo. (*Set respondet in Devon' in rotulo sequenti.*[i]) + Rannulfus Cancellarius debet CCC m. de misericordia foreste. Warinus de Quedich' debet xv m. pro dissaisina. Henricus de la Pomeraie debet lvij li. et dim. m. de iij^{bus} debitis contentis in rotulo vj^{o}. (*Set respondet in Devon' in rotulo sequenti.*[i]) + Willelmus de Heauton' debet v m. et dim. de misericordia foreste. Johannes f. Ricardi debet xiiij s. de minutis particulis foreste (*Set respondet in Devon' in rotulo sequenti.*[i]) dum fuit Vic. sicut continetur in rotulo xvj^{o}. + Thomas de Pollerch' debet x s. pro mendacio.

[I] The heading *CORNUBIA* is written on the left hand side of the membrane instead of in the normal centre position. Probably the original heading was *Debita Comitatus Cornubie pertinentia ad R.*, which is written centrally. The sentence *et non fit hic mentio ... placuerit*, does not fit grammatically with that heading, and must be an afterthought, with *Cornubia* added at the left of the line for clarification.

[R]adulfus Bloio r.c. de liij s. de scutagio Pict'. In thes. xx s. Et debet xxxiij s.

Henricus de Boderinga Vic. predicti comitis r.c. de xliij s. et x d. de hominibus de Lanzaveton'. Et de iiij li. de hominibus de Helleston'. Et iterum de iiij li. et xvj s. de Burgo de Helleston'. Et de C s. de Yvone f. Ascelin'. Et de ij m. et dim. de Priore de Sancto Germano. Et de xxx s. de Priore de Bodmine. Et de xj s. de Edwardo de Wotholcan. Et de dim. m. de Jordano de Trevagan. Et de dim. m. de Roberto Breino.[1] Et de ij m. de hominibus de Climeston' de j palefrido. Et (de[i]) vij s. et viij d. de Johanne de monte acuto de scutagio de Mungumeri. In thes. lib.

Et Q.E.

Willelmus f. Ricardi r.c. de xxiiij li. et viij s. et iiij d. de pluribus debitis contentis in rotulo vj. In thes. iiij li. xij s. et ix d. Et debet xix li. xv s. et vij d.

(Radulfus[c]) (Nicholaus[i]) de Heauton' (r.c.[d]) et Willelmus de Heauton' r.c. de ij m. pro recto foreste. In thes. dim. m. per Nicholaum. Et debent xx s.

Idem Nicholaus r.c. de C s. et j m. quia duxit Rosamundam sine licencia. I[n] thes. iiij li. et j m. Et debet xx s.

Episcopus Exon', barones, milites et omnes de Comitatu Cornub' (*Set episcopus respondet in Devon' in rotulo sequenti.*[i]) debent xviij li. et x s. et vj d. ut R. constituat eis Vicecomitem sicut continetur in rotulo vj^{o}. (+[i]) Ricardus Pucin et Sunehold' uxor eius debent dim. m. pro habendo pone sicut continetur ibidem. (+[i]) Willelmus de Dunham debet vij li. et x s. pro habendo judicio sicut continetur in rotulo xiij^{o}. Heres Ricardi f. Yvonis debet ij s. et xj d. de scutagio de Biham. Radulfus de Trublevill' debet xviij s. et ix d. de eodem. *Set respondet in Devon' in rotulo sequenti.*

Hugo de Bello campo r.c. de xxxvj s. et viij d. de ij^{bus} debitis contentis in rotulo vj^{o}. In thes. xxiij s. et iiij d.[2] Et debet j m.

Episcopus Exon', barones, milites et omnes de Comitatu Cornub' r.c. de CCCC et quater xx et xv li. et v s. et v d. pro deaforestatione sicut continetur ibidem. In thes. C et quater xx et xiiij li. et xiiij[3] s. et xj d. Et debent CCC li. x s. v[d.][4] (*Set respondent infra.*[i])

Robertus de Cardinan r.c. de xxvj li. et j m. pro Jacobo Judeo sicut continetur in rotulo vij^{o}. In thes. x m. Et debet xx li.

[J]ohannes f. Ricardi r.c. de quater xx et iiij li. et iiij s. et vj d. de pluribus debitis sicut continetur in rotulo de dimidio anno xvij^{o}. In thes. xx li. Et debet lxiiij li. et iiij s. et vj d. (*Set respondet in Devon' in rotulo sequenti.*[i])[5] per annum x li.

Andreas de Bodmine r.c. de ij m. et dim. pro habenda justic' sicut continetur in rotulo vij^{o}. In thes. xxx s. et ij d. Et debet iij s. et ij d.

Willelmus Pococ debet terciam partem de CC et xx m. pro summonendo

[1] In *NS 54*, p. 245 he is almost certainly shown as *Robertus* (*Brunus*[i]) *butillier*.
[2] Altered from *iij*.
[3] Altered from *xiij*.
[4] The *d* is hidden under a mending strip running down the right hand edge.
[5] This clause was written in a gap in the text which was not quite large enough, and the last few words are slanted upwards over the start of *per annum*.

Ricardo de Wica ad reddendum ei debitum illud. Rollandus de Penwore et Willelmus de Tikembrec escaetores debent respondere de exitibus terre Willelmi de Boterell' et (Cadwallan'[i])[1]

Episcopus Exon' et alii supra contenti r.c. de CCC li. et x s. et vj d. sicut supra continetur. In thes. nichil. Et Simoni f. Ricardi iij m. ad expensas suas ad quintamdecimam colligendam. *Et debent CC et quater xx et xvii[j]*[2] *li. et x s. et vj d.*[3]

DE OBLATIS

Robertus de Cardinan debet j palefridum pro habenda mercata sicut continetur in rotulo viijº. Radulfus Bloiho debet C et iij s. et viij d. de scutagio de Mungumeri. Predictus Robertus del Kardinan debet liiij li. et xl d. de eodem.

Idem Vic. r.c. de xvj s. et viij d. de Willelmo f. Ricardi de scutagio de Mungumeri. Et de viij s. et iiij d. de Huardo de Biskel' de eodem. Et de xvj s. et viij d. de Bartholomeo Turet de eodem. In thes. lib. Et Q.E.

Johannes f. Ricardi et Stephanus de Croy debent DCC et xxij li. et v s. et iiij d. de remanenti firme staminarie Cornubie sicut continetur in rotulo viij. *Set respondent infra per partes.*

Stephanus de Croy r.c. de xiiij li. ix s. et iiij d. de firma staminarie Cornubie de anno vº et vjº. Et de x m. de anno vijº et viijº de eadem staminaria. Et C et xxiij li. et j m. de eadem firma de dim. anno ixº antequam staminaria traderetur comiti Ricardo fratri R. Summa C et xliiij li. et xvj s. In thes. nichil. Et pro robis emptis ad opus R. in nundinis Sancti Edmundi et Winton' lxxix li. et ix s. et vij d. et ob. per breve R. Et debet lxv li. vj s. et iiij d. et ob. Idem r.c. de eodem debito. In thes. xv li. et iij s. et viij d. et ob. Et debet l (li.[i]) et ij s. et viij d. *Set respondet infra.*

Johannes f. Ricardi debet xxxiiij li. ix s. et iiij d. de predicta firma staminarie de anno vº et vjº. Et [*blank*] M m. de anno vijº et viijº de eadem firma. Et [*blank*] C et xxiij li. et j m. de eadem firma de dim. anno ixº antequam traderetur predicto fratri R. Summa DCCC et xxiiij li. et xvj s. *Set respondet in Devon' in rotulo sequenti.*
[*One line blank*]

NOVA OBLATA

Robertus de Cardinan [*blank*] C s. de prestito ei facto apud Bedeford'.

Ricardus de Wika debet C s. pro habenda j feria apud manerium suum de Wika. Simon Pincerna debet j m. pro habenda inquisitione versus Margaretam de novo burgo.

Andreas de Bomine r.c. de dim. m. quia retraxit se sicut continetur in rotulo viijº. In thes. lib. Et Q.E.

[Alexan]der de Sabrichteworðe clericus r.c. de x li. et x s. et xj d.

1 Rest of the name lost under the mending strip.
2 Rest of the pounds lost under the mending strip.
3 Probably written later: *Et debent ... xviij* are on a slightly different alignment from the rest of the line, and the rest of the entry is written on the same line as the next heading *De Oblatis*.

de remanenti denariorum quos habuit in custodia in obsidione castri de Byham. In thes. v m. Et debet x m. et x s.[1] et xj d. per annum v m.

Stephanus de Croy r.c. de l li. et ij s. et viij d. de remanenti firme staminarie sicut supra continetur. In thes. xxvij li. et dim. m. Et debet xxij li. et xvj s. Idem r.c. de eodem debito. In thes. nichil. Et in elemosinis constitutis episcopo Exon' xxij m. et dim. de iiij^or annis et dim. per preceptum H. de Burgo Justiciarii. Et debet vij li. et xvj s. Idem r.c. de eodem debito. In thes. lib. Et Q.E.

[*Endorsed*] CUMBERLAND ET NORRHANTESIR' (emend' totum[i]) ET NORHUMBERLAND' (iterum emend' totum[i]) ET CORNUBIA[2]

[*Rot.* 4 *Mem.* 1][3]

LINC'

Hugo episcopus Linc' Radulfus f. Reginaldi pro eo ut custos r.c. de DCCC et xxxvj li. et xx d. bl. Et de C et xl li. num. de firma Comitatus. In thes. C et xxx li. et xvj s. et ix d. bl. Et C et xvj (li.[i]) xiij s. ix d. ob. num.

Et in elemosinis constitutis militibus de Templo ij[4] m. Et in terris datis militibus de Templo xj li.[5] bl. in Eccles. Et in civitate Linc' C et xl li. bl. de quibus cives respondent infra. Et ecclesie de Semplingeham viij li et x s. bl. in soca de Castr'. Et comiti Bolon' CC li. bl. in Kirketon'. Et Henrico de Neovill' de Burreðe xv li. bl. in Askeby et Teinton' membris de Hornecastr'. Et W. comiti Warenn' l li. bl. in Stamford'. Et monachis de Becco vij s. in Hornecastr'. Et Waltero de Baduent vj li. et xiiij s. in Marun soca de Hornecastr'. Et monialibus de Torkes' ij m. in Torkesia quas solebant reddere R. Et canonicis de novo Loco lxvj s. in Husum. Et in villa de Grimesby C et xj li. num. de quibus homines ville respondent infra. Et Radulfo de Rodes xx li. et dim. m. in Hornecastr'. Et eidem l li. in Hornecastr' quas Ricardus Revel habuit per R. Ricardum. Et infirmis Linc' xlvj s. et viij d. in Askeby membro de Hornecastr'. Et Willelmo f. Roberti xl s. in soca de Castr'. Et R. comiti Cestr' et Linc' xx li. de tercio denario Comitatus sicut continetur in rotulo iiij^o. Et Radulfo de Rodes iiij li. et dim. m. in Hornecastr' quas Willelmus de Lisuris tenuit. Et Willelmo f. Galfridi falconar' xxx s. in Clipesby membro de Castr'. Et Radulfo falconario et filie Anketilli f. Turgisii viij li. in soca de Castr'. Et in Castr' cum soka xxxviij li. et vij s. et x d. bl. quibus homines ville respondent infra per breve R.

[*One line blank*]

1 Altered from *xj s*.
2 Docket written reverse way up at the foot of the membrane.
3 There are a couple of holes towards the bottom right hand edge of the membrane which have been fixed by tape. There is also a strengthening tape down the right hand edge of the membrane which has masked some of the clerk's handwriting.
4 Written as *jj*.
5 It looks as though the clerk originally wrote *m.* and then erased the last leg of the *m* but not too well such that it is still visible. The *l* was added later as well.

Et Willelmo de Insula x m. ad expensas suas ad placita R. tenenda cum M. de Pateshill' et sociis suis per breve R.[1] Et Jordano de Esseby constabulario castri Linc' C s. ad operationes eiusdem castri per breve R. Et in reparatione seldarum ferie Sancti Botulphi de Hoyland' lxiiij s. per breve R. et per visum Gilleberti de Tudenham et Gilleberti Hoppecrawe. Et Ricardo Duket[2] x m ad se sustentandum in servicio R. cum M. de Pateshill' et sociis suis per breve R. Et debet xx s. et j d. bl. (extensos ad xx s. et vij d. num.[i]) Et xxiij li vj s. et ij d. et ob. num. Idem r.c. de eodem debito. In thes. nichil. Et in superplus quod habet infra (in tercia linea[i]) viij li. et v s. et xj d. et ob. Et in superplus quod habet in dorso rotuli de misericordiis hominum viij li. et viij s. et xj d. Et in superplus quod habet ibidem de catallis fugitivorum vj li et xj s. et iiij d. Et debet xx s. et viij d. num. Idem r.c. de eodem debito. In thes. lib. Et Q.E.

Idem Vic. r.c. de xxvij li. et xiiij s. et ob. num. de remanenti firme Comitatus de anno preterito. In thes. nichil. Et ipsi R. in garderoba sua xxxvj li. ad expensas suas adquietandas per breve R. Et habet de superplus viij li et v s. et xj d. et ob. qui locantur ei supra.

f' Idem Vic. r.c. de [C][3] li. de proficuo Comitatus[4] de hoc anno et anno preterito. In thes. lib. Et Q.E.

[*One line blank*]

f' Rogerus Grossus r.c. de xij d. de firma terre in Haconesby. In thes. lib. Et Q.E.

f' Alanus elemosinarius r.c. de x s. de firma terre que fuit Roberti de Bassingeburn' in Grimesby et Bradel' quam idem Robertus dedit eidem Alano coram baronibus de scaccario. In thes. lib. Et Q.E.

f' Abbas de Grimesby r.c. de xl s. de firma propresturarum in Grimesby. In thes. lib. Et Q.E.

f' Johannes f. Walteri de Braitoft r.c. de xl s. de firma de Suffliet. In thes. lib. Et Q.E.

f' Radulfus de Bradel' r.c. de lx s. de firma terrarum quas tenet de R. in Bradel'. In thes. xxxviij s. et viij d. Et in terris datis Radulfo fleccario xiiij s. et viij d. Et Galfrido de Neovill' dim. m. in Bradel' et quietus est.

(f' Homines de[e]) [*rest of line blank*]

f' Homines de Grimesby r.c. de C et xj li. de firma ville sue. In thes. xxxviij li. xvij s. et iiij d. Et in terris datis Radulfo de Bradel' lx s. Et monialibus de Grimesby xxvij s. et iiij d. Et Johanni f. Galfridi de Neovill' xxx li. et x s. in Lesseby et Cotes et Bradel'. Et Waltero fleccario viij m. Et in decimis constitutis canonicis de Grimesby xj li. Et in Scarthhou xx li. Et canonicis de Grimesby x s. de quibus Vic. respondet supra pro eis. Et in propresturis quas Radulfus de Bradel' tenuit viij s. et viij d. de quibus Alanus elemosinarius respondet supra. Et Q.S.

1 This is probably at the eyre of 1226–9 which started at Lincoln on 9 September 1226 and concluded on 13 October 1226 with Martin of Pattishall as the leading justice. William de Lisle was also one of the justices. The ten marks would be for his expenses at the eyre in Lincoln.

2 Richard Duket or Ducket was also a justice at the eyre in Lincoln.

3 The clerk has either written a zero here or he made a mistake and closed up the 'C'.

4 The clerk has blotted what looks like 'nn' where he should have written 'mi'.

[*One line blank*]

Idem homines r.c. de xx s. et iiij d. de remanenti eiusdem firme de anno preterito. In thes. lib. Et Q.S.

f' Idem homines r.c. de xxiij li. et xij s. de firma propresturarum de Grimesby. In thes. x li. et v d. et ob. Et abbati de Grimesby vj li. et xij s. Et templariis iij s. et iiij d. Et abbati de Ruchford' ij s. et vj d. Et Alano elemosinario iiij li. et xv s. et ob. Et Johanni de Neovill' xxvj s. et ij d. Et monialibus de Ormesby xij s. et vj d. Et Q.S.

[*One line blank*]

f' Cives Linc' r.c. de C et quater xx li. num. de firma civitatis. In thes. C et xlj li. et vij s. et j d. Et in elemosinis constitutis militibus de Templo j m. Et in decimis constitutis canonicis Linc' xviij li. Et debent xix li. et xix s. et vij d.

[*One line blank*]

Idem cives r.c. de DCC et liij li. et vj s. et ij d. de pluribus debitis contentis in rotulo precedenti. In thes. C m. Et debet DC et quater xx et vj li. et xij s. et x d. per annum C m.

f' Telarii Linc' r.c. de vj li. pro gilda sua. Et de xx s. de eadem de anno vij°. In thes. vj li. Et debent xx s.

f' Willelmus f. Warnerii r.c. de vj d. de quadam propresturа. In thes. lib. Et Q.E.

f' Renerius f. Johannis r.c. de vj d. de quadam propresturа. In thes. lib. Et Q.E.

f' Radulfus fleccarius r.c. de xx flechiis de firma terre sue de Bradel' In thes. nichil. Et ipsi R. xx flechie. Et Q.E.

f' Homines de Soca de Castr' r.c. de xxxviij li. et vij s. et x d. bl. et (de[i]) xj li.[1] et xij s. et ij d. num. de firma (ville[d]) soke sue quam dominus R. eis concessit quamdiu sibi placuerit cum omnibus placitis et aliis ad eam pertinentibus tenendam per l libras annuatim reddendas per manum suam videlicet ad scaccarium Pasche xxv li. et ad scaccarium Sancti Michaelis xxv li. De quibus L li. reddent xxxviij li et vij s. et x d. bl. et residuum num. sicut predictum est. In thes. xxxvj li et xv s. et xj d. bl. Et xj li. et xij s. et ij d. num. Et debent xxxj s. et xj d. bl. Idem r.c. de eodem debito.

Radulfus de Bradel' r.c. de viij li. et xv s. et iij d. de pluribus debitis contentis in rotulo iij°. In thes. iiij m. Et debet vj li. et xxiij d. per annum iiij m.

Alexander de Pointon' r.c. de xvij li. et xiij s. et ij d. de pluribus debitis contentis in rotulo viij. In thes. vij li. et x s. Et debet x li. et iij s. et ij d. per annum C s.

Baldewinus (Hugo[i])[2] Wac r.c. de C et quater xx et xvij li. et xj s. et iiij d. de pluribus debitis contentis in rotulo precedenti. In thes. xxv li. Et debet C et lxxij li. et xj s. et iiij d. per annum xxv li.

R. episcopus Saresbir' debet x m. pro Simone de Lindon' pro habendo

1 *et (dei) xj li.* written over an erasure.

2 This interlineation occurs after the 'B' in *Baldewinus*. *NS 54*, p. 51 has Baldwin.

recto sicut continetur in rotulo x^{mo} R. Ricardi. Gillebertus de Turon' debet CCC m. pro habenda terra Hamonis de Mascy sicut continetur ibidem.

Oliverius de Vallibus r.c. [de] xxv [li.] pro v palefridis contentis in rotulo precedenti. Et de vj li. de iiij^{o} scutagio R. J. pro Willelmo de Longo campo. In thes. lib. Et Q.E.

Templarii r.c. de lvij li. et v s. pro Margareta de Percy sicut continetur in rotulo x R. Ricardi. In thes. l s. Et debet liiij li. et xv s. per annum l s.

Nicholaus de Chavincurt r.c. de xix li. et xvj s. et ij d. de debitis Guidonis de Véér sicut continetur in rotulo primo R. J. In thes. x li. Et debet ix li et xvj s. et ij d.

Johannes f. Jukell' r.c. de C et xvj s. et v d. de pluribus debitis contentis in rotulo precedenti. In thes. j m. Et debet C et iij s. et j d.

H. episcopus Linc' r.c. de C et quater xx et xiij li. et xiij s. et ij d. pro herede Petri de Amundevill' sicut continetur in rotulo iiij. In thes. x m. Et debet C et quater xx et vj li. et xix s. et x d. per annum x m.

Colinus de iiij^{or} maris r.c. de lxxij li. et xvij s. et vij d. pro eodem herede sicut continetur ibidem. In thes. iiij li. Et debet lxviij li. et xvij s. et vij d. per annum iiij li.

Hamelinus decanus r.c. de quater xx et x li. et xiij s. et vj d. et ob. de debitis Ááron. In thes. ij m. per abbatem de Kirkested'. Et ix s. et viij d per abbatem de Parco Lude. Et xliiij s. et iij d. per alios tenentes terras que fuerunt eiusdem Hamelini. Et debet quater xx et vj li. et xij s. et xj d. et ob.

Hugo de Neovill' crassus r.c. de quater xx et xij li. et v s. et viij d. pro Waltero de Neovill' de debitis Judeorum. In thes. xx m. Et debet lxxviij li. et xix s. per annum xx m.

Prior de Bulinton' r.c. de xlvij li. et x s. de debitis Ááron. In thes. C s. Et debet xlij li. et x s. per annum C s.

Willelmus de Humez debet lxxv m. pro maritagio sicut continetur in rotulo ij^{o}. Nicholaus Morel debet C li. et ij partes duarum Mil. marcarum sicut continetur in rotulo xij^{o} R. J. (+^{i}) Petrus archidiaconus Linc' debet x li. de remanenti compoti episcopatus Linc'.

Normannus de Arescy r.c. de ix m. pro iij accipitribus.[1] In thes. lib. Et Q.E.

Willelmus de Scoteinn' debet xvij li. et ij d. de pluribus debitis contentis in rotulo vij^{o} (set respondet infra^{i}).

Philippus de Kyme r.c. de DC et xxxj li. et v s. et iij d. et j osturco premente de pluribus debitis contentis in rotulo precedenti. Et de CC et lvj li. et j m. de tribus debitis Elye Materin Judei per tres cartas. Et de lx li. de duobus debitis predicti Elye et Pictavi generi sui per ij cartas. Summa DCCCC et xlvij li. et xviij s. et vij d. In thes. l li. Et debet DCCC et quater xx et xvij li. et xviij s. et vij d. et j osturcum prementem. per annum C li.

Henricus Foliot r.c. de xxv li. et xix s. et iiij d. et j palefrido pro habenda custodia sicut continetur in rotulo v^{o}. In thes. x m. Et debet xix li. et vj s. et j palefridum. per annum x m.

[1] In *NS 54*, p. 52 Norman accounts for three goshawks, not sparrowhawks.

Willelmus f. Roberti r.c. de ij m. pro habenda j carrucata terre in Glentewurðe. In thes. lib. Et Q.E.

Thomas f. Thome f. Eust' r.c. de C et ix li. et ix s. de pluribus debitis patris sui contentis in rotulo iij°. In thes. v m. et dim. Et debet C et v li. et xv s. et viij d. hoc anno xl s.

Simon le Brett r.c. de C s. et xxij d. de ij debitis contentis in rotulo v. In thes ij m. Et debet lxxv s. et ij d.

Rogerus de Fraxinet' r.c. de xxiij s. et iiij d. pro crasso pisce. In thes. lib. Et Q.E.

Radulfus de Wileweby r.c. de xxx li. et dim. (m.[i]) et ij palefridis de pluribus debitis contentis in rotulo vij°. In thes x li. Et debet xx li. et dim. m. et ij palefridos. per annum x li.

Thomas de Scoteinn' r.c. de xlvj li. et x s. et vij d. de pluribus debitis contentis in rotulo precedenti. In thes. v m. Et debet xliij li. et iij s. et xj d. per annum v m.

Walterus de Evermou r.c. de xxij li. et j m. de ij^{bus} debitis contentis in rotulo iij°. In thes. v m. Et debet xix li. et dim. m.

Hugo Dodd debet iij m. pro summonendo Radulfo Cossmann' ad reddendum ei debitum. Radulfus de Wium debet xx s. et j palefridum pro habenda terra in Wium.

Nicholáá de Haya r.c. de xxxij li. de scutagio Pict'. In thes. vij li. et vij s. Et debet xxiiij li. et xiij s.

Reginaldus de Landa r.c. de xxxviij m. et xl d. de misericordia. In thes. dim. m. Et debet xxxvij m. et x s. per annum dim. m.

Malgerus de Asegaresby r.c. de xviij li. et xiij s. et viij d. pro eodem. In thes. dim. m. Et debet xviij li. et vij s. per annum dim. m.

[*Rot.* 4 *Mem.* 2]

[*One line blank*]

Robertus Moisant r.c. de C et xj s. et viij d. pro deliberatione sua. In thes. x s. Et [debet] C et j s. et viij d. per annum x s.

Idem Vic. r.c. de j m. de Henrico f. Walteri. Et de xx s. de Fulcone de Oyri. Et de lxxiij s. de Radulfo f. Stephani. In thes. lib. Et Q.E.

Walterus de Marton' r.c. de v m. de misericordia. In thes. ij m. Et debet iij m. per annum ij m.

Oliverius de Aencurt r.c. de xxxij li. et j m. de iij^{bus} debitis contentis in rotulo precedenti. In thes. xviij li. Et debet xiiij li. et j m. de scutagio.

Gillebertus de Gand' r.c. de M et quater xx et iij li et xv s. et ix d. et ob. de pluribus debitis contentis in rotulo precedenti. In thes. l m. Et debet M et l li. et ix s. et iij ob. per annum l m.

Radulfus de Trublevill'[1] [*blank*] lxxv s. de catallis Outi prepositi hominis ipsius fugitivi pro malo retto de quibus idem R. debet respondere ad voluntatem R.

[1] The hand which drafts this name is noticeably different to that which drafted the previous entries on this membrane.

DE PRESTITO PICTAVIE

Henricus de Neovill' de Burreðe debet xx s. de eodem. Waleram de Rocheford' debet xij m. de eodem. Otuelus de Insula debet xj m. de eodem. Johannes de Neovill' debet x m. de eodem. Normannus de Aresci debet xj m. de eodem.

Hugo de Verly r.c. de CCCC et xxxvij li. et ij s. de ij^{bus} debitis contentis in rotulo iij^{o}. In thes. xxv li. Et debet CCCC et xij li. et ij s.

per annum xxv li.

Robertus Lupus [*blank*] xx m et ij palefridos pro Henrico archidiacono.

Idem de exit[1] [*blank*] de exitibus episcopatus Cestr' dum habuit custodiam.

Hugo de Maidewell' r.c. de lxiij s. et viij d. de Baldrico f. Oseb'. In thes. dim. m. Et debet lvij s. per annum dim. m.

Adam de Hasceby r.c. de xiij s. et vj d. pro habenda gratia R. J. In thes. dim. m. Et debet vj s. et x d.

Idem Vic. r.c. de j m. de Roberto le Thus. Et de xxiij s. et iiij d. de Waltero Frost. In thes. lib. Et Q.E.

Henricus Bech r.c. de xviij m. et x s. de ij^{bus} debitis contentis in rotulo vij^{o}. In thes xx s. Et debet xvij m. et xl d.

Johannes Blanchard' r.c. de xxiij s. et iiij d. pro habenda gratia R. J. In thes. xx s. Et debet xl d.

Robertus de Amundevill' r.c. de xij m. et dim. et j palefrido pro eodem. Et de x li. pro debitis Judeorum. In thes. C s. Et debet xx m.[2]

per annum C s.

Willelmus de Baiocis r.c. de xix li. et xl d. et j palefrido pro eodem. In thes. xl s. Et debet xvij li. et xl d. et j palefridum.

Herebertus de Neovill' r.c. de xix m. et j palefrido pro eodem. In thes ij m. Et debet xvij m. et j palefridum.

Nigellus de Pincobecc' r.c. de xvj s. et vijj d. Et de x m. pro ij^{bus} palefridis pro eodem. In thes. C s. Et debet l s.

Ricardus de Berking' r.c. de xxiiij s. et viij d. pro Willelmo de Rowell'.

Ricardus de Beningeworðe debet lx m. et j dextrarium pro habenda gratia R. J. Margareta filia Alani de Dunnhéé debet xl s. pro habendo precipe sicut continetur in rotulo ij^{o}. Margareta de Stikeswald' debet xx s. pro eodem.

Petrus de Orivall' r.c. de xl m. et dextrarium pro Roberto de Basingeham. In thes x m. Et debet xxx m. et j dextrarium.

[3] Idem Vic. r.c. de v s. et iiij d. de Galfrido de Angoteby. Et de xl d. de Willelmo f. Rogeri. Et de vj s. et iiij d. de Henrico f. Ricardi. In thes. lib. Et Q.E.

Robertus Greslé et Michael de Swineheved debent j m. pro habendo brevi sicut continetur in rotulo iiij^{o}. + Robertus de Wileweby debet dim.

1 *Sic.*

2 He also owes a palfrey.

3 There is a symbol shaped like a key between the previous line and this one. There is a broken line from this 'key' to another one 10 lines below, the last line of this section and which appears to suggest that this line should be inserted here. There is no obvious reason why it should so it has been ignored and the lines kept as shown in the membrane. There is another footnote when this other 'key' appears.

m. quia non est prosecutus. + Willelmus de Colevill' debet viij li. de ij^{bus} debitis contentis in rotulo vij^{o}.

Thomas de Monte Begonis r.c. de lviij s. et iiij d. pro summonendo Thoma. In thes. viij s. Et debet l s. et iiij d.

+ Henricus de Messingeham debet dim. m. pro summonendo priore. + Hugo f. Galfridi debet ij m. pro licencia concordandi cum Roberto de Sancto Amando. Robertus Lupus debet vj s. de catallis Odonis sicut continetur in rotulo precedenti.

Radulfus de Normanvill' r.c. de vij li. et xvj s. et viij d. de iij debitis. In thes. v m. Et debet iiij li. et viij s.

Joslanus de Neovill' r.c. de lx s. de relevio suo. In thes. xx s. Et debet xl s.

Walterus Bech' r.c. de lvj li. et xvij s. de pluribus debitis contentis in rotulo v^{o}. In thes. xv li. Et debet xlj li. et xvij s.

Simon de Ryeby[1] r.c. de x m. et dim. et iij palefridis pro habenda gratia R. J. In thes. v m. Et debet v m. et dim. et iij palefridos.

Willelmus de Rowell' debet dim. m. pro licencia concordandi cum Alicia de Bordell'. Hugo de Gretford' debet dim. m. pro licencia concordandi cum Thoma de Tholethorp per plegium Osberti de Tikecot'.[2]

Radulfus de Haya debet x m. pro plegio Bertrami de Aubeinni. Hugo f. Radulfi debet v m. pro Roberto de Sancto Amando. (Walterus Frost (debet^{c}) (r.c. de^{i}) xxiij s. et iiij d. pro Hugone de Trikingeham. In thes. lib. Et Q.[E.]^{i})[3]

DE PRIMO SCUTAGIO R.

Osbertus de Vallibus r.c. de l s. de eodem. In thes. lib. Et Q.E.[4]

Johannes de Baiocis r.c. de xvj li. et xvij s. et viij d. de eodem. In thes. x m. (et iiij s. et iiij d.^{i}) Et debet x li. Idem r.c. de eodem debito. In thes nichil. Et ipsi Johanni pro custodia castri de Plinton' (per breve R.^{i}) de tribus partibus anni xj. (Et Q. [E.]^{i}).

Thomas f. Eustachii r.c. de dim. m. de eodem de honore de Chokes. In thes. lib. Et Q.E.[5]

Galfridus f. Galfridi de Neovill' r.c. de xxx s. de iij^{bus} debitis contentis in rotulo precedenti. Et de vj m. de scutagio de Mungumeri. Et de xx s. de scutagio Pict' de dim. feodo Johannis Malherbe. Et de v s. de scutagio de Biham de eodem feodo. Et de j m. de scutagio de Mungumeri de eodem

[1] In *NS 54*, p. 56 and *NS 56*, p. 118 he is shown as *Simon de Driby*. There is a place called Driby and another called Riby in Lincolnshire.

[2] This is where the other symbol shaped like a key, mentioned in n. 2 above, is placed.

[3] This has been inserted here but is not shown above the line. It is uncertain where the insertion actually comes from. The word *E.* for *Est* is under the tape at the right hand side of the membrane.

[4] It looks as though the clerk got this on the wrong line, that is the line below. This is because the person in the line below was also quit of the debt. He also gets out of alignment again in the next but one line.

[5] This should be on the same line as the first statement but the clerk has written a bit out of line here.

feodo. Et de vj m. de scutagio de Bedef'. Et de x li. et x s. de wardis de Richemund' de vij annis preteritis. Et de xxx s. de eisdem de hoc anno. In thes. l s. Et debet xx li. xviij s. iiij d. (per annum C s.[c])

Idem r.c. de eodem debito. In thes l s. Et debet xviij li. et viij s. et iiij d. per annum C s.

Robertus Marmiun debet xxij m. et xij s. de eodem. Hugo episcopus Linc' debet iiij m. de eodem.

Jeronimus de Normanneby r.c. de xj li. et j palefrido pro habenda gratia R. J. In thes. j m. Et debet x li. et dim. m. et j palefridum.

Johannes Coleman r.c. de xliij li. et viij s. et iiij d. pro eodem. In thes. iiij m. Et debet xl li. et xv s.

Idem Vic. r.c. de iij m. et de v m. pro j palefrido de Willelmo camerario. Et de iij s. et vj d. de Galfrido Wind. In thes. lib. Et Q.E.

Johannes frater Ade de Iseinn' r.c. de xxv m. pro eodem. In thes. v m. Et debet xx m.

Willelmus Bastard' r.c. de xxv s. de misericordia. In thes. iij s. Et debet xxij s.

+ Rogerus de Angoteby debet ij s. pro eodem. + Hugo de Arescy debet ij s. et iiij d. pro eodem. + Hugo de Hundegat' debet v s. de eodem. (t[i]) Robertus f. Willelmi debet dim. m. pro dissaisina.

Walterus f. Haldan' et socii sui r.c. de j m. pro defalta. In thes. x s. Et debent xl d.

Robertus f. Turoldi r.c. de dim m. pro falso clamore. In thes. xl d. Et debet xl d.

Ricardus de Norf' r.c. de vj m. pro novis consuetudinibus. In thes. j. m. Et debet v m.

Jordanus de Eisseby r.c. de xij m. et dim. de iij[bus] debitis contentis in rotulo iiij. In thes. j m. Et debet xj m. et dim.

+ Hugo Panchard' debet dim m. pro plegio. + Walterus de Norðkime debet ij m. et dim. pro transgressione. + Robertus f. Walteri debet dim. m. pro licencia concordandi. Walterus f. Galfridi debet dim. m. pro eodem. + Magnus forestarius debet dim. m. pro [eodem].[1] + Radulfus frater Alexandri debet dim m. pro eodem. Alanus Karesman debet iiij s. et viij d. pro licencia concordandi. + Robertus f. Gerebricht debet dim. m. pro eodem. + Willelmus Turpin debet dim. m. pro dissaisina.

Adam Pasdelu r.c. de j m. pro dissaisina. In thes. xl d. Et debet x s.

Idem Vic. r.c. de dim. m. de Adam [*sic*] f. Thome. Et de xl d. de Johanne de Osegoteby. Et de xx d. de Roberto Wassepoke. Et de xx d. de Waltero Caperun. Et de v s. de Thoma Achard'. In thes. lib. Et Q.[E.]

+ Elyas f. Ricardi debet xv s. pro dissaisina. + Hamo le Chat debet dim. m. pro plegio. + Adam f. Ricardi de Angoteby debet dim. m. quia retraxit se. + Galfridus homo Johannis debet dim. m. pro vino vendito. Livina relicta Radulfi de Claxeb' debet dim. m. quia non est prosecuta. + Walterus de Kelleby debet dim. m. quia non habuit. + Hugo de Totinton' debet dim. m. pro eodem. + Thomas de Totinton' debet dim. m. pro eodem. Rogerus prepositus debet dim. m. pro vino vendito. + Galfridus de Beningworðe

1 The right hand edge has been strengthened and has gone over the last word of this text. UV indicates that the last word is *eodem*. This is what is in *NS 54*, pp. 59, 120.

debet j m. de ij^{bus} debitis contentis in rotulo vij^{o}. + Godwinus f. Turstani debet dim. m. quia non habuit. + Alanus de Fereby debet j m. pro novis consuetudinibus. + Henricus f. Dionis' debet dim. m. quia non est prosecutus. + Radulfus f. Saive debet dim. m. quia non habuit. + Brianus de Fuglestow' debet dim. m. pro eodem. + Rogerus f. Galfridi debet dim. m. pro eodem. + Robertus de Harpewell' debet xij d. de catallis Walteri. + Willelmus de alta ripa debet xiiij s. de catallis Badde. + Galfridus f. Alani debet dim. m. quia non habuit. + Radulfus Brunus debet dim. m. pro eodem. + Radulfus Bule debet dim. m. pro eodem. + Tadyat de Roppel' debet dim. m. pro eodem. + Alanus f. Simonis debet dim. m. pro vino vendito. Simon Bere debet dim. m. pro eodem. + Robertus de Bliton' debet dim. m. pro eodem. + Ricardus frater Roberti [de Bliton'] debet dim. m. pro eodem. Prior de Simpingeh' debet x m. pro dissaisina. + Constancia Ridel debet j palefridum pro summonendo Willelmo sicut continetur in rotulo v^{o}. Johannes de Colemere debet j m. quia non habuit. Willelmus de Waspré debet dim. m. [pro defalta].[1]

Robertus Greslé r.c. de xl m. pro dissaisina. In thes. v m. Et debet xxxv m.

Willelmus de Ros de Tidd r.c. de xxxviij li. et xix s. et viij d. de pluribus debitis contentis in rotulo v. In thes C s. Et debet xxxiij li. et xix s. et viij d. per annum C s.

Robertus Marmiun iunior r.c. de lxxviij li. et iij s. et iiij d. de pluribus debitis contentis in rotulo vij^{o}. In thes. xl m. Et debet lj li. et x s.

Alexander f. Johannis capellani debet x s. pro stallagio de Dunham (set respondet infra[i]). Ricardus f. Johannis debet ij m. quia retraxit se per plegium Rogeri Gat et Johannis de Bulehill' et Godefridi de Kinebir'.

Heres Alexandri de Neovill' r.c. de CCC et lij li. et xiiij s. et iij d. et ij palefridis de pluribus debitis contentis in rotulo v^{o}. In thes. xx m. Et debet CCC et xxxix li. et vij s. et vij d. et ij palefridos. per annum xx m.

Robertus Marmiun senior debet C et lxxj li. et j m. pro habenda custodia castri de Tameworðe sicut continetur in rotulo vij. Set comes[2] respondet inde inter alia debita sua in dorso rotuli.

Abbas de Parco Lude r.c. d xl m. de catallis que fuerunt Rogeri de Neovill'. In thes. xx m. Et debet xx m.

Idem Vic. r.c. de x s. de Roberto de Arcubus. Et de iiij m. de Abbate de Seleby. Et de x s. de Radulfo preposito. Et de j m. de Roberto de Otteb[y]. In thes. lib. Et Q.E.

Tria feoda et dimidium de honore de Eya in hoc Comitatu r.c. de vj li. et xxj d. et ob. de scutagio Hibernie sicut in rotulo precedenti. In thes. iiij li. et xl d. Et debet xxxviij s. et v d. et ob.

Willelmus de Sancto Laudo [*blank*] xv li. de debitis Judeorum.

Willelmus de Scoteinn' [*blank*] C et xiij s. et iiij d. de scutagio de Mungumeri. Et de xvij li. et ij d. de pluribus debitis contentis in rotulo vij^{o}. Et xl li. de debitis Judeorum.

[1] This is at the right hand edge of the membrane which is considerably rubbed and there is also some strengthening tape which has obscured the reason for the entry. The reason has been supplied from *NS 54*, p. 60.

[2] Perhaps the earl of Chester.

Radulfus de Trihampton' r.c. de ij m. de scutagio de Mungumeri. In thes. lib. Et Q.E.

Henricus de Neovill' de Burreðe [*blank*] C et iij s. et iiij d. de pluribus scutagiis contentis in rotulo precedenti.

f' Willelmus de Well' [*blank*] xx s. de scutagio de Mungumeri. Et dim. m. de scutagio de Bedeford'.

Robertus de Mustiers [*blank*] ij m. de scutagio de Mungumeri. Et ij m. de scutagio de Bedeford'.

Robertus de Morton' r.c. de xlj s. et viij d. de pluribus scutagiis contentis in rotulo precedenti. In thes. xl s. et iiij d. Et debet xvj d.

Robertus de Hasceby [*blank*] xvj s. et viij d. de ij^{bus} scutagiis contentis in rotulo precedenti.

Robertus camerarius debet ij m. et dim. de scutagio de Mungumeri.

Radulfus de Berevill' r.c. de xv s. et viij d. de iiij scutagiis contentis in rotulo precedenti. In thes. lib. Et Q.E.

Alexander f. Johannis capellani r.c. de x s. pro stallagio sicut supra continetur. In thes. v s. Et debet v s.

RESPICE IN TERGUM

[*Rot.* 4d *Mem.* 1]

Eudo de Lungviliers r.c. de xxxviij s. et iiij d. de iij^{bus} scutagiis contentis in rotulo precedenti. In thes xx s. Et debet xviij s. et iiij d.

Willelmus de Albinneio r.c. de MMM(M^{e}) et CCC et xliiij li. et xiiij s. et iiij d. et ob. et j palefrido de pluribus debitis contentis in rotulo viij^{o}. Et de v m. de misericordia foreste per B. de Insula. In thes. x li. Et debet MMM et CCC et xxxviij li. et xij d. et ob. et j palefridum.

per annum x li.

Ricardus de Helingeie r.c. de dim. m. ut scribatur. In thes. lib. Et Q.E.

Hugo de Stowe r.c. de xlviij li. et xviij s. et iiij d. de debitis Judeorum. In thes. xx s. Et debet xlvij li. et xviij s. et iiij d. per annum xl s.

Otuel de Insula (d^{e})r.c. de ij m. de primo scutagio R. In thes. lib. Et Q.E.

DE OBLATIS

Walterus de Hoiland' debet dim. m. pro summonendo Willelmo sicut continetur in rotulo precedenti.

Idem Vic. r.c. de dim. m. de Willelmo f. Jordani. Et de xxxv s. de Adam Painel. Et de xl s. de Henrico de Ortiaco. Et de ij m. de Otuel' de Insula de primo scutagio R. In thes. lib. Et Q.E.

Osbertus Arsic r.c. de ij m. pro licencia concordandi sicut continetur ibidem. In thes. j m. Et debet j m.

Herveus de Pinkeinn' r.c. de j m. pro dissaisina. In thes. dim. m. Et debet dim. m.

DE WARDIS MILITUM DE HONORE RICHEMUND' DE VIJ ANNIS PRETERITIS

Picot de Lacell' r.c. de vj li. et et v s. de eadem. In thes. xxv s. Et debet C s.

Robertus le Thus r.c. de vij li. et x s. de eadem. In thes. l s. Et debet C s. (Set inde quietus est de lxxv s. scilicet de warda trium annorum quia fuit in exercitibus de Byham, Mungumery et Bedef' in servicio R. Et debet de remanenti xxv s.[i])[1]

Radulfus de Trihamtun' r.c. de C et v s. de eadem. In thes. lxx s. Et debet xxxv s. Joslanus de Neovill' r.c. de lxx s. de eadem. In thes. xviij s. et iiij d. Et debet lj s. et viij d.

Robertus de Monasteriis r.c. de lxx s. de eadem. In thes. iij m. et dim. Et debet xxiij s. et iiij d.

Thomas de Muleton' [*blank*] lxx s. de eadem.

Willelmus de Well' r.c. de lij s. et vj d. de eadem. In thes. xij s. et vj d. Et debet xl s.

Radulfus de Hoiland' r.c. de xxxv s. de eadem. In thes. lib. Et Q.E.

Henricus Teutonicus debet xxxv s. de eadem. Johannes Maresc' debet xvij s. et vj d. de eadem.

Picot de Lacell' [*blank*] xij li. et x s. de relevio suo sicut continetur in rotulo precedenti.

Robertus de Brettevill' senior r.c. de iiij s. pro defalta. In thes. lib. Et Q.E.

Jordanus de Esseby debet dim. m. pro defalta sicut continetur ibidem.
[*One line blank*]

DE EISDEM WARDIS DE HOC ANNO

Idem Vic. r.c. de xxv s. de Picot de Lacell' de eadem. Et de xxv s. de Roberto le Tus de eadem. Et de xx s. de Radulfo de Trihampton' de eadem. Et de x s. de Jodlano de Neovill' de eadem. Et de x s. de Roberto de Monasteriis de eadem. Et de vij s. et vj d. de Willelmo de Welles de eadem. Et de v s. de Radulfo de Hoiland' de eadem. In thes. lib. Et Q.E.

Thoams de Muleton' [*blank*] x s. de eadem.

Henricus Teutonicus debet v s. de eadem. Johannes Maresc' debet ij s. et vj d. de eadem.

Thomas de Muleton' [*blank*] D et lxj li. et vij s. et j d. de pluribus debitis contentis in rotulo precedenti de quibus Robertus de Ros debet eum adquietare de lxxix li. et x s. (Set respondet in Cumberland'.[i]) quas Alanus de Kaldebec ballivus suus recepit de fine Ade Morevill' contento in predicto debito sicut recognoscit. Et Willelmus de Lancastr' heres Gilleberti f. Reinfridi de xxxix li. xiiij s. et v d. (Set respondet in Lanc'.[i]) quas Adam de Yeland' ballivus eius recepit de eodem fine sicut recognoscit. Et debet T[homas] CCCC et xlij li. ij s. viij d.[2] per annum C li.

Yllaria Trussebut debet x li. et viij s. et vij d de pluribus scutagiis contentis in Everwikesir' que requirebatur ibidem.

[1] This insertion is written on the line below.
[2] It should be CCCC li. xij s. viij d.

Johannes f. Galfridi de Neovill' r.c. de DCCCC et quater xx et xj li. et v s. et iiij d. de pluribus debitis contentis ibidem. In thes. l s. Et debet DCCCC et quater xx et xviij li et xv s. et iiij d. per annum C s.
[*One blank line*]

NOVA OBLATA

Gillebertus de Gand' debet dim. m. pro habendo brevi de attingendis xij iuratoribus nove dissaisine de tenemento in Hal et Hekenton'. (*t*[i]) Thomas de Ormesby debet dim. [m.] pro habendo brevi de attingendis xij juratoribus assise nove dissaisine de tenemento in Thorp. (*d*[i]) Elyas de Houton' debet dim. m. pro habendo brevi de attingendis xij juratoribus assise nove dissaisine capte apud Linc' coram Roberto de Laxinton' et sociis suis inter Willelmum f. Willelmi et ipsum Elyam de tenemento in Houton'. (*t*[i]) Petrus f. Lewelini debet dim. m. pro habendo brevi de attingendis xij juratoribus in Halinton'.

Idem Vic. r.c. de dim. m. de Simone f. Rann' pro habendo precipe versus priorem de Spalding' de terra in Muleton'. Et de dim. [m.] de Roheis' de Kyme pro habendo pone contra priorem de cruce Roheis'. Et de dim. m. de Thoma de la Felde pro habendo brevi de attingendis xij. In thes. lib. Et Q.E.

t Homines de Grimesby r.c. de lx m. et ij palefridis pro habenda villa de Grimesby in manu sua sicut eam prius habuerunt usque in iij annos a die Sancti Michaelis anno ix^{o}. In thes. xl m. Et debet xx m. et ij palefridos.

t Gillebertus de Riggeby r.c. de v m. pro j palefrido pro licencia concordandi cum Simone Hanselin de verberationibus et imprisonamento et toltis factis eidem. In thes. xl s. Et debet ij m. per plegium Jodlani de Neovill' [et] Willelmi de Welles.

Homines magistri Alberti de Tragarthorp et de Sutton' r.c. de xv m. pro habendo brevi quod teneant terram suam per easdem consuetudines et eadem servicia per que eam tenuerunt tempore Galfridi Baiard'. In thes. lib. Et Q.S.

f' Marg' que fuit uxor Radulfi de Diva r.c. de iiij li. de termino Sancti Michaelis huius anni pro habenda terra que fuit Radulfi de Diva mariti sui in Corby que fuit in manu R. ratione terre que fuit Rogeri de Torpel de quo predictus Radulfus terram suam tenuit tenendam usque ad etatem filii sui heredis ipsius Radulfi reddendo inde annuatim viij li. ad scaccarium ad ij^{os} terminos. In thes. iiij m. Et debet ij m.

Idem Vic. r.c. de lxx s. et viij d. de exitibus eiusdem terre dum fuit in manu R. In thes. lib. Et Q.E.

Henricus falconarius r.c. de iiij li. pro relevio suo de iiij libratis terre in Keleby quas tenere debet de R. In thes. lib. Et Q.E.

Prior de Spalling' debet xx s. pro habendo pone contra abbatem de Croiland'. Walterus de Hal' debet dim. m. pro habendo brevi de recordo coram justiciariis in proximo adventu suo in partes illas de terra in Cle.

Alanus f. Hacon' debet dim. m. pro habendo (pone[c]) brevi de attingendis xij de tenemento in Tedeltorp. Willelmus f. Alexandri debet dim. m. pro habendo brevi de attingendis xij juratoribus contra abbatem de Barling'.

Henricus de Munegeden' proximus heres Rogeri de Montebegon' [*blank*] pro relevio suo.

Simon Lostricier debet dim. m. pro habendo brevi de attingendis xij de tenemento in Halton'. Prior de Sixle debet dim. m. pro licencia concordandi cum Willelmo de Baiocis. Ricardus f. Willelmi de Pincebec debet C s. ut tradatur in ballio.

Homines de Grimesby [*blank*][1] quater xx m. ut M. de Pateshill' et socii sui justiciarii itinerantes in Comitatu Linc' eant usque Grimesby ad capiendas omnes assisas et tenenda omnia placita ad villam de Grimesby et libertates eiusdem ville spectancia.

Normannus de Arescy r.c. de j m. pro faciendo mentione in brevi suo de tempore H. R. avi. In thes. lib. Et Q.E.

Magnus f. Turgod' debet dim. m. pro transgressione per plegium Willelmi de Beningworðe. Prior de Sempingeh' debet dim. m. pro licencia concordandi cum Gilleberto de Gand'.

Johannes de Aencurt r.c. de j m. pro dissaisina de quadam assisa capta coram Jordano de Eisseby et sociis suis per preceptum R. in eodem Comitatu. In thes. lib. Et Q.E.

Robertus f. Agnetis unus heredum Rogeri de Neovill' r.c. de ij m. pro debitis ipsius Rogeri. In thes. lib. Et Q.E.

Willelmus de Redburn' alius heredum eiusdem r.c. de ij m. de debitis eiusdem. In thes. lib. Et Q.E.

Idem Vic. r.c. de ij s. et viij d. de Willelmo f. Walteri de Haconeby de primo scutagio R. de x^{a} parte feodi j^{us} militis in Haconeby. Et de ij s. et viij d. de eodem de scutagio de Mungumeri. Et de ij s. et viij d. de eodem W. de scutagio de Bedef'. In thes. lib. Et Q.E.

Rogerus de Neovill' heredes ipsius pro eo r.c. de DCCCC et lxxv li. et v s. et vj d. de pluribus debitis contentis in rotulo de dimidio anno xvij R. J. In thes. nichil hic. Et in rotulo vij R. In thes. per abbatem de Parco Luðe de catallis ipsius R. que habuit in custodia xx m. Et per eundem Abbatem in rotulo viij eiusdem xx m. Et per eundem Abbatem in rotulo ix eiusdem xx m. Et per eundem Abbatem ex alia parte huius rotuli xx m. Et in rotulo anni vj R. per Robertum f. Agnetis qui est unus heredum ipsius Rogeri j m. Et in anno vij^{o} R. per eundem Robertum in thes. lvj s. et viij d. Et in anno viij^{o} R. per eundem Robertum in thes. xxvj s. Et in anno ix R. per eundem Robertum in thes. ij m. Et ibidem de exitu terre Willelmi f. Alicie alterius heredis ipsius Rogeri ij m. Et supra per Robertum f. Agnetis in thes. ij m. Et ibidem per Willelmum de Redburne. In thes. ij m. Et debet DCCCC et xj li. et xvj s. et ij d.

Petrus de Paris' r.c. de x li. de debitis Elye Marterin Judei Lincoll'. In thes. xx s. Et debet ix li. per annum xl s.

DE AMERCIAMENTIS PER ROBERTUM DE LAXINTON'[2] ET SOCIOS SUOS

Idem Vic. r.c. de CC et xxij li. et j m. de misericordiis hominum et villarum quorum nominibus preponitur littera *t* in rotulo quem predicti

[1] There is something rubbed out here.

[2] This must have been an assize and/or gaol delivery as the eyre in September to

liberaverunt in thesauro. In thes. CC et xxj li. et ij s. et iij d. in C et xxviij taleis. Et Willelmo de Ebor' clerico x li. ad expensas suas adquietandas per breve R. Et habet de superplus viij li. et viij s. et xj d. quod locatur ei supra post corpus comitatus.

Idem Vic. r.c. de CC et lij li. et viij s. et viij d. et ob. de catallis fugitivorum et suspensorum de eodem itinere quorum nominibus preponitur littera *t* in predicto rotulo quem ipsi liberaverunt in thesauro. In thes. CC et lix li. et ob. in CCC et xlvij taleis. Et habet de superplus vj li. et xj s. et iiij d. quod locatur ei supra post corpus comitatus.

Idem Vic. r.c. de xiiij s. et vj d. de catallis Willelmi de Brancewell' suspensi. Et de ij s. de catallis Simonis Bercarii suspensi. Et de vj s. de catallis Becce de Lafford' suspense. Et de xv s. de catallis Galfridi Torfot suspensi. In thes. nichil. Et H. episcopo Linc' xlvij s. et vj d. de catallis villanorum suorum pro malefactis contra pacem quos idem episcopus habuit coram justiciariis ad standum recto per breve R. Et Q.E.

Idem Vic. r.c. de iij s. de catallis Alani de Toftis fugitivi. Et de ix s. et viij d. de catallis Galfridi Prentut fugitivi. Et de dim. m. de catallis Roberti f. Ailmund' fugitivi. Et de dim. m. de catallis Roberti f. Hugonis fugitivi. Et de j m. de catallis Ricardi Cote fugitivi. Et de vj d. de catallis Rogeri hominis Sancti Leonardi fugitivi. Et de j m. de catallis Willelmi f. Leiard' fugitivi. Et de x s. de catallis Johannis f. Leiard' fugitivi. Et de viij s. de catallis Roberti Longi fugitivi. Et de dim. m. de catallis Willelmi Widmer' fugitivi pro dissaisina. In thes. lib. In ix taleis. Et Q.E.

Oliverius de Vallibus r.c. de v m. de fine. In thes. lib. Et Q.E.

[1]*t* Simon f. Jacobi r.c. de dim. m. quia non habuit. In thes. xl d. Et debet xl d.

[*Rot.* 4d *Mem.* 2]

[*One line blank*]

d Hugo f. Willelmi r.c. de dim. m. pro dissaisina. In thes. xl d. Et debet xl d.

t Henricus f. Walteri r.c. de dim. m. quia non habuit. In thes. xl d. Et debet xl d.

t Galfridus Helle r.c. de dim. m. pro dissaisina. In thes xl d. Et debet xl d.

t Guido de Wainfliet r.c. de j m. pro eodem.

t Willelmus de Rasne r.c. de xx s. pro habenda jurata. In thes. x s. Et debet x s.

t Sewal' f. Walteri r.c. de iij m. pro dissaisina. In thes. ij m. Et debet j m.

d Radulfus f. Fulconis r.c. de xx s. pro eodem. In thes. dim. m. Et debet j m.

d Hamo piscator r.c. de dim. m. pro eodem. In thes. xl d. Et debet xl d.

d Willelmus f. Milonis r.c. de j m. pro eodem. In thes. viij s. iiij d. Et debet v s.[2]

October 1226 was led by Martin of Pattishall. See Crook, *Records of the General Eyre*, p. 79.

1 The following entries are written on the left hand side of the membrane.

2 The words *In thes. viij s. iiij d. Et debet v s.* are written in a more faded tone of ink than the rest of this entry.

t Ricardus f. Walteri r.c. de dim m. pro eodem. In thes. xl d. Et debet xl d.
t Nicholaus f. Willelmi r.c. de j m. pro defalta. In thes. dim. m. Et debet dim. m.
t Willelmus frater Pere de Lubrac r.c. de dim. m. pro eodem. In thes. xl d. Et debet xl d.
t Alanus de Mof r.c. de j m. pro eodem. In thes dim. m. Et debet dim. m.
t Thomas camerarius r.c. de xx s. pro eodem.
t Radulfus ad aquam r.c. de dim. m. pro eodem. In thes. ij s. et ij d. Et debet iiij s. et vj d.
d Rannulfus de Welles r.c. de dim. m. pro eodem. In thes. xl d. Et debet xl d.
t Johannes de Saltereia r.c. de dim. m. pro eodem. In thes. xl d. Et debet xl d.
t Lucas de Bulefeld' r.c. de dim. m. pro eodem. In thes. v s. Et debet xx d.
t Johannes Branche r.c. de dim. m. pro eodem. In thes. xl d. Et debet xl d.
t Alanus f. Roberti r.c. de dim. m. pro eodem. In thes. xl d. Et debet xl d.
f' Robertus f. Alani debet de (dim.^{d}) j[1] m. pro eodem.
t Willelmus frater Jordani de Hocton' r.c. de dim. m. In thes. ij s. et vj d. Et debet iiij s. et ij d.
t Thomas Muchard' r.c. de dim. m. pro eodem. In thes. xl d. Et debet xl d.
t Henricus Leveske r.c. de v m. pro transgressione. In thes. ij m. et dim. Et debet ij m. et dim.
[2]*t* Villata de Grantham r.c. de C s. pro receptamento. In thes. l s. Et debet l s.

[*Rot.* 4d *Mem.* 2]

[*One line blank*]
t Robertus Coffin r.c. de v m. de[3] catallis. In thes. lvij s. ij d. Et debet ix s. et vj d.
t Villata de Claipol r.c. de iij m. pro receptamento. In thes. xxxviij s. et v d. Et debet xix d.
t Villata de Naveneby r.c. de xl s. pro eodem. In thes. xxxvj s. et vj d. Et debet iij s. et vj d.
t Idem Vic. r.c. de xxx s. et v d. ob. de catallis Alani. In thes xxviij s. iiij d. ob. Et debet ij s. et ob.[4]
t Francoplegium Briani de Insula r.c. de j m. pro fuga. In thes dim. m. Et debet dim. m.
t Robertus de Tateshal' r.c. de xxiij s. pro eodem. In thes. xx s. Et debet iij s.
t Villata de Bliburc r.c. de j m. pro receptamento. In thes. ix s. ij d. Et debet iiij s. et ij d.

1 The amount is very indistinct here after considerable rubbing out. The *dim.* can just be made out with u/v and the badly written '*j*' written over.
2 The following entries are written on the right hand side of the membrane. This entry is above the stitching at the very foot of membrane 1 but is clearly the head of this second column.
3 The 'd' has been altered from a 'p'.
4 The clerk has made a mistake in his arithmetic. The amount is *ij s. et j d.*

t Villata de Filingeh' r.c. de ij m. pro eodem. In thes. xvj s. et viij d. Et debet x s.

Idem Vic. r.c. de liiij s. et viij d. de catallis Alani Spere. In thes. lib. Et Q.E.

t Francoplegium Hugonis Dispensarii r.c. de j m. pro fuga. In thes. dim. m. Et debet dim. m.

t Francoplegium Alexandri de Point' r.c. de j m. pro eodem. In thes. dim. m. Et debet dim. m.

t Nicholaus de Radeb' r.c. de j m. pro falsa inquisitione. In thes. dim. m. Et debet dim. m.

t Matheus f. Milonis r.c. de xl s. pro eodem. In thes. xx s. Et debet x s.[1]

p Eudo de Hawurðing'ham r.c. de C s. pro eodem. In thes. xx s. Et debet iiij li.

t Willelmus de Well' r.c. de ij m. ut Simon sit sub plegio. In thes. xx s. Et debet dim. m.

Radulfus de Trublevill' r.c. de lxxiij s. et v s.[2] de catallis Outi f. Reginaldi fugitivi. In thes. nichil. Et ipsi Radulfo lxxiij s. et v d. de dono R. per breve eiusdem. Et Q.E.

Tincturarii et textores Linc' r.c. de v m. pro licencia concordandi cum civibus. In thes. lib. Et Q.S.

e*tsi* Hugo Maresc' r.c. de dim. m. pro dissaisina. In thes. v s. Et debet xx d.

t Osbertus f. Nigelli r.c. de iij m. pro pluribus amerciamentis. In thes. xx s. Et debet xx s.

Lin. Johannes[3] de Beufou r.c. de xxxiij s. de debitis Ááron. In thes. ij s. Et debet xxxij[4] s.

Willelmus le Merveillus r.c. de vij li. xvj s. et vj d. de eodem. In thes. iiij s. Et debet vij *li.*[5] xij s. et vj d.

Walterus de Neweton' r.c. de vij li. iij s. et x d. de misericordia. In thes. iij s. Et debet vij li. et x d.

Marg' filia Rogeri[6] r.c. de xvj s. et viij d. pro summonendo Petro. In thes. dim. m. Et debet x s.

[7] [...][8] Idem Vic. r.c. de dim. m. de Willelmo f. Turkil, quia non habuit. Et dim. m de Lamberto de Weston' pro dissaisina. Et de dim. m. de Widone f. Ulfis quia non est prosecutus. Et de dim. m. de Ulfo de Pincebec quia non habuit. Et de dim. m. de Willelmo f. Ulfi pro eodem. Et de dim. m. de Waltero f. Simonis pro eodem. Et de xx s. de francoplegio abbatis Andeg' pro fuga Roberti. Et de j m. de francoplegio prioris de Spalding' pro fuga Walteri. Et de ij m. de francoplegio Thome de Muleton' pro fuga Alani Horn. Et de v m. de francoplegio prioris de Spalding' pro fuga Simonis

1 *x s. written for xx s.*
2 *Sic.* The clerk should have written a *d* for pence.
3 There are lines linking this entry and the next three entries.
4 *xxxij s. written for xxxj s.*
5 The clerk has written an *s.* for shilling and has then overwritten *li.*
6 There is some staining or blots over this name which makes it difficult to read.
7 The following entries are written right across the membrane.
8 Uncertain reading. There is something in the margin here but this is all that can be deciphered, even with u/v.

mercatoris. Et de C s. de francoplegio eiusdem prioris pro fuga Willelmi f. Willelmi et aliorum. Et de xx s. de francoplegio abbatis Andeg' pro fuga Alani pistoris. Et de x m. de francoplegio predicti prioris pro fuga Huberti. Et de xiij s. et ij d. de Joslano de Bradehus de catallis Hugonis suspensi. Et de x m. de francoplegio prioris de Spalding' pro fuga Ricardi f. Willelmi. In thes. nichil. Et priori et monachis de Spalding' xxviij li. et vj s. et vj d. per libertatem cartarum R. Et Q.E.

Idem Vic. r.c. de dim. m. de Galfrido f. Goscelini pro falso clamore. Et de dim. m. de Simone f. Roberti pro dissaisina. Et de dim. m. de Willelmo f. Eimerici pro falso [clamore]. Et de dim. m. de Radulfo f. Agnetis quia non habuit. Et de dim. m. de Willelmo f. Radulfi de Croxeby[1] pro defalta. Et de dim. m. de Alano de Toreswei pro eodem. Et de j m. de Willelmo la Haye pro eodem. Et de dim. m. de Thoma pistore pro eodem. Et de j m. de Nicholao f. Saher' pro defalta. Et de dim. m. de Ricardo de Ros pro eodem. Et de dim. m. de Willelmo f. Clementis pro eodem. Et de ij m. de Willelmo de Manneby pro falsa inquisitione. In thes. nichil. Et fratribus hospitalis Jer'l'm viij m. et dim. per libertatem carte R. Et Q.E.

Idem Vic. r.c. de dim. m. de Willelmo f. Radulfi pro dissaisina. Et de j m. de Radulfo de Ormesby pro iniusta detentione. Et de dim. m. de Adam de Blakenay pro dissaisina. Et de iij m. de Roberto Manwat quia fuit convictus. Et de iiij m. de Willelmo f. Galfridi pro eodem. Et de x m. de Johanne f. Oseberti pro eodem. Et de C s. de Johanne f. Galfridi pro eodem. Et de dim. m. de Willelmo de Tracy pro defalta. Et de dim. m. de Andrea homine templariorum pro eodem. Et de dim. m. de Alano templario pro eodem. Et de dim. m. de Willelmo Parlebien pro eodem. Et de dim. m. de Eudone de Spanneby pro eodem. Et de j m. de Roberto de Cukewald' pro eodem. Et de dim. m. de Simone f. Henrici pro defalta. Et de dim. m. de Simone f. Pere pro eodem. Et de j m. de francoplegio templi in Burton'[2] pro fuga Alani. Et de j m. de francoplegio eorundem pro fuga Willelmi. Et de j m. de francoplegio eorundem in Graham pro fuga Walteri. Et de dim. m. de francoplegio eorundem in Rouceby pro fuga Willelmi. Et de dim. m. de francoplegio eorundem in Burton' pro fuga Willelmi de Schirle. Et de dim. m. de francoplegio eorundem in Teueleby pro fuga Johannis. Et de dim. m. de Waltero de Belesby pro fuga Walteri Suspir'. Et de dim. m. de francoplegio eorundem in Orresby pro fuga Walteri. In thes. nichil. Et fratribus militie templi xxxviij m. per libertatem carte R. Et Q.E.

-ri-[3] Idem Vic. r.c. de j m. de priore de Sixle pro falso clamore. Et de dim. m. de Motekan' de Neweton' quia non habuit. Et de dim. m. de Alur' de Limberg' pro eodem. Et de j. m. de hominibus prioris de Ormesby in Ormesby pro fuga. Et de dim. m. de Roberto de Crokehol pro eodem. Et de dim. m. de francoplegio prioris de Simplingeh' in

[1] Uncertain reading.

[2] I have found no reference to a house of the Knights Templars in Burton in Lincolnshire, or any other Burton.

[3] There is something in the margin but not all can be determined, even with u/v.

Lechton'[1] pro fuga Willelmi. Et de j m. de francoplegio prioris de novo loco in Kadenay pro defalta. Et de dim. m. de francoplegio prioris de Ormesby pro eodem. Et de dim. m. de francoplegio eiusdem in Freskenai pro fuga Alani. Et de j m. de francoplegio prioris de Sixle in Ludford' pro fuga Rogeri. Et de xl s. de Waltero homine fratris Lamberti de Simplingeh' pro receptamento. In thes. nichil. Et monialibus de Simplingeham x m. per libertatem carte R.

Et Q.E.

Soc-ham[2] Idem Vic. r.c. de dim. m. de Gunwad' f. Jordani pro dissaisina. Et de dim. m. de Ricardo f. Jordani pro eodem. Et de dim. m. de Abraham f. Jordani pro eodem. Et de dim. m. de Hugone le Bret pro falso clamore. Et de dim. m. de Alano clerico pro defalta. Et de dim. m. de Willelmo de Waltham pro eodem. Et de dim. m. de Roberto falconario pro eodem. In thes. nichil. Et Abbati de Waltham iij m. et dim. per libertatem carte R.

Et Q.E.

Idem Vic. r.c. de dim. m. de Roberto f. Presbiteri quia non habuit. Et de x s. de Roberto *le prestre* pro defalta. In thes. nichil. Et canonicis de cruce Roheis' xvj s. et viij d. per libertatem carte R. Et Q.E.

+ Walterus f. Ricardi debet lxvj s. de debitis Ááron. + Willelmus f. Johannis debet xlij s. et iiij d. de eodem. + Robertus f. Martini debet vij li. et xviij d. de eodem. (*lin.*[i]) Willelmus nepos Warneri debet C et l m. pro habenda gratia R. + Gillebertus f. Nigelli debet dim. m. pro vino vendito. + Willelmus le Bas debet dim. m. pro eodem. + Stephanus Hurel debet dim. m. pro eodem. (*lin.*[i]) Nicholaus f. Brictij debet dim. m. pro vino vendito. + Ricardus Maresc' debet dim. m. pro transgressione. + Johannes f. Radulfi Nick debet v s. et viij d. pro[3] vino vendito. Galfridus de Marton' debet x s. pro dissaisina. Willelmus dispensator debet dim. m. quia non habuit. (*t*[i]) Henricus de Northorp debet dim. m. pro eodem. (*t*[i]) Radulfus f. Petri debet dim. m. pro eodem. (*t*[i]) Alicia que fuit uxor Walteri de Leiseby debet dim. m. pro dissaisina. (*p*[i])[4] Hamo Trunn et Alicia uxor eius debent dim. m. pro eodem. Robertus nepos de Denton' debet dim. m. quia non habuit. (*p*[i]) Willelmus f. Roberti de Glanvill' debet dim. m. pro eodem. (*t*[i]) Willelmus de Rasne de Ledenham debet dim. m. pro dissaisina. (*t*) Ricardus de Cotesbroc debet dim. m. quia non habuit. (*d*[i]) Radulfus f. Gille debet dim. m. pro eodem. (*p*[i]) Simon f. Roberti de Raðeby' debet dim. m. quia non est prosecutus. (*d*[i]) Robertus de Yrreby debet dim. m. quia non habuit. (*d*[i]) Walterus Rodkal debet dim. m. pro dissaisina. (*t*[i]) Alanus f. Ailwini debet dim. m. quia non est prosecutus. (*d*[i]) Walterus de Hilton' debet dim. m. pro dissaisina. (*t*[i]) Nicholaus de Raðeby debet dim. m. pro eodem. (*t*[i]) Jordanus de Markeward' debet dim. m. quia non habuit. (*t*[i]) Radulfus f. Gilleberti debet dim. m. pro falso clamore. (*Linc'*[i]) Ricardus de Neuport debet dim. m. quia non habuit. (*Linc'*[i]) Alexander de Bichc debet dim. m. pro eodem. (*p*[i]) Adam de Kingesbir' debet dim. m. pro dissaisina. (*t*[i])

[1] There is no Leighton in Lincolnshire. See *NS 54*, p. 291 which suggests this is Leighton Buzzard in Bedfordshire.

[2] There is something in the margin and this is the most likely reading even with u/v.

[3] *Pro* altered from *de*.

[4] This looks like a 'p'.

Simon le Bret debet j m. pro eodem. (*t*[i]) Ricardus f. Reginaldi debet dim. m. pro eodem. (*d*[i]) Robertus f. Reginaldi debet dim. m. quia non habuit. (*t*[i]) Willelmus de Rasne debet j m. de fine. (*t*[i]) Ricardus de Houton' debet dim. m. quia non est prosecutus. (*t*[i]) Hugo f. Rannulfi debet dim. m. quia non habuit. (*t*[i]) Alanus f. Roberti de Keles debet dim. m. pro dissaisina. (*t*[i]) Radulfus f. Goscelini debet dim. m. pro falso clamore. Willelmus f. Hugonis (*t*[i])[1] de Malbertorp debet dim. m. pro eodem. (*p*[i]) Ricardus Giffard' debet (dim.[c]) (j[i]) m. pro pluribus transgressionibus. (*p*[i]) Robertus de Ingoldeby debet dim. m. pro dissaisina. (*t*[i]) Thomas f. Matill' debet dim. m. (quia non habuit.[i]) (pro dissaisina.[c]) (*p*[i]) Hugo Sliet debet dim. m. pro dissaisina. (*t*[i]) Galfridus f. Henrici debet dim. m. quia non habuit. (*t*[i]) Willelmus f. Willelmi Nig debet dim. m. pro eodem. (*t*[i]) Robertus f. Tiece debet dim. m. pro eodem. (*p*[i]) Willelmus Bondenier debet dim. m. pro eodem. (*t*[i]) Alanus de Wandeford' debet dim. m. pro eodem. (*t*[i]) Ricardus de Turri de Morton' debet j m. pro eodem. (*t*[i]) Walterus f. Turstani debet dim. m. pro eodem. (*t*[i]) Robertus[2] Magnus debet dim. m. pro eodem. (*t*[i]) Johannes de Cotton' debet dim. m. pro eodem. (*t*[i]) Francoplegium Gerardi de Faencurt debet dim. m. pro fuga Walteri. (*t*[i]) Francoplegium Gerardi de Huwell' debet dim. m. pro fuga Ade Pichier. (*d*[i]) Francoplegium Huberti de Burg' debet xv s. et ix d. de catallis Johannis et duorum aliorum. (*d*[i]) Idem Francoplegium debet xl s. pro fuga eorundem. Francoplegium (*t*[i]) Hugonis de Neovill' grassi[3] in Ingoldeby debet dim. m. pro fuga Goscelini. (*d*[i]) Johannes Bonet debet x m. de catallis Ricardi f. Osberti. (*d*[i]) Idem Johannes debet ij m. de catallis Bocce de Cokerinton'. (*t*[i]) Petrus de Edelinton' debet ij s. et vj d. de catallis Hugonis f. Simonis. (*t*[i]) Simon de Seis debet iij s. pro habenda terra Dunwald' per j annum. (*t*[i]) Robertus de Tateshal' debet xvij s. de catallis Willelmi f. Astin'. (*t*[i]) Villata de Cotingeham debet j m pro receptamento. (*t*[i]) Francoplegium Nicholai de Chavincurt debet dim. m. pro fuga Simonis. (*t*[i]) Jordanus de Eisseby debet xj s. et vij d. de catallis Rogeri Blund'. (*d*[i]) Francoplegium Roberti Gresle debet xl s. pro fuga Willelmi. Ballivi Linc' debent iiij d. de catallis Baggard'. Idem ballivi debent ij s. et vj d. de catallis Walteri le potier. (*t*[i]) Francoplegium comitis Brittann' debet iiij m. pro fuga Willelmi f. Roberti. (*t*[i]) Alexander de Pointon' debet xl s. pro transgressione. (*d*[i]) Ranulfus de Villi debet C s. pro receptamento. (*d*[i]) Herbertus capellanus debet dim. m. pro dissaisina.

Ballivi Linc' r.c. de iij s. pro terra Johannis Maimund'. Et de v s. de catallis Willelmi cóópertoris. Et de x s. de textoribus Linc' de catallis Simonis Licherenave. Et de xij s. et vj d. de catallis Ruiges suspensi. Et de xlv s. de catallis Hugonis Gobinel fugitivi. In thes. lib. Et Q.E.

Rannulfus comes Cestr' [*blank*] xxxij li. et xix s. et viij d. et ob. de remanenti firme de Salop'sir' de anno vijº. Et xxj li. et xviij s. et iij d. et ob. de remanenti eiusdem firme de iiijª parte anni viij. Et xxxj s. et iiij d. de minutis firmis eiusdem comitatus contentis in rotulo viijº. Et xvij s. et iiij d. de cremento Novi burgi de iiij annis, scilicet iiijº, vº, vjº, vijº, sicut

[1] The letter 't' put above *Hugonis*.
[2] The clerk has altered the name to *Robertus* from *Rogerus*.
[3] In *NS 48*, p. 147 he is shown as *crassus*.

continetur in Salop'sir' in rotulo precedenti. Et lxxvj li. et dim. m. bl. de remanenti firme comitatus de Stafford' de anno vj^{o} et vij^{o}. Et xxj li. et viij s. et iij d. bl. de remanenti eiusdem firme de iiij^{a} parte anni viij qui sunt ei extensi ad C li. et xj s. et xj d. num. Et xix li. et iiij s. et vj d. de pluribus firmis et crementis contentis in rotulo viij^{o}. Et Dv m. pro Hugone de Logiis quos Willelmus de Erdinton' ballivus suus recepit. Et iiij li. et xvij s. de remanenti firme comitatus Lancastr' de iiij^{a} parte anni viij. Et xl s. pro abbate de Cokersand' de firma ij^{arum} carrucatarum terre de (ij^{i}) annis.[1] Et xl s. pro Rogero f. Roberti sicut continetur in Lanc' in rotulo precedenti. Et xxix li. et ij s. de firma terre Willelmi Marmiun de anno septimo, viij et ix^{o} (sicut continetur in hoc comitatu in rotulo precedenti.^{i}) Et ix li. et xiiij s. de eadem firma hoc anno. Et l m. pro dissaisina sicut continetur in rotulo viij^{o}. Et quater xx et xj li. et j m. de primo scutagio R. sicut continetur in rotulo v. Et ij dextrarios optimos et pulcherrimos et iij palefridos optimos pro Petro de Pratell' sicut continetur in rotulo viij^{o}. Et xvij m. et xij s. pro Roberto Marmiun seniore cuius terram habet de primo scutagio R. Et C et lxxj li. et j m. pro eodem Roberto pro habenda custodia castri de Tameworðe.[2] Et iiij m. de primo scutagio R. de ij^{bus} feodis in Onne qui requirebant (de^{i,d})[3] in Buk' in rotulo precedenti. Et iij equos dextrarios pro Ruald' f. Alani quos recognovit se recepisse de ipso R.[4] qui requirebantur de ipso R. in Everwikesir' in rotulo precedenti. Et C et xxj m. et v s. et iiij d. de primo scutagio R. de medietate honoris comitatus Leircestr'. Et de xx m. et viij s. et iiij d. de eodem de eadem medietate de parvis feodis Mauriton' quod scutagium requirebatur in Warew' et Leirc'[5] in j summa. Et l s. de carrucagio assiso ad ij s. in comitatu Glovern' qui requirebatur[6] in rotulo de carrucagio. Summa in denariis preter equos et dextrarios DC et xxxvj li. et (x^{d})xj[7] s. et ix d.
[*Nine lines blank*][8]

[*Endorsed*] emendatus et iterum emendatus

Lincolneschir'[9]

[*Rot.* 5 *Mem.* 1]

1 The last two letters of *annis* squeezed in.
2 The 'r' in '*Tameworðe*' is just visible under strengthening tape. The remainder, i.e. *ðe* is also just visible on the next line of the membrane.
3 This is rubbed out here.
4 This is probably from Ranulf earl of Chester, not the king.
5 This is at the right hand edge of the membrane and some has been obscured by the tape placed on this edge for strengthening purposes.
6 A stain or possibly even burn marks over this word and the next few words.
7 There is another *x* at the front of the number of shillings which is only partially rubbed out.
8 Printed '8' at the left hand side of the membrane.
9 The county name is preceded and followed by three vertical dots. It is written upside down to the rest of the membrane.

SUHANTESCIR

Ricardus episcopus Sar' Bartholomeus de Kemes' ut custos pro eo r.c. de DC et vj li. et iij s. bl. de firma comitatus. In thes. nichil.

(Et in elemosinis constitutis militibus de templo j m.[c]) (*quia infra*[i]). Et in terris datis Johanni Biset xl li. bl. et xl s. num. in Rokesburn'. Et Turstano dispensatori xv li. bl. in Worðie. Et Willelmo Briewerr' xxxvj li. et vj s. bl. in Sumburne. Et priori de Suðewic' v m. bl. in Colemere. Et eidem viij li. et j m. bl. in Colemere de quibus respondet infra. Et Ade de Gurdun xij li. bl. in Tisted'. Et Aimerico de Saceio xlij li. bl. in Berton' quamdiu R. placuerit. Et eidem lxj s. bl. in Seleburne. Et in Basingestok' lij li. bl. de quibus homines ville respondent infra. Et in civitate Wint' quater xx li. bl. de quibus cives respondent infra. Et monachis de Waverlay xxxvij li. et j m. num. in Nietham. Et H. de Burgo xxxv li. iiij s.[1] bl. in Odiham de quibus debet respondere. Et Ade de Bendenges xij li. in Lisse. Et eidem C s. in Odiham. Et monialibus de Ambresbir' xxxvij li. in Walhape. (Et in liberatione constituta Matheo de Walhape iiij li. et xj s. et iij d.[c]) (*quia infra*[i]). Et heredi Rogeri de Berneval xx li. in Husseburne. Et Cecil' de Clere C et xvij s. et viij d. et ob. in Eling'. Et in terra quam Cobbe faber tenuit in nova foresta xxij s. et vj d. (Et in liberatione Andree capellani ministrantis in capella Wint' l s.[c]) (*quia infra*[i]). Et Johanni de Stappel xxxvij s. in Stappel'. Et Johanni de Leonibus xxiiij li. in Husseburne. Et Yvoni de Fiffhið heredi Nicholai camerarii Lx s. in Walhop'. Et in Awelton' Lx li. bl. de quibus homines ville respondent infra. Et in Andour' quater xx li. bl. de quibus homines ville respondent infra. Et magistro Stephano de Luci iiij li. in Seleburne per breve R. quamdiu R. placuerit (*de quibus debet respondere*[i]). Et habet hic de superplus (xiij li. et xj s. et x d. et ob.[c]) (*vij li. et iiij s. et xj d. et ob.*[i]) bl. qui non debent ei allocari quia excrescunt per extensionem maneriorum et ipse respondet ut custos et nullum habet manerium in manu sua.

[*One line blank*]

Et pro xx barillis ad ponendas in quolibet barillo D m. de thesauro R. mittendas in Wasconiam per Henricum de Cornhill' et Thomam de Haya ad Ricardum fratrem R. et in locatione xx caretarum ad deferendum thesaurum illum usque Portesm' xxvj s. et iiij d. et ob. per breve R. Et in carriagio iij milium marcarum de quintadecima liberatarum Thome de Haya per manus R[icardi] Sar' episcopi et missarum usque Turrim Lond' ad opus eiusdem Ricardi xj s. et ix d. per breve eiusdem. Et in cariagio M librarum quas idem vicecomes recepit a predicto carriatarum usque Lond' et liberatarum E. Lond' episcopo de predicta quintadecima xvij s. et ij d. per breve eiusdem. Et pro barillis ad imponendum thesaurum R. quem Henricus de Cornhill' et Godefridus de Crawecumb' fecerunt carriari a Wint' usque Portesm' et pro carriagio eiusdem thesauri xviij s. et xj d. per breve eiusdem. Et in carriagio D m. liberatarum Henrico de Cornhill usque Evermue ad liberationes faciendas militibus et servientibus et balistariis missis in Wasconiam ad Ricardum fratrem R. xiij d. per breve R. Et in carriagio M et CCCC marcarum missarum in Wasconiam ad opus

[1] *iiij s.* written in margin.

Ricardi predicti per predictum Henricum usque Porecestr' ij s. et ij d. et ob. per breve eiusdem. Et in carriagio duorum milium[1] cere a Porrecestr' usque Lond' x s. et ix d. per breve eiusdem. Et in operatione CC et xxxvj cleiarum in balliva de Sumburne et carriandis usque Wint' et ibidem locatis et cóópertis et in D cleíís factis in balliva de Andeur' et in xv cleíís de eisdem CC carriatis usque Porrecestr' et in quater xx cleíís factis in nova foresta et carriatis usque Suhant' et in ix pontibus factis in bosco de Porrecestr' et carriatis usque Porrecestr' iiij li. (per breve eiusdem[c]) et viij s. et iiij d. per breve eiusdem. Et in CC et xxviij pontibus et M et DC et xv cleíís coadunatis et cóópertis in castro de Porrecestr' xxvij s. per idem breve. Et in reparatione cuiusdam turris in castro de Porrecestr' iiij li. ij s. et ix d. per idem breve. Et pro v hachíís et CCCC et xx quarrellis emptis et positis in castro Wint' et in D quarrellis carriatis á castro Divisarum usque Wint' viij s. et j d. per idem breve. Et in discarcatione v doliorum vini apud Porrecestr' et positorum[2] in[3] eodem castro et in j dolio circulando ij s. et ix d. per idem breve. Et in carriagio D et xl li. a Winton' usque Portesm' et pro barillis ad denarios illos imponendos iij s. et ix d. et ob. per idem breve. Et in emendatione castri Wint' Lxj s. et ix d. Et in emendatione castri de Porrecestr' xxxv s. et vj d. Et in elemosinis constitutis militibus de templo j m. Et Matheo de Walhop' in liberatione constituta iiij li. et xj s. et iij d. Et Andree capellano ministranti in capella castri Wint' l s. Summa xxvij li. et xij s. et ix d. et ob. que summa tota locatur ei infra in pluribus debitis.

f' Idem Vic. r.c. de lxx li. et xxj d. de proficuo comitatus hoc anno. Et de iiij li. et j m. de proficuo Judaismi hoc anno. In thes. nichil. Et episcopo Sar' pro custodia castri de Porrecestr' x li. per breve R. Et eidem pro custodia comitatus xx li. per idem breve. Et eidem pro custodia castri Wint' xliiij li. et xv s. et j d. per idem breve. Et Q.E.

f' Prior de Suðewic' r.c. de vij li. et xviij s. et v d. de firma de Colemere. In thes. lib. Et Q.E.

Johannes de Venoiz r.c. de quater xx et vij li. et ij s. et iij d. de pluribus debitis contentis in rotulo viij. Et de viij li. et xvj s. de remanenti firme de Axiesholt de anno v. In thes. x m. Et iterum x m. Et debet quater xx et ij li. xj s. vij d. per annum (xx m.[i]).

f' Idem Johannes [*blank*] j m. de firma foreste de Lindwude. Et j m. de eadem firma de anno preterito.

f' Johannes filius Roberti et Ela uxor eius r.c. de l s. de firma terre sue quam tenent in Awelton'. In thes. lib. Et Q.S.

f' Idem Vic. r.c. de iiij s. et ij d. de firma Alexandri de Munfichet. Et de xviij d. de firma Walteri forestarii. Et de iij s. de firma Willelmi de Ketehó. Et de xviij d. de firma Augustini forestarii pro vj acris et dim. frussandis. In thes. lib. Et Q.E.

f' Matheus de Monasterio r.c. de xij d. pro j acra claudenda. In thes.

f' Willelmus de Sancto Johanne r.c. de xij d. pro quadam pastura in Schireburne. Et de xij d. de eadem de anno preterito. In thes. lib. Et Q.E.

1 The unit is missing. Probably *librarum*, 2,000 lbs of wax.

2 *positorum* altered from *positis*.

3 *in* repeated.

f' Abbas de Waverle r.c. de j m. de firma grave que vocatur Kingesgrave. In thes. lib. Et Q.E.

f' Walterus de Everle r. c. de xix d. de firma j^{us} virgate terre in hundredo de Andeur' de (dimidio^{c}) (*hoc*^{i}) anno. In thes. lib. Et Q.E.

Idem W. debet xj s. et ix d. de eadem firma de pluribus annis preteritis. Set non debet summoneri quia comes Saresberie illos recepit quolibet anno dum habuit villam in manu sua et respondet in Wiltesir' in rotulo sequenti.

Idem W. [*blank*] dim. m. pro dissaisina.

(*f'* Homines de Basingestok' [*blank*] lij bl. [*sic*] et de xviij li. num. de firma ville sue quam R.[1] eis concessit per talem firmam (cum hundredo intrinseco^{i}) quamdiu ei placuerit tenendam, salvis R. v hundredis forinsecis^{c}) *quia infra.*

f' Homines de Basingestok' r.c. de xxvj li. bl. de firma ville sue de hoc ultimo dim. anno quam villam R. eis concessit pro lij li. bl. annuis cum hundredo intrinseco quamdiu sibi placuerit et xviij li. num. de cremento, salvis R. v hundredis forinsecis sicut villa fuit extensa per S. de Pateshill' et socios suos. In thes. xxiiij li. et xiiij s. bl. Et debent xxvj s. bl. [*Paler ink*] *Idem r.c. de eodem debito. In thes. lib. Et Q.S.*

f' Idem homines r.c. de ix li. num. de cremento de predicto dim. anno. In thes. lib. Et Q.E.[2]

Idem homines r.c. de xxij li. et vj s. de eadem firma de dim. anno x^{mo} de termino Pasche precedentis. In thes. lib. Et Q.E.

Idem homines r.c. de C et quater xx et xvj li. et iiij s. de ij debitis contentis in rotulo precedenti. In thes. x li. Et debent C et quater xx et vj li. et iiij s. per annum xx li.

f' Homines de Awelton' [*blank*] xxx li. bl. de firma ville sue de hoc ultimo dim. anno quam villam R. eis concessit cum intrinseco hundredo quamdiu sibi placuerit pro lx li. bl. annuis et xx li. num. de cremento, salvis R. iiij hundredis forinsecis sicut villa fuit extensa per Simonem de Pateshill' et socios suos.

f' Idem homines r.c. de x li. num. de cremento ville sue de predicto dim. anno.

Idem homines r.c. de Lxj li. et x s. de firma ville sue de dim. anno x^{mo} de termino Pasche.

Idem homines r.c. de CC et ij li. et iij s. et iiij d. de remanenti eiusdem firme de pluribus annis preteritis. Et de iiij li. et x s. et viij d. de veteri tallagio.

f' Homines de Portesmuðe r.c. de xviij li. de firma ville sue. In thes. xvj li. et iiij s. et viij d. Et Ricardus de Landa xxxv s. et iiij d. Et Q.S.

Idem homines r. [*blank*] xx m. de veteri tallagio. Et [*blank*] j tonell' vini sicut continetur in rotulo viij.

f' Homines de Andeur' r.c. de xl li. bl. de firma ville sue de hoc ultimo dim. anno quam villam R. eis concessit cum hundredo quamdiu sibi placuerit pro quater xx li. bl. et xx li. num. de cremento per annum sicut continetur in carta R. J. quam inde habent. In thes. xxxviij li. et j m. bl.

[1] *Rex* written on an obliteration.

[2] *Quietus Est* written for *Quieti Sunt*; so also in the next entry.

Et debent ij m. bl. Idem r.c. de eodem debito. In thes. nichil. Et in terra (uxoris[i]) Carbonell' iiij[or] s. Et debent xxiij s. et xj d. et ob. bl. Idem r.c. de eodem debito. In thes. lib. Et Q.S.

f' Idem homines r.c. de x li. num. de cremento eiusdem ville de eodem dim. anno. In thes. lib. Et Q.S.

Idem homines r.c. de xl li. bl. et x li. num. de eadem firma de primo dim. anno. In thes. iiij li. xv s. et x d. bl. et x li (num.[i]). Et W. comiti Saresburie xxx(v[i]) li. bl. (et v li.[c]) num. dum vixit. Et debent iiij s. et ij d. bl. Idem r.c. de eodem debito. In thes. lib. Et Q.(S.[i])

Idem homines [*blank*] lxvij li. et xix d. num. de firma ville sue de anno xvj. Et xv li. num. de eadem firma de iij[bus] partibus anni xvij[mo]. Et x li. de ultimo tallagio R. J.

f' H. de Burgo respondet in compoto suo de[1] firma de Odiham. Et idem respondet ibidem de eadem firma de anno preterito scilicet in rotulo compotorum.

f' Idem Vic. r.c. de xxv li. et iij s. et ix d. et ob. de padnagio de Axiesholt hoc anno. In thes. nichil. Et in summa misarum suarum quam habet supra xxv li. et iij s. et ix d. et ob. Et Q.E.

COMPOTUS NOVE FORESTE

f' Johannes de Monem' r.c. de[2] xxv li. de censu nove foreste. In thes. x li. et x s. Et in decimis consitutis canonicis de Saresbir' l s. Et W. Briewerr' xl s. in foresta de Beiri de dono R. Ricardi. Et Abbati de novo Loco[3] R. x li. ad operationem ecclesie sue quamdiu R. placuerit per breve R. Et Q.E.

Idem J. debet iiij li. de remanenti eiusdem firme de ij[bus] annis preteritis contentis in rotulo viij[o] [*rest of line blank*]

f' Idem J. r.c. de xv li. de firma x vaccariarum. In thes. xiij li. et x s. Et in decimis constitutis canonicis Saresbir' xxx s. Et Q.E.

f' Idem J. r.c. de xxx s. de censu buccorum. In thes. xxvij s. Et predictis canonicis iij s. Et Q.E.

f' Idem J. r.c. de j m. de consuetudine salinarum. In thes. nichil. Et ad saliendum lardarium R. apud Clarendon' xxx quarteria salis pro predicta marca per breve H. de Neovill'. Et Q.E.

f' Idem J. r.c. de ij s. de firma terre Roberti le harpur. In thes. lib. Et Q.E.

f' Idem J. r.c. de lxviij s. de firma veteris turbarie hoc anno. Et de iiij li. et xvj s. de padnagio eiusdem foreste hoc anno. In thes. lib. Et Q.E.

f' Idem J. r.c. de iiij li. et xvj s. de firma nove turbarie hoc anno. In thes. nichil. Et Ricardo Archerio iiij li. et xvj s. ad porcos emendos ad opus R. per breve H. de Neovill'. Et Q.E.

1 *suo de* squashed in; *suo* is in darker ink.

2 *de* repeated.

3 According to *NS 54* and *NS 48* in the index *Novo Loco* is Newstead, although which Newstead is not differentiated. It has not been possible to locate a religious house in any Newstead that has an abbot at its head. There is a priory at Newstead in Nottinghamshire and a priory at Newstead on Ancholme in Lincolnshire. An alternative is that this may be a reference to Beaulieu abbey in Hampshire, which was often referred to as 'bellus locus Regis'.

Johannes Blancbuilli debet dim. m. pro falso appello qui requirebatur in Wiltesir.

f' Hamo venator r.c. de j m. de firma cuiusdam essarti in Schireburn'. In thes. lib. Et Q.E.

E. de Ciconiaco (r.c.[i]) de[1] lxij li. et x s. bl. de firma de Odiham de anno vij^{o} et iiij^{a} parte anni viij. In thes. nichil. Et in perdona ipsi Engelardo lxij li. et x s. bl. per breve R. Et Q.E.

Willelmus de Sancto Johanne [*blank*] de proficuo comitatus de dim. anno xv^{o} R. J. Et [*blank*] de anno xvj. Et [*blank*] tribus partibus anni xvij.

f' Cives Wint' r.c. de quater xx li. de firma civitatis sue. In thes. xxviij li. et x s. et viij d. et ob. Et in elemosinis constitutis militibus de Templo j m. Et in firmis super montem lx s. Et Henrico Joseph ministranti in capella Sancti Judoci xl s. Et Willelmo Summatario de Butelleria R. xxx s. et v d. Et Waltero Longo xxx s. et v d. Et Cristiane nutrici R. lx s. et x d. Et Johanni carpentario xxx s. et v d. Et in carriagio cere R. usque Lond' et pro j dolio vacuo ad imponendum ceram illam[2] v s. et iij ob. per breve R. Et pro speciebus ad opus R. missis ei usque Merleberg' xix s. et ij d. per breve R. Et pro quibusdam rotis ad longam caretam R. et pro veteri ferro quod fuit super veteres rotas eiusdem carete ponendo in illis rotis x s. et ij d. per breve eiusdem. Et in superplus quod habent in anno preterito xxxvj li. et ix s. et viij d. Et Q.S.

Idem cives debent lxiiij li. et xvij s. et j d. de firma civitatis sue de dim. anno xvij^{o}. Et xlix li. bl. et iij d. bl. de remanenti firme civitatis de anno[3] xv^{o} et xvj^{o}. Et CC m. de veteri tallagio. Et x dolia vini pro def[alta] in foresta.

f' Adam Cawet' r.c. de iiij d. de firma cuiusdam propresture in magno vico Wint'. In thes. lib. Et Q.E.

Fullones Wint' debent xl s. de remanenti firme gilde sue. Telarii Wint' debent xxvij li. de remanenti firme gilde sue. Ricardus fusor et Willelmus Hugeline debent C et iij[4] li. de misericordia.

[*Rot.* 5 *Mem.* 2]

Homines de Suhanton' r.c. de CC li. de firma ville sue. In thes. quater xx et xiij li. Et in elemosinis constitutis militibus de templo j m. Et in decimis constitutis monachis de Lyra ix li. et v s. Et monachis de Cormeill' viij li. et xv s. Et leprosis de Suhant' xxiij s. et ij d. Et canonicis Sancti Dionisii vij s. et ij d. in terra de Porteswude. Et in Kingesland' quam predicti canonici habent C s. Et pro ij doliis vini emptis et liberatis Willelmo de Haverhill' et Russell' de Sancto Maxentio xl s. per breve R. Et in carriagio et carcagio eorum usque Wint' contra Natale domini anno x^{mo} xxxj d. et ob. per idem breve. Et in carcagio et carragio aliorum duorum tonellorum vini de prisa R. usque Clarendon' contra predictum Natale xxxj d. et ob. per breve eiusdem. Et pro iiij tonellis vini de prisa R. emptis que

1 Erasure after *de*.
2 Gerund *imponendum* with direct object *ceram* written.
3 *anno* written for *annis*.
4 *iij* altered from *iiij*.

sunt in cellario R. apud Suhant' iiij li. per breve eiusdem. Et in carriagio xx tonellorum vini usque Winton' contra predictum Natale xxiij s. et iiij d. (per breve R.[i]). Et in carcagio eorundem et minutis custis xlv d. per idem breve. Et pro j dolio vini de prisa R. empto et liberato magistro Nicholao de Farnham de dono R. xx s. per breve eiusdem. Et in carcagio et carriagio vj doliorum vini quorum duo missa fuerunt usque Clarendon' et quattuor usque Merleberg' xij s. et v d. et ob. per breve eiusdem. Et pro xvij doliis vini de prisa R. emptis et missis usque Merleberg' xvij li. per breve eiusdem. Et in carcagio et carragio eorundem xxxix s. iij d. et ob. per idem breve. Et in carcagio et carragio viij tonellorum usque Merleberg' xx s. et ij d. per breve eiusdem. Et in carragio j tonelli vini usque Sunning' quod R. reddid[it][1] episcopo Saresburie xxxj d. per breve eiusdem. Et pro v carettatis plumbi emptis et liberatis Galfrido de Lucy ad operationes castrorum in Insulis de Geres' et Gernes' viij li. et xiiij s. et v d. et ob. per breve eiusdem. Et in carragio j[us] tonelli vini missi usque Neubir' ij s. et vj d. et ob. per breve eiusdem. Et in locatione j[us] navis conducte ad deferenda lx dolia vini usque Westm' et aliis minutis custis vij li. et ij s. et ix d. et ob. per breve eiusdem. Et in carragio xv doliorum vini usque Winton' et vj doliorum vini usque Guldeford' et iiij doliorum vini usque Clarendon' et iiij doliorum vini usque Odiham et v doliorum vini usque Porrescestr' liij s. et x d. et ob. per breve eiusdem. Et in windagio (lx[i]) tonellorum vini que fuerunt in navi Vincentii de Hasting' et qui[2] Ricardus frater[3] R. comes Pictavie misit R. et in custo posito ad reponenda ea in cellario R. xv s. et ix d. per breve eiusdem. Et pro j tonello vini de prisa R. empto et liberato H. de Cornhill' de dono R. xx s. per breve eiusdem. Et in carragio x tonellorum vini usque Winton (et minutis custis[i]) xiij s. et vj d.[4] (et ob.[i]) per breve eiusdem. Et in carragio vij tonellorum vini usque Windles' (de eadem prisa R.[i]) et ij usque Odiham (de eadem prisa[i]) et j[us] usque Brehull' (de eadem prisa[i]) et iiij tonellorum de vinis que Ricardus frater R. ei misit usque Divisas et ij[orum] usque Gillingeh' et ij[orum] usque Lutegareshal' et j[us] usque Brehull' lvj s. et x d. per breve. Et pro x predictis tonellis vini de prisa R. emptis x li. per breve eiusdem. Et (in loco[c]) Jacobo Flandr' pro locatione j[us] cellarii per xv septimanas videlicet á vigilia Natalis domini anno x usque ad diem mercurii proximam post festum Sancti Ambrosii anno eodem ad vina R. de empto reponenda xv s. per breve eiusdem. Et Benedicto Asce et Cecil' de Puteo pro locatione ij[orum] cellariorum per xix septimanas ad alia vina R. de empto reponenda videlicet á predicta vigilia usque ad diem mercurii proximam post Inventionem Sancte crucis anno eodem xxviij s. et vj d. per breve eiusdem. Et ad hospitandum[5] et carriandum eadem vina de littore maris usque in cellaria predicta scilicet C et l dolia vini et ad religandum et barrandum et custodiendum predicta vina bermannis et carpentariis xxv s. per idem breve scilicet de quolibet dolio

[1] Final syllable written (*-id'*) squashed in.
[2] *qui* written for *que*.
[3] The word *frater* is preceded by a heavy dot.
[4] *xiij s. et vj d.* written over an erasure.
[5] Gerund written in full; subsequent expressions in this passage therefore also extended as gerunds rather than gerundives.

ij d. Et in reparatione Kaii R. apud Suhanton' et in operatione cuiusdam appenticii supra hostium cellarii R. ibidem xl s. per breve eiusdem. Et in carragio x tonellorum de vinis que R. frater R. ei misit usque Corf xxij s. et iij d. per breve eiusdem. Et in carragio iiij tonellorum vini de empto usque Rading' x s et vij d. per idem breve. Et in carragio xxj tonellorum vini missorum per plura maneria R. et minutis custis iiij li. et iiij s. et iij d. et ob. per breve eiusdem. Et pro iiij tonellis vini de prisa R. iiij li. per idem breve. Et debent lxiiij s. et j d. Idem r.c. de eodem debito. In thes. iij s. et iij d. Et debent lx s. et x d. Idem r.c. de eodem debito. In thes. nichil. Et talliatori lx s. et x d. Et Q.E.[1]

Idem homines r.c. de xviij li. et x s. et x d. de remanenti firme ville sue de anno preterito. In thes. lib. Et Q.E.[2]

Idem homines r.c. de x li. et xij s. et vij d. et ob. et iij^{bus} doliis boni vini. In thes. x li. et xij s. et vij. d. et ob. Et debent iij dolia boni vini sicut continetur in rotulo v^{o}.

Idem homines debent xl m. de misericordia foreste. Vidua Roberti Halveking debet x s. pro vino vendito. + Willelmus de Suwell' debet dim. m. quia non est prosecutus.

Simon de Sancto Laurencio r.c. de xix li. et xij s. et ij d. de remanenti firme de Suhant' dum fuit ballivus sicut continetur in rotulo v^{o}. In thes. xx s. Et debet xviij li. et xij s. et ij d. per annum xx s.

Josceus de Hampton' r.c. de x li. et v s. et vj d. de remanenti eiusdem firme de eodem anno dum fuit ballivus. In thes. xx s. Et debet ix li. et v s. et vj d. per annum xx s.

Willelmus de Rokesdon' r.c. de dim. m. pro dissaisina. In thes. xl d. Et debet xl d. Idem r.c. de eodem debito. In thes. lib. Et Q.E.

Henricus de capella debet xl s. de j palefrido qui requirebatur in Middelsex'.

+ Willelmus Finamur debet xxix s.[3] et viij d. pro vinis R. + Willelmus de Pratell' debet j m. de firma grave que vocatur Kingesore sicut continetur in rotulo precedenti.

Henricus de Braiboef [*blank*] xxv m. pro v palefridis de ij^{bus} debitis contentis in rotulo v^{o}. Et [*blank*] xxij li. et x s. de debitis Judeorum. Et [*blank*] iij m. pro licencia concordandi. Et [*blank*] j m. de ij debitis contentis in rotulo viij.

Eimericus de Sace debet vij li.[4] et x s. et x d. pro Willelmo de Bertona sicut continetur in rotulo vj^{o}. Robertus de (+[i]) Buddebrige debet dim. m. pro summonendo Jacobo clerico. Petrus de Werewell' debet C m. pro habenda benevolentia R. J. + Matheus de Brocherst debet iij s. de (misericordia[i]).[5]

Rogerus de Limes' r.c. de CCC et xiiij li. et xv s. de misericordia patris sui. In thes. dim. m. Et debet CCC et xiiij li. et viij s. et iiij d. per annum dim. m.[6]

1 *Quietus Est* written for *Quieti Sunt*.
2 *Quietus Est* written for *Quieti Sunt*.
3 First *x* of *xxix* squashed in.
4 *li.* altered from *s.*
5 Inserted above line at end of line with extended capitulum mark to the left.
6 It would take nearly a thousand years to pay off a debt of £314 8s. 4d. by yearly

Stephanus filius Ricardi r.c. de xiiij li. et xvj s. pro patre suo. In thes. xx s. Et debet xiij li. et xvj s.

Willelmus de Warburton' r.c. de C et xxxviij li. et vij s. et viij d. de pluribus debitis contentis in rotulo v. In thes. C s. Et debet C et xxxiij li. et vij s. et viij d. Et ij m. et dim. de scutagio de Mungumeri.

per annum x li.

Rogerus Butt[1] r.c. de C et quater xx et xv li. et xj s. de pluribus debitis contentis in rotulo precedenti. In thes. xx s. Et debet C et quater xx et xiiij li. et xj s. per annum xx s.

Pars terre Ricardi de Solariis quam Thomas Peverell'[2] denuit[3] debet xxxj li. de debitis ipsius Ricardi contentis in rotulo v^{o}. + Rogerus Pratt debet vj s. pro dissaisina. Benedictus niger debet xlix s. et iiij d. de ij^{bus} debitis contentis in rotulo v^{o}.

Oliverus de Ponchardun r.c. de xxviij li. et iiij s. et vj d. et ij m. auri de debitis ipsius Ricardi. In thes. xl s. Et debet xxvj li. et iiij s. et vj d. et ij m. auri. per annum xl s.

Stephanus de Bendeng' r.c. de xxv li. et dim. m. de debito Mauricii patris sui. Et de xxxiij li. et xij s. de debitis Judeorum. In thes. v m. Et debet lv li. et xij s. per annum v m.

P. Wint' episcopus debet j tonellum vini (*Set respondet post Warewic'.*[i]) sicut continetur in rotulo xj^{o}. Et ij^{o} cóópertoria de Geneciis (*Set respondet ibidem.*[i]) pro quietantia scutagii Wallie. Willelmus[4] de Edmundestrop' debet v m. pro habenda balliva de Witlingelee qui requirequirebatur[5] in Cornub' in rotulo viij.

Idem P. debet xxix li. et xviij s. et vj d. de scutagio Pictavie (*Set respondet ibidem.*[i]) de honore de Berchamsted. Et xlix li. et xix s. et j d. (*Set respondet ibidem.*[i]) de scutagio Wallie de medietate honorum de Toteneis sicut continetur in Devon' in rotulo v. Et vj m. (*Set respondet ibidem.*[i]) de primo scutagio R. de feodis Roberti de Esseby sicut continetur in Noting' in rotulo viij^{o}. Et xlix li. et xl d. (*Set respondet ibidem.*[i]) de scutagio Reginaldi de Valle torta. Et ij m. de j magno feodo (*Set respondet ibidem.*[i]) eiusdem sicut continetur in Cornub' in rotulo xiiij. Et ij m. (*Set respondet ibidem.*[i]) pro Gilleberto palmerio qui requirebatur in Oxon' in rotulo v.

Idem debet lix li. et xxij d. (*Set respondet ibidem.*[i]) de misericordiis plurium hominum suorum in diversis comitatibus contentis in rotulo precedenti. Et C et xxij li. et j m. (*Set respondet ibidem.*[i]) de debitis Reginaldi de Valle torta qui requirebatur in Devon'.

Idem debet ij palefridos pro essarto qui requirebatur in Oxon' (*Set respondet post Warewic.*[i]) in rotulo viij. Et ij dextrarios (*Set respondet ibidem.*[i]) pro habenda custodia sicut continetur in hoc comitatu in rotulo precedenti.

---

instalments of 6s. 8d.

1 Blot at end of word.

2 *Peverell* squashed in before *tenuit*.

3 *denuit* written for *tenuit*.

4 G written at start of the name *Willelmus*, but erased.

5 *requirequirebatur* written for *requirebatur*.

Jacobus de Scures r.c.[1] de lxviij li. et xvj s. et ij d. pro transgressione patris sui. In thes. j m. Et debet lxviij li. et ij s. et x d. per annum j m.

Willelmus de Ywerst r.c. de vj m. ut Suspirus tradatur in custodia. In thes. dim. m. Et debet v m. et dim.

Robertus de Cleuesdon' debet ij m. pro deliberatione sua. Walterus Luberi debet dim. m. pro dissaisina. Robertus le Heiward debet ij m. pro licencia concordandi. + Galfridus de Kalec' clericus debet j tonellum vini pro habendo brevi. Henricus de Cumb' debet xx s. pro deliberatione sua. + Ricardus Luberi debet dim. m. pro eodem. Willelmus Salvagius debet dim. m. pro eodem. Johannes de Garland' debet j m. pro eodem. Hugo filius Semanni debet dim m. pro eodem. Ysabell de Turkilleston' debet dim. m. pro habendo brevi.

Ricardus de Leicr' debet[2] quartam partem de xx m. pro justiciando Simone de Sancto Laurencio sicut continetur in rotulo primo. Johannes filius Walkelini debet j m. de ij debitis contentis in rotulo precedenti. Johannes de Cumpton' debet dim. m. pro eodem sicut continetur in rotulo ij^{o}.

Abbas de Hida r.c. de xij li. de scutagio Pictavie. In thes. vj li. Et debet vj li.

Engelardus de Cyconiaco r.c. de viij m. et dim. pro Johanne de Stappel' pro habenda terra. In thes. lib. Et Q.E.

Johannes Biset r.c. de C et quater xx et xiiij li. et xiiij s. et v d. et ob. de pluribus debitis contentis in rotulo viij^{o}. Et de C et xvj li. et j m. pro Thoma Basset de debitis Judeorum. In thes. xx li. Et debet CC et quater xx et xj li. vij s. et ix d. et ob. per annum xx [li.][3]

Gillebertus de Dene debet xl s. pro justiciando Willelmo de Pratell'. Set non debet summoneri quia non habuit nec habere potuit pro quo promisit. Willelmus Briewerr' debet x m. (*Set respondet ex alia parte rotuli.*[1]) pro Ricardo de Warneford' sicut recognovit.

Ricardus de Wareneford' r.c. de xl li. et j palefrido pro habenda villa de Essetenton'. Et de dim. m. de misericordia. In thes. ij m. et dim. Et debet xxxviij li. et j m. et j palefridum. per annum v m.

Hugo de forest' r.c. de xvij s. et x d. pro dissaisina. In thes. lib. Et Q.E.

Johannes de Windlesor' r.c. de xx m. pro habenda custodia sicut continetur in rotulo precedenti. In thes. v m. Et debet xv m.

Robertus Sexi debet xiij s. pro vino vendito. Philippus cuvarius debet xx d. Galfridus clericus de Awelton' debet vj s. Ricardus de Theddon' debet dim. m. pro plegio. Bartholomeus Britto debet xx s. pro vino vendito. Johannes de Portesm' debet v m. pro eodem. Heres comitis de Insula debet xl s. de catallis fugitivorum. Willelmus de Esselea debet dim. m. pro plegio. Willelmus Scurdi debet dim. m. pro plegio. Johannes de Escumb' debet dim. m. pro dissaisina. Willelmus Sellarius debet dim. m. pro eodem. Homines comitis de Gloec' debent vij m. de ij^{bus} debitis contentis in rotulo viij^{o}. Homines de Odiham debent v m. de eodem sicut continetur ibidem. Walterus capellanus debet ij s. Andreas de Welhop' debet ix s.

1 *r.c.* repeated.
2 *debet* written on alteration.
3 The right edge of the membrane has been lost at this point.

pro vino vendito. Willelmus Goldfinch debet viij d. pro habendo pone. Johannes Joseph debet dim. m. pro dissaisina. Walterus de Cadamo debet dim. m. pro plegio. Robertus Segrim debet dim. m. pro eodem. Homines de Andour' quorum nomina annotantur in rotulo iiij^{o} debent xv m. et viij d. de amerciamento.

Galfridus f. Turberti r.c. de xl d. In thes. lib. Et Q.E.

Willelmus de Sancto[1] Johanne r.c. de D (et xviij li. et x s. et iij d. et ob.[c]) (*lj li. et xvij s. et xj d. et ob.*[i]) et j bono palefrido de pluribus debitis contentis in rotulo vj^{o}. In thes. l m. Et iterum l m. Et debet CCCC et quater xx et v li. et iiij s. et vij d. et ob. (set respondet in dorso rotuli [i e]) (et j bonum palefridum[i]) per annum C m.

Ricardus de Siffrewast r.c. de vj li. pro habenda terra sicut continetur in rotulo vij^{o}. In thes. xl s. Et debet iiij li.

Matheus f. Herberti r.c. de lvj li. et iij s. et iiij d. de pluribus debitis contentis in rotulo viij. In thes. x m. Et debet xlix li. et x s.

Hamo venator r.c. de lxxiij s. pro habendo essarto contento in rotulo precedenti.

Vmfridus f. Rogeri debet j m. pro habenda vaccaria.[2] Osbertus Strug debet j m. pro habendo pone sicut continetur in rotulo precedenti. Petrus de Lavinton' debet xxxviij li. de tallagio sicut continetur ibidem. Willelmus de Insula debet j m. pro transgressione.

Thomas de Cormeill' r.c. de xj m. de ij debitis sicut continetur in rotulo precedenti. In thes. ij m. Et debet ix m.

Elyas f. Jordani et Editha uxor eius debent dim. m. pro habendo brevi de attingendis xij. Elyas Goding debet xl d. pro licencia concordandi. + Petrus Levesune debet xl d. quia non est prosecutus. Rogerus Swein debet (dim. m. per plegium Galfridi Salvagii[3].[i]) quia prosecutus est in curia christianitatis.[4]

Galfridus de Insula r.c. de xlvj li. et j m. pro habenda custodia sicut continetur in rotulo precedenti. In thes. xx m. Et debet xxxiij li. et dim. m. per annum xl m.

Gillebertus f. Agnetis de Popham r.c. de lxx s. de relevio suo contento ibidem. In thes. ij m. Et debet xliij s. et iiij d.

Johannes de Burne r.c. de iiij s. et viij d. pro dissaisina. In thes. xij d. Et debet iij s. et viij d.

Herbertus Sellator et Andreas Reinfr' r.c. de ij s. et viij d. In thes. x d. Et debent xxij d.

Nicholaus de quercu r.c. de xl d. pro falso clamore. In thes. lib. Et Q.E.

Robertus le Neuman r.c. de dim. m. pro dissaisina per plegium Johannis de Herierd. In thes. xl d. Et debet xl d.

Johannes de Brackel' r.c. de dim. m. pro falso clamore. In thes. lib. Et Q.E.

Willelmus Francesius r.c. de dim. m. pro eodem. In thes. lib. Et Q.E.

1 Word blotted.

2 *Th* written after *vaccaria*, then struck through.

3 Part of this name is under the strengthening tape at the right hand side but the letters are visible under the tape.

4 The first two letters of *christianitatis* are in Greek form.

Willelmus de Lusthill', Radulfus falconarius, Alexander de Wike et Henricus blundus debent xxxvj s. et iij d. de padnagio de Chette set Johannes de Herierd debet eos inde adquietare qui eos recepit sicut recognovit et reddidit illos in anno[1] (sub nomine Thome Croc et sociorum suorum. Et Q.E.[i])

Adam Ringstan r.c. de dim. m. pro transgressione. In thes. xl d. Et debet xl d.

Willelmus francesius et socii sui r.c. de xij s. et vij d. de padnagio anni iiij. In thes. vj s. et iiij d. Et debent vj s. et iij d.

Abbas de Hyda r.c. de xl m. de scutagio de Mungumeri. In thes. xl s. Et debet xxxvij m.

Willelmus de Pontdelarche [*blank*] ij m. de eodem.

[*One line blank*]

DE OBLATIS

Nicholaus de Sirlé r.c. de v m. pro appello sicut continetur in rotulo precedenti. In thes. nichil. Et Robertus de Meisy ad operationes castri de Merleberg' et Lutegareshal' per breve R. Et Q.E.

[*One line blank*]

RESPICE IN TERGUM

[*Rot.* 5d *Mem.* 1]

Thomas de Venoiz r.c. de x m. pro Ysabella que fuit uxor Roberti Maudoit in uxorem.[2] In thes. v m. et debet v m.

Idem Vic. r.c. de l s. et vj d. et ob. de remanenti compoti sui pro pluribus contentis[3] in rotulo precedenti. (In thes. nichil.[i]) Et in summa misarum ex alia parte rotuli xlix s. Et debet xviij d. et ob.

[W]illelmus[4] de Shorewell' [*blank*] xiiij li. et v s. et iij d. de padnagio de Axiesholt de anno vj^{o}. Et [*blank*] vij li. et xiiij s. de eodem padnagio de anno vij^{o}.

Idem W. debet respondere de xxxvj porcis precii xlij s.

Robertus de Belaunnei debet xl d. de scutagio de Bedeford' de viij^{va} parte j^{us} feodi de feodis comitis de Insula, qui requirebatur in compoto Walerandi teutonici in rotulo de carrucagio. Ricardus de Ripariis debet viij s. et x d. scutagii de[5] Bedeford' de tercia parte j^{us} feodi de feodis eiusdem comitis, qui requirebatur ibidem.

1 The rest of the sentence is written at the end of the line below.

2 Conflation of two expressions: *que fuit uxor Roberti*, and *quam Robertus duxit in uxorem*.

3 *contentis* written in error for *debitis*.

4 Initial capital obscured by repair to the membrane.

5 The rest of this entry is written alongside *Nova Oblata* in the line below.

NOVA OBLATA

Magister Stephanus de Lucy r.c. de iiij li.[1] de firma terre R. in Seleburn' que fuit in manu Vic. quam R. ei concessit (per breve suum[i]) quamdiu sibi placuerit ad respondendum inde ad scaccarium per manum suam de eadem firma de qua Vic. respondere consuevit. In thes. lib. Et Q.E.

Idem Vic. r.c. de ij s. et v d. et ob. de exitu terre Roberti de Pourton' dum habuit custodiam. In thes. lib. Et Q.E.

[T]homas[2] de Warblinton' [*blank*] x li. pro relevio suo de terris que fuerunt Willelmi patris sui.

Idem Vic. r.c. de liiij s. et v d. et ob. de exitu v hundredorum forinsecorum (de Basingestok'[i]) que R. retinuit in manu sua.

[I]dem[3] Vic. r.c. de xviij s. et viij d. de exitu (iiij[i]) hundredorum forinsecorum de Aulton' que Rex similiter [retinuit] in manu sua.

[J]ohannes[4] blancbuilli r.c. de dim. m. pro licencia concordandi. In thes. lib. Et Q.E.

Willelmus de Sancto Johanne debet CCCC et quater xx et v li. et iiij s. et vij d. et ob. et j bonum palefridum sicut continetur ex alia parte rotuli, de qua summa W. Briewerr' senior debet eum adquietare de xviij li. (*Set respondet infra.*[i]) de firma de Portesm' de anno xvij° R. J. quas recepit per inquisitionem inde factam. Et de lxj li. et ij s. et vj d. (*Set respondet infra.*[i]) de firma de Awelton' de tribus partibus anni predicti quas recepit per eandem inquisitionem. Et debet W. [de] Sancto Johanne CCCC et vj li. et ij s. et iij. ob. et j bonum palefridum. per annum C m.

W. briewerr' senior debet lxxix li. et ij s. et vj d. de ij debitis pro debitis W. de Sancto Johanne. Et x m. pro Ricardo de Warneforð sicut continetur ex alia parte rotuli, de quibus R. Cicestr' episcopus R. cancellarius debet eum adquietare sicut recognovit pro custodia terre et heredum[5] Dunecan' de Lacell' quam idem ei dimiserat in vita sua. Et quam Willelmus f. et heres eius postmodum ei concessit coram baronibus de scaccario pro C li. usque ad etatem heredum cum maritagiis eorundem computatis in fine C li. predictarum ij debitis predictis. *Set respondet in Buking' in rotulo sequenti.*

[*Four lines blank*]

BEDEFORD' ET BUKING'

Walterus[6] de Pateshill' ut custos r.c. de CCC et lxix li. et xix s. et xj d. bl. Et de C et viij li. num. de firma comitatuum. In thes. lxvij li. et j m. num.

Et in elemosinis constitutis militibus de templo ij m. Et fratribus hospitalis de Witsand' xxx s. et v d. Et Ade f. Militis xxx s. et v d. Et in terris datis monachis de Woburn' xxxij s. in molendino de Lecton'. Et monialibus de fonte Ebrold' xlviij li. et viij s. in Lecton'. Et eisdem iiij li. in Radenache.

1 *r.c. de iiij li.* repeated, with the *iiij li.* inserted above the line.
2 Initial capital obscured by repair to the membrane.
3 Initial capital obscured by repair to the membrane.
4 Initial capital obscured by repair to the membrane.
5 Altered from *heredis*.
6 Oversized initial capital.

Et eisdem xxxij s. in Brichill'. Et W. Marescall' quater xx li. bl. in Luiton'. Et in manerio de Brehill' xx li. bl. de quibus compotus redditur per se. Et in villa de Bedeford' xl li. bl. de quibus homines ville respondent infra. Et in villa de Ailesbir' l li. bl. de quibus Willelmus de Mandevill' respondet infra. Et fratribus hospitalis de Witsand' xl s. in Luiton'. Et Willelmo de Fiednes lx li. in Wendour'. Et fratribus militie templi x li. in Radenache. Et Hugoni de Gurnac' xl li. bl. in Hocton'. Et Henrico de Braibroc cum filia et herede Wiscard' Leidet xxx s. in hida de Hulmo.

Et Willelmo filio Warini xx m. per breve R. ad operationem castri de Rokingeh'. Et pro justicia facienda x s. et vj d. Et debet vij d. bl. Et xl li. et dim. m. num. Idem r.c. de eodem debito. In thes. vij d. bl. Et debet xl li. et dim. m. num. Idem r.c. de eodem debito. In thes. lib. Et Q.E.

[*One line blank*]

Idem vicecomes r.c. de C et viij li. et iij s. et vj d. de proficuo comitatuum. In thes. lxxiiij li. et xvj s. et ix d. et ob. Et debet xxxiij li. et vj s. et viij d. et ob. Idem r.c.[1] de eodem debito. In thes. lib. Et Q.E.

[*One line blank*]

Burgenses de Bedeford' r.c. de xl[2] li. bl. de firma burgi. In thes. xxxiiij li. xiij s. et viij d. bl. Et Ricardo de Landa xlv s. et vij d. et ob. Et Priori de Newenham[3] lx s. in terra de Sele et prato quod vocatur Kingesmede quamdiu R. placuerit de quibus respondent infra. Et debent v s. et viij d. et ob. bl. Idem r.c. de eodem debito. In thes. lib. Et Q.S.

Idem Burgenses r.c. de lx s.[4] bl. de remanenti eiusdem firme de anno viij. [*Darker ink*] In thes. nichil. Et in perdona eisdem burgensibus lx s. per breve R. quia pratum et terra destructa fuerunt per obsidionem castri Bedef'. Et Q.S.

Idem Burgenses debent xviij li. et xviij s. et ij d. et ob. bl. de firma burgi de dim. anno xvij^{s}.[5]

Idem Vic. r.c. de x li. de cremento de Buking'. Et de iiij m. de alio cremento pro accipitribus. Et de xl s. de dim. hundredo de Stambrig'. Et de iiij s. de firma de Hanewic'. Et de iij s. de firma terre Lambricti de Claidic. Et de iiij s. de firma j^{us} virgate terre in Eversholt. In thes. lib. Et Q.E.

Willelmus de Mandevill' r.c. de lx li. de firma de Ailesbir'. In thes. lib. Et Q.E.

Magister Simon cocus R. r.c. de xx li. bl. de firma ville de Brehill' quam villam R. ei commisit cum domibus suis ibidem custodiendam quamdiu ea bene custodierit. Ita quod de debito quod Walterus Buistard' debet R. pro arreragiis que ab eo exiguntur per summonitionem scaccarii de firma eiusdem manerii reddet idem Simon singulis annis quamdiu predictum manerium habuerit in manu sua v m. per breve R. In thes. ix li. et x s. et

1 Not abbreviated, but written as *reddit comp.*

2 The space left for *r.c. de* was not large enough, and the *de* is squashed against the *xl*.

3 There was a priory of Augustinian Canons at Newnham or Newenham by Bedford according to D. Knowles and G. Hadcock, *Medieval Religious Houses* (Harlow, 1971), p. 167.

4 *f'* written originally (for *firma*?) and changed to *s*.

5 *xvij s.* written for *xvijo*.

vj d. bl. [*blank*] Et predicto Simoni coco lx s. et x d. Et fratribus hospitalis de Witsand' in Lutegareshal' lx s. et v d. Et in defalta bosci de Hildesden' lx s. Et in liberatione capellani de Brehill l s. Et habent de superplus x s. et viij d. bl. qui sunt eis extensi ad xj s. num. et locati infra.

Idem Simon r.c. de xvj li. et x s. et vij d. pro Waltero Buistard' de pluribus crementis et tallagiis eiusdem manerii contentis in rotulo viij. Et de xlv s. et v d. pro eodem de ij^{bus} debitis contentis in rotulo precedenti. In thes. xij s. Et debet xviij li. et[1] iiij s. per annum v (m.^{i})

Homines de Brehill' debent[2] C et vj s. et j d. de remanenti firme et crementi de Brehill' de dim. anno xvij R. J. Et xxvj li. et x s. et x d. de pluribus tallagiis contentis in rotulo viij^{o} (*et fine de Burstall'*^{i}).[3] *Set respondet infra.*

Predictus Simon r.c. de xl s. de cremento ville de Bruhill'. Et de iiij s. de quodam essarto in Bruhill'. Et de viij s. et iiij d. de prato de Aclay. In thes. xij s. et iiij d. Et in superplus quod habet supra xj s. Et debet xxix s.

Prior de Neweham r.c. de lx s. de firma de la Sele et de prato quod vocatur Kingesmede sicut continetur in rotulo precedenti. In thes. lib. Et Q.E.

Hugo de Hosdeng' r.c. de xxx li. et viij s. et iiij d. pro Waltero de Windlesor' sicut continetur in rotulo vij^{o}. In thes. lx s. Et debet xxvij li. et viij s. et iiij d. per annum lx s.

Comes Simon debet l li. super Purnewic et Bludeie sicut continetur in rotulo ij^{o} R. J. Turstanus Scotus debet xlv m. et vij s. et iiij d. quia fuit convictus. Radulfus de Norewiz clericus debet ij m. et dim. de vinis R.

Willelmus de Windlesor' debet quater xx et x li. et xiij s. et vij d. de ij^{bus} debitis contentis in rotulo viij^{o}. *Set respondet in Berkesir'.*

Petrus de Goldinton' r.c. de quater xx et j li. et j sparvario de pluribus debitis contentis in rotulo iij^{o}. In thes. x m. Et debet Lxxiiij li. et dim. m. et j sparvarium. per annum x m.

G. comes Gloec' debet C et xix li. et xvj s. et iij d. et ij osturcos pro Waltero de Trailli sicut continetur in rotulo vj^{o}. Willelmus de Bello campo debet xxiiij li. et dim. m. de auro Regine.

Radulfus f. Galfridi r.c. de lx s. pro transgressione. In thes. xx s. Et debet xl s.

Willelmus de bosco debet xij li. et xviij s. quia fuit convictus. Idem Vic. debet vj li. (et xvj s. et ij d.^{i}) de minutis particulis foreste. + Moyses Wobode debet j osturcum sicut continetur in rotulo xvj^{o}. Gervasius de Schirinton' debet j m. pro defalta.

Henricus f. Gosce r.c. de xxj li. et vj s. pro eodem. In thes. dim. m. Et debet xx li. et xix s. et iiij d. per annum dim. [m.]

Osbertus de Wotton' debet xvj li. et vij s. et vj d. quia fuit convictus. Set non debet summoneri usque ad voluntatem R. pro nimia paupertate sua.

Hugo de Bathon' r.c. de C (s.^{i}) pro hominibus de Bedeford' sicut

1 Rest of the entry written at the end of the previous line.
2 *debent* perhaps erased.
3 Inserted above the line in darker ink.

continetur in rotulo precedenti. In thes. xx s. Et debet iiij li. de quibus Willelmus de Lond' clericus debet eum adquietare sicut recognovit.
per annum xl s. per breve R.

Idem Hugo debet xl li de[1] hidagiis et sectis comitatuum sicut continetur in rotulo viij°.

Willelmus f. Warini debet xij li. et v s. et viij d. de ij^{bus} scutagiis contentis in rotulo precedenti de quibus Godescall' de Machelin' debet eum adquietare (*Set respondet infra.*[1]) de C et xix s. qui illos recepit sicut recognovit. Et debet W. vj li. et dim. m. *Set respondet infra*.

Godescall' de Machelin' debet C et xix s. de primo scutagio R. pro Willelmo filio Warini sicut supra continetur. Henricus de Braibroc (*Set respondet infra.*[1]) debet C s. de scutagio Pictavie quos recepit sicut continetur in rotulo vij°. Alexander de Burton' debet j m. pro habendo brevi contra Roheis' Pippard'. Ignorius de Sancto Claro debet xl s. pro habendo brevi qui requirebatur in Lond'.

Willelmus de Sancto Edwardo r.c. de xxix li. et xiiij s. de debitis Judeorum. In thes. xx s. Et debet xxviiij li. [*sic*] et xiiij s. per annum xx s.

Homines de Brehull' r.c. de xxxj li. et xvj s. et xj d. de ij^{bus} debitis supra contentis. In thes. ij m. per j talliam de ante guerram locatam precepto H. de Burgo Justiciarii coram R. Cycestr' episcopo R. cancellario et W. Carleo[l'][2] episcopo. Et in operatione cuiusdam palicii lxv s. et ix d. per breve R. Et Roberto de Droes liiij s. et ij d. de anno primo R. post guerram dum habuit custodiam per breve eiusdem. Et debent xxiiij li. et x s. et iiij d. *Set respondent infra*.

Willelmus f. Hamonis debet xvj li. et vij s. de prestito (Pictavie[1]). Willelmus de bello campo debet xxij m. de eodem. Robertus Maudoit debet ij m. de eodem. Ricardus de Siffrewast debet xiiij m. de eodem pro filio suo. Hugo de Gornac' debet C m. de eodem. Walterus de Trailli debet v m. de eodem. Willelmus Hosatus debet ij m. de scutagio de Mungumeri. Et ij m. de scutagio de Bedef', qui requirebatur in Noting' in rotulo precedenti de j feodo in Upton'.

W. Marescallus Comes de Pembr' r.c. de CCCC et lxix li. et xviij s. et iij d. et ob. de pluribus debitis contentis in rotulo precedenti in rotulo compotorum. In thes. l li. Et debet CCCC et xix li. et xviij s. et iij d. et ob.

Idem W. r.c. de xx m. pro Bartholomeo de Mortemer sicut continetur in rotulo vij°. In thes. nichil. Et in perdona Matheo nepoti et heredi predicti Bartholomei xx m. per breve R. Et Q.E.

Simon de Berevill' r.c. de xviij s. et vj d. et ob. pro justiciando Willelmo. In thes. ix s. Et debet ix s. et vj d. et ob.

Simon[3] Druell r.c. de xxvij m. et dim. (et j palefrido[1]) pro patre suo pro habendo officio sicut continetur in rotulo primo R. In thes. x m. Et debet xvij m. et dim. et j palefridum. per annum x m.

Johannes de Bello campo r.c. de CCCC et xxx li. et xviij s. et iiij d. de pluribus debitis contentis in rotulo viij°. In thes. xx li. Et debet CCCC et x li. et xviij s. et iiij d. per annum xx li.

[1] Written on an alteration.
[2] The rest of this word is covered by the mending strip.
[3] Simon Druell is shown as William in *NS 54*, p. 94.

Homines de Bruhill' r.c. de xxiiij li. et x s. et iiij d. de pluribus debitis supra contentis. In thes. xxiij s. et iiij d. Et debent xxiij li. et vij s. *Set respondent post Warewic' et Leicr' quia non erat hic locus.*[1]

DE PRIMO SCUTAGIO REGIS

([2]Willelmus f. Warini r.c. de vj li. et dim. m. de ij scutagiis sicut supra continetur. In thes. nichil. Et in perdona ipsi Willelmo vj li. et dim. m. per breve R.[i]) (Et Q.E.[i])

Willelmus de Fiednes debet iiij m. de eodem. Comes de Ferrar' debet j m. de eodem pro Willelmo de Vernone sicut continetur in rotulo precedenti. Set respondet in Norhantesir'. Willelmus de Canterlu junior debet x m. de eodem de feod' Leonie de Stutevill'.

Willelmus f. Hamonis r.c. de xiiij li. et vj s. et vj d. de ij^{bus} scutagiis contentis in rotulo precedenti. In thes. x m. Et debet vij li. et xiij s. et ij d.

[*Rot.* 5d *Mem.* 2]

Jordanus[3] francesius r.c. de iiij li. et vij s. et ix d. de eodem. In thes. xx s. Et debet lxvij s. et ix d. per annum xx s.

Johannes de Mikeleham debet x li. et vij s. et j palefridum pro habenda gratia R. J. *Set respondet in Surr'.*

Robertus de ferrar' debet CC et quater xx m. pro habenda Johanna sicut continetur in rotulo ij^{o} (*Set respondet infra.*[i]). Rogerus de Argentoem debet xxv m. et dim. pro dissaisina. *Alicia de Torneie que manet apud Eure debet dim. m. pro falso clamore que requirebatur in Middelsex'.*

Bogo de Knovill' r.c. de ix li. et j m. pro Gerardo de Graenvill' sicut continetur in rotulo iij^{o}. In thes. j m. Et debet ix li. per annum j m.

Nicholaus de Keinesham debet dim. m. pro dissaisina. + Nicholaus f. Reginaldi debet dim. m. pro eodem. + Petrus f. Willelmi debet dim. (m.[i]) quia non est prosecutus. + Morinus Vinitor debet ij m. pro vino vendito. + Milo de Kilpaec debet vij s. pro dissaisina.

+ Rogerus de Cundecot' debet ij m. pro vino vendito. + Henricus de la Hill' debet iiij s. et viij d. pro eodem. + Nicholaus f. Galfridi (et Radulfus f. Stephani[i]) debent dim. m. pro licencia concordandi. + Johannes f. Rodlandi debet dim. m. pro habendo pone. Willelmus f. Warini debet C s. pro habendo j mercato sicut continetur in rotulo iij^{o}. Willelmus de Turevill' debet ij palefridos pro habenda saisina. + Simon le Bigod debet dim. m. pro vino vendito. Henricus de Curten' debet x m. pro dissaisina.

Josceus de Chelvesdon' r.c. de dim. m. de fine sicut continetur in rotulo iij^{o}. In thes. lib. Et Q.E.

Johannes de Horsedenn' debet j m. pro iniusta detentione. Ricardus de

1 Perhaps here *resp'* is standing for *respice* rather than *respondent*.

2 This entry begins beside the heading *DE PRIMO SCUTAGIO REGIS*. The quittance is an interlinear of an interlinear item.

3 The mending strip on the left edge partly covers the initial letters of the first eight lines of this membrane.

Argentoem de Clendon' debet dim. m. pro Matillide Duredent. Willelmus de Fiednes debet xx s. de scutagio de Biham. Henricus de Hamslap' debet xl d. quia non habuit.

Willelmus Maudoit r.c. de quater xx et v. li et xvij s. et vj d. de iij^bus debitis sicut continetur in rotulo viij. In thes. x li. Et debet lxxv li. et xvij s. et vj d. *Et iiij m. que requirebantur in Berkes' in rotulo precedenti super Yuur.*[1] (*Et ij s. et ij d. et ob. de scutagio de Mungumeri per eadem qui*[2] *summa requirebatur in Buk'sir.*[1]) per annum xl m.

Comes Gloecestr' debet dim. m. pro Waltero de Trailly pro licencia concordandi sicut continetur in rotulo vj^o. + Willelmus de Mixebir' debet dim. [m.] pro licencia concordandi per plegium Ricardi filii Petri.

Galfridus de Pichelestorn' [*blank*] dim. m. pro dissaisina.

Johannes de Wadelaw' r.c. de iiij li. pro iij^bus dissaisinis. In thes. xx s. Et debet lx s.

Cecilia que fuit uxor Willelmi de Sancto Remigio r.c. de iiij m. pro habenda custodia sicut continetur in rotulo viij. In thes. lib. Et Q.E.

Osbertus de Santerdon' r.c. de xl s. de scutagio Pictavie. Et de C s. de fine passagii in Pictaviam. In thes. ij m. Et debet viij m. et dim. per annum ij m.

Radulfus de Puteham r.c. de xxx s. de predicto fine passagii. In thes. j m. Et debet xvj s. et viij d.

Beatricia de Karun r.c. de xiiij li. pro habenda custodia sicut continetur in rotulo viij^o. In thes. lib. Et Q.E.

Adam Wille debet dim. m. pro dissaisina. + Robertus Longus debet dim. m. pro eodem.

Robertus[3] de Croinden' r.c. de xx s. de ij^bus misericordiis per plegium Alani Basset. In thes. lib. Et Q.E.

Ricardus de Rothomag' r.c. de j m. pro eodem per plegium eiusdem Alani. In thes. lib. Et Q.E.

Willelmus f. Ricardi de Stanes r.c. de j m. pro eodem per plegium eiusdem. In thes. lib. Et Q.E.

Idem vic. r.c. de j m. de Ricardo de Turri. Et de j m. de Rogero de Penna. Et de dim. [m.] de Willelmo de Windlesor'. In thes. lib. Et Q.E.

Hugo de Bathon' r.c. de xx m. pro redemptione Johannis de Grasmednill'. In thes. ij m. Et debet xviij m. *de quibus Willelmus de Lond' (clericus*[1]*) debet eum adquietare sicut recognovit.* per annum iiij m. per breve R.

Ricardus de Turovill' debet x li. de parte sua de ij feodis in Chalfhunt' de fine D m. Et xl s. de scutagio Pictavie. Set non debet summoneri. Quia inde quietus est in rotulo xv R. J.

Walterus de Woketon' r.c. de j m. pro dissaisina sicut continetur in rotulo precedenti. Et de ij m. de fine suo sicut infra continetur. In thes. ij m. et iterum j m. Et Q.E.

Willelmus de Baiocis [*blank*] dim. m. pro eodem sicut continetur ibidem.

1 Uncertain reading. Name hard to read.

2 *qui* written for *que*.

3 This line is bracketed in the left hand margin to the one below, with a margination *-il'* cut off on the left side.

Radulfus Tirel r.c. de dim. m.[1] de scutagio de Mungumery. In thes. lib. Et Q.E.

G. Comes Gloec' debet iiij m. de eodem de feodo Walteri de Trailli. Willelmus de Fiednes debet iiij m. de eodem. [*Darker ink*] Idem W. et Henricus de Trublevill' debent xxiiij m. de scutagio de Mungumeri de feod' comitis de Gisnes dum habuerunt saisinam.

Hugo de Hosdeng r.c. de ix m. et ix d. de eodem. In thes. xx s. Et debet C et j s. et viij d. per annum xx s. (qui requirebantur in Essex' in rotulo precedenti[i]).[2]

Radulfus Tirel r.c. de j m. de scutagio de Bedeford'. In thes. lib. Et Q.E.

Willelmus Hoese r.c. de C et xiij s. et iiij d. de pluribus scutagiis contentis in rotulo precedenti in Norh'tesir'. In thes. lib. Et Q.E.

Comes Gloecr' debet iiij m. de eodem. Mauricius de Borham et Odo Burnard heredes Alexandri filii Geroldi debent xlij s. et iiij d. de debitis Áárон pro eodem Alexandro qui requirebantur in Essex'.

Willelmus Maudoit debet C li. pro Alicia Comitissa de Warewik' que requirebatur in Gloecestr' in rotulo precedenti. Stephanus le bel debet dim. m. pro dissaisina qui requirebatur in Oxon' in rotulo precedenti.

DE OBLATIS

Idem vic. r.c. de dim. m. de Waltero de Bergeveny. Et de xxxix s. et vij d. de catallis Falkesii de Breautéé. In thes. lib. Et Q.E.

Johannes f. Fulconis de Hida debet xxxvij s. (et iij ob.[i]) de relevio suo sicut continetur in rotulo precedenti. Rogerus de Ho debet j m. pro habenda inquisitione sicut continetur ibidem. Johannes f. Ricardi Scurnel debet (xl s. pro[i]) eodem per plegium Johannis de Wiggehal' et Ricardi filii Henrici de Lenn'. Walterus de Woketon' debet ij m. de fine suo (*Set respondet supra.*[i]) pro transgressione sicut continetur ibidem. Alexander de la Broche debet dim. m. pro licencia concordandi sicut continetur ibidem.

Rogerus Burnard' r.c. de (x[c]) (vij[i]) m. de fine suo pro falso clamore. In thes. iiij m. et dim. Et debet ij m. et dim.

Sibilla de Kauresfeld' r.c. de dim. m. pro licencia concordandi sicut continetur ibidem. In thes. iij s. Et debet iij s. et viij d.

Winda de Windlesor' debet j m. pro falso clamore que requirebatur in itinere Simonis de Hal et sociorum eius. Simon f. Arnulfi de Aschwell' debet dim. m. pro dissaisina qui requirebatur ibidem.

NOVA OBLATA

Willelmus f. Warini r.c. de lx m. sicut infra continetur. In thes. nichil. Et in perdona ipsi W. lx m. per breve R. Et Q.E.[3]

Willelmus f. Warini attornatus Reginaldi de Sancto Walerico r.c. de lx

[1] *m.* repeated.

[2] Written at the end of the preceding line.

[3] The beginning of this entry written on the same line as the heading *Nova Oblata*.

m. quas manucepit coram R. pro ipso Reginaldo reddendas cum debito quod idem Reginaldus debet R. pro habenda saisina de manerio de Aspel' ad opus ipsius Reginaldi. Set respondet supra.

Johanna de Ferraríís r.c. de C m. pro habenda licencia maritandi se cuicumque voluerit preterquam inimicis R. per plegium Willelmi de Averench' de xx m., Stephani Haringod' de x m., Hugonis de Clohall' de xx m., Roberti de Hucham de x m., Galfridi de Luci de x m., Ricardi de Stokes de x m., Roberti de Aubervill' de x m., Cecil' de Abrincis de x m. In thes. l m. Et debet l m.

Idem vicecomes r.c. de j m. de Roberto Amaur' pro licencia concordandi cum Thoma Poinnant. Et de dim. m. de Radulfo de Goudinton' pro eodem cum Petro de Coudinton'. Et de j m. de Jordano Lenveisie pro habendo pone. Et de dim. m. de Galfrido de Querendon' pro eodem cum Willelmo Russell'. Et de dim. m. de Johanne de Gatesden' pro eodem cum Thoma de Ravelingeham. Et de dim. m. de Rogero le Brun pro eodem cum Nicholao bruno. In thes. lib. Et Q.E.

Ricardus f. Odard r.c. de xl s. quia retraxit se per plegium Roberti de Brocton' et Galfridi filii Petri forestarii. In thes. x s. Et debet xxx s.

Robertus de Ferrar' debet CC et quater xx m. pro habenda Johanna sicut supra continetur de quibus Johannes draparius de Windles' debet respondere de lij li. pro blado de Sipeham quod fuit predicti Roberti et respondet in Berkes'. Et debet R. C et xxxiiij li. C et j m.[1]

AMERCIAMENTA FACTA PER SIMONEM DE HAL' ET SOCIOS SUOS IN COMITATIBUS BED' et BUKING'

Idem vicecomes r.c. de C et iij li. et xvj s. et ij d. de misericordiis hominum villarum et hundredorum et catallis fugitivorum et suspensorum quorum nominibus preponitur littera t in rotulo quem predicti liberaverunt in thesauro. In thes. lib. MCC et xlij t[otalis]. Et Q.E.

Willelmus[2] Integal' r.c. de j m. pro dissaisina. In thes x s. Et debet xl d.

Robertus Neweman r.c. de dim. m. pro falso clamore. In thes xl d. Et debet xl d.

Willelmus f. Ailwine r.c. de x s. pro plegio. In thes. v s. Et debet v s.

[D]ecena Willelmi Wischard r.c. de j m. pro fuga. In thes. dim. m. Et debet dim. m.

[W]illelmus Burdun (Norh[i]) r.c. de j m. pro transgressione. In thes. dim. m. Et debet dim. m. (*Set respondet in Norht in rotulo sequenti.*[i])

[P]etrus molendinarius r.c. de j m. pro dissaisina. In thes. x s. Et debet xl d.

[W]alterus de Bergaveni r.c. de xl s. quia retraxit se. In thes. xx s. Et debet xx s.

[H]undredum de Stok' r.c. de iiij m. pro transgress'. In thes. ij m. Et debet ij m. Set respondet infra.

1 *C et j m.* written after the heading on the following line.

2 This entry and those following are written on the left hand side of the membrane. Marginal notations are therefore invisible under the mending strip.

[H]undredum de Dustebereg' r.c. de j m. pro eodem. In thes. dim. m. Et debet dim. m.

[Ra]nn' f. Baldewini r.c. de dim. m. quia non habuit. In thes. ij s. Et debet iiij s. et viij d.

[G]odefridus blundus r.c. de dim. m. pro eodem. In thes. xl d. et debet xl d.

[R]ann' Cobbe r.c. de dim. m. pro eodem. In thes. xl d. Et debet xl d.

[W]illelmus Russel r.c. de dim. m. pro eodem. In thes. xl d. Et debet xl d.

[R]ein' f. Willelmi r.c. de dim. m. pro eodem. In thes. xl d. Et debet xl d.

[Hu]ndredum de Wottesdon' r.c. de ij m. pro transgressione. In thes. xvj s. et viij d. Et debet x s.

[V]ic. r.c. de xlix s. de catallis Ricardi Pain suspensi. In thes. xxix s. Et debet xx s.

[?Willelmus] Pinel r.c. de dim. m. pro defalta. In thes. xl d. Et debet xl d.

[Ra]d' Pinel r.c. de dim. m. pro eodem. In thes. xl d. Et debet xl d.

[Wi]llelmus dispensator r.c. de dim. m. pro dissaisina. In thes. xl d. Et debet xl d.

[W]alterus essartator r.c. de dim. m. pro eodem. In thes. xl d. Et debet xl d.

[R]obertus f. Johannis r.c. de dim. m. pro eodem. In thes. vj. s et j d. Et debet vij d.

[...]e? f. Johannis r.c. de dim. m. pro eodem. In thes. xl d. Et debet xl d.

[W]illelmus de Kaldecot' r.c. de dim. m. pro eodem. In thes. xl d. Et debet xl d.

[.]n' Meriet? r.c. de x s.[1] pro dissaisina. In thes. v s. Et debet v s.

d Hugo[2] Halidai r.c. de dim. m. pro dissaisina. In thes. xl d. Et debet xl d.

p Elyas folkard' et Robertus de Abbatia r.c. de dim. m. pro eodem. In thes. xx d. Et debent v s.

d Ricardus f. Ailwini et Robertus f. Gilleberti r.c. de dim. m. pro eodem. In thes. v s. Et debent xx d.

d Ricardus Banin r.c. de dim. m. pro eodem. In thes. xl d. Et debet xl d.

d Johannes Gatesher r.c. de dim. m. pro eodem. In thes. xl d. Et debet xl d.

t Willelmus Folcard et Robertus f. Bernard' r.c. de dim. m. pro eodem. In thes. v s. Et debent xx d.

d Rannulfus Malgor et Ricardus f. Petri r.c. de dim. m. pro eodem. In thes. v s. Et debent xx d.

d Willelmus Lenfant et Hugo f. Petri r.c. de dim. m. pro eodem. In thes. v s. Et debent xx d.

p Rogerus prepositus et Walterus Balle r.c. de dim. m. pro eodem. In thes. xx d. Et debent v s.

p Willelmus banin et Petrus f. Roberti r.c. de dim. m. pro eodem. In thes. xx d. Et debent v s.

d Rann' forestarius r.c. de dim. m. pro eodem. In thes. xl d. Et debet xl d.

Robertus f. Wigor r.c. de dim. m. pro eodem. In thes.[3] lib. Et Q.E.

1 *dim. m.* underlined for deletion, and *x s.* written above *dim.*

2 The following entries are written on the right hand side of the membrane.

3 *In thes.* repeated.

p Walterus f. Muriel' et Robertus blundel r.c. de dim. m. pro eodem. In thes. xx d. Et debent v s.
d Johannes fitun et Hugo fitun r.c. de dim. m. pro eodem. In thes. xl d. Et debent xl d.
d Ricardus f. Winem' r.c. de dim. m. pro eodem. In thes. xl d. Et debet xl d.
d Robertus f. Hugonis et Nicholaus f. Willelmi r.c. de dim. m. pro eodem. In thes. xx d. Et debent v s.
p Willelmus et Johannes filii Siward' r.c. de dim. m. pro eodem. In thes. xx d. Et debent v s.
d Walterus Cortehacher et Radulfus carpentarius r.c. de dim. m. pro eodem. In thes. v s. Et debent xx d.
d Tovi[1] Selibern et Ricardus f. Ailwardi r.c. de dim. m. pro eodem. In thes. xl d. Et debent xl d.
d Willelmus Huber et Godefridus Bauin r.c. de dim. m. pro eodem. In thes. xl d. Et debent xl d.
d Ricardus f. Gregorii r.c. de dim. m. pro eodem. In thes. xl d. Et debet xl d.
p Rogerus f. Gregorii et Robertus de Wik' r.c. de dim. m. pro eodem. In thes. xx d. Et debent v s.

Idem vicecomes r.c. de x s. de catallis Johannis de Bledelaw' suspensi. In thes. nichil. Et monachis de becco x s. per libertatem carte. Et Q.E.

Ricardus f. Roberti r.c. de xx d. pro dissaisina. In thes. lib. Et Q.E.

[Hu]ndredum[2] de Stok' r.c. de ij m. sicut supra continetur. In thes. nichil. Et canonicis de Merton ij m. per libertatem carte. Et Q.E.

Willelmus de Cantilup' debet xx m. pro ij^{bus} dissaisinis de itinere Henrici de Braibroc et Thome de Haiden'.[3]

[Idem Vi]c. r.c. de dim. m. de Decena Andree filii Radulfi fugitivi. Et de dim. m. de Decena Walteri le franceis fugitivi. In thes. nichil. Et S. Archiepiscopo Cant' j m. per libertatem carte. Et Q.E.

[...]n de Braibroc debet C s. de scutagio Pictavie de feodo Roberti de Albineio sicut supra continetur. Set non debet summoneri quia protestatum est[4] per inquisitionem inde factam precepto R. quod illos recepit. Set continetur in summa xxiiij li. (et s.[5] et ix d.^{i}) quos idem Henricus liberavit in thesauro de ...[6] predicti Roberti sicut continetur in rotulo xvj^{o} R. J. Et tunc restabant solvende xxv li. et xj s. de quibus Willelmus de Sancto Maxentio (ballius P. Wint' episcopi^{i}) recepit xxij li. et xj s. sicut constat per eandem inquisitionem et de quibus predictus episcopus habuit quietum per breve R. in (anno^{c}) (rotulo^{i}) v^{o} de ... li. et xj s. Et debet idem episcopus xl s. Et debet residuum feod[orum] predicti Roberti (iiij li. et xij s. et viij d.^{c}) lx s. scilicet de Johanne de Merston' x s. De Waltero de Gisnet' xx s. de dim. feodo in Welewe. Et de Henrico de Albineio xx s. de dim. feodo [in ...]

1 Or *Toni*? *Tom*?
2 This line and the following lines go right across the membrane.
3 This entry is written on the same line as the previous one, with an insertion sign before it, but it is not apparent where else it belongs.
4 *protestatum est* repeated.
5 No figures given for shillings.
6 Extreme left hand of some lines lost under the mending strip.

eford. Et ij s. et viij d. de xv[a] (parte[i]) j feodi in Aldolvestr' sicut continetur in eadem inquisitione. Et restant solvendi vij s. et iiij d. qui requirendi sunt de predictis feodis.
[*Endorsed*] SUHAMPTESCHIR (emend'[i]) ET BEDEFORDSCHIR' (emend'[i]) ET BUKINGEH' (emend' et iterum emend' totum[i])

[*Rot.* 6 *Mem.* I][1]

[*Seven lines blank*]

BERKESIR'

Henricus[2] de Scaccario ut custos r.c. de CC et lxx li. xiiij s. et ij d. bl. de firma comitatus de dim. anno. In thes. nichil.

Et in terris datis monachis de Rading' xxviij li. in Bleobir'. Et eisdem xij li. et x s. in Henred'. (Et eisdem xx s. in forinseco hundredi de Rading'.[c]) (quia non sunt de corpore comitatus.[i]) Et monachis de Cluniaco l m. in Ledecumb'. Et W. Maresc' xxv li. bl. in Waneting'. Et Josceo de Pluggenay xj li. et x s. bl. in Lamburn'. Et [*blank*][3] xj li. et x s. bl. in eadem villa. Et Ricardo Walensi C s. bl. in Estbir' cum filia et herede Radulfi de Lanval'. Et Willelmo de Lanval' l s. bl. in Blakegrave. Et Willelmo Brieguerr' C s. bl. in Uplamburn'. Et [*blank*] xxvj li. bl. in Schriveham. Et in Cocham et Bray lx li. bl. de quibus compotus redditur per se. Et monachis de monte Drogon' lxx s. in Mighal'. Et monachis de Noyun xxx s. in Grafton'. Et Henrico f. Geroldi xvj li. in Speresholt'. Et Roberto de Curten' xxv li. in Sutton'. Et Ricardo Walensi lxxv s. in Uplamburn'. Et Bertramo de Garcly vij li. et x s. in Gainge quamdiu R. placuerit. Et habet hic de superplus xxv s. et vj d. (bl.[i]) que excrescunt per extensionem maneriorum. Et ideo non debent ei allocari.
[*One line blank*]

Et in carriagio viij doliorum vini (per aquam[i]) á Walingeford' usque Oxon' et aliorum viij doliorum vini á Wallingeford' usque Wudestok' et eisdem carcandis et discarcandis xx s. per breve R. Et in operatione muri iuxta pontem corneicium castri de Walingeford' dum habuit custodiam C et vij s. et v d. et ob. per breve R. Et in liberatione Hugonis de Seuekeworðe probatoris et (custodia[i]) armata eiusdem et in custo posito ad mittendum xv prisones á Walingeford' usque Lond' xl s. per breve eiusdem. Et in emendatione castri de Warengeford' et domorum in castro C s. de toto anno. Summa xiij li. vij s. v d. et ob. qui debent allocari ut idem. H. Vic.

[1] The bottom left hand edge of the membrane on the dorse side has been fixed by tape. This has obscured some of the writing by the clerk. There is something written at the top of the dorse of the membrane in a different hand to that of the face. It is difficult to make out what it is but it looks like *Hic Inci*[*pit*].

[2] The 'h' in *Henricus* is a majuscule 'h' which extends over three lines.

[3] This *blank* also appears in *NS 54*, p. 221, *NS 56*, p. 163, and *NS 48*, p. 1.

voluerit de quibus x li. et xvj s. et vij d. et ob. locantur ei (*infra. Et restant ei locande*[1] *l s. et x d. et preca totum infra.*[i])[2]

f' Idem Vic. r.c. de xl m. de proficuo comitatus de hoc dim. anno. In thes. xxxv m. Et in summa misarum quod habet supra in proxima linea v m.

Et Q.E.

[*Two lines blank*]

Hugo Dispensarius ut custos r.c. de CC et lxx li. xiiij s. et ij d. bl. de firma comitatus de alio dim. anno. In thes. nichil.

Et in terris datis monachis de Rading' xxviij li. in Bleobir'. Et eisdem xij li. et x s. in Henred'. (Et eisdem xx s. in forinseco hundredi de Rading'.[c]) (quia non sunt de corpore comitatus.[i]) Et monachis de Cluniaco l m. in Ledecumb'. Et W. Marisc' xxv li. bl. in Waneting'. Et Josceo de Pluggen' xj li. et x s. bl. in Lamburn'. Et [*blank*] xj li. et x s. bl. in eadem villa. Et Ricardo Walensi C s. bl. in Estbir' cum filia et herede Radulfi de Lanval'. Et Willelmo de Lanval' l s. bl. in Blakegrave. Et Willelmo Briegerr' C s. (bl.[i]) in Uplamburn'. Et [*blank*] xxvj li. (et x s.[c]) bl. in Schiriveham. Et in Cocham et Bray lx li. bl. de quibus compotus redditur per se. Et monachis de monte Drogon' lxx s. in Mighal'. Et monachis de Noyun xxx s. in Grafton'. Et Henrico f. Gerold' xvj li. in Speresholt. Et Roberto de Curten' xxv li. in Sutton'. Et Ricardo Walensi lxxv s. in Uplamburn'. Et Bertramo de Garcly vij li. et x s. in Gange quamdiu R. placuerit. Et habet hic de superplus xxv s. et vj d. bl. qui excrescunt per extensionem maneriorum. Et ideo non debent Vic. allocari.[3]

[*One line blank*]

Et in elemosinis constitutis militibus de Templo j m. Et pro viij quarteriis et quarta parte unius quarterii de mestilione et j quarterio frumenti emptis ad dominicum R. seminandum (apud Watlinton'[i]) xxix s. et iiij d. per breve R. Et pro vj bobus et iiij equis emptis ad predictum dominicum de Watlinton' instaurandum lxiij s. et vj d. per idem breve. Et in reparatione ij^{orum} molendinorum R. de Walingeford' iiij li. et xvij^{e} s. et iiij d. per idem breve. Et pro ferro et ascere ad carrucas de Watlinton' et ferratura affrorum et pro forragiis et carris et aliis necessariis utensilibus xxx s. et iij ob. Et pro prato R. de Walingeford' falcando et carriando et blado de Merston' metendo et (prato[i]) falcando xxiij s. et iiij d. Et habet de superplus xij li. xvj s. et xj d. et ob. quod totum locatur ei infra in prima linea.

f'[4] Idem Vic. r.c. de xxij li. et xxij d. et ob. de proficuo comitatus de hoc dim. anno. In thes. x li. Et in predicto superplus quod habet supra xij li. xvj s. et xj d. et ob. Et habet hic de superplus xv s. et iij ob.

f' Hugo de Sotesbroc [*blank*] xij d. de firma molendini de Henlik'.

f' Reginaldus de Benetfeld' [*blank*] vj d. de firma sua. Et vj d. de eadem firma de anno preterito.

[1] This should be *locandi*.

[2] This interlineation is very faint. It is uncertain as to what *preca totum* or *precarotum* means but either appear to be possibilities for what is written.

[3] The whole of this paragraph is a repeat of the second paragraph above. The final sentence is drafted in a notably darker ink.

[4] The left hand edge of the membrane is much rubbed from here on. An '*f*'' can be supplied from *NS 54*, p. 222.

f' Jordanus de Lond' r.c. de v m. de firma avalagii Tamisie. In thes. lib. Et Q.E.

f' Alanus Basset r.c. de xx li. de firma de Wicumb'. In thes. xviij li. et viij s. et viij d. Et in elemosinis constitutis monachis de Becco xviij s. Et ecclesie illius ville j m. Et Q.E.

Idem A. [*blank*] ix li. et iiij s. et iiij d. de eadem firma sicut continetur in rotulo iiij.

f' Heres Michaelis de Sancto Phileberto [*blank*] xij d. de firma sua. Et ij s. de eadem firma de ij^{bus} annis preteritis.

f' Galfridus de Baggeset' r.c. de xij d. de firma iiij acris[1] in Cruchefeld'. In thes. lib. Et Q.E.

f' Idem Vic. r.c. de xxiij s. et viij d. de quadam domo escaeta in Oxon'. In thes. xxij s. et vj d. Et in defalta cuiusdam domus vaste xiiij d. Et Q.E.

f' Robertus mapparius r.c. de iij s. pro j mappa. In thes. lib. Et Q.E.

f' Idem Vic. r.c. de xl s. de remanenti firme de Uplamburne de terra que remansit in manu R. post extensionem terre Ricardi Walensis. In thes. x s. Et item xxx s. Et Q.E.

f' Henricus f. (Yvonis[c]) (Eudonis[i])[2] r.c. de dim. m. de firma j^{us} virgate terre in Clopcot'. Et de iij m. de eadem firma de vj annis preteritis. In thes. xl d. Et debet xliij s. et iiij d. Idem r.c. de eodem debito. In thes. lib. Et Q.E.

Engelardus de Cyconiaco debet xj m. et vij s. et iiij d. pro herede Galfridi de Baggeset' sicut continetur in rotulo viij.

Willelmus de Leghe r.c. de vij li. et iij s. et iiij d. pro Matheo de Bixtrop'. In thes. xlvij s. et ix d. Et debet iiij li. et xv s. et vij d. per annum xlvij s. et ix d.

Josceus de Pluggenai debet xj li. et xviij s. et ix d. de ij^{bus} debitis contentis in rotulo viij^{o}.

E. Lond' episcopus r.c. de xxv li. et x s. et viij d. pro W. quondam Cestr' episcopo pro habenda custodia sicut continetur in rotulo xv^{o}.

Willelmus de Windles' [*blank*] quater xx et x li. et xiij s. et viij d. de tribus debitis contentis in rotulo viij^{o} in Buking' et Bed' qui requirebatur ibidem per plegium Willelmi de Mara.

DE PRESTITO PICTAVIE

Milites Warini f. Geroldi debent xij m. de eodem. Robertus f. Amaurici debet xiiij m. de eodem. Walterus Foliot debet xvj m. de eodem. Amauricus f. Roberti debet xj m. de eodem.

Heres Radulfi de Auvers debet j m. de scutagio Pictavie. + Leviva de Worðe debet xviij d. et ob. quia retraxit se. Robertus de Bergefeld' debet xl m. pro pluribus transgressionibus contentis in rotulo ij^{o}.

Robertus Cuvarius r.c. de xviij s. et viij d. de misericordia. In thes. ij s. Et debet xvj s. et viij d. per annum iiij s.

Radulfus Russel debet xvij m. et dim. de primo scutagio R. (Set non debet summoneri donec R. preceperit.[c]) (amodo summoneatur et

1 *Sic. Recte* acrarum.

2 In *NS 54*, p. 223 Henry is shown as being the son of Yvo.

respondeat in Sumerset'.[i]) Rogerus f. Pagani debet dim. m. pro iniusta detentione. + Adam de Rupe debet x s. pro eodem. (+[i]) Cecilia relicta Petri debet j m. pro dissaisina.

[*One line blank*]

DE OBLATIS

Willelmus de Capell' debet dim. m. pro iniusta detentione. + Radulfus de Crikelad' debet j m. de prestito ei facto in Anglia tempore R. J. + Henricus Serviens debet dim. m. pro mala custodia. + Rogerus Kuddere debet dim. m. quia non habuit.

Oto f. Willelmi r.c. de viij m. pro habenda uxore sicut continetur in rotulo ij. In thes. iiij m. Et debet iiij m.

Vincentius de Lamburn' r.c. de iij s. et viij d. quia non est prosecutus. In thes. xij d. Et debet ij s. et viij d.

Willelmus f. Rogeri r.c. de x s. pro dissaisina. In thes. lib. Et Q.E.

Thomas Croc r.c. de xliij s. et iiij d. de relevio suo. In thes. j m. Et debet xxx s.[1]

Fulco f. Warini r.c. de M et xlj li. et xvij s. et iiij d. de pluribus debitis contentis in rotulo viij^{o}. In thes. l m. Et debet M et viij li. et x s. et viij d. *Et C et viij li. de debitis Judeorum, quamdiu R. placuerit.*[2] per annum l m.

Idem F. debet iij dextrarios de precio et iij palefridos et j osturcum et j tercellum et ij espainellos. Edelina et Cecilia filie Rogeri debent dim. m. pro habendo pone sicut continetur in rotulo vij^{o}.

Milites et liberetenentes de foresta de Berkesir' r.c. de lxxviij li. et x s. et j d. et iiij palefridis pro habenda custodia sicut continetur in rotulo vj^{o}. In thes. xxviij li. et vij s. et iiij d. et ob. Et debent l li. ij s. viij d. et ob. et iiij palefridos.

[*One line blank*]

Ballivi de Waneting' r.c. de xij li. de carrucagio et hidagio de Berkesir' quas ipsi receperunt. In thes. vj s. Et debent xj li. et xiiij s.

Robertus de Burnebu et Johanna uxor sua r.c. de x li. et xvj s. et viij d. et j palefrido pro habenda rationabili parte sua sicut continetur in rotulo vij^{o}. In thes. C s. Et debent C et xvj s. et viij d. et j palefridum. per annum C s.

Johannes brunus et Alicia uxor eius r.c. de viij li. et dim. m. et j palefrido pro eodem. In thes. C s. Et debent v m. et j palefridum. per annum C s.

Radulfus de Wedon' et Laurentia uxor eius r.c. de v m. pro j palefrido de fine suo pro eodem. In thes. lib. Et Q.S.

Bartholomeus de Rakinton' et Matillis uxor eius r.c. de (de[c]) xxv li. et j palefrido pro eodem. In thes. l s. Et debent xxij li. et x s. et j palefridum. per annum iiij li.

[1] There are two dots at the end of the drawn line of this item, at the right edge of the membrane.

[2] It looks as though this is an additional item that has been written after the line had been completed, possibly by a different clerk. The ink appears darker than that for the rest of the entry.

Matheus (Robertus^i)[1] Brand r.c. de xl m. pro habenda custodia sicut continetur in rotulo vij^o. In thes. x li. Et debet xvj li. et j m.

Osbertus Giffard [*blank*] quater xx et xiij li. et dim. m. pro habenda custodia sicut continetur in rotulo viij^o.

Gillebertus de Brettenioles[2] r.c. de xl s. de scutagio Pictavie. Et de C s. de fine passagii. In thes. x s. Et debet vj li. et x s. per annum xx s.

Robertus Nigell' [*blank*] l s. de fine passagii.

Johannes Belet r.c. de xx s. pro relevio suo. In thes. lib. Et Q.E.

Idem Vic. r.c. de xl d. de Unfrido Visdelu. Et de v m. de Willelmo de Burmingeh'. Et de xx s. de villata de Maidenecot'. Et de dim. [m.] de Radulfo de Kameis. Et de j m. de Willelmo de Esseteford'. In thes. lib. Et Q.E.

Idem Vic. r.c. de dim. m. de Roberto Kibe de Lawude. In thes. nichil. Et in summa misarum quam habet supra i m. Et Q.E.

Milites et liberi homines de Bruningemere r.c. de vij li. et xviij s. pro habendo respectu [foreste].[3] In thes. xxxvj s. et vij d. Et debent vj li. et xvij d.

Villata de Purlé r.c. de dim. m. pro defalta. In thes xl d. Et debet xl d. Eadem r.c. de eodem debito. In thes. lib. Et Q.E.

Osmundus de Acle viridarius debet xviij s. et iiij d. quia fuit convictus. + Beniaminus Capellanus de Merkeham debet dim. m. pro defalta. Willata de Lekhamsted' debet dim. m. pro eodem. Johannes Francesius debet iij m. ut sit quietus. Thomas de Eleton' de Brai debet dim. m. pro defalta. Jacobus de Hinedon' debet iiij m. (ut sit q^c) pro habenda saisina. Ricardus Bulloc et Ricardus de Cornevill' debent j m. pro habendo breve sicut continetur in rotulo precedenti.

[*One line blank*]

DE SCUTAGIO DE MUNGUMERI DE HONORE DE WALINGEF'

Idem Vic. r.c. de ij[4] m. de Roberto de Cestreton' de eodem. Et de xx s. de Willelmo de Archis de eodem. Et de xx s. de Yrveo Malet de eodem. In thes. lib. Et Q.E.

Robertus de Valeines r.c. de j m. de eodem. In thes. dim. m. Et debet dim. [m.] Idem r.c. de eodem debito. In thes. lib. Et Q.E.

Johannes de Kaisnet' (r.c. de^c) et Alicia de Bella aqua r.c. de xlj s. et x d. de eodem. In thes nichil. Et in predicta summa misarum xlj s. et x d. Et Q.E.

Henricus de Taiden' r.c. de xx s. de eodem. In thes. dim. m. Et debet j m.

Robertus de Burnebu r.c. de xx(vij^i) s. et iij d. de eodem. In thes. xvj s. et iiij d. Et debet x s. et xj d.

Willemus Pippard' (debet^c) r.c. de vj li. et xvij d. de ij^bus debitis in rotulo precedenti. In thes. xlj s. et j d. Et debet iiij li. et iiij d. Idem r.c. de eodem debito. In thes. lib. Et Q.E.

Willelmus Painel debet xij s. et vij d. de eodem. Walterus Croc debet ij

1 The clerk has not crossed out *Matheus*. Also *Matheus* is the name in *NS 54*, p. 226 for this item. It could be a later annotation.

2 In *NS 54*, p. 227 he is shown as *Gillebertus de Brittenot*.

3 This addition comes from *NS 54*, p. 227.

4 'L' erased before '*ij*'.

m. de eodem. Galfridus de Chausi debet j m. de eodem. Galfridus f. Angot' debet dim. m. pro eodem. Ysabella Basset debet ij s. et ij d. et ob. de eodem. (Set respondet in Buk'.[i]) Walterus de Ayvill' debet ij m. de eodem. Villata de Chaugrave debet ij m. de eodem.

Johannes de Kesn' r.c. de xxxj s. et iij ob. de scutagio de Bedef' sicut infra continetur. In thes. nichil. Et in predicta summa misarum xj s. et vj d. Et debet J. xix s. et vij d. et ob.

DE SCUTAGIO DE BEDEF' DE EODEM HONORE

Hugo de Druvall' r.c. de xliiij s. et x d. et ob. de eodem. In thes. lib. Et Q.E.

Willelmus Painel debet viij m. de eodem. Ysabella Basset debet xv s. et vj d. et ob. de eodem. (Set W.(illelmus[c]) Maudoit respondet inde in Buk'.[i]) Chaugrave debet ij m de eodem. Johannes de Kesn' debet xxxj s. et iij ob. de eodem. (Set respondet supra.[i]) Willelmus Basset debet dim. m. de eodem. Robertus Corbet debet ij m. de eodem.

Willelmus Pippard' r.c. de C et xiij s. et iiij d. de eodem. In thes. ij m. et dim. Et debet iiij li.

DE OBLATIS

Willelmus de Ferrar' r.c. de C et viij li. et dim. m. pro habenda custodia sicut continetur in rotulo viij°. In thes. nichil. Et in allocatione feodi ipsius W. xxv li. per breve R. quas R. ei concessit recipiendas per annum de eodem debito sicut continetur in eodem brevi. Et debet quater xx et iij li. et dim. m.
[*Two lines blank*]

[*Rot.* 6 *Mem.* 2]

Willelmus Pippard' r.c. de xxx li. pro relevio suo de feodis vj militum que Rogerus pater eius tenuit in capite de honore de Walingef'. In thes. x li. Et debet xx li.

Robertus de Tacheham et Helewis uxor eius r.c. de dim. m. pro habendo brevi sicut continetur in rotulo precedenti. In thes. lib. Et Q.E.[1]

Reginaldus de Benetfeld' [*blank*] iiij s. de minutis particulis foreste.

Merston' et Linlée non respondent hic quia R. concessit ea[2] Amabil' que fuit uxor Radulfi de Vernay ad sustentationem suam et puerorum suorum usque ad festum sancti Michaelis anno xij° R. per breve R.
[*One line blank*]

NOVA OBLATA

Willelmus Maudoit[3] de relevio suo de terris quas Ysabell' Basset

1 *Quietus Est* written for *Quieti Sunt*.
2 *ea* written for *eas*.
3 There is a large blank space after this name but nothing further is required for the sense.

mater eius cuius heres ipse est de R. tenuit in capite et de quibus R. cepit homagium ipsius.
[*One line blank*]

DE BANCO

Idem Vic. r.c. de j m. de Radulfo de Alre pro licencia concordandi. Et de ij m. et dim. de Abbate de Rading' pro eodem cum Petro f. Herberti. Et de j m. de Willelmo capellano de Winkefeld' pro eodem. (Et de dim. m. de Adam Witcolt pro eodem.[c]) (quia infra[i]). (Et de dim. m. de Rogero de Cuserig' quia retraxit se.[c]) (*quia infra*[i]). In thes. lib. Et Q.E.

Petrus f. Herberti debet ij m. et dim. pro licencia concordandi cum Abbate de Rading'. Johannes Blancbuilli debet dim. m. (set respondet in Suhantesir'[i]) pro (eodem cum Matheo de Be…[c]) (falso appello.[i]) Reginaldus de Benetleg' debet dim. m. pro vj acris excolendis de friesche in Asserug' de feodis comitisse Sar' in Heinton'. Adam Witcolt debet dim. m. pro licencia concordandi. Rogerus de Cuserig' debet dim. m. quia retraxit se.
[*One line blank*]

Homines de Walingeford' r.c. de xl li. bl. de firma ville sue de Walingeford'. In thes. xxxvj li. et vij s. iij d. bl. Et Abbati de Dorcestr' ij s. Et monialibus de (Dorcest[c]) Garing' xij s. Et in liberationibus constitutis Hugoni de Barentin xxx s. et v d. Et debet xxx s. et vij d. bl. Idem r.c. de eodem debito. In thes. lib. Et Q.E.
[*One line blank*]

Henricus de Scaccario r.c. de lxvj s. et vij d. et ob. (bl.[i]) de remanenti firme ville de Walingeford' de anno vij° et viij° R. In thes. nichil. Et in predicta summa misarum lxix s. et xj d. et ob. num. pro lxvj s. vij d. et (ob. bl.[i]) Et Q.E.

Hugo dispensator r.c. de ix s. et vj d. de exitu maneriorum de Linleg' et de Merston' ante quam traderotur[1] Amabil' que fuit uxor Radulfi de Vernai per breve R. In thes. lib. Et Q.E.

Walterus Mantel r.c. de j libra cimini. In thes. lib. Et Q.E.

Stephanus de Stall' r.c. de iiij d. de firma j acre terre. In thes. lib. Et Q.E.

Henricus archiepiscopus Dublin' r.c. de l m. de firma ville de (Linléé[c]) Wattlinton' de anno x°. Et de l m. de feno et blado eiusdem manerii e[2] vendito Et de x li. et viij s. (et viij d.[c]) de stauro eiusdem manerii ei vendito. Et de C li. quas recepit de thesauro R. in festo Cathedre[3] sancti Petri anno R. x. (Et[c]) In thes. nichil. Et ipsi archiepiscopo in parte solutionis debiti (quia R. ei debet[i, d]) DCCC li. et j m. quod R. ei debet[4] C et lxxvij li. (et xvij li.[c]) et ij s. et ij d. per breve R. Et debentur eidem archiepiscopo DC et xxiij li. et xj s. et ij d. de quibus ipse vel executores sui vel

1 *traderotur* written perhaps for *traderentur*.
2 *e* written for *ei*.
3 The first letter of *Cathedre* has been corrected from an *S*.
4 The clerk has rubbed out the underlining here.

ecclesia Dublinensis percipient si de eo humaniter[1] contingerit ante quam predictum debitum persolvatur annuatim C li. de firma de Limeric. Et l m. de firma civitatis (Dublin' l m. donec predictum debitum persolvatur sicut continetur in rotulo de Cancellaria.[i])[2]

AMERCIAMENTA PER M. DE PATESHILL' ET SOCIOS SUOS

Idem Vic. r.c. de xlv m. ix s. et iiij d. de misericordiis hominum, villarum, teðeringarum et francoplegiorum quorum nominibus proponitur littera *t* in rotulo quem predicti liberaverunt in thesauro. In thes. xlij m. et vj s. in lxvj taleis. Et debet iij m. et xl d. de quibus Henricus de Scaccario debet respondere sicut recognovit. Idem H. r.c. de eodem debito. In thes. nichil. Et in predicta summa misarum xliij s. et iiij d. Et Q.E.

[3]*t* Radulfus de Gainch' r.c. de dim. m. quia non habuit. In thes. xl d. Et debet xl d.

p Radulfus f. Hugonis r.c. de dim. m. pro eodem. In thes. nichil. Et in predicta summa xl d. Et debet R. xl d.

p (*t*[i]) Radulfus f. Ailred' r.c. de dim. m.[4] pro eodem. In thes. nichil. Et in predicta summa xl d. Et debet R. xl d.

p (*t*[i]) Radulfus f. Willelmi r.c. de dim. m. pro eodem. In thes. nichil. Et in predicta summa xl d. Et debet R. xl d.

[5]*p* (*t*[i])[6] Osmundus Illing r.c. de dim. m. quia non habuit. In thes. nichil. Et in predicta summa xl d. Et debet O[smundus] xl d.

t[7] Willelmus f. Anketill' r.c. de x s. pro transgressione. In thes. dim. m. Et debet xl d.

[8] Idem Vic. r.c. de ix s. de catallis Edwardi. In thes. ix d. Et debet viij s. et iij d. de quibus H. de Scaccario debet respondere (et respondet infra.[i])

Idem Vic. r.c. de dim. m. de catallis Willelmi le Grant. In thes. iiij s. iiij d. ob. Et debet (i[d]) ij s. iij d. et ob. de quibus idem H. debet respondere (et respondet infra.[i])

[9] Francoplegium Henrici Ailwin' in Kenedebir' r.c. de j m. pro fuga Rogeri Pol. In thes. nichil. Et monialibus de fonte Ebrold' j m. per libertatem carte R. Et Q.E.

Godefridus Schort r.c. de x s. pro dissaisina. In thes. nichil. Et fratribus hospitalis Jer'l'm x s. per libertatem carte R. Et Q.E.

t (-ini)[10] Francoplegium Roberti portarii in Bestenham debet dim. m. pro

1 An interlinear mark is shown under the 'i' of *humaniter* but nothing is shown above the word.

2 This interlineation is written to the right of the heading below.

3 The following entries are written at the left hand side of the membrane only.

4 The beginning of the letter 'm' is written with a flourish. It looks like a '*j*' which might mean the clerk was intending to write '*j m.*' that is for 'one mark' then realised his mistake.

5 The following entries are written at the right hand side of the membrane only.

6 The '*t*' has been partially rubbed out.

7 The '*t*' has been partially rubbed out. This may have been the clerk's intention.

8 There is something rubbed out here but it is undecipherable.

9 The following entries are written across the whole membrane.

10 There is a line from this line to the last line of the paragraph. There is also

fuga Ricardi Wint'. Robertus de Erburgefeld' debet dim. m. pro dissaisina per plegium Ricardi f. Elene. Radulfus de la Wifald' debet j m. pro eodem. Henricus de Winkefeld' et alii villani abbatis de Abbendon' de Winkefeld' debent ij m. pro habenda inquisitione. Alexander de Wodemannecot' debet j m. pro dissaisina. Ricardus Bulloc debet j m. pro eodem. Willelmus del Broc de Windlesor' debet j m. pro eodem per plegium (Nigelli[c]) Galfridi f. Nigelli, Nigelli Trenchevent et Sigar' carpentarii. Willelmus Waker debet dim. m. pro eodem per plegium eorundem. Willelmus le Gersere debet dim. m. per plegium eorundem (set respondet infra.[i]) Adam Pera de Sheingefeld' debet dim. m. pro dissaisina. Adam f. Rogeri debet dim. m. pro eodem per plegium Willelmi de Benetfeld'. Willelmus de la Cumb' et (Osbertus f. Osberti de Bochurst et Hugo cuparius debent[c]) Edwardus de la More debent dim. m. quia retraxerunt se. Henricus de Benetfeld', Osbertus f. Osberti de Bochurst et Hugo cuparius debent j m. per plegium eorundem. Robertus de Burcham debet dim. m. quia retraxit[I] per plegium Ricardi Bulloc. Radulfus de Wolveleg' et Ricardus Hoc debent dim. m. per plegium eorundem. Kipping f. Ailric' de Wokingeham debet dim. m. quia retraxit se. Lucas clericus et Willelmus f. Eilric' debent dim. m. pro plegio eiusdem.

t Radulfus Blundus de Goseie debet x s. quia non habuit Robertum Longum quem manucepit. (*t*[i]) Radulfus de Wolveléé debet lxj s. et viij d. de catallis Ysáác de Wolveie suspensi. (*d*[i]) Josceus de Pluggenay debet dim. m. pro defalta et transgressione. Et C s. pro transgressione de libertate sua. (*t*[i]) Rogerus le Wie debet dim. m. pro transgressione. (*t*[i]) Elyas caretarius de Sutton' debet dim. m. pro dissaisina. Henricus de Scaccario tunc Vic. debet vj s. de catallis Roberti Longi fugitivi. Set respondet infra.

Idem Vic. r.c. de liij s. et ij d. de catallis Mathei forestarii suspensi. In thes. nichil. Et Bartholomeus Pechie liij s. et ij d. de dono R. per breve R. Et Q.E.

p Willelmus de Seuekeworðe r.c. de xxvj li. et x s. de debitis Judeorum. In thes. xl s. Et debet xxiiij li. et x s. per annum xl s.

Reginaldus clericus de Hodicot' r.c. de x s. pro falso dicto suo. In thes. lib. Et Q.E.

f' Hugo dispensarius r.c. de C et xij s. de proficuo honoris de Walingeford' de dim. anno dum fuit Vic. In thes. lib. Et Q.E.

Henricus de Scaccario r.c. de vj [s.] de catallis Roberti Longi sicut supra continetur. In thes. nichil. Et in predicta summa misarum vj s. Et Q.E.

COMPOTUS DE BLADO DE LINLÉÉ DE ANNO X^{O} DUM FUIT IN MANU R.

Idem Vic. (r.c.[i]) de ix quarteriis et dim. et quarta parte j^{us} quarterii frumenti de exitu eiusdem manerii (quod totum[i]) apud Watlinton' fuit seminatum. Et Q.E.

---

something illegible written above the '*t*'.

[I] This word is split over two lines. The second part of the word is on the last line of this item and has the line as mentioned in the preceding footnote from the beginning of the item.

Idem Vic. r.c. de vj quarteriis et quarta parte de mestilione de quibus j quarterium et dim. fuit seminatum ibidem et totum residuum in liberatione servientum ibidem. Et Q.E.

Idem Vic. r.c. de iij quarteriis et dim. de avena eiusdem manerii quod totum liberatum fuit Hugoni de Bathon' unde ipse debet respondere. Et Vic. Q.E.

Idem Vic. r.c. de vj quarteriis frumenti de quadam consuetudine apud Wallterton'[1] quod vocatur Chircheschet quod totum fuit seminatum ibidem. Et Q.E.

Henricus de Scaccario r.c. de x s. de catallis duorum supra contentorum. In thes. nichil. Et in predicta summa xviij d. Et debet ix s. et ob. Idem r.c. de eodem debito. In thes. lib. Et Q.E.

Willelmus le Gersere r.c. de dim. m. pro plegio sicut supra continetur. In thes. nichil. Et in perdona ipsi Willelmo quia cruce signatus est et pro paupertate sua dim. m. per breve R. Et Q.E.

Johannes draperius de Windles' debet lij li. pro Roberto de Ferrar' de fine eiusdem Roberti pro habenda Johanna pro blado de Sipeham quod emit de predicto Roberto que locantur eidem R. in Buking'. In thes. lib. Et Q.E.

[*Three lines blank*]

DE AMERCIAMENTIS HOMINUM DE HONORE DE WARENGEF' IN BUKING' AMERCIATIS PER SIMONEM DE HAL ET RICARDUM DUKET ET SOCIOS EORUM QUI REQUIREBANTUR IN PREDICTO COMITATU IN EODEM ITINERE

H. de Scaccario custos predicti honoris r.c. de dim. m. de decenna Philippi f. Baldewini de Cherdeston'. Et de j m. de decenna Galfridi de Em'ton' fugitivi. Et de x(vj[i]) s. de catallis Reginaldi Adelard' suspensi. Et de dim. (m.[i]) de Radulfo molendinario de Wicumb' pro plegio. Et de xl s. de villata de Wicumb' pro transgressione. Et de j m. de decenna Ade f. Radulfi Blund' fugitivi. Et de dim. m. de decenna Roberti prepositi de Messenden' fugitivi.
Et de dim. m. de Willelmo de Hedesore pro defalta. Et de dim. m. de Ricardo de Rothomago pro eodem. In thes. lib. Et Q.E.

Turstanus Basset clericus r.c. de xl s. pro dissaisina. In thes. dim. m. Et debet ij m. et dim.

Willelmus de Stanes r.c. de C s. de fine quem fecit cum R. pro habenda custodia terre et heredis Matillidis que fuit uxor Simonis Hokede et maritagio ipsius heredis. In thes. l s. Et debet l s. Idem r.c. de eodem debito. In thes. lib. Et Q.E.

[*Eleven lines blank*]

[1] There is a blot after the first 't' which obscures the second 't'. The clerk may also have blotted out a superfluous 'e' here.

WAREWIKESCIR' ET LEIRCESTR'SCIR'

Robertus Lupus ut custos r.c. de C et xxviij li. et ij s. bl. de firma comitatus de Warew'. Et de quater xx et v li. et xvj s. et iiij d. bl. de firma comitatus Leircestr'. In thes. nichil.

Et in elemosiniis constitutis militibus de Templo ij m. Et in terris datis in Warewicsir' monachis de Bordeslé xiiij li. et xij s. in Budiford'. Et monachis de Rademor' xvij li. et xv s. in Stanleia. Et eisdem in eodem manerio xx li. et ij s. et vj d. de dono. Et Galfrido[1] [f.] Willelmi coci xx s. in Staverton'. Et Galfrido Salvag' x li. in Neweton'. Et in quietantia terre Radulfi f. Radulfi iiij s. in Tameworðe. Et Radulfo f. Roberti pincerne x s. in Budiford'. Et in terris datis in Leixcestr'sir' Willelmo de la Basoche et heredibus Galfridi Luterell' xv li. in Roelay'. Et Stephano de Segrave xij li. in Kinton' de quibus respondet infra. Et Luelino principi Norwall' vij li. et xij s. in Budiford' in maritagio cum Johanna uxore sua. Et Ricardo f. et heredi Willelmi de Harocurt xvj li. in soca de Stratton'. Et Radulfo de Trublevill' viij li. in Kinton'. Et fratribus militie Templi x li. in soca de Roleia quamdiu R. placuerit. Et Johanne uxori Luelini xxv li. in Roeleia quamdiu R. placuerit. Et Willelmo de Cantilupo vij li. x s. in Bugeden' et Haverberg'. Et in suo superplus quod habet in anno preterito xxiij li. et xviij s. bl. Et debet xxxij li. et xij s. et xj d. bl.

[2][*Rot.* 6d *Mem.* I]

f' Idem Vic. [*sic*]

f' Idem Vic. [*blank*] xl li. de veteri cremento comitatuum. Et xl li. de eodem cremento de anno preterito.

f' Idem Vic. r.c. de ij s. et ij d. de j bovata terre in Tilton'. Et de x s. et viij d. de firma de Skeftinton'. Et de xlviij s. de xxij bovatis terre in soca de Rolea, in Twiford'. In thes. lib. Et Q.E.

f' Idem Vic. r.c. de xl s. de essartis de Rolea. In thes. nichil. Et Johanne uxori Luelin' xl s. quamdiu R. placuerit. Et Q.E.

f' Idem Vic. r.c. de xlvij s. et ix d. de firma ij^{arum} carrucatarum terre in Medburne quas Rogerus Orget tenuit. In thes. nichil. Et Willelmo extraneo[3] illas ij carrucatarum terre quamdiu R. placuerit. Et Q.E.

f' Stephanus de Segrave r.c. de xij li. de firma de Kinton'. In thes. lib. Et Q.E.

f' Olenta que fuit uxor Walteri de Rudes r.c. de xl s. de firma terre de Brome. Et de xx s. de remanenti eiusdem firme. In thes. xx s. Et debet xl s.

Ricardus f. Willelmi de Harocurt r.c. de CCC et lxj li. et vj s. et iiij d. et ob. et ij dextrariis et x osturcis de pluribus debitis contentis in rotulo precedenti. In thes. xx m. Et debet CCC et xlvij li. et xix s. et viij d. et ob. et ij dextrarios (et x osturcos. per annum xx m.[i])[4]

1 It looks as if the clerk began to write the next item, realised that there was an item missing so included it, but forgot to cross out *Galfrido*.

2 There is a '6' in pencil in the middle of the bottom of the membrane.

3 William the stranger appears to be William de Cantilupe. See *NS 54*, p. 197.

4 This interlinear is on the line below.

Nicholaus de Verdon' [*blank*] v m. pro j palefrido et j dextrario de pluribus debitis contentis in rotulo xj° R. J.

Idem N. debet xij m. de prestito Pictavie. Milites honoris comitis Leircestr' debent lv li. de auxilio Vic. Comes Leircestr' debet j tonellum vini. Heres comitis Simonis de Munforti debet lx li. de catallis Foberti de Dovorr'.

Heredes Amabil' de Limes' [*blank*] CC et xliiij li. et xiiij s. et x d. et iij palefridos de remanenti finis ipsius Amabil' ut non distringatur ad se maritandam sicut continetur in originali de anno vj° R. J.

[*Two lines blank*]

Hugo de Oddingeseles et Basilia uxor eius [*blank*] C et quater xx et xiiij li. et j m. de ij^bus debitis contentis in rotulo precedenti. Et xv s. (de parte sua^i) de scutagio Pictavie qui requirebantur super heredes Amabil' de Limes' in rotulo precedenti. Et x s. de sut'[1] de Biham qui requirebantur ibidem super eosdem. Et ij m. de primo scutagio R. qui requirebantur ibidem super eosdem.

[*One line blank*]

David f. (et heres^i) David de Lindes' qui habuit unam de sororibus predicte Amabil' [*blank*] v m. de parte sua de fine et scutagiis predicte Amabil' de vj scutagiis R. J. Et xv s. de parte sua de scutagio Pictavie. Et x s. de parte sua de scutagio de Biham. Et ij m. de parte sua de primo scutagio R. que iiij^or debita requirebantur super heredes predicte Amabil' in rotulis precedentibus.

Willelmus de Sancto Michaeli de Ichenton' r.c. de xvj li. et iiij s. pro defalta. In thes. ij s. et vj d. Et debet xvj li. et xviij d.

Petrus f. Willelmi medici r.c. de lj li. et x s. de debitis Ááron.[2] In thes. xx s. per Petronillam de Belegrave. Et x s. per Agnetem de Bissech'. Et debet l li. per annum xxx s.

Rogerus de Quency [*blank*] M et C et vij li. et iij s. de pluribus debitis contentis in rotulo iiij°.

Idem R. r.c. de CC et quater xx li. et xviij s. et xj d. de debitis Judeorum contentis in rotulo iiij°. In thes. xl li. Et debet CC et xl li. et xviij s. et xj d. per annum xx li.

Alicia Sorel debet xv m. et j palefridum pro habenda dote. Johannes de Bracebrige debet C et v s. et iiij d. pro habenda inquisitione. Willelmus f. Ordrici debet xxxj s. et vij d. de misericordia.

Petrus Burdet [*blank*] iiij m. de misericordia.

Comes de Warewic' r.c. de xxxj li. et ix s. et vij d. de pluribus debitis contentis in rotulo vij°. Et de xlix li. et xij s. et v den' de scutagio de Mungumeri. In thes. xvij li. et x s. Et debet lxiij li. et x s. Idem r.c. de eodem debito. In thes. xiij li. et xix s. et vij d. Et debet xlix li. et xij s. et v d. de scutagio de Mungumeri.

Willelmus f. Reginaldi de Musel' r.c. de lxxiiij s. de pluribus scutagiis contentis in rotulo precedenti. In thes. viij s. et iiij d. Et debet lxv s. et viij d. Idem r.c. de eodem debito. In thes. xx d. Et debet lxiiij s.

per annum x s.

[1] *sut'* written for *scut'*.

[2] There is something rubbed out following this name.

Robertus de Wivill' r.c. de xvj m. et dim. de ij^{bus} debitis contentis ibidem. In thes. ij m. Et debet xiiij m. et dim.

R. comes Cestr' debet quater xx et xiiij li. et xiij s. et viij d. de ij^{bus} scutagiis contentis ibidem. Set respondet in Linc'sir.

[*One line blank*]

Philippus de Kinton' debet x m. pro Ricardo Laban' sicut continetur in rotulo precedenti. Hamo f. Odonis falconar' debet xl (s.^{i}) pro passagio in Hiberniam. + Henricus de Branteston' debet dim. m. quia retraxit se.

Henricus des Asceaus r.c. de v s. pro habendo pone. In thes. lib. Et Q.E.

+ Robertus de Alnet' debet j palefridum pro habenda saisina terre in Burton' sicut continetur in rotulo vij^{o}. Geroldus de Normanvill' debet xxij m. de prestito Pictavie. Willelmus f. Galfridi et socii sui debent x s. ut possint esse sub plegio.

Willelmus de Turevill', Robertus de Mesnill', Gillebertus de Pirie et Simon Bude r.c. de viij m. et x s. pro habendo brevi sicut continetur in rotulo xvj^{o} [R. J.] In thes. xj s. per Willelmum. Et xl d. per Robertum. Et debent C et ij s. et iiij d.

Alexander de (Neovill'^{c}) (Noers^{i}) et Juliana uxor eius r.c. de iij m. pro habendo brevi. In thes. v s. Et debent xxxv s.

Robertus de Tateshall' [*blank*] xv li. et j palefridum pro Ysouda de Baskervill' pro habenda dote.

Ricardus Illing' et socii sui r.c. de xlij s. et viij d. pro dissaisina. In thes. xxx s. Et debent xij s. et viij d.

Yvo de Dien et Robertus de Leicr' r.c. de C et xxiiij li. et vij s. et j d. et ij palefridis pro Regin[aldo] Basset. In thes. x m. per Robertum. Et de[bent] C et xvij li. et xiij s. et ix d. et ij palefridos.

[*One line blank*]

Prior de Covintr' r.c. de xv li. de scutagio Pictavie. In thes. l s. Et debet xij li. et x s.

Willelmus f. Roberti de Edwalton' r.c. de xv s. de eodem. In thes. lib. Et Q.E.

Hugo de Assebroc r.c. de dim. m. pro licencia concordandi. In thes. lib. Et Q.E.

[1] Ricardus f. Ricardi debet dim. m. pro habendo pone. + Elyas de Nunneleg' debet dim. m. quia retraxit se. + Willelmus de Buking' debet xx s. pro dissaisina. + Walterus de la Hille debet dim. m. pro eodem. + Hugo f. Rimild' debet dim. [m.] pro eodem. + Wimundus molendinarius debet dim. m. pro eodem. + Walterus Evesune[2] debet dim. m. pro eodem. Jacobus f. Keneward' debet dim. m. pro eodem. + Willelmus le Hoppere debet dim. m. pro eodem. (+^{i}) Osbertus de Westbir' debet dim. m. quia non est prosecutus. Walterus mercator debet dim. m. pro dissaisina. + Walterus f. Herewardi debet dim. m. pro eodem. + Johannes Wint' debet dim. m. pro eodem. + Henricus f. Hugonis prepositi debet dim. m. pro eodem. + Felicia de Saukevill' debet quartam partem de xx m. sicut continetur in

1 There is something rubbed out in the margin. It is just a line.

2 In *NS 54*, p. 200 and in *NS 56*, p. 8 Walter is shown as '*f. Evesune*', though here he is just *Walterus Evesune*.

rotulo iij°. + Galfridus Cunein debet dim. m. quia non habuit. + Rogerus Slatere debet dim. m. pro eodem. + Wimarc f. Willelmi debet dim. m. pro eodem. + Alicia de Hout debet xl d. pro d[issaisina].[1]

Heres Hugonis de Asting' r.c. de x li. et viij s. et viij d. sicut continetur in rotulo iiij°. In thes. j m. Et debet ix li. et xv s. et iiij d.

Susanna filia Galfridi r.c. de x s. de ij^bus^ debitis. In thes. lib. Et Q.E.

Idem Vic. r.c. de xl d. de Roberto de Thorp. Et de iiij s. et ij d. de Roberto de Mesnill'. Et de xl d. de Elya de Beleton'. Et de xl d. de Josceo de Wastineis. Et de v s. de Ricardo de Coleshill'. Et de iiij s. de Willelmo de Albineio. In thes. lib. Et Q.E.

[2] Hundredum de Gudlakestan' r.c. de viij s. et viij d. In thes. iiij s. Et debet iiij s. et viij d.

Robertus pincerna r.c. de j m. In thes. dim. m. Et debet dim. m.

[3] Bartholomeus Basset r.c. de xxxvj s. et viij d. In thes. dim. m. Et debet xxx s.

Robertus f. Ricardi r.c. de j m. In thes. dim. m. Et debet dim. m.

Edricus f. Camoc, Radulfus f. Terrici, Radulfus f. Radulfi, Radulfus f. Roberti de Eccon', Ricardus f. Roberti et Terricus frater eius r.c. de xx s. per plegium. In thes. xv s. Et debent v s.

Johannes de Linleg' debet v s. Dunewald de Herdeby debet xl d. Willelmus de Croxton' debet xl d. Radulfus f. Galfridi debet xl d. Simon carettarius de Bucmenistr' debet dim. m. quia non est prosecutus. Adam frater eius debet dim. m. pro plegio. Alicia de Gand' debet lx s. de debitis Judeorum. Rogerus f. Willelmi debet xl d. pro plegiio. Hugo f. Willelmi de Haverberg' debet dim. m. pro dissaisina. Ricardus Sprogan[4] debet xvj d. pro habendo pone.

Alexander Rex Scottorum debet C m. pro habenda custodia terrarum comitis David.[5]

Ricardus de Martiwast r.c. de xlj li. (et dim. m.^i^) de debitis Judeorum. In thes. lx s. Et debet xxxviij li. et dim. m. per annum C s.

Willelmus de Hautsted debet C et liij li. et xiij s. et vij d. de debitis Judeorum.

DE SCUTAGIO MILITUM DE PARTE HONORIS COMITIS LEIRCESTR' DE SCUTAGIO PICTAVIE ET DE FINE PASSAGIORUM

Henricus de Pecco r.c. de xx s. de eodem[6] sicut continetur in rotulo viij°. In thes. lib. Et Q.E.

[1] *Dissaisina* supplied from *NS 54*, p. 200.

[2] The following entries are written at the left hand side of the membrane only.

[3] The following entries are written at the right hand side of the membrane only.

[4] In *NS 54*, p. 202 he is shown as *Ricardus Scrogan*.

[5] This is David, earl of Huntingdon, who had died in 1219.

[6] For this item, and the next three, the reason for the debt and/or account could be any one of the items in the heading or for all three or any combination. The reference to *NS 54*, p. 202 does not reveal what it is for only that it concerns the sum from Bitteswell in Leicestershire.

Radulfus pincerna debet xij li. de eodem sicut continetur ibidem. Radulfus de Turevill' debet x li. de eodem sicut continetur ibidem.

Idem Vic. r.c. de iiij s. et ij d. de Lacton' de eodem. Et de xij s. de Willelmo f. Roberti de Edwalton' de eodem. In thes. lib. Et Q.E.

Ricardus de Boresworðe r.c. de C et xxxvj li. et xvij s. et xj d. de debitis Judeorum. In thes. xxx s. Et debet C et xxxv li. vij s. et xj d.
per annum lx s. quia pauper est.

DE OBLATIS

Abbas de Mirisvallibus r.c. de xx m. pro habenda pastura (de Stanesfeld'[i])[1] sicut continetur in rotulo viij. In thes. v m. Et debet xv m.
per annum v m.

Simon Pepin r.c. de xiiij s. et viij d. pro defalta. In thes. v s. Et debet ix s. et viij d.

Comitatus Leircestr' r.c. de xxxvij li. v s. et ix d. et ob. pro contemptu Curie. In thes. xiiij li. et xvij s. Et debet xxij li. et viij s. et ix d. et ob.

Robertus de Hardredeshill' r.c. de CCCC et lv(ii[d]) li. et vij s. et v d. de ij[bus] debitis contentis in rotulo precedenti. In thes. xx m. Et debet CCCC et xlij li. et ix d. per annum xx m.

Alanus de Bladis r.c. de xxxv li. de debitis Judeorum. In thes. ij m. per ipsum A. Et j m. (per[c]) de[2] Abbate de Bordesle qui ita redderet annuatim donec debitum persolvatur. Et debet xxx(iij[i]) li. de quibus Walterus Pohier debet (CCij [li.][i]) per a[nnum].[3]

Idem Vic. r.c. de ij s. de Sokemannis de Crowenham. Et de ij s. de Roberto David. (Et de ij s. de Willelmo de Weliden'.[c]) Et de ij s. de Willelmo de Waleden'. Et de ij s. de Herberto de Kaithorp'.[4] Et de iiij s. de villata de Norton'. Et de iij d. de Hugone de Karinton'. Et de iiij s. et x d. et ob. de Roberto de Wivill'. Et de ij s. et vj d. de Edmundo de Stanton'. Et de xviij d. de Waltero de Preston'. Et de iiij d. et ob. de Alicia de Haya. Et de iiij d. et ob. de Nicholao f. Simonis. Et de xij d. de Johanne f. Simonis. Et de iij d. de Roberto f. David. Et de ix s. et ix d. de priore de Landa. Et de vj d. et ob. de Roberto de Bláåston'. Et de vij d. et ob. de Radulfo de Neovill'. Et de vj d. de priore de Belueér. In thes. lib. Et Q.E.

Reginaldus de Welleford' debet ij s. pro (ij acris frumenti in Norton'[c]) (transgressione[i]). (Edmundus de Skeftinton' debet ij s. pro eodem.[c]) Robertus de Bláåston' debet ij s. pro novo essarto. Robertus de Woleward' debet xx d. pro defalta. Robertus de Alnet' debet viij m. pro summonendo Hugone de Morewic'. Rogerus de Welleford' debet ij s. pro ij [acris] frumenti[5] in Norton'. Edmundus de Skeftinton' debet ij s. pro eodem et xij d. pro ij acris avene.

1 In *NS 54*, p. 203 it is shown as *Manistonesfeld'*. There is a Stansfield in Suffolk and Yorkshire.

2 *per* converted into *de* by prolonging the right hand side of the round part of 'p' and adding 'e'. The next word is abbreviated *Abbe* with suspension marks that could be extended to either *Abbatem* (for *per*) or *Abbate* (for *de*).

3 The end of the text is obscured by the strengthening tape down the right hand edge.

4 There is a Caythorpe in Nottinghamshire and another in Lincolnshire.

5 An omission before *frumenti*, probably *acris*.

Willelmus de Cantilupo senior debet respondere de exitibus terrarum comitis Simonis de monte forti sicut continetur in rotulo precedenti qui requirebatur in Kent in rotulo precedenti.

Nicholaus f. Ordrici debet iij m. pro justiciando Ricardo de Siffrewast. Comes Leircestr' debet xx s. de primo scutagio R.

Willelmus de Francton' burgensis de Covintr' [*blank*] ij m. et ij s. de promisso pro justiciando Radulfo de Wikewan'.

Willelmus de Francton' dominus de Francton' [*blank*] ij m. et ij s. de eodem pro eodem.

[*One line blank*]

DE SCUTAGIO DE MUNGUMERI

Prior de Covintr' [*blank*] j m. de eodem.

Feodum Rogeri de Turlaveston' [*blank*] dim. m. de eodem. Et dim. m. de scutagio de Bedeford'.

[*Two lines blank*][1]

[*Rot.* 6d *Mem.* 2]

Ricardus f. Roberti de Harocurt debet iiij m. de eodem. Archiepiscopus Ebor' debet dim. m. de eodem. Willelmus Bardulf' debet iiij m. de eodem de firma Leicr'. Et iiij m. de scutagio de Bedeford'.

Galfridus Salvagius r.c. de xlj s. et viij d. de eodem. In thes. xxvj s. Et debet xv s. et viij d.

Hugo Dispensarius debet xv s. et x d. de pluribus scutagiis contentis in rotulo (precedenti[c]) viij. Et dim. m. de scutagio de Bedef'. Ricardus f. Roberti de Harocurt' debet iiij m. de scutagio de Bedef'. Ricardus f. Willelmi de Harocurt debet iiij m. de eodem. Set non debet summoneri quia tenet de comite Warewic' qui habet inde quietantiam per breve R. in rotulo (anni[i]) viij.

[*One line blank*]

NOVA OBLATA

Willelmus Taske r.c. de xl s ut tradatur in ballio sicut continetur in rotulo precedenti. In thes. lib. Et Q.E.

Robertus f. David de Roppel [*blank*] dim. m. ut scribatur sicut continetur in rotulo viij°.

Idem Vic. r.c. de ij m. de Nicholao de Creddeworðe. Et de v m. de Johanne de Tisshó. Et de x s. de Ricardo de Kaldecot'. In thes. lib. Et Q.E.

Willelmus f. Willelmi r.c. de dim. m. pro licencia concordandi. In thes. xl d. Et debet xl d.

Rogerus de Crest [*blank*] xv li. et xvj s. de debitis Judeorum. Et C et ix s. de eodem qui requirebantur infra super Abbatem de Pippwell'.

[1] There is the number 'II' stamped in the left margin.

Rogerus de Herdeberg' [*blank*] xij li. et v s. de eodem pro predicto Rogero sicut continetur in rotulo precedenti.

Abbas de Pippwell' debet C et ix s. de eodem pro eodem sicut continetur ibidem. Set non debet summoneri quia R. de Crest respondet inde supra et idem abbas tenet feodum a quo debitum illud exigebatur in elemosinam.

Abbas de Gerewedon' r.c. de C et ix [s.] pro eodem sicut continetur ibidem. In thes. iiij li. Et debet xxix s.

Abbas de Cumb' r.c. de xl s. de eodem sicut continetur ibidem. In thes. lib. Et Q.E.

Abbas de Miris Vallibus r.c. de xl m. pro pastura de Fairfeld' sicut continetur in rotulo precedenti. In thes. x m. Et debet xxx m. per annum x m.

Rogerus Lazuche debet j palefridum pro habenda j feria sicut continetur ibidem. Homines comitis Wint' manentes in suburbio Leicr' debent viij m. de blado sicut continetur in rotulo precedenti. Set respondent infra in proxima linea.

Homines comitis Wint' suprascripti r.c. de viij m. sicut supra continetur. In thes. lib. Et Q.S.

NOVA OBLATA

Henricus de Hasting' r.c. de l m. pro habenda saisina[1] de tota terra quam Willelmus pater eius cuius heres ipse est de R. tenuit in capite et que ipsum Henricum hereditarie contingit et R. eius inde homagium cepit. Et preceptum est Vic. War' et Leicr' quod capiat de ipso securitatem de predictis l m. reddendis ad hos terminos, videlicet ad Pascham anno x° xij m. et dim. et ad festum sancti Michaelis anno eodem xij m. (et dim.[i]) Et ad Pascham anno xj° xij m. et dim. et ad festum sancti Michaelis anno eodem xij m. et dim. Catalla etiam ipsius W. in eadem terra inventa executoribus testamenti ipsius W. habere faciat salvo R. debito suo si quod ei debuit. In thes. xxv m. Et debet xxv m.

Vic. debet respondere de misericordia in quam vel abbas de Croxton' vel Philippus de Gand' inciderunt de loquela que fuit coram R. inter eos (coram R.[s]) de iniuriis eidem abbati factis per predictum Philippum unde quedam lex adiudicata fuit predicto Philippo facienda in comitatu Leicr'.

Idem Vic. [*blank*] x li. de misericordia in quam Robertus Pincerna incidit bis per judicium comitatus sui de iniusta vexatione abbati predicto ab eodem Roberto facta ut dicit.

[*One line blank*]

Radulfus Barun debet dim. m. pro habendo pone contra Amiciam filiam Radulfi surdi in parva Glen. Galfridus Vdard' debet dim. m. pro eodem de terra in Ilenedon'.

Nicholaus de Verdon' [*blank*] xx m. quia non habuit Sampsonem qui fuit de manupastu suo.

Henricus comes Warew' debet xx s. pro habenda jurata apud Westm'. Gieva de Covintr' debet dim. m. pro querendo pede cyrographi. Rannulfus f. Henrici debet dim. m. pro licencia concordandi cum Johanne de

[1] This is a partial copy of the fine shown in the *Calendar of Fine Rolls*, II, 1224–34, pp. 71–2, no. 83.

Wauk'geham.[1] Idem Johannes debet dim. m. pro eodem. Henricus comes Warew' debet j m. pro licencia concordandi cum priore hospit'.[2]

Willelmus de Graenvill' r.c. de dim. m. pro licencia concordandi cum Willelmo de Stutevill'. In thes. lib. Et Q.E.

Willelmus de Grafton' r.c. de dim. m. pro eodem. In thes. lib. Et Q.E.

Gillebertus f. Ricardi debet dim. m. pro habendo pone coram justiciariis itinerantibus contra Robertum pincernam et Agnetem filiam eius de terra in Eyton'.

Adam vinetarius de Covintr' debet j dolium vini pro habendis pannis suis quietis captis in nundinis de Hoyland'.

[*Nineteen lines blank*]

[3] Homines de Brehull' r.c. de xxiij li. et vij d. de ij^bus^ debitis contentis in Buking'. In thes. nichil. Et in perdonis ipsis hominibus xiij li. (et vij s.^i^) per breve R. de fine quem fecerunt cum R. J. pro Burstall' quam non habuerunt nisi per j annum et dimidium sicut continetur in eodem brevi. Et debent x li. et xij d.[4] per annum xx s. per idem breve.

COMPOTUS PETRI WINTON' EPISCOPI QUI REQUIREBATUR IN SUHANTESCIR'

Petrus Winton' episcopus r.c. de j (bono^c^) dolio boni vini quia non reduxit ad memoriam R. J. de quadam zona danda. Et de ij^bus^ cóópertoriis de Geneciis pro quietantia scutagii Wallie tempore predicti R. Et de xxix li. et xv[*iij*][5] s. et vj d. de scutagio Pictavie de honore de Berchamsted' de tempore R. eiusdem. Et de xlix li. et xix s. et j d. de scutagio Wallie de medietate honoris de Toteneis de tempore eiusdem in comitatu Devon'. Et de vj m. de primo scutagio R. huius de feodis Roberti de Eisseby in comitatu Notingeh'. Et de xlix li. et xl d. de vj^o^ R. J. de feodis Reginaldi de Valletorta. Et de ij m. de j magno feodo eiusdem in comitatu Cornub'. Et de ij dextrariis pro habenda custodia de servicio feodi j militis quod Rogerus f. Henrici tenuit de R. In thes. nichil. Et in perdona ipsi episcopo pro bono et fideli servicio quod fecit J. R. patri R. et ipsi R. et qui in terrram sanctam peregre profectus est j dolium boni vini et ij^o^ cóópertoria de Geneciis et C et xxxiiij li. et vij s. et vij d. et ij dextrarios per breve R. quod est in forulo marescalli in Suh'tesir'. Et Q.E.

Idem r.c. de ij palefridis pro essarto facto in comitatu Oxon'. In thes. nichil. Et (ipsi episcopo^c^) in perdona ipsi episcopo ij palefridos per breve R. Et Q.E.

Idem P. r.c. de lix li. et xxij d. de misericordiis plurium hominum suorum in diversis comitatibus contentis in rotulo viij^o^. Et de C et xxij li.

[1] There is something written under the strengthening tape after the 'k', but it is not possible to determine it.

[2] No name given for the hospital.

[3] Strengthening tape on the left hand side of the membrane has partially obscured some of the text at the beginning of each line for the remainder of the membrane.

[4] It should be £9 13s. 7d.

[5] There are some letters missing from this number under the right hand strengthening tape. They are supplied from *NS 54*, p. 9.

et j m. de debitis Reginaldi de Valletorta qui requirebatur in Devon'. Et de ij m. de Gilleberto palmerio qui requirebatur in Oxon' in itinere M. de Pateshill'. Summa C et quater xx et iij li. et xxij d. In thes. nichil. Et in superplus quod habet in Suhantes' post corpus comitatus C et quater xx et iij li. et xxij d. Et Q.E.

Gervasius de Aldermannebir' r.c. de (l^d) ij m. et dim. pro defalta in itinere Simonis de Hal et sociorum suorum in Essex' qui requirebatur ibidem. In thes. nichil. Et ipsi Gervasio ij m. et dim. per libertatem carte R. in qua continetur quod Gervasius nec heredes sui si in misericordiam inciderint non debent amerciari ultra dim. marcam et amerciatus fuit hic predictus Gervasius ad xl s. de quibus pacavit dim. m. in predicto itinere in Essex'. Et Q.E.

[*Endorsed*] Berkeschir' (emend' totum et sufficit[i]) et Warewik' et Leircestreschir'[1]

There is a printed '12' in the bottom left hand corner of the membrane.

[*Rot.* 7 *Mem.*1]

GLOECESTRESIR'

Willelmus de Putot ut custos r.c. de CCC et lxxij li. et xiij s. et vj d. bl. de firma comitatus. In thes. nichil.

Et in elemosinis constitutis militibus de templo j m. Et in decimis constitutis monachis de Ferléa xxij s. in piscaria de Gern et de Raddeia. Et in liberationibus constitutis Matheo Brazdefer xlv s. et vij d. et ob. Et Helene nutrici R. lx s. et x d. Et Simoni de Cambray manco xlv s. et vij d. et ob. Et Waltero de Turri xj s. et iiij d. et ob. de quarta parte anni per breve R. in liberatione que fuit Johannis fortis et amodo totum scilicet iij ob. per diem. Et Roberto Blundo xlv s. et vij d. et ob. Et Galfrido Salvag' xlv s. vij d. et ob. Et in decimis constitutis monachis de Cormeill' xl s. Et in terris datis infirmis de Dudestan' xx s. in Bertona. Et monachis de Flexleia vj li. in Dimmoc. Et Waltero f. Walteri Blundi xx s. in Aure. Et canonicis de Lanton' xj s. in Chiltham. Et eisdem xx s. in piscaria de Horsepul. Et Waltero de Essel' xiiij li. in Chiltham. Et Roberto de Amenevill' xxviij li. in Betton'. Et Willelmo de Gamach' vij li. in Muena quam Willelmus Turpin tenuit. Et eidem viij li. in Dimmoc. Et heredi Walteri de Stradewi xx s. in j virgata terre in Upton'. Et Amaurico de parco xx s. in j virgata terre in Brewern'. Et monachis de Stanleia viij li. in Wappeleia. Et in Slochtres xxiiij li. de quibus Vic. respondet infra. Et in Dimmoc xvj li. de quibus homines ville respondent infra. Et in Neweham x li. de quibus Vic. respondet infra. Et Willelmo Foukeram heredi Alicie de Gundevill' xv s. in Steriden' membro de Winterburn' de quibus respondet infra. Et Ricardo Walensi xxij li. in Winterburn'. Et G. comiti Glovern' xx li. de

1 There are three vertical dots before and after *Berkeschir'*, after *Warewik'*, and after *Leircestreschir'*.

tercio denario comitatus. Et canonicis de Sancta Barbara xxx li. (bl.[i]) in Beckeford'. Et canonicis de Cyrecestr' xxix li. bl. in Cyrecestr' de quibus respondent infra de xxx li. num. cum vij hundrediis et dimidio. Et Fulconi f. Warini x li. bl. in Aloestan'. Et Waltero blundo xvj li. bl. in Aure de quibus respondet infra. Et in villa de Gloecestr' l li. bl. de quibus burgenses respondent infra. Et in Kaerliun xl s. bl. Et in Chiltham cum Hundredo et Westhal' xxvij li. et ix s. bl. de quibus homines ville respondent infra. Et in Winchecumb' cum hundredis annotatis in rotulo viij xxviij li. de quibus idem abbas respondet infra.

Et pro xxiiij salmonibus bonis et friscis emptis ad opus R. contra Natale et missis usque Winton' vj li. iiij s. et x d. et ob. per breve R. Et pro xl salmonibus tam salsis quam friscis et xxiiij lampredis emptis ad opus R. et missis usque Lond' contra diem cinerum viij li. et iiij s. et iij d. per breve eiusdem de emendis lx salmonibus et xx lampredis. Et pro xx lampredis in pane positis et missis post R. in partes Norf' liij s. et iij ob. per breve eiusdem. Et in operatione et reparatione domorum in Castro Gloecestr' in forinseco ballio x li. et v s. et j d. per breve R. et per visum Johannis draparii et Thome Ovenad'. Et ipsi Vic. de dono R. pro custodia castri predicti l m per idem breve. Et in recisione et reparatione jarulli circa castrum predictum vento prostrati et fracti C s. et vij d. per breve eiusdem. Et in operatione pontis de Gloecestr' xvj li. et xvj s. et viij d. per breve eiusdem et per visum predictorum. Et in reparatione camere R. in castro Gloecr' iiij li. et xvj s. et ob. per breve eiusdem et per visum predictorum. Et habet de superplus lxxvij li. et xvij s. et viij d. bl. qui sunt ei extensi ad quater xx et j li. et xix s. et ij d. num. De quibus lxviij li. et xiiij s. et iiij d. locantur ei infra in proficuo comitatus. Et in firma de Neweham x li. Et restant ei hic locande[1] lxviiij s.[2] et x d.

[*Six lines blank*]

f Idem Vic. r.c. de lxviij li. xiiij s. et iiij d. de proficuo comitatus hoc anno. In thes. nichil. Et suo superplus quod habet supra lxviij li. et xiiij s. et iiij d.

Et Q.E.

[*One line blank*]

Radulfus Musard respondere[3] debet de proficuo comitatus de anno preterito et iij^{bus} partibus anni preteriti. Set respondet inde in rotulo precedenti.

[*One line blank*]

Idem debet respondere de propresturis ville Glovernie de viij^{to} annis preteritis scilicet de lij s. per annum. Summa xx li. et xvj s.

f' Idem Vic. [*blank*] de eisdem propresturis de hoc anno.

f' Burgenses Gloecestr' r.c. de l li. bl. de firma Burgi. Et de lxxiij s. et iiij d. bl. de remanenti eiusdem firme de anno preterito. In thes. xlij li. et x s. et viij d. bl. Et Ricardo Burgensi et David[4] Dunning' et Willelmo de Samford' et Ade Croc xx li. et x s. pro x doliis vini emptis ad opus R. per

[1] *Locande* written, although both *solidi* and *denarii* are masculine.

[2] *s*. repeated.

[3] Two oblique strokes are written each side of the word *respondere*.

[4] Written as *DD* with a horizontal suspension mark through the uprights.

breve eiusdem. Et habuit de superplus viij li. et vj s. et x d. bl. qui sunt eis extensi ad viij li. et xij s. et iiij d. et ob. num. quod totum locatur eis infra.
f' Idem burgenses debent C s. bl. de veteri cremento eiusdem burgi sicut continetur in rotulo precedenti. Et respondent inde in rotulo xviij^{o} R.E. f. R.E. in adhuc Item Glouc'.[1]
f' Idem burgenses r.c. de x li. num. de novo cremento burgi. Et de x li. de eodem cremento de anno preterito. In thes. x li. Et in suo superplus quod habent supra viij li. et xij s. et iiij d. et ob. Et debent xxvij s. et vij d.
f' Willelmus Fukeram r.c. de xv s. de firma terre sue de Steriden'. Et xv s. de eadem firma de anno preterito. In thes. xv s. Et debet xv s.
f' Walterus Blundus r.c. de xvj li. bl. de firma de Aure. Et de ij m. bl. de remanenti eiusdem firme de anno preterito. In thes. xvj li. et xv s. et x d. bl. Et debet x s. et x d. bl. Idem r.c. de eodem debito. In thes. lib. Et Q.E.
f' Idem W. r.c. de iiij li. num. de cremento eiusdem ville. In thes. lib. Et Q.E.
f' Idem Vic. r.c. de j m. de firma terre de Sandherst. In thes. lib. Et Q.E.
f' Philippus de Aura r.c. de j m. de redditu ij^{arum} virgatarum terre in Aure. In thes. lib. Et Q.E.
f' Burgenses Glovernie r.c. de ij s. de Guihall' in Glovernia. In thes. lib. *f'* Abbas Cyrecestr' r.c. de xxx li. num. de firma de Cyrecestr'. In thes. lib. Et Q.E.
f' Amauricus de parco r.c. de xij d. de j virgata terre in Briwern'. In thes. lib. Et Q.E.
f' Idem Vic. r.c. de xxiiij li. de firma de Slochtres (*Set respondet ut custos in dorso rotuli.*[1]). Et de x li. de firma de Neweham. In thes. nichil. Et in predicto superplus x li. Et Q.E.
f' Idem Vic. [*blank*] debet [*blank*] de proficuo eorundem maneriorum. Set respondet in dorso rotuli de Slochtres ut custos.

Homines de Dimmoc r.c. de l m. de firma ville sue. In thes. lib. Et Q.S.
f' Homines de Chiltham r.c. de lxiiij li. de firma ville sue cum Hundredo et Westhall' sicut continetur infra. In thes. lib. Et Q.S.
f' Abbas de Winchecumb' r.c. de l li. de firma ville de Winchecumb'. Et de l li. de eadem firma de anno preterito. In thes. quater xx et ij li. et dim. m. Et debet xvij li. et j m. Set respondet infra.
f' Osbertus Giffard' de Brimefeld' r.c. de lx s. de firma terre de Pichelecumb'. Et de vj li. de eadem firma de ij^{bus} annis preteritis. In thes. ij m. Et debet vij li. et j m.

Radulfus de Wiliton' debet xxvj li. et xij s. et ix d. de remanenti compoti sui de Bertona et Chascia de anno viij^{o}. Set respondet in dorso rotuli.

Humfridus de Bohuin debet l m. et j palefridum pro patre suo preter l m. et j osturcum quas[2] prius promiserat. Et xxij li. et j m. de scutagio Pictavie.

[1] This whole line, including the marginal *f'*, is squashed in between two other lines and written in a hand dating to about 100 years later, as the reference to the roll of 18 Edward II also indicates. See Introduction, p. 187.

[2] The 50 marks have been more influential than the goshawk in determining the gender of the relative pronoun.

Philippus de Aura r.c. de xxix li. et xvij s.[1] et l lampredas [*sic*] de ij^{bus} debitis contentis in rotulo vij^{o}. In thes. xl s. Et debet xxvij li. et xvij d. et l lampridas [*sic*]. per annum xl s.

Rogerus f. Nicholai r.c. de liiij li. et xv s. et x d. de pluribus debitis contentis in rotulo iiij^{o}. In thes. x li. Et debent xliiij li. et xv s. et x d. per annum x li.

Paganus de Katurciis r.c. de xxviij li. de ij^{bus} scutagiis contentis in rotulo vj^{o}. In thes. x li. Et debet xviij li.

Willelmus Crassus iunior debet xxx m. pro dissaisina. Thomas Bloet debet D m. sicut continetur in rotulo xiiij^{o} R. J. Predictus Willelmus Crassus debet j m. pro viridi in Essex sicut continetur in rotulo precedenti.

Burgenses Gloec' [*blank*] CC et quater xx lampredas ut non distringantur.

Willelmus Avenel r.c. de xix li. et dim. m. pro Radulfo patre suo pro Petronilla de Dene sicut continetur in rotulo xij^{o}. Et de xx m. de proprio debito suo pro habenda terra qui requirebatur in Sumerset in rotulo precedenti. In thes. xx m. Et debet xix li. et dim. m. per annum xx (m^{i}).

Willelmus Crassus senior debet C m. de primo scutagio R. de feodo Radulfi de Sumeri sicut continetur in rotulo precedenti.

Henricus de Scrupes [*blank*] dim. m. de remanenti plurium debitorum contentorum in rotulo viij^{o}.

Robertus f. Willelmi de Berkel' [*blank*] C et lxxvj li. de tribus debitis contentis in rotulo iij^{o} de quibus Radulfus Musard debet eum adquietare de xlvj li. xvj s. et viij d. (*Set respondet infra.*^{i}) pro viij libratis terre quam de eodem Roberto tenet in Cutbrichteleg' per finem factum coram R. et baronibus de Scaccario. Et debet Robertus C et xxix li. et iij s. et iiij d. de quibus (Ricardus^{i}) de Harocurt debet eum adquietare de lxxvj li. et xv s. et iiij d. pro (xv^{c}) (xiij^{i}) libratis terre quas tenet in Endrefeld'. Et respondet in Wigorn'. (*Et debet R. lij li. et viij s.*^{i})

Radulfus Musard [*blank*] xlvj li. et xvj s. et viij d. pro Roberto de Berkel' sicut supra continetur per pleiagium Radulfi de Wiliton' et Galfridi de Longo campo, Osberti Giffard de Gloecestr'sir', Willelmi de la Mare. [*One line blank*]

Idem Radulfus r.c. de lxij li. et xvij s. et j d. de remanenti compoti sui de firma maneriorum de Slochtres et de Neweham contenti in rotulo precedenti. In thes. nichil. Et in superplus quod habet infra xlv s. et vij d. et ob. Et debet lx li. et xj s. et v d. et ob.

Idem Radulfus r.c. de xviij li. et v s. de liberatione Johannis (Fortis^{i}) de viij^{to} annis male computatis in corpore comitatus (dum fuit Vic.^{i}) post mortem ipsius Johannis. In thes. xx li. et x s. et vij d. et ob. Et habet de superplus xlv s. et vij d. et ob. quod locatur[2] ei supra.

Idem Radulfus [*blank*] lij m. pro G. comite Gloecr' de fine Willelmi Bloet sicut continetur in rotulo primo.

Ricardus de Muscegros r.c. de lj li. et iiij s. de ij^{bus} debitis contentis in rotulo iij^{o}. In thes. iiij li. Et debet xlvij li. et iiij s. Idem r.c. de eodem debito. In thes. xx s. Et debet xlvj li. et iiij s.

Johannes Cotele r.c. de iij m. pro matre sua. In thes. lib. Et Q.E.

[1] *s.* altered from *d.*

[2] *locatur* written as *lacatur*.

Alicia de Hale r.c. de dim. m. sicut infra continetur. In thes.

DE PRESTITO PICTAVIE

Paganus de Katurciis debet lviij m. de eodem. Robertus de Amenevill' debet xlvj s. et viij d. de eodem.

Simon f. Henrici (deb[c]) et socii sui debent C s. ut habeant pacem sicut continetur in rotulo primo. Galfridus de Mandevill' debet CCCC et l li. et viij d. de scutagio (Pictavie[i]) de f[eodis] honoris Glovernie.

Robertus de Welleboef' debet xxx m. et j bonum chascur' ut deliberetur a prisona sicut continetur in rotulo vij°. (*Set respondet infra.*[i]) + Samuel de Burton' debet ij m. pro habenda saisina. Walterus de Clyfford' debet CCC capones pro deliberatione Gilleberti de Mortem' (Set non debet summoneri[i]) donec R. preceperit. + Willelmus de Wititon' debet dim. m. pro falso clamore. Walterus de Stanton' debet j m. pro defalta. + Johannes molendinarius debet j m. ut tradatur in custodiam. Alicia de Hale debet dim. m. pro habendo pone. Set respondet supra.

Philippus de Banton' [*blank*] xlvij li. et j m. pro habenda saisina terre Henrici de Stanton'.

Willelmus clericus Glovernie r.c. de lxx s. pro habenda saisina sicut continetur in rotulo iij°. In thes. j m. Et debet lvj s. et viij d.

Abbas de Winchecumb' r.c. de xvij li. et j m. de remanenti firme sue[1] sicut supra continetur. In thes. xvj li. Et debet ij m. et dim.

[*Rot.* 7 *Mem.* 2]

Villata Gloecr' r.c. de l s. de tallagio. In thes. x s. Et debet xl s.

Idem Vic. r.c. de x s. et iiij d. de (Johanne del maris[c]) (*Galfrido de Longo campo*[i]). Et de ij s. et iiij d. de Waltero del maris. Et de lx s. de Waltero Hadewolf'. In thes. lib. Et Q.E.

Ricardus de Briewes [*blank*] xx m. pro habenda custodia sicut continetur in rotulo ij°.

Thomas frater Roberti de Berkel' [*blank*] CCC et quater xx et vj li. de ij[bus] debitis contentis in rotulo vj°.

Galfridus Basset et socii sui r.c. de lxxij s. et x d. pro morte hominis. In thes. xxxj s. et iiij d. Et debent xlj s. et vj d.

Hundredrum de Cyrecestr' debet viij s. et iiij d. pro misericordia. + Addam cloddarius debet dim. m. ut possit esse sub plegio. + Robertus f. Cecil' debet dim. m. quia non est prosecutus. + Willelmus de Weston' debet dim. m. pro plegio eiusdem.

Ricardus Burgensis r.c. de ij m. de catallis Henrici. In thes. dim. m. Et debet xx s.

Willelmus cisor r.c. de x s. et viij d. pro justiciando Rogero. In thes. nichil. Et in superplus quod prepositus Bristoll' habet in rotulo precedenti x s. et viij d. Et Q.E.

Willelmus de Busset' [*blank*] xx s. ut possit esse sub plegio.

Reginaldus Carpentarius debet dim. m. pro plegio.

[1] *sue* repeated.

Willelmus Senesc' [*blank*] dim. m. pro eodem.

+ Robertus Toppe debet xxv s. de fine. + Johannes de Bristoll' debet medietatem de lvj m. sicut continetur in rotulo iij°.

Robertus Sellator, Adam Bercarius et Robertus de Harpetrie r.c. de iiij s. et viij d. pro pleiag'. In thes. ij s. Et debent ij s. et viij d.

Walterus de Hurst r.c. de xx s. ut possit esse sub plegio. In thes. lib. Et Q.E.

Ricardus Noel r.c. de dim. m. pro licencia concordandi. In thes. iij s. Et debet iij s. et viij d.

Aluredus Carettarius r.c. de xxiiij s. pro carettis suis removendis. In thes. ij s. Et debet xxij s.

Radulfus de Sulleg' r.c. de liiij li. et j m. pro relevio suo sicut continetur in rotulo vj. In thes. xx m. Et debet xlj li. et dim. m. per annum xx m.

Villata de Gloecr' [*blank*] lx m. de tallagio.

Willelmus de Dene r.c. de iij m. pro habenda justicia sicut continetur in rotulo viij°. In thes. j m. Et debet ij m. Idem r.c. de eodem debito. In thes. lib. Et Q.E.

Radulfus Juvenis r.c. de dim. m. pro habendo pone sicut continetur ibidem. In thes. xl d. Et debet xl d.

Willelmus de Campeden' et Matill' uxor eius et Eva de Horton' r.c. de dim. m. pro habendo pone sicut continetur ibidem. In thes. xl d. Et debent xl d.

Abbas de Cyrecestr' r.c. de xxx s. ut possit respondere sicut continetur in rotulo viij. In thes. lib. Et Q.E.

Duo feoda Ricardi de Harocurt de Quenton' et Weston' [*blank*] xiiij li. de fine et passagio Pictavie.

Archiepiscopus Ebor' debet vj m. et iiij s. et v d. de scutagio de Mungumeri. Set inde quietus est in rotulo ix° in Everwikesir' ubi respondet de omnibus scutagiis suis.

David le Moinne debet j m. quia retraxit se. (*Set respondet infra.*[i])
Laurencius Mercerius debet terciam partem de xxxv m. pro summonendo Johanne de Kenn' sicut continetur in rotulo precedenti.

Robertus de Welleboef' r.c. de xxx m. et j bono chascuro sicut supra continetur. In thes. v m. per Thomam de Baskervill' qui fuit plegius de tanto. Et debet R. xxv m. et j chascurum de quibus Johannes de Báálun' debet eum adquietare de x m. (*Set respondet infra.*[i]). Et debet R. xv m. et j chascurum.

DE SCUTAGIO DE BEDEFORD'

Thomas de Berkel' [*blank*] x m. de eodem.

Robertus de Amenevill' [*blank*] ij m. de eodem.

Galfridus de Norton' et Elyas de Yrnham, Petrus de Lata grava[1] et Adam de Bidiford' r.c. de v m. pro j palefrido ut appellum[2] sicut continetur in rotulo precedenti. In thes. xvj s. et (iiij[c]) (viij[i]) d. per Adam de Budiford'. Et debent alii l s.

[1] In *NS 54*, p. 44 and *NS 56*, p. 74 he is shown as *Petrus de la Leegrave*.
[2] Verb missing. Supply e.g. *haberent*.

Engelardus de Cyconiaco debet l li. et xj s. et iiij d. de tribus debitis contentis in rotulo viij in Hereford' Wall' qui requirebatur ibidem in rotulo (precedenti^c) *vij*^o.

DE OBLATIS

Ricardus Walensis r.c. de l m. pro relevio suo de manerio de Winterburn'. In thes. xv li. Et debet xviij li. et dim. m.

Homines de Cyrecestr' r.c. de x m. pro habenda inquisitione sicut continetur in rotulo precedenti. In thes. lib. Et Q.S.

Abbas de Cyrecestr' r.c. de xx m. pro eodem. In thes. xj li. et j m. Et debet ij m. et dim. Idem r.c. de eodem debito. In thes. lib. Et Q.E.

Johanna de Bocland' debet dim. m. pro habendo brevi sicut continetur ibidem. Set respondet in Berkesir' in rotulo sequenti.

Idem Vic. r.c. de xx s. de Petro Croc pro habendo brevi. Et de dim. m. de abbate de Kingeswode. Et de dim. m. de Waltero Cumin. In thes. lib. Et Q.E.

Walterus serviens [*blank*] ij m. quia retraxit se[1] per plegium Gilleberti f. de Hida[2] qui manet in comitatu Oxon'.

Mauricius de Gandino r.c. de C m. pro habendis pluribus precipe. Et de C s. pro habendo j mercato apud Radewic. Et de CCCC et xxiij li. et xv s. et vj d. de debitis Judeorum pro Henrico de Oylly. Et de iij m. de scutagio Wall'. Et de j m. pro licencia concordandi cum Thoma de Berkelay. Summa CCCC et quater xx et xviij li. ij s. et ij d. In thes. quater xx m. Et debet CCCC et xliiij li. et xv s. et vj d. per annum quater xx m.

Johannes de Báálun r.c. de x m. pro plegio Roberti de Oildeboef'[3] sicut supra continetur. Et debet ix m. reddendas infra ij annos.

COMPOTUS FORESTE DE DENE

f' Rogerus de Clyfford' Nicholaus clericus pro eo r.c. de x li. de firma predicte foreste. In thes. iiij li. et iiij s. Et Willelmo Maresc' xlvij s. in redditu castri Godricy. Et in venatione R. salianda et custodienda iij s. per breve R. Et in carriagio x aprorum usque Winton' xij s. per breve R. Et debet liiij s.

[*One line blank*]

f' Idem R.[4] de xj li. et xiij s. et x d. de redd[itu] hominum nove foreste quorum nomina annotantur in rotulo iij^o. Et de v s. et ix d. de redd[itu] aliorum de novo cremento quorum nomina annotantur in rotulo vij^o. Et de vj s. de Roberto Balle et sociis suis. Summa xij li. v s. et vij d. In thes. lib. Et Q.E.

f' Idem R. r.c. de xxiiij s. et vj d. de redd[itu] aliorum de novo cremento quorum nomina annotantur in rotulo precedenti. In thes. xxxiiij s. et vj d. Et habet de superplus x s qui locantur ei infra.

1 *quia retraxit se* repeated.

2 No forename given.

3 See above p. 124 for the original entry. The surety written is as shown here but this must be the same surety as shown above. He is indexed as such.

4 No space is left after *R*.

Idem R. r.c. de x s. et iiij d. de remanenti compoti sui de anno preterito. In thes. lib. Et Q.E.

f' Idem R. r.c. de iij s. de Johanne de Stanton' pro xij acris novi essarti per breve R. Et de ij s. de Hugone Wolwine pro viij acris essarti per idem breve. Et de ij s. de Waltero f. Waltering' pro viij acris novi essarti per idem breve. Et de xij d. de Maciana que fuit uxor Walding' f. Johannis minatoris R. qui mortuus fuit in servicio R. apud Bedeford' (iiij acris essarti per breve R.[i]). Et de ij s. de Nigello le Bret pro viij acris essarti per breve R. Summa x s. In thes. nichil. Et in superplus quod habet supra x s.[1] Et Q.E.

f' Robertus de Wakering' clericus r.c. de dim. m. de firma xl acrarum essarti in Greneweie[2] extra magnum cóópertum R. sicut continetur in rotulo precedenti. In thes. lib. Et Q.E.

Johannes de Monemuth' debet C et iij s. et xj d. de remanenti compoti sui sicut continetur ibidem. Et j palefrido de remanenti venditionis cablicii sicut continetur ibidem. Set non debet summoneri quia inde quietus est in rotulo viij[o].

f' Hugo de Kinardesle [*blank*] xviij s. de firma essart[3] lxxij acrarum terre in foresta de Dene in Welinton' qui requirebatur in Hereford' in Wall'.

f' Burgenses[4] Bristoll' r.c. de CC et xlv li. de firma ville sue á festo Sancti Michaelis anno ix[o] usque ad festum Sancti Michaelis anno x[o]. In thes. vij li. et xviij s. et vij d. Et in elemosinis constitutis militibus de templo j m. Et eisdem iiij li. in denariis. Et eisdem ij m.[5] et dim. in redditu cuiusdam domus in villa de Brist' quam R. eis dedit. Et monachis de Theokebir' lx s. de redditu molendini Bristoll'. Et eisdem xiiij li. et x s. in denariis. Et Radulfo de Wiliton' constabulario Bristoll' ad expensas consanguineé R. et familie sue in castro Bristoll' per preceptum R. commorantis lvij li. et x s. scilicet a die sabbati proxima post festum Sancti Michaelis usque ad diem sabbati ante festum Sancti Gregorii utraque die computata scilicet qualibet die sabbati l s. per breve R. Et eidem R. á (predicto[c]) die sabbati post festum Sancti Gregorii usque ad diem sabbati ante festum Sancti Michaelis utraque die computata ad expensas predictorum scilicet per xxviij septimanas lxx (ij[i]) li. (et x s.[i]) per breve eiusdem. Et xx servientibus peditibus qui sunt in castro Bristoll' per preceptum R. quorum decem capiunt singuli per diem iij d. et ob. et alii x capiunt (singuli[i]) per diem iij d. xvj li. et xv s. et x d. per breve eiusdem de liberationibus suis a die Epiphanie usque ad dominicam proximam ante festum Sancti Gregorii utraque die computata scilicet lxij dies. Et eisdem a crastino predicte dominice usque ad diem Sancti Gregorii utraque die computata scilicet per iiij[or] dies xxj s. et viij d. per breve eiusdem. Et Alienore cognate R. ad elemosinas suas faciendas v m. per breve R. de remanenti

1 Each line of this passage is preceded by a marginal *f'*.
2 See *Calendar of Fine Rolls*, II, 1224–34, p. 33, no. 219 for the fine to which this relates.
3 No suspension mark is shown at the end of this word.
4 The B of *Burgenses* is written large, so that it takes up some of the space required for the initial H of *Hugo* in the line above; this shows that this space must have been blank when the B was written.
5 *m.* repeated.

xx m. quas R. precepit ei dari ad elemosinas suas. Et pro ix ulnis de viridi ad capam et (penı^c)[1] tunicam et pallium ad opus Ranulfi de Hurle cum furrura de agnis ad capam et penulam de cuniculis ad pallium xxxv s. per breve R. Et pro robis vij^tem vigilum et aliorum plurium commorantium in predicto castro quorum nomina annotantur in breve R. quod est in forulo marescalli C et vj s. per idem breve. Et in emendatione et reparatione domorum in castro Bristoll' xxj li. et ix s. et xj d. per breve eiusdem et per visum Johannis Sellarii et Roberti[2] la Warr'. Et xx servientibus peditibus commorantibus in castro predicto quorum x capiunt singuli per diem iij d. et ob. et alii x capiunt singuli per diem iij d. xij li. et iij s. et ix d. per breve R. pro liberatoribus suis a festo Sancti Gregorii usque ad clausum Pascha[3] utraque die computata. Et eisdem servientibus a die Jovis proxima ante festum Sancte (Margar'^i) usque in crastinum Nativitatis beate Marie utraque die computata scilicet per lvij dies xv li. (viij^i) s. et ix d. per breve eiusdem. Et pro j dolio vini ad opus Rogeri de Portes de dono R. ij m. et dim. per breve eiusdem. Et pro iij doliis vini emptis et liberatis Radulfo de Wiliton' ad ponendum in castro predicto C et viij s. per breve eiusdem. Et in carriagio xxv d[oliorum] vini á Bristoll' usque Wigorn' per aquam carriatorum ad opus R. xxvj s. per breve eiusdem. Et pro lineo panno empto ad opus Alienore cognate R. xlv s. per breve eiusdem. Et in superplus quod habuit in anno predicto v s. et iiij d. habend[os] de superplus C s. et vj d. de quibus C s. locantur eis ex alia parte rotuli. Et restant eis locandi[4] vj d.

Martinus de Bristoll' debet iiij m. pro summonendo[5] Matheo de Guneton' et aliis sicut continetur in rotulo precedenti.

David Monachus r.c. de j m. sicut supra continetur. In thes. x s. Et debet xl d.

NOVA OBLATA

Galfridus de Stratton' r.c. de dim. m. pro habendo brevi de attingendis xij versus Agnetem de Cardonvill' de ten[emento] in Stratton'.[6] In thes. lib. Et Q.E.

Arnoldus f. Hamonis et Johannes de Kaerdif burgenses Bristoll' debent iiij^or dolia vini pro habendis pannis suis quietis qui capti fuerunt in nundinis Hoyland' eo quod non fuerunt de assisa.

Homines de Chiltham debent iij dolia vini de promisso pro habenda villa sua ad firmam sicut supra continetur a festo Sancti Michaelis anno x^o usque in iiij annos sequentes.

Henricus Flandr' debet j m. pro habendo brevi de attingendis xij

1 The cancelled word ends in three minims, and presumably is the beginning of *penulam*.
2 Name on rubbed right hand edge of membrane, and very difficult to read.
3 *Pascha* written in full and very clearly. As this cannot be a genitive form, presumably the clerk regarded it as indeclinable.
4 Final *-i* written over original final *-e*.
5 *summonendo* written in full.
6 See *Calendar of Fine Rolls*, II, 1224–34, p. 55, no. 363 for the writ to which this relates.

iuratoribus nove dissaisine de tenemento in Risendon'. Willelmus de Audebir' debet dim. m. pro licencia concordandi cum Rogero f. Philippi per plegium eiusdem R.

Henricus ruffus r.c. de xx m. de fine quem fecit cum R. pro saisina sua recuperanda de iij virgatis terre quas habuit in Berton' Gloecr' que capte fuerunt in manum R. eo quod cum ipse teneret terram illam de predicta Bertona eam tenere[1] de Umfrido de Bohun comite Hereford'. Ita quod idem Henricus reddet R. de eadem terra per annum dim. m. et faciet sectam ad curiam R. de prefata Bertona et salvis R. tallagiis suis. In thes.

Robertus Marmiun iunior r.c. de xx s. pro habendo termino R. de feodo suo quod Hugo Cuteman et Robertus Tuleward' suspensi tenuerunt de eo. In thes. lib. Et Q.E.

Homines de Sancto Briavell' et de nova terra [*blank*] xx m. pro essartis suis in pace habendis que habuerunt tempore Hugonis de Neovill' per liberationem suam et Johannis de Monem' et Rogeri de Clyfford' unde annuum redd[itum][2] ad scaccarium ita quod nullus constabularius Sancti Briavell' de essartis illis se intromittat nisi a domino R. inde speciale habuerit mandatum. Et inde habent litteras[3] R. patentes si ei placuerit.

Hugo Giffard [*blank*] v m. de scutagio de Mungumeri. Et v m. de scutagio de Bedef' qui requirebatur in Hereford' in rotulo precedenti.

AMERCIAMENTA PER M. DE PATESHILL' ET SOCIOS SUOS

Idem Vic. r.c. de quater xx et x m. et vj s. et iiij d. et ob. de misericordiis hominum et catallis fugitivorum et suspensorum quorum nominibus proponitur[4] littera *t* in rotulo quem predicti liberaverunt in thes. lib. Et Q.E.

RESPICE IN TERGUM

[*Rot.* 7d *Mem.* 1]

ADHUC DE EODEM ITINERE

p Willelmus[5] de Leicr' r.c. de dim. m. quia non habet. In thes. xl d. Et debet xl d.

t Henricus Chepman f. eius r.c. de j m. pro eodem. In thes. dim. m. Et debet dim. m.

d Idem Vic. r.c. de xxj s. et xj d. de catallis Radulfi de Schireburne. In thes. dim. m. Et debet xv s. et iij d.

d Nicholaus f. Rogeri r.c. de xx s. pro habendo termino R. In thes. j m. Et debet dim. m.

[1] Finite verb missing. Perhaps *debuit tenere*, 'ought to have held'?

[2] These two words are difficult to read. The finite verb is missing – perhaps *solvunt*?

[3] *Ritteras* originally written and then altered to *Litteras*.

[4] Written as *propronuntur*.

[5] This entry and the next five are written on the left hand side of the page.

t Idem Vic. r.c. de xxij s. de catallis Walteri ruffi. In thes. j m. Et debet viij s. et viij d.
d Ricardus de Gardino [*blank*] dim. m. quia non est prosecutus. In thes. [*blank*]. Et debet [*blank*].

Willelmus[1] Camerarius r.c. de dim. m. quia non est prosecutus. In thes. lib. Et Q.E.

Idem Vic. r.c. de iiij s. et j lorica et j haubergello et j cóópertorio ferreo de catallis Heine de Bernieres suspensi. In thes. iiij s. Et debet j loricam et j haubergellum et j cóópertorium ferreum. Set Walterus Cotele debet inde respondere sicut continetur in rotulo predicto et respondet infra.

Walterus Cotele debet j loricam et j haubergellum et j cóópertorium ferreum sicut supra continetur.

Idem Vic. r.c. de j m. de francoplegio ville de Westerle pro fuga Thome f. Susanne. In thes. nichil. Et J. episcopo Bath' j m. per libertatem carte R.[2] Et Q.E.

Brist'.[3] Burgenses Bristoll' r.c. de C s. pro transgressione. In thes. nichil. Et in suo superplus quod habent ex alia parte rotuli C s. Et Q.S.
p Hugo Pincerna debet lj s. de catallis Ricardi Russell'. (*d*[1]) Francoplegium ville de Fairford' debet ij m. pro fuga Roberti Burgensis et Roberti f. Clementis et Willelmi Sparke. (*d*[1]) Reginaldus f. Serlonis debet dim. m. pro dissaisina.

Radulfus Musard tunc Vic. debet vij s. de catallis Roberti Toui. Et ij s. de catallis Henrici de Hagenepenne suspensi. Et j m. de catallis Roberti Burgensis qui abiuravit regnum. Et x s. et x d. de catallis Reginaldi Brente fugitivi. Et xxij s. de catallis Walteri f. Oseberti fugitivi. Et xxiij s. et vj d. de catallis Gilleberti de Stockwell'. Et vj d. de catallis Willelmi Maresc' fugitivi. Et v s. de catallis Willelmi f. Henrici de[4] Witinton'. Summa iiij li. et iiij s. et ij d.

Idem Vic. r.c. de j m. de francoplegio Rogeri de Smethefeld' in Gate pro fuga Willelmi Mar'. In thes. nichil. Et in perdona Radulfo de Wiliton' j m. per breve R. Et Q.E.

Heres Henrici de Ferrariis debet quater xx et xij li. et xv s. et viij d. de tercio scutagio R. Ricardi qui requirebatur in Devon'.

AMERCIAMENTA DE ITINERE R. DE ASSISIS CORAM EO CAPTIS

Idem Vic. r.c. de xxxiij m. et dim. de misericordiis hominum quorum nominibus proponitur littera *t* in rotulo de eodem itinere liberato in thesauro. In thes. lib. Et Q.E.
t Robertus Malregard r.c. de xx [s.] pro dissaisina per plegium Johannis Gerard' et Walteri de Solariis. In thes. x s. Et debet x s.
t Willelmus de Bosco r.c. de j m. pro licencia concordandi cum Ricardo de Bosco per plegium eiusdem Ricardi. In thes. dim. m. Et debet dim. m.

1 This entry and the next five are written on the right hand side of the membrane.
2 *carte R. Et Q.E.* written at the end of the following line.
3 Lines written right across the membrane from now on.
4 *de* written over *fi.*

p Henricus Flandr' r.c. de C s. pro dissaisinis per plegium Bartholomei Labanc et Laurencii de Lascell'. In thes. xl s. Et debet lx s.
p Petrus Achard' de Abbenesse [*blank*] dim. m. pro plegio Ricardi de Abbenesse servientis per plegium eiusdem servientis.
Glo' d[1] Reginaldus f. Serlonis [*blank*] dim. m. pro falso clamore per plegium Roberti Juvenis et Roberti Lorimar'

Adam Espare[2] r.c. de dim. m. quia non est prosecutus. In thes. lib. Et Q.E.

Glo' d Petrus f. Johannis [*blank*] dim. m. pro plegio eiusdem.
d Hugo Bagge [*blank*] j m. pro eodem.
Brist' (*t*ⁱ) Laurencius carnifex [*blank*] xl s. quia non est prosecutus per plegium Nicholai f. clerici et Hugonis le Grant.
SerA' t Ricardus de Manton' (*Stanton'*)[3] [*blank*] xx s. pro licencia concordandi cum Waltero Walding' per plegium eiusdem Walteri.

Nicholaus le seculior r.c. de xl s. pro dissaisina. In thes. nichil. Et in perdona ipsi Nicholao xl s. per ij^{o} brevia R. Et Q.E.

Johannes de Monemue r.c. de iiij li. et x s. de carrucagio assiso ad ij s. Qui requirebatur in rotulo de carrucagio. In thes. lib. Et Q.E.

[*One line blank*]

f' Idem Vic. ut custos r.c. de C et x s. et vj d. et ob. de redditu assiso de manerio de Slochtres de toto anno. Et de xxij s. de placitis et perquisitis de eodem termino. In thes. nichil. Et pro xviij bobus emptis ad iij carrucas R. ibidem instaurandas vj li. et iij s. Et pro ij affris ibidem emptis xix s. et vj d. Et pro ij carretis scilicet j ferrata et alia non ferrata viij s. et viij d. Et pro iij^{bus} carrucis et cultris et vomeribus et aliis necessariis ad carruc' dim m. Et in stipendiis j^{us} servientis et ij^{orum} hominum caretariorum totum annum xij s. Et habet de superplus xxxvij s. iij d. et ob.

[*One line blank*]

Radulfus de Wiliton' r.c. de xxvj li. et xij s. et ix d. de remanenti compoti sui sicut continetur ex alia parte rotuli. Et de xv li. et vij s. et iij ob. de redditu assiso de Bertona Bristoll' de anno R. ix^{o}. Et de xxxij s. de redditu mobili de eodem anno. Et de viij li. de placitis et perquisitis de Bertona de eodem anno. Et de iiij s. de quadam consuetudine que vocatur Chirchschet de eodem anno. Et de xv s. et viij d. de lana et pellibus, sepo et j corio venditis anno eodem. Et de CC li. et l s. receptis de firma Bristoll' a die sabbati proxima post festum Sancti Gregorii anni eiusdem usque ad diem sabbati proximum[4] ante festum sancti Michaelis anni x^{mi} utraque die computata. Et de xx li. receptis de firma predicta per breve R. anno eodem. Summa CC et lxxv li. et xviij d. et ob.

Idem r.c. de xx li. (et iiij s. et viij d.ⁱ) de redditu assiso de Bertona de anno x^{mo}. Et de xxxj s. de redditu mobili eodem anno. Et de x li. et x s. et x d. de placitis et perquisitis de Bertona anno eodem. Et de xxix s. et iiij d. de misericordiis Judeorum per predictum tempus (scilicet anno ix et x^{o}

1 The 'd' is on the line below.
2 The 'p' is written over a capital 'G' partially rubbed out.
3 *Stanton* written above *Manton*, which is not cancelled in any way.
4 *proximum* written clearly, as is the preceding *proxima*: the clerk is inconsistent here.

i). Et de xxix s. et x d. de padnagio anno eodem. Et de iiij s. de quadam consuetudine que vocatur Chirchschet anno eodem. Et de xxij s. et ij d. de stipendiis servientum peditum recentis[1] in absentia ipsorum. Et de xiij s. de lana vendita anno eodem. Summa xxxvij li. iiij s. et x d. Summa summarum CCC et xij li. et vj s. et iiij d. et ob. In thes. nichil.

Et in expensis Alienore cognate R. cum familia sua et alterius familie moram facientis in castro tam equitum quam peditum numero xxxv hominum et xx equorum preter familiam predicte Alienore per totum predictum tempus scilicet per j annum et xxix septimanas CC li. et lxv li. et ix s. et iiij d. et ob. Et in minutis et forinsecis et necessariis expensis Barton' et castri per totum predictum tempus xvj li. et viij s. et ij d. Et pro C et lxij ovibus emptis de quibus xliiij mortue sunt et de pellibus xv est responsum supra viij li. et xij d. Et in expensis suis et clerici et prepositi qui venerunt ad reddendum compotum xxx s. Summa CC et quater xx et xj li. et viij s. et vj d. et ob. Et debet xx li. et xvij s. et ix d. et ob.

Idem debet respondere de xxix pellibus ovium predictarum mortuarum. Et de C et xviij ovibus vivis que remanserunt apud Bertonam. Preterea expensum est in castro Bristoll' per predictum tempus instaurum subscriptum scilicet C et xxv quarteria frumenti precii xxxj li. et v s. Et ij^{o} dolia vini que remanserunt in castro. Et xxviij dolia vini per brevia R. unde unum remansit in castro. Et carnes xxxj boum que remanserunt in castro precii iiij li. et xiij s. Et xxiiij bacones qui remanserunt in castro precii xxx s. Et C et xlviij casei precii xxx s. et x d. et remanserunt in castro C et xxxij casei.

[*Eight lines blank*]

COMPOTUS WALERANDI TEUTONICI DE TERRIS COMITIS DEVON' EXTRA INSULAM DE WICHT

Idem Walerandus r.c. de ix li. et xxij d. de redditu assiso Burgi de Cristchirche de toto hoc anno. Et de iiij li. iij s. et iiij d. de redditu assiso de Bureton' membro de Cristchirche. Et de xiiij li. et xv s. et ob. de redditu assiso de Holeherst membro eiusdem. Et de iiij li. et ij s. et viij d. de redditu assiso manerii de Edbrichton' cum molendino. Et de vij li. et vij s. et ix d. et qu. de redditu assiso manerii de Bremmor'. Et de vij li. et ix s. et iij d. de redditu assiso manerii de Brumbrig'. Et de xliiij s. et vj d. de burgagio de Limiton'. Et de C et xij s. et viij d. de redditu assiso manerii de Limiton'. Et de lx s. de redditu assiso de tercio denario thelonei ville de Dorcestr'. Summa lvij li. et xvij s. et ob.

Idem W. r.c. de lxx s. de exitu prepositure Burgi de Cristchirche de eodem termino. Et de xxx s. de auxilio assiso eiusdem Burgi. Et de iiij li. et v s. de placitis et perquisitis curie de Cristchirche cum hundredo forinseco. Et de lxvj s. de perquisitis nundinarum de Cristchirche preter xx sol. annuos quos Prior de Cristchirche percipit de predictis nundinis nomine

[1] *recentis* written, but it cannot be correct, as there is nothing for it to agree with. Should it be *receptis* = (wages) received? Or *recenti* = recent (absence)?

elemosinarum. Et preter j m. quam W. quondam comes Devon' dedit per cartam suam cuidam pauperi vidue in elemosinis matri scilicet abbatis de Quarrera tenendam in vita ipsius vidue. Et preter x s. quos Huge[1] Chauvel tenet de dono predicti comitis per cartam ipsius. Et de xl s. de exitu piscariarum de Cristchirche. Et de xl s. de feno ibidem vendito. Et de xij s. de auxiliis et perquisitis de Buriton'. Et de lxj s. et viij d. de auxiliis et perquisitis de Holeherst. Et de xxiiij s. de viij quarteriis siliginis ibidem venditis. Et de viij s. de xij quarteriis avene ibidem venditis. Summa xxj li. et vj s. et viij d.

Idem W. r.c. de v s. et vj d. de placitis et perquisitis de Edbrichton'. Et de lxxij s. de xviij quarteriis frumenti ibidem venditis. Et de xiij s. et iiij d. de x quarteriis avene ibidem venditis. Et de xxij s. et vj d. de ix quarteriis ordei ibidem venditis. Summa C et xiij s. et iiij d.

Idem W. r.c. de ix s. de placitis et perquisitis de Brummor'. Et de iiij li. et viij s. de xxij quarteriis frumenti ibidem venditis. Et de xvj s. et viij d. de xiiij quarteriis avene ibidem venditis. Et de xxxv s. de xiiij quarteriis ordei ibidem venditis. Summa vij li. et viij s. et viij d.

Idem W. r.c. de vij s. et vj d. de placitis et perquisitis de Bumbrige. Et de v s. de feno ibidem vendito. Et de xiij li. de sale vendito apud Limiton'. Summa xiij li. et xij s. et vj d. Summa summarum C et v li. xviij s. et x d. et ob.

DE TERRIS INFRA INSULAM

Idem W. r.c. de xj li. et iiij s. et vj d. de redditu assiso manerii de Bocumb' preter l s. quos prior de Carebroc percipit annuatim nomine elemosine.[2] Et de lxxiij s. et x d. de redditu assiso de Wrokeshal'. Et de lxx s. et ix d. et ob. de redditu assiso de Torleg'. Et de xiij s. et ij d. de redditu assiso de Bulenor'. Et de l s. et v d. de redditu assiso de Welleg'. Et de iiij li. et ix s. et j d. de redditu assiso de Eremue. Et de viij s. et iiij d. de redditu assiso quem homines de Bulenor' reddunt annuatim eidem manerio. Et de xvj s. de quadam consuetudine annuatim in Eremue. Et de iiij li. de redditu assiso terre Walteri de Hanou. Et de xiij li. de redditu assiso novi burgi. Et de xj li. et dim. m. de redditu assiso prepositure burgi eiusdem preter j m. quam infirmi de Carebroc habent nomine elemosinarum. Summa lv li. et xij s. et ix d. et ob.

Idem W. r.c. de xx s. de exitu molend' de Bocumb'. Et de xx s. de placitis et perquisitis ibidem. Et de viij li. et xvij s. et ix d. de xxxix quarteriis et dim. frumenti ibidem venditis. Et de xl s. de xxx quarteriis avene ibidem venditis. Et de xl s. de xvj quarteriis ordei ibidem venditis. Et de xx s. (et viij d.[i]) de viij quarteriis pisorum ibidem venditis. Summa xv li. et xliiij s. et v d.

Idem W. r.c. de j m. de placitis et perquisitis de Wroxhal'. Et de lxxij s. de xvj quarteriis frumenti ibidem venditis. Et de xxj s. et iiij d. de xvj quarteriis avene ibidem venditis. Et de xxxvij s. et vj d. de xv quarteriis ordei ibidem venditis. Et de vij s. et vj d. et iij quarteriis pisorum ibidem

[1] Name clearly written.
[2] Singular *elemosine* written in full.

venditis. Et de vij s. de j pondere casei ibidem vendito. Et de j m. de lana ibidem vendita. Et de ij s. de pellibus ovium ibidem venditis. Et de v s. de pellibus agnorum ibidem venditis. Summa viij li. et xix s.

[*Rot.* 7d *Mem.* 2]

Idem W. r.c. de x s. de placitis et perquisitis de Torleg'. Et de viij li. et xj s. de xxxviij quarteriis frumenti ibidem venditis. Et de xxxvij s. et iiij d. de xxviij quarteriis avene ibidem venditis. Et de xl s. de xvj quarteriis ordei ibidem venditis. Et de xv s. de vj quarteriis pisorum ibidem venditis. Summa xiij li. et j m.

Idem W. r.c. de xij s. de placitis et perquisitis de Welleg'. Et de C et viij s. de xxiiij quarteriis frumenti ibidem venditis. Et de xvj s. de xij quarteriis avene ibidem venditis. Et de xxij s. et vj d. de ix quarteriis ordei ibidem venditis. Et de vij s. et vj d. de iij quarteriis pisiorum[1] ibidem venditis. Summa viij li. et vj s.

Idem W. r.c. de x s. de placitis et perquisitis de Eremue. Et de lxiij s. de placitis et perquisitis de Carebroc. Summa iiij li. et iij s. Summa summarum infra Insulam C et vj li. et xij s. et vj d. et ob. Summa summarum extra Insulam et infra CC et xij li. xj s. et v d. In thes. C et lx li.

Et pro j careta empta (cum apparatu[i]) contra autumpnum apud Cristechirch' et in precariis carruc[ariorum] ibidem v s. et ix d. Et in pratis falcandis et levandis et bladis metendis et colligendis xix s. et v d. Et in stipendiis j herciatoris et iiij carrucariorum et prepositi et forestarii ibidem xxiiij s. et ij d. per totum annum. Et in piscariis reparandis ibidem xxj s. Summa lxx s. et iiij d.

Et pro j careta empta cum apparatu et in locatione caretarum ad attrahendum scilicet apud Limiton' et saccis emptis ad salem imponendum xx s. Et in pratis falcandis et levandis ibidem xij d. Et in stipendiis prepositi et bedelli ibidem vij s. per totum annum. Summa xxviij s.

Et in elemosinis constitutis per comitem altari Sancti Eustachii de Edbrichtinton' viij d. Et pro j careta empta cum apparatu ibidem iij s. Et pro ferro et ascero ad carrucas ibidem et pro carrucis emptis vj s. et iiij d.

Et pro j equo caretario et ij bobus emptis ibidem xx s. et iij d. Et in pratis falcandis et levandis et precariis autumpnalibus ibidem xx s. Et in compannagio et stipendiis ij servientum et j ancille et j^{us} herciatoris et prepositi et hewardi et ij^{orum} carrucariorum ibidem xxj s. et xj d. Et in compannagio j^{us} servientis custodis manerii eiusdem xv s. Summa iiij li. et vij s. et iij d.

Et pro j careta cum apparatu apud Brummor' iij s. Et pro ferro et ascero cum carrucis emptis ibidem viij s. et vj d. Et in pratis falcandis et levandis et bladis sarclandis metendis et colligendis et precariis autumpnalibus ibidem xv s. Et pro j bove empto ibidem vj s. et ix d. Et in stipendiis ij carrucariorum et ij caretariorum ibidem et j^{us} herciatoris et j ancille et prepositi et heiward' xxiiij s. (et xj d.[i]) per totum annum.

[1] *pisiorum* written for *pisorum*.

Et in companagio j^{us} servientis custod[is] manerii xv s. Et in stipendiis prepositi et bedelli de Bumbrig' v s. Summa lxxviij s. et ij d.

Et pro j careta cum apparatu empta apud Bocumb' ijj s. Et pro ferro et ascero cum carrucis emptis ibidem viij s. et vj d. Et in pratis falcandis et levandis et bladis sarclandis metendis colligendis et precariis autumpnalibus xviij s. et vij d. Et in stipendiis iij carrucariorum et j herciatoris et j ancille et in stipendiis j^{us} prepositi et ij bedellorum et j^{us} heiward' et custodis grangiarum et j^{us} forestarii et iij caretariorum xl s. et vij d. Et pro j mola ibidem xx s. Summa iiij li. x s. et viij d.

Et pro j careta cum apparatu empta apud Wroxhal' iij s. Et pro iij bobus emptis ibidem xv s. et vj d. Et pro ferro et ascero cum carrucis emptis cum apparatu et stipendiis fabri fabricantis ferramentum carruce per annum xiij s. et x d. Et in pratis falcandis et levandis et bladis sarclandis metendis et colligendis et precariis autumpnalibus xj s. et ix d. Et pro feno empto ibidem ij s. et vj d. Et in stipendiis prepositi heiwardi et ij carrucariorum et ij caretariorum xix s. Et in companagio servientis manerii xv s. Summa iiij li. et vij d.

Et pro j careta cum apparatu empta apud Torleg' iij s. Et pro ij bobus emptis ibidem x s. et iiij d. Et pro ferro et ascero cum carrucis et earum apparatu ibidem xij s. et vij d. Et in pratis falcandis levandis et bladis sarclandis metendis et colligendis et precariis autumpnalibus xj s. et ix (d.[i]). Et in stipendiis iij carrucariorum j ancille j herciatoris prepositi et heiwardi et ij caretariorum ibidem xxxiij s. et iiij d. Et in companagio servientis manerii per annum xv s. qui etiam custos fuit de Torleg' et Welleg'. Summa iiij li. et vj s.

Et pro j careta cum apparatu empta apud Welleg' iij s. Et pro ferro et ascero cum carrucis emptis cum apparatu ibidem iij s. et vj d. Et in pratis falcandis et levandis et bladis sarclandis metendis et colligendis et precariis autumpnalibus xiij s. et vj d. Et in stipendiis ij carrucariorum j herciatoris prepositi haiwardi et j caretarii xvij s. Summa xxxvij s.

Summa summarum xxvij li. xvij s. et xj d.[1]

Et ipsi Walerando xx li. de hoc anno pro custodia castri de Carebroc per breve R. Et eidem Walerando lx s. (et x d.[i]) de hoc anno pro custodia castri de Cristchirch' per idem breve. Et in emendatione domorum et grangiarum maneriorum extra insulam xxij s. Et in emendatione domorum et grangiarum infra insulam xxxij s. Et iterum ipsi Walerando C et vj s. et v d. et ob. pro custodia castri de Cristchirch' de tribus partibus anni viij et toto anno ix^{o} per breve R. Et in stipendiis custodis turris de Cristchirch' et ij^{orum} hominum suorum et equi sui xx s. Et in stipendiis j^{us} forestarii equitis itinerantis per insulam j m. Et in stipendiis $iiij^{or}$ servientum custodum maneriorum scilicet ij^{orum} infra insulam et ij^{orum} extra xl s. scilicet cuilibet eorum x s. per annum. Et in stipendiis ij^{orum} forestariorum peditum infra insulam x s. scilicet utrique v s. per annum.

(*Et restant ei locandi xiiij s. et vij d.*[c])[2] Summa xxxv li. iiij s. et vij d. et

[1] This summation is written on the right hand side of the line.
[2] The words deleted here are written again in the following line.

ob. Et habet de superplus x li. et xj s. et iij ob. de quibus ix li. et xvj s. et vj d. locantur ei infra.

Et restant ei locandi xiiij s. et vij d.

Idem r.c. de ix li. et xvj s. et vj d. et ob. de remanenti compoti sui de anno preterito. In thes. nichil. Et in superplus quod habet supra ix li. et xvj s. et vj d. et ob. Et Q.E.

Idem r.c. de quater xx quarteriis et xiij frumenti de exitu horreorum de Edbrichtiton' et Brimmor' maneriorum extra insulam. De quibus xl quarterii seminati fuerunt in predictis maneriis. Et xl quarterii venditi de quorum precio respondet supra. Et in victualibus servientum per maneria xiij quarterii. Et Q.E.

Idem r.c. de xiij quarteriis siliginis de exitu predictorum maneriorum. De quibus v quarterii fuerunt seminati ibidem. Et viij quarterii venditi sunt de quorum precio respondet supra. Et Q.E.

Idem r.c. de quater xx quarteriis ordei de exitu eorundem maneriorum. De quibus xx quarterii (et dim.[1]) fuerunt ibidem seminati. Et xxij quarterii et dim. venditi de quorum precio respondet supra. Et in liberatione j^{us} servientis (caretarii[1]) et iiij carrucariorum xxv quarterii. Et in liberatione ij^{orum} herciatorum iiij quarterii. Et in liberatione ij ancillarum viij quarterii. Et Q.E.

Idem r.c. de C et xx quarteriis avene de exitu eorundem horreorum. De quibus lxvj quarterii [*line ends here*].

Idem r.c. de CC et quater xx et iij quarteriis et dim. frumenti de exitu horreorum infra insulam. De quibus C et xl quarterii fuerunt seminati per maneria infra insulam. Et C et xvij quarterii et dim. venditi de quorum precio respondet supra. Et in liberatione servientum et forestariorum infra insulam xxvj quarterii. Et Q.E.

Idem r.c. de C et lix quarteriis [ordei][1] de exitu eorundem horreorum. De quibus xliiij quarterii seminati fuerunt ibidem. Et lvj quarterii venditi de quorum precio respondet supra. Et in liberationibus viij servientum xl quarterii. Et in liberationibus iij ancillarum per maneria xiij quarterii. Et in liberationibus vj herciatorum per maneria vj quarterii. Et Q.E.

Idem r.c. de CC et xxxij quarteriis et dim. avene de exitu eorundem maneriorum. De quibus C et xxij quarterii et dim. fuerunt seminati. Et quater xx et vj quarterii venditi de quorum precio respondet supra. Et in prebenda affrorum per maneria xxiiij quarterii. Et Q.E.

Idem r.c. de xxxiij quarteriis pisorum de exitu eorundem horreorum. De quibus xiij quarterii fuerunt seminati. Et xx quarterii venditi de quorum precio respondet supra. Et Q.E.

[*The rest of the membrane is blank.*]

[*Endorsed*] emend' semel et satis

Gloucestresir Et Compotus Walerandi Teutonici de terris comitis Devon' infra Insulam et extra.

[1] Word for the grain missing and supplied by comparison with other grain accounts here.

[*Rot.* 8 *Mem.* I]

WILTESIR'

Willelmus comes Saresbir', Adam de Alta Ripa ut custos pro eo r.c. de CC et lxx li. et xiiij s. et xj d. (bl.[i]) de firma comitatus de dim. anno. In thes. nichil. Et in elemosinis constitutis (milit'[c]) canonicis de monasterio Hederoso ministrantibus in capella de Clarendon' xv s. et ij d. et ob. Et priori de monasterio Hederoso xxij s. et ix d. et ob. Et monachis de Maumesbir' lxv s. pro sciris et hundredis. Et in liberatione constituta Matill' uxori Gilleberti Fael xxx s. et v d. Et W. comiti Saresbir' xj li. et viij s. et iij d. et ob. de tercio denario comitatus de hoc dimidio anno. Et in liberatione capellani de Clarendon' xxv s. Et Johanni de Chieresburg' vj li. in Seinde. Et Thome Benun cum herede Thome Rufi iiij m. in Imedon'. Et Willelmo de Cantilupo vij li. et x s. in Kalne et in Caleston' quamdiu R. placuerit de quibus respondet infra. Et monachis de Cheppeham l s. in Lokeswell. Et Waltero de Paueilly C s. in Cheppham que fuit Reginaldi de Paueilly. ¶ Et Margar' de Ripariis xvij li. bl. in Worðe.[1] Et Galfrido de Mandevill' de Coc C et xv s. bl. in Worðe. Et Willelmo de Mandevill' comiti Essex' xj li. bl. in Cyriel. Et monachis de Ferleg' l s. bl. in Worðe. Et Hugoni de Neovill' crasso x li. et x s. bl. in Ambresbir'. (Et Hugoni de Champania x li. bl. in Cheppeham[c]) (*quia infra*[i]). Et (Hugoni de Neovill'[c]) (*quia supra*[i]). Et in Westcumb' et Bedwinde xiiij li. bl. de quibus W. Maresc' respondet infra. Et Thome Maudoit xx li. bl. in Wermenistr' cum hundredo. Et W. comiti Sar' et canonicis Cenoman' xxv li. bl. in Ambresbir'. Et Hugoni de Champania x li. (bl.[i]) in Chepeham quamdiu R. placuerit. Et Waltero f. Walteri de Dunestanvill' xx li. bl. in Hechtredebir'. Et ad custodiam castri de Saresbir' iiij li. et xv s. bl. in Saresbir'. Et Roberto de Turevill' C s. bl. in Worðam. Et Luce de Drumar' xviij li. bl. in Mere quamdiu R. placuerit. Et Hugoni de Stamford' iiij li. bl. in Cheleworðe. Et in Merleberg' xvj li. bl. de quibus compotus debet reddi per se. Et in Cosseham et Gatestert membro eius x li. de quarta parte anni per breve R. de quibus homines ville respondent infra.

[*One line blank*]

Et in calumpnia de Merleberg' ix li. bl.

Et in emendatione domorum in castro Saresbir' l s. Et debet xxv li. et x s. et iiij d. et ob. bl. Idem r.c. de eodem debito. In thes. nichil. Et Ele comitisse Sar' xj li. et viij s. et iij d. et ob. de tercio denario comitatus (de dim. anno sequenti. Et debet xiiij li. et xiij s. et vj d. bl.[i])[2]

Idem Vic. [*blank*] de proficuo comitatus in ij^{bus} annis et dim.

[*One line blank*]

[1] The sign is usually written to indicate the insertion of an entry which belongs to the line below into an available space on the line above, but this entry seems to be in its correct place.

[2] From *de dim. anno* to the end of the sentence written on the line above.

Simon[1] de Hal ut custos r.c. de CC et lxx li. et xiiij s. et xj d. bl. de firma comitatus de alio dim. anno. In thes. nichil.

Et in elemosinis constitutis militibus de Templo (dim.[c]) j m. Et canonicis de monasterio Hederoso ministrantibus in capella de Clarendon' xv s. ij d. et ob. Et priori de monasterio Hederoso xxij s. ix d. et ob. Et monachis de Maumesbir' lxv s. pro sciris et hundredis. Et in liberatione constituta Matill' uxori Gilleberti Fael xxx s. et v d. Et in liberatione capellani de Clarendon' xxv s. Et Johanni de Chieresburg' vj li. in Seinde. Et Thome (de[i]) Reinny[2] cum herede Thome Rufi iiij m. in Imedon'. Et Willelmo de Cantilupo vij li. et x s. in Kalne et in Caleston' quamdiu R. placuerit de quibus respondet infra. Et monachis de Chepeham l s. in Lokeswell. Et Waltero de Pauelly C s. in Cheppeham que fuit Reginaldi de Paueilly. ¶ [3] Et Margar' de Ripariis xvij li. bl. in Worðe.[4] Et Galfrido de Mandevill' de Coc C et xv s. bl. in Worðe. Et Willelmo de Mandevill' comiti Essex' xj li. bl. in Ciriel. Et monachis de Ferleg' l s. bl. in Worðe. Et Hugoni de Neovill' crasso x li. et x s. bl. in Ambresbir'. Et in Westcumb' et Bedewinde xiiij li. bl. de quibus W. Maresc' respondet infra. Et Thome Maudoit xx li. bl. in Wermenistr' cum hundredo. Et Ele comitisse Saresbir' et canonicis Cenomanensibus xxv li. bl. in Ambresbir'. Et Hugoni de Champania x li. (bl.[i]) in Chepeham quamdiu R. placuerit. Et Waltero f. Walteri de Dunestanvill' xx li. bl. in Hechtredebir'. Et ad custodiam castri de Saresbir' iiij li. et xv s. (bl.[i]) in Saresbir'. Et Roberto de Turevill' C s. bl. in Worðam. Et Luce de Drumar' xviij li. bl. in Mere quamdiu R. placuerit. Et Hugoni de Stamford' iiij[or] li. bl. in Cheleworðe. Et in Merleberg' xvj li. bl. de quibus compotus debet reddi per se. Et in Cosseham et Gatestirt membro eius xx li. de quibus homines ville respondent infra.

[*One line blank*]

Et in calumpnia de Merleberg' ix li. bl.

Et in eadem calumpnia de lv annis dum comes Patricius et alii tenuerunt comitatum M et CC[5] et vij li. bl.

Et in emendatione domorum in castro Saresbir' l s. Et in custo posito ad claudendum parcum de Clarendon' xviij li. et iiij d. per breve R. et (per[i]) visum Walteri de Langeford et Ricardi de Hairez. Et in operatione D cleiarum et carragio earum usque ad pontem de Radbrig' C et ix s. et iiij d. per breve R. Et debet lxxviij s. et v d. bl.

[*One line blank*]

Idem Vic. [*line ends here*]

[*One line blank*]

1 The S of *Simon* is written two lines deep, and the initial E of *Et*, the first word in the second line, is written within the lower curl of the S in such a way that it appears that the S was written first.

2 *Beinun* written, then altered in different ink to *Reinny*. In the first paragraph he is written as *Thome Benun*, but in *NS 54*, p. 153 he is shown as *Thome de Reinni*.

3 From here to 'Et in calumpnia de Merleberg' ix li. bl.' is repeated from the same paragraph on the previous page also beginning 'Et Margar' de Ripariis xvij li. bl. in Worðe' etc. Why this is the case it has not been possible to determine. Perhaps one of the texts was supposed to be crossed out and the clerk did not do it.

4 See n. 2 in page above.

5 *Sic*.

W. Briewerr' senior [*blank*] de firma de Divisis et Rudes de anno preterito. Et [*blank*] de censu foreste de Cheppeham de eodem anno.
[*One line blank*]

Nulla fit hic mentio de villa de Wilton' quia Thomas de Cyrecestr' respondet inde in compoto suo.

f' Michael de Columbar' r.c. de[1] lx s. de brulliis de Andoeur' de hoc anno. Et de lx s. de eisdem de anno preterito. In thes. lib. Et Q.E.

f' Philippus de Lya [*blank*] x s. de censu foreste de Westbir'. Et [*blank*] x s. de eodem censu de anno preterito.

f' Willelmus Burnel [*blank*] x s. de firma de Westbir'.

Idem W. r.c. de x s. de eadem firma de anno preterito. In thes. lib. Et Q.E.

Nulla fit hic mentio de Westcumb' et Bedewind' quia W. Marescallus respondet inde in compoto suo in rotulo compotorum in rotulo precedenti.

f' Rogerus de Bereford r.c. de x s. de censu foreste de Graveling'. In thes. ix s. Et canonicis Sar' xij d. Et Q.E.

f' Walterus nepos et heres Philippi de Caleston' r.c. de lviij s. et iiij d. de firma de Caleston'. In thes. lib. Et Q.E.

f' Willelmus de Cantilupo senior r.c. de xv li. de firma de Calne. In thes. vij li. et x s. Et debet vij li. et x s. Idem r.c. de eodem debito. In thes. lib. Et Q.E.

Idem Willelmus r.c. de xvj s. de eadem firma de anno preterito. In thes. lib. Et Q.E.

Willelmus le Brett [blank] *x m. pro habenda assisa de morte antecessoris de terra de Berleg' qui requirebatur in Sumerset in rotulo precedenti.*[2]

MERLEBERG'

f' Homines de Merleberg' r.c. de l li. de firma ville sue. In thes. xxxviij li. et j m. Et Simoni Horn ij m. de dono R. per breve R. Et Roberto de Meisy x li. ad operationem castri de Merleberg' per breve eiusdem. Et Q.E.

f' Willelmus de Rughedon' r.c. de ij s. de firma molendini fulerez extra Merleberg'. In thes. lib. Et Q.E.

Idem W. r.c. de j pari calcarium deauratorum pro eodem molendino. *In thes. lib. Et Q.E.*[3]

Mattheus f. Herberti debet CCC m. pro habenda terra sicut continetur in rotulo precedenti. Hamo de Bachampton'[4] debet lxj s. et iiij^{or} d. pro transgressione patris sui. Willata de Wilton' (*Set respondet infra.*[i]) debet xxxiiij li. et xxij d. et ob. de veteri tallagio.

Margar' de Kesnet' r.c. de xij li. et viij s. et ix d. de misericordia Michaelis de Clopcot' pro perjurio. In thes. iij m. Et debet x li. et viij s. et ix d.

Galfridus Salvagius r.c. de xxx li. et xiiij s. et viij d. de ij^{bus} debitis

1 *de* repeated.
2 This line written in thinner writing, presumably added later.
3 *In thes. lib. Et Q.E.* written later.
4 The -*ch*- is written on a fold. Perhaps Bathampton?

sicut continetur in rotulo precedenti. In thes. C s. Et debet xxv li. xiiij s. et viij d. per annum x li.

Hugo Hosatus debet D m. pro deliberatione sua sicut continetur in rotulo viij. Set non debet summoneri quia R. mandavit per litteras suas (que sunt in forulo Marescalli^{i}) quod idem Hugo pacavit Willelmo de Harocurt C m. de fine illo et residuum ad scaccarium Dublinense preter xxix li. de quibus heredes ipsius Hugonis satisfacient ad predictum scaccarium baronibus ibidem residentibus terminis eis statutis. Et sic hic Q.E.

Radulfus de Sancto Germano r.c. de iiij li. et xl d. pro habendo brevi versus Robertum de Venoiz. In thes. xx s. Et debet lxiij s. et iiij d. per annum j m.

Godefridus de Alno [r.c.] de xv li. et xx d. de ij^{bus} debitis contentis in rotulo precedenti. Et de x s. de scutagio de Biham. In thes. xxv s. Et debet xiiij li. et dim. m. per annum C s.

Umfridus de Sancto Vigore [*blank*] j m. de primo scutagio R. Et [*blank*] j m. de scutagio de Mungumeri. Et j m. de scutagio de Bedef'. Et v s. de scutagio de Byham.

Villata de Wilton' r.c. de xxxiiij li. et xxij d. et ob. de veteri tallagio. In thes. lib. per j taleam de ante guerram allocatam precepto H. de Burgo Justiciarii coram baronibus de scaccario. Et Q.E.

DE PRESTITO PICTAVIE

Willelmus de Neovill' debet v m. de eodem pro Johanne de Cardovill' milite suo. Ricardus de Grimsted debet iiij m. de eodem. Walterus de Unstanvill' debet xxxviij m. de eodem. Willelmus de Feritate debet j m. de eodem. Thomas Maudoit debet xxj m. de eodem. Eustachius de Balleol' debet j m. de eodem. Thomas de Samford' debet xvj m. de eodem pro Ricardo filio suo.

Thomas Burel debet dim. m. pro habendo pone contra Robertum de Middelton'. Eustachius de Balleol' debet xl s. de scutagio Pictavie. Sibilla de Bosco debet dim. m. pro habendo pone sicut continetur in rotulo ij^{o}.

Galfridus de Mandevill' de Worðie r.c. de xij li. xix s. et viij d. et j palefrido de iij^{bus} debitis contentis in rotulo iiij^{o}. In thes. ij m. et dim. Et debet xj li. vj s. et iiij d. et j palefridum.

Magister Robertus de Lavinton' debet dim. m. pro summonendo Petro[1] sicut continetur in rotulo vj^{o}. Johannes fusor debet xxj li. pro summonendo Thoma Maudoit sicut continetur in rotulo ij^{o}.

Henricus Hosatus r.c. de xix li. et dim. m. (et ij palefridis^{i}) de ij^{bus} debitis contentis in rotulo vij^{o}. In thes. xx m. Et debet vj li. et ij palefridos. Et xxij li. et x s. deb'[2] Judeorum. per annum x m.

Mattheus (de^{c}) Wac debet x s. de scutagio de Byham. Set postea habuit quietantiam per breve R.

Hugo de Samford' r.c. de x m. pro relevio suo sicut continetur in rotulo vij^{o}. In thes. v m. Et debet v m.

1 According to *NS 51*, p. 220 this is Peter de Lamar'.

2 Possibly for *debita*, as another object of *debet*, but it is perhaps more likely that the clerk has omitted *de* by haplography, and it should read *de debitis Judeorum*.

[*Rot.* 8 *Mem.* 2]

Willelmus Talebot debet xxxiiij m. quas recepit de Walerando de Rokeford' sicut continetur in rotulo viij. Habet respectum per breve R. donec inquiratur per rotulos qui sunt apud Corf' si illas pacavit in warderoba R. J.

Willelmus de Ponte del Arch' r.c. de v m. pro habenda saisina sicut continetur ibidem. In thes. lib. Et Q.E.

Thomas de Wica debet dim. m. pro Jordano de Wica qui requirebatur in Hereford' in Wallia in rotulo precedenti.

DE PLACITIS FORESTE

Villata de Sernecot' r.c. de dim. m. pro defalta. In thes. lib. Et Q.E.

Homines Alani Basset (deb[c]) in Wititon' debent j m. pro defalta de qua Adam de Alta Ripa debet eos adquietare sicut Johannes clericus suus recognovit. Henricus de Karevill' debet xx s. pro eodem.

Villata de Eiton Meisi debet dim m. pro defalta. Ricardus Passem' debet dim. m. pro eodem. Alanus f. Warini debet dim. m. pro eodem. Villata de Tockeham debet dim. m. pro eodem.

Merleberge[1] Willelmus de Meisi de Merston' debet dim. m. pro defalta. Hugo de Kilpaec debet dim. m. pro eodem. Mildenhal' debet dim. m. pro eodem. Nicholaus de Barbefloe debet dim. m. pro habenda inquisitione. Hugo de Henton' debet dim. m. pro brullo suo sicut continetur in rotulo precedenti. Robertus f. Nigelli de Langeford debet iij[2] m. pro eodem.

Idem Vic. r.c. de j m. de villata de Luditon'. Et de v m. de villata de Periton' Abbatis. Et de dim. m. de Nicholao de Wiltesir'. In thes. lib. Et Q.E.

...*er*[3] Okeburn' Prioris r.c. de j m. pro defalta. In thes. nichil. Et abbati de Becco j m. per libertatem carte R. Et Q.E.

Gillebertus de Lasci (clericus[i]) debet x m. pro falso clamore.

DE SCUTAGIO DE MUNGUMERI

Idem Vic. r.c. de ij m. de Henrico Hosat' de Fikelden' de eodem. Et de ij m. de Radulfo Russell' de eodem. In thes. lib. Et Q.E.

Mattheus Wac debet dim. m. de eodem. Galfridus Hosatus debet ij m. de eodem. Henricus Hosatus de Littleton' debet ij m. de eodem. (*Set respondet infra.*[i]) Robertus Maudoit debet viij s. et x d. de eodem. Willelmus Cumin debet viij s. et x d. de eodem. Hugo de Champania debet dim. m. de eodem. Albreða de Boterell' habet quietantiam per breve R. de hoc scutagio. (Thomas de Sancto Vigore debet j m. de eodem[c]) *quia supra*.

Eva de Tracy r.c. de ij m. de eodem. (In thes. nichil[c]) Et de ij m. de scutagio de Bedeford'. In thes. nichil. Et Gilleb[erto] de Clara com[iti] Hereford'[4] et Glovernie iiij m. per breve R. qui habet heredem in custodia. Et Q.[5] E.

1 *Merle* / *berge* written on two lines in the margin.
2 *iij* written on alteration.
3 Margination mostly illegible, but may possibly be *Merleberge* again.
4 The clerk made a mistake here, this should be Hertford and not Hereford.
5 This word is *quieta*, and so refers back to Eva de Tracy, confirming that *Gilleb'* is

Henricus Hosatus de Littleton' r.c. de ij m. sicut supra continetur. In thes. lib. Et Q.E.

DE SCUTAGIO DE BEDEFORD'

Robertus Maudoit debet viij s. et x d. de eodem. Willelmus Cumin debet viij s. et x d. de eodem. Galfridus Hosatus debet ij m. de eodem. Hugo de Campania debet dim. m. de eodem. Godefridus[1] Escudemor debet x m. de eodem.

Henricus Hosatus (r.c.[c]) de Littleton' r.c. de ij m. de eodem. In thes. lib. Et Q.E.

Robertus de Turevill' habet quietantiam per breve R. (Thomas de Sancto Vigore debet j m. de eodem[c]) *quia supra.*

R. Sar' episcopus r.c. de lxix li. et viij d. de pluribus debitis et scutagiis contentis in rotulo precedenti. In thes. nichil. Et in perdona ipsi episcopo pro expensis quas fecit in servicio R. lxix li. et viij d. per breve R in quo particule predicti debiti continentur. Et Q.E.

Willelmus quondam comes Saresbir' r.c. de MM et C et lvij li. et xvj s. et j d. de pluribus debitis firmis et scutagiis contentis in rotulo precedenti. Et lviij li. et xv s. et v d. de debitis et catallis plurium hominum villarum teðingarum et hundredorum quorum nominibus preponitur littera *t* cum puncto preposito in rotulo quem Martinus de Pateshill' et socii sui liberaverunt in thesauro. In quo etiam continentur debita predictorum et cause debitorum. Et [*blank*] ix li. et iij s. et viij d. de partialibus debitis subscriptorum[2] in eodem itinere sicut ibidem annotatur. Et [*blank*] j m. de hundredo de Rughebergh'[3] sicut infra continetur. Et [*blank*] liiij s. et vij d. de catallis plurium contentorum ex alia parte rotuli. Et de xxxv s. et iij d. de remanenti firme comitatus de anno preterito. Et de C m. de primo scutagio R. de feodo Radulfi de Sumeri qui requirebatur in comitatu Staff' in rotulo precedenti. Et vj li. et xiiij s. quas Robertus de Crievequer Vic. suus recepit de exitibus ville de Calne dum illam habuit in manu sua sicut continetur in rotulo precedenti. Et xxx li. et xij s. bl. de firma de Ludingeland' de hoc dimidio anno qui sunt ei extensi ad xxxj li. et ix s. et ix d. num. qui requirebatur in Norf'. In thes. CC m. Et fratri Simoni Templar' apud novum templum Lond' die sabbati proxima post octabas apostolorum Petri et Pauli[4] anno R. x per manum Thome f. Rannulfi clerici. De R. Scotorum M li. ad opus R. per breve R. Et debet M et CC li. et xlviij s. et ix d. Et iiij li. et iiij s. de carrucagio assiso[5] ad ij s. in Dunewic' terra Eustachii de Vesci qui requirebatur in rotulo de carrucagio.

[*Four lines blank*]

---

for Gilleberto (dative case).

1 *Godefridus* written on alteration.

2 That is of the people listed in the roll delivered by Pateshill and his associates into the treasury.

3 The modern form of this hundred is shown as 'Potterne and Cannings' in Helen Cam, *The Hundred and the Hundred Rolls* (London, 1930), p. 284.

4 Saturday 11 July 1226.

5 *assiso* repeated.

Robertus de Maysi r.c. de xlj li. ij s. et ob. de remanenti compoti sui sicut continetur post Devon' qui requirebatur ibidem. In thes. nichil. Et in liberatione Simoni Horn de tribus annis qui habet iij d. per diem a festo Cathedre[1] Sancti Petri[2] anno regni R. viij^{o} usque ad eundem terminum anno eiusdem[3] xj^{o} xiij li. et xiij s. et ix d. per breve R. Et debet xxvij li. et viij s. et iij d. et ob.

DE OBLATIS

+ Walterus Wineman debet dim. m. pro quadam loquela ponenda coram Justic[iariis] sicut continetur in rotulo precedenti.

Idem Vic. r.c. de dim. m. de Johanne f. Simonis pro habendo pone. Et de dim. m. de Ricardo de la Folie pro licencia concordandi. In thes. lib. Et Q.E

[*One line blank*]

NOVA OBLATA

f' Homines de Corsham r.c. de xxx li. de firma ville sue de tribus partibus anni quam villam R. eis concessit cum pertinenciis tenendam ad firmam quamdiu sibi placuerit reddendo ad scaccarium per manum suam per annum xl li. In thes. lib. Et Q.S.

Idem homines debent respondere R. de C acris imbladatis ibernagio quas receperunt imbladatas post mortem Galfridi de Neovill' (sine instauro[i]) quando R. manerium illud recipiet.

Jacobus f. et heres Philippi de Lya [*blank*] xx s. pro relevio suo de terra quam tenere debet in capite de R. in Lya unde R. cepit homagium predicti Jacobi.

Walterus nepos et heres Philippi de Caleston' [*blank*] v s. (pro relevio suo[c]) pro habenda saisina terre quam idem Philippus tenuit de R. in capite in Caleston'.

Jacobus de Lavinton' [*blank*] j m. pro licencia concordandi cum Willelmo Segin.

Willelmus f. Brichtive, Reginaldus de Bosco et Johannes de Puteo r.c. de xx s. pro transgressionibus. In thes. lib. Et Q.E.[4]

Robertus de Camera qui habet filiam Rogeri Forestarii de Gravelling' [*blank*] xx s. pro habenda balliva sua in pace que eum contingit ex parte uxoris sue quam comes[5] Sar' ei dedit.

[*One line blank*]

AMERCIAMENTA DE ITINERE M. DE PATESHILL' ET SOCIORUM SUORUM

f' Hundredum de Crikelad' r.c. de xx s. pro murdro. In thes. nichil. Et

1 Initial *C* altered from *S*.
2 Thursday 22 February 1224.
3 Monday 22 February 1227.
4 *Quietus Est* written for *Quieti Sunt*.
5 Initial *C* altered from *S*.

W. comiti Sar' (xv s.[c]) xv s. et iij d. de quibus respondet supra. Et debet hundredum iiij s. et ix d.
f' Hugo Bagger r.c. de j m. de fine suo pro transgressione. In thes. nichil. Et predicto comiti dim. m. de qua respondet supra. Et debet H. dim. m.
f' Hundredum de Stappel' r.c. de xx s. pro murdro. In thes. nichil. Et predicto comiti j m. Et de[1] qua respondet ibidem. Et debet hundredum dim. m.
f' Teoðinga de[2] Kinton' com'[itis] r.c. de xx s. pro fuga Baldewini Kirie. In thes. nichil. Et predicto comiti j m. de qua respondet supra. Et debet teoðinga dim. m.
t Hundredum de Swaningberg' r.c. de ij m. pro murdro. In thes. vj s. et vj d. Et predicto comiti xvij s. et vij d. de qua respondet ibidem. Et debet hundredum ij s. et vij d.

Adam de Alta ripa r.c. de lxxvj s. de catallis Radulfi Cole. In thes. nichil. Et predicto comiti lxxvj s. de quibus respondet supra. Et A. Q.E.

Hundredum de Ambresbir' r.c. de xx s. pro murdro. In thes. iij s. Et predicto comiti xvij s. de quibus respondet supra. Et hundredrum Q.E.
f' H(un[c])eredes Egidii Hosatii et Luce de Kaning' r.c. de xlix s. quos patres eorum coronatores receperunt de placitis corone. In thes. nichil. Et predicto comiti xxiiij s. et vj d. per Galfridum filium et heredem Egidii de quibus respondet supra. Et debent heredes Luce xxiiij s. et vj d.

Idem Vic. r.c. de dim. m. de warda Willelmi fabri in Merleberg' pro fuga Roberti Taburel. Et de dim. m. de parva Cheverel pro fuga Thome Schortfrend. Et de ij m. de hundredo de Domerham pro murdro. Et de viij d. de catallis Nicholai Britton'. Et de dim. m. de teoðinga de Tudpitte pro fuga Johannis le Niwe. Et de j m. de villa de Merden' quia non habuit Nicholaum f. Gilleberti. Et de iiij s. de Roberto de Veteri Ponte tunc Vic. de catallis Godefridi Herm. Et de xx d. de catallis Osberti forestarii fugitivi. In thes. lib. Et Q.E.

Hundredum de Rugeberghe r.c. de ij m. pro murdro. In thes. nichil. Et episcopo Sar' j m. per libertatem carte R. Et predicto comiti j m. de qua respondet supra. Et hundredum Q.E.
t Teðinga de Immere r.c. de j m. pro fuga Ricardi de Immere et sociorum eius. In thes. xij s. et iiij d. Et debet xij d.

Robertus de Meisy constabularius de Merleberg' debet ij m. de hundredo de Selkele pro murdro (*Set respondet in compoto suo.*[i]). Et dim m. de teoðinga de Shaghe pro fuga Sirich' (*Set respondet ibidem.*[i]). Et dim. m. de teoðinga ville de Kenete Thom' pro fuga Edwardi de Kenet'. (*Set respondet ibidem.*[i]) Et dim. (m.[i]) de Berton' de Merleberg' pro fuga Roberti de Bischopeston' quem recepit sicut recognoscit. (*Set respondet ibidem.*[i])
d Overton'[3] Prioris Wint' debet j m. pro fuga Walkelini Golding' et Philippi

1 Altered from *deb*.
2 Altered from *r'*.
3 Some of the land was used by the bishop of Winchester to support the monks of Winchester Old Minster. This land was known as 'East Overton' but this name has since disappeared from the map. See *V.C.H. Wilts*, ii, p. 120 and *V.C.H. Wilts*, xi, 'Parishes: Overton', pp. 181–203.

Pistoris. (*d*[i]) Villata de Noneton' eiusdem prioris debet x s. pro receptamento Roberti blund' extra teoðingam.

Villa de Okeburn' Prioris r.c. de j m. pro concelamento et quia non fecit presentationem de quodam mortuo. In thes. nichil. Et abbati de Becco j m. per libertatem carte R. Et Q.E.

Villa de Merleberg' debet ij m. quia sepelierunt homines occisos sine visu coronatoris. Set constabularius respondet in compoto suo post Devon'.

Idem Vic. r.c. de j m. de Petro f. Simonis de Lavinton' quia non habuit Willelmum f. Simonis de manupastu suo. Et de j m. de teoðinga de Kanning episcopi pro fuga Willelmi Bercarii. Et de dim. m. (de teoðinga[i]) de Hocon' pro fuga Radulfi Angod'. Et de xx s. de catallis Roberti f. Rogeri suspensi. Et de x s. de theoðinga de Fiffhide Nicholai pro fuga Simonis. Et de dim. m. de Johanne f. Nigelli quia non habuit quem plegiavit. Et de dim. m. de Gervasio f. Margerie pro eodem. Et de dim. m. de Asce Lamberd pro eodem. Et de dim. m. de teoðinga de Poterne pro fuga Arnoldi fabri. Et de xxx s. et x d. de catallis eiusdem Arnaldi. Et de viij s. de catallis Edmundi del Broc fugitivi. Et de vij d. de catallis Willelmi Cuherde. Et de xx s. de hundredo de Rammesbir' pro murdro. Et de dim. m. de teoðinga de Beidon' pro fuga Gervasii de Beidon'. Et de xviij d. de catallis eiusdem Gervasii. Et de dim. m. de teoðinga de Bisshopeston' pro fuga Willelmi Dairemunt. Et de dim. (m.[i]) de Roberto de Cerisi quia non habuit quem plegiavit. Et de dim. m. de teoðinga de Wiveleford' pro fuga Walteri. Et de dim. m. de teoðinga de Veteri Saresbir' pro fuga Johannis. In thes. nichil. Et episcopo Saresbir' ix li. iiij s. et iiij d. per libertatem carte sicut continetur in rotulo vj^{o} R. J. in Gloec' et in rotulo viij eiusdem in Dorset' et Sumerset. Et Q.E.

[*One line blank*]

RESPICE IN TERGUM

[*Rot.* 8d *Mem.* I]

Idem Vic. r.c. de vj s. de catallis Philippi f. Roheis' suspensi. Et de xl d. de catallis Philippi f. Hugonis et Johannis Bieve et de exitibus terre eorum de termino R. Et de xxvij d. de catallis Roberti Sticoriis qui abiur[avit].[1] Et de xxxiij s. de catallis Walteri Grunin extra teoðingam. Et de iiij s. de catallis Willelmi Sparke fugitivi. Et de xij d. de catallis Hugonis de Wivelesford' fugitivi. Et de v s. de catallis Walteri Wad' et Rogeri Longi fugitivorum. In thes. nichil. Et W. comiti Saresbir' liiij s. et vij d. de quibus respondet ex alia parte rotuli.

Radulfus de Ralleg' debet x s. de catallis Johannis le Niewe fugitivi. Teðinga de (Petrus[i])[2] Stanton'[3] debet dim. m. pro fuga Hugonis fabri.

1 An opaque mending strip down the right hand edge of the membrane obscures the end of some lines. Possible losses are shown here as […].

2 The clerk has forgotten that this name should be in the ablative; so also with the second inserted *Petrus* a few words further along.

3 Perhaps *de* missing prior to '*Stanton*' and also prior to '*Tockham*' a few words

(*d*[i]) Teoðinga de (Petrus[i]) Tockham debet dim. m. pro fuga Hugonis de Tocham et sociorum eius. (*d*[i]) P... f. Herberti debet xx s. de catallis eiusdem Hugonis. (*γ*[i])[1] Teoðinga de Stanlegh' debet dim. m. pro fuga Willelmi Parmentarii. (*d*[i]) Teoðinga de Cumb' debet x s. pro fuga Walteri et Ricardi parcar[iorum].[2] Radulfus Gernun (*Set respondet in Essex.*[i]) debet xx s. ... de catallis Walteri le Cunte fugitivi. (*d*[i]) Hundredum de Ellestubbe (*Com' Cestr'*[i]) debet xx s. pro murdro. (*d*[i]) (Hundredum[c]) (Villata[i]) de Hakeneston' (*Com' Cestr'*[i]) debet dim. m. pro fuga Henrici Godmann. Teoðinga (*Winton' priorum*[i]) de Enedeford' debet dim. m. pro fuga ... friend. (*d*[i]) Heres Thome de Cormeilles debet vj s. de catallis Willelmi de Tudeworðe fugitivi. (*d*[i]) Teoðinga (*Com' Cestr'*[i]) de Fiffhide (debet[c]) in Ellestubbe debet dim. m. pro fuga Rogeri King et Stephani f. Ascelini. Teoðinga de Neðerehavene debet dim. m. pro fuga Willelmi Herberti. (*p*[i]) Hundredum de Kunbrige debet j m. pro murdro. (*t*[i]) Teoðinga de Maidenton' debet dim. m. pro fuga Galfridi Maloulvert. (*d*[i]) Jordanus Cocus debet dim. m. de fine suo pro falso appello per plegia Rogeri Picot et Radulfi Hervi. (*t*[i]) Teoðinga de Rolveston' debet dim. m. pro fuga Josephi f. Lieve. (*t*[i]) Teoðinga de Cumb' prebende debet dim. m. pro fuga Philippi de Cumb'.

Idem Vic. r.c. de xx s. de Teoðinga de Bultingeford' pro receptamento Ernaldi Bercarii extra teoðingam. Et de dim. m. de Teoðinga de Ambresbir' pro fuga Osberti le Beghe. In thes. nichil. Et monialibus de fonte Ebrold' ij m. per libertatem carte R. Et Q.E.

Robertus Guiun debet dim. m. pro transgressione.

Ricardus Saresbir' episcopus r.c. de xxx li. de firma de Divisis et de Rudes de toto anno. In thes. nichil. Et (in liberatione[i]) ij[or] forestariorum custodientibus[3] forestas de Chippeham et Melkesham quorum uterque habuit per diem iij ob. ab viij[o] die Januarii anno R. x[o] per totum annum integrum iiij li. et xj s. et iij d. per breve R. Et in operatione castri de Divisis xxiiij[or] li. et xiij s. et v d.[4] per breve eiusdem et per visum Nicholai prepositi et Henrici aucupis. Et debet xv s. et iiij d.

Idem episcopus r.c. de lx s. de censu foreste de Cheppeham de predicto anno. In thes. nichil. Et canonicis Sar' xij s. Et debet xlviij s.

REQUIRE COMPOTUM DE MERLEBERG' POST DEVON' QUIA NON ERAT HIC LOCUS

Humfridus de Bohun debet xl li. pro Humfrido avi sui[5] de debitis Judeorum de ij[bus] debitis Ysáác f. Cresselin'.

along as there are a two villages called Stanton St. Bernard and Stanton St. Quentin and also the village of Tockenham in Wiltshire. Note: the tithing is amerced for the flight of Hugh of Tockenham.

1 A branching sign for which this is an equivalent symbol.

2 If this denotes the men's occupation, then the extension is *parcariorum*; if their surname then *parcar'*.

3 *forestariorum* altered from *forestariis*, but *custodientibus* left unchanged.

4 Something obliterated in the middle of *v d.*

5 *avo sui* written for *avo suo*.

[*Five lines blank*]

SALOPESIR'

[J]ohannes Bonet ut custos r.c. de CC et lxv li. et xv s. de firma comitatus. In thes. nichil.

Et in elemosinis constitutis militibus de Templo j m. Et monachis de Malverne ij s. Et infirmis de Salopesbir' xxx s. Et in terris datis monachis de Weneloc xj li. in Dudinton'. Et Abbati de Haghhemann' lxxj [s.] et iiij d. in Walecot'. Et in quietantia terre de Corfham quam Walterus de Clyfford' habet per breve R. xxvij li. Et Alicie de Harocurt et Johanne sorori sue C et x s. in Alviðele. Et in villa de Bruges C s. de quibus Burgenses respondent infra. Et in villa de Salopesbir' xx li. de quibus Burgenses respondent infra. Et Roberto de Girros xxxv s. in Claverlay. Et Johanni Extraneo xj li. et x s. in Nesse et Chesseworðin. Et canonicis de Hagheman xl s. in molendino de Wrocworðin. Et monachis de Salopesbir' lx s. in terra de Eston'. Et Johanni Extraneo xij li. in terra de Wrocworðin de quibus respondet infra. Et Willelmo de Gameches xiiij li. et iij s. in Stotesdon'. Et monachis de Crokesdon' xlij s. et viij d. in Edwineie. Et in Welington' vij li. Et P. Wint' episcopo xvij li. et dim. m. in Hales ad faciend[am] ibidem domum relligionis. Et Luelino Walensi x li. in Ellemere. Et Henrico de Aldiðeleg' l s. de quarta parte anni in Egemedon'. Et in eadem villa vij li. et x s. de tribus partibus anni de quibus Vic. respondet infra. (Et in liberatione portar[ii] et vigil[um] castri de Salopesbir' x s. et x d. Et in liberatione portar[ii] et vigil[um] castri de Bruges xxx s. et v d.[c]) (*cancellantur coram baronibus quia constabularii castrorum habent certa stipendia pro custodia castrorum*[i]). Et in defalta instaur' maneriorum xxviij li. et dim. m. Et H. de Burgo Justiciario xl s. in Stratton' de dim. anno et amodo totum quamdiu R. placuerit per breve R. de quibus debet respondere. Et in reparatione turris de forinseco muro castri de Bruges que nuper cecidit et similiter veteris chimineie magne camere R. in eodem castro xiij li. xjv s. et ix d. per breve R. (et per visum Hamonis Palmerii et Ricardi Bernard'.[i]) Et Thome Maudoit constabulario castri de Bruges xxxiij li. et xj s. et iiij d. ad custodiam castri eiusdem per iij brevia R. Et eidem Thome viij m. in molendino de Werrefeld' in parte solutionis xl m. quas percipit per annum pro custodia predicta per [breve] R. Et in amputatione capitum utlaghorum x s. Et pro ferramento prisonum et justicia facienda xxiiij s. Et pro saccis et barillis ad imponendam quintamdecimam de Salopesir' et Staffordsir' et in custo posito ad ipsam quintamdecimam á Bruges usque Winton'[1] xlviij s. et viij d. per breve R. Et in emendatione castrorum de Bruges et Salopesbir' et domorum in eisdem castris x li. Et habet de superplus xix s. et j d. qui locantur ei infra in Staffordsir'.

Idem Vic. r.c. de C m. de proficuo comitatus hoc anno. (In thes.[c]) In thes. lib. Et Q.E.

Idem Vic. [*blank*] iiij li. xj s. et iij d. de ij debitis in rotulo precedenti contentis.

[1] A gerundive such as *cariandum* should be supplied here.

Burgenses de Bruges r.c. de x m. de firma ville sue. In thes. vj li. et iij s. et iiij d. Et canonicis de Bruges x s. Et Q.[S].

Burgenses de Salopesbir' r.c. de xx li. de firma ville sue. Et de x m. pro vj fugatoribus de veteri cremento eiusdem burgi. Et de v m. de novo cremento eiusdem burgi. In thes. lib. Et. Q.[S].

Idem Vic. r.c. de xvj d. de firma de Pikethorn'. Et de xij d. de Kingesland'. Et de ix s. de Bardesle. Et de iiij s. et iiij d. de minutis particulis de Claverlay. In thes. lib. Et Q.E.

Idem Vic. r.c. de iiij s. et iiij d. de cremento de novo burgo. Et de iiij s. et iiij d. de eodem cremento de anno preterito.

Johannes extraneus r.c. de C et lxiij li. de firma de Wrocworðin de pluribus annis preteritis contentis in rotulo precedenti. In thes. nichil. Et in perdona ipsi Johanni pro fideli servicio suo quod Johannes extraneus senior fecit R. J. patri R. tempore suo et postea ipsi R. tempore suo et pro magnis expensis quas temporibus predictis fecit et pro dampnis sibi illatis in servicio ipsius patris R. et R. C et lxiij li. per breve R. Et Q.E.

Idem Johannes r.c. de xij li. de eadem firma de hoc anno. In thes. nichil. Et ipsi Johanni xij li. ad se sustentandum in servicio R. quamdiu R. placuerit per idem breve. Et Q.E.

H. de Burgo [*blank*] de firma de Stratton' de dim. anno quamdiu R. placuerit.

Idem Vic. r.c. de dim. m. de Radulfo f. Willelmi. Et de dim. m. de Yerverð f. Ithel'. Et de dim. m. de Emon' fratre suo. Et de dim. m. de Ricardo de Lopinton' de scutagio de Mungumeri. In thes. lib. Et Q.E.

[*One line blank*]

[V]illata de Ellemere debet xx s. pro defalta. +Ysabell' de Ledewic debet dim. m. pro falso clamore. + Nicholaus frater Philippi de Ugeford' debet j palefridum ut sit extractus á prisona. +Richerius de Schagebir' debet v m. pro perdonatione fuge.

Willelmus f. Willelmi f. Alani [*blank*] x milia marcarum pro habenda terra patris sui sicut continetur in rotulo xvj^{o}.

Hugo de Mortuo Mari [*blank*] CCCC et xl li. et ij osturcos et j dextrarium precii xxx m. de ij^{bus} debitis contentis in rotulo precedenti. Et D et xlj li. et xv s. et viij (d.^{i}) de ij debitis contentis ibidem.

Homines de Bruges r.c. de x li. pro habenda carta de libertatibus. In thes. liberaverunt per ij taleas de ante guerram (allocatas^{i})[1] percepto[2] H. de Burgo Justiciarii coram (P. Wint' et^{c}) J. Bathon' episcopis[3] et aliis baronibus scaccarii. Et Q.[S].

Philippus de Ugeford' r.c. de v m. ut sit extractus a prisona. In thes. x s. Et debet iiij m. et xl d. per annum x s.

Walterus de Clyfford' [*blank*] x m. pro relevio suo sicut continetur in rotulo precedenti.

Gervasius Bernel et Willelmus Corbet r.c. de iij m. ut possint esse sub plegio. In thes. ij m. Et debent j m.

[J]ohannes vinitarius de Bruges debet dim. m. pro vino vendito. + Adam

[1] Perhaps altered from *allocatarum*?

[2] *percepto* written for *precepto*.

[3] Perhaps altered to *episcopo*?

de Stanford' debet dim. m. pro dissaisina. +Radulfus f. Willelmi debet dim. m. quia retraxit se. +W. Covintr' episcopus debet xx s. de catallis Roberti de Rodes fugitivi.

[T]homas Corbet r.c. de quater xx et j li. de relevio suo. In thes. xx m. Et debet lxvij li. et j m.

[A]licia de Harocurt et Johanna soror sua [*blank*] j m. de scutagio de Mungumeri.

[T]homas de Baskervill' [*blank*] v m. pro habenda inquisitione sicut continetur in rotulo vij°.

[G]odescallus de Machelin debet x li. pro abbate de Cumhir[1] sicut continetur in rotulo precedenti.

Idem Vic. r.c. de v s. et iiij d. de Baldewino Wischard' de scutagio de Mungumeri. Et de iij s. et ij d. de Thoma de Cheriton' de scutagio de Bedef'. Et de j m. de Ricardo de Chesthill' de eodem. Et de ij m. de Ricardo de Lopinton' de eodem. Et de ij m. de herede Guidonis extranei de eodem. In thes. lib. Et Q.E.

Heres Guidonis extranei debet ij m. de scutagio de Mungumeri. Adam de Brinton' debet ij m. de eodem. (Hugo de Wlenklawe (r.c.ⁱ) de j m. de scutagio de Bedeford'. In thes. lib. Et Q.E.ⁱ)[2]

Radulfus de Sanford' r.c. de j m. de eodem. In thes. dim. m. Et debet dim. m.

Idem Vic. debet vij li. et x s. de firma de Egemedon' de tribus partibus anni. Set respondet infra.

DE OBLATIS

[*Rot.* 8d *Mem.* 2]

Willelmus Pantolf r.c. de xxv li. de relevio suo contento in rotulo precedenti. In thes. C s. Et debet xx li.

Stephanus Walensis r.c. de j m. pro licencia concordandi. In thes. dim. m. Et debet dim. m.

[*One line blank*]

NOVA OBLATA

Idem Vic. r.c.[3] de vij li. et x s. de firma de Egemedon' de tribus partibus anni dum fuit in manu R. Et [*blank*] de proficuo eiusdem.

Hugo de Mortuo mari [*blank*] xx m. pro dissaisina.

Willelmus de Hodenet r.c. de xl m. pro habenda custodia terre et heredis

[1] This is what is written in the roll but in *NS 54*, p. 37 the *Abbas de Cumbir'* is shown as owing £11 for having seisin of lands in two unknown vills. This may be a reference to the abbey of Cymmer in Radnorshire in Wales.

[2] This entry is written to the right of the previous one, with an insertion mark squeezed in before it.

[3] *r.c.* repeated.

Baldewini de Hodenet quam idem B. tenet de R. in capite de honore de Mungumeri. In thes. lib. Et Q.E.

AMERCIAMENTA DE ITINERE R. CORAM R. CYCESTR' EPISCOPO ET WILLELMO DE (HOBRIG'[c]) LOND'

Idem Vic. r.c. de C s. (et dim. m.[i]) de misericordiis hominum quorum nominibus preponitur littera *t* in rotulo quem predicti liberaverunt in thesauro. In thes. lib. in xvj taleis. Et Q.E.

Hugo de Beckebir' r.c. de ij m. pro dissaisina. In thes. j m. Et in perdona ipsi Hugoni j m. per breve R. Et Q.E.

Baldewinus de Hodenet r.c. de iij m. pro eodem. In thes. xx s. Et in perdona ipsi Baldewino xx s. per breve R. Et Q.E.

Willelmus f. Galfridi de Tetteshill' debet dim. m. pro dissaisina.

[*One line blank*]

AMERCIAMENTA CORAM R. PER ROBERTUM DE LAXITON' ET WILLELMUM DE LOND'

Idem Vic. r.c. de xxvij m. et dim. et iij s. et xj d. de misericordiis hominum quorum nominibus preponitur littera t in rotulo quem predicti liberaverunt in thesauro. In thes. lib. Et Q.E.

[*Seven lines blank*]

STAFFORDSIR'

Johannes[1] Bonet ut custos r.c. de C et xl li. bl. de firma comitatus. In thes. lxxvj li. iiij s. et xj d. (et ob.[i]) bl.

Et in elemosinis constitutis militibus de Templo j m. Et eisdem xliij s. et iiij d. bl. in Kyel. Et monachis de Bordeslé x li. bl. in Terdebigge. Et canonicis de Trentham C s. in Blorton' et Cokenache. Et Willelmo de Herovill' lx s. in Wodnebir'. Et in pastura quam R. concessit Johanni extraneo viij s. et viij d. Et in vasto foreste de Sethill' ix s. Et Henrico de Waleton' xxx s. in Cestreton'. Et Willelmo de Gamach' iiij li. in Tettenhall'. Et archiepiscopo Dublinensi x li. in Pencriz. Et R. comiti Cestr' xx li. in villa novi castri sub Lima. Et gaiolario Stafford' xl s. pro liberatione sua. Et Rogero Moysant servienti itineranti per comitatum j m. Et debet vj li. et v s. et ob. bl. (Idem r.c. de[c]) qui sunt ei extensi ad vj li. et viij s. et viij d. num. Idem r.c. de eodem debito. In thes. nichil. Et in superplus quod habet supra post corpus comitatus Salopensis xix s. et j d. Et debet C et ix s. et vij d. num.

f' Idem Vic. r.c. de lx m. de proficuo comitatus hoc anno. In thes. nichil. Et ipsi Vic. pro custodia castri de Salopesbir' et comitatus lx m. Et Q.E.

[*One line blank*]

[1] The initial *J* spreads over six lines.

f' Johannes f. Philippi r.c. de ix li. de firma de Kenefar'. In thes. lib. Et Q.E.

Idem Johannes r.c. de xiij li. et dim. m. pro Rogero Gernet. In thes. xl s. Et debet xj li. et dim. m.

f' Idem Vic. r.c. de dim. m. de firma vivarii de Stafford'. Et de j m. de firma de Ruelea. Et de iij s. de exitu molendini de Craddel'. Et de C s. de cremento de Swinford' et Clent et Mere. Et de j d. de redditu Ricardi de Puteo pro j acra excolenda. In thes. lib. Et Q.E.

f' Hugo de Loges r.c. de x m. de censu foreste de Kanot. In thes. lib. Et Q.E.

f' Rogerus de Sumervill' r.c. de C s. de cremento de Alrewas.

Johannes f. Alani r.c. de C et xxxiiij li. et xij s. et ix d. de precio instauri et pro defalta instauri sicut continetur in rotulo xjº R. J. In thes. lx li. Et debet lxxiiij li. et xij s. et ix d.

Rogerus de Sumervill' r.c. de C s. de remanenti compotus sui de cremento de Alrewas sicut continetur in rotulo precedenti.

(Heres Thome de Erdinton' r.c. de MMM et CCCC et xxix li. et xiiij s. et v d. et ob.[c]) *quia infra per partes*.

Heres Thome de Erdinton' debet quinque milia marcarum pro habenda custodia sicut continetur in rotulo xvjºjº in Salopesir' per plegia scilicet comitis R. Cestr' de D m. (*Set respondet in Linc' in rotulo sequenti.*[i]), Huberti de Burgo de CCC m (*Set habet quietantiam per breve R.*[i]), Hugonis de Bailloel de C m. (*Set respondet in Norhumb' in rotulo sequenti.*[i]), Henrici de Tracy de C m. (*finivit*[1] *in Devon'*[i]), Brianum[2] de Insula de xxx m., Fulconem f. Warini de C m. (*Set respondet in Bercsir' in rotulo sequenti.*[i]) Willelmum de Huntingefeld de C m. (*mortuus est*[i]), Rob' de Roppel' de C m. (*mortuus est*[i]), Phil' de Kime de C m. (*Set respondet in Linc' in rotulo sequenti.*[i]), Galfr' de Lucy de C m. (*finivit*[i]), Nich' de Verdon' de xxx m. (*Set respondet in Warrw' in rotulo sequenti.*[i]), Walterum[3] de Dunestanvill' de CC m. (*Set respondet in Salop'.*[i]), Ric' de Munfichet de C m (*mortuus est*[i]), Walterus[4] de Clifford' de C m. (*mortuus est*[i]), Willelmum[5] de Mandevill' de C m. (*mortuus est*[i]), Johannem de Monem' de C m., Hug' de Mortemer de lx m. (*mortuus est*[i]), Rogerum Lazuche de lx m., Henr' de Véér de xx m. (*mortuus est*[i]), Willelmum Rufum de xxx m., Walterum de Lascy de CC m., Johannem f. Hugonis de C m. (*mortuus est*[i]), Rob' Marmiun de C m. (*mortuus est*[i]) sicut annotatur in originali anni xv.

Idem heres r.c. de vj li. et xvj s. et viij d. bl. de remanenti firme de Stafford' extensis ad vij li. et vij d. num. de (dim.[i]) anno xvij. Et de dim. m.

1 *finivit* written in full (and again for Geoffrey de Lucy below). This shows that in this passage at least the abbreviation *resp'* (which is extended here to the traditional *respondet*) may in fact be the past tense *respondit*.

2 *Brianum* written for *Briani*; the next two names, *Fulconem* and *Willelmum*, are also in the accusative, but the four following names are too abbreviated to show case endings.

3 Written in the accusative: *Walt'm*.

4 Written in the nominative: *Walt's*.

5 Written in the accusative: *Will'm*. Several of the following names are also clearly accusative.

de firma de Rueleg' de eodem dim. anno. Et de xviij d. de exitu molendini de Craddeleg' de eodem termino. Et de viij li. et ix s. et ij d. de firma terre de Burford' sicut continetur in rotulo xvj°. Et de xxx li. pro habenda custodia terre Ricardi de Stratton'. Et de v m. pro Johanne de Samford' pro dissaisina. Et de ix li. et vij s. et x d. de minutis particulis foreste. Et de C et xiij s. et iij ob. de remanenti firme comitatus de Salopesir' de dim. anno xvij. Et de xviij li. de scutagio Pictavie de feodis Galfridi de Véér. Et de xvj li. de feodis eiusdem de novo feffamento. Et de C s. pro Willelmo Pantolf'. Et (de[i]) lxx s. et viij d. de catallis plurium. Summa C et vj li. et ij d. et ob. In thes j m. Et in ij^{bus} rotulis precedentibus xvj s. et viij d. de eadem summa. Et debet C et iiij li. et x s. et ij d. et ob.

Magister Johannes de Rammesbir' debet iij palefridos pro habendis litteris. + Anora Mauban debet xx m. pro habendo precipe versus Thomam Basset.

Herveus Bagod r.c. de v m. pro dissaisina. In thes. lib. Et Q.E.

Idem Vic. r.c. de j m. de Ricardo de Puteo. Et de lxiij s. et iiij d. de Roberto de Sardon'. Et de dim. m. de francoplegio Nicholai Cuvarii. Et de dim. m. de Nicholao de Dokeseia. Et de xvij s. et vij d. de hundredo de Offelawe. Et de xx s. de Petronilla que fuit uxor Walteri de Keningeford' que requirebatur in Wigorn' in rotulo precedenti. Et de iiij li. de Thoma Corbet pro relevio suo. In thes. lib. Et Q.E.

Jordanus de Kanot [debet][1] ij s. et viij d. ut deliberetur a prisona. +Simon f. Henrici debet xiij li. et xix s. et v d. pro habendo brevi. Heres Willelmi de Canvill' debet ij m. de primo scutagio R. Henricus de Aldiðeleg' debet j spervarium mutarium ut scribatur. Villata de Peinchill' debet ij s. et iiij d. pro murdro. Francoplegium Ricardi de Porta debet dim. m. pro fuga. Francoplegium Johannis carrucarii in Tunstal' debet dim. m. pro fuga Roberti.

Heres Rogeri de Benetleg' r.c. de iij m. ut deliberetur a prisona. In thes. dim. m. Et debet ij m. et dim. per annum dim. m.

Unfridus de Branteston' r.c. de xx s. quia retraxit se. In thes. dim. m. Et debet j m.

Henricus de Aldiðeleg' [*blank*] iiij li. et xij s. et ix d. de catallis plurium.

Ricardus Fleghe debet dim. m. pro dissaisina. + Adam Bidulf' debet xx s. ut sit sub plegio. Ricardus de Puteo debet j m. pro habenda inquisitione versus Robertum de Puteo. Henricus de Bermundescot' r.c. de x s. pro pluribus transgressionibus. In thes. xl d. Et debet dim. m.

H. archiepiscopus Dublinensis r.c. de C m. pro Willelmo de Cusac sicut continetur in rotulo viij°. In thes. nichil quia J. Furnensis[2] episcopus thesaurarius R. in Hibernia significavit R. per litteras suas patentes quod predictus Willelmus reddidit ad scaccarium R. Dublinense tempore quo G.[3] de Mariscis fuit alias Justiciarius hibernie C m.

Ideo hic Q.E. per breve.[4]

[1] No space left for a verb, which is supplied here by comparison with those in the rest of the section.

[2] John de St. John was Lord High Treasurer of Ireland 1217–32 and bishop of Ferns 1223–53.

[3] This is Geoffrey de Marisco who was justiciar of Ireland from 1215 to 1221.

[4] *Ideo hic Q.E.* spread out at the end of the line in the same format as *In thes. nichil*

Hugo de Logis r.c. de lx s. de remanenti firme sue de anno preterito. In thes. ij m. et dim. Et debet ij m.

Idem H. debet viij m. et dim. de ij debitis contentis in rotulo viij.

Ricardus de Pakinton' r.c. de xviij s. et v d. de padnagio. In thes. dim. m. Et debet xj s. et ix d. per annum dim. m.

Idem R. et heredes Rogeri de Lisewis r.c. de C et xix s. et iiij d. de padnagio. In thes. xl s. Et debent lxxix s. et iiij d. per annum xl s.

[*One line blank*]

AMERCIAMENTA CORAM R. PER ROBERTUM DE LAXITON'

ET WILLELMUM DE LOND'

Idem Vic. r.c. de xxv m. et dim. de misericordiis hominum quorum nominibus preponitur littera t in rotulo quem predicti liberaverunt in thesauro. In thes. lib. Et Q.E.

Robertus pistor de Burton' debet dim. m. pro plegio Henrici f. Willelmi.

[*Endorsed*] Wilteschire: (emend'[i]) Et in Dorso Salopesir': (emend[i]) Et Staffordschire: (emend' et iterum emend' totum[i])

[*Rot.* 9 *Mem.* 1]

[*The writing on the bottom right hand edge of the membrane has been obscured by tape.*]

LANCASTR'

Willelmus[1] comes de Ferrar', Robertus de Muntiai ut custos r.c. de C et (lviij li. et ij s. et viij d.[c]) (lxxiiij li. et vij s. et xiiij d. et ob.[i]) de firma honoris de Lancastr'. In thes. nichil.

Et in terris datis Roberto f. Roberti Salvag' ix li. in Steineby. Et Willelmo de Greseleg' iiij li. et xvj s. in Drakelawe. Et Willelmo Maresc' xxij li. in Kartmel. Et Ricardo f. Yerverð de Hilton' xxiiij s. in Penelton'. Et Rogero de Huntingefeld' xv li. in Mendham. Et in villa de Lancastr' xx m. de quibus homines ville respondent infra. Et heredibus Willelmi de Valoinnes x li. in Corfho'. Et Turstano Banastr' xj li. et xj s. et iiij d. in Makeresfeld'. Et Willelmo Colmose xxiiij s. in Hamelton' quamdiu R. placuerit. Et in duabus carrucatis terre quas R. J. dedit canonicis de Cokersand' xvj s. de quibus respondet infra. Et in vasto ville de Smethedon' quam R. J. vastavit pro haya de Tocstaðe j m. Et Galfrido Balistario xliiij s. in Haconeshou et Pessore. Et in Wellingore in terra que fuit Victoris de Wellingore lviij s. Et in Croxton' in terra que fuit (Roberti[c]) (Hugsonis[i])[2] janitoris xiij li. Et ibidem in terra que fuit Willelmi de Sancto Albino x m. (et dim.[c]) Et Anselmo de Watenes xiij

---

Et Q.E. is arranged.

[1] The first letter is two lines high and has been written with a flourish.

[2] There is what appears to be a letter *s* between the 'g' and the 'o' in *Hugonis. NS 56*, p. 140 has *Hugonis* for Hugh.

li. in Naveneby de ballio R. sicut continetur in brevi eiusdem quod est in forulo marescalli in anno v°. (Et comiti de Dereb' x li. de tercio denario comitatus quas Vic. Lanc' solebat recipere per annum per manum Vic. de Notingeh' ad firmam comitatus Lancastr' sicut continetur in rotulo primo R. J[c]) (quia infra[i]). Et Ricardo f. Yerverð de Hilton' xviij s. in Boulton'. Et heredibus Ricardi f. Rogeri in Birstathbrening' xvj s. Et eisdem xij s. in Kelgrimesareghe que duo sunt membra de Sengelton'. Et monachis de Deulacresse C s. in pastura de Rosshale quamdiu R. placuerit. Et in defalta x li. quas Vic. Lancastr' solebat recipere per annum per manum Vic. de Notingeh' ad firmam comitatus Lancastr' que date sunt comiti de Ferrar' sicut continetur in rotulo primo R. J. x li. Et in quietantia terre Johannis constabularii Cestr' lxx s. de Sakefech. Et Ricardo de Mide iiij li. et x s. in Hales de quibus respondet infra. Et Henrico de Waleton' xl s. in Waleton' de quibus respondet infra. Et Roberto de Crosseby x s. de quibus respondet infra. Et Robertus Malet vij s. et vj d. ibidem de quibus respondet infra. Et Gilleberto de Waleton' xx s. in Wavretre de quibus respondet infra. Et Henrico de Waleton' xxviij s. in Forneby de quibus respondet infra. Et in burgo de Preston' vj li. de quibus homines ville respondent infra. Et priori de Lithum ix s. et ij d. et ob. in Lithum de dono R. J. Et Q.E.

f' (*Wap' de Salford'*)[1] Idem W.[2] r.c. de xxiij s. de villa de Salford' de redditu assiso. Et de xlviij s. de redditu assiso de Burton'. Et de xxxij s. de redditu assiso de Ordeshal'. Et de iiij s. de redditu assiso de Cadewallessiet'. Et de ij s. de redditu assiso de Schoresworðe. Et de iiij s. de Tonge de eodem. Et de xxvj s. de firma terre Augustini de Barton'. Et de xvij s. et viij d. de firma terre Willelmi de Radeclive. Et de j m. de firma terre Rogeri de Middelton' in Chetham. Et de xxiiij s. de firma terre Roberti de Prestewich' in Prestwich' et Heton'[3] et Selesworðe. Et de x s. de firma terre Alexandri de Pilkinton' in Runton'. Et de v s. de firma terre Jordani decani in Overholm et Slorenholm. Et de x s. de firma terre Ade de Pennebir' in Pennebir'. Et de vj s. de firma terre Willelmi f. Rogeri de Radich' in Radich'. Et de xx s. de firma terre Gospatric in Cherlton'. Et de v s. de firma terre Roberti f. Radulfi de Traford' in Trafford'. Et de xxiiij s. de firma terre Willelmi f. Willelmi de Ricton' in Ricton'. Et de xx s. de firma terre Willelmi de Jeovill' et Gerardi de Canvill'. Et de x s. de firma medietatis de Flixton'. Et de xx s. de firma terre Hugonis Norrensis in Blacrode. Et de viij s. de firma de Clyfton'. Summa: xvj li. et xij s.

f' Idem W. r.c. de x s. de Sakfie de terra Rannulfi f. Rogeri. Et de ij m. de eodem de feodo Rogeri de Monte begonis. Et de xviij d. de eodem de medietate de Flixton'. Et de lx s. de eodem de terra Roberti Greslé. Summa: iiij li. et xviij s. et ij d.

[1] This appears in the margin underneath '*f*''. It is on three separate lines with *Salford'* spread onto two lines.

[2] That is William Earl Ferrers.

[3] *a* or (less likely) *o* blotted after *e*.

IN WAPENT' DE WEST DEREB'

f' Idem W. r.c. de iiij li. et xvj s. de redditu assiso de Overton' cum exten(sione[i]) operum villanorum eiusdem ville de terris quas tenent in villenagio in eadem villa. Et de lx s. de redditu assiso de Waleton'. Et de C et v s. de villenagio R. in Crosseby. Et de x s. de redditu assiso Roberti de Crosseby qui libere tenet[1] in eodem manerio. Et de vij s. et vj [d.] de redditu assiso Roberti Malet qui tenet eodem modo ibidem. Et de (vij li. d.[c]) iiij li. et x s. de redditu assiso de Hales quam Ricardus de Mide tenet per cartam R. J. Et de l s. de[2] cremento eiusdem manerii. Et (de[i]) xx s. de redditu assiso de Wavertre. Et de dim. m. de cremento eiusdem. Et de ix li. de redditu assiso de Lieverpol. Et de lxxij s. et vj d. de redditu assiso de West Dereb'. Et de xx s. de redditu assiso in Lathum pro theinagio. Et de xxj s. et iiij d. de redditu assiso[3] de Bolde pro theinagio. Et de xx s. de redditu asssiso de Ditton' pro theinagio. Et de xx s. de redditu assiso de Gerstan' pro theinagio. Et de j m. de theinagio de Thingwell'. Et de (xx[c]) (x[i]) s. de Ricardo Walensi de theinagio in Upletherland'. Et de xxij s. de Henrico de Melling' de theinagio in Melling' et Uppholand'. Et de xx s. de (Ricardo[c]) (Adam[i]) de Mulinell' de theinagio de Litherland'. Et de xviij s. de Alano de Hoiland' de theinagio de Hoiland' et Aintre et Barton'. Et de v s. de Alano f. Bernolf' de theinagio in Bikerstath. Et de j m. de Ricardo f. Rogeri de theinagio in Forneby et Bolde. Et (He[c]) de xxviij s. de Henrico de Waleton' de redditu assiso de Forneby quam tenet per cartam R. J. Et de dim. m. de eodem H[enrico] de cremento. Summa: xlv li. et xv s. et v d.[4]
f' Idem r.c. de xj s. et x d. de Sakefie de feodo Willelmi pincerne. Et de iij s. de eodem de feodo Bussell' in Kirkedal'. Et de vj s. de eodem de Adam de Molinell'. Summa: xx s. et x d.
[*One line blank*]

IN WAPENT' DE AUGMODERNESS'

f' Idem Vic. r.c. de xv li. de redditu assiso burgi de Preston' per cartam R. H. secundi. Et de iij s. de firma cuiusdam domus qui fuit Hervei suspensi. Et de xxviij s. de dominico de Singelton'. Et de ix s. de (dominico[c]) (redditu assiso[i]) de Riggeby. Et de vj s. de redditu assiso de Wra. Et de iiij li. et x s. et x d. de redditu assiso de Brocton' cum extensione operationum et consuetudinum. Et de xx s. de redditu abbatis de Cokersand' pro ij carrucatis terre de Neubigging'. Et de x s. de redditu Theobaldi Walteri quos reddere debet per annum vel j osturcum sorum. Et de xx s. de redditu Henrici de Lea. Summa: xxiiij li. vj s. et x d.
f' Idem W. r.c. de xl s. de Waltero f. Osberti de iij carrucatis terre in Salewic et Clifton' et v carrucatis terre in Plumton' et Westby et ij carrucatis terre in Berton' quas tenet in theinagio. Et de xvij s. et v d. et ob. de heredibus Ricardi f. Rogeri in Plumton' de iiij carrucatis terre quas tenet in theinagio. Et de xx s. de Roberto de Winequike de v carrucatis terre

1 *liberetenet* written as one word.
2 There is writing over something rubbed out from the beginning of this line.
3 There is another sign here of uncertain significance.
4 Really £45 5s. 4d.

in Torrenton' et dimidia carrucata in Stainhol quas tenet in theinagio. Et de x s. de Petro de Stalmin de iij carrucatis terre in Stalmin de theinagio. Et de xviij s. et viij d. de heredibus Roberti f. Bernardi quem redditum sic reddere debet per annum vel xij s. cum j osturco soro vel dim. m. pro eo de xij bovatis terre in Gosannesareghe de theinnagio. Et de xvij s. de Rogero de Heton'. Et de v s. de Swano de Hudereshal'. Et de iiij (s.[i]) de Petro de Burnhul de dim. carrucata terre in Alston' de theinagio. Et de viij s. de Henrico de Hoiland' in Ribbelton' de theinagio. Et de viij[1] s. de Elya de Hoton' de dimidia carrucata in Middelarghe de theinagio.[2] Et de x s. de herede Arthuri de Aschton' de j carrucata in Aschton' de Drengag'. Et de ij s. de Alano de Singelton' in Billesburg' in Drengag'. Et de v s. de Johanne de Steinhol' de j carrucata in Steinhol' de Dreng'. Et de ij s. de Ricardo de Halechton' de ij bovatis terre in Dreng'. Summa: viij li. vij s. et iij ob.
f' Idem. r.c. de dim. m. de feodo Willelmi Pincerne de Sakefie. Et de j m. de feodo Theberti Walteri de eodem. Et de ij s. de Adam de Mereton' de eodem. Summa: xxij s.

WAPENT' DE LONESDAL'

f' Idem. r.c. de vij s. et vj d. de redditu assiso de Overton'. Et de ij m. de redditu assiso de Middelton'. Et de vij s. et vj d. de redditu assiso x bovatarum terre in Skerton'. Et de lxxij s. de redditu assiso de Sline membra de Skerton'. Et de iij m. et dim. de redditu assiso de Boulton'. Et de xx s. de redditu molendini de Boulton'. Et de (Stapelthier[c]) xl s. de redditu assiso de Stapelthiern'. Et de viij s. de redditu assiso de Hest. Et de xx s. de Caton'. Et de v s. de Bolrum. Et de v s. de redditu terre molendini de Lanc'. Et de x s. de terra Gilleberti de Croft (de theinagio[i]) . Et de xv s. de redditu Ade f. Osberti et Willelmi f. Orm (de eodem[i]). Et de xvj s. de redditu de Bar (de eodem[i]) . Et de iiij s. de redditu de Clahtun' (de eodem[i]). Et de iij s. et iiij (d[i]) de redditu terre Gillemichhiel. Et de xv s. de Waltero de Parles in Poulton'. Et de x li. de redditu Michaelis de Forneis'. Et de xviij s. de Tatham et Ireby de heredibus Ricardi f. Walthief' de j carrucata in Tatham et j carrucata in Irreby. Et de xxx s. de redditu vaccariarum positarum ad firmam. Et de dim. m. de firma de Luceldal'. Et de lxij d. de firma cuiusdam domus escaete in Lanc'. Et de viij li. de (firma[c]) exitu molendini Lanc' hoc anno. Summa: xxxvj li. xvij s. et iiij d.
f' Idem. r.c. de x s. de redditu assiso j^{us} carrucate terre in Wapent' de Lailondesir' quam Ricardus de Thorp' tenet. Summa: x s. Summa summarum: C et xxxix li. et ix s. et viij d. et ob.

[3]In thesauro: C et xxxj li. et xvj s. Et iterum xv li. et iiij (s.[i]) de iiij firmis contentis in rotulo precedenti. Et habet de superplus vij li. et x s. et iij d. et ob. qui locantur ei infra.
[*One line blank*]

[1] It looks as if the clerk wrote something like 'Wiij' here. It is possible that he meant 'xviij'.
[2] There is a large smudge over the 'g' in '*theinag*''. It is possible this was intended, or was a later rubbing out.
[3] This line starts considerably more indented than the others so it is shown as such.

Idem. r.c. de Cl m. de proficuo comitatus de anno preterito et tribus partibus anni viij. In thes. nichil. Et ipsi comiti pro custodia castrorum de Lancastre et West Dereb' et comitatus de predicto tempore C m. per breve R. Et debet (l^{i})[1] m. Set respondet infra in (prima linea^{i}).
(*f'* Idem Vic. r.c. de lxx m. de proficuo comitatus hoc anno. Et de l m. de proficuo comitatus sicut supra continetur. In thes. nichil. Et ipsi comiti pro custodia predictorum castrorum et comitatus quater xx li.^{c}) quia infra.

Idem Vic. r.c. de lxx m. de proficuo comitatus de hoc anno. Et de l m. de remanenti proficui sicut supra continetur. Et de C et xiiij li. de wardis militibus (deb'^{c}) eiusdem honoris debitis de hoc anno et ij annis preteritis. In thes. nichil.

[2]Et comiti de Ferrar' C li. pro custodia castrorum predictorum C li. de hoc anno (et sicut^{c}) per breve R. in quo continetur quod sic locentur ei C li. singulis annis quamdiu predictus comitatus et predicta castra fuerint in manu sua per preceptum R.

Et debet quater xx et xiiij li. Idem r.c. de eodem debito. In thes. nichil. Et in superplus quod habet supra vij li. et x s. et iij d. et ob. Et debet quater xx et vj li. et ix (d^{c}) (s.^{i}) (et ob.^{c}) et viij d. et ob.

Idem Vic. r.c. de CC et xliiij li. et xxiij d. et ob. de supra scriptis firmis eiusdem honoris de tribus partibus anni viij et toto anno preterito. In thes. in anno preterito de firma eiusdem honoris xliij li. et viij d. de predicto tempore. Et vj s. de firma ij burgagiorum in Preston' de predicto tempore. Et xl s. de firma abbatis de Cokersand' de eodem tempore. Et xxviij li. de cremento maneriorum de predicto tempore. Et ij s. de redditu cuiusdam domus in Lancastr' de eodem tempore. Et in emendatione castrorum de Lancastr' et West Dereb' xvij li. et x s. sicut continetur in rotulo precedenti. Et debet C et liij li. et iij s. et iij d. et ob.
[*One line blank*]
f' Homines de Lancastr' r.c. de xx m. de firma ville sue. In thes. lib.
Et Q.E.[3]
f' Willelmus de Lancastr' r.c. de iij m. et dim. de firma de Neuby in Westmeriland'. In thes. lib. Et Q.E.

R. comes Cestr' debet iiij li. et xvij s. de remanenti firme comitatus de quarta parte anni preteriti. Et xl s. pro abbate de Cokersand'. Et xl s. pro Rogero f. Roberti pro habenda saisina sicut continetur in rotulo precedenti. Set respondet post Linc' de omnibus hiis debitis.

Homines de Lanc' debent xiij m. de remanenti firme ville sue de anno xvij R. J.

Willelmus de Lanc' r.c. de viij milibus et CCCC et lxvj li. et iiij s. et vj d. et ob. de pluribus debitis contentis in rotulo precedenti. In thes. lxxv m. Et debet viij milia et CCCC et xvj li. et iiij s. et vj d. et ob.
per annum l m.
+ Johannes del Hec debet dim. m. de misericordia foreste. Ricardus de Riblecestr' debet xx li. et dim. m. de ij debitis contentis in rotulo vj^{o}.

1 This is written above an erasure.
2 This line and the next in the text both start considerably more indented than the others.
3 *Quietus Est* written for *Quieti Sunt*.

+ Alexander le Wilde debet j m. de misericordia. Alexander de Folrich debet iiij s. pro falso clamore. Ysabella que fuit uxor Rannulfi de Meresia debet xxvij m. et j palefridum ut non distringatur per plegium Hugonis de Neovill' forestarii sicut continetur in originali anni ix R. J. + Adam f. Elye debet ij s. et viij d. pro falso clamore. + Rogerus Lespiecier debet dim. m. pro vino vendito. + Willelmus Rufus debet dim. m. pro dissaisina. + Wilekinus Rufus debet ij s. pro eodem. + Thomas de Bedeford' debet xij d. pro eodem. Henricus f. Elye debet ij s. pro iniusta detentione. Hamo de Mascy debet x m. pro dissaisina. Turstanus Banastr' (set respondet infra[i]) debet quater xx et x m. pro habenda saisina sicut continetur in rotulo iij[o]. Adam de Penebir' debet x m. pro habenda ballia, set non debet summoneri quia non habuit nec habere potuit pro quo promisit. Brunus frater Ricardi Coci debet dim. m. pro dissaisina. + Hugo Ybain debet dim. m. pro eodem. + Thomas Dogget debet dim. m. pro eodem.

Milites de honore de Lancastr' debent quater xx et xvij li. et j d. de scutagio Pictavie. Et liij li. et xv s. et ij d. de primo scutagio R.

DE SCUTAGIO DE MUNGUMERI

Idem Vic. r.c. de iiij m. de Willelmo Esturmi de eodem. Et de iiij m. de Ricardo de Preston' de eodem. Et de ij m. de Philippo de Hasting' de eodem. Et de j m. de Willelmo de Valeines de eodem. In thes. lib.

Et Q.E.

W. episcopus Carleol' r.c. de j m. pro Ricardo de Fornell' de eodem. Et de j (y[d]) m. de (Ricardo[c]) de scutagio de Bedef'[1] pro eodem. Et de iiij s. et v d. et ob. pro eodem. R. de vj[a] parte j feodi in Wellingore. Et de iiij s. et v d. et ob. de scutagio de Bedeford' pro eodem. In thes. nichil. Et (ipsi[c]) in perdona ipsi episcopo xxxv s. et vij d. per breve R. Et Q.E.

[*Rot.* 9 *Mem.* 2]

[*One line blank*]

[2]Radulfus Frasier r.c. de j m. de eodem. In thes. dim. m. Et debet dim. m.

Willelmus pincerna debet (dim.[c]) ij m. et dim. de eodem. Galfridus Trussebut debet (dim.[c]) (j[i]) m. de eodem sicut continetur in rotulo precedenti. Leonius de Maunoers debet iiij m. de eodem. Philippus de Aubineio debet ij m. de eodem pro Galfrido monacho. Robertus f. Willelmi debet ij m. de eodem. Radulfus de Sancto Georgio (debet[c]) et Johannes de Isennii et Willelmus de la Basoche debent xvj s. et x d. et ob. de eodem. Willelmus Esturmi debet ij m. de eodem de j feodo quod non recognoscit. Thorp Bussel debet ij m. de eodem. Adam de Cokefeld' debet j m. de eodem. Thomas de Muleton' debet ij m. de eodem pro Ricardo de Fliet' (set postea habuit quietantiam per breve R. in Lincolnesir'[i]). Rogerus de Huntingef'

[1] There is some stitching below here which affects the next line as well. The stitching was done after the original writing as one of the stitches has been made over one or more words in the text.

[2] There is a fold here across most of the membrane. It obscured some of the text.

debet ij m. de eodem. Galfridus de Saukevill' iiij m. de eodem de ij feodis que non recognoscit. Robertus de Quency debet ij m. de eodem de j feodo quod non recognoscit. Heredes Galfridi Luterell' debent xvij s. et ix d. de eodem. (DE SCUTAGIO DE BEDEFORD[c])

Idem Vic. r.c. de j m. de Henrico falconario de (scutagio de Mungumeri[i].) Et de iiij[1] s. et v d. de Ricardo de Hilton' de eodem. Et de xxiij d. de Adam de Middelton' de eodem. In thes. lib. Et Q.E.

[2]*t* Galfridus Carbonel r.c. de j m. de (scutagio de Bedeford'[i]). In thes. dim. m. Et debet dim. m.

t Advocatus de Betun r.c. de j m. de eodem. In thes. dim. m. Et debet dim. m.

t Radulfus Frasier' r.c. de j m. de eodem. In thes. dim. m. Et debet dim. [m.]

[3]*d* Ricardus de Preston' r.c. de iiij m. de eodem. In thes. xl s. Et debet j m.

d Willelmus Esturmi r.c. de iiij m. de eodem. In thes. xl s. Et debet j m.

d Idem debet ij m. de j feodo quod non recognoscit.

[4]*d* Hugo Malet debet ij m. de eodem. (*d*[i]) Galfridus Trussebut debet j m. de eodem. (*d*[i]) Thorp Bussel debet ij m. de eodem. (*d*[i]) Adam de Cokefeld' debet j m. de eodem. (*d*[i]) Rogerus de Huntingefeld' debet ij m. de eodem. (*d*[i]) Galfridus de Saukevill' debet iiij m. de[5] eodem de ij feodis que non recognoscit. (*d*[i]) Robertus de Quency debet ij m. de eodem de j feodo quod non recognoscit. (*d*[i]) Hubertus de Burgo debet xvij s. et ix d. de eodem in Croxton'. Robertus de Crevequer habuit quietantiam per breve R. de j feodo quod Philippus de Hasting' tenet.

Radulfus de Sancto Georgio et Johannes de Iseinny r.c. de ix s. et viij d. et ob. de eodem. In thes. iiij s. et v d. per Radulfum. Et debet (d[i]) Johannes v s. et iij d. et ob.

Rannulfus de Sules [*blank*] C li. pro venatione inventa.

Turstanus Banastr' r.c. de quater xx et x m. pro habenda saisina sicut supra continetur. In thes. liberavit per ij^{as} tal' factas ante guerram et allocatas per preceptum R. et H. de Burgo justiciarii coram baronibus de scaccario. Et Q.E.

NOVA OBLATA

Simon f. Willelmi debet C s. pro relevio[6] suo de feodo j militis quod tenet in capite de R. in Gringelthorp.

Willelmus de Carleton' avunculus Ricardi f. et heredis Margar' de Torint'[7] r.c. de vj m. pro habenda custodia terre et heredis ipsius M. que de R. tenet in capite cum maritagio eiusdem heredis. In thes. lib. Et Q.E.

[1] The 'g' of 'Mungumeri' interferes with the numbers of shillings, but this is definitely '*iiij s.*'.

[2] The following entries are written on the left hand side of the membrane.

[3] The following entries are written on the right hand side of the membrane.

[4] The following entries are written right across the membrane.

[5] The word *de* is repeated on separate lines.

[6] For the fine giving Simon his relief, see *Calendar of Fine Rolls*, II, 1224–34, p. 64, no. 33.

[7] For the fine giving William of Carlton his lands that his mother Margaret of

Idem Vic. r.c. de dim. m. de Galfrido monacho de scutagio de Bedef'. Et de j m. de abbate de Grimesby et monialibus de Cotum de eodem. Et de j m. de Willelmo de Valeines de eodem. Et de iiij s. et v d. de Ricardo de Hilton' de eodem. Et de xxiij d. de Adam de Middelton' de eodem. In thes. lib. Et Q.E.

Willelmus de Lancastr' heres Gilleberti f. Reinfr' debet xxxix li. xiiij s. et v d. pro Thoma de Muleton' quos Adam de Yeland' ballivus eiusdem Gilleberti recepit de fine Ade de Morevill' sicut rec' sicut continetur in Linc' in rotulo precedenti. Et j osturcum pro habenda feria sicut continetur in rotulo precedenti in Everwicsir'.

[*Six lines blank*]

KANTIA

Hubertus de Burgo Rogerus de Grimeston' ut custos pro eo r.c. de CCCC et xij li. et vij s. et vj d. bl. Et de C et lxv li. et j m. num. de firma de Kent. In thes. nichil. Et in superplus quod habet infra C et lxv li. et j m. num.

Et in elemosinis constitutis militibus de Templo ij m. Et monachis de Sancto Augustino x li. in Middelton'. Et infirmis de Roffa xlj s. et v d. in servicio Stephani de Norwud'. Et in liberationibus constitutis portario civitatis Cant' xx s. quia facit justiciam civitatis.[1] Et in terris datis militibus de Templo vj li. bl. in Dele. Et eisdem xiij li. bl. in Stroda. Et in villa de Derteford' abbati de Sancto Johanne x li. bl. Et heredibus Willelmi Malet C et viij s. bl. in Derteford'. Et monachis de Favresham C li. bl. in Favresham. Et canonicis Sancti Bernardi viij li. bl. in Chiselherst. Et in Dovor' xxiiij li. bl. de quibus compotus debet reddi per se. Et militibus de Templo xx s. in Kingeswode. Et canonicis de Meriton' xxx s. in Sutton'. Et Alicie de la Barbecan' v s. pro escambio terre sue. Et monialibus de Scapeie xxxix s. et iij d. in consuetudinibus terre Joscelini. Et ecclesie Christi Cant' xxv li. in Middelton'. Et eidem ecclesie xxxvij s. in Berkesores. Et infirmis de Herebaudon' xx m. Et hospitali de Blien C s. in Leiesdon' ad inveniendos ij capellanos et clericos eorum imperpetuum in obsequio hospitalis. Et Osberto Giffard' xxxij li. in Ailesford'. Et hospitali Sancte Marie de Strode xij d. in ij^{bus} partibus bosci qui est iuxta Malling'. Et monachis ecclesie Christi Cant' l s. in bosco de Blien. Et monialibus de Fonte Ebroldi iiij s. in Middelton' in servicio Henrici de Schorn'. Et canonicis de Liesnes xx s. in terra que fuit Gilleberti de Focarmund'. Et Thome f. Willelmi de Moriston' l s. in Middelton' sicut continetur in rotulo iiij^{o} R. J. Et fratribus hospitalis Jer'l'm in Sutton' vij li. et v s. bl. in terra quam G. f. Petri dedit Willelmo de Wrotham. Et eisdem fratribus C s. bl. in Derteford'. Et eisdem iiij li. in terra que fuit Gilleberti de Focarmunt. Et in willa de Derteford' quater xx et iij li. (et x s.[i]) bl. de quibus Thomas de Gillingeh' respondet infra.

Et Willelmo de Hardr' constabulario Cant' x m. per breve R. de termino Sancti Michaelis anno R. ix^{o} de xx m. quas á R. percipit per annum pro

---

Thornton held in chief see *Calendar of Fine Rolls*, II, 1224–34, p. 64, no. 75.

1 In *NS 54*, p. 143 it is shown as *civitatis* as above but in *NS 48*, p. 200 and in *NS 56*, p. 94 it is *comitatus*.

custodia castri Cant'. Et ballivis portus Dovor' xviij s. quos [posuerunt][1] in passagio Magistri Petri socii Magistri Oton' nuncii pape revertentis de Anglia ad ipsum Oton' in partes transmarinas et in passagio ipsius Oton' usque in Angliam per breve eiusdem. Et in conductu j^{us} navis ad opus Walerand' teutonici et Colm' de Mol' transfretantium in nuncium R. iij m. et dim. per breve eiusdem. Et in conductu j^{us} navis ad opus Oton' nuncii pape transfretantis in partes suas xxxiiij s. et ob. per breve eiusdem. Et in ligatura et reparatione vij ingeniorum R. ferro ligatorum vij li. et x s. et iij ob. per breve eiusdem. Et in liberationibus Willelmi de Langham, Albini et Willelmi de Cantuar' servientium R. per C et xl dies videlicet a die Sancti Michaelis anno R. viij^{o} ad purificationem beate Marie anno eiusdem ix^{o} ad castrum Cant' custodiendum vj li. et vj s. per breve R. Et eisdem xx s. ad robas emendas per idem breve. Et in liberationi et conductu Erkembaud' probatoris á Rofa usque Lond' xij s. per breve eiusdem. Et in operatione turris castri Roffe xx li. et xij d. per breve R. Et in emendatione Dispense et Butillerie aule castri predicti (viij li.[i]) xviij s. et vj d. per idem breve. Et magistro Roberto de Hocot xl s. per idem breve in parte solutionis liberationum suarum per idem breve. Et Simoni fabro pro operatione ferramentorum que fecit ad ingenia R. de castro predicto liganda xl s. per idem breve. (Et in conductu j^{us} navis ad opus episcopi Covintr' transfretantis in servicium R. xviij s. per breve eiusdem.[c]) (Cancellatur quia non fuerunt pacate.[i])[2] Et incluse de Sutton' que habet per diem j d. viij s. et ij d. per breve R. scilicet á xvj^{o} die Jan[uarii] anno R. ix usque in ix septimanas et v dies sequentes. Et in operatione Turris[3] Roffe C li. per breve eiusdem et per visum Willelmi Potin et Johannis anglici. Et item in eadem operatione l li. per breve eiusdem et per visum eorundem. Et in emendatione domorum in castro Rofe Lj s. Et in emendatione domorum in castro Cant' xl s. Et habet de superplus C et lv li et ((xvj s. et [–][4] d. (nu'[c]) bl.[c])) iij s.[5] bl. qui sunt ei extensi ad C et lviij li. et xvj[-][6] s. numero. Et in superplus quod habet in anno preterito xxxviij li. et xv s. et viij d. Et est summa totius superplusagii CC li. xxxiiij s. et viij d. de quibus C et lxv li. et j m. locantur ei supra in firma numero et totum residuum infra in proficuo.

f' Idem Vic. r.c. de C et xxxix li. et iiij s. de proficuo comitatus hoc anno. In thes. lxij li. et iiij s. et viij d. Et in expensis eiusdem Vic. xl li. Et in superplus quod habet supra xxxvj li. et xvj d.[7] Et debet xviij s. Idem r.c. de eodem debito. In thes. lib. Et Q.E.

f' Homines de Rouecestr' r.c. de xxv li. de firma ville sue. In thes. xix li. et vj s. et x d. Et debet C et xiij s. et ij d.

1 *perosuerunt* written.

2 This relates to the preceding passage of text which was underlined to show cancellation.

3 A capital 'T' for *Turris* written over a capital 'B'.

4 Something erased, now illegible.

5 This has been inserted over an erasure.

6 Something erased, perhaps *j*.

7 This is on a separate line and considerably indented from the norm, but it obviously belongs with the previous paragraph.

f' Idem Vic. r.c. de v s. et j d. de pluribus minutis firmis contentis in rotulo precedenti. Et de xx s. de lastag' de Sandwic'. In thes. lib. Et Q.E.

Ricardus de Chileham r.c. de xxviij li. pro Foberto de Dovor' sicut continetur ibidem. In thes. lxxix s. Et debet xxiiij li. et xij d.

Willelmus de Abrincis debet j osturcum pro habenda feria sicut continetur in rotulo xvj R. J. Godefridus de la Dene debet quater xx et xj li. et x s. pro habenda gratia R. J.

Simon de Chelefeld' r.c. de vij li pro Leticia matre sua. In thes. xl s. Et debet C s. Idem r.c. de eodem debito. In thes. xx s. Et debet iiij li. per annum xl s.

Warinus de Munchansi r.c. de CCCC et lxxviij li. et iij s. et iiij d. de pluribus debitis contentis in rotulo iiij^{o}. In thes. quater xx li. Et debet CCC et quater xx et xviij li. iij s. et iiij d. per annum quater xx li.

Hugo de Bosco debet DCCCC et lxxvj li. et xij s. et vij d. de pluribus debitis contentis in rotulo x^{o} R. J. Vicecomites qui tenuerunt comitatum per xlix annos debent xlix li. de lestagio de Sandwic'.

Rogerus de Leiburn' r.c. de xxix li. et xvij s. de pluribus debitis contentis in rotulo vij^{o}. In thes. xx m. Et debet xvj li. et x s. et iiij d. per annum x m.[1]

Radulfus f. Thome f. Bernardi r.c. de CCC et xxvij li. et xv s. et iij d. de iij^{bus} debitis contentis in rotulo vij. In thes.[2] xiiij li. et j m. Et debet CCC et xiij li. et xxiij d. per annum xx m.

Idem debet xl m. pro Wandreg' de Corcell' que sunt in respectu sicut continetur ibidem, set preceptum est quod summoneatur. (et respondet in Surr'. Et debet T. xvij li. xij s. et iij d. per annum x m.[i])

Thomas de Bavelingeham r.c. de xxiiij li. et v s. et vij d. de parte sua de debitis S. de Turneham. In thes. v m. Et debet xx li. xviij s. et xj d. de quibus Johannes de Gatesden' debet eum adquietare de v m. sicut [recognovit.]

Adam de Bendeng' r.c. de xviij li. et ij s. et iij d. de parte sua de debitis eiusdem S. In thes. x m. Et debet xj li. et viij s. et xj d. per annum x m.

Reginaldus de Cornhill' r.c. de MM et CCCC et xxxij li. et ix s. et ij d. de pluribus debitis contentis in rotulo precedenti. In thes. xl li. Et debet MM et CCC et quater xx et xij li. ix s. et ij d. per annum xx m. per breve R.

Henricus de Cobbeham r.c. de xix li. et x s. et j palefrido de ij^{bus} debitis contentis in rotulo xj^{o} R. J. In thes. xv li. Et debet iiij li. et x s. et j palefridum. Idem r.c. de eodem debito. In thes. lib. Et Q.E.

Reginaldus de Ludesdon' r.c. de C et lxx li. et xx d. pro impressione sigilli. In thes. v m. Et debet C et lxvj li. et xv s.

Willelmus cocus r.c. de CCCC li. et ij s. et iiij d. pro habenda gratia R. J. In thes. iiij s. Et debet CCC et quater xx et xix li. xviij s. et iiij d.

Hugo de Stanherst r.c. de C s. et iiij d. pro impressione sigilli. In thes. iiij s. Et debet iiij li. et xvj s. et iiij d.

Johannes f. Alulphi r.c. de xxxvij s. et vj d. pro eodem. In thes. xxiiij s. et ij d. Et debet j m. Idem r.c. de eodem debito. In thes. lib. Et Q.E.

1 *x* over an erasure.

2 There is an insertion mark prior to the money but there is no insertion shown above the line of text.

Walterus telarius r.c. de lxviij s. et ij d. pro eodem. In thes. iiij s. Et debet lxiiij s. et ij d.

Bartholomeus de Lunesdon' r.c. de iiij li. et xiiij s. et ij d. pro eodem. In thes. iiij s. Et debet iiij li. et x s. et ij d.

Homines de Roffa r.c. de vij li. et v s. et ix d. pro transgressione. In thes. C s. Et debent xlv s. et ix d.

Hamo de Gatton' r.c. de CC et vij li. et dim. et iiij palefridis pro habenda terra que fuit patris sui. In thes. xx m. Et debet C et quater xx et xiiij li.
per annum xx m.

Matillis que fuit uxor Terrici aurifabri et Reginaldus f. eius debent xlij li. et dim. m. pro habenda terris. Theophania de Westland' debet medietatem de CC et xij m. pro justiciando Jacobo de Fugheleston'.

RESPICE IN TERGUM

[*Rot.* 9d *Mem.* 1]

Stephanus Haringot debet xl m. pro herede Rogeri de Mereworðe sicut continetur in rotulo ij°. Et j canem vulpecularem sicut continetur in rotulo viij°. Et lij m. de prestito Pictavie. + Robertus de Abbendon' debet xx m. pro dissaisina.

Cecilia uxor Rogeri Wastehoese r.c. de iiij li. et xv s. et iiij d. de remanenti firme Roffe sicut continetur in rotulo viij°. In thes. lx s. Et debet xxxv s. et iiij d.

Johannes f. Petri de Stanford' debet xx s. pro habendo precipe versus Jacobum fratrem suum qui requirebatur in Essex'. Willelmus Rufus de Delce debet dim. m. pro iniusta detentione qui requirebatur ibidem.

DE PRESTITO PICTAVIE

Robertus Arsic debet xv li. et v s. et viij d. de eodem. Albricus de Marines debet iiij li. de eodem. + Cristiana de Fenglesham debet j m. pro habendo precipe. Osbertus Giffard' debet C s. pro habendo mercato. (Set non debet summoneri quia non habuit nec habere potuit pro quo promisit.[i])

Hamo de Valoinnes r.c. de vj li. et iiij s. et viij d. de remanenti firme de Cantebr'. In thes. C s. Et debet xxiiij s. et viij d. Idem r.c. de eodem debito. In thes. lib. Et Q.E.

Willelmus de Abrincis [*blank*] xxxvj s. et viij d. de primo scutagio. Et xj li. de ij scutagiis de tempore R. J. sicut continetur in rotulo precedenti.

Comitissa Augi r.c. de C et xxv m. de primo scutagio R. In thes. xij li. Et debet C et vij m. Eadem r.c. de eodem debito. In thes. xxxj li. et dim. m. Et debet xl li.

Hamo de Crevequer r.c. de quater xx et iij li. et xix s. et viij d. de pluribus debitis contentis in rotulo vj°. In thes. xx li. Et debet lxiij li. et xix s. et viij d. per annum xx li.

Willelmus de Longo Campo r.c. de xliij s. de ij partibus debiti patris sui sicut continetur in rotulo iiij°. In thes. lib. Et Q.E.

Andreas Carpentarius r.c. de iij s. pro defalta. In thes. xiij d. Et debet xxiij d.

Walterus de Herberdesfeld' r.c. de iiij s. et viij d. pro iniusta detentione. In thes. lib. Et Q.E.

Matheus f. Bartholomei r.c. de dim. m. pro falso appello. In thes. xij d. Et debet v s. et viij d.

Aluredus Maresc' debet dim. m. pro eodem. Thomas Gernun debet j m. pro falso clamore. Ysáác de Westheia debet dim. m. pro iniusta detentione. Willelmus de Clisci debet dim. m. pro dissaisina. Ranulfus de Reinni debet xl s. pro summonendo Galfrido sicut continetur in rotulo iij°. Homines de quinque portubus debet xxxj li. et dim. m. de misercordiis hominum v^{que} portuum, quorum nomina annotantur in rotulo iij°. Guido de Castelione debet C li. de relevio suo. (Set respondet in Essex.^{i}) + Johannes de Grenewiz debet terciam partem de hoc quod perquirere poterit de lx li. pro justiciando Hamone Brand sicut continetur in rotulo viij. + Willelmus Parvus de Lond'[1] debet dim. m. pro licencia concordandi cum Elya de Bello.

Feodum de [W]illelmi[2] de Turevill' in Hastingel' r.c. de vij li. de fine passagii et scutagio. In thes. ij m. Et debet C s. et j m. de[3] *quibus heres Roberti de Hereford' debet respondere et respondet in Norf'.*

Feodum eiusdem Willelmi in Godwineston' [*blank*] vij li. de eodem.

Robertus de vij Vannis *debet*[4] xxxj s. et ob. de scutagio de Mungumeri. Radulfus f. Bernardi debet ij m. de eodem qui requirebatur in Sumerset' in rotulo precedenti. Et C s. quia non venit ad regardum foreste coram B. de Insul' (qui requirebatur ibidem.^{i})[5]

Hamo de Crievequer [*blank*] xij m. de eodem.

Bertram de Crioil r.c. de C et xxxvij li. de debitis Judeorum. In[6] thes. l s. Et debet C et xxxiiij li. et x s. per annum l s.

Robertus de Coddham barbator debet dim. m. pro falso clamore.

Radulfus f. Nicholai [*blank*] C li. pro com'[7] Gloecr' sicut continetur in rotulo precedenti.

Warinus de Munchansi r.c. de v m. pro habenda jurata. In thes. lib. Et Q.E.

Idem Vic. r.c. de dim. m. de Gervasio de Aldermannebir'. Et de dim. m. de Roberto Amaur'. In thes. lib. Et Q.E.

Thomas et Johannes f. Hugonis [*blank*] dim. m. pro licencia concordandi cum Magistro Adam de Roffa per plegium Petri de Mareworðe.

Willelmus Potin et Johannes Anglicus r.c. de iiij d. et ob. de remanenti compoti de anno preterito. In thes. lib. Et Q.S.

1 In *NS 54*, p. 149 William Parvus is shown as coming from Cheriton in Kent.

2 In *NS 54*, p. 149 he is shown as *Willelmi de Turevill'* but here the clerk has put in a '*T*' as in *Tillelmi*.

3 From here to the end added later.

4 This word is written in a different hand.

5 This is written on the line above.

6 There is a different hand from this point onwards for this item only. It also appears to have been slightly rubbed and may be in a different ink.

7 This could be *comitatu* or *comite* for the county or the earl of Gloucester.

Rogerus de Lenham persona de Hardr' r.c. de C et lxxix m. et xij s. et iiij d. pro habenda gratia R. J. In thes. ij s. Et debet C et lxxix m. et x s. et iiij d.

Thomas de Gillingeham [*blank*] quater xx et iij li. et x s. de firma ville de Derteford' per breve R.

Bertram de Crioil debet C li. pro monachis Sancti Augustini Cant' pro habenda custodia Abbatie sue vacantis.

NOVA OBLATA

Willelmus de Orlaveston' r.c. de dim. m. pro habendo pone contra priorem de Horton'. In thes. lib. Et Q.E.

Johannes Turce [*blank*] xv m. pro habenda custodia cunei de Cantuar' et Alexander de Dorset' debet respondere de securitate.

Ysabell' de Curton' r.c. de dim. m. pro licencia concordandi cum Juliana. In thes. lib. Et Q.E.

Reginaldus de Cornhill' Iunior qui fuit camerarius [*blank*] C (s.[i]) pro defalta qui requirebatur in Lond' in itinere[1] M. de Pateshill' inter placita corone.

Petrus Pict' debet xl (-b-[d])[2] s. pro vino vendito qui requirebatur ibidem. (Set respondet in London'.[i]) Petrus Dagun debet j m. pro eodem qui requirebatur ibidem. Warinus de Munchansi debet xl m. pro falso clamore versus priorem de Hertford'.

Amicia de Horkeden' [*blank*] xviij li. et iiij s. et ij d. de debitis Judeorum de quibus Constantinus Iuvenis debet eum adquietare sicut recognovit. per annum xl s.

S. archiepiscopus Cant' [*blank*] CCC et xj li. et ij s. et iij d. de pluribus debitis contentis in Surr' de quibus reddet ad festum Sancti Michaelis anno R. xj° l m. Et ad Pascham anno xij° l m. et ita in anno sequenti C m. ad eosdem terminos per breve R. salvo tamen quod celerius reddet sicut continetur ibidem. Ita tamen quod solutis CC m. idem archiepiscopus de residuo reddet C li. per annum.

[*One line blank*]

Ricardus de Argentoem et Johanna uxor eius [*blank*] CC m. pro predicto archiepiscopo sicut continetur ibidem de quibus reddent ad festum Sancti Michaelis anno R. xj l m. et ad Pascham anno xij° l m. et ita in anno sequenti C m. ad eosdem terminos per predictum breve R.

Willelmus de Aineford [*blank*] CCC et l li. pro S. Cantuar' archiepiscopo sicut continetur in Surr' qui requirebatur ibidem.

[*Three lines blank*]

[1] According to Crook in *Records of the General Eyre*, p. 79 the London Eyre took place from 9 March 1226 to 23 April 1226 with Martin of Patteshall as the leading judge.

[2] There is a gap here and some rubbing out.

HEREFORD' IN WALLIA

Radulfus[1] f. Nicholai, Henricus frater eius ut custos pro eo r.c. de C et lxiiij li. et xvj s. et v d. bl. de firma comitatus. In thes. nichil.

Et in elemosinis constitutis militibus de Templo j m. Et in decimis constitutis monachis de Lyra xij li. Et monachis de Cormeilles xij li. Et Priori de Hereford' lx s. et x d. (Et infirmis de Hereford' xij d.[c]) (quia infra in civitate[i].) Et Margarete nutrici Ysabelle sororis R. lx s. et x d. Et Willelmo nuncio xv s. et ij d. et ob. de dim. anno. Et Johanni de Lysewis xv s. et ij d. et ob. de alio dimidio anno et amodo totum per breve R. Et Johanni Braz lx s. et x d. Et Simoni de Cambray xxx s. et v d. Et Simoni Pict' et Rogero capellano vij li. et xij s. et j d. Et in terris datis Gilleberto Talebot xvj li. et x s. bl. in Linton'. Et Willelmo de Cantilupo cum herede Henrici de Longo campo xvj li. et x s. bl. in Wiliton' super Waie et Caples. Et in civitate Hereford' xl li. bl. de quibus cives respondent infra. Et Hugoni Pantolf' C s. in Stanford'. Et fratribus hospitalis Jer'l'm x s. et vj d. in Abboderade et Belestan' et Freðendal. Et Willelmo f. Warini xl s. in molendino de Maworðin de quibus respondet infra. Et in tercio denario comitatus Umfrido comiti Hereford' xx li. per breve R.

[*One line blank*]

Et in carriagio vj doliorum vini á Bristoll' usque Hereford' repositorum in castro Hereford' ad opus R. xx s. et vij d. per breve R. Et in carriagio x doliorum vini á Bristoll' usque Hereford' ad opus R. xxxiiij s. et xj d. per breve eiusdem. Et in liberatione Willelmi fleccarii qui singulis diebus solebat percipere iij d. á crastino Sancti Michaelis anni ix^{ni}[2] usque Dominicam proximam post epiphaniam anni x^{mi}[3] scilicet per C et iiij dies utraque die computata xxvj s. scilicet per C et iiij dies.[4] Et eidem Willelmo á crastino predicte Dominice usque ad diem Sancti Michaelis anno eodem utraque die computata scilicet per CC et lxxj dies iiij li. et x s. et iiij d. scilicet per diem iiij d. per breve R. Et Willelmo fabro et Johanni fratri suo qui sunt apud Hereford' ad quarrellos fabricandos qui convencionaverunt R. quod facient singulis diebus operabilibus C quarrellos et habent per diem ix d. xiij li. et xiij s. et ix d. per breve R. a die Sancti Michaelis anni x^{mi}[5] usque ad diem Sancti Michaelis anni xj^{mi}[6] utraque die computata. Et pro ferro et ascero fusto carbone (et barillis ad imponendum non dum quarrellos[i]) emptis ad predictos quarrellos fabricandos et in flechiandos x li. et ij s. et iij d. et ob. per breve R. per totum tempus predictum. Et in emendatione domorum in castro C s. Et habet de superplus xij li. et xvj d. et ob. bl. qui sunt ei extensi[7] ad xij li. et xiij s. et v d. num. quod totum locatur ei infra in pluribus debitis.

f' Idem Vic. r.c. de C et xxxv li. et xv s. de proficuo comitatus de anno viij, ix^{o} et hoc anno. In thes. nichil. Et Radulfo f. Nicholai pro custodia

1 The first letter in this word is three lines high and has been written with a flourish.
2 Tuesday 30 September 1225.
3 Sunday 11 January 1226.
4 Written over rubbing out.
5 Tuesday 29 September 1226.
6 Wednesday 29 September 1227.
7 A double xx written here and then the first x altered to an 'e'.

comitatus et castri de Hereford' C et xxv li. et xv s. per breve R. de allocandis sibi de predicta custodia quolibet predictorum trium annorum C m. Et restant ei (locande[c]) (reddende[i]) per predictum breve, lxiiij li. et v s. de quibus xxv li. vij s. et iij ob. reddite[1] *sunt in rotulo anni xjj sequenti in duobus locis in debitis plurium. Et restant ei adhuc reddende xxxviij li et xvij s. et x d. et ob. qui redduntur ei in rotulo xij*[o].

[*One line blank*]

Idem Vic. r.c. de x li. de remanenti compoti sui de tercio denario comitatus de anno preterito. In thes. nichil. Et in predicto superplus x li. Et Q.E.

Idem Vic. r.c. de vij li. et iij s. et vij d. bl. de remanenti firme comitatus de anno viij[o]. In thes. vj li. et xix s. et vj d. bl. (Et debet iiij s. et j d. bl.[i]) Idem r.c. de eodem debito. In thes. lib. Et Q.E.

f' Cives Hereford' r.c. de. xl li. bl. de firma civitatis sue. Et de lvij s. et viij d. bl. de remanenti eiusdem firme de anno preterito. In thes. xxxvj li. xvij s. et ij d. bl. Et in cimiterio Hereford' vij s. Et in firma Hereford' ij s. de anno preterito et hoc anno qui in rotulis precedentibus computantur in corpore comitatus. Et debent C et xj s. et xj d. et ob. Idem r.c. de eodem debito. In thes. liiij s. et iij ob. bl. Et debent lvij s. x d. (bl.[i])

f' Willelmus f. Warini r.c. de ij s. de firma molendini de Maworðin. In thes. lib. Et Q.E.

f' Nicholas Scleraris r.c. de x s. de firma cuiusdam essarti in Maworðin. In thes. lib. Et Q.E.

f' Cives Hereford' r.c. de xxv s. et iiij d. de firma propresturarum. In thes. lib. Et Q.S.

Willelmus de Stutevill' r.c. de xx s. et ij palefridis … de remanenti debiti sui contenti in rotulo precedenti.[2]

[*Rot.* 9d *Mem.* 2]

[*Two lines blank*]

Abbas de Straflur debet DCC m. sicut continetur in rotulo xiiij R. J. Johannes de Luston' debet ij s. pro quodam apro. Robertus falconarius et Robertus f. Oriold' debent xiiij m. pro quercubus emptis sicut continetur in rotulo vij[o]. Hoelus de Kaerliun debet CC et l m. ut habeat filium suum et domum suam. + Rogerus le harpur debet dim. m. pro dissaisina. + Hugo Blisse debet dim. m. pro plegio. + Willelmus f. Ricardi debet dim. m. pro eodem. Episcopus Hereford' debet xxxv s. de scutagio de Byham de feodis que non recognoscit.

Johannes de Báálun r.c. de lx s. pro habenda custodia sicut continetur in rotulo xij[o]. In thes. xxx s. Et debet xxx s.

Walterus de Baskervill'[3] r.c. de C et lxvij li. et xiiij s. et iiij d. de debitis Judeorum. In thes. x m. Et debet C et lxj li. et xij d. per annum x m.

[1] The remainder of this paragraph was added later possibly by a different hand.

[2] There is some stitching across the membrane causing overlapping of the two halves, which obscures some of this entry.

[3] In *NS 54*, p. 248 he is identified as 'Walter the s. of Walter de Baskervill'.

Radulfus Torel r.c. de xlvij li. et xvj s. et viij d. de eodem. In thes. ij m. Et debet xlvj li. et x s. per annum ij m.

Willelmus de Furcis r.c. de vj li. et x s. de eodem. In thes. xl s. Et debet iiij li. et x s. per annum xl s.

Thomas de Capes [*blank*] xlix li. et iij s. de eodem.

Canonici de Hereford' r.c. de lxx s. de parte sua de eodem pro Waltero de Eglinton'. In thes. xxx s. Et debet xl s. per annum xl s.

Walterus de Hida [*blank*] vj li. xix s. et x d. de parte sua de eodem debito.

DE PRESTITO PICTAVIE

Johannes de Monem' debet xliij li. de eodem. Walterus de Clyfford' debet xxiij li. et vj s. et vij [d.] de eodem. Rogerus de Clyfford' debet xxvj li. de eodem. Robertus de Mortuo mari debet ix m. de eodem.

Willata de Hereford' debet lxxiij li. et xij s. de ij^{bus} debitis contentis in rotulo iiij^{o}. Thomas de Aneyse debet xx s. pro Rogero f. Aitropi sicut continetur in rotulo viij. Willelmus f. Henrici de Longo campo debet l li. et xvj s. et viij d. pro habenda gratia R.

Rogerus de Clyfford' r.c. de xxxiiij m. de ij^{bus} scutagiis contentis in rotulo vj^{o} per plegium Roberti de Marisco et Willelmus [*sic*] de Halham [et][1] Willelmi f. Petri de terminis servandis. Et de viij s. de catallis fugitivorum. In thes v m. Et debet xix li. et xiiij s. et viij d. per annum v m.

Reginaldus de Breosa debet xxxiij li. et ix s. et j d. de ij^{bus} debitis contentis in rotulo viij^{o}. Cives Hereford' debent x m. pro habenda feria die Sancti Dionis'. + Adam le Wilde debet dim. m. pro habendo brevi.
[*One line blank*]

DE PRIMO SCUTAGIO R.

Walterus de Lascy r.c. de xvj li. et j m. de ij^{bus} debitis contentis in rotulo viij^{o}. In thes. iiij li. et j m. Et debet xij li.

Feoda Roberti de Candos debet xxj m. et iiij s. et v d. et ob. de eodem. Episcopus Hereford' debet vij m. de eodem de feodis que non recognoscit.
·[2] Johannes de Monemue (Vic. pro eo^{i}) r.c. de lj s. et ix d. de eodem.. In thes nichil. Et in superplus quod Vic. habet supra lj s. et ix d. Et Q.E.
· Hugo de Kilpaec r.c. de xl s. de cablicio de ballia sua sicut continetur in rotulo vij^{o}. In thes xx s. Et debet xx s. Idem r.c. de eodem debito. In thes. nichil. Et in predicto superplus xx d. Et debet H. xviij s. et iiij^{or} d.
[*One line blank*]

DE SCUTAGIO DE MUNGUMERY

Idem Vic. r.c. de ij m. de Gilleberto Talebot de eodem. Et de ij s. et viij d. de Roberto Malherb' de eodem. Et de ij s. et viij d. de Radulfo de Bray de eodem. Et de iij s. et viij d. de j^{o} scutagio et scutagio de Byham de eodem

[1] *et* omitted.

[2] A dot written in the margin here and also in front of Hugo on the next line down.

R. Et de ij s. et viij d. de Roberto Malherbe de scutagio de Bedeford'. Et de ij s. et viij d. de Radulfo de Bray de eodem. In thes. lib. Et Q.E.

Hugo le Pohier [*blank*] v m. de eodem de feodo de Cormeilles. Et v m de scutagio de Bedeford'.

Gillebertus Talebot debet ij m. de scutagio de Bedeford'. Reginaldus de Breosa debet xlv m. et vij s. et j d. de eodem.

Robertus de Tresgoz debet xx li. et j m. de pluribus scutagiis de honore Bolon' qui requirebatur in Essex'.

Robertus de Furcis r.c. de xxx s. de debitis Judeorum pro Waltero de Eglindon'. In thes x s. Et debet xx s. per annum x s.

Elyas de Birstall' r.c. de xij s. de eodem debito. In thes. lib. Et Q.E.

[*One blank line*]

DE OBLATIS

Hugo de Kinardesle r.c. de xv m. pro habenda licencia frussandis lxxij acris terre in Welinton' sicut continetur in rotulo precedenti. In thes. lib. Et Q.E.

Idem H. debet xviij s. de firma eiusdem terre sicut continetur ibidem. Set respondet in Gloecr' quia terra est in eodem comitatu.

Walterus de Baskervill' r.c. de v m. pro j palefrido pro habend' j mercato et j feria sicut continetur ibidem. In thes. iij m. et debet ij m.

Otewicus le Pohier debet dim. m. pro licencia concordandi sicut continetur ibidem.

Hugo le Pohier debet vij li. et ij s. de pluribus scutagiis contentis ibidem. Ranulfus f. et heres Rogeri le Pohier debet v m. pro transgressione. Querebantur in Notingehamsir' super Rogerum patrem suum.

Idem Vic. r.c. de vj s. de catallis Ade le Thressere suspensi. In thes. lib. Et Q.E.

NOVA OBLATA

Willelmus f. Warini [*blank*] j palefr' pro habendo j mercato singulis septimanis per diem mercurii apud manerium de Prestemed' et j feriam[1] singulis annis ibidem duraturam in vigilia Sancti Andree et ipso die usque ad etatem R.

[*One blank line*]

Hugo Decanus de Beysham debet xx (s.[i]) pro habendo brevi de attingendis xij juratoribus nove dissaisine de tenemento in Perestowe.

[*One line blank*]

DE AMERCIATIS IN ITINERE R. PER R. EPISCOPUM CYCESTIR', R. CANCELLARIUM ET WILLELMUM DE LOND' ET SOCIOS EORUM

Idem Vic. r.c. de xxxj m. de misericordiis hominum quorum nominibus proponitur littera *t* in rotulo quem predicti liberaverunt in thesauro. In thes. lib. Et Q.E.

[1] *Sic. mercato* and *feriam* written.

Rogerus de Leiburn' r.c. de xl s. pro dissaisina. In thes. xx s. Et in perdona ipsi Rogero xx s. per breve R. Et Q.E.

Roaldus Maubanc r.c. de j m. pro eodem. In thes. dim. m. Et debet dim. m.

Gillebertus de Herdewic (debet[c]) et Radulfus le porter debent dim. m. quia non habuerunt quem plegiaverunt. Hunith' f. Johannis debet dim. m. pro falso clamore per plegium Sexill' f. Johannis et Mathei Rugga.

Engelardus de Cyconiaco r.c. de CC li. quas Petrus de Cancell' dum fuit constabularius Bristoll' recepit tempore J. R. patris R. de fine abbatis de Strafflur sicut continetur in rotulo xiij° R. J. In thes. nichil. Et in perdona ipsi Engelard' CC li. per breve R. Et Q.E.

[*One line blank*]

RESIDUUM SUSSEX' QUIA NON ERAT IBI LOCUS

Willelmus de Sancto Johanne r.c. de D m. pro habendis bruliis Cycestr' cum pertinenciis ad assartandum et excelendum.[1] Ita quod reddet inde ad festum Sancti Michaelis anno x[mo] C li. et ad Pascham anno xj° C li. et ad festum Sancti Michaelis anno eodem C m. et ad Pasch' anno xij° C m. Et ad festum Sancti Michaelis anno eodem vij li. et x s. Et ad Pasch' proximo sequens vij li. et x s. Et sicut deinceps singulis annis xv li. de redditu assiso.

f' De quibus D m. R. episcopus Cycestr' cancellarius R. qui habet medietatem eorundem brulliorum de voluntate R. et permissione dicti Willelmi debet eum adquietare (et respondet infra[i]) de CC m. et xxx s. ad terminos sibi datos sicut ambo recognoverunt coram baronibus de scaccario. In thes. lxv li. et iij s. et iiij d. Et debet C et xxxiij li. et vj s. et viij d. De quibus predictus R. episcopus Cycestr' qui etiam habet alteram medietatem eorundem brulliorum de voluntate R. et eiusdem Willelmi debet adquietare sicut recognovit *et*[2] *reddere firmam supradictam xv li. ad terminos suprascriptos et respondet infra de* [*debito*][3] *superdicto.*

[*One line blank*]

R. Cycestr' episcopus r.c. de CC m. et xxx s. pro Willelmo de Sancto Johanne sicut supra continetur. In thes. xxxiij li. et vj s. et viij d. Et debet C et j li. et x s. Et preterea C et xxxiij li. et vj s. et viij d. pro eodem Willelmo sicut supra continetur in secundo fine. Idem[4] r.c. de eodem debito. In thes. nichil. Et in perdona ipsi episcopo CC m. per breve R. Et debet C et j li. et x s.[5]

1 This fine is also shown in *Calendar of Fine Rolls*, II, 1224–34, p. 90, no. 218.

2 From here to the end of the line it is written in a different hand and ink and has a squashed appearance even though it does not reach the end of the line on the membrane.

3 The clerk may have made a mistake here as he wrote *beb'* but *debito* appears to make more sense.

4 The ink is fainter here almost to the end of the line.

5 This is the point where the ink becomes distinct again. The clerk has not written the usual *s.* for shillings but an old fashioned 's' in a Carolingian minuscule script.

[*Sixteen blank lines*]

[*Endorsed*] emendatus et iterum emendatus totus
Lancastr' et Kantia et Hereford'[1] in Wallia

[*Rot.* 10 *Mem.* 1]

[*There is strengthening tape down the right hand side of the membrane. Down the left hand side near the bottom there is some wearing which has taken some of the marginalia from the text. There is an area torn off at the bottom left hand side of the membrane which has taken a small portion of the text.*]
[*Six lines blank*]

NORFOLK' ET SUFFOLK'

Hugo Rufus ut custos r.c. de DCC et quater xx et x li. et ij s. bl. de firma comitatuum. In thes. xxj li. xiij s. et xj d. bl.

Et in elemosinis constitutis militibus de Templo iij m. Et fratribus hospitalis de Norewic iiij li. et xj s. et iij d. Et infirmis de Sancto Edmundo xxx s. et v d. in Tieford'. Et monialibus de Tieford' xxx s. et v d. in eadem villa. Et in terris datis heredibus (Radulfi[c]) (Rogeri[i]) de (Tóóni[c]) (Akoinni[i]) C s. in Holkham. Et W[illelmo] comiti Sar' cum custodia terre que fuit Hugonis Bigod'[2] x li. et xvj s. et viij d. in Aclay de dim. anno.[3] Et A[lexandro] R. Scottorum x li. et xvj s. et viij d. in eadem villa de alio dim. anno. Et predicto W[illelmo] comiti [Sar'] viij li. in Bergeria de dim. anno. Et predicto A[lexandro] R. [Scottorum] viij li. ibidem de alio dim. anno. Et predicto W[illelmo] comiti xj li. et v s. in Halvergat' de dim. anno. Et predicto A[lexandro] R. xj li. et v s. ibidem de alio dim. anno. Et predicto W[illelmo] comiti x li. in Walesham de dim. anno. Et predicto A[lexandro] R. x li. ibidem de alio dimidio anno. Et predicto W[illelmo] comiti C et

[1] There are three vertical dots before and after *Lancastr'*, after both instances of *et* and after *Hereford'* and a stamped figure 18 at the bottom left hand side of the membrane.

[2] This is probably Earl Hugh II Bigod who died in February 1225. It is known that, as his three children were all under age at that time, the inherited lands were first given into the wardship of William Longespee, earl of Salisbury, until his death in March 1226. Thereafter, the wardship was purchased by Alexander II, king of Scotland, on behalf of the eldest son and heir of Hugh II, Roger III Bigod and his wife Isabella, who was the sister of Alexander II. See Marc Morris, *The Bigod Earls of Norfolk in the Thirteenth Century* (Woodbridge, 2005), pp. 4–6. The other possibility is that Hugh Bigod is in fact Hugh III Bigod who was the second son of Hugh II Bigod. However, Morris makes clear that these lands belonged ultimately to Roger III Bigod the eldest son.

[3] Presumably this is from the day after the feast of St. Michael on 29 September 1225 until Easter 1226. However, the earl was dead before then. The king of Scotland took over the obligation for the lands for the second half-year for Acle and all subsequent lands mentioned in relation to Hugh Bigod with the possible exception of one – Stockton.

x s. bl. in Eresham de dimidio anno. Et predicto A[lexandro] R. C et x s. bl. ibidem de alio dimidio anno. Et predicto W[illelmo] comiti viij li. bl. in Dikingeham de dimidio anno. Et predicto A[lexandro] R. viij li. bl. de alio dimidio anno. Et predicto W[illelmo] comiti xij li. bl. in Stocton'. Et predicto A[lexandro] R. xij li. bl. ibidem de alio dim. anno. Et predicto W[illelmo] comiti xj li. bl. in dimidio hundredo de Eresham. Et predicto A[lexandro] R. xj li. bl. ibidem de alio dimidio anno. Et W[illelmo] comiti Maresc' et comiti de Warenn' xliiij li. et xvj (s.^{i}) et iij d. bl. in Folesham cum pertinenciis. Et in villa de Norewiz C et viij li. bl. de quibus homines ville respondent infra. Et in Gipeswiz xxxv li. bl. de quibus homines ville respondent infra. Et in Gernemue xl [li.] bl. de quibus homines ville respondent infra. Et W. comiti Saresberie xxx li. et xij s. bl. in Ludingeland' de dim. anno de quibus debet respondere. Et Rogero f. Osberti xxx li. et xij s. bl. ibidem de alio dimidio anno de quibus respondent infra per breve R. in quo continetur quod R. concessit ei manerium illud cum pertinenciis á Pascha[1] proximo preterito anno scilicet x^{o} usque in iij annos completos, solvendo inde per annum quater xx li. ad scaccarium. Et heredibus Ricardi de Lucy xx li. bl. in Disce. Et W[illelmo] comiti Warenn' xxiij li. et xix s. et ij d. bl. in Tieford' pro escambio de Columbar' et aliarum terrarum de Toreinni. Et Willelmo Pippard' xvj li. et j m. bl. in Hintlesham. Et[2] Ade f. Hervei et Juliane uxori sue filie et heredi Johannis f. Hugonis xvj li. bl. in Ormesby de quibus respondent infra. Et in Ailesham xl li. et xij s. bl. de quibus H. de Burgo debet respondere. Et Willelmo Talebot xvj li. et j m. bl. in Hintlesham quamdiu R. placuerit. Et monachis de Sancto Edmundo lxxvj s. in Beccles. Et eisdem x li. in Ailesham ad luminare ecclesie Sancti Edmundi. Et canonicis de Tieford' xx s. in Bliburc. Et monachis de Becco xiij s. in Blakeham. Et Willelmo May xx s. in Causton'. Et Roberto Mai xl s. in Stanhó. Et in defalta monetariorum in Tieford' iiij li. Et canonicis de Buttel' lij s. in Schelfleg' sicut continetur in rotulo vj R. J. Et Willelmo Britton' xx s. in Cattel'. Et heredibus Ricardi Vetule xxiiij s. in sokemannis cum hundredo. Et heredibus Henrici de Kemesec xx li. in Ixning'. Et Ricardo de Argentoem xl s. ibidem. Et Ysáác f. Abraham de Felmingeham xxviij s. in Felmingeham. Et Huberto de Burgo xxj li. in Causton'. Et Thome de Haya x li. in Ixning' in terra que fuit Willelmi de Dunse. Et Willelmo de Mandevill' lx s. in Ixning'. Et Waltero delacr' x li. ibidem. Et Margar' de Creissi xiij li. in Bliburg'. Et Radulfo de Tóóni xxvj li. et viij s. et viij d. in Saham. Et comiti Bolon' x li. in Ixning'. Et Johanni Maresc' xxv li. et xvij s. et vj d. in Heingeham quamdiu R. placuerit. Et Waltero de Evermou x li. in Ixning' quamdiu R. placuerit.

Et Gilleberto de Hauvill' ij m. ad j runcinum emendum per breve R. Et eidem xx s. ad expensas suas de dono R. per idem breve. Et pro j dolio vini empto ad opus R. et carriato usque Walsingeham xliiij s. et j d. per breve eiusdem. Et in carriagio vini R. per diversa loca xiij s. et ij d. per breve eiusdem. Et pro ij^{bus} palefridis emptis ad opus R. ix m. et ij s. et vj d. per breve eiusdem. Et in liberationem j^{us} probatoris ij s. Et debet xiij s. bl. Idem r.c. de eodem debito. In thes. lib. Et Q.E.

1 *Pascha* written in full – very unusual.
2 *Et* is repeated.

[*One line blank*]

f' Idem Vic. r.c. de C et xx li. et xvij s. et vj d. de proficuo comitatuum hoc anno. In thes. lib. Et Q.E.

f' H. de Burgo [*blank*] xl li. et xij s. de firma de Ailesham. Et xl li. et xij s. de eadem de anno preterito.

[*One line blank*]

f' Cives de Norewic' r.c. de C et viij li. bl. de firma ville sue. In thes. quater xx et xvj li. et v s. bl. Et monialibus de Carrho xxv s. et in defalta vj monetariorum vj li. Et debent iiij li. et xvij s. et iij d. bl. Idem r.c. de eodem debito. In thes. Et Q.S.

f' Homines de Gipeswic r.c. de xxxv li. bl. de firma ville sue. In thes. xx li. et vj s. bl. Et P.[1] Norewic' episcopo x li. in Wica. Et defalta iiij monetariorum iiij li. Et debent xxviij s. bl. Idem r.c. de eodem debito. In thes. lib. Et Q.S.

f' Idem homines r.c. de C s. num. de cremento ville sue. Et de vj li. et xl d. de (remanenti eiusdem^{i}) crementi[2] de pluribus annis preteritis. In thes. C s. Et debent vj li. et xl d.

Idem homines [*blank*] x li. et xvij s. bl. de firma ville sue de dim. anno xvij R. J.

f' Homines de Donewiz r.c. de C et xx li. et j m. de firma ville sue. In thes. xliij li. et xvj d. Et in perdonis ipsis hominibus xl li. per finem quem fecerunt cum R. J. Et in decimis constitutis monachis de Eyé xij li. Et monachis de Ely j m. et eisdem xxiiij milia allecis. Et militibus de Templo x s. Et debent xxiiij li. et viij s. et viij d. Idem r.c. de eodem debito. In thes. lib. Et Q.S.

f' Homines de Gernemue r.c. de lv li. de firma ville sue. In thes. lib. Et Q.S.

Homines de Donewiz [r.c.] xxxiij li. et xv s. de firma ville sue de dim. anno xvij R. J. In thes. nichil. Et in perdonis ipsis hominibus pro fideli servicio suo facto R. J. patri (R.^{c}) (nostro et nobis^{i}) tempore guerre xxxiij li. et xv s. per breve R. Et Q.S.

f' Ricardus Agoillun r.c. de (v^{c}) (xl^{i}) m. de (remanenti^{c}) firma de Oreford'. Et de xvj [s.] et viij d. de remanenti eiusdem firme de anno preterito. In thes. iiij m. Et ad custodiam castri de Oreford' xxx m. Et debet iiij li. xvj s. et viij d. Idem r.c. de eodem debito. In thes. nichil. Et in operatione castri de Oreford' xxxiiij s. Et debet lxij s. et viij d.

Thomas de Burgo r.c. de v m. de remanenti firme de Oreford' de dim. anno viij. In thes. ij m. et dim. Et debet ij m. et dim.

f' Willelmus comes Saresberie debet xxx li. et xij s. bl. de firma de Ludingeland' de dim. anno. Set respondet in Wiltes' cum aliis debitis suis.

f' Rogerus f. Osberti r.c. de xl li. num. de eadem firma de alio dim. anno. In thes. lib. Et Q.E.

f' Idem Vic. r.c. de v s. et vij d. de firma terre Willelmi Tonitrui. Et de iiij s. de firma de Waðe. In thes. lib. Et Q.E.

1 This would be Pandulf who had been legate of the pope to King John and Henry III.

2 *Cremento* altered to *crementi*.

f' Idem Vic. r.c. de c s. de firma de Berchholt. In thes. xx s. Et in elemosinis constitutis militibus de Templo iiij li. Et Q.E.

f' Robertus de Hauvill' [*blank*] xvj li. de firma de Westhall'. Et de[1] exitu eiusdem manerii ultra firmam hoc anno.

f' Idem Vic. r.c. de C li. de veteri cremento comitatuum. In thes. lib. Et Q.E.

f' Bartholomeus de Creic r.c. de xxij li. et dim. m. de firma de Camb'. Et de xxx s. de scutagio annuo. In thes. lib. Et Q.E.

f' Adam f. Hervei et Juliana uxor eius r.c. de xvj li. de firma de Ormesbi. In thes. lib. Et Q.S.

f' Abbas de Sancto Edmundo r.c. de xx s. pro[2] j osturco soro de terra de Berton' sicut continetur in rotulo viij. In thes. lib. Et Q.E.

Walterus Pippard' debet l li. bl. de firma de Hintlesham sicut continetur in rotulo iiij R. J. Rogerus f. Osberti debet ij osturcos mutarios sicut continetur in rotulo vij R. J.

ed Thomas de Gedding' r.c. de xxxviij li. et xvij s. et vij d. de ij debitis contentis in rotulo precedenti. In thes. xl s. Et debet xxxvj li. et xvij s. et vij d. per annum xl s.

Heredes Willelmi le Veautr' r.c. de lxix li. de debitis Aaron. In thes. v m. Et debet lxv li. et j m.

Theobaldus Walteri r.c. de xij li. de ij^{bus} debitis contentis in rotulo iiij^{o}. In thes. C s. Et debet vij li. per annum C s.

Willelmus Brito r.c. de quater xx et ix li. et xj s. et viij d. de pluribus debitis contentis in rotulo precedenti. In thes. xij li. Et debet lxxvij li. et xj s. et viij d. per annum xij li.

Gip' Johannes Prikehert r.c. de xlix m. et xl d. de cambio de Gipeswiz. In thes. xij d. Et debet xlix m. et ij s. et iiij d.

Willelmus de Warenn' de Wermegai debet C et lxiiij li. et j d. de iij^{bus} debitis contentis in rotulo iiij^{o}. Hubertus de Burgo debet DC et quater xx et iij li. et dim. m. de pluribus debitis contentis in rotulo v^{o}.

Rogerus de Creissi r.c. de xlij li. et dim. m. de iij debitis contentis in rotulo viij^{o}. In thes. x m. Et debet xxxv li. et j m. per annum x m.

Adam de Badvent r.c. de liiij s. et vj d. pro patre suo pro retto foreste. In thes. lib. Et Q.E.

Villata de Gipeswiz r.c. de xvj li. et xix s. et viij d. et ij osturcis de pluribus debitis contentis in rotulo v. In thes. viij li. et j m. Et debet viij li et vj s. et iiij d. et ij osturcos.

Burgenses de Gernemue r.c. de vj doliis vini. Et de x milibus allecis. In thes. nichil. Et in perdonis ipsis burgensibus pro bono et fideli servicio suo vj dolia vini et x milia allecis per breve R. Et Q. S.

Fulco Bainnard' r.c. de xx s. de j osturco pro habenda inquisitione. In thes. lib. Et Q.E.

Gip' Alexander f. Baldric' r.c. de iiij li. et viij s. et x d. et ob. scilicet de tercia parte de xx m. pro justiciando Elya. In thes. xij d. Et debet iiij li. et vij s. et x d. et ob.

[1] There is a blank space here and the following word is difficult to make out because of a crease.

[2] The clerk has formed the abbreviated 'pro' from 'de' but has not crossed out 'de'.

+ Galfridus de Melsa debet lxxiiij s. et viij d. ut deliberetur a prisona. + Godefridus de Waur' debet xl s. et j palefridum pro habenda inquisitione. + Lambertus Teutonicus debet j tonellum vini Autisiodorum.

Petrus de Nereford' r.c. de xx li. de pluribus debitis contentis in rotulo iiij°. In thes. C s. Et debet xv li.[1] per annum C s.

Magister Henricus de Gernemue debet CC et lxvij li. (et ix s. et viij d.ⁱ) pro habenda gratia R. Daniel de Merlai debet CC m. pro dissaisina. Rannulfus Putrel debet liiij li. et xij s. et x d. pro habenda gratia R.

ed Willelmus de Kentewell' [*blank*] xliij li. et vij s. et iiij palefridos de pluribus debitis contentis in rotulo v°.

Matheus de Guneton' r.c. de CCC et (xⁱ)xxviij li. et ij s. et xj d. pro Roberto de Castr' pro habenda gratia R. In thes. C s. Et debet CCC et xxxiij li. et ij s. et xj d. per annum C s.

ed Hubertus de Munkansi r.c. de xlix li. et iij s. et iiij d. pro patre suo pro habendo recto de Staverton'. In thes viij li. Et debet xlj li. et iij s. et iiij d.

ed Thomas de Burgo [*blank*] xxxiiij m. et dim. et ij palefridos et ij osturcos sicut continetur in rotulo v.

Benedictus de Blakeham r.c. de iij m. pro j osturco sicut continetur in rotulo ix°. In thes. lib. Et Q.E.

ed Henricus de Illeg' r.c. de xxj li. et ij s. et j d. de iij^{bus} debitis contentis in rotulo viij. In thes. xx s. Et debet xx li. et ij s. et j d. per annum xx s.

Johannes de Risses r.c. de (dim. m.ᶜ) (xiij s.ⁱ) pro (habendo precipeᶜ) xiij s.[2] pro licencia concordandi. In thes. iij s. Et debet x s.

Johannes f. Radulfi r.c. de dim. m. pro habendo precipe. In thes. lib. Et Q.E.

Homines de Norewiz debet vj palefridos pro habendis libertatibus suis. Willelmus Pippard' debet xx m. pro habenda terra patris sui. Homines episcopi Elyensis debet ix m. pro dissaisina. Radulfus de Bunewell' debet xx s. pro eodem.

[*One line blank*]

[*Rot.*10 *Mem.* 2]

Ger'[3] Jordanus f. Willelmi r.(c.ⁱ) de viij s. pro habenda jurata. In thes. ij s. et viij d. Et debet v s. et iiij d.

Ricardus de Caleston' r.c. de xx li. et viij s. de debitis Ysáác Judei sicut continetur in rotulo xvj°. In thes. j m. Et debet xix li. et xiiij s. et viij d.

Rogerus de Rieburg r.c. de xl s. pro habendo brevi. In thes. dim. m. Et debet ij m. et dim.

Margar'[4] et Alicia et Agnes sorores r.c. de x s. de iij^{bus} debitis contentis in rotulo xvj°. In thes. ij s. Et debent viij s.

Margar'[5] de Creissi r.c. de D et lxvj li. et j m pro habenda hereditate

[1] There are two items rubbed out on this line. One item looks like a capital 'S' and the other looks like a drawing of a face in profile.

[2] This is written over an erasure and in effect it has been duplicated.

[3] The word is under the stitching and hard to read. It might be *Ber'*.

[4] *NS 54*, p. 176 has Margareta.

[5] *NS 54*, p. 176 also has Margareta.

sicut continetur ibidem. In thes. l li. Et debet D et xvj li. et j m. Et v m. et dim. de ij^{bus} scutagiis de feodis Andree de Helyun que requirebantur in Essex in rotulo (precedenti.[i])

Gip' Turstanus de Gipeswiz debet lx s. et j osturcum pro patre suo ut homines de Gipeswiz distringantur.

Nicholaus de Ely de Lond' r.c. de dim. m. pro licencia concordandi cum Hugone de Gurnac'. In thes. lib. Et Q.E.

Alexander Rex Scottorum r.c. de D m. pro habenda custodia heredum comitis Hugonis le Bigod' sicut continetur in dorso rotuli. In thes. lib. Et Q.E.

Heres Roberti de Nereford' debent C (s.[i]) et j m. de passagio et scutagio de feodo Willelmi de Turevill' in Hastingel' qui requirebantur in Kent super predictum feodum.

DE PRESTITO PICTAVIE

Willelmus de Hasting' debet xxix m. de eodem pro se et militibus suis. Walterus del acr' debet xx s. de eodem. Ricardus de Fresingfeld' debet vij m. de eodem. Hugo Talemasch' debet xiij m. de eodem.

Nicholaus de Nereford' r.c. de xl s. pro patre suo pro imbladiamento facto in Bercsir'. In thes. lib. Et Q.E.

Idem N. debet x m. et viij s. quos pater suus recepit de manerio de Brede[1] abbatis de Fiscamo dum habuit custodiam.

Hugo Rufus[2] tunc Vic. debet lx li. et ix s. et iiij d. de remanenti carrucagii de Norf' et Suff' sicut continetur in rotulo de carrucagio. Hugo abbas Sancti Edmundi debet lxxv (li.[i]) de eodem carrucagio infra viij hundreda et dim. sicut ibidem.

DE SCUTAGIO PICTAVIE

Henricus Dux Lovan' debet C et xl li. et xl d. de eodem sicut continetur in rotulo precedenti.

Robertus de Saham [*blank*] lxv s. de v scutagiis contentis in rotulo viij^{o}.

Edmundus de Tudeham [*blank*] viij li. et xiiij s. et vij d. et ob. de pluribus scutagiis contentis ibidem.

Willelmus Blundus r.c. de xiiij li. de eodem. In thes. v m. Et debet x li. et j m.

Johannes de Cornerðe r.c. de CCCC et lxxvj li. et xvij s. et ij d. de pluribus debitis contentis in rotulo viij. In thes. x m. Et debet CCCC et lxx li. et iij s. et ij d. per annum x m.

Robertus Agoillun r.c. de xvj li. et v s. et x d. de pluribus debitis contentis ibidem. In thes. x m. Et debet ix li. et xij s. et vj d. per annum x m.

1 The abbot of Fecamp had custody over the vill of Brede in Sussex. See *NS 54*, p. 165.

2 Hugh Rufus was actually appointed as deputy, or undersheriff, for Norfolk and Suffolk in June 1225. Hubert de Burgh was the actual sheriff from September 1217 until April 1227. Herbert de Alencun was then appointed as sheriff of Norfolk and Suffolk.

Willelmus f. Jordani debet j m. pro summonendo Rogero sicut continetur in rotulo precedenti. Bartholomeus Bainnard' debet xx (s.[i]) quia retraxit se versus priorem de Lewes de ultima presentatione ecclesie de Riston' sicut Oliverius de Vallibus et socii sui justiciarii assignati ad assisam illam capiendam per litteras suas mandaverunt.

DE CONVICTIS

[1]*p* Willelmus f. Rannulfi r.c. de xv li. et xv s. In thes ij s. Et debet xv li. et xiij s

p Brictiva uxor Johannis r.c. de xv li. et xvij s. et iiij d. In thes. ij s. Et debet xv li. et xv s. et iiij d.

p Simon de Flichham r.c. de xxix li. et xviij s. et iiij d. In thes dim. m. Et debet xxix li. et xj s. et viij d.

p Robertus summetarius r.c. de ix li. et (iiij[c]) (ix[i]) et iiij d. In thes. iiij s. Et debet ix li. et v s. et iiij d. per annum (iiij s.[i]).

p Reginaldus Carpentarius r.c. de C et iiij s. et vj d. et ob. In thes. ij s. Et debet C et ij s. et vj d. et ob.

p Bartholomeus f. Philippi r.c. de xxxvj li. et xviij d. In thes. v s. et iij d. Et debet xxxv li. et xvj s. et iij d.

p Rogerus de Bradebec r.c. de viij li. et xvj s. et ij d. In thes. iij s. Et debet viij li. et xiij s. et ij d.

p Adam f. Willelmi r.c. de C et (vj[c]) (iij[i]) s. In thes. iij s. Et debet C s.

[2]*p* Willelmus de Muleton' r.c. de xviij li. et ix s. et iij d. In thes. xij d. Et debet xviij li. et viij s. et iij d. per annum (xij d.[i])

p Robertus f. Herberti r.c. de xxx li. et xix s. et vj d. In thes. ij s. Et debet xxx li. et xvij s. et vj d. per annum (ij s.[i])

p Odo de Appelton' r.c. de xvij li. et v s. et ij d. In thes. dim. m. Et debet xvj li. et xviij s. et vj d. per annum (dim. m.[i])

p Walterus de Berton' r.c. de (lxxiij s. et viij d.[c]) (xxxvij s.[i]) In thes. vj s. et vj d. Et debet xxx s. et vj d.

p Joscelinus de Ereswell' r.c. de x li. et v s. et viij d. In thes. x s. et iiij d. Et debet ix li. et xv s. et iiij d.

p Henricus Hache r.c. de lv s. et iiij d. In thes. vj s. Et debet xlix s. et iiij d.

p Radulfus Truve debet lxxiij s. et viij d. + Rannulfus Algar debet ix li. et ij s. quia fuit convictus. Set non debet summoneri usque (ad voluntatem R.[i])[3] + Johannes Brunmann debet xviij li. pro eodem. + Johannes Gallicus debet lxiij li. et xiij s. et v d.

+ Gillebertus de Lenn' debet terciam partem de liiij li. et j m. pro justiciandis debitoribus suis. Robertus de Ingeworðe r.c. de j m. pro iniusto impedimento. In thes. xl d. Et debet x s.

+ Robertus f. Willelmi debet dim. m. pro habendo pone sicut continetur

[1] The following entries are written at the left hand side of the membrane only.

[2] The following entries are written at the right hand side of the membrane only.

[3] This is not shown as an interlinear but is written in the middle of the line below as though following on from the line on the right hand side. From now on the entries are written across the whole membrane.

in rotulo viij°. Nigellus de Gipeswic' debet j palefridum pro deliberatione navis sue. (+[i]) Willelmus f. Leticie debet dim. m. pro attingendis xij.

Hamo Passelewe r.c. de vij li. et iij s. pro comite de Warewic' sicut continetur in rotulo vij°.[1] In thes. C et iij s. Et debet xl s.

Prior de (Norewiz[c]) Tieford' r.c. de C s. pro defalta foreste. In thes. C s. Et debet ij m. et dim.

Elyas Chubbe r.c. de iiij m. pro justiciando Rogero de Creissi. In thes. viij s. Et debet xlv s. et iiij d.

Bartholomeus f. Rannulfi r.c. de ij s. pro habendo brevi. In thes. lib. Et Q.E.

Robertus f. Michaelis de Oreford' r.c. de ij m. et dim. et ij[bus] doliis vini. In thes. ij m. et dim. Et debet ij° dolia vini.

Johannes de Wauton' r.c. de lviij [s.] et x d. et ob. pro justiciando Roberto Toly.[2] In thes xx s. Et debet xxxviij s. et x d. et ob. per annum xx s.

Robertus marescallus comitis Bolon' d[ebet] j bonum (palefridum[c]) equum pro habenda uxore sua.

ed Willelmus de Godingeham debet xx s. per plegium Ricardi Agoillun. (*ed*[i]) Adam de Cateshill' debet dim. m. pro habendo brevi. (*ed*[i]) Rogerus Drie debet dim. m. pro eodem. + Adam f. Simonis et Johannes f. Gilleberti debent dim. m. pro eodem.

du'[3] Edmundus f. Bernardi r.c. de v m. pro summonendo Johanne Haðewn.[4] In thes. dim. m. Et debet lx s.

+ Robertus de Mouton' debet (dim.[c]) (j[i]) m. pro habendo brevi (du'[i]). + Robertus Brunus debet xx s. pro habendo brevi. Willelmus Wiard'[5] debet dim. m. pro eodem. Galfridus de Aldwarton' debet dim. m. pro eodem. + Walterus de Skeggeness' debet iij m. pro vino vendito.

Robertus de Maisy [*blank*] x m. de primo scutagio R. de feodis Richemund'.

Rogerus de Huntingefeld' r.c. de xvj m. de debitis Judeorum sicut continetur ex alia parte rotuli. In thes. xl s. Et debet xiij m. per annum xl s.

DE AMERCIAMENTIS

Idem Vic. r.c. de iij s. et vij d. de Ricardo de Birun. Et de iij s. et viij d. de Willelmo Goki. Et de xj s. et ij d. de catallis.[6] Et de ij s. et viij d. de Simone Bruning'. Et de iiij s. de Arnaldo Fillekann'. Et de xx d. de Radulfo de Stocton'. Et de xx d. de Johanne Rufo. Et de ij s. et ij d. de Simone de Peski. Et de xx d. de Hugone Wage. Et de iij s. de Roberto Hurtevent. Et de ij s. (et viij d.[i]) de Waltero f. Bernardi. Et de iij s. de Agnete filia Roberti. Et de xx d. de Willelmo pictore. Et de xx d. de Willelmo f. Galfridi. Et de

1 In *NS 56*, p. 83 Hamo is paying the first scutage of the king for the Earl of Warwick.
2 In *NS 54*, p. 179 Robert is shown as the son of Toly.
3 In *NS 56*, p. 84 there is only a marginal entry of *d*. It is possible that this is actually *ou'*.
4 In *NS 56*, p. 84 his surname is shown as Haðewis'.
5 In *NS 56*, p. 84 he is shown as the son of Wiard.
6 The clerk does not indicate if they are the chattels of William Goki or some other individual.

xl d. de Willelmo parcario. Et de iiij s. et viij d. de Willelmo Heiward'. Et de dim. m. de Turstano de Bekewell'. Et de ij s. et j d. de Willelmo f. Radulfi. Et de v s. de Thoma fabro. Et de xl d. de Galfrido f. Galfridi. Et de dim. m. de Johanne Rodland'. Et de dim. m. de Willelmo de Kentewell'. Et de dim. m. de Matill' Mai. Et de dim. m. de Hugone f. Galfridi. Et de dim. m. pro Thoma Grim. Et de dim. m. de Willelmo f. Radulfi. Et de dim. m. de Willelmo f. Radulfi[1] pro plegio. Et de dim. m. de Philippo f. Ricardi. Et de dim. m. de Rogero Marisco. In thes. lib. In xxx taleis. Et Q.E.

[2]*p* Galfridus de Fercles r.c. de iiij m. In thes. j m. Et debet iij m.

t Robertus Francesius r.c. de j m. In thes. dim. m. Et debet dim. m.

t Ricardus f. Willemi r.c. de iij s. et viij d. In thes. xx d. Et debet ij s.

t Nicholaus Rote r.c. de iiij s. In thes. xx d. Et debet ij s. et iiij d.

Alexander[3] Cachevache r.c. de iij s. et viij d. In thes. xij d. Et debet ij s. et viij d.

Willelmus f. Ade camerar' r.c. de iiij s. et viij d. In thes. xij d. Et debet iij s. et viij d. Robertus de la Hill' r.c. de xxx s. In thes. x s. Et debet xx s.

Emma relicta Willelmi r.c. de ix s. et iiij d. In thes. ij s. Et debet vij s. iiij d.

[4]*t* Rogerus Salom' r.c. de iiij s. et viij d. In thes. ij s. et viij d. Et debet ij s.

Don', ɣ Philippus Arnoldus r.c. de lvij s. et xj d. In thes. (ij s.[c]) v s. Et debet (iij s.[c]) lij s. et xj d.

t Hugo de Kanc' r.c. de xl s. et iij ob. In thes. (v[d]) (x[i]) s. Et debet xxx s. et iij ob.

Nor, ɣ Ricardus de Becc' r.c. de v s. In thes. xx d. Et debet xl d.

t Robertus Bridd r.c. de dim. m. In thes. iij s. Et debet iij s. et viij d.

p Ricardus f. Johannis r.c. de dim. m. In thes. ij s. Et debet iiij s. et viij d.

t Stephanus de Buthorp r.c. de dim. m. In thes. iij s. et iiij d. Et debet iij s. et iiij d.

d Willelmus pincerna r.c. de v s. In thes. ij s. Et debet iij s.

[5] Stephanus Vicarius debet vij s. (*d*[i]) Simon f. Yvon' debet xl d. *p* Willelmus Scurell' debet dim. m. pro transgressione. (*d*[i]) Rogerus Ailmer debet dim. m. pro eodem. + Godefridus de Waure debet j m. quia recordatus est sine licencia. + Radulfus de Castr' debet dim. m. pro falso clamore. *d* Ricardus de Stanham debet dim. m. pro dissaisina. (*d*[i]) Bartholomeus (dim. m.[c]) de Creic debet xx s. pro eodem. (*d*[i]) Gerardus f. Galfridi debet dim. m. quia retraxit se. (*p*[i]) Willelmus Orpede debet dim. m. pro eodem. (*d*[i]) Johannes persona de Rissemere debet ij m. pro dissaisina. + Johannes de Bendevill' debet dim. m. quia retraxit se. (*d*[i]) Willelmus de Castro debet dim. m. quia noluit iurare. + Daniel faber debet dim. m. pro falso clamore. (*d*[i]) Willelmus de Ingeham debet j m. quia non est prosecutus. + Willelmus Chieure debet iiij s. et viij d. pro eodem. (*d*[i]) Friede caretarius debet dim. m. pro dissaisina. + Alexander Columbel debet iiij s. et viij d. pro vino

1 A repeat of the previous entry.

2 The following entries are written down the left hand side of the membrane.

3 There are some marginalia prior to this name but the left hand side is so worn it is impossible to say what they are. The same applies to the next five entries.

4 The following entries are written down the right hand side of the membrane.

5 The following entries are written right across the membrane.

vendito. + Bernardus Berd debet dim. m. pro appello suo non prosecuto. + Reginaldus f. Semann' debet j m. pro plegio. + Willelmus Gillot debet dim. m. quia non est prosecutus. (*d*[i]) Walterus f. Eustachii debet C s. pro licencia concordandi de appello et pace fracta. (*d*[i]) Johannes f. Walteri debet dim. m. pro dissaisina. + Rogerus clericus debet dim. m. pro falso clamore. (*d*[i]) Ernoldus f. Rogeri debet dim. m. pro plegio. (*d*[i]) Robertus f. Galfridi de Dalling' debet dim. [m.] ɼ, (*Nor*[i]) Galfridus de Kirkested' debet dim. m. pro plegio. (*d*[i]) Johannes f. Roberti debet (dim.[c]) (j[i]) m. de precio j[us] bane que requirebatur super Vic. in rotulo precedenti. + Gillebertus Stuterell' dim. m. quia non est prosecutus. + Willelmus f. Roberti Arkengier et Thomas Arkengier et Petrus de Folesham debent ij m. pro vino vendito. (*d*[i]) Reginaldus f. Hugonis debet dim. m. pro plegio. (+[i]) Robertus Bridd debet dim. m. pro dissaisina. Radulfus de Lond' debet dim. m. pro vino vendito. + Willelmus f. Stephani debet dim. m. pro dissaisina. (*d*[i]) Henricus de Wica debet dim. m. pro eodem. + Reginaldus le Oiselur debet dim. pro eodem. *p* Ailwardus molendinarius debet dim. m. pro eodem. + Galfridus de Hasting' debet xl s. pro eodem. (*d*[i]) Willelmus frater eius debet dim. m. pro eodem. (*d*[i]) Nicholaus f. Huberti debet dim. m. quia non est prosecutus. (*d*[i]) Walterus forestarius debet dim. m. pro plegio. (*d*[i]) Galfridus f. Thome debet dim. m. pro plegio. + Eustachius f. Olavi debet dim. m. pro eodem. + Elyas de Frivill' debet dim. m. pro plegio. + Willelmus f. Radulfi de Eresham[1] debet dim. m. pro dissaisina. (*d*[i]) Johannes f. Normanni debet dim. m. pro plegio. (*d*[i]) Ricardus f. Werebod' et Petrus f. Rogeri debent j m. pro licencia concordandi. (*d*[i]) Walterus f. Hervici debet dim. m. pro eodem. (*d*[i]) Willelmus f. Petri debet dim. m. pro eodem. (*d*[i]) Ricardus f. Galfridi debet j m. pro eodem. + Alexander f. Helewis' debet dim. m. quia non est prosecutus. (+[i]) Galfridus f. Ailwini debet dim. m. pro plegio. (*d*[i]) Simon cocus debet dim. m. pro dissaisina. (*d*[i]) Walterus frater Alexandri Gunter debet dim. [m.] pro eodem. (*d*[i]) Robertus de Suddon' debet dim. m. pro eodem. (*d*[i]) Sampson Carpentarius [debet] dim. m. pro eodem. (*d*[i]) Willelmus f. Galfridi debet dim. m. pro falso clamore. (*d*[i]) Ricardus et Paganus de Walesham debent dim. m. pro eodem. (*d*[i]) Ricardus f. Henrici debet dim. m. quia non est prosecutus. (*d*[i]) Willelmus Chieur' debet dim. m. pro dissaisina. (*d*[i]) Lucas vinitor debet dim. m. pro vino vendito. (*d*[i]) Willelmus f. Simonis debet dim. m. quia non est prosecutus. + Galfridus Salvagius debet dim. pro plegio. (*d*[i]) Willelmus de la Riole de Notton'[2] debent x s. pro dissaisina. (*d*[i]) Jordanus de Kailli debet dim. m. quia non est prosecutus. (*d*[i]) Nicholaus f. Willelmi de Illeg' debet dim. m. pro plegio.

1 In *NS 56*, p. 89 and in *NS 54*, p. 185 he is shown as William son of Ralph of Earlham in Norfolk as opposed to Earsham in Norfolk here.

2 The clerk may have left out a name here. *NS 56*, p. 91 has *Stephanus de Norton* as well as *Willelmus de la Riole*.

RESPICE IN TERGUM[1]

[*Rot.* 10d *Mem.* 1]

d Willelmus f. Fulconis debet dim. m. pro falso clamore. *d* Henricus vinitor debet dim. m. quia non est prosecutus. + Walterus f. Linote debet dim. [m.] pro eodem. (*d*^{i}) Willelmus de la Hoese debet dim. m. pro eodem. (*d*^{i}) Osebertus f. Radulfi debet dim. m. pro eodem. + Petrus Walterus et Willelmus et Nicholaus debent j m. pro eodem. *d* Rannulfus f. Henrici debet dim. m. pro eodem. *d* Hugo de Blafeld' debet dim. m. pro eodem. *d* Rogerus et Martinus de Bodekesham debent dim. m. pro eodem. + Rogerus Drie debet dim. m. pro dissaisina. + Willelmus Esthard' debet dim. m. pro plegio. (*d*^{i}) Walterus f. Simonis debet (dim.^{i}) m. pro dissaisina. *d* (*Nor'*^{i}) Radulfus Maresc' debet dim. m. pro plegio. + Walterus Cnott debet dim. m. pro dissaisina. (*d, Nor'*^{i}) Stephanus (Gust^{i}) debet C s. pro eodem.[2]
Episcopus Nor' Idem Vic. debet C et v li. et xiij s. et xj d. de misericordiis hominum episcopi Norewic' quorum nomina annotantur in rotulo vij^{o} in itinerantibus justiciariorum.
ed Idem Vic. debet xiij m. et ix s. et ij d. de misericordiis decenarum et villarum et catallis fugitivorum abbatis Sancti Edmundi ann[otatis] ibidem.
Ely Idem Vic. debet xxxix li. et xvj s. et viij d. de misericordiis hominum episcopi Elyen' quorum nomina annotantur in rotulo v^{o} de itinere justiciarorum.
t[3] Sewalus Buggel r.c. de xl d. In thes. xx d. Et debet xx d.
p Willelmus de Reimereston' r.c. de v s. et vj d. In thes. ij s. Et debet iij s. et vj d.
t Adam Barat r.c. de iiij s. et viij d. In thes. xx d. Et debet iij s

Idem Vic. r.c. de xl d. de Roðe de Norewic. Et de dim. m. de Roberto Blundo. In thes. lib. Et Q.E.

p[4] Willelmus f. Savie r.c. de vij s. et x d. In thes ij s. Et debet v s. et x d.
p Reinerus de Burgo (de^{c}) r.c. de dim. m. In thes. xl d. Et debet xl d.
p Robertus Wenge r.c. de x s. et iiij d. In thes. xl d. Et debet vij s.
t Herbertus de Cimiterio r.c. de xl d. pro proprestura. In thes. xx d. Et debet xx d.
[5]*Nor* (*di*) Thomas f. Bunde debet dim. m. pro licencia concordandi. (*d*^{i}) Eustachius f. Copman[6] debet dim. m. quia non est prosecutus. (*d*^{i}) Galfridus de Kirkested' debet dim. m. pro falso clamore. (*d*^{i}) Simon Spich debet j m. pro vino vendito. (*d*^{i}) Rogerus de Weston' debet dim. m. pro plegio. (*d*^{i}) Odo f. Sampsonis debet xl d. quia non est prosecutus. (*d*^{i}) Robertus capellanus

1 There is a pencilled '10' in the middle of the membrane.
2 In *NS 54*, p. 186 the amercement is shown as being for false claim instead of disseisin as here.
3 There is a line, or bracket, from this line to the next line, but then the line proceeds for another two lines. These four lines contain two items per line and the following four items are on the left hand side of the membrane.
4 The next four items are on the right hand side of the membrane.
5 The following entries are written across the whole membrane.
6 In *NS 54*, p. 186 he is shown as *Eustachius Copman*, not the son of Copman.

debet dim. m. pro eodem. (*d*[i]) Johannes Dorat debet j m. pro vino vendito. (*d*[i]) Robertus illuminator debet dim. m. quia non est prosecutus.

Nicholaus de Stutevill' r.c. de j m. pro habenda inquisitione. In thes. lib. Et Q.E.

Willelmus de Arcubus r.c. de dim. m. pro habendo pone. In thes. lib. Et Q.E.

Len Galfridus f. Asketin debet j m. pro vino vendito. Wolmerus Lamb et socii sui debent iiij s. de catallis Willelmi de Linc'. Willelmus de Plesset' debet j m. pro eodem. Stephanus Hurel debet j m. pro eodem. Nicholaus de Gernemue debet C s. ut possit se retrahere.

Dun[1] Augustinus f. Burchard' r.c. de x s. pro plegio. In thes. xl d. Et debet dim. m.

Ricardus f. Rogeri r.c. de dim. m. pro plegio. In thes xx d. Et debet v s.

Robertus f. Ricardi r.c. de xl s. pro transgressione. In thes. dim. m. Et debet ij m. et dim.

Robertus f. Reginaldi r.c. de dim. m. quia retraxit se. In thes. xx d. Et debet v s.

Edwardus f. Ricardi debet x s. pro dissaisina. Vincentius vinitor debet dim. m. pro vino vendito. Bernardus de Dunewiz (debet[c]) et Swanild' uxor eius debent x s. pro dissaisina.

[2]*Gip'* Johannes f. Nicholai r.c. de v s. pro plegio. In thes. lib. Et Q.E.

Stephanus Tailliator r.c. de dim. m. quia retraxit se. In thes. xl d. Et debet xl d.

+ Goldingus f. Edmundi debet dim. m. pro dissaisina. + Radulfus cocus debet dim. m. pro falso clamore.

[3]*Ger* Angerus nepos Gilleberti r.c. de iiij s. et viij d. de misericordia. In thes. xx d. Et debet iij s.

Eche sutor r.c. de v s. pro falso clamore. In thes. xx d. Et debet xl d.

Turbertus plumbarius r.c. de xl d. quia non est prosecutus. In thes. xx d. Et debet xx d.

Simon de Lond' r.c. de v s. pro vino vendito. In thes. ij s. Et debet iij s.

Alexander Wolbald' r.c. de xvj d. quia noluit iurare. In thes. lib. Et Q.E.

+ Brianus f. Rogeri debet dim. m. pro falso clamore. Alexander Columbel debet dim. m. pro vino vendito. Willelmus f. Toly debet dim. m. pro falso clamore. Ricardus de Covintr' debet dim. m. pro defalta. Milo vinitor debet dim. m. pro vino vendito. Robertus Dogget debet x s. quia non est prosecutus.

ed Willelmus Hervei r.c. de vij li. et x s. et j palefrido pro habendis terris sicut continetur in rotulo vij°. In thes. x s. Et debet vij li. et j palefridum.

Hugo le Bigod r.c. de lxxj li. et xiiij s. et viij d. de pluribus debitis contentis in rotulo vij°. In thes. nichil. Et W. comes Warenn' quater xx li. de catallis ipsius H. captis in manerio R. pro predicto debito et venditis ipsi W. comiti de quibus quater xx li. idem comes Warenn' respondebit ad

1 This line and the next four lines are bracketed together. Presumably they all relate to Dunwich.

2 This line and the next two lines are bracketed together.

3 This and the next five lines are bracketed together.

scaccarium in summa debiti quod idem comes Warenn' debet R. per finem quem fecit cum R. reddendi ei per annum C m. de eodem debito per breve R. Et habet H. de superplus viij li. v s. iiij d.

Robertus de Saham debet v s. de scutagio de Biham. Edmundus de Tudeham debet x s. de eodem. Ricardus Duket tunc Vic. debet xij s. et ix d et ob. de baconibus sicut continetur in rotulo v°.

Lambertus de Muleton' debet lx s. et j d. de misericordia sicut continetur in rotulo iiij per plegium Thome de Muleton' patris sui. Set respondet in Cumberland' in rotulo sequenti.

ed. Galfridus f. Roberti debet dim. m. pro falso clamore. Warinus clericus debet dim. m. pro dissaisina. Andreas f. Johannis debet dim. m. pro habendo pone. Nicholaus de Scrouteby debet dim. m. pro defalta. Johannes Fluri debet iij m. pro habenda terra sicut continetur in rotulo v°.

P. Norewic' episcopus r.c. de v m. pro j palefrido pro habendo mercato sicut continetur ibidem. In thes. lib. Et Q.E.

Alexander de Bassingeburne [*blank*] xxx li. et xix s. et j d. de exitibus ville de Costesie sicut continetur in rotulo v°.[1]

Villata de Norewiz r.c. de xxxvj li. de tallagio. In thes. xviij li. et xv s. Et debet xvij li. et v s.

Willelmus de Camera r.c. de x m. ut possit esse sub plegio Johannis Maresc'. In thes. dim. m. Et debet ix m. et dim.

Hugo de Braham debet x s. pro habenda inquisitione sicut continetur in rotulo vij°. Radulfus de Boilund' debet iij s. et iiij d. de misericordia. Hugo de Mildehal' debet j m. pro iniusto impedimento sicut continetur ibidem.

Willelmus de Sapeston' r.c. de ix m. pro habenda justicia sicut continetur in rotulo vij°. In thes. j m. Et debet viij m.

Villata de Gernemue [*blank*] xxxij li. et j m. de tallagio.

Villata de Donewiz r.c. de xxviij li. de eodem. In thes. nichil. Et in perdonis ipsis hominibus pro fideli servicio suo facto R. J. patri R. et ipsi R. tempore guerre xxviij li. per breve R. Et Q.S.

Ricardus f. Umfridi r.c. de dim. m. (de[c]) pro habendo pone. In thes. lib. Et Q.E.

Ricardus f. Roberti de Bedef' debet v m. de primis denariis pro justiciando Gerardo sicut continetur (ibidem[c]) in rotulo viij°. Henricus de Walepole debet dim. m. pro dissaisina qui requirebatur in Oxon' in rotulo de itinere M. de Pateshill'.

Willelmus de Wutton' [*blank*] xl m. scilicet de tercia parte quater xx li. pro justiciandis Willelmo Blome (et alios[i])[2] sicut continetur ibidem.

Willelmus de Burdeleis r.c. de ij m. de relevio suo. In thes. lib. Et Q.E.

Martinus de Bella Fago r.c. de xl s. pro habenda justicia sicut continetur in rotulo viij. In thes. lib. Et Q.E.

Hamo Passelew' [*blank*] xij m. et dim. pro Roberto Passelew' fratre suo sicut continetur ibidem.

[1] There is no reference to this in the Pipe Roll for 5 Henry III but it appears in *NS 51*, p. 182, where it indicates that the revenue is from year five. It therefore looks as though the clerk has made an error of reference here.

[2] *Alios* written for *aliis*.

Arnoldus de Mandevill' r.c. de xvj li. et j m. pro Roberto de Burgat' sicut infra continetur. In thes. vj li. Et debet x li. et j m. per annum vj li.

DE SCUTAGIO DE MUNGUMERI

Edmundus de Tudeham debet ij m. de eodem. Et duas m. de scutagio de Bedef'.

Henricus de Illeg' debet vj m. de eodem de feodis Andree de Heliun. Robertus de Saham debet j m. de eodem. Willelmus f. Willelmi de Kayhú debet vij li. et xv s. de pluribus scutagiis contentis in rotulo viij. Nicholaus de Bello Campo debet v m. de eodem de feodis Gilleberti de Tany. Thomas de Longa Villa debet j m. quia non est prosecutus qui requirebatur in itinere Simonis de Hal in Essex'.

Warinus clericus de Subir' debet dim. m. pro dissaisina. Petrus de Nereford' debet dim. m. pro eodem qui duo requirebantur in Essex' in itinere Simonis de Hal et sociorum eius.

DE SCUTAGIO DE BEDEFORD'

Idem Vic. r.c. de xxj s. et iiij d. de abbate de Hulmo de eodem. Et de ij m. de Margar' de Creissi de eodem. In thes. lib. Et Q.E.

Henricus de Illeg' debet vj m. de eodem. Robertus de Saham debet j m. de eodem. Willelmus f. Willelmi de Kayhú [debet] iij m. de eodem.

Robertus f. Walteri r.c. de lxvj li. et xviij s. et viij d. de scutagio Pictavie. In thes. xij d. per Robertum de Havill' de xl^{ma} parte j^{us} feodi. Et xl s. per Willelmum de Witewell' et Willelmum de Skeggeton'. Et ij s. per Nigellum de Rifflec'. Et iij s. et iiij d. per Robertum de Munteinni. Et viij s.[1] per Walterum Malet. Et dim. m. per Philippum de Snaring'. Et x s. per Galfridum de Snaring'. Et xx s. per Robertum de Presseinny. Et debet lxij li. et vij s. et viij d.

Bartholomeus de Creic r.c. de quater xx et xv li. et ij s. et viij d. de debitis Judeorum. In thes. xx li. Et debet lxxv li. et ij s. et viij d. per annum xx li.

Elyas de Burum r.c. de lxvj li. et xiij s. et viij d. de eodem. In thes. vij li. et x s. Et debet lix li. et iij s. et viij d.

Radulfus de Clere r.c. de CC li. et v m. de eodem. In thes. v m. Et item xxxv m. Et debet C et lxxvj li. et xiij s. et v d.[2] per annum xl m.

Willelmus de Pinkeinni r.c. de xx li. de eodem. In thes. xl s. Et debet xviij li. per annum xl s.

Robertus de Chieurevill' r.c. de lxiiij li. et j m. de eodem. In thes. xl s. Et debet lxij li. et j m. per annum xl s.

Galfridus de Wenaveston' r.c. de ix li. de eodem. In thes. xl s. Et debet vij li. per annum xl s.

Dionisius de Lechesham r.c. de xiiij li. et iij s. et x d. et ob. de eodem. In thes. xl s. Et debet xij li. et iij s. et x d. et ob. per annum xl s.

Arnoldus de Mandevill' r.c. de xviij li. et j m. de eodem pro Roberto de

[1] The 'v' is almost like a 'w' or one 'v' overlying another.

[2] The total owing to the treasury is £176-13s-4d not £176-13-5d.

Burgat'. In thes. xl s. Et debet xvj li. et j m. Set respondet supra.

per annum vj li.

Willelmus Juvenal r.c. de viij li. de eodem. In thes. v m. Et debet vij m.

per annum v m.

Rogerus de Huntingefeld' clericus debet xvj m. de eodem. (Set respondet ex alia parte rotuli.[i]) Willelmus Juvenal debet C s. pro panno vendito qui requirebatur in Lond' in rotulo de itinere M. de Patheshill' et sociorum eius.

Ricardus Duket [*blank*] xiij li. de remanenti carrucagii de Norf' et Suff' quas recepit dum fuit Vic. ibidem sicut recognovit, qui requirebatur in rotulo de carrucagio.

DE OBLATIS[1] (Willelmus Juvenal debet j m. pro habendo precipe qui requirebatur in London'[i]).

[*Rot.* 10d *Mem.* 2]

Ricardus de Brumford' r.c. de vij m. pro transgressione (sicut continetur infra[i]). In thes. xx s. per Vic. Essex' de Ricardo Bataill' plegio suo. Et debet v m. et dim.

Idem Vic. r.c. de j m. de Willelmo de Heingeham. Et de dim. m. de Alexandro de Poringeland'. Et de dim. m. de Galfrido le Brett. Et de dim. m. de Willelmo de Wigorn'. Et de dim. m. de Warino le Utlage. Et de dim. m. de Margar' de Colevill'. Et de v m. pro j palefrido de Willelmo de Stutevill'. Et de j m. de Henrico coco. Et de ij m. de Radulfo de Sunderland'. Et de dim. m. de Johanne de Flegg. Et de dim. m. de Alano de Ekingeham pro licencia concordandi. In thes. lib. Et Q.E.

Prior de Norewic' r.c. de x m. pro ij^{bus} palefridis pro habendis ij^{bus} mercatis sicut continetur in rotulo precedenti. In thes. v m. Et in quietantia ipsius prioris quia non habuit nec habere potuit pro quo promisit v m. per breve R. Et Q.E.

[2] Adam f. Walteri r.c. de xx s. pro pone. In thes. j m. Et debet dim. m.

p Radulfus de Sunderland' r.c. de C s. pro saisina. In thes. xx s. Et debet iiij li.

p Baldewinus de Pateford' r.c. de iiij m. pro sacramento. In thes. ij m. Et debet ij m.

p Henricus f. Radulfi r.c. de ij m. pro eodem. In thes. dim. m. Et debet xx s.

t Rogerus f. Radulfi r.c. de iij m. et dim. pro eodem. In thes. ij m. et dim. Et debet j m.

p Galfridus de Denton' r.c. de lx s. pro eodem. In thes. xiiij s. Et debet xlvj s.

1 There is an insertion which is almost impossible to read alongside the heading because of the overlapping stitching and membranes. It is not possible to determine which particular line of the text this is an insertion. However, William Juvenal is also shown in the item two lines above so it might be a continuation of that line as the clerk could not fit this inserted text into the space left.

2 The following entries are written at the left hand side of the membrane only.

p Rogerus f. Rannulfi r.c. de xxiij s. et iiij d.[1] In thes. x s. Et debet j m.
Thomas de Kirkeby r.c. de ij m. et dim. In thes. ij m. Et debet dim. m.
[2]*t* Willelmus f. Main r.c. de xl s. pro eodem. In thes. xx s. Et debet xx s.
p Robertus de Gelverton' r.c. de xl s. pro eodem. In thes j m. Et debet ij m.
t Galfridus Grimbald' r.c. de ij m. et dim. In thes. xx s. Et debet j m.
t Hugo March r.c. de ij m. et dim. pro eodem. In thes. xx s. Et debet j m.
t Johannes Midsumer r.c. de ij m. et dim. In thes. xx s. Et debet j m.
t Rogerus de Baddeslé r.c. de v m. pro transgressione. In thes. xl s. Et debet ij m.
p Robertus de Laundr' r.c. de vj m. et dim. pro falso presentatione. In thes xx s. Et debet v m.
d[3] Robertus Cornet debet dim. m. pro dissaisina. (*d*[i]) Robertus f. Henrici de Cokefeld' debet j m. pro habendo brevi. (*d*[i]) Willelmus nuncius debet dim. m. pro habenda inquisitione. (*d*[i]) Nicholaus f. Hugonis et Hugo et Henricus et Galfridus fratres eius debent dim. m. pro habenda jurata. (*d*[i]) Thomas de Schotford' debet dim. m. pro licencia concordandi.
[4] Robertus de Meisi debet xv li. de warda de Richemund' de vj annis preteritis. (*d*[i]) Alexander de Bassingeburn' debet lxv s. de catallis Rogeri Sirich' quos recepit dum fuit constabularius Merleberg' qui requirebatur in rotulo (de itinere[i]) M. de Pateshill' (in Wiltesir'[i]).[5]

Petrus Leverot [*blank*][6] de catallis Roberti Decani de Norton'

Johannes Maresc' r.c. de D et xlvj li. et viij s. et ix [d.] de remanenti plurium debitorum contentorum in rotulo vij° de quibus finem fecerat per C marcas annuatim per C m.[7] et reddidit in anno preterito CC m. scilicet de anno ix° et hoc anno. Et de lxx li. et xiiij s. et xj d. de pluribus aliis debitis contentis in rotulo viij° de quibus finem non fecerat. Et de xx m. pro plegio Henrici filii comitis sicut continetur in Devon' in rotulo iiij° R. J.[8] Et (de[i]) C et v s. quos Ballivi sui receperunt de Philippo de Hambir' sicut continetur in Wigorn' in rotulo precedenti. Et xvij s. et vj d. de wardis Richemund' in Linc'. Et x m. de abbate de Bordesleg' pro assartis suis in pace habendis in Ballia de Fekeham sicut continetur in rotulo de perquisitis foreste dum fuit justiciarius foreste quem liberavit in thesauro per manum R. Cycestr' episcopi cancellarii. Et de vj m. de eodem abbate pro quadam domo in pace habenda quam levavit in foresta predicta unde non habuit warant' nisi Galonem tunc legatum et W. Maresc' seniorem sicut continetur ibidem. Et de xl m. quas recepit de Wigorn' episcopo et W. de Bello Campo pro saisina habenda de foresta de Amberleg' et

1 For this and the next item there is no reason for the debt provided.
2 The following entries are written at the right hand side of the membrane only.
3 It looks as though the clerk overwrote a 'p' with a 'd'. Also, this item starts on the right hand side of the membrane and continues on the next line across the membrane.
4 There is some strengthening tape down the left hand side of the membrane which may have obscured some marginalia.
5 This is actually on the line below.
6 There is a gap of at least three inches before the completion of the text.
7 100 marks repeated.
8 This is Henry s. of Reginald, earl of Cornwall. See Carpenter, *The Minority of Henry III*, pp. 120–2. Henry actually died in 1222.

Horewell' deaforestata per consilium R. sicut continetur ibidem. Et de xx m. quas recepit de eisdem pro saisina habita et libertate illa concessa in pace utenda sicut continetur ibidem. Et de x m. quas recepit de predicto episcopo pro protectione habenda ne gravaretur á forestario vel aliis sicut continetur ibidem. Et de viij m. de abbate de Bordeseg' pro protectione et per sic quod servientes foreste sicut forestar' de feod' nec alii illos vexarent de essartis suis nec intrarent in grangiis suis ad manducandum sicut continetur ibidem. Et de ij m. de cellerario de Evesham pro habendo brevi de protectione. Et de C s. de perquisitis per manum Willelmi de Eston' sicut continetur ibidem. Et de vj m. de perquisitis per Henricum Dairel sicut continetur ibidem. Et de v m. per manum dicti Willelmi de perquisitis sicut continetur ibidem. Et de C s. de Matill' de Chauz pro auxilio habendo ad ballivam de foresta habendam in Noting' sicut continetur ibidem. Et de xl m. de militibus comitatus Noting' et Dereb' pro auxilio habendo ad deaforestandam id quod debet deaforestari per cartam R. secundum perambulationem factam per preceptum R. per litteras suas sicut continetur ibidem. Et de x m. de eisdem pro de[1] altera de ambulatione per preceptum R. sicut continetur ibidem. Et de x m. de abbate de Dora pro assartis suis de Trivel in Herefordsir' in pace habendis secundum tenorem carte R. J. Et de v m. de eodem abbate pro protectione et bona pace et (Et[i]) de j palefrido de eodem abbate pro eodem. Et de v m. et j palefrido de Margar' de Lascy apud Lond' receptis. Et de ij m. de Waltero de Aschel' de promisso pro assarto suo iuxta Hayam R. Et de xl m. de hominibus comitatus Gloec' pro auxilio habendo ad forestam comitatus deaforestandum secundum perambulationem factam per preceptum R. Et de xx m. de hominibus comitatus de Berkesir' pro auxilio habendo ut predictum est et pro libertate foreste secundum cartam R. tenenda. Et de v m. de abbatissa de Warewell' pro essarto suo in Sudhantesir' in pace habendo. Et de xlij s. de perquisitis in ballia de Pemberge per Robertum de Braiboef. Et de xv s. et j d. de perquisitis apud Lond' pacatis. Et de xvj s. et iij d. de perquisitis apud Oxon'. Et de xx m. de hominibus comitatus Hunted' pro predictis auxiliis et libertate carte tenendis. Et de x m. (de eisdem[i]) pro saisina habenda per preceptum R. illis concessa. Et de ij m. de hominibus Hereford' manerii R. pro pastura sua habenda in bosco de Sappel' quam solent habere. Et de v m. de hominibus de Wimundel' et Weston' et Ailinton' et Wolflé et Branton' pro pastura sua in Wichewode. Et de xl m. de militibus foreste de Galtris pro auxilio habendo et libertate carte tenenda Et de xl m. de militibus foreste inter Usam et Derewent pro eodem. Et de v m. de perquisitis foreste de Gautris per Ricardum de Lond'. Et item de v m. de perquisitis per eundem R. Et de ij m. de perquisitis per[2] Galfridum de Cumpton' de ballia sua. Et de x m. de militibus comitis Cumberland' pro auxilio habendo ut predictum est et libertate carte tenenda. Et de x m. de priore hospitalis Jer'l'm pro essartis in pace habendis unde habet cartam R. H. scilicet de C acris. Et de xx s. de perquisitis de Willelmo de Erlawe per Rogerum clericum. Et de xl s. de priore Sancti Andree pro bosco suo de Kingesbir' claudendo. Et de j m. de Willelmo de Horton'

1 This passage is corrupt. Either the *pro* or the *de* is redundant, as is the second *de*.
2 The clerk has corrected the 'p' from a 'd', which is still showing.

forestario de saliceto pro essarto suo in saliceto in pace habendo. Et de iij m. de Engelmund de Dummarc pro pastura bosci de Baggel' habenda. Et de j m. de Willelmo de Haumund' pro bosco suo de Bruschawe claudendo. Et de ij m. de Amabilia de Bello Campo pro viij acris assarti in Bosco de Wottun'. Et de ix m. de hominibus comitatus Buking' pro auxilio ut predictum est. Et de j dolio vini rubei raspati de Radulfo Hareng' pro assartis ij acrarum. Et de j alio dolio vini de eodem ut Thomas de Sancto Walerico perhaberet lx acras secundum tenorem carte R. Et de xiij m. de Johanne f. Nigelli pro assarto suo. Et de xx s. de Ricardo et Willelmo de Doddeford' pro bosco suo de Doddeford' assartando. Summa DCCCC et xxx li. et vj s. et ij d. et ij palefridos et j dolium vini rubei raspati et j aliud dolium vini. In thes. nichil. Et in perdona ipsi J. CC et xj m. per breve R. Et debet DCC et quater xx et ix li. et xij s. et x d. et ij palefridos et ij dolia vini ut predictum est. per annum C m. per breve R. *Respondet infra.*

Idem J. r.c. de garnistura castri de Divis[is][1] quam recepit cum eodem castro post mortem R. J. patris R. Et de exitibus episcopatus Coventr' vacantis et in custodia J. existentis tempore predicti R. J. De quibus omnibus Dominus Rex quietum clamavit ipsum Johannem per breve suum quod est in forulo marescalli. Et Q.E.

Idem J.[2] r.c. de DCC et quater xx et ix li. et xij s. et x d. et ij palefridis et ij doliis vini de pluribus debitis supra contentis. In thes. xx s. per Ricardum et Willelmum de Dodeford'. Et debet DCC et quater xx et viij li. et xij s. et x d. ij palefridos et ij dolia vini. (per annum C m.[c])

[3] Idem debet vj m. et dim. de debitis Judeorum qui requirebantur in Linc' in iudaismo.

Idem J. r.c. de eodem debito.[4] In thes. ij per cellerarium de Evesham. Et debet DCC et quater xx et vij li. et vj s. ij d. et ij palefridos et ij d[olia vini.][5]

NOVA OBLATA

Ranulfus de Shelton' et Katerina uxor eius r.c. de xv m. pro habenda saisina de feodis trium militum que fuerunt Henrici de Illeg' patris ipsius Katerine cuius heres ipsa est et que ipsam contingunt hereditar' in Illeg' unde R. cepit homagium eius. In thes. xx s. Et debet xiij m. et dim. De quibus reddet singulis annis xx s., scilicet ad Pasch' x s. et ad festum Sancti Michaelis x s. donec totum persolvatur.

Willelmus Bainnard' debet j m. pro habendo pone de tenemento in Raveningeham et Vic. respondeat de securitate. Walterus de Rising'

1 There are a two abbreviation symbols following this word.
2 This is John Marshal.
3 The next two lines are on the same line as the heading '*Nova Oblata*'. However, they relate to the previous section and for the sake of clarity the heading has been shown on a separate line.
4 This item is a follow on to the item prior to the previous one. It may be the reason for the possible crossed out attermination.
5 There is a piece of the membrane missing here, which has been strengthened by some tape.

debet dim. m. pro habendo pone de terra in Rising' et Vic. respondeat de securitate.

Rogerus de Kentewell' debet quinquaginta li. pro relevio suo de terra que fuit Gilleberti de Kentewell', scilicet de feodis x militum unde idem Gillebertus saisitus fuit die quo obiit et que ipsum R. iure[1] contingit hereditarie [et] Vic. respondeat de securitate. Radulfus de Burgo debet x m. pro relevio suo de terra que fuit Rogeri de Burgo in Burgo. Robertus f. Henrici et Willelmus et Ricardus fratres eius debent v m. pro habenda inquisitione quis sit proprinquior (heres[i]) Arnoldi Ise qui mortuus est et Vic. respondeat de securitate. Willelmus Cachehare de Tieford' debet j m. pro habendis v pieciis pannorum qui capti fuerunt in nundinis de Hoiland' eo quod non fuerunt de latitudine. Willelmus de Haverhill' et Willelmus scissor respondeat de securitate. Alexander Rex Scottorum (debet[i]) D m. (Set respondet ex alia parte rotuli[i])[2] reddendas ad mediam quadrag[esimam] pro habendis sibi vel eius assignatis usque ad etatem heredum H. le Bigod' comitis Norf' wardis maritagiis et escaetis que exciderunt de terris et feodis militum et aliorum qui tenuerit de eodem comite per servicium militare et quos R. in manu sua retinuit quando terras et feoda predicta concessit predicto R. Et pro habendo l m. annuatim de comitatu Norf' usque ad etatem predictorum heredum quas predictus comes recipere solebat singulis annis de comitatu Norf' nomine eiusdem comitatus. Et pro habendis presentationibus ecclesiarum ad eosdem heredes spectantium ita quod ad eas presentet predictus R. vel eius assignati cum eas vacare contigerit. Et pro habendis l libratis terre quas R. retinuit in manu sua ad custodiam castri de Framelingeham reddendo singulis annis de cetero xx li. usque ad etatem eorundem heredum ad custodiam eiusdem castri quod R. reddidit Rogero filio et heredi predicti comitis custodiendum per manum H. de Burgo usque ad etatem eiusdem Rogeri. Decena Alling' butarii in Sééng' debet dim. m. pro fuga Johannis Ferling' qui requirebatur in Hertfordsir' in rotulo Simonis de Hal et sociorum suorum.

Idem Vic. r.c. de dim. m. de Rogero f. Osberti[3] pro licencia concordandi cum Rogero de Ludham. Et de dim. m. de Roberto de Blundeston' pro eodem. Et de dim. m. de Willelmo Rusteng' pro eodem. Et de dim. m. de Waltero de Rising' [pro eodem]. Et de ij m. et dim. de Hugone de Plaiz pro eodem. Et de dim. m. de Rogero de Hales pro eodem. Et de dim. m. de Rogero de Sudfeld' pro eodem. Et de dim. m. de Johanne de Halegton' pro eodem. Et de dim. m. de Willelmo de Giselham pro eodem. Et de v m. de Herberto de Alencun pro eodem. Et de xx s. de Warino de Monchansi pro eodem. Et de xx s. de Willelmo de Franchevill' pro eodem. Et de dim. m. de Willelmo Salvag' pro eodem. Et de j m. de Hugone de Grentenhagh' pro eodem. Et de j m. de Rogero de Aldham pro eodem. Et de j m. de Waltero f. Ade pro eodem. Et de j m. de Vincentio de Navelton' pro eodem. Et de dim. m. de Huberto Espervier pro eodem. Et de dim. m. de Augustino de Blakenham pro eodem. Et de dim. m. de Bartholomeo Brittone pro eodem. Et de dim. m. de Oseberto Georg' pro eodem. Et de dim. m. de Radulfo f.

1 The word *iure* is repeated.
2 This is very faint but the writing appears to be in the same hand.
3 'O' written over 'A'.

Martini pro eodem. Et de dim. m. de Roberto de Graveny. Et de xl s. de Priore de Lewes pro eodem. Et de xv m. de Henrico de Véér pro eodem. Et de xl s. de Adam de Kailly pro eodem. In thes. lib. Et Q.E.

[1] Simon de Saham r.c. de xx s. pro transgressione. In thes. dim. m. Et debet j m.

Goda que fuit uxor Haldan' r.c. dim. m. pro attornato per breve. In thes. xl d. Et debet xl d.

Ricardus de Brumford' r. c. de C s. pro transgressione. In thes. dim. m. Et debet vij m. Set respondet supra.

[2] Hubertus de Nereford' r.c. de j m. pro transgressione. In thes. dim. m. Et debet dim. m.

Ernoldus f. Ricardi et fratres eius r.[c.] de ij m. pro transgressione. In thes. xx s. Et debet dim. m.

Willelmus Painel debet ij m. et dim. pro licencia concordandi cum Hugone de Plaiz. Robertus de Haltsted' debet dim. m. pro eodem cum Willelmo de Neref'.

[*One line blank*]

AMERCIAMENTA FACTA PER SIMONEM DE HAL ET SOCIOS EIUS.

Idem Vic. r.c. de xxvij li. et vj s. et x d. de misericordiis hominum Decenarum et villarum quorum nominibus preponitur littera *t* in rotulo quem predicti liberaverunt in thesauro. In thes. lib. In j talea. Et Q.E.

Stephanus de Weðeresden' r.c. de dim. m. quia retraxit se. In thes. xx d. Et debet v s.

Andreas de Guneware (debet[c]) et Johannes Balle debent dim. m. quia non habuerunt Adam de Cote quem plegiaverunt. Willelmus de Boxton' debet dim. m. pro dissaisina. Willelmus f. Oseberti de Gedding' debet dim. m. quia non habuit quos plegiavit. Decena Simonis f. Alani fugitivi debet dim. m. pro fuga ipsius S. Gillebertus f. Nigelli debet dim. m. pro falso clamore. Thomas de Blumvill' debet C li. pro habenda custodia terre et heredum Oliverii Avenel et maritagium eorundem heredum et maritagium Agnetis uxoris eius.

[*Six lines blank*]

There is a printed '20' in the fifth blank line.

[*Endorsed*] emend' et iterum emendat'

Norfolk et Suffolk[3]

[*Rot.* II *Mem.* I]

[1] The following entries are written at the left hand side of the membrane only.

[2] The following entries are written at the right hand side of the membrane only.

[3] There are three vertical dots before and after *Norfolk*, after *et*, and after *Suffolk*.

NOTINGEHAM ET DEREBISIR[1]

Radulfus f. Nicholai ut custos r.c. de CC et lxxix li. et v s. et xj d. bl. Et de xl li. et x s. num. de firma comitatuum. In thes. nichil.

Et in elemosinis constitutis militibus de Templo ij m. Et in villa de Notingeh' lij li. bl. de quibus homines ville respondet infra. Et in villa de Dereb' xl li. bl. de quibus homines ville respondent infra. Et in Ernhal' cum pertinenciis xij li. et xiiij d. bl. de quibus Hugo de Neovill' respondet infra. Et in Snointon' Willelmo Briewerr' viij li. bl. Et eidem xiij li. et iiij s. bl. in Cestrefeld'. Et in Karelton' viij li. et dim. m. num. de quibus Vic. respondet infra. Et in Mammefeld' xxxvj li. et vij s. et vj d. de quibus idem respondet infra. Et in Derleton' x li. de quibus idem respondet infra. Et in Edwinestowe vj li. et vij s. et vj d. de quibus idem respondet infra. Et canonicis de Scirewode v s. in Pappelwic. Et eisdem C s. in Oswardebecc'. Et canonicis de Haverholm iiij li. in Stanton' et Turverton'. Et priori de Novo loco vij li. et vj d. in Wakeringeham et Scheperton' et Misterton'. Et Thome de Lanum iiij m. in duabus Tilnis. Et canonicis de Wellebecc' xij s. et vj d. in Hungerclune. Et Willelmo de Aubineio xxvj li. in Oskinton'. Et comiti Bolon' l li. in Dunham. Et heremite Sancti Edwini de Haia de Birchwude xl s. Et Henrico Corbin ij m. et dim. in Karelton'. Et Marine uxori Roberti f. Hugonis xxxvij s. et iiij d. in Claworðe nomine dotis. Et Rogero de Monte Begon' xxxviij li. et xix s. in manerio de Oswardebecc'. Et Willelmo de Hardredeshill' lvj s. de tribus partibus anni in Claworðe. Et in eadem villa xviij s. et viij d. de quarta parte de quibus Vic. respondet infra. Et heredibus Philippi de Ulecot' lxxv s. et iij d. in Oswardebecc'. Et abbati de Wellebecc' xl s. in molendino de Radford a festo Sancti Michaelis anno x^{o} in iiij annos sicut continetur in rotulo precedenti de quibus respondet infra.

[*One line blank*]

Et in carriagio x tonellorum vini á Linc' usque Notingeh' reponendorum in castro de Noting' et in carcagio et discarcagio eorundem xlij s. et viij d. per breve R. Et in quintadecima de Notingehamsir' conducenda á Notingeh' usque Wint' xxxviij s. et ij d. per breve eiusdem. Et in ferramento prisonum vij s. et x d. Et in emendatione castri et domorum in castro de Notingeh' C et xvij s. et x d. Et habet de superplus xix li. et ix s. et ix d. num. quod totum locatur ei infra in pluribus debitis.

f' Idem Vic. r.c. de C et x li. et vij s. et v d. de proficuo comitatus[2] de hoc anno. Et de iiij li. et vij s. et vij d. de proficuo honoris Peverell'. In thes. nichil. Et Radulfo f. Nicholai pro custodia comitatus et castri de Noting'[3] C li. per breve R. de hoc anno. Et debet xiiij li. et xv s. et v d.[4] Idem r.c. de eodem debito. In thes. nichil. Et in superplus (quod habet supra^{i}) xxviij s. et xj d. Et debet xiij li. vj s. et j d.

f' Idem Vic. r.c. de xvj li. de remanenti proficui de anno preterito. In thes. nichil. Et in superplus quod habet in anno preterito xiij li. et vj s. et ij

1 There are three dots after *Derebesir*.
2 *Comitatus* written for *comitatuum*.
3 Mending strip obscures end of line.
4 Sum of money squashed into space left by obliteration.

d. Et debet liij s. et x d. Idem r.c. de eodem debito. In thes. nichil. Et in superplus quod habet supra liij s. et x [d.] Et Q.E.[1]

Homines de Notingeh' r.c. de lij li. bl. de firma ville sue. In thes. xlv li. et xij s. et ij d. bl. Et in elemosinis constitutis militibus de Templo vj d. Et monialibus de Dereb' C s. Et debent xxij s. et iiij d. bl.

Idem r.c. de eodem debito. In thes. xj s. et viij d. bl. Et in superplus quod telarii habent in rotulo precedenti ix (s.[i]) et viij d. et ob. bl. Et debent x s. et xj d. et ob. bl. Idem r.c. de eodem debito. In thes. lib. Et Q.[S].

Idem homines debent xlvj s. bl. (*Set respondent infra.*[i]) de remanenti eiusdem firme de anno preterito. Et xvj li. et x s. et iiij d. bl. (*Set respondent in dorso rotuli.*[i]) de remanenti eiusdem firme de pluribus annis preteritis contentis in rotulo iiij[o].

f' Idem homines r.c. de xxiij s. et vj d. de censu domorum. Et de ix s. de toftis monetariorum. In thes. xxv s. et xx d. Et Ysoude de Gray dim. m. pro domo quam amisit per fossatum castri de Notingeh' usque ad etatem R. Et Q.S.

f' Telarii de Notingeh' r.c. de xl s. pro gilda sua. In thes. lib. Et Q.S.

f' Burgenses de Dereb' r.c. de xl li. bl. de firma ville sue. In thes. xxxiij li. viij s. v d. et ob. bl. Et Ricardus f. Petri de Sandiacr' C s. in Lutchirche. Et canonicis de Dereb' x s. Et debent xxvij s. et ob. (bl.[i]). Idem r.c. de eodem debito. In thes. lviij s. et v d. Et habent de superplus xxxj s. et iiij d. et ob. bl. qui locantur eis infra in proxima linea.

Idem burgenses r.c. de xxxj s. et iiij d. et ob. bl. de remanenti firme ville sue de anno preterito. In thes. nichil. Et in superplus quod habet supra xxxj s. et iiij d. et ob. Et Q.S.

f' Idem burgenses r.c. de[2] x li. num. de cremento ville sue. Et de xl s. de remanenti eiusdem crementi de anno preterito. In thes. x li. Et debent xl s.[3]

f' Hugo de Neovill' r.c. de x li. de firma de Ernhal'. In thes. lib. Et Q.E.

(*f'* Idem Vic. r.c. de xj li. et xij s. et ij d. de firma de Meleburn' de dim. anno. In thes. nichil. Et Philippo Marc xj li. et xij s. et ij d. ad se sustentandum. Et Q.E.[c]) (*quia in dorso*[i])

(*f'* Walterus episcopus Carleol'[4] [*blank*] xj li. et xij s. et ij d. de eadem firma de alio dim. anno per breve R. quamdiu R. placuerit[c]) *quia in dorso*.

f' Willelmus comes de Ferrariis r.c. de quater xx li. bl. de firma de Werkeworðe et Esseburne. In thes. lxxvij li. et j m. bl. Et debet iij m. et dim. Idem r.c. de eodem debito. In thes. lib. Et Q.E.

f' Idem comes r.c. de xl li. num. de firma eorundem maneriorum. In thes. lib. Et Q.E.

f' Idem Vic. debet xx li. et v s. et vj d. de veteri cremento maneriorum. Et xx li. et v s. et vj d. de eodem cremento de anno preterito. Set non debet summoneri quia non habet maneria in manu sua.

f' Idem Vic. r.c. de xv li. (*et iiij s. sicut continetur in rotulo ij[o] R. J.*[i]) de firma de Lindeby. In thes. nichil. Et Laurencio de Sancto Michaeli vj li.

1 *Et Q.E.* written at end of line above.

2 *de* repeated.

3 Written centrally on an obliteration.

4 There is an obliteration after *Carleol'*.

et vij s. de parte sua in eadem villa.[1] Et monachis de Lenton' l s. Et in superplus quod habet supra vj li. et vij s. Et Q.[E.]

f' Idem Vic. r.c. de xxiij s. de veteri cremento de Lindeby. Et de iiij s. de novo cremento. Et de xviij s. et viij d. de firma de Claworðe de iiij[a] parte anni. In thes. xviij s. et viij d. Et in predicto superplus xxvij s. Et Q.E.

f' Hugo de Neovill' [*blank*] viij li. de firma de Clipeston' (de anno viij[o] et anno ix[o]).[2]

f' Laurencius de Sancto Michaeli r.c. de j pellicia grisia de vij fessiis de firma terre sue de Lindeby. In thes. nichil. Et ipsi R. j pelliciam grisiam[3] de vij fessiis. Et Q.E.

f' Idem Vic. r.c. de xij d. de firma terre Godefridi Spigornell'. Et de vj d. de firma terre Johannis de Burn'. In thes. lib. Et Q.E.

f' Homines de Bulewell' r.c. de C s. de firma ville sue. In thes. nichil. Et Philippo Marc C s. ad se sustentandum quamdiu R. placuerit salvis R. tallagiis et auxiliis. Et Q.S.

f' Idem Vic. ut custos r.c. de x li. de firma de Derleton'. Et de viij li. et dim. m. de firma de Carleton'. Et de xxxvj li. et vjj s.[4] et vj d. de firma de Mammefeld' cum soca. Et de vj li. et vij s. et vj d. de firma de Edenestow'. Et de vj s. de firma de Raghenild'. Summa lxj li. et vij s. et viij d. In thes. liij li. xiiij s. et viij d. Et debet vij li. et xiij s. Idem r.c. de eodem debito. In thes. nichil. Et in predicto superplus vij li. et xiij s. Et Q.E.

Philippus Marc debet proficuum comitatuum de anno viij. Set non debet summoneri quia R. perdonavit ei illud proficuum pro expensis quas fecit in obsidione castri de Bedef' et in custodia castri de Noting' per breve suum. Et Q.E.

Idem P. r.c. de iiij li. et xix s. et viij d. de remanenti firme de Meleburn' de anno vij. Et de xx li. et v s. et vj d. de veteri cremento maneriorum de anno viij[o]. Et de xxxij s. et viij d. de remanenti firme de Derleton' de eodem anno. Et de vij li. et dim. m. de remanenti firme de Carleton' de eodem anno. Et de xvj li. et xv s. et viij d. et ob. de remanenti firme de Mammefeld' de eodem anno. Et de ij m. pro Ricardo le Herre qui vocatur Ricardus Flandr' in rotulo precedenti. Et de ij m. pro Huberto f. Radulfi. Et de x li. (de[i]) tallagio de Mammefeld'. Summa lxiij li. et xiij s. et vj d. et ob. In thes. nichil. Et in suo superplus quod habet in rotulo viij[o] lxiij li. et xiij s. et vj d. et ob. Et Q.E.

Idem P. debet iiij li. et xiij s. et viij d. de remanenti firme de Meleburn' de anno viij[o]. Set respondet infra[5] in summa.

Idem P. r.c. de xix li. et viij s. et x d. quos recepit de carrucagio de Derebisir' sicut continetur in rotulo precedenti. Set respondet in rotulo de carrucagio de x li. et xij s. et x d. Et debet viij li. et xv s. et xj d. Set respondet ibidem in eadem summa.

Idem P. r.c. de[6] xlix li. et xj s. et j d. de remanenti compoti sui contenti

[1] Part written on alteration.
[2] Written on alteration and blotched.
[3] *pelliciam grisiam* in the accusative (written -*ā*).
[4] Second *j* added in darker ink.
[5] *infra* repeated.
[6] *r.c. de* written on alteration and above the line.

in rotulo v°. In thes. nichil. Et in perdona ipsi Philippo pro fideli servicio suo quod fecit R. J. patri R. et ipsi R. xlix li. et ij s. et j d. per breve R. Et Q.E.

Idem P. r.c. (de[i]) xx s. pro comitatu de Noting' pro habendo respectu sicut continetur in rotulo precedenti. Et lv s. pro duobus comitatibus de alio fine pro habendo respectu sicut continetur ibidem. Set respondet ibidem in eadem summa.

Idem P. debet xxxvj s. pro[1] comitatu Derebis' de tercio fine pro eodem. Et xxj li. et xj s. et x d. de minutis particulis[2] foreste dum fuit Vic. sicut continetur in rotulo xiiij° de quibus Eustachius de Ludham debet eum adquietare de vj li (*Set respondet infra.*[i]). Et restant solvende[3] super Philippum xv li. et xj s. et x d. Set quietus est per Justiciarios de predictis xv li. et xj s. et x d. per (summam[i]) C s. (*Set respondet infra in eadem summa.*[i]) pro paupertate hominum super quos remanens debiti predicti [oneratum?][4] fuit.

(*...pot'*)[5] Agnes la Corniere debet v m. de tallagio. + Simon f. Fulconis debet dim. m. pro habenda terra. + Willelmus Lappareillur debet dim. m. pro vino vendito. + Herbertus Francesius debet dim. m. pro transgressione. + Gervasius de Clifton debet iij m. pro falso dicto.

Radulfus f. Ascer' r.c. de dim. m. de misericordia pro propresturis. In thes. nichil. Et in perdona ipsi Radulfo dim. m. per breve R. Et Q.E.

Radulfus le Pohier (per Vic.[i]) debet v m. pro transgressione. Set requirendus est in Hereford' in Wall' super Ranulfum heredem Rogeri.

Jordanus f. Willelmi de Appecot r.c. de ix li.[6] et j m. de debitis Judeorum. In thes. xl s. Et debet vij li. et j m. per annum xl s.

Ricardus de Bello Campo [*blank*] x s. de pluribus debitis contentis in rotulo iij°.

Ricardus f. Gervasii de Wiverton' r.c. de quater xx et xiij li. et j m. de debito Ááron. In thes. xx s. Et debet quater xx et xij li. et j m.

W. comes de Ferrariis [*blank*] CC et lvij li. et dim. m. et xx li. pro ij^{bus} dextrariis de pluribus debitis contentis in rotulo ij°.

Ricardus f. Petri de Sandiacr' r.c. de iiij s. et j d. pro habenda terra patris sui. In thes. lib. Et Q.E.

Petrus Picot r.c. de xvj li. et iiij s. et viij d.[7] pro habenda terra patris sui. In thes. iiij li. Et debet xij li. iiij s. et viij d. per annum iiij li.

Eustachius de Ludham debet vj li. pro Philippo Marc de minutis

1 Initial *p* altered from *d*?
2 The clerk began to write *forest'*, and altered it to *particulis*.
3 *solven* written at the end of the line, which is then obscured by the mending strip so that it is impossible to see if anything more was written here. The letters *de* begin the next line. Grammatically, the clerk should have written *solvendi*, but the feminine *solvende* does appear for *solvendi* elsewhere on this roll. *De* as a separate word would not make good sense here.
4 Word illegible under fold in the membrane. *Oneratum*, 'charged' would make good sense.
5 There is something written in the margin, but it has partially been cut off in the left hand margin of the roll.
6 *ix* written on alteration.
7 Written over erasure.

particulis foreste sicut supra continetur. Set respondet in Everwicsir' in rotulo sequenti.

DE PRESTITO PICTAVIE

Adam de novo mercato debet xxxj m. de eodem. Yvo de Heriz' debet viij m. de eodem.

f' Idem Vic. respondet de proficuo maneriorum supra contentorum in proficuo comitatus.

Thomas (Basset[c]) (dispensarius[i]) debet vj li. de scutagio Pictavie. Thomas Basset debet x m. pro justiciando Yvone de Dien. Ricardus de Mariscis debet CC et lxvj li. et j m. pro habenda terra sicut continetur in rotulo viij°.

Johannes de Lee (r.c. de[i]) ij m. et dim. ut sit quietus sicut continetur in rotulo ij°. In thes. lib. Et Q.E.

Henricus f. Ernold debet dim. m. pro justiciando Yvone de Dien.[1] Hubertus de Burgo debet l m. de primo scutagio R. de feod' Dodon' Bardulf'. Henricus de Bailleol' debet ij m. pro dissaisina. Elyas de Boeles debet xxij s. de catallis Mathei mercatoris.

Eustachius de Ludham debet xxv s. de primo scutagio pro Huberto f. Radulfi sicut continetur in rotulo precedenti. Set respondet in Everwikesir' in rotulo sequenti.

Robertus de Walleia r.c. de xj m. pro habenda carta. In thes. j m. Et debet x m.

Heredes Philippi de Ulecot' r.c. de xl s. de scutagio Pictavie sicut continetur in rotulo precedenti. In thes. lib. Et Q.S.

\+ Henricus de Radnesse debet x s. quia non venit. + Ricardus de Wisho debet dim. m. pro vino vendito. +[2] Rogerus de Bramléé debet dim. m. quia non habuit. + Galfridus de Raveneston' debet dim. m. pro defalta.

Willelmus Basset r.c. de xj li. et xviij s. et x d. pro habenda terra sicut continetur in rotulo iiij°. In thes. l s. Et debet ix li. viij s. et x d. Idem r.c. de eodem debito. In thes. l s. Et debet vj li. xviij s. et x d. per annum C s.

Nicholaus de Wiliton' debet xxij li. de iij^bus debitis contentis in rotulo viij. Cecil[ia] de Hilton' debet dim. m. quia non est prosecuta. Herbertus Fot debet dim. m. pro vino vendito. Willelmus cementarius de Derebisir' debet xx s. ut possit esse sub plegio. Henricus f. Nicholai debet dim. m. quia non est prosecutus. + Laurencius de Trou debet xxx s. de padnagio.

Comitatus de Noting' debet xl s. pro habendo respectu sicut continetur in rotulo iiij°. Willelmus de Boeles debet x li. pro dissaisina sicut continetur in rotulo vij°. Set respondet infra.

Comitatus de Noting' et Dereb' (debent[i]) lviij s. et iij d. de alio fine pro habendo respectu.

Laurencius de Sancto Michaeli [*blank*] x li. et j m. de pluribus debitis contentis in rotulo precedenti. Et xliiij s. et v d. et ob. de tercia parte x m. de debito Walteri Croc. per annum xx s.

[1] or *Dieu*?

[2] The upright stroke of the + is written like the upright for the capital letter R.

Rogerus Brito r.c. de xviij li. (et x s.[i]) de relev…o[1] contento in rotulo viij[o]. In thes. ij m. Et debet vij li. et xl d.[2] per annum ij m.

[*Rot.* II *Mem.* 2]

Willelmus[3] de Boeles r.c. de x li. sicut supra continetur. In thes. nichil et in perdona ipsi Willelmo x li. per breve R. Et Q.E.

DE SCUTAGIO DE MUNGUMERI

Idem Vic. r.c. de (ij[c]) (dim.[i]) m. de (eodem[c]) Johanne de Aencurt. Et de ij m. de Nicholao f. Hugonis de Haveresham de eodem de honore Peverell. Et de j m. de Radulfo de Wileweby. In thes. lib. Et Q.E.

Radulfus de Gresel' r.c. de iiij m. de eodem de predicto honore. In thes. j m. Et debet iij m.

Robertus de Pauilli r.c. de vj m. et xvj d. de eodem de predicto honore. In thes. ij m. Et debet iiij m. et xvj d.

Willelmus de Vernone debet iij m. de eodem de predicto honore. (*Postea habuit quietantiam per breve R.*[ic]) Eustachius de Moret' debet xl s. de eodem de predicto honore. Willelmus de Sancto Patricio debet v m. de eodem de predicto honore. Petrus de Goldinton debet v m. de eodem de predicto honore.

Willelmus Avenel debet iij m. de eodem de predicto honore. (*Postea habuit quietantiam per breve R.*[ic]) Johannes de Monte acuto debet ij m. de eodem de predicto honore. Hugo de Neovill' debet ij m. de eodem de predicto honore. Robertus Amaur' debet ij m. de eodem de predicto honore. (*Set respondet in Oxon' in rotulo sequenti.*[i]) Hospitalarii debent ij m. de eodem.

Robertus de Chaurces r.c. de ij m. de eodem de predicto honore. In thes. lib. Et Q.E.

Robertus Brito [*blank*] ij m. de eodem de predicto honore.

Willelmus f. Roberti de Esseby [*blank*] iij m. de eodem de predicto honore.

Homines de Notingeham r.c. de xlvj s. bl. de remanenti firme ville sue de anno preterito sicut supra continetur. In thes. lib. Et Q.S.

DE SCUTAGIO DE BEDEFORD'

Robertus f. Willelmi de Esseby [*blank*] iiij m. de eodem.

Willelmus de Vernone debet iij m. de eodem. Willelmus de Sancto Patricio debet vj m. de eodem. Radulfus de Wileweby debet j m. de eodem. Johannes de Monte acuto debet ij m. de eodem. Robertus Amaur' debet ij m. de eodem. (*Set respondet in Oxon' in rotulo sequenti.*[i]) Hospitalarii debent ij m. de eodem. Nicholaus f. Hugonis de Haveresham debet ij m. de eodem.

1 *relev*[*i*]*o* or *relev*[*io su*]*o*. Word(s) obscured by a tag.

2 *xviij li.* clearly written, but the arithmetic requires it to be *ix li.*

3 The first word of this line is indented by 1½ inches.

Willelmus de Briewerr' [*blank*] v m. de eodem (de dominico[c]) de Bolesores.

[*One line blank*]

Walterus de Godardvill' debet CC m. pro habenda Johanna in uxorem sicut continetur in rotulo viij.

Brianus de Insula [*blank*] de firma de Pecco de quarta parte anni viij. Et [*blank*] de firma de Bolesores de quarta parte eiusdem anni.

f' Idem B. r.c. de iiij li. de firma de Clypeston' per breve R. quam R. ei concessit per talem firmam quamdiu R. placuerit.[1] In thes. lib. Et Q.E.

DE PLACITIS FORESTE

Idem Vic. r.c. de ij s. de Nicholao Duredent. Et de x d. de Roberto Wirroc. Et de x s. de Henrico de Stavenebi. Et de viij d. de Hugone le Melere. Et de dim. m. de Thoma de Cellario. Et de dim. m. de Turemoð' de Linton. Et de ij s. de Walerando f. Akeman'. Et de iij s. de Ada de Keleburn'. Et de xij d. de Waltero textore. Et de iij s. de Osmund. Et de xij d. de Rogero f. Orm. Et de xij d. de Radulfo de Wudeburg'. Et de xij d. de Roberto de Crois. Et de iij s. de Rogero de Aufertun'. Et de ij s. de Rogero Colling'. Et de vj d. de Rogero Cnotting'. In thes. lib. Et Q.E.

(*p*) Hugo[2] f. Edwardi r.c. de xx s. pro misericordia. In thes. ij s. Et debet xviij s.

Adam le Wine r.c. de viij m. pro essarto. In thes. iiij m. Et debet iiij m.

t Henricus de Chedesdon r.c. de dim. m. pro eodem. In thes. xl d. Et debet xl d.

t Henricus capellanus r.c. de j m. pro murdro. In thes. v s. Et debet viij s. et iiij d.

t Robertus[3] de bella aqua r.c. de dim. m. pro viridi. In thes. xl d. Et debet xl d.

t Hugo de Wermoteworð r.c. de ij m. pro essarto. In thes. dim. m. Et debet xx s.

Thomas de Streton' r.c. de xxiijj s. et viij d. pro regardo. (In[c]) In thes. lib. Et Q.E.

t Rogerus de Norf' debet xij d. pro viridi. (t[i]) Villata de Chedesden' debet iij s. pro novo vasto. + Ricardus f. Swani debet dim.[4] m. pro defalta. (*d*[i]) Rogerus plumbarius debet xij d. pro plegio. Radulfus de Morleg' debet xij d. pro eodem. (*d*[i]) Galfridus Blundus debet ij s. pro eodem. (*t*[i]) Willelmus f. Roberti de Stanl' debet xij d. pro eodem. (*d*[i]) Hugo de Neuton' forestarius debet ij s. pro eodem. (*t*[i]) Hugo f. Philippi de Dereb' debet j m. quia non habuit. (*t*[i]) Galfridus capellanus de Auferton' debet xij d. pro eodem. (*d*[i]) Alexander f. Radulfi de Halum debet ij s. pro eodem. (*d*[i]) Adam f. Hugonis de Tibbeschelf debet ij s. pro eodem. (*d*[i]) Walterus f. Walteri de Neuton' debet ij s. pro eodem. Ricardus de Loftsco debet ij s. pro eodem.

1 This entry is in slightly thinner writing.

2 This and the next three entries are written on the left hand side of the membrane.

3 This and the next three entries are written on the right hand side of the membrane.

4 *dim.* written on the left; this and the subsequent lines are written right across the membrane.

(*t*[i]) Walle de Bigginge debet iij s. pro novo essarto. (*t*[i]) Radulfus f. Radulfi de Sumercot' debet dim. m. pro eodem. (*t*[i]) Robertus Molendinarius de Auferton' debet xij d. pro eodem. (*t*[i]) Willelmus f. Liolf' debet vj d. pro j acra avene. (*d*[i]) Thomas Barri debet iij d. pro dim. acra. (*t*[i]) Willelmus de Wichenor' debet vj d. pro j acra. (*d*[i]) Hugo f. Ascelot' debet vj d. pro eodem. (*t*[i]) Johannes le grant debet vj d. pro eodem. (*p*[i]) Willelmus f. Huberti debet iiij s. pro defalta. (*p*[i]) Andreas de Riparia debet v s. pro eodem.

t Robertus Malluvel r.c. de iij m. pro licencia concordandi. In thes. xxiij s. et iiij d. Et debet xvj s. et viij d.

Require compotum Roberti de Laxinton' de Bolesores[1] de dim. anno in rotulo compotorum.

DE OBLATIS

Idem Vic. r.c. de iij m. de Waltero Malet. Et de j m. de Henrico de Burun. In thes. lib. Et Q.E.

Homines de Edenestowe r.c. de viij m. pro habenda pastura sicut continetur in rotulo precedenti. In thes. iiij m. Et debent iiij m.

f' Idem homines [*blank*] dim. m. de firma eiusdem pasture sicut continetur ibidem.

Johannes de Heriz [*blank*] xx li. de relevio suo.

Rogerus f. Alexandri debet dim. (m.[i]) pro habendo brevi sicut continetur ibidem. Stephanus Meverel et Alicia de Lockeleg' debent j m. pro eodem sicut continetur ibidem.

Homines de villa et soca de Mamefeld' debent xx m. ut teneant terras suas sicut continetur ibidem. Set non debent summoneri quia de hoc fine quieti sunt in rotulo anni v.

f' Abbas de Wellebec r.c. de x li. de firma molendinorum de Radford sicut continetur ibidem. In thes. lib. Et Q.E.

Willelmus Briewerr senior debet respondere de firma de Bolesor' de toto anno ix°. Et de blado eiusdem manerii et instauro contento in rotulo viij° scilicet xxiiij bobus. Set respondet in rotulo compotorum.

Robertus de Tateshal' [*blank*] de firma de Bolesores de dim. anno priusquam Robertus de Laxinton illud dimisit.

NOVA OBLATA

Radulfus Musard [*blank*] xv m. pro habendis terris quas Walterus de Godardvill' et Johanna [uxor][2] eius soror Ysabell' uxoris predicti Radulfi tenuerunt que ipsam Ysabell' hereditarie contingunt de quibus R. cepit homagium predicti Radulfi et concessit per hunc finem quod habeat saisinam de predictis terris per plegium Willelmi de Meisnil de iij m., Henrici de

1 This must be the account for Bolsover Castle. Robert of Laxton (Lexington) was keeper of Bolsover Castle and The Peak.

2 *uxor* must be supplied to make sense of this entry.

Cubbeleg' de iij m., Rogerus[1] f. pape (?)[2] de iij m., Rogeri parmentarii de ij m., Willelmi f. Hugonis de ij m., Johannis de Bosco de ij m.

Robertus de Hardredeshill' [*blank, including* deb *erased*] xl s. pro relevio suo et pro habenda saisina terre quam Willelmus pater eius tenuit de R. in capite in Claworðe et que ipsum Robertum hereditarie contingunt,[3] de qua terra R. cepit homagium suum. Plegii de fine Walterus de Claworðe, Adam f. Johannis de Claworðe, Willelmus ad aulam, Johannes f. Alexandri.

Abbas de Burton' r.c. de dim. m. pro habendo pone versus Thomam Tuschet et Nicholaum de Wiliton'. In thes. lib. Et Q.E.

DE BANCO

t Prior de Reppendon' debet dim. m. pro licencia concordandi cum Nicholao de Wilinton'. (*t*[i]) Amauricus de Noers debet dim. m. pro eodem cum Elya de Amundevill'. (*d*[i]) Robertus de Aciour' debet j m. pro licencia concordandi cum Leodegar' de Diva.

[*One line blank*]

DE PLACITIS HUGONIS DE NEOVILL'

f' Homines R. de Derleton' et Ragenild' et de soka de Dunham et de Marcham [*blank*] v m. pro habenda pastura sua usque ad cóópertum bosci de Kingesleg' sicut habuerunt antequam palicium quod modo prostratum est factum esset circa boscum.

Hugo le Bel r.c. de j m. pro iij acris et dim. terre essartandis et excolendis de tenui Buissinet'[4] in campo de Noting' iuxta Tikehall et Foxhol'[5] reddendo per annum x d. de redditu ad festum Sancti Michaelis pro quietantia regardi. In thes. dim. m. Et debet dim. m.

Idem H. r.c. de x d. de censu eiusdem terre. In thes. lib. Et Q.E.

Henricus f. Ricardi [*blank*] xl s. de fine facto ut sit quietus de instauro sicut continetur in rotulo compotorum in compoto R. de Laxinton'.

AMERCIAMENTA FACTA PER ROBERTUM DE LAXINTON' ET SOCIOS SUOS

Idem Vic. r.c. de C et lxj m. et ix d. et ob. de misericordiis hominum et villarum et francoplegiorum quorum nominibus preponitur littera *t* in rotulo quem predicti liberaverunt in thesauro. In thes. lib. in C et lj taleis. Et Q.E.

1 *Rogerus* written for *Rogeri*.

2 Written as *pp* with one horizontal suspension mark over both letters possibly for *prepositi*, 'reeve'.

3 *contingunt* written for *contingit*.

4 Of thin brushwood? *Buissinet*' is not traceable but could be from a form **buissinetum*, ultimately deriving from *busca*.

5 There are a number of places in Nottinghamshire called Fox Holes but none, as far as can be ascertained, near Nottingham, see *The Place-Names of Nottinghamshire*, ed. J. E. B. Glover, A. Mawer & F. M. Stenton (EPNS, Cambridge, 1979), pp. 46, 192, 239.

p Henricus[1] de Buketon r.c. de iij m. quia retraxit se. In thes. j m. Et debet ij m.
t Rogerus f. Alexandri r.c. de liij s. pro dissaisina. In thes. xlvj s. iiij (d.[i]) Et debet dim. m.

Robertus f. Willelmi de Harestan r.c. de xl s. pro habenda jurata. In thes. xx s. Et debet xx s.
p Robertus de Viliers r.c. de xl s. pro dissaisina. In thes. ij m. Et debet j m.
p Rogerus f. Alexandri r.c. de v m. quia non[2] est prosecutus. In thes. j m. Et debet iiij m.
p Radulfus[3] de Gresel' r.c. de v m. pro falso clamore. In thes. j m. Et debet iiij m.
t Villata de Blie[4] r.c. de j m. pro fuga Roberti Kachetaval. In thes dim. m. Et debet dim. m.
t Ricardus Blundus r.c. de xxj s. et iij d. pro fuga eiusdem. In thes. xvj s. Et debet v s. et iiij d.[5]
t Magister Stephanus de Raðklive r.c. de xj s. de catallis Thome. In thes. v s. Et debet vj s.
t Villata de Esseburn' r.c. de ij m. pro fuga Petri. In thes. xxij s. et iiij (d.[i]). Et debet xl d.

Philippus[6] Marc [*blank*] xx s. pro dissaisina. Et xxiij li. et vjj d. de vj debitis supra contentis.
t Comes de Ferrariis [*blank*] xx s. de catallis Ricardi de Bardeslaw' suspensi. Et ij s. de catallis Rogeri fabri suspensi. Et iiij s. de catallis Ricardi f. Thome de Beuteshill' suspensi.
t Robertus de Carleol' [*blank*] ij s. et vj d. de catallis Gilleberti Trutt suspensi.

Idem Vic. r.c. de vij s. et ix d. de catallis Ricardi Godpurs suspensi. Et de j m. de villata de Bauðinton' pro fuga Radulfi f. Hervic'. Et de vj li. xij s. et v d. de catallis aliorum hominum (suorum[c]) (episcopi Linc'[i]) suspensorum et fugitivorum quorum nomina non annotantur hic quia non sunt annotata in predicto rotulo quem predicti Justiciarii liberaverunt in thesauro. In thes. nichil. Et episcopo Linc' vij li. xiij s. et vj d. per breve R. Et Q.E.
d Robertus f. Galfridi et Robertus f. Roberti debent dim. m. quia non habuerunt quem plegiaverunt. *t* Hugo de Stredl' debet j m. pro habendo respectu. *t* Reginaldus Marc debet xl s. pro dissaisina per plegium Petri Marc et Galfridi Gyun. (*t*[i]) Radulfus de Sancto Paulo debet dim. m. pro dissaisina. (*p*[i]) Petrus Marc'[7] debet xx s. pro eodem per plegium Philippi Marc.
(*t*[i]) Rogerus f. Gunnild' debet dim. m. pro defalta. (*t*[i]) Galfridus de Akour' debet dim. m. pro falso clamore. (*t*[i]) Radulfus f. Thome de Turlaveston' debet dim. m. quia non habuit. (*t*[i]) Arnoldus de Winefeld debet dim. m. pro falso clamore.

1 This and the next four lines are written on the left hand side of the membrane.
2 *non* repeated.
3 This and the next four lines are written on the right hand side of the membrane.
4 Name unclear.
5 *iiij d.* written for *iij d.*
6 This and subsequent lines go right across the membrane.
7 Name hard to read at the end of the line.

t Thomas f. Thome de Wilfrint' debet iiij d. de catallis Roberti Walensis fugitivi. (*t*[i]) Robertus de Kelesholt debet vj d.[1] de catallis Hugonis de Hill'. (*d*[i]) Radulfus f. Nicholai Vic. debet viij s. de catallis Roberti generi Petri. (*t*[i]) Robertus f. Fulcherii debet iiij s. et iiij d. de catallis Henrici cementarii fugitivi. (*t*[i]) Villata de Clivedon (Regis[i]) debet dim. m. pro receptamento Thome Capelein. (*p*[i]) Villata de Hikeling' debet dim. m. pro fuga Galfridi Scot. (*t*[i]) Villata de Screveton' deb[2] parte domine debet dim. m. pro fuga Willelmi. (*t*[i]) Alanus Malet debet dim. m. pro habenda terra quam Herebertus de Roby suspensus tenuit de ipso.

(*t*[i]) Henricus f. Matill' debet dim. m. pro dissaisina per plegium Henrici de Wallegh' et Henrici de Clyve. (*d*[i]) Stephanus f. Johannis et Johannes Rudde debent dim. m. pro eodem. (*d*[i]) Unfridus de Olleton' et Willelmus frater eius debent dim. m. pro eodem. (*d*[i]) Adam f. Radulfi et Rogerus frater eius debent (dim. m. pro eodem.[3] (*d*[i]) Willelmus f. Lefwine et Henricus Kidewilde debent dim. m. pro eodem.[i])

[*One line blank*]

RESPICE IN TERGUM[4]

[*Rot.* IId *Mem.*I]

Robertus de Tateshall' r.c. de xv li. de firma de Bolesor' de dim. anno, scilicet á secundo die Maii usque ad diem Sancti Michaelis quam villam cum castro et cum pertinenciis R. commisit ei custodienda[5] quamdiu sibi placuerit redddendo[6] per annum xxx li. sicut Robertus de Laxinton' reddere[7] per litteras R. patentes quas idem Robertus de Tateshall' habet. In thes. x li. Et debet C s.

Homines de Notingeh' r.c. de xvj li. et x s. et iiij d. bl. de remanenti firme ville sue de pluribus annis preteritis ante guerram sicut continetur ex alia parte rotuli. In thes. xvj li. et xiij d. bl. per iiij taleas de ante guerram allocatas per H. de Burgo Justiciarium coram baronibus de scaccario. Et debent ix s. et vij d. bl. In thes. lib. Et Q.S.

f' Idem Vic. r.c. de xj li. et xij s. et ij d. de firma de Meleburne de dim. anno. In thes. nichil. Et in elemosinis constitutis canonicis de Chalke xij d. Et Johanni f. Willelmi l s. in Chelardeston'. Et Philippo Marc viij li. xiiij

1 Written over erasure.

2 *deb* written for *de*.

3 Last four words written at end of preceding line.

4 Three long down-strokes, the first two like the top half of the letter Y, appear to the left of this instruction.

5 *custodienda* written for *custodiendam*; or perhaps the clerk is including *castrum* and *pertinencia* in the keeping, and therefore choosing the neuter plural form.

6 End of line I obscured by mending strip, but the line ends *redd*, and line 2 begins *dendo*; it would appear that not only is nothing lost, but the clerk has used three [d]s to complete the word *reddendo*.

7 *reddere* written for *reddidit* (or a word such as *consueverat* 'was accustomed' omitted).

s. et (x denarios[i]) ad se sustentandum in servicio R. Et Petro de Derby vj s. et iiij d. in Normanton. Et Q.E.

f' W. episcopus Carleolensis r.c. de xj li. et xij s. et ij d. de eadem firma de alio dim. anno. In thes. nichil. Et in elemosinis constitutis canonicis de Chalke xij d. Et predicto Johanni l s. Et Petro de Dereby vj s. et iiij d. in Normanton'. Et ipsi episcopo viij li. et xiiij s. et x d. per breve R. ad se sustentandum in servicio R. Et Q.E.

[*Three lines blank*]

WIGORN'

Walterus de Bello campo Thomas de Wigorn' ut custos pro eo r.c. de CC et xv li. et x s. et iiij d. (bl.[i]) de firma comitatus. In thes. nichil.

Et in terris datis monachis de Bordesleia vj li. et iij s. in Holeweia. Et eisdem x s. in piscaria de Mertleia. Et in villa de Wigorn' xx li. bl. de quibus cives respondent infra. Et Willelmo de Frusa xxxiij li. in Mertleia. Et Willelmo de Fornell' xliij li. bl. in Bremmesgrave quamdiu R. placuerit de quibus respondet infra. Et Hugoni de Neovill' xv li. in Feckeham de quibus respondet infra. Et in manerio de Wiz quater xx li. bl. de quibus homines ville respondent infra. Et Luelino principi Norwall' xxx li. in Suckeleg'. Et habet de superplus xij li. et xiij s. qui excrescunt per extensionem maneriorum. Et ideo non debent Vic. allocari. Et in elemosinis constitutis militibus de templo j m. Et incluse de Stok' xxx s. et v d. Et monachis de Cormeilles lxxv s. Et monachis Glovern' xx s. Et in liberatione constituta capellano de Feckeham l s. Et in suo superplus quod habet in anno preterito ix li. et xiiij s. et vj d. Summa xix li. et iij s. et iij d. qui debent allocari Vic. ubi voluerit ...[1] de qua summa locantur ei infra xij li. et dim. m. in pluribus debitis. Et restant ei locande[2] vj li. et xvj s. et vij d.

Idem Vic. [*blank*] de proficuo comitatus de hoc anno. Et de [*blank*] de eodem proficuo de anno preterito. Et de [*blank*] de eodem de iij^{bus} partibus anni viij.

[*One line blank*]

f' Cives Wigorn' r.c. de xxiiij li. bl. de firma ville sue. In thes. xxj li. v s. et iiij d. (bl.[i]) Et item (xvj s. et viij d. bl.[i]) Et in carriagio xv tonellorum (vini[i]) missorum per aquam (festinanter[i]) a Wigorn' usque Salop'sir' ad opus R. xl s. per breve R. Et Q.S.

f' Idem cives r.c. de xv d. de propresturis ville Wigorn'. Et de xij d. de firma cuiusdam domus escaete in Wigorn'. In thes. lib. Et Q.S.

[*One line blank*]

f' Willelmus de Fornell' r.c. de xliij li. bl. de firma de Bremesgrave. In thes. xlj li. vij s. et ix d.[3] bl. Et in elemosinis constitutis monachis de Bordesleg' xxiiij s. Et debet ix s. et v d. bl. Idem reddit compotum[4] de eodem debito. In thes. lib. Et Q.E.

1 *ubi voluerit* ... written under a crease in the membrane. A word may be lost here.
2 *locande* written for *locandi*.
3 *d* written over *b*.
4 *reddit compotum* written in full.

f' Idem W. r.c. de vij li. de cremento eiusdem ville. Et de xx m. de cremento facto per H. Bardulf'. In thes. xviij li. Et debet xlvj s. et viij d. Idem r.c. de eodem debito. In thes. lib. Et Q.E.

[*One line blank*]

Hugo de Neovill' r.c. de xv li. bl. de firma ville de Feckeham. Et de vj li. et vj d. de remanenti eiusdem firme de anno preterito sicut infra continetur. In thes. xxj li. xiij d. et ob. bl. Et in elemosinis constitutis monachis de Lyra xxx s. Et habet de superplus xxix s. et iij ob. bl.[1]

f' Idem H. [*blank*] xx li. de firma foreste de Fekeham. Et xl li. de eadem firma de ij^{bus} annis preteritis.

f' Homines del Wiz r.c. de C li. de firma ville sue.

f' Idem Vic. [*blank*] xiij li. de veteri cremento comitatus pro j summario et j austurco. Et lxvj li. de v annis preteritis.

[*One line blank*]

Idem Vic. r.c. de xl d. de Nicholao de Radestan'. Et de dim. m. de comit[atu] Wigorn' de fine.[2] Et de j m. de Hawisia filia Alienore. Et de xx s. de Thoma Rup pro transgressione. Et de dim. m. de abbate de Hal' pro licencia concordandi. In thes. nichil. Et in summa misarum quam habet supra l s. Et Q.E.

Alienor relicta Huberti r.c. de ij m. et dim. pro habenda inquisitione. In thes. nichil. Et in predicta summa misarum j m. Et debet A. xx s.

Manerium de Hanleg' debet iiij m. pro murdro. + Robertus f. Alexandri debet xl d. pro dissaisina. + Willelmus f. Avicie debet j m. pro eodem. + Johannes Leg debet xl d. pro eodem. Walterus de Aiton' debet dim. m. pro eodem. + Ricardus de Hulcrombe debet dim. m. pro falso clamore. Jordanus de Wikewan debet j m. pro iniusta detentione. Petrus f. Petri f. Edwin' debet terciam partem de xxvij li. pro justiciando Willelmo de Stutevill'. + Willelmus Capra debet xx d. pro vino vendito.

Pars abbatis de Persore in hundredo de Persore (debet[c]) (r.c. de[i]) ij m. et dim. pro murdro. In thes. nichil. Et ipsi abbati ij m. et dim. per libertatem carte R. per preceptum Justic'. Et Q.E.

Willelmus le blake debet j m. pro habendo brevi. Eustachius ruffus et Sabina uxor eius et Oliva de Wigorn' et Johanna que fuit uxor Philippi de Witeleg' debent xl s. pro habendo pone.

Burgenses del Wiz [*blank*] iiij li. et ij s. pro habenda carta sicut continetur in rotulo viij.

Abbas de Westm' r.c. de vij s. et v d. de remanenti compoti sui. In thes. lib. Et Q.E.

Heres (Rogerus[i]) Roberti de la Berghe [*blank*] xxxj li. et j m. de debitis Judeorum.

Walterus de Bello campo r.c. de CCCC et quater xx et viij li. de debitis Judeorum. In thes. iiij li. et j m. Et debet CCCC et quater xx et iij li. et dim. m.

Hugo de Neovill' debet vj li. et vj d. bl. de remanenti firme ville de Feckeham sicut continetur in rotulo precedenti. Set respondet supra.

[*One line blank*]

1 *xxx s. ... bl.* written at the end of the following line.

2 There was no earl of Worcester at this date, so it must be *comitatu* not *comite*.

DE PLACITIS FORESTE PER H. DE NEOVILL'

Thoki de Estwude [*blank*] xvj s. pro proprestura ij acrarum quam clauserat in pace habenda ita tamen quod faciat pacem de communa cum vicinis.

Petrus de Feckeham r.c. de j m. pro ij acris de frusseto excolendis iuxta terram suam de Rueding'. In thes. lib. Et Q.E.

f' Idem P. [*blank*][1] viij d. de censu eiusdem terre.

Henricus de parco [*blank*] iij m. pro viij acris de dominico R. habendis et excolendis iuxta domum suam pro quibus essartis finem fecit prius cum Johanne Maresc'.

Idem H. [*blank*] xxxij d. de censu pro quieto regardo.

[*One line blank*]

AMERCIAMENTA PER ROBERTUM DE LAXINTON' ET WILLELMUM DE LOND'

Idem Vic. r.c. de xxiij m. de misericordiis hominum quorum nominibus preponitur littera *t* in rotulo quem predicti liberaverunt in thesauro. In thes. lib. in j talea. Et Q.E.

Ricardus[2] Strech' r.c. de j m. pro dissaisina. In thes. vj s. et ij d. Et debet vij s. et ij d. Set respondet infra.

Johannes le Pohier r.c. de dim. m. pro eodem. In thes. xl d. Et debet xl d. Set respondet ibidem.

Hamo crassus r.c. de v m. pro eodem. In thes. xxj s. x d. Et debet xliiij s. et x d. Set respondet ibidem.

Robertus[3] Coleking' et socii sui r.c. de xxx s. pro eodem. In thes. xxij s. et debent viij s. Set respondent infra.

Petrus de Torendon r.c. de dim. m. pro licencia concordandi. In thes. xl d. Et debet xl d. Set respondet infra.

Ysabell' de Hanleg' r.c. de dim. m. quia retraxit. In thes. xl d. Et debet xl d. Set respondet infra.

Idem[4] Vic. r.c. de viij m. et dim. de misericordiis hominum quorum nominibus preponitur littera *t* cum littera *d* in predicto rotulo quem predicti liberaverunt in thesauro. In thes. nichil. Et in summa misarum quam habet supra viij m. et dim. Et Q.E.

Idem Vic. r.c. de vij s. et ij d. de Ricardo Strech. Et de xl d. de Johanne le Pohier. Et de xliiij s. et x d. de Hamone Crasso. Et de viij s. de Roberto Coleking'. Et de xl d. de Petro de Torindon'. Et de xl d. de Ysabell' de Hanleg' sicut supra continetur.[5] In thes. nichil. Et in predicta summa misarum quam habet supra lxx s. Et Q.E.

[1] P. is followed by what may be the start of the letter [d] for *debet*.

[2] This and the next two lines are written on the left hand side of the membrane.

[3] This and the next two lines are written on the right hand side of the membrane.

[4] This line and subsequent lines are written right across the membrane.

[5] The order of names given in lines 51–2 suggests that when entries are written in two columns the names are to be read down the left hand column before beginning on the right hand one; that is, the name on the right of the first line comes after the last name on the left hand side. This has implications for interpreting *pro eodem*. In this

Ricardus de Harocurt [*blank*] lxxvj li. et xv s. et iiij d. pro Roberto f. Willelmi de Berkel' pro xiij libratis terre quas tenet in Enderfeld' qui requirebatur in Glovernia.

Abbas de Hales debet dim. m. pro licencia concordandi cum Thoma le Cordwaner. (Ricardus de Harocurt debet lxxvj li. et[d])

DE ITINERE R. DE AMERCIATIS[1] IN GLOECESTRESIR'

Henricus f. Nicholai de Bradeweye debet dim. m. quia non est prosecutus. Willelmus francolanus debet dim. m. pro plegio eiusdem. Henricus f. Philippi de Bradeweie debet dim. m. pro eodem. Robertus Marmiun de Bradeweie debet j m. pro falso clamore per plegium Roberti de Percham et Elye de Winiecot'.

[*12 lines blank*]

[*Rot.* 11d *Mem.* 2]

SUDSEXIA

Matheus f. Herberti, Herbertus f. Walteri pro eo ut custos r.c. de xl li. de firma comitatus. In thes. xxvj li.

Et in elemosinis constitutis militibus de Templo j m. Et in xx pontibus factis et carriatis usque Portesm' xx s. per breve R. (Et in conductu quintedecime R. usque Winton' xxv s. per breve eiusdem[c]) (*quia in anno precedenti*[i]). Et custodi heredis comitis Arundell' xx m. de tercio denario comitatus nomine comit[is][2] de Sussex per breve R. Et habet de superplus xx s. qui locantur ei infra in proficuo.

Idem Vic. r.c. de xxx li. et xvij s. et iiij d. de proficuo comitatus de anno preterito. Et de xxvij li. et x s. et iij d. de eodem proficuo de hoc anno. Summa lxiij li. et vij s. et vij d. In thes. nichil. Et ipsi Vic. xx m. ad expensas suas adquietandas quas fecit in anno ix^{o} in custodia comitatus (per breve R.[i]). Et item eidem xx m. ad expensas suas pro eadem custodia hoc anno per breve eius.[3] Et idem eidem pro custodia gaiole Cycestr' hoc anno lx s. et x d. per idem breve. Et in superplus quod habet supra et infra lxij s. et viij d. Et debet xxx li. et x s. et ix d. Idem r.c. de eodem debito. In thes. nichil. Et pro custodia predicte gaiole anno ix^{o} lx s. et x d. per breve. Et debet xxvij li. ix s. et xj d.[4]

---

example, it makes no difference, as all would appear to be paying for disseisin; but if Hamo crassus had been amerced, say, *pro transgressione*, Robertus Coleking, amerced *pro eodem*, would have paid for trespass, and not for disseisin, the reason why Richard Strech was amerced.

1 *amerciatis* 'people amerced' written, not the more usual *amerciamentis*, 'amercements'.

2 Probably *comitis*, i.e. the under-age earl of Arundel. 'Until 1243 the titles of the earl of Arundel, Chichester and Sussex were used indifferently'. See F. M. Powicke and E. B. Fryde, *Handbook of British Chronology, 2nd edn* (London: Royal Historical Society, 1961), p. 452.

3 *eius* written for *eiusdem.*

4 Last clause written at the end of the third line below this line.

Idem Vic. r.c. de xj li. et iiij s. de remanenti firme comitatus de anno preterito. In thes. nichil. Et heredi comiti Arundell' xx m. de tercio denario comitatus de anno preterito per breve R. Et habet de superplus xlij s. viij d. qui locantur ei supra in proficuo.[1]

Compotus de Boseham de hoc anno non redditur hic quia respondet inde in rotulo compotorum in anno predicto.

Cives Cycestr' [*blank*] xxxviij li. et x s. de firma ville sue. In thes. [*blank*]. Et in quietantiam hominum archiepiscopi lx s. Et in quietantiam episcopi et canonicorum Cycestr' lx s. Et in quietantiam hominum de Portesm' dim. m. Et in defaltis iiij^{or} croftorum qui sunt inclusi in Brull' Cycestr' xl d. Et in elemosinis constitutis monachis Arundell' xl s.

[*One line blank*]

Idem cives [*blank*] x m. de remanenti veteris tallagii.

Herbertus de Baddebir' [*blank*] xxxij li. et xvj s. pro dissaisina.

Thomas de Wilardeby debet lxx m. de ij^{bus} debitis contentis in rotulo vj^{o}. + Robertus de Yham debet j tonellum vini pro habendo brevi. + Jacobus f. Alard' debet CCC m. pro falso clamore. + Willelmus f. Roberti debet v m. pro eodem.

W. comes Warenn' [*blank*] CCC et xv li. et xv s. et ij bonos palefridos et j alium palefridum et j osturcum de pluribus debitis contentis in rotulo precedenti. Et quater xx li. de catallis Hugonis le Bigod ei venditis sicut continetur in Norf' qui requirebatur ibidem. per annum C m. per breve R.

Matill' de Lund'ford r.c. de xliiij [li.] et iij s. et iiij d. et ob. pro Hugone de Lund'ford sicut continetur in rotulo iiij^{o}. In thes. xl s. Et debet xlij [li.] et iij s. et iiij d. et ob. per annum xl s.

Willelmus de Milliers [*blank*] xxv m. pro habenda saisina.

Reginaldus de Berneual r.c. de xxx m. de relevio Willelmi de Bodiham sicut continetur in rotulo xv^{o}. In thes. nichil. Et in perdona ipsi Reginaldo C s. per breve R. Et debet xv li. [*blank*] de quibus per annum C s. per idem breve.

Abbas de Bello r.c. de xlj li. pro habenda confirmatione. In thes. xv li. Et debet xxvj li.

Willelmus Aguillun r.c. de CCC et quater xx m. pro habenda uxore sicut continetur in rotulo xv^{o}. In thes. xx m. Et debet CCC et lx m.
per annum xx m.

Abbas de Fiscam' r.c. de quater xx m. de ij^{bus} debitis contentis in rotulo viij. In thes. lib. Et Q.E.

Ailwinus de la Hulle debet xl d. pro dissaisina. Robert de Ellested' debet xij canes vulpeculares sicut continetur in rotulo iij^{o}. + Reginaldus f. Willelmi debet iiij s. et viij d. pro dissaisina.+ Willelmus Brunman debet dim. m. pro eodem.

Robertus Salvagius r.c. de xxx li. de pluribus debitis contentis in rotulo vj^{o}. In thes. vj li. Et debet xxiiij li.

Hugo Esturmi r.c. de iiij m. et dim. de ij palefridis contentis in rotulo xvj^{o}. In thes. ij m. Et debet ij m. et dim.

Heres comitis Arundell' [*blank*] xlviij s. et iiij d. et ob. et j bonum

[1] *viij d. ... proficuo* written at the end of the second line below this line.

palefridum non in denariis et ij bonos osturcos de pluribus debitis contentis in rotulo precedenti.
[*One line blank, at the start of which 'Rad' was written and then obliterated*]

DE PRESTITO PICTAVIE

Radulfus f. Briani debet xj m. de eodem. Petrus de Scoteinn' debet xij m. de eodem. Willelmus de Bodiham debet ij m. de eodem. Rogerus la Zuche debet ix m. de eodem. Simon de Ethingeh' debet xiiij m. de eodem. Galfridus de Sancto Leodegar' debet ij m. et dim. de eodem. Robertus de Buscy debet iij m. et dim. de eodem. Johannes le Cunte debet iiij m. de eodem. Roelendus Bloet debet iiij li. de eodem. Et x m. et dim. de catallis plurium maneriorum Willelmi de Braiosa.

Johannes Wadeng' debet dim. m. pro habendo pone sicut continetur in rotulo primo. Villata de Schorham debet xv m. de tallagio. Magister Robertus de Gloec' debet CC et ix li. ix s. et iiij d. et viij dolia vini et lxxvj bacones de pluribus [debitis].[1]

Henricus de Marisco r.c. de j m. pro dissaisina. In thes. v s. et x d. Et debet vij s. et vj d.

Stephanus le Pohier (*Set respondet infra.*[1]) debet xix li. pro habenda saisina sicut continetur in rotulo primo. Ricardus de Kahaign' debet xvj s. et viij d. de primo scutagio R. de parvis feodis Morit[anie]. S. episcopus Exon' debet xv m. de eodem de feodo capellarie de Boseham.

Executores testamenti Rannulfi quondam episcopi Cycestr' [*blank*] xlv li. et xj s. et iiij d. de scutagio episcopatus Norewic' dum idem R. habuit custodiam.

Stephanus le Pohier r.c. de xix li. pro habenda saisina sicut supra continetur. In thes. xx s. Et debet xviij li.

DE AMERCIAMENTIS

Idem Vic. r.c. de x s. de remanenti debitorum plurium pro quibus respondit in rotulo precedenti. Et de ij s. et ij d. de Henrico de Marisco. Et de xl d. de Roberto Wisbelin. Et de dim. [m.] de Ricardo de Horsted. In thes. lib. Et Q.[E].

Alicia de Wakeherst r.c. de xl d. pro dissaisina. In thes. xij d. Et debet xxviij d.

Ricardus f. Wolmar' r.c. de dim. m. pro falso clamore. In thes. iiij s. Et debet ij s. et viij d.

Godwinus fleccarius debet v s. et viij d. pro falso clamore. + Johannes de Rocheford debet xl d. pro plegio. + Alicia de Wincheles' debet iij s. et vj d. pro iniusta detentione. + Osbertus Speche debet ij s. et iiij d. pro panno vendito. + Farmannus de Esseburn debet xiiij s. pro transgressione. + Willelmus Luneking' debet v s. et v d. quia retraxit se. + Engelram de Pikes debet medietatem de xviij m. sicut continetur in rotulo ij°. + Willelmus Luve debet xl d. quia non est prosecutus. + Johannes Hose

[1] Last word invisible under mending strip.

debet ij s. quia non habet. + Jacobus le Tac debet dim. m. pro panno vendito. + Johannes f. Rogeri debet xl d. pro dissaisina. + Clemens de Porta debet xx d. pro eodem. Rogerus de Moncell' debet xl d. quia non est prosecutus. + Henricus (de^{c}) Brand debet dim. m. pro defalta. + Michael Rufus debet dim. m. pro eodem. + Robertus blundus debet xx s. pro panno vendito. + Ricardus de Wica debet dim. m. pro eodem. + Johannes f. Reginaldi debet dim. m. pro defalta. + Rogerus Testard debet j m. de ij debitis contentis in rotulo iij^{o}. + Willelmus de Stokes debet xx s. pro vino vendito. + Matill' Lempereiz debet ij m. pro eodem. + Roelendus Bloet debet C s. quia non habet. + Radulfus de Gueres debet xix s. pro eodem. + Ricardus Caboc[he][1] debet dim. m. pro plegio. + Sperlingus piscator debet dim. m. pro eodem. + Rogerus f. Sabine debet dim. m. pro eodem. + Gervasius molendinarius debet dim. m. pro eodem. + Radulfus Witlac debet dim. m. pro eodem. + Walterus Wriðer debet dim. m. quia non habet. + Woluricus de Horsted' debet dim. m. quia retraxit se. + Willelmus f. Ricardi de Batel' debet dim. m. pro dissaisina. Ricardus Bigge debet dim. m. pro eodem. Gunnora que fuit uxor Ailnoð debet dim. m. pro eodem. + Simon f. Roberti debet dim. m. pro eodem. + Ricardus f. Simonis debet dim. m. quia non est prosecutus. + Rogerus f. Umfridi Fresteng debet dim. m. pro defalta. + Stephanus de novo ponte debet dim. m. pro eodem. + Willelmus f. David debet dim. m. quia non est prosecutus. Willelmus f. Ade debet dim. m. pro plegio. + Juliana de Cnoll' debet dim. m. pro eodem. + Galfridus Nobilis debet dim. m. pro transgressione.

Margar' de Burgo debet j spervarium ut scribatur sicut continetur in rotulo vij^{o}. Ricardus de Brom debet xix li. xv s. et iiij d. de pluribus debitis contentis in rotulo iijj^{o}. It[em] debita de itinere Justic[iariorum].[2]
[*One line blank*]

DE OBLATIS

Idem Vic. r.c. de v sol. de Sibill' de Burcherse. Et de iij s. et viij d. de Jacobo de Were. In thes. lib. Et Q.E.

Ricardus de Kahaign' [*blank*] vj li. et v s. de scutagio de Mungumeri de parvis feodis Morit'[anie].

Radulfus de Tóóni habet quietantiam per breve de eodem de ij feodis.

Episcopatus Exon' [*blank*] xv m. de eodem de f[eodo][3] capellarie de Boseham.

Ricardus de Kahaign' debet vj li. et v s. de scutagio de Bedef'. (Willelmus^{c})

Willelmus de Sancto Johanne r.c. de dim. m. pro habenda inquisitione sicut continetur in rotulo precedenti. In thes. lib. Et Q.E.
[*One line blank*]

[1] Ending of name obtained from *NS 54*, p. 168.

[2] This is presumably the heading under which the *plura debita* of Richard de Brom must be sought in roll 7.

[3] Or *firma*?

NOVA OBLATA *Cancellata hic quia (finis iste*[i]*) melius et evidentius post Hereford' in Wall' ubi finis iste requirendus est.*

(Willelmus de Sancto Johanne debet dim. m. pro habendis brulliis Cycestr' cum pertinenciis suis ad assartandum et excolendum. Ita quod reddet inde ad festum Sancti Michaelis anno x° C li. et ad pasch' anno xj° C li. et ad scaccarium [ad festum] S[ancti] Mich[aelis] anno eodem C m. et ad pasch' anno xij° C m. et ad scaccarium [ad festum] S[ancti] Mich[aelis] anno eodem vij li. et x s. et ad scaccarium[1] proxim° sequens vij li. et x s. et sic deinceps singulis annis xv li. de redditu assiso de quibus D m. R. episcopus Cycestr' R. cancellarius debet eum adquietare de CC m. et xxx s. pro habenda medietate brulliorum predictorum ad terminos sibi datos sicut ambo recognoverunt coram baronibus de scaccario.[c])[2]

Idem Vic. r.c. de dim. m. de Alexandro de Horsie pro licencia concordandi. Et de dim. m. de Roberto falconario pro querendo pede.[3] Et de dim. m. de Radulfo de Ellemere pro habendo pone. Et de dim. m. de Willelmo Bernehus pro licencia concordandi. Et de dim. m. de Andrea Peverel pro eodem. Et de dim. m. de Willelmo de Benefeld pro eodem. Et de dim. m. de Roberto (Peverel[i]) pro eodem. Et de dim. m. de Rannulfo del Broc pro eodem. In thes. lib. Et Q.E.

Ricardus Basoc r.c. de j m. de fine. In thes. dim. m. Et debet dim. m.

Ricardus de la Helde r.c. de ij m. et dim. pro licencia concordandi. In thes. ij m. Et debet dim. m.

Willelmus le Frie r.c. de v m. pro licencia concordandi. In thes. j m. Et debet iiij m. (R. Cycestr' episcopus debet CC m. et xxx s. pro W. de S. Johanne sicut supra continetur[c]) *quia respondet post Heref' in Wall'*.

[*Centred*] Require residuum huius comitatus post Heref' in Wall' quia non erat hic locus.
[*7 lines blank*]

[*Endorsed*]
emendum totum et iterum emendum totum
Notingehamsir' et Derebisir' Et Wigornia Et Sussexia

[*Rot.* 12 *Mem.* 1][4]

[*There is strengthening tape down the right hand side of the membrane. Down the left hand side near the bottom there is some wearing which has taken some of the marginalia and text, possibly through tears or just worn away over the years.*]

1 *scaccarium* written for *pasch*'? This sentence is awkwardly expressed, which lends point to the comment that is to be found '*melius et evidentius*' elsewhere. There would appear to be no 'treasury of St. Michael', so perhaps *die* should be supplied.
2 This passage, written on three lines, is cancelled by diagonal crossed lines.
3 Presumably he is seeking a foot of fine.
4 There is a pencilled '12' centred at the top of the membrane on the first line but partially obscured by the folds of the other membranes. There is also a pencilled '12' centred near the bottom of the membrane but just above the last line of text.

[*One line blank*]

CANTEBRIG' ET HUNTEDON';

Galfridus de Haðfeld' ut custos r.c. de CCC et lxxiij li. et ix s. et iiij d. bl. de firma comitatuum. In thes. quater xx et xij li. et iiij s. et x d. bl.

Et in elemosinis constitutis militibus de Templo ij m. Et in liberationibus constitutis Willelmo caretario R. lx s. et x d. Et Magistro Hugoni de Barentin carpentario xxx s. et v d. Et Roberto Dentdefer xxx s. et v d. Et in terris datis in Cantebrig'sir monialibus de Littlemor' xl s. in Bergeia. Et Petro f. Petri Picot C s. in Wilburgeham. Et in Gudmecestr' l li. bl. de quibus homines ville respondent infra. Et Galfrido Flandr' x li. bl. in Fordham. Et Henrico de Kemesec x li. bl. in Fordham. Et in villa de Cantebrig' xl li. bl. de quibus homines ville respondent infra. Et in villa de Huntedon' xxxv li. bl. de quibus homines ville respondent infra. Et in Cestreton' xx li. bl. de quibus canonici de Bernewell' respondent infra. Et Waltero f. Johannis de Merc x li. in Cumberton'. Et Huberto de Burgo xxxviij li. in Saham. Et Rannulfo comiti Cestr' et Linc' cum custodia filii et heredis comitis David xl li. in Branton' et Alcmundebir' usque ad etatem ipsius heredis. Et Paulino de Taiden' vij li. et x s. in Wilburgeham in terra quam Petrus de Malo alneto habuit de dim. anno per breve R. Et fratribus militie Templi vij li. et x s. in eadem terra de alio dimidio anno per breve R. et amodo totum.

[*One line blank*]

Et Gilleberto de Hauvill' xl s. ad vadia sua adquietanda[1] de dono R. per breve R. Et Henrico de Hauvill' xl s. ad custodiam avium R. per breve eiusdem. Et in carriagio viij tonellorum vini a Jakel' usque Rokingeh' v et usque Clive iij[2] xj s. et ij d. per breve eiusdem. Et pro justicia facienda v s. et x d. Et debet xvij d. bl. Idem r.c. de eodem debito. In thes. lib.

Et Q.E.

[*One line blank*]

f' Idem Vic. r.c. de xl m. de proficuo comitatuum hoc anno. In thes. lib.

Et Q.E.

f' Homines de Huntedon' r.c. de xxxv li. bl. de firma ville sue. In thes. xxxj li. ij s. et v d. bl. Et in elemosinis constitutis canonicis de Huntedon' xl s. Et monialibus de Huntindon' xiiij s. et x d. Et debent xxv s. et v d. bl.

Idem homines [*blank*] xiij s. et ij d. bl. de remanenti eiusdem firme sue de anno preterito. Et xxiiij s. (et ij d. bl.[i]) de remanenti eiusdem firme de anno vij^{o}.

f' Idem homines r.c. de x li. de cremento eiusdem ville. Et de xxxv s. de remanenti eiusdem crementi de ij^{bus} annis preteritis. In thes. x li. Et debet xxxv s.

Idem homines r.c. de xviij li. et iij s. de pluribus debitis contentis in rotulo viij. In thes. viij li. Et debent x li. et iij s.

1 'a' written over a 'd' at the beginning of this word.

2 That is of the 8 casks of wine from Yaxley 5 were carried to Rockingham and 3 to King's Cliffe in Northants.

f' Idem homines r.c. de vj s. de terra Radulfi Sokemann' de Branton'. In thes. lib. Et Q.S.

f' Telarii Huntindon' [*blank*] xl s. pro gilda sua.

f' Homines de Cantebrig' r.c. de xl li. bl. de firma ville sue. In thes. xxxiij li. et vj s. et ij d. Et in quietantia terre Willelmi Rufi xvj s. et viij d. Et Willelmo de Mortemer in terra de Neweham quam fratres hospitalis de Cantebr' habent C s. sicut continetur in rotulo xiiij R. J. Et debent xxiij s. bl. Idem r.c. de eodem debito. In thes. xiiij s. et viij d. bl. Et debent viij s. et iiij d.

f' Idem homines r.c. de xx li. de cremento ville sue. In thes. lib. Et Q.S.[1]

Idem homines [*blank*] C s. bl. de remanenti firme ville sue de dim. anno xvij^{o}.

f' Idem homines r.c. de ij s de terris Simonis de Insula in Cantebrig'. Et de iij s. et iiij d. de terris Angeri. Et de vij s. et viij d. de eisdem firmis de pluribus annis. In thes. lib. Et Q.S.

f' Idem Vic. r.c. de xx s. de terra Hamelini de Badburgeham. Et de xvj d. de v acris terre in eadem villa. Et de iiij s. de xv acris terre quas Simon clericus tenuit in Abbinton'. Et de ij s. et viij d. de servicio forestarie de Wilburgeham. In thes. lib. Et Q.E.

f' Homines de Gudmecestr' r.c. de C et xx li. de firma ville sue. In thes. lib. Et Q.S.

f' Canonici de Bernewell' r.c. de xxx li. bl. de firma ville de Cestreton'. In thes. xxix li. et ij s. et vj d. bl. Et debent xvij s. et vj d. bl. Idem r.c. de eodem debito. In thes. lib. Et Q.S.

Radulfus f. Fulconis r.c. de C et xlv li. et iij s. et ij d. et iij palefridis de pluribus debitis patris sui contentis in rotulo xv R. J. In thes. C s. Et debet C (et xl^{c})[2] (xl^{i}) li. et iij s. et ij d. et iij palefridos. per annum C s.

Homines Alienore regine et aliorum qui annotantur in rotulo vj R. J. debent C m. ut divise perambulentur sicut continetur ibidem. Comes David debet ij osturcos norrenses sicut continetur in rotulo xiij^{o}. Et x m. de ij scutagiis contentis in rotulo viij^{o}.

Homines de Cantebr' r.c. de x li. et xix s. et vij d. de pluribus tallagiis contentis in rotulo vij^{o}. In thes. C s. Et debent C et xix s. et vij d. Set respondent infra.

Stephanus de Hochton' r.c. de viij s. et iiij d. de tallagio. In thes. v s. Et debet xl d.

Idem Vic. r.c. de ix s. et iiij d. de fine suo. Et de xvj s. de Thoma de Capell'. Et de viij m. de Baldewino de Rosay. In thes. lib. Et Q.E.

Radulfus de Broiera r.c. de D et xxiiij li. et xvij s. et ij d. et j palefrido de iij^{bus} debitis contentis in rotulo viij^{o}. In thes. xx m. Et debet D et xj li. x s. et vj d. et j palefridum de quibus Walterus de Leicr' (debet eum adquietare sicut recognovit^{i}.) per annum xx m.

Galfridus de Haðfeld' r.c. de xxj li. et xiiij s. de pluribus debitis. In thes. C s. per priorem de Bernewell'. Et debet xvj li. et xiiij s. per annum C s.

[1] The strengthening tape at the right hand side of the membrane obscures the 'S' of *sunt* but it can be seen under the tape.

[2] The 'x' has been inserted afterwards and is repeated as an interlinear.

Walterus f. Roberti r.c. de xlvj li. et xl d. de pluribus debitis. In thes. xl s. Et debet xliiij li. et xl d. per annum xl s.

Vitalis Engainne debet iij vulpecularios. (+[i]) Eudo f. Agnet' debet x m. pro habenda assisa. + (Stephanus[c]) (Galfridus[i]) persona de Stanton' debet xx s. pro eodem. Stephanus le Bloy debet vj m. de prestito Pictavie.

Simon de Sancto Licio r.c. de x li. et xvj s. et viij d. et j palefrido de ij[bus] debitis contentis in rotulo iij[o]. In thes. ij m. Et debet ix li. et x s. et j palefridum. per annum ij m.

Hugo Malebisse r.c. de xxij li. et vij s. et xj d. pro habenda gratia R. In thes. C s. Et debet xvij li. et vij s. et xj d.

Nicholaus f. Willelmi le Moinne r.c. de xxxviij s. et viij d. pro habenda saisina. In thes. xx s. Et debet xviij s. et viij d.

Galfridus f. Hugonis de Scalar' r.c. de CC et iiij li. et vij s. et xj d. de pluribus debitis in rotulo viij. In thes. xx m. Et debet C et quater xx et iiij li. vij s. et xj d. per annum xx m.

Abbatia de Rammes' debet viij li. de scutagio Pictavie.

Robertus de Insula qui habet j heredum Johannis de Wahill' debet vj li. et dim. m. de eodem sicut continetur in rotulo precedenti. (+[i]) Mauricius capellanus debet j palefridum pro deliberatione Ricardi Bastard' sicut continetur in rotulo ij[o].

Hubertus de Brumford r.c. de xxiij s. et ix d. et ob. de ij scutagiis in rotulo precedenti. In thes. x s. Et debet xiij s. et ix d. et ob.

Elyas de Amundevill' r.c. de viij li. et iij s. et iij ob. de pluribus debitis contentis in rotulo viij. In thes. iiij li. Et debet iiij li. et iij s. et iij ob.

Willelmus Patric' r.c. de lij s. et j d. de pluribus debitis contentis ibidem. In thes. xxxv s. Et debet xvij s. et j d.

Hamo Pechie r.c. de lviij li. et viij s. et xj d. de scutagio Pictavie.

Ricardus f. Willelmi de Scalar' r.c. de xxxj li. et xviij s. et iiij d. de pluribus debitis contentis ibidem. In thes. x li. Et debet xxj li. et xviij s. et iiij d. per annum x li.

Abbas de Thornie r.c. de xl li. et xix s. et v d. de pluribus debitis pro Adam [*sic*] f. Drogonis sicut continetur in rotulo iiij[o]. In thes. x m. Et debet xxxiiij li. et vj s. et j d. per annum x m.

Henricus Leveske r.c. de xx m. pro habenda custodia sicut continetur in rotulo precedenti. In thes. x m. Et debet x m.

Ricardus f. Simonis [*blank*] v m. pro habenda inquisitione sicut continetur in rotulo ij[o].

+ Robertus f. Roye debet dim. m. quia non est prosecutus. Episcopus Elyensis debet xxiiij m. et dim. de primo scutagio R. de feodis que non recognoscit. Robertus de Mara (set respondet infra[i]) debet dim. m. pro justiciando Roberto le Bloy. + Ricardus de Widipol debet dim. m. pro f[also clamore].[1]

Willelmus de Gimeges r.c. de ij m. de relevio suo. In thes. lib. Et Q.E.

Homines comitatus Hunted' r.c. de xiij li. et ij s. et iiij d. pro deaforestatione sicut continetur in rotulo ij[o]. In thes. viij m. Et debet viij li. et xv s. et viij d.

Hundredum de Hurtlingestan' [*blank*] iij m. pro murdro.

[1] *falso clamore* supplied from *NS 54*, p. 76.

Edelina que fuit uxor Willelmi f. Arnaldi de Cristeshall' debet dim. m. quia non est prosecuta. + Sibilla filia Alani de Childerlé debet dim. m. pro eodem. + Willelmus de Kancia debet dim. m. quia non habuit. + Rogerus f. Baldric' debet dim. m. pro dissaisina. + Durandus debet dim. m. quia non servavit diem. + Rogerus carettarius debet iij s. pro viridi. Warinus de Haneton' debet dim. m. pro licencia concordandi cum Henrico Leveske.

Villata de Ketelstan' r.c. de j m. pro veteri vasto. In thes. lib. Et Q.E.

Willelmus de Offord' r.c. de x m. pro Baldewino de Riparia sicut continetur in rotulo precedenti. In thes. xxij s. et iiij d. Et debet C et xj s.
per annum xliiij s. et v d.

Hamo Pechie [*blank*] x m. de prestito.

Nicholaus de Breautéé r.c. de xlvij s. et ix d. pro blado sicut continetur ibidem. In thes. lib. Et Q.E.

Robertus Passelewe [*blank*] iiij li. et xiij s. de catallis plurium sicut continetur in rotulo precedenti.

Rogerus de Torpel r.c. de j m. de scutagio de Mungumeri. In thes. lib.
Et Q.E.

Willelmus f. Warnerii Engainne r.c. de ij m. de scutagio de Mungumeri et Bedeford'. In thes. j m. Et debet j m.

Radulfus de Bray r.c. de C et xxv li. pro habenda gratia R. sicut continetur in rotulo viij. In thes. xxv li. Et debet C li. Idem r.c. de eodem debito. In thes. xxv li. Et debet lxxv li. per annum l li.

Robertus de Mara r.c. de dim. m. pro justiciando Roberto le Bloy sicut supra continetur. In thes. lib. Et Q.E.

DE OBLATIS

Homines de Cantebr' r.c. de xx m. pro habenda domo que fuit Beniamin sicut continetur in rotulo precedenti. In thes. x li. Et debet v m.

f' Idem homines r.c. de j m. de firma eiusdem domus. In thes. lib.
Et Q.S.

Sibilla de Trumpinton' r.c. de dim. m. quia retraxit se. In thes. lib.
Et Q.E.

Burgenses de Cantebrig' r.c. de xxxvij m. et dim. de fine suo pro libertate sua habenda. In thes. xv li. Et debet x li.

Idem Vic. r.c. de dim. m. de Alano f. Gunnild'. Et de dim m. de Willelmo de Burdeleis. Et de j m. de Ricardo f. Simonis. Et de j m. de (Henrico[c]) (Waltero[i]) Corde. Et de dim. m. de Henrico Leveske. In thes. lib. Et Q.E.

Adam f. Eustachii Dunning' r.c. de xl s. pro plegio. In thes. lib.
Et Q.E.

Homines de Cantebr' r.c. de C et xix s. et vij d. de pluribus tallagiis sicut supra continentur. In thes. xxxvij s. per j taleam de ante guerram[1] allocatam precepto H. de Burgo coram baronibus de scaccario. Et debent iiij li. et ij s. et vij d.

[1] This is written as all one word by the clerk.

DEBITA VILLE DE CANTEBR'

Homines de Cantebr' r.c. de xij s. de Ricardo Wolward'. Et de iiij s. et viij d. de Hugone Heldecuppe. Et de iiij s. et iiij d. Yvone Carnifice. Et de xj s. et viij d. de Simone Bagge. Et de iiij[1] s. de Adam telar'. Et de iiij s. et iiij d. de Willelmo de Scheldford'. Et de xviij d. de Alexandro le Fittere. Et de ix s. de Ricardo Legelin'. Et de v s. de Henrico f. Elye. Et de xvj s. et iiij d. de Yvone f. Absalon'. Et de ij s. et vj d. de Reginaldo Schortcnicht. Et de iij s. et vj d. de Galfrido de Clait. Et de v s. et vj d. de Ketell' mercatore. Et de xiiij d. de Childmanno. Et de iiij s. et iiij d. de Frere. Et de xviij d. de Johanne fabro. Et de ij s. de Petro Criket. Et de iiij s. et x d. de Radulfo Pirle. Et de iiij s. et vj d. de Huberto piscatore. Et de x s. de Warino f. Anketill'. Et de vj s. de Adam le Wanc'. In thes. lib. Et Q.S.

[2]*t* Galfridus Wolward' r.c. de vij s. In thes. iiij s. Et debet iij s.
t Johannes f. Seled' r.c. de xj s. et ij d. In thes. vj s. Et debet v s. et ij d.
t Ricardus f. Ricardi r.c. de v s. et viij d. In thes. iij s. et ij d. Et debet ij s. et vj d.

[*Rot.* 12 *Mem.* 2]

[*One line blank*]
p Martinus Wolward' r.c. de xlj s. et viij d. In thes. v s. Et debet xxxvj s. et viij d.
t Radulfus f. Galfridi r.c. de x s. In thes. iiij s. Et debet vj s.
p Kailli le Tannur r.c. de xxviij s. In thes. iiij s. Et debet xxiiij s.
t Walterus f. Colice r.c. de vj s. In thes. ij s. Et debet iiij s.
p Reginaldus de Abbinton' r.c. de xv s. et vj d. In thes. v s. Et debet x s. et vj d.
t Thomas de Oy r.c. de x s. et viij d. In thes. ij s. Et debet viij s. et viij d.
p Reginaldus f' Alur' r.c. de xxix s. et viij d. In thes. j m. Et debet xvj s. et iiij d.
p Jordanus Niker r.c. de xxvj s. et iiij d. In thes. vj s. et vj d. Et debet xix s. et x d.

[*Rot.* 12 *Mem.* 1]

[3]*p* Edwardus f. Edwardi r.c. de xlv s. et viij d. In thes. xvj s. Et debet xxix s. et viij d.
t Renerius de Winebold' r.c. de vj s. et vj d. In thes. ii j. Et debet iiij s. et vj d.
p Willelmus Wolsi r.c. de xxvj s. In thes. iiij s. Et debet xxij s.
[*A line of stitching joins the two membranes*]

[*Rot.* 12 *Mem.* 2]

1 There is a crease here in the membrane which partially obscures some of this sum.
2 The following entries are on the left hand side of the membrane only.
3 The following entries are on the right hand side of the membrane only.

t Robertus le Wanc' r.c. de vj s. et x d. In thes. ij s. Et debet iiij s. et x d.
p Johannes Lane r.c. de xij s. et viij d. In thes. ij s. Et debet x s. et viiij d.
p Herveus f. Salede r.c. de xxvij s. In thes. iiij s. Et debet xxiij s.
p Willelmus Carnifex r.c. de iiij m. In thes. ij s. Et debet l s. et iiij d.
d Reginaldus Godscó r.c. de l s. et viij d. In thes. v s. Et debet xlv s. et viij d.
p Brictnodus Tanur[1] r.c. de v m. In thes. xj s. et viij d. Et debet lv s.
p Walterus Blundus r.c. de xiiij s. et viij d. In thes. v s. Et debet ix s. et viij d.
p Ricardus Paiwomb' r.c. iiij s. et viij d. *p* Simon Niger debet ij s. et viij d. + Andreas de Winepol debet v s. et ij d.
[2] + Basilia uxor Godwini[3] debet xxij d. (*d*[i]) Walterus Carpentarius debet ij s. et viij d. (*d*[i]) Godefridus f. Godefridi debet dim. m. pro habendo brevi. (*d*[i]) Herveus de Burgat' debet xl d. pro licencia concordandi. (*d*[i]) Henricus f. Albr' debet xl d. pro eodem. (*d*[i]) Walterus Saliung debet dim. m. quia non est prosecutus. (+[i]) Robertus Twislet debet j m. pro vino vendito. (*d*[i]) Thomas Pupelot' debet ij s. et vj d. de veteri tallagio. (*d*[i]) Yvo f. Matillidis debet iiij s. et x d. (+[i]) Ricardus Guder[4] debet xix s. et ij d. (+[i]) Ricardus de Bernewell' debet lxxvj s. et viij d. Ricardus Wolward debet xxxj s. et viij d. (*d*[i]) Johannes f. Helene debet vij s. et iiij d. (+[i]) Johannes Crocheman debet xxxviij s. et viij d. (*d*[i]) Benedictus feltrarius debet vj s. et x d + Simon le Taillur[5] debet xij s. et viij d. (+[i]) Radulfus Prutfot debet lvj s. (*d*[i]) Simon Niger debet xxij s. et iiij d. (+[i]) Fulco Crochemann debet lv s. (+[i]) Walterus Sissard' debet xj s. (*d*[i]) Henricus Telarius debet vij s. et iiij d. (+[i]) Ricardus Gibelot debet xxxiiij s. (+[i]) Ricardus le Peinnier debet vj s. et x d. + Godricus le Hawre debet ix s. et iiij d. (+[i]) Simon f. Godrici debet xxiiij s. et viij d. (+[i]) Sumer debet vij s. et iiij d. (+[i]) Walterus Ere debet xxiiij s. + Walterus Billing debet xxxviij s. et viij d. + Johannes de Estfliet debet xxx s. + Ricardus Curtesius debet xxiiij s. et viij d. (+[i]) Gillebertus Curtesius debet xv s. (*d*[i]) Willelmus Prest debet vij s. et x d. (*d*[i]) Robertus Custance debet xj s. (*d*[i]) Robertus Vivien debet xlvj s. + Ricardus de Storteford' debet xxij s. + Gunilda de Gravel' debet dim. m. ut replegietur. + Hugo Telarius debet dim. m. quia non est prosecutus. + Decena Acharii debet dim. m. pro fuga Albini. + Albricus Longus debet xv s. pro vino vendito.

Comes (--oui-ll-[i,d])[6] Simon debet C et quater xx et xvj li. de pluribus debitis Ááron Judei contentis in rotulo precedenti.
[*One line blank*]

1 In *NS 54*, p. 78 he is shown as *Bartholomeus Tanur*.
2 The following entries are written across the whole membrane.
3 In *NS 54*, p. 75 this person is shown as *Basilius filius Godwini* but the amount of money is the same.
4 In *NS 54*, p. 78 he is shown as *Ricardus Gudred'*.
5 In *NS 54*, p. 78 he is shown as *Simon cisor*.
6 This is faint writing above the line, possibly erased.

DE TENENTIBUS TERRAS [*SIC*] QUE FUERUNT SIMONIS DE TURRI DE DEBITIS JUDEORUM

Galfridus f. Simonis de Turri r.c. de xxiij li. et xiij s. et viij d. de debitis Judeorum pro Simone patro suo. In thes. xx s. Et debet xxij li. et xiij s. et viij d. per annum xx s.

Willelmus de Burdeleis r.c. de xxxv. li. de debitis Judeorum qui requirebatur in Judaismo. In thes. xl s. Et debet xxxiij li. per annum xl s.

DE MILITIBUS HONORIS RICHEMUND' IN HOC COMITATU DE SCUTAGIO DE MUNGUMERI QUI TENENT DE COMITE BRITANN' QUIA COMES NEC ALIQUIS PRO EO FUIT IN EXERCITU

Idem Vic. r.c. de iiij m. de Everard' Francesio de eodem de ij feodis. Et de ij m. de Hugone Malebisse de j feodo. Et de iiij m. de Thoma de Burgo de ij feodis. Et de j m. de Johanne f. Henrici de dim. feodo. Et de iiij m. de Thoma de Valeines de ij feodis. Et de ij m. de Hamone Lenveisie de ij militibus. Et de j m. de Alano de Mean(a[i])y de dim. feodo. Et de j m. de Alano Folifet de dim. feodo. Et de dim. m. de Radulfo f. Fulconis de quarta parte j[us] feodi. Et de ij m. de Anketill' Váássore de j feodo. Et de j m. de Galfrido de Scalar' de dim. feodo. Et de dim. m. de Ricardo de Scalar' de quarta parte j[us] feodi. In thes. lib. Et Q.E.

Ysabella comitissa Oxon' r.c. de xviij m. de eodem de ix feodis eiusdem honoris. In thes viij li. (que tenet de predicto comite.[i]) Et in perdona Hamoni Pechie vj m. (per breve R.[i]) de iij feodis qui tenet de ipsa comitissa. Et Q.E.

Eadem comitissa r.c. de ij m. de eodem de j feodo quod W. de Mandevill' comes Essex de ea tenet in Linton' (de eodem honore.[i]) In thes. nichil. Et in perdona ipsi comitisse ij m. per breve R. Et Q.E.

DE HIIS QUI REMANSERUNT R. IN PARTE SUA DE EODEM HONORE QUANDO PARTITIO FACTA FUIT INTER IPSUM ET PREDICTUM COMITEM

Warinus de Saham r.c. de j m. de eodem de dim. feodo quod recognoscit. In thes. lib. Et Q.E.

Idem debet j m. de dim. feodo quod non recognoscit.

Michael de Fornell' r.c. de xiiij m. de vij feodis eiusdem honoris de eodem. In thes. viij m. Et debet vj m.

[*One line blank*]

DE SCUTAGIO DE BEDEFORD' DE EODEM HONORE

Comes Brittann' habet quietantiam (per breve R.[i]) de omnibus feodis suis suprascriptis.

DE PARTE R. DE EODEM HONORE

Warinus de Saham r.c. de j m. de eodem de dim. feodo quod recognoscit. In thes. lib. Et Q.E.

Idem W. debet j m. de dim. feodo quod non recognoscit.

Michael de Fornell' r.c. (de[i]) xiiij m. de eodem. In thes. vj m. Et debet viij m.

Hamo Pechie habet quietantiam per breve R. de j f[eodo].

[*One line blank*]

DE WARDIS EIUSDEM HONORIS DE PARTE R.

Warinus de Saham r.c. de xxx s. de eodem de dim. feodo quod recognoscit de vj annis preteritis scilicet per annum v s. In thes. xxiiij s. Et debet vj s.

Idem W. debet xxx s. de dim. feodo quod non recognoscit de eodem de eisdem vj annis.

Michael de Fornell' r.c. de (fornell' j[c]) xxj li. de eodem de vij feodis de predicto termino scilicet de quolibet feodo x s. per annum. In thes. lx s. Et debet xviij li.

Hamo Pechie [*blank*] lx s. de eodem de j feodo de eodem termino.

Nicholaus f. Radulfi de Bello campo [*blank*] C et xvij li. et iij s. et iiij d. pro patre suo de ij[bus] debitis contentis in rotulo vij[o] qui requirebatur in Essex' super predictum Radulfum.

NOVA OBLATA

Walterus f. Roberti r.c. de v m. pro habenda licencia claudendi boscum[1] suum de Ellinton' ad parcum faciendum antequam perambulatio facta fuit de foresta. In thes. j m. Et debet iiij m.

Helewis' que fuit uxor de Coldham[2] [*blank*] dim. m. pro habendo brevi coram justiciariis apud Westm' contra Ricardum de Melkesham et Gervasium de Straham[3] (de tenemento[i]) in Ely et Thefford'.[4]

Ricardus le Taillur et Roheis' uxor sua debent dim. m. pro habendo brevi de attingendis xij juratoribus nove dissaisine coram justiciariis assignatis de tenemento in Cumberton'. Alexander iuvenis debet j m. pro habendo brevi contra Adam de Laxfeld' de debito ix m.

Reginaldus Morel r.c. de dim. m. pro licencia concordandi cum Lucya que fuit uxor Roberti le Bloy. In thes. lib. Et Q.E.

[1] See *Calendar of Fine Rolls*, II, 1224–34, p. 29, no. 194.

[2] See *Calendar of Fine Rolls*, II, 1224–34, p. 40, no. 258 where she is shown as the wife of Eustace of Coldham.

[3] This might be Stretham in Cambridgeshire, which is very near Little Thetford in Cambs.

[4] See *Calendar of Fine Rolls*, II, 1224–34, p. 40, no. 258 where the place is called Elm Thefford. This might still refer to Little Thetford as in this fine there is only a reference to one tenement as there is here. Perhaps the clerk has made a mistake in this roll as the fine would need to be very accurate if both parties are to agree the location.

Jordanus Lenveisie r.c. de dim. m. pro mentione facienda de tempore H. R. avi R. In thes. lib. Et Q.E.

Homines comitatus Hunt' debent xx m. pro libertate carte tenenda. Et x m. pro saisina sua habenda per preceptum R. illis concessa. Homines de Herford' manerio R. debent ij m. pro habenda pastura sua in bosco de Sappel' habenda[1] quam solent habere. Homines de Wagmundel' et Westun' et Helinton' et Wulfel' et de Branton' debent v m. pro pastura sua in Wichewud'. Philippus de Parnes de Mordon' debet dim. m. pro falso clamore qui requirebatur in Essex' in itinere Simonis de Hal.

Willelmus Marisc' de Tidd debet dim. m. quia non est prosecutus in Linc' coram Roberto de Laxinton' et sociis suis qui requirebatur ibidem.

AMERCIAMENTA FACTA PER SIMONEM DE HAL ET SOCIOS SUOS

Idem Vic. r.c. de C et xj m. et v s. de misericordiis hominum et decenarum quorum nominibus preponitur littera *t* in rotulo quem predicti liberaverunt in thesauro. In thes. lib. in C et quater xx^{ti} taleis. Et Q.E.

ā Alanus Wiclof r.c. de dim. m. pro defalta. In thes. iiij s. Et debet ij s. et viij d.

t Galfridus Flameng de Fordham debet dim. m. pro dissaisina. Willelmus (*Cani*^{i}) de Colecestr' debet dim. m. pro dissaisina. (*t*) Ricardus f. Osberti de Pappeworðe debet x s. pro dissaisina per plegium Walteri f. Elvinis et Roberti de Cnappewell'. Idem Vic. debet xv s. de catallis Simonis Gulias suspensi, (de quibus Magister Willelmus de Banocis debet respondere sicut rec[ognoscit]^{i}.) Decena Henrici de Kingeston' debet x s. pro fuga ipsius (de quibus de[2] debet respondere.^{i}) (*t*^{i}) Decena Willelmi Rotecorn fugitivi debet dim. m. pro fuga ipsius. (*d*^{i}) Willelmus f. Simonis debet dim. m. pro defalta. (*t*) Decena Ricardi Sparewe fugitivi debet dim. m. pro fuga ipsius (Bedef'.^{i}) Decena Roberti de la Forde debet dim. m. pro fuga ipsius (Hun^{i}) Decena Willelmi Babel debet dim. m. pro fuga ipsius.

[E]ly episcopus' Idem Vic. r.c. de dim. m. de decena Ricardi f. Rogeri de Sneilewell' pro fuga ipsius. Et de dim. m. de decena Hugonis de la Reche de Swafham pro fuga. Et de dim. m. de decena Johannis f. Sibill' de Sheldford' quia non habuit quem plegiavit. Et de dim. m. de Henrico aliquid[3] pro dissaisina. Et de dim. m. de Radulfo f. Bartholomei de Coteham pro defalta. Et de j m. de Joscel' de Pidel' pro fuga. Et de x s. de Asceo de Colne pro eodem. Et de xx s. de Adam f. Hervei pro eodem. In thes. nichil. Et G. Elyen' episcopo v m. et x s. per libertatem carte R. Et Q.E.

C(ui)v –Ro.[4] Idem Vic. r.c. de ij m. de medietate ville de Cruce Roheis' pro receptamento Gilleberti Hoggesfot latronis. In thes. nichil. Et canonicis de Cruce Roheis' ij m. per libertatem carte R. Et Q.E.

1 *habenda* repeated.
2 Extra *de* written in error.
3 *Sic.*
4 The membrane has worn away at least one of the initial letters of each line of the marginalia. It is possible that the second line has '*Ro*' for Roheis. The first line might be 'Cruce'.

+ Idem Vic. r.c. de dim. m. de decena Rogeri Gaillard' de Stilton' pro fuga. Et de dim. m. de decena Martini Rotecorn' fugitivi. In thes. nichil. Et fratribus militie Templi j m. per libertatem carte R. Et Q.E.
d Johannes de Croxton' debet dim. m. pro dissaisina. (*d*[i]) Rogerus le Diable debet j m. pro defalta, qui duo requirebantur in itinere Simonis de Hal et sociorum suorum in Essex'.

ITEM NOVA OBLATA

Prior de Sancto Neoto r.c. de xxx m. quas receperat de denario Willelmi Martel. Et de x m. quas receperat de Ernis' de Bonevill'. In thes. xxv m. Et debet xv m.

Abbas de Rammes' [*blank*] C m. pro dissaisina qui requirebatur in itinere Simonis de Hal per R. amerciatus.

Willelmus de Bokesworðe et Philippus f. Johannis debent xx s. de remanenti carrucagii Cantebrig'sir sicut continetur in rotulo de carrucagio. Galfridus de Hemmingeford' et Robertus de Wassingel' debent vij s. et vj d. de remanenti compoti de Huntindonesir' sicut continetur in rotulo de carrucagio.
[*Three lines blank*]

OXON'

[*Both the left and right-hand sides of the membrane are very rubbed and there are some parts torn off. Dots indicate where text is missing.*]

Walterus Foliot ut custos r.c. de quater xx et et j li. et xiij s. et ij d. bl. de firma comitatus de quarta parte anni. In thes. nichil.

Et in elemosinis constitutis infirmis Sancti Bartholomei extra Oxon' iiij li. et xviij s. et x d. de eodem termino. Et eisdem ad pannos xvj s. et iij d. Et monachis de Bordeslé xxv s. in porcaria de Benton'. Et in terris [datis] Waltero de Verdon' C s. bl. in Blockesham. Et abbatisse de Godestow' xxv s. bl. in Hedindon'. Et canonicis de Osen' iij[1] (x[d]) s. bl. ibidem. Et comiti Bolon' xv li. et v s. bl. in Banton'. Et canonicis Sagien[sibus] [...] s. bl. in Brichtelmeston'. Et Engelard' de Ciconiaco[2] xiiij li. et vij s. bl. in Bensinton' quamdiu R. placuerit. Et abbati de Osen' ij s. et iiij d. et ob. in villa Oxon'. Et in Blockesham C s. bl. de quibus Vic. [*respondet* ([...]cora.[i])][3] Et Waltero Boistard' vij s. et vij d. (et ob.[i]) ad custodiam domorum R. Oxon'. Et monachis de Tama xv s. in Wifald'. Et canonicis de Sancta Frideswiða xij s. et iij ob. in Oxon'. Et Petronille que fuit uxor Galfridi [flecc]arii xij s. et vj d. de molendino de Hedindon' quod vocatur Kingesmuln'. Et abbati de Osen' xix d. in Bensinton'. Et infirmis de Walingeford' ix d. ibidem. Et capellano de Wudestok' xij s. et vj d. [de libera]tione sua. Et abbatisse de Godestow' xxv s. in Bensinton'. Et Willelmo capellano Oxon' xij s. et vj d. de liberatione sua. Et Waltero Foliot v s. et x d. in Bensinton'. Et ecclesie Sancte Marie Oxon' viij [...]

1 Perhaps written over an erasure.
2 There is some smudging or blotting over this word.
3 *Respondet* supplied from *NS 54*, p. 20.

[…]ton’. Et comiti de Warewic et particibus suis, heredibus Thome Basset x li. et xij s. et vj d. in Hedindon’ de quibus respondent infra. Et Mauricio f. Reginaldi andeg’ l s. in Bensinton’.
[*One line blank*]

[Et in repar]atione domorum in castro Oxon’ et aule et camerar’ R. et capelle R. extra castrum Oxon’ et domorum et capelle R. iiij li. et vj s. et vij d. per breve R. Et debet ix li. et xv s. (iiij d.[i]) et ob. bl. qui sunt ei extensi […][1] (et v s. et iij ob. bl. Set respondet in dorso.[i])[2]

Idem debet xiij li. et xix s. et v d. bl. de remanenti firme comitatus de dim. anno preterito qui sunt ei extensi ad xiiij li. et vij s. et vj d. num. (Set respondet in dorso.[i])

Et W. debet C et xiiij s. de proficuo comitatus de hac quarta parte anni. (Set respondet in dorso.[i]) Et xiiij li. (de[c]) et x d. de proficuo comitatus de dim. anno preterito. (Set respondet in dorso.[i])
[*One line blank*][3]

RESPICE IN TERGUM

[*Rot.* 12d *Mem.* 1]

Idem W. debet xxij li. et iij s. et viij (d.[i]) de remanenti exitus maneriorum de dim. anno preterito. Et xxvj (li.[i]) et v s. (et v d.[i]) de remanenti eiusdem exitus de (quarta parte[i]) de hoc anno.[4]

Idem W. debet iiij li. et x s. de exitu de Littlemor’ de dim. anno preterito. Et xv s. de eodem exitu de quarta parte huius anni. Summa omnium debitorum suorum prescriptorum. Summa liij li. xiiij s. et ij d. Set respondet infra.

Predictus Walterus r.c. de x li. et v s. et iij ob. de remanenti firme comitatus Oxon’ sicut continetur ex alia parte rotuli post corpus comitatus. In thes. nichil. Et in defalta firme ville Oxon’ de eadem quarta parte anni quam non recepit et de qua Godefridus de Crawecumb’ debet respondere super compotum suum x li. Et debet W. v s. et iij ob. et respondet infra.

Idem W. r.c. de v s. et iij ob. sicut supra continetur. Et (de[i]) xiiij li. et vij s. et vj d. de remanenti firme comitatus de dim. anno preterito. Et (de[i]) C et xiij s. de proficuo comitatus de quarta parte huius anni sicut supra continetur. Et (de[i]) xiiij li. et x d. de proficuo eiusdem de dim. anno preterito. Et de xxij li. et iij s. et viij d. de remanenti exitus maneriorum de dim. anno preterito. Et de xxvj li. et v s. et v d. de remanenti eiusdem exitus de quarta parte anni huius sicut continetur in rotulo compotorum. Et de iiij li. et x s. de exitu de Littlemor’ de dim. anno preterito. Et de xv s. de eodem exitu de quarta parte huius anni sicut supra continetur. Summa quater xx et viij li. et vj d. et ob. In thes. nichil. Et ipsi W. pro custodia castri Oxon’ et de Wudestok’ et comitatu per idem tempus (xix li. et xiij s. et x d.[c]) (xxviij li.

1 Perhaps this is all that is written.
2 This has been inserted on the line below.
3 There is the number ‘12’ written in pencil in the middle of this line.
4 The clerk has overwritten a ‘j’ with the ‘o’ of *anno*.

et vj d. et ob.[i]) per breve R. Et debet lx li. Idem r.c. de eodem debito. In thes. xxx li. Et debet xxx li. [1]Idem r.c. (O[d]) de eodem debito (et [...] bl.[i]) In thes. xx li. Et debet x li.

Godefridus[2] de Crawecumb' Robertus de Haya ut custos pro eo r.c. de CC et xliiij li. et xix s. et vj d. et ob. bl. de firma comitatus de tribus partibus anni. In thes. nichil.

Et in elemosinis constitutis militibus de Templo j m. de toto anno. Et xiij infirmis Sancti Bartholomei extra Oxon'[3] xiiij li. xvj s. vj d. et ob. de (tribus partibus anni.[i]) Et eisdem ad pannos xlviij s. et ix d. Et monachis de Bordesle lxxv (s.[i]) in porcaria de Benton'. Et in terris datis Waltero de Verdon' xv li. bl. in Blockesham. Et abbatisse de Godestowe lxxv s. bl. in Hedendon'. Et canonicis de Os[e]neia[4] ix s. bl. in Hedendon'. Et comiti Bolon' xlv li. et xv s. bl. in Banton'.[5] Et canonicis Sagiensibus vij li. et x s. bl. in Brichthelmeston'. Et Engelard' de Cyconiaco xliij li. et xij d. (et[i])[6] in Bensinton' quamdiu R. placuerit. Et abbati de Oseneie in donis vij s. et ob. in villa Oxon'. Et custodi domorum R. xxij s. et ix d. et ob. Et monachis de Tama xlv s. in Wifalda. Et canonicis de Sancta Freðeswiða xxxvj s. et iiij d. et ob. Et Petronille que fuit uxor Galfridi fleccarii xxxvij s. et vj d. in molendino de Hedindon' quod vocatur Kingesmuln'. Et abbati de Oseneie iiij s. et ix d. in Bensinton'. Et infirmis de Walingeford' ij s. et iij d. ibidem. Et capellano de Wudestok' xxxvij s. et vj d. Et abbatisse de Godestowe lxxv s. in Bensinton'. Et (Willelmo[c]) (Roberto[i]) capellano Oxon' xxxvij s. et vj d. de liberatione sua. Et Waltero Foliot xvij s. et vj d. in Bensintone. Et ecclesie Sancte Marie Oxon' ij s. de eodem termino. Et comiti de Warew' et participibus suis heredibus Thome Basset xxxj li. et xvij s. et vj d. in Hedendon' de quibus respondet infra. Et Mauricio f. Reginaldi Andeg' vij li. et x s. in Bensinton'. Et in Blockesham xv li. bl. de quibus Vic. respondet infra.

[*One line blank*]

Et in carriagio braonis R. capti in parco de Beckel' carriati ab Oxon' usque London' iiij s. et ix d. per breve R. Et in justicia facienda et prisonibus carriandis vij s. et vj d. Et Godefrido de Crawecumb' xix li. (de predicto termino[i]) per breve R. in quo continetur quod allocentur (per[d]) (hoc[i]) anno xl li. pro custodia castri et comitatus. Et in reparatione capelle R. Oxon' et operatione j[us] butillarie nove et j[us] dispense nove et camini parvi garderobe et cameris R. cóóperiendis et turris castri Oxon' plumbate et reparatione domorum eiusdem castri et partis illius Barbecane que fracta fuit et reparatione domorum R. de Wudestok' tam superioris quam inferioris ad fontem C et lxiiij li. et iiij d. per breve R. et per visum Walteri

1 There has been some rubbing out on this line with a small number of letters or words still extant.

2 The initial letter is spread over two lines and is very elaborate.

3 From here to the end of the line and from a similar position on the line below to the right hand edge of the membrane there has been considerable rubbing out.

4 The 'e' in the middle of *Oseneia* has been affected by the rubbing out. It looks as though it could be a capital 'E', or 'l', or 'c', or 't'.

5 There has been considerable rubbing out here as well.

6 This is a superfluous word inserted by the clerk.

Caperun et Ricardi Mai de operatione de Wudestok' et Benedicti Mercerii et Andree de Wulgarigut' de operatione Oxon'. Et habet de superplus C et xliij li. et xvij s. et iiij d. et ob. bl. qui sunt ei extensi ad C et lj li. viij s. iiij d. et ob. num. de quibus quater xx et xj li. et vij s. et vij d. et ob. locantur ei infra in pluribus debitis. Et restant ei locand' lx li. et ix d. quod totum locatur ei in rotulo sequenti.

f' Idem Vic. r.c. de xxiiij li. et x s. de proficuo comitatus de tribus[1] partibus anni. In thes. nichil. Et in superplus quod habet supra xxiiij li. et x s. Et Q.E.

f' Telarii Oxon' r.c. de vj li. pro gilda sua pro j m. auri. In thes. lib. Et Q.E.

f' Corvasarii Oxon' r.c. de xv s. pro gilda sua pro j uncia auri. In thes. lib. Et Q.E.

f' Idem Vic. r.c. de xviij d. de iij^{bus} fabricis in Oxon'. Et de viij d. de propresturis. In thes. lib. Et Q.E.

f' Comes [de] Warewic' r.c. de xx li. de firma de Hedindon'. In thes. lib. Et Q.E.

f' Thomas de Langeleg' r.c. de vij li. de censu foreste de Corneberi. In thes. vj li. et vj s. Et in decimis constitutis canonicis Linc' xiiij s. Et Q.E.

Idem T. r.c. de xiij li. et xvj s. et viij d. de remanenti eiusdem firme de pluribus annis preteritis. Et de xliiij li. et xl d. et j bono palefrido pro habenda custodia sicut continetur in rotulo vj^{o}. In thes. lx s. Et debet lv li. et j bonum palefridum.

f' Idem Vic. r.c. de C li. de firma de Bensinton'. In thes. nichil. Et Engelardo de Ciconiaco C li. ad se sustentandum quamdiu R. placuerit. Et Q.E.

Walterus archiepiscopus Ebor' r.c. de M et CC m. de pluribus (annis^{c}) debitis contentis in rotulo precedenti. In thes. CC m. Et ipsi R. in garderoba sua apud Rading' C m. per breve R. Et debet DCCCC m. de quibus per annum C m. et respondet in Everwikesir'.

Johannes de Gray custos Oliverii de Aiencurt debet lxx li. de scutagio Pictavie sicut continetur in rotulo vij^{o}.

Radulfus Hareng' r.c. de lxij li. et vj d. de ij^{bus} debitis contentis in rotulo precedenti. In thes. xij li. et j m. Et debet xlix li. et vij s. et ij d. per annum xvj m.

Robertus Maudoit r.c. de xxxiij li. et x s. et vj d. de ij^{bus} debitis Radulfi Murdac contentis ibidem. In thes x m. Et debet xxvj li. et xvij s. et ij d. per annum x m.

Comes Bolon' debet M m. pro dissaisina. Robertus de Bello campo debet xx m. quia non habuit homines suos ad rectum. Heres Gerardi de Canvill' debet j m. de scutagio Wall'. Villata de Bernecestr' debet ij m. pro vasto. Hugo Crumpe debet quartam partem de xxiiij m. pro habendo precipe sicut continetur in rotulo ij^{o}. + Radulfus Piket debet j m. pro licencia concordandi. + Henricus de Littleton' debet j m. pro iniusta detentione. Ricardus de Hamedon' debet j. m. pro licencia concordandi.

Otuel f. Rogeri r.c. de dim. m. de misericordia patris sui. In thes. lib. Et Q.E.

[1] The *t* is written over a *p*.

Gillebertus de Stanford' r.c. de ij m. de fine. In thes. xv s. Et debet xj s. et viij d.

Johannes de Bassingeburn' r.c. de CCC et xxxix li. et xj s. et j d. de pluribus debitis contentis in rotulo viij°. In thes lx li. Et debet CC et lxxix li. et xj s. et j d. per annum lx li.[1]

Robertus Arsic [*blank*] quater xx et vj li. et xl d. et j palefr' de pluribus debitis contentis ibidem.

Heredes Johannis f. Hugonis [*blank*] lxxvj (s.[i]) et x d. de ij^{bus} debitis eiusdem J. contentis ibidem.

Henricus Doyilli[2] r.c. de C et quater xx et xij li.[3] et viij s. et xj d. de pluribus debitis contentis in rotulo ij°. In thes. xx s. Et debet j m. Idem r.c. de eodem debito. In thes. lib. Et Q.E.

Magister militie Templi r.c. de ij m. et dim. pro Willelmo Grimbald' sicut continetur in rotulo xiiij° R. J. In thes. xx s. Et debet J m. Idem r.c. de eodem debito. In thes. lib. Et Q.E.

Henricus Doilly [*blank*] xxiij li. de scutagio de Mungumery sicut supra continetur.

DE PRESTITO PICTAVIE

Andreas de Bello campo debet xx m. de prestito Pictavie. Elyas de Bello campo debet xx m. de eodem.

Stephanus Croc [*blank*] dim. m. pro licencia concordandi.

Idem Vic. r.c. de xl d. de Johanne de Cruce pro falso clamore. Et de dim. m. de Willelmo cultellario. Et de j m. de Willelmo archidiacono Richemund'. In thes. lib. Et Q.E.

Walot r.c. de[4] dim. m. pro vino vendito. In thes. ij s. Et debet iiij s. et viij d.

Wal. Willelmus Swein debet dim. m. quia non habuit. Radulfus persona de Stok' debet xl d. pro defalta. Willelmus de la Wose debet iiij s. et viij d. quia non est prosecutus. Gillebertus Rufus debet dim. m. quia retraxit se. Willelmus Morin debet l s. de relevio suo.

Villata de Cauresham [*blank*] xl s. pro murdro.

Willelmus de Wigorn' debet C s. quia non habuit. + Willelmus Wimbel debet dim. m. pro eodem. + Radulfus vinitarius debet dim. m. pro vino vendito. + Walterus falconarius debet dim. m. quia non est prosecutus. + Absalon de Bureford' debet dim. m. pro plegio. Hugo f. Ricardi debet dim. m. pro falso clamore. + Robertus Piedurs debet dim. m. pro vino vendito. + Galfridus f. Hugonis aurifabri debet dim. m. pro eodem. + Radulfus Cusinet debet dim. m. pro eodem. + Petrus cultellarius debet dim. m. pro eodem. (+[i]) Philippus f. Radulfi debet dim. m. quia non est prosecutus. + Gillebertus f. Willelmi debet v m. pro summonendo Henrico Doylli.

Prior hospitalis Jer'l'm [*blank*] l m. pro dissaisina.

1 In *NS 54*, p. 22 he is shown as owing 100 marks per year, or £66 13s. 4d.

2 In *NS 54*, p. 23 he is shown as *Henricus Doilli.*

3 It looks as though the clerk has written something, possibly a 'd' on either side of the 'l' in 'li.'. However, the amount as shown is correct.

4 *De* is repeated.

Radulfus de Caueresham et Muriell' uxor eius [*blank*] xxx m. et dim. pro justic[ianda] Cecil'[1] de Langetot.

Hugo de Gornac [*blank*] C et quater xx et xiij li. et dim. m. et ij^bus^ doliis vini de pluribus debitis contentis in rotulo viij^o^.

Willelmus de Bouen'[2] r.c. de l s. pro magistro hospitalis Sancti Bartholomei Lond'. In thes. x s. Et debet xl s.

Alexander de la Thierne et Gillebertus Taillard' agistores foreste de Wichewode debent xxviij li. et xiij s. et v d. de padnagio de[3] pluribus annis R. J. et R. huius sicut continetur per partes in rotulo precedenti respondent infra per partes.

Walterus de Verdone [*blank*] C et quater xx li. et xiij d. de pluribus debitis contentis in rotulo vj^o^.

Rannulfus f. Rogeri r.c. de xxij s. scilicet tercia parte lxvj s. pro summonendo Manassero. In thes. lib. Et Q.E.

+ Godefridus f. Martini debet dim. m. pro habendo pone. + Philippus de bello monte debet j m. pro licencia concordandi sicut continetur in rotulo precedenti.

[4] Galfridus de Mora r.c. de dim. m. pro licencia concordandi. In thes. lib. Et Q.E.

Matheus de Bixtrope r.c. de iij m. et dim. pro habenda gratia R. sicut continetur in rotulo viij. In thes. ij m. Et debet xx s.

Johanna que fuit uxor Ade pincerne r.c. de v m. pro habenda saisina sicut continetur ibidem. In thes. ij m. Et debet iij m. Eadem r.c. de eodem debito. In thes. xx s. Et debet xx s.

Robertus de Droes r.c. de CCCC et quater xx li. et vj s. de pluribus debitis contentis ibidem. In thes. l li. Et debet CCCC et xxx li. et vj s.

Idem Vic. r.c. de j m. de Roberto Arsic de scutagio de Mungumeri. Et de ij m. de herede Guidonis de Diva de eodem. In thes. lib. Et Q.E.

Johannes de Harocurt [*blank*] ij m. de eodem. Et ij m de scutagio de Bedeford'.

Willelmus de Alcrinton' r.c. de dim. m. de scutagio de Bedeford'. In thes. lib. Et Q.E.

Eva de Gray [*blank*] viij (m.^i^) de eodem de iiij f[eodis] comitis Devon' que requirebatur in compoto Walerand'[5] teutonici in rotulo de carrucagio.

1 In *NS 54*, p. 224 this item comes under Berkshire and Caversham is shown as in Berkshire. It used to be in Oxfordshire before being transferred to Berkshire in a local Governement split in 1911 and is now incorporated into Reading.

2 This might be Boveney in Buckinghamshire.

3 The latter half of the word *padnagio* and the word *de* are very faint. It looks as if there has been some rubbing out here.

4 There was a hole in the middle of the line which partially goes onto the next line. The clerk worked round it. There is now some strengthening tape on the back of the membrane to ensure the hole does not get any larger.

5 An original flaw on the membrane between this name and 'teutonici'. The clerk appears to have worked round it.

DE OBLATIS

Petronilla que fuit uxor Galfridi fleccarii r.c. de x m. pro habendo j molendino quod vocatur Kingesmuln' in vita sua sicut continetur in rotulo precedenti. In thes. lib. Et (Quietus)[1] Est.

Roheis' de Cokefeld' r.c. de C s. pro Henrico f. Henrici sicut continetur ibidem. In thes. lib. Et (Quietus) Est.

Margar' de Ripariis r.c. DC li. et lj s. et v d.[2] (et duobus doliis vini andeg'[l]) de pluribus debitis Falkes' de Breautéé contentis in rotulo precedenti. In thes. CC li. Et debet CCCC [li.][3] et lj s. et v d. et ij^{o} dolia vini andeg' per annum CC li.

Idem Vic. r.c. de ij m. et dim. de (Willelmo[c]) (Wano[l])[4] de Penedoc. Et de xx s. de abbate Sancti Ebrolf'. Et de dim. m. de Roberto de Auvers. In thes. lib. Et Q.E.

Ricardus de Ripariis (tunc vicecomes[l]) r.c. de xlij li. et xj d. de remanenti redditus villarum de Blockesham et Wudestok' sicut continetur in rotulo viij^{o}. Et de vij li. et ij s. et vij d. et ob. de remanenti compoti sui de medietate ville de Blockes-[5]

[*One line blank*]

[*Rot.* 12d *Mem.* 2]

[6] -ham sicut continetur in rotulo precedenti. Et de lxx s. et xj d. et ob. de[7] remanenti compoti sui de manerio de Wudestok' cum membris ad manerium de Wudestok' pertinentibus sicut continetur ibidem. Summa lij li. xiiij s. et vj d.

[*One line blank*]

Alexander de la Thierne et Gillebertus Taillard' et Rogerus Gulafr' agistores foreste de Wichewode debent vij li. xviij s. et viij [d.] de padnagio anni xiiij^{mi} R. J.

Idem debent vij li. et vij s. pro C et xlvij porcis eiusdem anni appreciatis sic per Brianum de Insul' anno v R. huius.

Idem debent iiij m de predicto padnagio de anno xvj^{o} R. J. de quibus

[1] *Quietus* written for *Quieta* and in the next item.

[2] There has been considerable rubbing out here as though the amounts changed on a number of occasions.

[3] The *li.* is missing from the text here but there has been considerable rubbing out here and for the rest of the amounts shown until the notification of the 2 casks of wine.

[4] This should be Walter of Pendock as the item refers to the fine shown in *Calendar of Fine Rolls*, II, 1224–34, p. 49, no. 318. This shows he did pay what was owed at the appropriate time.

[5] This is the end of the line. The name of the vill continues on the next line of text which is after the stitching across the membrane joining two membranes together.

[6] There is some strengthening tape down the whole left hand side of this half of the membrane which may have obscured some marginalia.

[7] There is some transparent paper stuck on the text which is approximately 7.5 centimetres wide and is 7 lines of text in length. The writing is visible through this paper.

Thomas de Langeleg' debet respondere qui illas recepit sicut recognovit sicut continetur in memor' anni viij et respondet infra.

Idem debent lij s. pro lij porcis et xx hoggastris[1] eius anni sic appreciatis per predictum B. anno eodem de quibus Willelmus Russell' debet respondere qui illas recepit sicut recognovit sicut continetur ibidem et respondet infra.

Idem debent lj s. de eodem padnagio de anno primo R. huius de quibus Ricardus de Henle clericus debet eos adquietare qui illos recepit sicut recognovit sicut continetur ibidem et respondet infra.

Idem debent C et xj s. et v d. de eodem padnagio de anno ij° R. huius.

Thomas de Langeleg' [*blank*] iiij m. pro Alexandro de la Thiern' et sociis suis sicut supra continetur.

Willelmus Russel' [*blank*] lij s. pro eisdem sicut continetur ibidem.

Ricardus clericus de Henle [*blank*] lj s. pro eisdem sicut continetur ibidem.

[*One line blank*]

NOVA OBLATA

Abbas de Einesham r.c. de v m. pro j palefrido pro habendo recordo coram Justiciariis de Banco de terra in Huston'. In thes. lib. Et Q.E.

Willelmus de Abrincis et Matill' uxor eius et Johanna que fuit uxor Roberti de Ferrar'[2] de relevio suo de tota terra quam Hawis' que fuit uxor Johannis de Bouill' tenuit de R. in capite et unde saisita fuit die quo obiit. Set respondent in Bedef' et Buk' in memor'.[3]

Johannes Luvel capitalis plegius Willelmi de Rumeliaco pro se et aliis plegiis ipsius Willelmi r.c. de C et xx m. quas predictus Willelmus debet R. In thes. (x^d^)x m. Et debet C et x m. per annum xx m.

Prior de Abbendon' r.c. de dim. m. pro j acra frisci de terra sua excolenda iuxta domum Reginaldi Pille. Et de vj m. pro claudenda quadam parva mora iuxta Stamford' ad pratum faciendum. Ita tamen quod fere possint intrare et exire et pro essartandis ij acris de costera bosci sui que vestite sunt roboribus tenuibus ad assidendum quendam iuvenem desuper ad custodiendum boscum suum et R. habebit robora ad quendam rogum faciendum ad firmandam villam suam Oxon' et debent liberari hominibus Oxon' de precepto R. In thes. lib. Et Q.E.

[*One line blank*]

AMERCIAMENTA FACTA PER M. DE PATESHILL' ET SOCIOS EIUS APUD OXON'

Idem Vic. r.c. de xl m. et xj s. et viij d. de misericordiis hominum et decenarum quorum nominibus preponitur littera *t* in rotulo quem predicti liberaverunt in thes. In thes. lib. in lxij taleis. Et Q.E.

1 These are hoggets, pigs, or boars in their second year.

2 There is a large blank space after this name as though another name should have been inserted. The text carries on as normal.

3 *memorandis*?

[1] Galfridus f. Walteri de Gersindon' r.c. de xx m. de fine suo quia retraxit se. In thes. viij m. Et debet xij m. per plegium annotatum in rotulo predicto.

Vivianus f. Radulfi et Ricardus Foliot r.c. de v s. de catallis Henrici de Neuport qui abiuravit regnum. Et de xxxvj s. de catallis Godefridi le Buc qui fecit idem. Et de xvj d. de catallis Ricardi de Essex' qui fecit idem. In thes. xxj s. et ij d. per Vivianum. Et debent xxj s. et ij d.

Johannes de Wotton' r.c. de ij m. pro dissaisina. In thes. j m. Et debet j m.

Ricardus Foliot r.c. de C s. pro licencia concordandi. In thes. lx s. Et debet xl s.

Willelmus f. Benedicti r.c. de dim. m. pro dissaisina. In thes. xl d. Et debet xl d.

Robertus de Harpeden' debet xl s. de fine suo pro transgressione per plegium Johannis de Sancto Johanne. (*Set respondet in Berkesir' in rotulo sequenti.*[i]) Decena Radulfi le Norreis in Berewic' debet dim. m. quia non habuit quandam brasciatricem citradictam. Radulfus f. Willelmi debet dim. m. quia retraxit se per plegium Ricardi de Acton'. Gregorius de la Hage debet dim. m. pro plegio Ricardi le Daneis qui retraxit se. Gillebertus de Bageruge et Geroldus de Hida debent dim. m. pro dissaisina. Willelmus de Mikelmere debet dim. m. pro eodem. Willelmus Iugeniator debet dim. m. pro eodem. Willelmus Luvekene (et Hugo le Duc[i]) debent dim. m. pro eodem. Willelmus Dec debet dim. m. pro eodem. Ricardus Colgrim debet dim. m. pro eodem. Willelmus de Hida et Johannes Ailard' et Ricardus Teissun debet dim. m. pro eodem. Willelmus Morin debet dim. m. pro plegio Roberti Nol qui retraxit se. Radulfus Sanzaveir debet dim. m. pro dissaisina. Rogerus Basse debet dim. m. pro eodem.

Robertus Amauri r.c. de xl s. pro quodam angulo vestito tenui querceto[2] In thes. nichil. Et in perdona ipsi Roberto pro bono et fideli servicio suo quod fecit in quintadecima colligenda xl s. per breve R. Et Q.E.

Abbas de Becco r.c. de dim. m. pro licencia concordandi cum Rogero f. Guidonis. In thes. lib. Et Q.E.

[*Two lines blank*]

COMPOTUS DE EXITU J^US MOLENDINORUM DE OXON'

Idem Vic. r.c. de xvj li. de[3] quater xx quarteriis frumenti de exitu eiusdem molendini vendit[is] de tribus partibus anni. In thes. nichil.[4] Et pro ij molis emptis ad idem molendinum iiij li. et ij s. et viij d. Et pro ferro empto ad idem molendinum et fabro fabricanti ferrum illud ij s. et iij d. Et in reparatione stagni ix s. et v d. et ob. Et in emendatione domus molendini et aliis minutis necessariis iiij s. et viij d. et ob.

1 It is impossible to tell if there is a letter *t* in the margin because of the strengthening tape down the left hand side of the membrane.

2 Literally 'a corner clad with thin oak' – *angulus* can be a plot of land at a corner – presumably this one was planted with oak saplings.

3 The *de* has been written over a *q*.

4 There is a large gap between the end of this sentence and the next one.

Summa iiij li. xix s. et j d. Et debet xj li. et xj d. Idem r.c. de eodem debito. In thes. nichil. Et in superplus quod habet supra post corpus comitis xj li. et xj d. Et Q.E.

Idem Vic. r.c. de xl li. viij s. iiij d. et ob. de remanenti compoti sui de medietate de Blockesham et de Wudestok' cum pertinenciis sicut continetur in rotulo compotorum. Et de xj li. et viij s. et iiij^{or} d. de exitu ville de Littlemor' de tribus partibus anni sicut continetur. In thes. nichil. Et in predicto superplus lv li. et xvj s. et viij d. et ob. Et Q.E.

[*Forty-five lines blank*]

[*The remainder of the roll is written upside down and is in larger writing. The first item shows the abbreviated names of the counties linked together by lines with the remaining part shown as being common to these three counties.*]

[*Endorsed*] CANTEBRIG' et HUNTEDON' (emendatur[i]) et Oxonefordschir'[1]

[*One line blank*]

Annus X^{us} R. H.

[*One line blank*]

Cant'
Hunt'
Oxon' → de anno x^{o} regis Henrici tercii

[*Rot.* 13 *Mem.* 1]

SURREIA #[2]

Willelmus de Warenn', comes Surr' Willelmus de Mara ut custos pro eo r.c. de C et lxxiiij li. et[3] vij s. bl. de firma comitatus. In thes. nichil.

Et in terris datis canonicis de Meriton' xvij li. et xvij s. in Ewell'. Et episcopo Sar' in Godelming' pro excambio de Divisis xxx li. Et heredibus Stephani de Turneham C s. in Erdinton' membro de Godelming'.[4] Et Eustachio de Eyl[5] xx li. in Gummeschelve. Et eidem x s. in Leddrede. Et in quietantia piscarie quam Radulfus de Hou tenuit iij s. Et Alano Basset

1 There is some very faded writing above the three counties but only one decipherable. There are also three vertical dots before and after *Cantebrig'*, after *et*, after *Huntedon'*, and after *Oxonefordschir'*.

2 Three lines written beside the heading in a different hand, preceded by the symbol #. They are in reverse order, i.e. the bottom line of the three is to be read first, then the second, and finally the top line. These lines are printed in the text where the symbol # occurs at the start of the third of these lines.

3 *et* repeated.

4 As far as can be determined Artington appears to be part of Guildford, not Godalming.

5 In both *NS 56*, p. 40 and *NS 54*, p. 250 he is shown as 'Eustace de Eys'.

ix li. et xvij s. in Woking'. Et in Kingeston' xxviij li. et x s. bl. de quibus homines ville respondent infra. Et Reginaldo de Braiosa xix li.[1] et xij s. in Gummeschelve. Et episcopo Lond' x li. in Stokes de dono R. J. Et abbati de Saviniaco xx s. in Hamme. Et R. episcopo Cycestr' xix li. et j m. in Waleton' et Hamme que fuerunt Amaur' de Croyun quoniam R. commisit eidem episcopo *ad se sustentandum*.[2] Et heredibus Briani hostiarii lxix s. et x d. in Leddred'. Et debet hic xv li. et xj s. et x d. bl. qui sunt ei extensi ad xvj li. et vij s. et v d.[3] num. et respondet infra.

Et in elemosinis constitutis militibus de templo j m. Et in liberationibus constitutis infirmis hospitalis Regine xxx s. et v d. Et Willelmo de Stiviton' xxx s. et v d. Et Ricardo Norrensi lx s. et x d. Et Willelmo et Nicholao filiis Johannis de Broc lx s. et x d. Et capellano leprosorum Cycestr' lx s. et x d. Et capellano ministranti in capella Sancte Katerine de Geldeford' l s. Et Helene nutrici R. vj li. et xx d. Et Radulfo de Rothomag' xxx s. et v d. Summa xxij li. et xviij s. et ix d. Et de remanenti summe misarum de anno preterito xxx li. et viij s. Et est summa omnium misarum liij li. et vj s. et ix d. num. de quibus locantur ei infra in proxima linea xvj li. et vij s. et v d.[4] Et xix li. et xix s. et iiij d. infra in debitis plurium. Et restant ei locande xvij li *de*[5] *quibus viij li. xij s. et viij d. allocantur ei in rotulo xij*^{o} *in Surr' in ij debitis.* #[6] (*Et restant allocande ix li. de quibus vj li. xviij s. viij d. allocantur ei in rotulo xvij in hoc comitatu. Et restant allocandi xlj s. et iiij d. De quibus j m. allocatur W. de Mara in rotulo xviij in hoc comitatu. Et xvj s. viij d. in hoc comitatu in rotulo xxiij in duobus debitis. Et restant xj s. iiij d.*^{i})

• Idem Vic. r.c. de xvj li. et vij s. et v d.[7] num. de remanenti firme comitatus. In thes. nichil. Et in summa misarum suarum supra contentarum xvj li. et vijj s. et v d.[8] Et Q.E.

f' Idem Vic. [*blank*] de proficuo comitatus de iij^{bus} partibus anni vij^{mi}. Et [*blank*] de eodem proficuo de anno viij^{o} et anno ix^{o} et (hoc^{i}) anno.

f' Homines de Kingeston' r.c. de xxviij li. et x s. bl. de firma ville sue. In thes. xxvij li. et xviij d. bl. Et debent xxviij s. et vj d. (bl.^{i}) qui sunt eis extensi ad xxix (s.^{i}) et xj d. num. et respondent infra.

[*One line blank*]

Idem homines debent xlj s. et x d. (num.^{i}) de remanenti veteris et novi crementi ville sue de anno preterito et anno viij. *Set respondent infra*.[9]

f' Idem homines debent xxj li. et x s. de veteri et novo cremento eiusdem ville. Set respondent infra.

f' Idem homines [*blank*] xx s. de terra Postelli de lana Regine dum eam

1 Altered from *xxix li.*

2 Written densely in darker ink on erasure in a different hand.

3 Altered from *vj*.

4 *vij* and *v* written on obliterations.

5 From now until end of line written in darker ink over an obliteration, and in the same hand as lines referred to in n. 6 below.

6 The symbol # inserted here to indicate the correct place for the three lines written beside the heading. They are printed here in the order in which they should be read.

7 *vij* and *v* written on obliterations.

8 *vijj* and *v* written on obliterations.

9 The last three words in slightly paler ink.

non collig[unt]. Et lxxix s. de eadem de pluribus annis preteritis sicut continetur in rotulo precedenti.
f' Idem Vic. debet x s. de firma propresturarum de hoc anno. Et xiiij li. et v s. de eadem de pluribus annis preteritis.

Pentecost' de Wendleswurðe [*blank*] xxxvj li. et vij s. et iiij d. de misericordia.
+ Remundus de Tiches debet j palefridum pro habendo brevi sicut continetur in rotulo xv R. J. Alicia Bataille debet dim. m. pro habenda assisa sicut continetur in rotulo ij^{o}.
Kin Willelmus de Fornell' *r.c. de* xviij li. et xiij s. et viij d. pro Gilleberto Prodomme. In[1] thes. j m. *Et debet xviij li. et iiij d.*
• Michael de Polsted r.c. de xxvj li. et ix s. et viij d. ut Willelmus de Windles' et pro transgressione. In thes. nichil. Et in summa misarum quam (Vic.[i]) habet supra xl s. Et debet Michael xxiiij li. et ix s. et viij d.

Alexander de Windles' debet v m. et dim. de ij^{bus} debitis contentis in rotulo precedenti. Alanus Basset debet xvj m. de prestito Pictavie. Ricardus Gulafr' debet dim. m. pro licencia concordandi. Willelmus de Wauton' debet viij m. de ij^{bus} debitis sicut continetur in rotulo vij^{o}. Ailnodus f. Wulmeri debet dim. m. quia non est prosecutus. Heres (kulg'[i]) Nicholai de Ditton debet dim. m. pro dissaisina. Walterus de Horle debet v s. de catallis.

Biatrix filia Stephani de Turneham r.c. de xxvij li. et xv s. et vj d. de debito patris sui sicut continetur in rotulo viij^{o}. In thes. C s. Et debet xxij li. et xv s. et vj d. per annum C s.

Abbas de Certes' [*blank*] xx m. de iiij^{or} scutagiis sicut continetur in rotulo vij^{o}. Et [*blank*] vj m. de scutagio de Mungumeri de feodis que recognoscit.
ar Willelmus iuvenis [*blank*] dim. m. pro habendo brevi sicut continetur in rotulo viij^{o}.
ar Willelmus Longus debet dim. m. pro habendo pone. Willelmus de Mara debet CC et xiij li. et xv s. et ix d. pro Henrico fratre suo sicut continetur in rotulo xv^{o} R. J. Et xxv li. et vj s. et ij d. de carrucagio comit[atus][2] sicut[3] continetur in rotulo de carrucagio.

Homines de Kingeston' r.c. de x li. et xv s. de veteri et novo cremento contento in rotulo vij^{o}. Et de xxv li. et xxj d. de iij^{bus} debitis supra contentis. In thes. xxxv li. Et debent xvj s. et ix d. Idem r.c. de eodem debito.[4] In thes. lib. Et Q.E.

Hundredrum de Amelberge debet xx s.[5] pro murdro. Set non debet summoneri quia amensuratum fuit precepto Justiciariorum coram S. de Segrave ad xx s. quos pacaverunt in rotulis (precedentibus[i]).

[1] Paler ink from *In* to the end of the line.
[2] Two small oblique lines and a caret written after this word to indicate that the sense is continued in the line above.
[3] Two small oblique lines written above this word to indicate that the sense is continued from the line below.
[4] A caret written below the line after *debito*. The final six words are at the end of the line below.
[5] There is an erasure before *xx s*.

Kin Gillebertus Fullo debet dim. m. pro plegio. Ricardi Barbator qui manet apud Ledred' debet dim. m. pro falso clamore qui requirebatur in Lond' in rotulo de itinere M. de Pateshill et sociorum eius.
Kin Willelmus f. Johannis debet dim. m. pro eodem. Abbas de Certes' debet iiij li. de carrucagio hominum suorum sicut continetur in rotulo de carrucagio. Homines de Kingeston debent lxxij s. de carrucagio hominum hundredi[1] de Kingeston' sicut continetur ibidem.
• Ricardus Rufus r.c. de xij s. pro dissaisina. In thes. nichil.[2] Et in predicta summa misarum ij s. Et debet R. x s.
• Johannes de Newenham r.c. de xxj s.[3] et viij d. ut replegietur. In thes. nichil. Et in predicta summa misarum xx d. Et debet J. xx s.

Hundredum de Reigat' debet xxx s. pro murdro. (*Set non debet summoneri propter amensurationem factam ad xj s. quia pacaverunt.*[i]) Willelmus frater Hugonis debet dim. m. pro dissaisina (*Set respondet infra.*[i])[4] Gillebertus f. Ade debet dim. m. pro eodem (*Set respondet infra.*[i]). Hugo Burchhard debet dim. m. pro eodem (*Set respondet infra.*[i]). Petrus f. Galfridi Capellani debet dim. m. quia non est prosecutus. Philippus de la Garston' debet dim. m. pro falso clamore. Willelmus de la Foxiere debet dim. m. pro defalta. Matillis de Dammartin debet dim. m. pro dissaisina. Rogerus de (Dorking[c]) (Cranford[i]) debet dim. m. quia non est prosecutus. Rogerus f. Willelmi de Dorking debet dim. m. quia retraxit se. Radulfus f. Mauricii debet dim. m. quia non est prosecutus. (*Set respondet infra.*[i]). Hugo Cumin (Meriton'[i]) de Ewell' debet dim. m. quia non est prosecutus. Petrus (King'[i]) de Taleworðe debet dim. m. de misericordia. Abbas de Certes' debet ij m. de scutagio de Mungumeri de j feodo quod non recognoscit. W. de Mara debet vj s. de carrucagio hominum comitis Warenn' sicut continetur in rotulo de carrucagio.
• Lucas Pratt r.c. de dim. m. pro licencia concordandi. In thes. nichil. Et in predicta summa misarum dim. m. Et Q.E.
• Prior de Meriton' r.c. de C et j m. pro Winterburn' Canonicorum sicut continetur in rotulo precedenti. In thes. nichil. Et in predicta summa misarum xx m. Et debet prior quater xx et j m.

Hugo de Windlesorum debet viij m. de ij^{bus} scutagiis contentis in rotulo precedenti. Rollandus de Acsted debet vj li. de scutagio de iij feodis qui requirebatur in Essex.

Sibilla de Fiednes debet xxxiij li. et viij d. de pluribus scutagiis contentis in Essex[5] (de honore Bolon'[i]) que requirebatur ibidem. Johannes de Mikeleham debet x li. et vij s. et j palefridum pro habenda gratia R. qui requirebatur in Buking'.

1 A caret is written after the word *hundredi*. The final five words are at the end of the line above.
2 *nichil* written on an erasure.
3 *xxj* written on an erasure.
4 William is called *fil' Hugonis* in the amercements section.
5 *Essex* followed by an erasure.

AMERCIAMENTA DE ITINERE M. DE PATESHILL ET SOCIORUM SUORUM

Willelmus f. Gile r.c. de dim. m. pro iniusta detentione.

Episcopi Win' Predictus Willelmus de Mara Vic. r.c. de xxviij d. de catallis Edwini le Bule suspensi. Et de vij s. et ij d. de catallis Herberti de Fernham suspensi. Et de xviij s. et iiij d. de catallis Willelmi Albi suspensi. Et de xij s. de catallis Elurich' de Sele suspensi.[1] (Idem Vic. r.c. de dim. m. de Willelmo f. Hugonis sicut supra continetur. Et de dim. m. de Gilleberto f. Ade sicut ibidem. Et de dim. [m.] de Hugone Burchhard sicut ibidem.[i])[2] Et de dim. m. de Radulfo f. Mauricii ut ibidem. In thes. nichil. Et in predicta summa ij m. Et Q.E.[i])[3]

Episcopi Sar' Idem W. r.c. de xiiij s. et vj [d.] de catallis Ricardi Neweman suspensi. Et de xvij d. de catallis Hemann' Fot suspensi.

Kin Homines de Kingeston' [*blank*][4] ij s. et vj d. de catallis Huberti de Cleigat' suspensi.

Ar Idem W. (r.c.[c]) de (d[ebet][i]) lxvij s. de catallis Willelmi Blundi suspensi. Abbas de Bello debet xviij s. de carrucagio hominum suorum in hoc comitatu sicut continetur in rotulo de carrucagio.

• Idem W. r.c. de viij s. de catallis Johannis Beluncle suspensi. In thes. nichil. Et in predicta summa misarum viij s. Et Q.E.

• Idem W. r.c. de xlvj s. et viij d. de catallis Edwardi de Totinges fugitivi. In thes. nichil. Et in predicta summa misarum xxxiiij s. et ij d. Et debet[5] xij s. et vj d. quod ponit super archiepiscopum Cant'.

• Idem W. r.c. de x s. et viij d. de catallis Hugonis de la Hethe fugitivi. Et de ij s. et x d. de catallis Roberti de Paris' fugitivi. In thes. nichil. Et in predicta summa misarum xiij s. et vj d. Et Q.E.

(Ricardus le Barbur debet dim. m. pro falso clamore.[c]) (*quia supra*[i]) Johannes de Gatesden debet v m. pro Thoma de Bavelingham qui requirebatur in Kent.

S. archiepiscopus Cant' r.c. de CC m. de prestito ei facto de thesauro R. anno R. vij°. Et de C m. de prestito ei facto de eodem thesauro anno R. viij°. Et de D et xxxij li. xviij s. et xj d. de quintadecima dominici sui et hominum suorum et hominum militum suorum. Et de C et lxj li. et x s. de quintadecima virorum relligiosorum parochie sue[6] in Kantia et hominum eorundem exceptis abbate Sancti Augustini et priore Sancte Trinitatis Cant' et hominibus ipsorum unde dicti abbas et prior debent per se respondere. De qua quintadecima episcopi Bathon' et Saresberie et socii eorum audierunt compotum a ballivis predicti archiepiscopi (*Set respondent in rotulo de quintadecima.*[i]). Summa DCCC et quater xx et xiiij li. et viij s. et xj d. de qua summa Willelmus de Einesford debet adquietare ipsum

1 *Suspensi* followed by an erasure.

2 This is shown as an interlinear entry on the line above *Et de dim. m. de Radulfo f. Mauricii... Et Q.E.* but the two entries belong together with *Idem Vic...* being the start.

3 *Et de dim.* to *Q.E.* written on the line below.

4 Followed by an erasure.

5 *debet* followed by an erasure.

6 *parochie sue* written in full.

archiepiscopum de CCCC li. per breve R. et respondet infra. Et debet idem archiepiscopus CCCC et quater xx et xiiij li. et viij s. et xj d. Idem r.c. de eodem debito. In thes. l li. Et debet CCCC et xliiij li. et viij s. et xj d. de quibus idem archiepiscopus debet reddere singulis annis C li. ad ij[os] terminos per breve R. in quo continetur quod si necesse habuit R. prefatus archiepiscopus omnem diligentiam apponet non obstante concessione ad predictum residuum debiti sui celerius R. reddendo de qua predicta summa Ricardus de Argent' et Johanna uxor debent eum adquietare de CC m per breve R. (*Set respondent in Kent.*[i]). Et debet predictus archiepiscopus CCC et xj li. et ij s. et iij d. (*Set respondet ibidem.*[i])

Predictus Willelmus r.c. de CCCC li. pro predicto archiepiscopo sicut supra continetur. In thes. l li. Et debet CCC et l li. de quibus debet predictus Willelmus reddere singulis annis C li. ad predictos terminos per breve R. Set respondet in Kent.

S. archiepiscopus predictus r.c. de CC et lxix li. et vj s. et iiij d. de parte quintedecime sue et hominum suorum et hominum militum suorum et quorundam virorum relligiosorum et hominum eorum preter particulas suprascriptas. In thes. nichil. Et ipsi R. in camera sua ad opus Ricardi fratris sui lxix li. et vj s. et iiij d. per litteras R. patentes que sunt in thesauro R. Et iterum eidem R. in camera sua ad opus eiusdem Ricardi C et quater xx et vi li. et v s. et viij d. per litteras eiusdem patentes que sunt ibidem quas attulit de computando sibi CCC m. de quibus CCC m. J. episcopus Bathon' respondet in rotulo quintedecime in compoto suo de xiiij li. et xiiij s. et iiij d. Et Q.E.

LONDON ET MIDDELSEX

Cives Lond', Rogerus le Duc et Martinus f. Willelmi pro eis r.c. de CCC li (bl.[i]) de firma comitatus. In thes. C et xxxvj li. et xvij s. et viij d. bl.

Et in elemosinis constitutis militibus de templo ij m. Et in liberatione constituta Roberto Caretario de Buteilleria R. xlv s. et vij d. et ob. Et Waltero capellano Sancti Stephani lx s. et x d. Et Johanni de Cantia nuncio xxx s. et v d. Et Roberto le Herberiur iiij li. et xj s. et iij d. Et Eve nutrici Ricardi fratris R. xxx s. et v d. Et eidem xlv s. et vij d. et ob. quos Willelmus de Eys percipere consuevit. Et Ade de capella R. xxx s. et v d. Et Cecil' Minnote lx s. et x d. Et Ricardo f. Roberti de Leveland x li. et xij s. et xj d. pro custodia domorum R. de Westm'. Et eidem vij li. et xij s. et j d. pro custodia gaiole de Fliete. Et pro oleo ad lampadem Regine xxx s. et v d. Et in elemosinis constitutis Matillidi de Herlave lx s. et x d. Et Petro Sarraceno civi Romano xx li. donec R. ei assignaverit xx libratas terre. Et in elemosinis constitutis fratribus hospitalis Jer'l'm pro animabus antecessorum R. et pro anima Roberti de Quency iiij li. et xj s. et iij d. sicut continetur in rotulo ij[o]. Et in quietantia terrarum episcopi Lond' C s. Et in quietantia canonicorum Sancti Pauli Lond' pro xxiiij hidis xl s.

[*One line blank*]

Et pro j roba de russeto scilicet tunica et supertunica cum furrura de agnis scilicet ulna xvj d. ad opus Ricardi f. Nigelli prisonis et ij lintheaminibus et ij[bus] paribus lineorum pannorum et j chalone precii iij s. ad opus eiusdem xxij s. et iiij d. per breve R. Et Ricardo Gurnard de Lond' pro j bargia ad sellam summar[ii] capelle R. et j huscia et aliis rebus minutis et necessariis ad summar[ium] capelle R. v s. et ob. per breve eiusdem. Et Reginaldo [f.][1] Willelmi ad j robam de viridi scilicet supertunica et pallio cum furrura de bissis xxx s. et ij d. per breve eiusdem. Et pro xx carratis plumbi emptis et carriatis usque Dovor' ad operati-

[*Rot.* 13 *Mem.* 2]

ones R. in castro Dovor' faciendas xlj li. et vij s. per breve eiusdem. Et in carriagio papilionum R. usque Porrecestr' xv s. per breve eiusdem. Et pro tela et fusteinia et cordis et aliis necessariis ad j papilionem faciendum ad capellam R. vij li. et xviij s. et vij d. per breve eiusdem. Et pro carbone ad operationes R. in turri Lond' faciendas xlij s. per breve eiusdem. Et in carriagio D m. ad opus R. usque Wigorn' vij s. et x d. per breve eiusdem. Et in carriagio thesauri R. usque Gloverniam vij s. et vij d. per breve eiusdem. Et in carriagio teldarum et heiriarum usque Portesm' ad magnam navem R. vij s. et vj d. per breve eiusdem. Et in reparatione ij coffrorum R. et selle summarii[2] capelle R. xxxv d. per breve eiusdem. Et in carriagio vinorum R. per diversa loca vij m. per breve eiusdem. Et in carriagio xx caratarum plumbi á turri Lond' usque Dovor' xxxj s. et viij d. per breve eiusdem. Et in carriagio harnasii Magistri Petri Balistarii usque Corf' dim. m. per breve eiusdem. Et pro panno ad scaccarium baronum xl s. et ij d. Et in carriagio robarum R. usque Winton' contra Natale iiij s. per breve eiusdem. Et pro xviij barillis ad imponendum thesaurum R. missum usque Wint' viij s. et vj d. per breve eiusdem. (Et pro xl ulnis de nigra burneta emptis ad opus R. contra Pentecost' C s. per breve eiusdem[c]) (*quia denarii redditi fuerunt per Willelmum de Haverhill'*[i]). Et pro vj caretatis plumbi emptis et liberatis Thome de Blumvill' ad novam turellam turris Lond' cooperiendam xij li. et iij s. per breve eiusdem. Et pro justicia facienda xviij s. Et iterum pro iiij caretatis plumbi ad predictam turrim Lond' cooperiendam viij li. et xix d. per predictum breve. Et Waltero Spigornell' servienti de capella R. ad duo paria cingulorum et alia necessaria ad summar[ium] capelle xij s. et iij d. ob. per breve eiusdem. Et pro carbone ad operationes quas Thomas facit in turri Lond' iij s. et xj d. per breve eiusdem. Et debent viij li. et vj s. et x d. bl.[3]

Idem Vic[ecomites] (Andreas Bukerell' et Johannes Travers[i]) r.c. de xxij li. et vj s. et ob. bl. de remanenti firme comitatus de anno preterito. Et de xxxviij li. et xix s. et v d. bl. de eadem de anno viij°. Idem r.c. de eodem debito. In thes. xxix li. et ij s. et vj. d. (bl[i]). Et debent xxxij li. et ij s. et xj d. et ob. bl.[4]

Willelmus Joinier et Thomas Lamberti r.c. de xvij li. et viij s. et v d. et ob. bl. de remanenti eiusdem firme de anno vij°. In thes. vj li. et xviij s. et iiij d. bl. Et debent CC et x s. et[5] iij ob. bl.

1 The text has *Regin' Willelmi.*

2 *sum(m)arii* written clearly and in full, and so not an adjective agreeing with *selle.*

3 The sum of money is written in paler ink.

4 *li. ... ob. bl.* written at the end of the previous line.

5 *et* repeated.

Ricardus Reingier Radulf r.c. de xv li. et xiiij s. de remanenti eiusdem firme de iij^{bus} annis. In thes. xiiij li. et x s. bl. Et debet xxiiij s. et v d. bl. Idem r.c. de eodem debito. In thes. lib. Et Q.E.

Nulla fit hic mentio de ripa Regine quia Thomas de Cyrecestr' custos honoris Berchamsted respondet inde in compoto suo.

f' Telarii Lond' r.c. de xx m. pro gilda sua. In thes. lib. Et Q.S.

f' Willelmus cocus r.c. de xx s. de redditu domus que fuit Radulfi vinetarii. In thes. nichil. Et Josceo specario xx s. quamdiu R. placuerit. Et Q.E.

f' Petrus f. Rogeri et Petrus f. Alani r.c. de vij s. de quadam terra escaeta que fuit Roberti f. Edith'. In thes. lib. Et Q.E.

f' Idem Vic. r.c. de ij s. et vij d. de gara Sancti Clementis. Et de j d. de terra Hervei. Et de iiij d. de gara in veteri vico quam Lambertus tenuit. Et de iiij d. de Henrico f. Alexandri goriurarii de quadam proprestura frustranda. In thes. lib. Et Q.E.

Alanus Bursarius r.c. de C et lvij m. de misericordia patris sui. In thes. j m. Et debet C et lvj m. per annum j m.

Martinus f. Willelmi r.c. de CC et lxx li. et x s. In thes. x li. Et debet CC et lx li. et x s. per annum x li.

Ydonea Bukerell' r.c. de lxxviij m. et dim. sicut continetur in rotulo iij^{o} R. J. In thes. iiij m. Et debet lxxiiij m. et dim. per annum iiij m.

Jordanus nepos Gervasii r.c. de lxj[1] m. pro uxore Ernisii Rufi. In thes j m. Et debet lx m. per annum j m.

Eborardus aurifaber r.c. de vij m. pro falso clamore. In thes. j m. Et debet vj m. per annum j m.

Abbas de Westm' debet lxx li. pro habenda custodia de Scheperton' (set non debet summoneri quia non habuit nec ipse habere potuit pro quo promisit[i]). Willelmus Blundus debet C et xvj s. et viij d. pro habenda terra (sicut continetur in Essex in rotulo vj^{o} R. J.[i]). Johannes Pera f. Normanni debet terciam partem de x m. sicut continetur in rotulo primo R. J.

Ricardus f. Roberti de Stanmere r.c. de xxij li. et xvj s. et viij d. pro patre suo pro habendo assensu curie. In thes. v s. Et debet xxij li. et xj s. et viij d. per annum v s.

Yda relicta Thome de Haverhill' r.c. de xiiij li. de debito predicti Thome pro Roberto Child'. In thes. dim. m. Et debet xiij li. et j m.

Johannes de Mascai r.c. de xl s. pro quodam leporario invento. In thes. v s. Et debet xxxv s. per annum xx s.

Martinus f. Ade Camerar' debet xxxv s. quia non habuit ad rectum Robertum de Watefeld'. Ricardus de Coudres debet j m. pro habendo brevi sicut continetur in rotulo primo. Ignorius de Sancto Claro debet xl s. pro habendo brevi sicut continetur in rotulo primo. (*Set respondet in Buk'*.[i]).

Ricardus de Leveland' (Vic. pro eo[i]) r.c. de xxv m. (pro viro suo[c]) pro habenda custodia. In thes. x m. Et debet xv m. per annum x m.

Stephanus f. Andree r.c. de xvij m. pro habenda saisina de Chiggewell'. In thes. dim. m. Et debet xvj m. et dim. per annum j m.

\+ Robertus de Abbendon' debet j m. pro habendo brevi sicut continetur in rotulo primo R. Willelmus de Windlesor' debet C li. pro habenda saisina terrarum sicut continetur in rotulo xiiij^{o}. (*Set respondet in Berkesir.*[i]) +

[1] Figure written over erasure.

Galfridus Rufus clericus debet x s. pro justiciando Henrico de Oilly sicut continetur in rotulo primo.

Robertus Junctor r.c. de xx s. pro Warino Longo. In thes. x s. Et debet x s.

Leticia filia Roberti Simplicis r.c. de ij m. et dim. In thes. dim. m. Et debet ij m. per annum dim. [m]

Andreas de Grendon' r.c.[1] de lv li. et x s. et ij d. et j palefrido pro Thoma de Barentin pro habendis terris sicut continetur in rotulo primo. In thes. xx s. Et debet liiij li. et x s. et ij d. et j palefridum. per annum xx s.

Nicholaus le Burgoinnun r.c. de v s. pro summonendo Johanne de Fraxinet'. In thes. lib. Et Q.E.

Matheus Blundus r.c. de C et lv li. et xviij s. et j d. de ij^{bus} debitis contentis in rotulo ij^{o}. In thes. iiij m. Et debet C et liij li. et iiij s. et ix d. per annum iiij [m.]

Willelmus Pollard r.c. de x s. pro habendo brevi. In thes. xl d. Et debet dim. m.

Philippus Walerand' r.c. de iiij li. et xiij s. pro eodem sicut continetur in rotulo primo. In thes. xx s. Et debet lxxiij s. per annum xx [s.]

Radulfus de Barbefloe et Willelmus Quarrell' debent vij s. et x d. pro falso judicio (*Set respondent infra.*[i]). + Andreas de Mimmes debet dim. m. pro habendo pone sicut continetur in rotulo iij^{o}. Radulfus de Westm' draparius debet j m. pro dissaisina, qui requirebatur in Essex in itinere Simonis de …[2]

Edwardus filius Yvon' r.c. de v s. pro habendo pone sicut continetur in rotulo iij^{o}. In thes. lib. Et Q.E.

Robertus Burel et Gillebertus de Aquila et Willelmus Hardel debent x li. de primis denariis solvendis pro summonendis Nicholao de Dunewic et aliis sicut continetur ibidem. + Galfridus aurifaber debet dim. m. pro transgressione.

Ricardus Besant r.c. de j m. pro summonenda priorissa de Strafford'. In thes. lib. Et Q.E.

Magister hospitalis Sancti Bartholomei Lond' r.c. de vij li. et v s. pro herede Johannis Le Borgoinn. In thes. x s. Et debet vj li. et xv s. per annum x s.

Willelmus le Vilein r.c. de xxv s. pro justiciando Albrico de Norhant'. In thes. x s. Et debet xv s. per annum x s.

Idem Vic. r.c. de xl d. de Nicholao de Sancto Albano. Et de xl d. de Johanne de Haneworðe. Et de xl d. de Alicia filia Rogeri. Et de dim. m. de Waltero f. Avicie. In thes. lib. Et Q.[E.]

Johannes[3] de Hille r.c. de ij s. et viij d. In thes. ij s. Et debet viij d.[4]

Drogo piscator r.c. de ij s. et viij d. In thes. ij s. Et debet viij d.

Godefridus messor r.c. de ij s. et viij d. In thes. ij s. Et debet viij d.

1 *r.c.* repeated.

2 Name lost at the end of the line. Probably Simon de Hal', who is shown on p. 34 above as taking an eyre in Essex.

3 This and the next two entries are written on the left hand side of the membrane.

4 The membrane is torn irregularly down the right hand side from now on.

Johannes[1] Keneward' r.c. de (xx^{c}) (xlij^{i}) d. In thes. xvj d. Et debet ij s. et ij d.

Johannes Cadel r.c. de ij s. et viij d. In thes. ij s. Et debet viij d.

Adam bubulcus r.c. de ij s. et viij d. In thes. ij s. Et debet viij d.

Hundredum de Spelethorn' r.c. de xxij d. pro mur[dro]. In thes. nichil. Et in perdona H. de Burgo Justiciarii per libertatem sedendi ad scaccarium xxij d. de terris suis. Et Q.E.

Garhundredum debet xx s. et xj d. pro murdro (*Set respondet infra.*^{i}). Willelmus Fige debet dim. m. pro dissaisina. Willelmus de Mohaut debet x s. pro vino vendito. Walterus Blundus cum decena sua debet x s. quia non habet (*Set respondet in Berkesir' in rotulo sequenti.*^{i}). Henricus f. Gerold' debet dim. m.[2]
+ Josceus le Newelier debet dim. m. pro eodem. Alicia de Tornie debet dim. m. pro falso clamore (*Set respondet in Buking.'*^{i}). Petrus f. Ade aurifabri debet dim. m. ut possit recedere a brevi. Didonius de Estwude debet dim. m. quia non est prosecutus (*Set respondet in Essex.*^{i}). [Gilbertus][3] grossus debet xx s. quia non habuit (*Set respondet ibidem.*^{i}). Radulfus f. Ricardi debet dim. m. pro eodem. Ricardus de Cruce debet dim. m. pro transgressione (*Set respondet in Berkesir' in rotulo sequenti.*^{i}). + Galfridus Rufus debet dim. m. pro eodem. + Joseph le Batur debet dim. m. quia non habuit. + Walter Coppen[ose][4] debet dim. m. pro eodem. + Johannes Bocointe debet iij m. et dim. de ij^{bus} debitis contentis in rotulo vij^{o}. Andreas Bukerell' debet v m. pro transgressione sicut continetur in rotulo v^{o}. Rogerus de Duay debet iij dolia vini ut R. wara[ntizet] (ei defaltam qui requirebatur in Norf' in rotulo precedenti^{i}).

Willelmus Hardel r.c. de xl s. de ij^{bus} doliis vini Andegavie. In thes. lib. Et Q.E.

Warinus f. Walteri debet dim. m. pro habendo brevi sicut continetur in rotulo iiij^{o}. (*Set respondet in Berkesir' in rotulo sequenti.*^{i}). + Jordanus le Prude debet terciam partem de xvij li. et xvij s. sicut continetur ibidem. Hamo f. Henrici debet dim. m. pro licencia concordandi. Galfridus f. Roberti debet dim. m. quia non est [prosecutus]. (*Set respondet in Berkesir' in rotulo sequenti.*^{i}).

Galfridus Molarius debet dim. m. quia non est prosecutus. Henricus de capella debet xij m. de bladis de Apsele qui requirebatur in Buking' in rotulo precedenti. *Set respondet in dorso rotuli.*

Robertus de Basingcurt debet xl s. pro vino vendito. Rogerus f. Roberti debet xx s. pro habendo brevi de j masag' in Lond'. Henricus de capella debet xl s. de j palefrido sicut continetur in rotulo vij^{o}. (*Set respondet in Suhantes'.*^{i}) Petrus Elinant debet x m. pro vino vendito.

Willelmus le viel r.c. de xx s. pro summonendo Warino sicut continetur in rotulo v^{o}. In thes. x s. Et debet x s. per Robertum de Bassingeburne.

Reginaldus de Lieges r.c. de C s. pro summonendo Nicholao de Kenet (sicut continetur in rotulo precedenti^{i}). In thes. xl d. Et debet iiij li. et xvj

1 This and the next two entries are written on the right hand side of the membrane.
2 End of line torn.
3 Name missing from end of line, supplied from *NS 54*, p. 87.
4 Ending supplied from *NS 54*, p. 87.

s. et viij d. Set non debet summoneri quia testatum est per justiciarios de Banco quod idem Reginaldus non habuit nec habere potuit xxiiij li. pro quibus fecit summoneri predictum Nicholaum nisi vij m. per concordiam inter eos factam de licencia justiciariorum. Et sic [Q.E.]

Benedictus Crespin r.c. de x m. pro xxiiij pedibus terre in Lond' sicut continetur in rotulo v. In thes. v m.[1] Et debet v m. Idem[2] r.c. de eodem debito. In thes. lib. Et Q.E.

Arnoldus de Mandevill' r.c. de ij m. et dim. de pluribus scutagiis contentis in rotulo viij. In thes. x s. Et debet xxxiij s. et iiij d.

Fulco draparius debet j m. pro licencia concordandi cum Roberto de Burgat' sicut continetur in rotulo vij. Petrus f. Alulph' debet C et xxij li. et vj s. de debitis Judeorum. Johannes Bocointe debet xv li. et viij s. de eodem. (*Set respondet in tergo.*ʲ) Ricardus de Lalinges (*Set respondet in dorso rotuli.*ʲ) debet dim. m. pro vino vendito. Hugo de Norf' debet v s. pro justicianda Matillide de Blancmustier. Cives Lond' debent MM m. de tallagio ad relaxationem interdicti. Et CC m. de prestito eis facto ad villam suam claudendam.

Elyas f. Benedicti Judei episcopi debet j m. de[3] misericordia sicut continetur in rotulo vij°. Petrus Pict' debet xl s. pro vino vendito qui requirebatur in Kent. Laurencius de Sancto Michaeli debet viij li. pro patre suo de debitis Judeorum. per ann[um][4]

Laurencius f. et heres Willelmi de Sancto Michaeli r.c. de j pellice grisia de vij fessiis de relevio suo sicut continetur in rotulo viij. In thes. nichil. Et ipsi R. j pellicem grisiam de vij fessiis. Et Q.E.

Hundredum de Osolvestan' r.c. de xxxiij s. et vj d. et ob. pro murdro. In thes. ij s. et viij d. Et debet xxx s. et x d. et ob. qui sunt super libertates archiepiscopi Cant' et episcopi[5] Lond' et aliorum.

Magister militum templi r.c. de CC et l li. in auxilium agendorum R. de dono. In thes. lib. Et Q.E.

Johannes de Westmuln' r.c. de xl d. quia non habuit. In thes. nichil. Et episcopo Lond' xl d. per libertatem carte R. Et Q.E.

Josceus f. David iudeus [*blank*] xl s. pro habendo respectu sicut continetur in rotulo viij°.

Tenentes terras et tenementa Rogeri f. Willelmi f. Ysabell' [*blank*] xxxvij li. et dim. m. de debitis Judeorum sicut continetur in rotulo precedenti.

Ricardus f. Ricardi de Lond' r.c. de xx s. pro summonendo Ricardo sicut continetur in rotulo viij°. In thes. j m. Et debet dim. m.

Willelmus Wite r.c. de iij m. pro licencia concordandi sicut continetur ibidem. In thes. lib. Et Q.[E.]

Judei Lond' [*blank*] C m. pro Bonevie Mutun Judeo.

Willelmus Juvenal r.c. de xx s. pro habendo precipe. In thes. dim. m. Et debet j m. Set respondet in Norf'.

1 *v m.* in fainter ink.
2 Darker ink again at *idem*.
3 A caret is written below the line after *de*, but there seems to be no insertion for it to refer to.
4 Sum lost at the end of the line.
5 *episcopi* written in full on alteration.

Rogerus de la Dune r.c. de xx s. pro dissaisina. In thes. dim. m. Et debet j m.

Willelmus de Bosco debet dim. m. ut loquela que est coram justiciariis itinerantibus ponatur coram justic[iariis] sicut continetur in rotulo precedenti. Ricardus de Hatton' debet dim. m. pro habendo brevi sicut continetur ibidem. + Walterus Travers debet terciam partem de xx m. [pro] Petro de Vallibus qui requirebatur in Norhumberland in rotulo (sequenti[c]) (*precedenti*[i]). Ricardus de Schireburne debet dim. m. quia non est prosecutus, qui requirebatur in Suhantes' in rotulo precedenti.

NOVA OBLATA

Garhundr[edum] r.c. de xx s. et xj d. sicut supra continetur. In thes. vij s. Et debet xiij s. et xj d. qui sunt super libertatem.[1]

Mercatores de Normannia qui habuerunt res et mercandisas suas in magna navi de Portigal' r.c. de CC m. de fine suo pro habendis omnibus rebus suis per plegia Willelmi Jouner et Petri de Rothom' per Petrum. Et xliiij li. et iij d. per Willelmum. Et pro j mil[le][2] cere empto ad opus R. per ipsum Willelmum et liberato Nicholao de Camera xxij li. et xiij s. et j d. per breve R.

Abbas Westm' r.c. de v m. pro licencia concordandi cum Gilleberto de Heindon'. In thes. lib. [Et Q.E.]

Idem Gillebertus r.c. de v m. pro eodem. In thes. j m. Et debet iiij m.

Johannes de Braintefeld' r.c. de j (m.[i]) pro licencia concordandi cum Willelmo Jouner per plegium eiusdem W. In thes. dim. m. Et debet dim. m.

RESPICE IN TERGUM

[*Rot.* 13d *Mem.* 1]

Ricardus de Lalinges r.c. de dim. m. pro vino vendito sicut continetur ex alia parte rotuli. In thes. lib. Et Q.E.

Prior Hospitalis Jer'l'm r.c. de D m. de dono in agend[o] negotiorum R. In thes. lib. Et Q.E.

Ricardus f. Willelmi r.c. de j m. pro licencia concordandi cum Thoma de Blenchenham per plegium Gilleberti de Hendon'. In thes. xl d. Et debet x s.

Willelmus f. Petri et Philippus de Leircestr' r.c. de dim. m. pro habenda inquisitione. In thes. lib. Et Q.S.

Galfridus le Criur r.c. de lx s. et j d. pro recreantisa sua. In thes. lib. Et Q.E.

Willelmus de Reimes [*blank*] dim. m. pro facienda mentione in brevi

[1] Entry written beside heading *Nova Oblata* with the insertion sign, but it is unclear where it fits in. Perhaps it was the last item, and should have been written at the foot of the membrane.

[2] Unit not shown, but *empto* written in full, as if *mille* were a noun rather than an indeclinable adjective.

suo de tempore R. H. avi. Willelmus Blundus debet dim. m. pro licencia concordandi cum Thoma de Burgo.

Radulfus de Barbefloe et Willelmus Quarrell' r.c. de vij s. et x d. pro falso judicio. In thes. iiij s. Et debent ij s. et x d.

AMERCIAMENTA PLACITORUM CORONE DE CIVITATE LOND' APUD TURRIM

CORAM M. DE PATESHILL ET SOCIIS SUIS

Idem Vic. r.c. de quater xx et v m. et xj s. et x d. et ob. de misericordiis hominum quorum nominibus preponitur littera *t* in rotulo quam predicti liberaverunt in thesauro. In thes. lib. in C et iiij taleis. Et Q.E.

Constantinus[1] Juvenis r.c. de C s. pro dissaisina. In thes. xxx s. Et debet lxx s. per annum xx s.

Jacobus Cissor r.c. de x s. quia non habuit. In thes. iiij s. Et debet vj s.

Edmundus[2] barbator r.c. de xx s. ut sit quietus. In thes. x s. Et debet x s.

Jacobus aurifaber r.c. de xx s. pro habendo termino. In thes. x s. Et debet x s.

Gillebertus de Aquila r.c. de C s. de fine suo pro quadam terra que fuit Radulfi Burewold'. In thes. xvj s. et viij d. Et debet xiij li. et iij s. et iiij d. Idem debet amodo [*blank*] ij m. et dim. per annum.

Willelmus le Viel debet dim. m. pro panno vendito. Willelmus Russel debet dim m. pro eodem. Gillebertus de Fakenham debet dim. m. pro eodem. Augustinus Mercerius debet j m. pro vino vendito. Ricardus de Hauvill' debet dim. m. pro eodem. Ricardus Matefelun debet dim. m. pro eodem. Wilekinus Chubbe debet dim. m. pro eodem. Robertus de Basingcurt debet dim. m. pro eodem. Rogerus villanus debet dim. m. pro eodem. Hugo vinetarius debet dim. m. pro eodem.

[*One line blank*]

Robertus de Turri r.c. de vj d. de cremento redditus de propprestura. In thes. lib. Et Q.E.

Idem R. et Radulfus Red et socii sui r.c. de xij d. pro eodem. In thes. lib. Et Q.E.[3]

Willelmus Brunus r.c. de j d. de eodem. In thes. lib. Et Q.E.

Edmundus f. Benedicti [r.c.] de j d. de eodem. In thes. lib. Et Q.E.

Johannes Durand [*blank*] j m. pro vino vendito.

Willelmus le Wite [*blank*] xxxiiij li. scilicet medietatem de lxviij li. quas ipse et Henricus f. Gerold[4] receperunt de xvij saccis lane de Andrea de Ypro receptis qui Henricus mortuus est sine herede et non habuit catalla vel terras nisi j domum in qua uxor eius manet in viduitate sua preceptum est[5] quod non distringatur.[6]

[1] This entry and the next are written on the left hand side of the membrane.
[2] This entry and the next are written on the right hand side of the membrane.
[3] *Quietus Est* written for *Quieti Sunt.*
[4] Altered from *Gerard.*
[5] A word such as *ideo* is needed before *preceptum est.*
[6] *vel ... distringatur* written at end of line above.

Cives Lond' r.c. de M li. et C m. de tallagio civitatis Lond' facto in anno vij^{o} R. coram ipso R. In thes. D li. Et debent D et lxvj li. et j m.

Abbas de Thama debet dim. m. ut scribatur in magno rotulo quod Simon f. et heres Gilleberti de Sancto Michaeli venit coram baronibus de scaccario et concessit et carta sua confirmavit deo et Beate Marie et monachis de Tame donationem quam Philippus de Cramford' patruus suus eis fecit de illa dim. hida terre cum pertinenciis suis in Cramford' que fuit maritagium Hersonte avie sue scilicet matris patris sui et similiter donationem quam idem Philippus eis fecit de illa virgata terre cum pertinenciis suis in Cramford' quam emerat de Willelmo de Cramford' tenend[as] ipsis monachis sicut carte ipsius Philippi quas inde (habent[i]) proportant et testantur. Et quod idem Simon remisit et de se et heredibus suis inperpetuum quietumclamavit prefatis monachis et etiam abiuravit totum jus et clamium quod in prefatis terris habuit aliquando et quod ipse et heredes sui in eisdem terris imposterum habere poterunt ita quod nullum jus in ipsis terris vel in eorum pertinenciis deinceps habere vel clamare poterunt. Et quod pro hac confirmatione et quietaclamantia dederunt prefati monachi ipsi Simoni xij m. argenti coram predicto scaccario.

Henricus de Capella r.c. de xij m. de bladis de Apsele sicut continetur ex alia parte rotuli. In thes. nichil. Et in perdona ipsi Henrico xij m. per breve R. Et Q.E.

Johannes Bocuinte debet xv li. et viij s. de debitis Judeorum sicut continetur ex alia parte rotuli de quibus Radulfus (de Wilicun'[i]) debet eum adquietare de x li., Henricus de Waltham clericus de xlij s., Johannes f. Willelmi camerar' de lxvj s. pro terris que fuerunt predicti Johannis sicut continetur in memorand'. *Require residuum huius comitatus post Dorset' et Sumerset' quia non erat hic locus.*

DEVONIA

Willelmus de Raleg' ut custos r.c. de CCC et xij li. et vij s. bl. de firma comitatus Devon'. In thes. xxj li. et xj s. et ij d. bl.

Et in elemosinis constitutis militibus de Templo j m. Et in maneriis Cornub' que pertinent ad firmam comitatus C et xxij li. et x s. bl. de quibus Vic. (Cornub'[i]) debet respondere. Et monialibus de Polshó C s. bl. in Culinton'. Et Willelmo Brieguerr' xvj li. bl in Axminstr' cum hundr'. Et in Cassewell' xij li. bl. de quibus Thomas de Cyrecestr' respondet infra. Et in Diepeford' viij li. et dim. m. bl. de quibus idem T. respondet ibidem. Et heredibus Thome Basset xx li. bl. in Culinton'. Et eisdem C et xvj s. bl. in eadem villa in terra que fuit Philippi le Brett. Et eisdem xx li. et vj s. bl. in Witeford'. Et monachis Sancti Nicholai Exon' l s. in Bradenham. Et in Branton' xx li. de quibus Thomas de Cyrecestr' respondet infra salvo R. hundredo. Et in Lideford' iiij li. et iiij s. ad faciendum ibi mercatum sicut antiquitus esse solebat. Et in elemosinis constitutis canonicis Sancte Trinitatis London' xxv li. et xij s. et vj d. in civitate Exon'. Et in civitate Exon' xij li. et xix s. de quibus Thomas de Cyrecestr' respondet infra. Et in tercio denario comitatus Devon' xviij li. et dim. m. de quibus idem Thomas respondet ibidem.

[*Indented*] Et debet xv s. et xj d. bl. Idem r.c. de eodem debito. In thes. lib. Et Q.E.

[*One line blank*]

Willelmus de Briewerr' Junior [*blank*] xxvij s. et ij d. bl. de remanenti firme comitatus de anno preterito.

Idem W. r.c. de xvj li. de proficuo comitatus de dim. anno viij. Et (de[i]) xxx li. de eodem proficuo de anno ix^{o}. Et de quater xx et xvj m. et viij s. et x d. de warda Novi Castri super Tinam de ij^{bus} annis preteritis. Et de xxxix li. et vj s. et j d. de primo scutagio R. de tercia parte feodorum comitis de Insula. Et de xl li. de proficuo comitatus de Norhumberland de anno viij^{o}. Et de C et l li. de exitibus manerii de Cassewell' per v annos scilicet quolibet anno xxx li. (Et [*blank*] C et vj li. et viij s. et iiij d. et ob. de remanenti compoti sui de catallis Falk' de Breautéé[c]) (*Set respondet infra.*[i]). Summa CCC et xxxix li. et xix s. et xj d. In thes. nichil. Et ipsi Willelmo xxx li. per breve R. pro custodia Novi Castri super Tinam anni R. viij m. Et debet CCC et ix li. et xix s. et xj d. Idem r.c. de eodem debito. In thes. xx li. Et debet CC et quater xx et ix li. et xix s. et xj d. Et xxix li. xv s. et ob. de remanenti compoti sui de catallis Falkas' de Breautéé contenti infra. per annum C m.

f' Idem Vic. r.c. de xl m. de proficuo comitatus hoc anno preter expensas ipsius scilicet xxx li.

f' Idem Vic. r.c. de quater xx et xj li. et j d. de firma maneriorum. In thes. vij li. xvj s. et ix d. Et Radulfus de Tóóny xiij li. in Ailrichescot' quod est membrum de (Ailrichescot'[c]) (Tauton'[i]). Et Willelmus Briewerr' senior lx s. in Wasfeld et Tiverton'. Et in Lifton' xv li. Et in Kenton' xxxiij li. Et in Wica ix li. Et in Ailrichescot' lx s. Et in feria Exon' lxj s. Et in lestagio eiusdem ferie lx s. Et in stallagio ferie Exon' j m. que fuit Willelmi de Helyun. Et in firma domus que fuit eiusdem Willelmi x s. quas viij firmas Y. Regina mater R. habuit in dotem et de quibus Thomas de Cyrecestr' respondet in compoto suo. Et Q.E.

f' Homines de Kenton' debet lx li. de firma ville sue de quibus predictus Thomas respondet in compoto suo.

f' Idem T. debet respondere de Cassewell' et Diepeford' et de Bramton' et de civitate Exon' et de tercio denario comitatus Devon' et …[1]

f' Henricus de Ponte Audomar' r.c. de xv li. de firma terre que fuit Luce f. Johannis. In thes. nichil. Et Eustachio de Curten' C s. nomine dotis. Et ipsi H. x li. quamdiu R. placuerit. Et Q.E.

Willelmus de Pinu r.c. de C et xij s. et viij d. sicut continetur in rotulo primo R. J. In thes. j m. Et debet iiij li. et xix s. et iiij d.

Henricus de la Pomeraie debet (de[i]) xxxiiij li. et xviij s. et x d. et ij osturcos de ij^{bus} debitis contentis in rotulo precedenti. Henricus f. comitis debet M et xviij li. et xij s. et vj d. (et ij palefridos[i]) de pluribus debitis contentis in rotulo precedenti per plegium illorum qui[2] (annotantur in rotulo iiij^{o} R. J.[i])

Walterus de Raleg' r.c. de xliij li. et xv s. et viij d. de misericordia Willelmi f. Johannis patris sui. In thes. j m. Et debet xliij li. et ij s. et iiij d. per annum j m.

[1] Line ends here.

[2] Caret written below the line, and the last six words inserted above the line.

Henricus de Tracy r.c. de C et xx li. et xiij s. et iij d. de iij^{bus} debitis contentis in rotulo precedenti. In thes. x li. Et debet C et x li. et xiij s. et ij d. per annum xx li.

Johannes Wac r.c. de D m. pro habenda gracia R. sicut continetur in rotulo precedenti. In thes. x m. Et debet CCC et xxvj li. et j m. per annum x m.

Robertus Burnard' debet xx m. pro habenda saisina sicut continetur in rotulo xiij. Henricus f. Simonis Lorimerii debet terciam partem de lv li. pro justiciando comite Devon'. Heres comitis de Insula debet quater xx et xiijj li. et xiv d. de pluribus debitis contentis ibidem.

Willelmus Painel r.c. de C et xxxj li. et vj s. de pluribus debitis contentis in rotulo precedenti. In thes. xx m. Et debet C et xvij li. et xix s. et vij d. per annum xx m.

Willelmus de Alba mar' et Muriel uxor eius r.c. de xxxj li. et xl d. ut ipse W. ducat eam in uxorem. In thes. ij m. Et debent xxix li. et xvj s. et viij d.

Robertus de Curten' r.c. de C et xxxviij li. et xv s. et iij d. et iiij m. auri de pluribus debitis contentis in rotulo viij^{o}. In thes. xxx li. Et debet C et viij li. et xv s. et iij d. Et C s pro transgressione qui requirebatur in[1] (Dorset in rotulo precedenti in itinere H. de Neovill'.[1]) per annum xxx li.

Idem R. debet xx m. de misericordia foreste sicut continetur in rotulo precedenti.

Christiana[2] filia Willelmi Chieure r.c. de vij li. et xix s. et vj d. et ob. pro habendo brevi sicut continetur in rotulo vij^{o}. In thes. xv s. Et debet vij li. et iiij s. et vj d. et ob.

Philippus Chaceboef debet v m. de fine sue.[3] Cives Exon' debent lxviij li. et x s. de veteri tallagio. Henricus de Ferrariis debet quater xx et xij li. xv s. et viij d. de tercio scutagio R. Ricardi sicut continetur in rotulo iiij^{o} R. (*Set requirend*[*us*] *est in Glovernia.*[1])

Hugo Painel debet xxxj m. de prestito Pictavie. Abbas de Tavistok' debet xx s. de eodem. + Edith que fuit uxor Ricardi King debet iiij^{tam} partem de x li. et iiij d. pro justiciandis debitoribus suis sicut continetur in rotulo ij^{o}.

Episcopatus Exon' debet xxxj li. de scutagio Pictavie de feodis que recognoscit. Et xxxv li. et viij s. de eodem de feodis que non recognoscit. Et xxxv m. de primo scutagio R. de feodis que non recognoscit.

Reginaldus de Valle torta debet DC m. pro patre suo pro habenda parte sua sicut continetur in rotulo vij^{o}. *Set respondet infra.*

Idem R. r.c. de CC et quater xx et xviij li. et vj s. et xj d. et ob. de pluribus debitis contentis in rotulo precedenti. In thes. *Set respondet infra per partes.*

Matheus de Thorinton' r.c. de xxvij li. de primo scutagio R. In thes. x li. Et debet xvij li. per annum x li.

Idem M. r.c. de C li. pro relevio suo per plegium annotatum in rotulo

[1] Caret written below the line, and the rest of the entry inserted at the end of the line above.

[2] Name written with the Greek letters Xρ for the first syllable.

[3] *sue* written for *suo*.

viij°. In thes. x m.[1] Et debet quater xx et xiij li. et dim. m. *Set respondet infra.*

(Idem M. debet xlix li. et vij s. et vij d. de ij scutagiis contentis in rotulo precedenti de quibus Willelmus de Briewerr' junior debet eum adquietare de lviij m. de scutagio de Bedef' sicut recognovit et respondet infra. Et debet Matheus x li. xix s. et iij d.[c]) (*quia infra per partes*[i])

(Willelmus Briewerr' junior debet lviij m. de scutagio de Bedeford' pro Matheo de Torinton' sicut supra continetur.[c]) quia infra super Matheum qui inde solvit partem in rotulo precedenti per Rogerum de Langeford.

Abbas de Tavistok' debet xliij s. et iiij d. de ij debitis contentis in rotulo precedenti.

Rogerus Barat r.c. de lxxvj s. et viij d. pro justiciando Willelmo sicut continetur in rotulo ij°. In thes. j m. Et debet lxiij s. et iiij d.

Oliverus de Campo Ernulph' r.c. de vj m. et xv d. de debitis Judeorum. In thes. ij m. Et debet iiij m. et xl d. per annum ij m.

Idem Vic. r.c. de iiij s. et vj d. de Wimundo de la Weie. Et de ij s. et vj d. de Willelmo de Torleg'. Et de xl d. de Ada de Medon'. Et de xl d.[2] de Willelmo de Medon'. In thes. lib. Et Q.E.

[*Rot.* 13d *Mem.* 2]

Ernaldus[3] de Swineston' debet v s. + Ricardus de Culeworð[4] debet xl d. + Henricus Husce (debet[c]) et Robertus Parmentarius debent ij s. et ix d. pro defalta. + Rogerus Barill' debet dim m. quia non est prosecutus. (+[i]) Willelmus f. Walteri debet dim. m. pro plegio. Ricardus Mudde Serviens hundredi de Plinton' debet dim. m. pro transgressione. Reginaldus de Wica debet dim. m. pro dissaisina. + Simon Hache debet dim. m. pro eodem. Johannes Cumin debet dim m. pro eodem. + Ricardus de Fugelhus debet dim. m. pro eodem. + Ricardus Aimer debet dim. m. pro eodem. + Ricardus de Toteneis debet dim m. pro vino vendito. + Ricardus le Moinne debet dim. m. pro eodem.

Robertus de Blacford' r.c. de xix m. et dim. pro Willelmo Briewerr' sicut continetur in rotulo iiij°. In thes. ij m. et dim. Et debet xvij m. Idem r.c. de eodem debito. In thes. ij m. et dim. Et debet xiiij m. et dim. per annum v m.

Walerandus teutonicus r.c. de C m. pro habenda staminaria sicut continetur in rotulo iijj°. In thes. lib. Et Q.E.

Hugo de Sancto Vedasto r.c. de xlvij li. de ij[bus] debitis contentis in rotulo vij°. In thes. C s. Et debet xlij li. per annum C s.

Idem Vic. r.c. de iij s. de Remundo de Leghe. Et de iiij m. de Rogero de Reimes. Et de x s. de Willelmo Flandr'. In thes. lib. Et Q.E.

Henricus de Trublevill' debet xvj li. de firma de Westhal' in Suff' sicut continetur in rotulo precedenti. Willelmus Talebot (et socii sui[i]) debent

1 *x m.* written above an ink blot.
2 Something is erased before the *d.*
3 This line is hidden under a fold in the membrane.
4 *NS 54*, p. 256 has *Ricardus de Cuneworðe.*

xxvij s. et vj d. de carrucagio huius comitatus sicut continetur in rotulo de carrucagio.

Matheus de Torinton' r.c. de quater xx et xiij li. et dim. m. de relevio suo sicut supra continetur. In thes. ij m. per Robertum de Bulkeworðe unum plegium. Et xxx s per Willelmum de Wideworðe alium plegium. Et debet M. quater xx et x li et x s.[1]

DE SCUTAGIO DE MUNGUMERI

Episcopatus Exon' debet xxxj m. de eodem de feodis que recognoscit. Et xxxv m. de feodis que non recognoscit. *Set respondet infra in summa omnium feodorum.*

Abbas de Tavistok' debet ij m. de j feodo quod non recognoscit. Episcopus Exon' debet xviij s. de carrucagio relligiosorum in hoc comitatu sicut continetur in rotulo de carrucagio.

Nicholaus Avenel r.c. de iiij s. et v d. de eodem. In thes. lib. Et Q.E.

Reginaldus de Valle torta et Johannes Biset [*blank*] ij m. de j feodo in Culinton'. Et ij m. de scutagio de Bedeford'.

Matheus de Torinton' [*blank*] lviij m. de eodem sicut supra continetur.

DE SCUTAGIO DE BEDEFORD'

Reginaldus de Alba mara debet j m. de eodem. Abbas de Tavistoke debet ij m. de eodem de j feodo quod non recognoscit.

W. episcopus Exon' r.c. de lxix li. viij s. et viij d. de firma plurium maneriorum et tallagiis (et scutagiis[1]). In thes. l li. Et debet xix li. et viij s. et viij d. Et preterea xxxv m. de scutagio de Mungumeri de feodis que non recognoscit.

Matheus de Torinton' [*blank*] x li. et xix s. et iij d. de eodem sicut supra continetur.

DE OBLATIS

Idem Vic. r.c. de dim. m. de Henrico f. Theobaldi. Et de j m. de Thoma Russell. Et de xl s. de Willelmo de Bikeleg'. In thes. lib. Et Q.E.

Willelmus Buzun r.c. de v m. pro habenda custodia sicut continetur in rotulo precedenti. In thes. ij m. Et debet iij m.

Burgenses de Plinton' debent xx m. de palefr[idis] content[is] in rotulo precedenti. *Set T. de Cyrecestr' respondet inde in compoto suo.*

Robertus de Chááluns debet v m. pro relevio suo sicut continetur in rotulo precedenti. *Set T. de Cyrecestr' respondet ibidem.*

Stephanus Flandr' debet xliij s. et ix d. de scutagio de Byham qui requirebatur in Cornubia in rotulo viij^{o}. Galfridus de Pridias debet ix s. et iiij d. pro licencia concordandi qui requirebatur ibidem. Predictus Stephanus Flandr' debet C et xvj s. et viij d. de scutagio de Mungumeri qui requirebatur ibidem. Et x m. de scutagio de Bedef' qui requirebatur ibidem.[2]

[1] *et x s.* inserted on the line below.

[2] *et ... ibidem* inserted after the heading *Nova Oblata.*

NOVA OBLATA

Edmundus de Tudeham [*blank*] iij palefrid' pro habendo brevi de assisa mortis antecessoris de manerio de Stanton' cum pertinenciis. Et xx s. pro licencia concordandi de eadem assisa per Warinum f. Johel' unum justiciariorum de eadem assisa. Ricardus f. Johannis debet dim. m. pro iniusta detentione versus Ricardum de Dun. Thomas f. Daniel' debet j m. pro mentione facienda in brevi de tempore H. R. avi.

Homines de comitatu Devon' r.c. de CC m. pro habendo Vic. de se ipsis usque in tres annos á festo Sancti Michaelis anno ix et Vic. ille habebit xxx li. per annum pro expensis suis et respondebit de omnibus exitibus et proventibus eiusdem comitatus. In thes. xliij li. et dim. m. Et debent quater xx et x li.

Willelmus Briewerr' (junior[i]) r.c. de C et vj li. et viij s. et iiij d. de tallagiis et aliis exitibus terrarum Falkasii de Breauteé contentis in rotulo compotorum de terris suis. In thes. nichil. Et W. episcopo Exon' lxxvj li. et j m. (per breve R.[i]) ad milites et servientes retentos ad obsidionem castri de Plinton' quam fecit per preceptum R. dum R. fuit ad obsidionem castri de Bedeford'. Et debet xxix li. et xv s. et ob. *Set respondet supra inter alia debita sua.*

Walerandus teutonicus r.c. de CC m pro habenda staminaria Devon' sicut continetur in rotulo v^{o}. In thes. C li. Et in perdona ipsi l m per breve R. ad se sustentandum in servicio R. quamdiu R. placuerit. Ita quod idem Walerandus de cetero reddet R. ad scaccarium pro stagnaria illa C li. per annum ad ij^{os} terminos scilicet ad pasch' anni huius l li. et ad festum Sancti Michaelis anno eodem l li. Et sic deinceps C li. quolibet anno ad eosdem terminos quamdiu stagnariam illam tenuerit per preceptum R. Et Q.E.

[P.] Winton' episcopus r.c. de DC m. supra contentis super Reginaldum de Valle torta. In thes. nichil. Et R. J. patri R. in garderoba sua C et lxj li. et vj s. et viij d. per breve R. in quo continetur quod protestatum est coram R. et consilio suo quod de predicto debito quod exigebatur ab ipso de fine quem Rogerus de Valle torta pater ipsius Reginaldi qui fuit in custodia predicti episcopi fecit cum R. J. patre R. pro habenda illa parte terrarum que remansit Henrico de Nonant de partitione facta inter ipsum Henricum et Willelmum de Braios[a] solvit predictas C et lxj li. vij s. et viij d. in predicta warderoba. Et debet C et xxij li. et j m. pro parte sua predicti debiti et (*Set respondet in Suhantesir.*[i]) dictus Reginaldus respondebit de residuo predicti debiti ad scaccarium pro parte sua (scilicet[i]) de C et xvj li. sicut continetur in eodem brevi et respondet infra.

Idem Reginaldus r.c. de C et xvj li. pro parte sua de predicto debito supra contento in prima linea. Et de lxvj m. et iij s. et ix d. de primo scutagio R. de medietate honoris de Toteneis. Et de lvj m. et iij s. et ix d. de scutagio de Mungumery de eadem medietate. Et de l m. de relevio suo de tercia parte terre que fuit Thome Basset. Et de v m. et xiij d. et ob. pro Petro Oliverii. Et de CC et xxiij li. et xiiij s. et iiij d. de debitis Judeorum pro Henrico de Nonant. Et de xlix li. et iij s. et iiij d. de scutagio de Mungumeri de feodis suis in Cornubia. Et de ij m. de eodem de j feodo in Culinton'. Et de C s. de prestito ei facto apud Bedef'. Summa D li. et lix s. et vij d. et ob. In thes. xxx li. Et debet CCCC et lxxij li. et xix s. et vij

d. et ob. de quibus solvit in rotulo precedenti l m. in summa deb[itorum]. Et debet CCCC et xxxix li. et xij s. et xj d. et ob. per annum lx m.
[*One line blank*]

COMPOTUS DE LA BERTON' ET HUNDR' DE MERLEBERG' Á FESTO SANCTI MATHIE APOSTOLI ANNI VIJ (R.[1]) USQUE AD FESTUM SANCTI MATHIE ANNO XJ° EIUSDEM

Robertus de Maisy ut custos r.c. de ix li. et v s. et xj d. de redditu assiso de la Berton' de iij^{bus} partibus anni viij et iiij^{a} parte anni ix. Et de ix li. v s. et xj d. de eodem de iij^{bus} partibus anni ix et iiij^{a} parte anni x. Et de ix li. (v s. et xj d. de iij^{bus} partibus anni x et iiij^{a} parte anni xj[1]).[1] Et de iiij li. et x s. et vj d. de redditu medietatis molendini fulerez de anno viij. Et de xxij s. et vij d. de redditu eiusdem medietatis de quarta parte anni antequam traderetur Reginaldo Basset per breve R. ad se sustentandum in servicio R. quamdiu R. placuerit. Et de lxxiiij s. et xj d. de herbagio anni viij. Et de x d. de lana vendita vij ovium que debentur R. de faldagio tempore Paschali scilicet de qualibet falda j ovis. Et de xj d. de teloneo. Et de ij s. et iij d. et ob. de padnagio debito quolibet anno. Et de vj li. et xj s. et vij d. et ob. de exitu molendinorum ij^{orum} ad bladum. Et de lxix s. et viij d. de placitis et perquisitis. Et de vij li. et xv s. et viij d. et ob. de quater xx et xj quarteriis et dim. et iij bussellis venditis scilicet ordei et avene quod Robertus Lupus eis dimisit. + Et de lxiij s. et iiij d. et ob. de herbagio anni ix. Et de lxij s. et x d. de lana et caseo C et quater xx et xix ovium emptarum et v de faldagio et vij de anno preterito. Et de viij d. de teloneo. Et de ix d. et ob. de padnagio. Et de vj li. et vj s. et iij ob. de exitu molendinorum. Et de xxxvij s. et iij d. de placitis et perquisitis. Et de iij s. et xj d. de v coriis affrorum venditis. Et de xxij li. et xiij s. et viij d. et ob. de quater xx et iiij quarteriis et dim. frumenti venditis. Et de xj li. et xv s. et vj d. de C et xlix quarteriis avene venditis. Et de lix s. et vj d. et ob. de herbagio hoc anno. Et de lxxvj s. et x d. de lana et caseo venditis ovium predictarum et xxiiij de novo emptarum et v de novo faldagio. Et de v d. de teloneo. Et de ix d. et ob. de padnagio. Et de viij li. et iij s. et vj d. de exitu molendinorum. Et de xlj s. et ix d. de placitis et perquisitis. Et de vj li. et viij s. et iiij d. de xxxviij quarteriis et iij bussellis frumenti venditis. Et de xx s. de iiij quarteriis et dim. ordei venditis. Et de xviij li. et xj s. et xj d. de CC et quater xx et vj quarteriis et dim. et j bussello avene venditis. Summa C et xlvij li. v s. et x d. et ob.

[Idem][2] r.c. de vij li. et xij d. de auxilio constabularii in hundredo de Selkel' pertinente ad castrum de Merleberg' de predictis tribus annis. Et de vj li. et vij s. de visu franciplegii de eisdem tribus annis. Et de iiij li. et xiij s. et vij d. de placitis et perquisitis in hundredo de eisdem tribus annis. Et

[1] *v s. ... anni xj* inserted after heading for this section.
[2] The left hand side of the membrane is torn away from this point on, with the loss of some letters at the start of the lines following. This loss is shown by [...] when the missing letters cannot be deduced.

de lv li. et dim. m. quas recepit de hominibus de Merleberg' de firma sua ad operationem castri. Summa lxxiij li. et viij s. et iij d.

[Idem] r.c. de dim. m. de Teðing' ville de Kenette pro fuga Godwin' de itinere M. de Pateshill'. Et de dim. m. de Bertona pro concelamento de eodem itinere. Et de ij m. de villata de Merleberg' quia sepelierunt homines de eodem itinere. In thes. lib. Et Q.E.

[Idem] r.c. de ij m. de hundredo de Selkel' pro misericordia. Et dim. m. de Teðing' de Sawe pro fuga Roberti. Et de xj li. et xiiij s. de censu censariorum de Savernac de predictis tribus annis scilicet per annum lxxviij s. Summa xiij li. et vij s. et iiij d.

[I]dem r.c. de xxxiij s. et v d. de redditu assiso de Lutegareshal' de anno viij^{o}. Et de xxvj s. et iij d. et ob. de redditu assiso eiusdem ville de iij^{bus} partibus anni noni antequam traderetur hominibus ville ad firmam pro xij li. quamdiu R. placuerit. Et de[1] [...] ij s. de padnagio anni ix^{mi}. Et de viij li. et iij d. de exitu fori de anno viij^{o}. Et de iiij li. et v s. et xj d. de exitu eiusdem fori a festo Sancti Mathie apostoli anni ix^{ni} usque ad festum Sancti Michaelis eiusdem anni. Et de ix s. et ij d. de perqui[sitis a]nni viij^{vi}. Et de x s. et xj d. de faldagio de Lutegareshal' eodem anno. Et de iiij s. de redditu Rannulfi Gobuten pro iiij^{or} acris terre. Et de xix s. et ij d. de frumento et avena ibi invento et vendito. Et de viij s. de perquisitis anni ix. Et [de] j m. de faldagio anni ix^{ni}. Et de iiij s. de redditu Rannulfi Gobute de eodem anno. Et de ij s. et ix d. de coriis ij^{orum} affrorum et j bovis venditorum. Et de iij s. et xj d. de j sue et iij porcellis venditis. Et de vj li. et [...] ij s. et viij d. et ob. de xxiiij quarteriis et ij bussellis frumenti ibidem venditis. Et de vij li. et x s. et ix d. et ob. de lj quarteriis et j bussello de hastivell' venditis. Et de iiij s. de ij quarteriis siliginis venditis. Et de xxij s. et viij d. de [...] quarteriis et dim. et ij bussellis ordei venditis. Et de iiij li. et xiij s. et viij d. et ob. de lxxij quarteriis et iij bussellis avene venditis. Et de xij s. et iij d. et ob. de faldagio anni x^{mi}. Et de xxxv s. et vij d. et ob. de x quarteriis [fr]umenti venditis. Et de xviij d. de dim. quarterio ordei vendito. Et de ix d. de ij bussellis pisorum venditis. Summa xlij li. et ij d. Summa summarum CC et lxxvj li. et xix d. et ob. In thes. nichil.

[*Indented*] Et pro ferro et ascero ad vij carrucas ad Bertonam et ferraturam affrorum et in aliis necessariis expensis ad carrucas per predictos tres annos vj li. et xiij s. et xj d. et ob. Et pro iiij^{or} bobus emp[tis ad] instaurand[as] carruc[as] xvj s. et vj d. et ob. Et in stipendiis vij bubulcorum et iij aliorum servientum herciatorum et caretariorum per predictos iij annos vij li. et xij s. et viij d. Et in pratis falcandis levandis et cariandis [...] bladis sarclandis metendis carriandis et salvo reponendis et cóóperiendis per predictum tempus xj li. et vj d. preter operationes debitas curie. Et pro C et v ovibus matricibus emptis et C et vj multonibus similiter emptis ...ij li. et xiij s. et x d. de quibus idem Robertus debet respondere. Et in reparatione falde et bercarie per predictum tempus vij s. et iiij d. Et in operatione j^{us} bovarie de novo facte apud Bertonam xxviij s. et ij d. Et in minutis expensis ad ...iariam per predictum tempus v s. Et in carriagio ij^{arum} molarum (a Suhanton'i) et emptione aliarum ij^{arum}

[1] A mending strip obscures the right hand edge from here until the bottom of the membrane.

molarum (Merlebergh'[i]) ad molendina de la Berton' et reparatione stagni et excluse vj li. et x s. et v d. et ob. Et in operatione baye magne vivarii apud Merleberg' xxix s. Et pro ij^{bus} baculis ad balistas faciend[as] iij s. et ij d. per breve R. Et in venatione R. salienda et carienda[1] usque Wint' á Merleberg' xiiij s. et vij d. per iij brevia R. Et in custo posito ad duos prisones [...] pro malo recto ducendos a Merleberg' usque Lond' et pro ferramentis eorum xviij s. ij d. et ob. per breve eiusdem. Et in custo posito ad exclusas faciendas circa castrum de Merleberg' ad aquam retinendam iiij li. xviij s. et vij d. et ob. [per] breve R. Et in operatione j^{us} nove coquine in castro et j^{us} furni cóóperiendi et eadem coquina lapide cóóperienda xj li. xv s. iiij d. et ob. per idem breve. Et in operatione j parve camere que lapide cooperta est lxxv s. et ix d. et ob. per [idem] breve. Et in emendatione graduum coram thalamo R. et in eis lapide cóóperiendis xxxj s. xvij d. et ob. per idem breve. Et in emendatione tresancie inter aulam et gradus xij s. et vij d. per idem breve. Et in operatione j^{us} bretaschie [...] thalamum Regine xlj s. et vj d. per idem breve. Et in emendatione camere Regine plumbate et listate et muro gabuli levando et coloribus et plumbo emptis et aliis emendationibus eiusdem camere et similiter fenestris ferr[o] reparandis vij li. xv s. et v d. per idem breve. Et in emptione petre ad j torellam retro cameram plumbatam faciendam continentem ij^{os} estagios et carriagio eiusdem petre et in maremio prostrando et carriando et sabulo fodiendo et [carr]iando xvij li. et vij s. et v d. et ob. per idem breve. Et in operatione et carragio j^{us} rogi C et xviij s. et x d. per idem breve. Et in cóópertura j camere cóóperte lapide et j^{us} coquine juxta portam et emendatione dispense et Bu[tilleri]e et aule et aliarum domorum in castro per tres annos predictos xxxvij li. xj s. viij d. et ob. per idem breve. Et in operatione j^{us} turelle apud Lutegareshal' juxta portam et fenestris vitreis emptis ad capellam et emendationem [...] domorum ibidem vj li. xiiij s. et vj d. Et pro ferro et ascero ad iiij carrucas de Lutegareshal' et operatione carruc[arum] ibidem (per predictum tempus[c]) ij annos et iiij^{tam} partem anni iiij li. et viij s. et ix d. et ob. Et in emptione [...]boum ibidem lxix s. et v d. et ob. Et in stipendiis iiij bubulcorum et j^{us} caretarii per predictum tempus liiij s. et ix d. et ob. Et in cibo servientum quem habent de die quo incipiunt seminare et die Natal' et die Pasch' [...]Et in blado sarclando metendo et colligendo et triturando per predictum tempus (apud Lutegareshal'[i]) iiij li. ix s. et iiij d. Et in emendatione j bovarie v s. et vj d. Et ipsi Roberto pro custodia castri de Merleberg' per predictum tempus [...] ii m. et dim. de pluribus exitibus ballie sue contentis in brevi R. quod est in forulo mareschalli preter xvij m. et dim. quas recepit in garderoba R. pro qua custodia recepit x m. per annum. Et pro blado seminando [...] per predictos iij annos iiij li. et xviij s. et iij d. et ob. Summa omnium predictarum expensarum CC et xxxiiij li. xix s. et vij d. et ...[2] Et debet xlj li. ij s. et ob. *Set respondet in Wiltesir'*.

[*Centred*] H. de Neovill' debet respondere de blado de Lutegareshal' de anno x^{o}.

[*Endorsed*]

[1] *carienda* written for *carianda*.

[2] Nothing written to complete the sense. Perhaps *ob.* is needed?

Surreia (emend'[i]) et London (emend'[i]) et Middelsexia (emend'[i]) et Devonia (emend'[i])
Et compotus de Merleberg' (emend'[i]) (quia …[i])[1]

[*Rot.* 14 *Mem.* 1]

DORSET'

Ricardus episcopus Saresbir', Gillebertus de Stappelbrige ut custos pro eo r.c. de quater xx et x li. bl. de firma comitatus de tribus partibus anni. In thes. lviij s. bl.

Et in terris datis Huberto de Burgo cum herede Willelmi de Lanvalet' vij li. et x s. (bl.[i]) in Schaftebir'. Et in hundredo de Piddelton' quod Willelmus de Monte acuto habuit per R. xl s. Et monachis de Binesdon' xv s. in molendino de Fordinton' quod habuit per R. Et eisdem xx s. in molendino extra Dorcestr'. Et in liberatione capellani de Dorcestr' xxxvij s. et vj d. Et Roberto Chantemerle lxiij s. et ix d. in Dalewude et Witewell' membris de Fordinton'. Et Abbati de Cerne (lx s.[i]) in Modberge et Tettecumb' de quibus respondet infra. Et in villa de Dorcestr' ix li. bl. de quibus homines ville respondent infra. Et in Gillingeh' xxx li. bl. de quibus Vic. respondet infra. Et in Fordinton' xx li. et v s. bl. de quibus Vic. respondet infra ut custos.

[*One line blank*]

Et in carriagio venationis decem cervorum usque Winton' ij s. et vj d. per breve R. Et in carriagio x milium quarrellorum usque Portesmuth' xj s. et vj d. per breve eiusdem. Et in operatione j[us] grangie facte apud Gillingeh' xiij li. et x s. et viij d. per breve eiusdem et per visum Johannis venatoris et Willelmi f. Reginaldi. Et in emendatione castri de Schireburn' de toto anno C s. Et in expensis servientum qui conduxerunt quintam decimam usque Winton' xviij s. et iiij d. per breve R. Et habet de superplus x li. et iij d. bl. qui sunt ei extensi ad x li. et ix s. et iij d. num. quod totum locatur ei infra in proficuo.

[*One line blank*]

Idem Vic. r.c. de xvij li. et xiiij s. et viij d. et ob. de proficuo comitatus de predictis tribus partibus anni. In thes. C et v s. et v d. et ob. Et in superplus quod habet supra xx li.[2] et ix s. et iij d. Et debet xl s.

(Idem Vic. [*blank*] iiij s. de exitu terre Willelmi le Brett[c]) *quia infra super alium Vic.*

Idem Vic. r.c. de xx li. de firma de Bere de tribus partibus anni. Et de lx s. de proficuo eiusdem manerii de eodem termino. In thes. lib. Et Q.E.

Idem Vic. r.c. de xxx li. (bl.[i]) de firma de Gillingeh' de predictis tribus partibus anni. In thes. xxix li. et ij s. et vj d. bl. Et debet xvij s. et vj d. bl. Idem r.c. de eodem debito. In thes. lib. Et Q.E.

Idem Vic. r.c. de xlix s. et vij d. de proficuo eiusdem manerii de eodem termino hoc anno. In thes. lib. Et Q.E.

1 Two very faint words inserted, of which the first is perhaps *quia*.
2 *supra xx* squashed in.

Idem Vic. r.c. de vj li. de firma de Pourstok' de tribus partibus anni. Et de xl s. de proficuo eiusdem manerii de eodem termino hoc anno. In thes. lib. Et Q.E.

Idem Vic. r.c. de xx li. et v s. (bl.[1]) de firma de Fordinton' de tribus partibus anni. In thes. xix li. xiij s. et ij d. et ob. bl. Et debet xj s. et ix d. et ob. bl. Idem r.c. de eodem debito. In thes. lib. Et Q.E.

Idem Vic. r.c. de lvij s. et[1] ix d. de proficuo eiusdem manerii de eodem termino. In thes. lib. Et Q.E.

Homines de Dorcestr' r.c. de xij li. bl. de firma ville sue de toto anno. Et de xij s. et vj d. bl. de remanenti eiusdem firme de anno preterito. In thes. xij li. et ij s. bl. Et debent x s. et vj d. bl.

[*Two lines blank*]

Willelmus f. Henrici ut custos r.c. de xxx li. bl. de firma comitatus de Dorset' de quarta parte anni. In thes. lxv s. bl.

Et in elemosinis constitutis militibus de templo j m. de toto anno. Et in terris datis Huberto de Burgo cum herede Willelmi de Lanval' l s. bl. in Schaftebir' (de quarta parte anni[1]). Et in hundredo de Piddelton' quod Willelmus de Monte acuto habuit per R. J. unam m. Et monachis de Binesdon' v s. in molendino de Fordinton' quod habent per R. Et eisdem vij s. et vj d. in molendino extra Dorcestr'. Et in liberatione capellani de Dorcestr' xij s. et vj d. Et Roberto Chantemerle xxj s. et iij d. in Daleswude et Wittwell' membris de Fordinton'. Et Abbati de Cerne xx s. in Modberge et Tetecumb' de quibus respondet infra. Et in villa de Dorcestr' lx s. bl. de quibus homines ville respondent infra. Et in Gillingeham x li. bl. de quibus Hugo de Neovill' respondet infra per breve R. Et in Fordinton' vj li. et xv s. bl. de quibus Vic. respondet infra. Et debet xxj d. bl.

[*Two lines blank*]

Idem Vic. r.c. de vj li. et (x[1])v s. de firma de Fordinton' de quarta parte anni. In thes. lib. Et Q.E.

Idem Vic. [*rest of the line blank*]

Idem Vic. r.c. de iiij s. de exitu terre Willelmi le Bretti de toto anno. In thes. lib. Et Q.E.

Idem Vic. r.c. de lx s. de firma de Bere de quarta parte anni. In thes. lib. Et Q.E.

H. d'[2] Neovill' [*blank*] x li. bl. de firma de Gillingeham de quarta parte anni.

[*One line blank*]

Idem H. [*blank*] xl s. de firma de Pourstok' de quarta parte anni. Et [*rest of line blank*]

Abbas de Cerne r.c. de iiij li. de firma de Modberge et Tetecumb'. In thes. lib. Et Q.E.

Idem Vic. r.c. de xl s. de remanenti de Winterburn' de toto anno. In thes. lib. Et Q.E.

Hugo de Gundevill' debet CCC m. et iij palefridos pro habenda recognitione sicut continetur in rotulo xj°. Et xv m. pro dissaisina.

Idem Hugo r.c. de xxij s. pro vinis R. venditis. In thes. lib. Et Q.E.

[1] *d.* changed to *et.*

[2] *d'* written for *de.*

Robertus de Barentin debet CC et quater xx et iij li. et iij s. et iiij d. pro habenda gratia R. J. Thomas de Neovill' clericus debet lxv m. et iiij s. et ij d. pro habenda custodia sicut continetur in rotulo xv°.

Rogerus f. Radulfi de Winesham r.c. de CC et lx li. et xviij s. et xj d. pro eodem. In thes. j m. Et debet CC et lx li. et v s. et vij d. per annum j m.

Aluredus de Linc' r.c. de dim. m. de j palefrido sicut continetur in rotulo iiij°. In thes. lib. Et Q.E.

Abbatissa de Sancto Edwardo [*blank*] xxiij li. et dim. m. de scutagio Pictavie.

Eadem abbatissa debet ix li. et xix s. de pluribus scutagiis contentis in rotulo precedenti de feodis que non recognoscit. Et iiij li. et xj s. de scutagio de Mungumeri de eisdem feodis.

Eadem abbatissa r.c. de lxx s. de scutagio de Byham de feodis que recognoscit. In thes. lib. Et Q.E.

Abbas de Cerne debet xxxvj li. de iiij^or^ scutagiis contentis in rotulo precedenti de feodis qui[1] non recognoscit.

Nicholaus archerius r.c. de lxj s. et viij d. pro habenda inquisitione. In thes. x s. Et debet lj s. et viij d.

Adam f. Roberti forestarii r.c. de iiij li. pro habenda ballia que fuit patris sui. In thes. lib. per j taleam de ante guerram allocatam precepto H. de Burgo Justiciarii coram baronibus de scaccario. Et Q.E.

Robertus del Estre debet vj s. de baconibus R. venditis. + Thomas de Kenefar' debet v m. quia fuit convictus. + Hamelinus de Mutford' debet ij m. pro habendo brevi sicut continetur in rotulo ij°.

Hugo Poinz debet vj m. de prestito Pictavie.

Galfridus f. Alexandri r.c. de j m. pro habendo pone. In thes. dim. m. Et debet dim. m.

Walterus de Turbervill' r.c. de CCC et xij li. de pluribus debitis contentis in rotulo viij. In thes. x li. Et debet CCC et ij li. per annum x li.

Robertus de Novo burgo [*blank*] viij m. de primo scutagio.

Idem Robertus [*blank*] iiij li. et x s. de scutagio de Byham.

Robertus de Andel' debet xxx s. pro dissaisina. + Aimericus de Maullai debet j m. pro eodem. + Avicia filia Roberti Britton' debet dim. m. pro falso clamore. (G^c^) Galfridus de Gisnes[2] debet xx s. pro vino vendito. + Philippus Britto debet dim. m. pro eodem. + Robertus d'aise[3] debet xx s. pro vino vendito. + Petrus Barre debet j m. pro eodem. + Ernaldus de Blanies debet j m. pro eodem. + Petrus de Lungevill' debet j m. pro eodem. + Ingulfus de Baiune debet j m. pro eodem.

Rogerus del Estane debet iiij m. pro transgressione. Hugo Poinz debet ij m. pro licencia concordandi. Cristiana Wác et Rogerus Martel debent j m. ut Johanna summoneatur sicut continetur in rotulo precedenti.

Aluredus de Linc' debet xij li. et xj s. et vij d. et ob. de scutagio de Biham. Henricus f. comitis[4] debet xx li. et x s. de eodem.

1 *qui* written for *que*.

2 The beginning of this word is written on an alteration.

3 In *NS 54*, p. 240 and *NS 56*, p. 3 he is shown as *Robertus de Aise*. There is a hint of an apostrophe after the 'd'.

4 In *NS 54*, p. 240 Henry is shown as being the son of the earl of Cornwall.

Walterus de Grava r.c. de xj li. et xl d. scilicet de quarta parte de l li. sicut continetur in rotulo iiij^{o}. In thes. xx s. Et debet x li. et xl d.
per annum xx s.

Willelmus de Esse et Margar' uxor eius r.c. de lvj s. et viij d. pro summonendo Johanne sicut continetur ibidem. In thes. xviij s. Et debent xxxviij s. et viij d.

Simon de Littleton' r.c. de xl s. de fine suo. In thes. xx s. Et debet xx s.

Robertus salsarius r.c. de xxx s. de predicto fine. In thes. j m. Et debet xvj s. et viij d.

Petrus de Medleto debet vij li. de fine passag' et scutag' Pictavie. Set non debet summoneri quia testatum est per inquisitionem inde factam per preceptum R. quod tenet feodum illud de quo debitum illud exigitur de comite Glovernie. Et ideo Q.E.

Robertus de Gouiz r.c. de D et xxxij li. de debitis Judeorum. In thes. C s. Et debet D et xxvij li. per annum C s.

Galfridus de Witchirche r.c. de v m. ut non distringatur sicut continetur in rotulo precedenti. In thes. xliiij s. Et debet xxij s. et viij d.

[*One line blank*]

DE OBLATIS

[*Rot.* 14 *Mem.* 2]

[*One line blank*]

Petrus de Ruvil' r.c. de v m. pro j palefrido pro habendo brevi de nova dissaisina sicut continetur in rotulo precedenti. In thes. lib. Et Q.E.

Hugo f. Willelmi et Matill' uxor eius r.c. de j m. pro habendo brevi sicut continetur ibidem. In thes. lib. Et Q.E.[1]

[*One line blank*]

DE PLACITIS DE BANCO

Idem Vic. r.c. de j m. de Aluredo de Linc' pro licencia concordandi. Et de dim. m. de Willelmo f. Ailnoði pro eodem. Et de j m. de priore de Cristchirche pro eodem. In thes. lib. Et Q.E.

Henricus Baret (debet^{c}) (r.c. de^{i}) j m. pro defalta coram B. de Insula de placitis foreste. In thes. nichil. Et episcopo Saresb' j m. per libertatem carte R. Et Q.E.

[*One line blank*]

DE PLACITIS FORESTE PER H. DE NEOVILL'

Paganus f. Willelmi r.c. de iij m. pro concelamento. In thes. xx s. Et debet xx s.

Galfridus Cribbe r.c. de xx s. pro recto foreste. In thes. v s. Et debet xv s.

Cecilia que fuit uxor Ade de Hertleg' r.c. de ix m. pro habenda custodia sicut continetur ibidem. In thes. ij m. Et debet vij m. per annum ij m.

[1] *Quietus Est* written for *Quieti Sunt.*

Idem Vic. r.c. de v m. de burgo de Warrham. Et de xx s. de Henrico de Ortiaco pro falsa presentatione. In thes. lib. Et Q.E.

Hundredum de Hundresberge debet xv s. pro stultiloquio. Winterburn' Fercles debet xx s. pro concelamento (*Set respondet infra.*[i]).

Idem Vic. r.c. de (Ada[c]) xij d. de Adam Abbe pro defalta. Et de ij s. de Hamone Croy. Et de iij m. de Hamone de Almodinton' quia non habuit. In thes. lib. Et Q.E.

Adam capellanus de Polham debet xij d. pro defalta. Walterus f. Godfridi de Gillingeham debet xij d. pro viridi.

Abraham de Dieuelespol r.c. de dim. m. pro defalta. In thes. nichil. Et episcopo Saresbir' dim. m. per libertatem carte R. Et Q.E.

Gillebertus de Stapelbrige [*blank*] xvij s. et iiij d. et ob. de remanenti compoti sui de Gillingeham sicut continetur in rotulo precedenti. Et de xvj s. de vj quarteriis de Drowe ibidem venditis.

Winterburn' Fercles r.c. de xx s. pro concelamento sicut supra continetur. In thes. lib. Et Q.E.

NOVA OBLATA

Willelmus de Ponte Arche r.c. de xx m. pro pl[egiando] Henr[ico] f. comitis Cornubie sicut continetur in rotulo iiij[o] R. J. in Devon' ubi omnes alii plegii ipsius Henrici annotantur. In thes. iiij m. Et pro C et xlvij baconibus emptis ab ipso Willelmo ad opus R. per Vic. Suhantesir' C s. per[1] breve R. Et debet viij m. et dim. (*Idem r.c. de eodem debito. In thes. lib. Et Q.E.*)

AMERCIAMENTA FACTA PER M. DE PATESHILL' ET SOCIOS SUOS

Idem Vic. r.c. de xliiij li. et xij s. et viij d. et ob. de misericordiis hominum villarum et Teðingarum et catallis fugitivorum et suspensorum quorum nominibus preponitur littera *t* in rotulo quem predicti liberaverunt in thesaurum. In thes. lib. Et Q.E.

Walterus del Hoc r.c. de dim. m. pro falso clamore. In thes. iij s. Et debet iij s. et viij d. per plegium Willelmi Daci.

Heimericus Buche r.c. de dim. m. pro ij[bus] dissaisinis. In thes. nichil. Et in perdona ipsi Heimerico dim. m. per breve R. Et Q.E.

Idem Vic. r.c. de dim. m. de Henrico de Cedindon' pro dissaisina. Et de dim. m. de Radulfo de Widioc pro falso clamore. Et de dim. m. de teðeringa de Netherbir' pro fuga Ricardi le Batur. Et de j m. de teðeringa de Cermenistr' pro fuga Radulfi filii Rogeri. In thes. nichil. Et episcopo Saresbir' ij m. et dim. per libertatem carte R. Et Q.E.

Idem Vic. r.c. de dim. de teðeringa de Wotton' pro fuga Edwardi Sutoris. In thes. nichil. Et episcopo Bathon' dim. m. per libertatem carte R. Et Q.E.

Idem Vic. r.c. de xix s. et vj d. de catallis Bude extra Teðeringam. In

[1] *per* written on an alteration.

thes. nichil. Et fratribus hospitalis Jer'l'm xix s. et vj d. per libertatem carte R. Et Q.E.

Gillebertus Guto et Jordanus frater eius debent dim. m. pro dissaisina per plegium Jordani Guto. Willelmus f. Alexandri debet dim. m. pro eodem. Idem Vic. debet v s. et iiij d. de catallis Manasseri de Blocksworde fugitivi. Et xij d de catallis Hugonis de Bledelawe fugitivi. Et iiij s. et catallis Simonis Prat fugitivi. Et v s. et iiij d. de catallis Willelmi Gule fugitivi. Et dim. m. de catallis Hugonis le Batur qui obiit in prisona.

Willelmus de Witefeld' r.c. de j m. pro dissaisina. In thes. dim. m. Et debet dim. m.

Galfridus Malregard' debet ij m. de j feodo com' Devon' de scutagio de Bedef' qui requirebatur in compoto Walerand' teutonici in rotulo de carrucagio. Prior de Cristchirch' debet j m. de dim. feodo eiusdem qui requirebatur ibidem. Walterus de Morba (debet[c]) et Prior de Pitenor' debent (dim.[c]) (j[i]) m. de dim. feodo eiusdem qui requirebatur ibidem.

[*17 lines blank*]

SUMERSET'

[J]oscelinus Bathon' episcopus, Willelmus de Schorewell' ut custos pro eo r.c. de CCC et lx li. bl. de firma comitatus. In thes. quater xx li. et xij s. et v d. bl.

Et in elemosinis constitutis militibus de templo j m. Et in terris datis fratribus de Chartus' residentibus apud Witham x li. bl. Et in Yvelcestr' xxviij li. bl. de quibus Thomas de Cyrecestr' debet respondere. Et heredi Roberti de Berkelay xxx li. bl. in Bedmenistr'. Et ecclesie Wellensi xiiij li. bl. in Norðcuri. Et in Ceddre et Axebrige H. episcopo Linc' xvj li. bl. de quibus respondet infra. Et Henrico de Ortiaco cum herede Ricardi Revel xl li. num. in Curi et Lamport. Et eidem lxxij s. et vj d. in quodam socagio in Sumerton'. Et Roberto filio Mauricii v s. in Alkesia. Et Henrico de Ortiaco l s. in manerio de Sumerton'. Et Roberto de Veteri ponte xxx li. in Meleburne. Et canonicis de Tanton' xvj d. in pastura et jalneto de Kingeshill. Et Oliverio Avenel cum Agnet' filia et herede Odonis de Wandestr' vij li. in Norðcuri. Et Radulfo Malet cum herede Willelmi f. Gilleberti de Norf' viij li. in Norðcuri. Et Roberto de novo burgo x li. in Herdecot'. Et Willelmo Brewer' xx s. in Kingeswere. Et Reginaldo de pontibus xl s. in hundredo de Norton'. Et J. Bathon' episcopo xxxv li. in Cungresbir' de quibus respondet infra. Et Huardo de Bikelay viij li. in Holewale membro de Meleburne. Et debet xl li. et xiij s. et vij d. bl. Idem r.c. de eodem debito. In thes. nichil. Et in emendatione gaole de Yvelcestr' xlj s. per breve R. Et debet xxxviij li. et xiiij s. et vij d. bl. de quibus Willelmus de Schorewell' debet respondere sicut recognovit.

[*Two lines blank*]

Idem Vic. debet de proficuo comitatus de hoc anno. Et de anno preterito. Set non debet summoneri quia nullum (habet[c]) (habuit[i]) proficuum.

J. Bathon' episcopus r.c. de vj li. et x s. et v d. bl. de remanenti firme comitatus de primo anno[1] preterito. In thes. lib. Et Q.E.

[1] Initial *a* altered from *p*.

[*One line blank*]

Non respondetur hic de Yvelcestr' quia Thomas de Cyrecestr' respondet inde in compoto suo.

Homines de Yvelcestr' [*blank*] x li. et iij d. bl. de remanenti firme ville sue de dim. anno xvij^{o} R. J.

Johannes de Erleghe r.c. de C s. bl. de firma de Pereton'. Et de v s. bl. de remanenti eiusdem firme de anno preterito. In thes. iiij li. et xv s. bl. Et debet x s. bl.

H. Linc' episcopus J. Bathon' episcopus pro eo r.c. de xx li. num. pro xvj li. bl. de firma de Ceddre et Axebrige. In thes. xvij li. iij s. et iiij d. Et fratribus de Chartus' xl s. in pastura de Ceddreford. Et debet xvj s. et viij d. in dorso (rotuli[i]) (*Set respondet infra.*[i])

Prior Bathon' r.c. de xx li. de firma de la Berton'. In thes. lib. Et Q.E.

J. Bathon' episcopus r.c. de xxxv li. de firma de Cungrebir'. In thes. nichil. Et ipsi episcopo C s. in Bageworðe in terra quam Willelmus f. Willelmi de Hamton' tenuit qui debent ei allocari anno xj^{o} et anno xij^{o} sicut continetur in rotulo precedenti. Et priori et monachis de Chartusa xxv m. de elemosinis R. constitutis de termino Sancti Michaelis (per breve R[i]). Et xx servientibus R. peditibus existentibus in castro Bristoll' de quibus decem capiunt singuli per diem iiij d. et alii x iij d. et ob. x li. et xvj s. et viij d. ad liberationes suas xl diebus per breve eiusdem. Et ad operationem ecclesie Wellensis v m. que debent ei allocari usque ad x annos (sequentes[i]) completos. Et habet de superplus xvj s. et viij d. qui locantur in dorso (rotuli[i]).

Prior Bathon' r.c. de xxx li. de firma civitatis Bathon' quam tenet per talem firmam quamdiu R. placuerit. In thes. lib. Et Q.E.

[Idem] Vic. r.c. de ij m. de hundredo de Brieweton'. Et de dim. m. de firma de Crendon'. Et de vj d. et j libra cimini et j par[1] cirotecarum de redditu de Cumpton Eust[achii] de Durevill' waivati.[2] In thes. lib. Et Q.E.

Willelmus de Mariscis r.c. de xv li. et iiij s. de ij^{bus} debitis contentis in rotulo precedenti. In thes. ij m. Et debet xiij li. et xvij s. et iiij d.

Radulfus f. Johannis Russell' debet liiij li. et xvij s. de debito Jacobi de novo mercato de relevio patris sui. Et xviij li. et dim. m. de auro Regine de eodem relevio. Et x li. et vij s. et vj d. de scutagio Wallie pro eodem Jacobo. Et xvij m. et dim. et x d. de primo scutagio de medietate feodorum ipsius Jacobi (*qui requirebatur in Berkesir.*[i]). Summa quater xx et xv li. et v s. et iiij d.

Hubertus de Burgo debet lx m. pro habenda confirmatione R. J. de conventione inter ipsum et comitem de Insula sicut continetur in rotulo iij^{o} R. J. in dorso rotuli iij^{ti} Item nova oblata. Et vj li. et xv s. et xj d. de

1 *pare* written for *par.*

2 *waivati* written in full. Presumably the rent of Compton Durville was waived but that would have been *waivato* to agree with *redditu*. So, it could be that Eustace has been waived the rent as it might agree with *Eustachii*. The other possibility is that *waivati* is masc. nom. pl. agreeing with the composite subject of *vj d. + libra cumini + j pare cirotecarum* as the bits of the rent that got waived. It is probable that Eustace refers to Eustace of Boulogne who held as tenant in chief one of the manors of Compton Durville.

remanenti firme de Dunes…[1] de anno iiij R. J. Et xix li. et xvj s. et ix d. et ob. de eadem firma de dim. anno R. J. v°. Et xj li. et xviij s. de remanenti firme de Bada de anno vj° eiusdem. Et lx li. pro habenda quietantia (*Set respondet infra*[i])[2] de CCCC m. de novo cremento de Dorset' et Summerset' sicut continetur in rotulo xij° R. J. Et l m. de prestito sicut continetur in rotulo ij° R. J. Et j m. de exitibus terre de Stoclinz sicut continetur ibidem. Et xxvj s. de vino Osberti f. Johannis capto propter falsum galonem …[3] et lxxiij li. et xij s. et viij d. et ob.

Juliana et Avicia heredes Henrici de Cultura r.c. de xj li. et v s. et viij d. de scutagio Hibernie. In thes. ij m. Et debent ix li. et xix s.

[Robertus][4] de Mandevill' r.c. de xx m. et ix s. et vj d. et j osturcum de ij[bus] debitis contentis in rotulo ij°. In thes. x m. Et debet x m. et ix s. et vj d. et j osturcum.

[Sava]ricus de Malo Leone debet l li. quas recepit de J. Bathon' episcopo sicut continetur in rotulo iiij°.

[Robertus de] Mucegros [*blank*] DC et xxxvj lli. et xvj d. de pluribus debitis contentis in rotulo precedenti.

RESPICE IN TERGUM[5]

[*Rot.* 14d *Mem.* 1]

Alanus Basset r.c. de CC et xx li. et iiij s. et iiij d. et ob. de pluribus debitis contentis in rotulo viij°. In thes. x li. Et debet CC et x li. iiij s. et iiij d. et ob. per annum x li.

Ricardus Luvel r.c. de CC et lj li. et xij s. et vj d. de pluribus debitis contentis (ibidem[c]) in rotulo iiij°. In thes. l m. Et debet C et quater xx et iiij li. et xix s. et ij d. per annum l m.

Rogerus Seinne debet x m. pro habendo (herede[i]) et custodia et maritagio heredis Giffard Witeng' (*set mortuus primo et nichil invenit ut de suo*[i]) sicut continetur in rotulo primo R. Johannes de Boterell' debet xvij m. et dim. de primo scutagio R. Willelmus Hosatus debet ix li. et iij s. et viij d. pro deliberatione sua. Willelmus Briegerr' debet x s. de firma de Kingeswerre de dim. anno xvij° R. J. + Alicia filia Roberti debet ij m. pro habendo precipe versus Ricardum Avenant. + Robertus de Dunmere debet xl s. pro habendo brevi sicut continetur in rotulo xvj°.

Willelmus de Morton' r.c. de ij m. et de v m. pro j palefrido pro habenda terra sicut continetur in rotulo xv R. J. In thes. xx s. Et debet v m. et dim.

Hamo de Linleg' debet iij m. ut deliberetur á prisona. + Simon le Hordier debet xxx s. de vinis R. venditis. Terricus teutonicus debet l li. et ij s. et xj d. et ob. de pluribus debitis contentis in rotulo precedenti

1 The second part of this name is illegible at the start of a line.
2 This insertion is very faint.
3 Word illegible at start of a line.
4 This name and the next two supplied from *NS 54*, p. 41.
5 Three dots drawn vertically each side of this instruction.

Hugo de Vivone [*blank*] CCCC et xvj li. et j m. de pluribus debitis Willelmi Malet. Et x m. de prestito Pictavie.
[*One line blank*]

DE PRESTITO PICTAVIE

Walterus de Essel' debet viij li. et iij s. et iiij d. de eodem. Robertus de Mandevill' debet vij m. de eodem. Willelmus de Mariscis debet viij m. de eodem pro Jordano filio suo.
ho[1] Villata de Yvelcestr' [*blank*] xix s. de tallagio.

Heres Willelmi f. Martini debet x li. de scutagio Pictavie. Ricardus de Mariscis debet xxiiij li. et iij s. de iij^{bus} debitis contentis in rotulo ij^{o}. + Michael f. Michaelis debet dim. m. pro habendo pone sicut continetur ibidem. Walterus f. Willelmi debet xx m. pro defalta in Cornubia.

Johannes de Monte acuto r.c. de xxv s. de scutagio Pictavie. In thes. lib. Et Q.E.

Gervasius Boschier r.c. de j m. pro habendo brevi. In thes. lib. Et Q.E.

Homines de Dorset' et Sumerset' r.c. de CC m. pro habendo Rogero de Forda Vic. In thes. lvj li. Et debent lxxvij li. et dim. m.

Galfridus de Barenton' r.c. de xix m. pro Thoma Foliot sicut continetur in rotulo ij^{o}. In thes. j m. Et debet xviij m. per annum j m.

Willelmus f. Johannis de Harpetree r.c. de C et xviij li. et xiiij s. et iiij d. de pluribus debitis contentis in rotulo precedenti. In thes. xxxiij li. Et debet quater xx et v li. xiiij s. et iiij d. per annum l m.

J. Bathon' episcopus r.c. de xvj s. et viij [d.] de remanenti firme de Ceddre et Axebrig' sicut supra continetur. In thes. nichil. Et in superplus quod idem episcopus habet in compoto suo de Cungrebir' xvj s. et viij d. Et Q.E.

Radulfuus de Suleniaco r.c. de l m. pro Roberto Arsic sicut continetur in rotulo iij^{o}. In thes. xx s. Et debet xlviij m. et dim. per annum xx s.

Henricus filius comitis debet quater xx et ij m. de primo scutagio R. de feodo Reginaldi de Moyun. + Robertus filius Roberti de Keinesham debet lxxij s. et vj d. pro vino vendito. + Rosellus de Hescecumb' debet dim. m. quia non est prosecutus. (per annum^{c})

Philippus de Albiniaco debet C m. per plegium Bertrami de Albiniaco.

Philippus de Fornell' r.c. de viij s. et viij d. pro dissaisina. In thes. lib. Et Q.E.

f' Idem Vic. r.c. de iij s. de exitu terre de Stoclinz'. In thes. lib. Et Q.E.

Thomas de Cyrecestr' [*blank*] vj s. de eodem exitu de ij^{bus} annis preteritis.

Robertus de Gurnac' r.c. de x m. pro Eva de Tracy ut non distringeretur sicut continetur in rotulo precedenti. Et de xxiij li. et viij s. et iiij d. pro licencia concordandi. Et de x m. de fine suo pro Henrico de Veym. Et de iij m. pro habendo cyrographo. In thes. lxx s. Et debet xxxv li. et v s. per annum lxx s.

[1] There is perhaps a letter before *ho*.

Johannes Dacus r.c. de ij s. et vj d. de scutagio de (Mun'[c]) Byham. Et de dim. m. de scutagio de Mungumeri. In thes. lib. Et Q.E.[1]

Johannes de Scalar' r.c. de xl s. pro Elya de Bello campo pro dissaisina. In thes. ij m. Et debet j m.

Willelmus le Pohier r.c. de l s. pro Ricardo f. Matillidis. In thes. lib. Et Q.E.[2]

Ricardus Revel r.c. de viij m. et dim. pro dissaisina. In thes. ij m. et dim. per Henricum de Ortiac'. Et debet vj m.

Executores testamenti Rogeri de Forda [*blank*] xiij li. et xvj s. et ix d. de debitis ipsius Rogeri.

[*One line blank*]

J. Bathon' episcopus [*blank*] j spervar' sor' ut scribatur in magno rotulo quod Henricus de Tracy venit coram baronibus de scaccario et recognovit quod ratam et gratam habet pro se et heredibus suis concessionem et donationem quam venerabilis pater Joscelinus Bathon' episcopus fecit bone memorie Willelmo Briewerre super advocatione ecclesie de Suðbovi (in Devensir'[i]) cum pertinenciis et concessionem et confirmationem quam idem Willelmus Briewerr' fecit fratribus hospitalis de Bruges et quod eam carta sua confirmavit.

f' Henricus de Ortiac' et Sabina uxor eius r.c. de j austurco soro pro lxxij solidatibus terre in Pettony et Wern' membris de Sumerton'.

[*One line blank*]

DE SCUTAGIO DE MUNTGUMERI

Heres Roberti f. Reginaldi debet ij m. de eodem. Johannes f. Ricardi debet (C et[i]) xviij s. et viij d. de eodem. Ricardus del Estr' debet v m. et v s. et vj d. et ob. de eodem.

Johannes del Monte acuto r.c. de xij m. et dim. De eodem. In thes. iiij li. Et debet vj m. et dim.

[*One line blank*]

DE SCUTAGIO DE BEDEF'

Heres Roberti f. Reginaldi debet ij m. de eodem. Guido de Cultura debet ij m. de eodem. Odo de Wandestr' debet j m. de eodem.

Ricardus del Estr' r.c. de v m. et v s. et vj d. et ob. de eodem. In thes. xx s. Et debet lij s. et ij d. et ob.

Hugo de Meriet' r.c. de xxv s. de eodem. In thes. lib. Et Q.E.

Hugo de Neovill' [*blank*] xxiiij m. et xj s.[3] et j d. de medietate feodorum de Curci de eodem scilicet de medietate xxiiij feodorum et dim. et tercia parte j feodi.

Idem Hugo [*blank*] xvj m. et dim. de medietate feodorum Willelmi le Meschin de eodem s[cilicet] de medietate de xvj feodis et dim.

1 The final *est* written very flamboyantly.

2 The final *est* also written flamboyantly.

3 *xj s.* written on alteration.

Margar' de Ripariis debet[1] xxiiij m. et xj s. et j d. de eodem de alia medietate feodorum de Curcy. *Set respondet in Oxon' in rotulo sequenti.*

Eadem M. debet xvj m. et dim. de (alia[1]) medietate feodorum Willelmi le Meschin de eodem. *Set respondet ibidem.*

Ricardus de Mucegros r.c. de lv li. pro Rogero de la Forde sicut continetur in rotulo viij. In thes. x li. Et debet xlv li.

Heres Willelmi de Wrotham debet respondere de exitibus staminarie Devon' et Cornub' de dim. anno xvij° R. J.

Henricus de Ortiaco et Sabina uxor eius [*blank*] pro relevio suo sicut continetur in rotulo precedenti.[2]

DE OBLATIS

Ricardus de Wrotham. r.c. de xl m. pro habenda saisina forestarie[3] sicut continetur in rotulo precedenti. In thes. x m. Et debet xxx m.

per annum x m.

Willelmus le Bret' [*blank*] x m. pro habenda assisa sicut continetur ibidem.

Idem Vic. r.c. de dim. m. de Willelmo de Germovill' pro licencia concordandi. Et de ij m. de Roberto Amaur' pro eodem. Et de ij m. de Abbate de Keinesham pro eodem. In thes. lib. Et Q.E.

Willelmus del Estr' r.c. de CC et quater xx et iij li. et j m. de ij debitis contentis in rotulo precedenti. In thes. iiij li. Et debet CC et lxxix li. et j m.

per annum vj m. quamdiu R. placuerit.

[*One line blank*]

DE PLACITIS FORESTE

Osbertus Bullepalle debet x s. pro defalta. Ranulfus Capellanus de Cnolle debet ij m. pro eodem. Elyas clericus de Chinnoc debet xx s. pro eodem. Johannes de Scalar' debet dim. m. pro transgressione.

Idem Vic. r.c. de x s. de Willelmo le Moinne pro transgressione. Et de iiij s. et viij d. de Willelmo Buche pro eodem. Et de iij m. de Willelmo Carbonel pro defalta. Et de xx s. de Simone de Cantelu pro eodem. Et de dim. m. de Thoma de Marisco. Et de j m. de Mauricio de Gandino. In thes. lib. Et Q.E.

Abbas de Alba Landa r.c. de j m. pro transgressione assise. In thes. dim. m. Et debet dim. m.

Henricus Caretarius r.c. de xl s. pro defalta. In thes. j m. Et debet ij m.

Hugo de Boullay r.c. de iij m. pro eodem. In thes. ij m. et dim. Et debet dim. m. Et dim. m. pro veteri vasto.

[*One line blank*]

DE MINUTIS PARTICULIS FORESTE EIUSDEM ITINERIS

Idem Vic. r.c. de liiij s. et vj d. de misericordiis hominum et villarum quorum nominibus proponitur littera *t* ante *d* litteram in rotulo quem B. de Insula liberavit in thesauro. In thes. lib. in xl taleis. Et Q.E.

[1] *debet* written out of alignment.

[2] This line is in heavier writing than those before it.

[3] *saisina forestarie* written clearly and in full.

Martinus de Middelton' r.c. de xij d. pro assarto. In thes. lib. Et Q.E.

[*Rot.* 14d *Mem.* 2]

+ Johannes de Lega debet xij d. pro eodem. + Reginaldus de Lega debet xij d. pro eodem. Walterus f. Ricardi debet ij s. pro eodem. Willelmus clericus de Dilinton' debet ij s. pro eodem. (+ⁱ) Emelota de Hescecumb' debet xij d. pro eodem. + Ricardus Longus debet xij d. pro eodem. + Adam de la Pille debet xij d. pro eodem. Adam prepositus debet xij d. pro eodem. + Willelmus Pilloc debet ij s. pro eodem. + Henricus de Langeford' debet xij d. pro eodem. + Thomas de Malling' debet xviij d. pro eodem.

Idem Vic. r.c. de dim. m. de Radulfo torto. Et de j m. de Galfrido de Fornell'. Et de dim. m. de Willelmo de Lucumb'. Et de dim. m. de Matheo de Linces. Et de dim. m. de Adam de Fernak'. Et[1] de dim. m. de Galfrido Blundo. In thes. lib. Et Q.[E.][2]

Hugo Sanzaveir (r.c.ᶜ) debet xl s. pro canibus habitis contra assisam.

Hugo de Meriet' r.c. de xxiij li. et ij s. et vj d. de debitis Judeorum. In thes. C s. Et debet xviij li. et ij s. et vj d. per annum C s.

Robertus de Blakeford r.c. de iiij m. de catallis Falkesíí. In thes. ij m. Et debet ij m.

[*One line blank*]

NOVA OBLATA

Henricus f. Ricardi [*blank*] xxxij m. et dim. pro relevio suo de sex parvis feodis et dim. de honore Mauritann' unde quodlibet feodum debet v m. reddendas infra ij^os annos videlicet viij m. et xx d. ad scaccarium [ad festum] Sancti Michaelis anno [x^o][3] et viij m. et xx d. ad scaccarium [ad festum] Pasch' anno xj^o. Et viij m. et xx d. ad scaccarium [ad festum] Sancti Michaelis anno eodem et viij m. et xx d. ad scaccarium [ad festum] Pasch' anno xij^o per plegium Godefridi de Crawecumb' et Hugonis Sanzaveir.

[*One line blank*]

Robertus de Cultura [*blank, with an obliteration*] ij m. et dim. pro relevio suo de tercia parte feodi j^us militis in Orcheleg' unde R. cepit homagium suum.

Huardus de Bickeleg' debet dim. m. pro licencia concordandi cum Margar' de Wodeton'. Eadem Margar' debet dim. m. pro eodem per plegium eiusdem Huardi. Willelmus de Eston' debet xx s. pro falso clamore versus Mauricium de Gandino per plegium Jordani de Bedeford'. Abbas de Keinesham debet j m. pro faciendo mentione in brevi suo de tempore Henrici R. avi. Galfridus de Fornell' debet dim. m. pro licencia concordandi cum Philippo Denebaud'.

Alexander de Dorset' r.c. de x m. pro dissaisina in itinere M. de

1 Thinner writing from *Et de* to the end of the line.

2 The *E* is under the reinforcing strip.

3 The figure is under the reinforcing strip, but may be inferred as *x*^o.

Pateshill’. In thes. nichil. Et episcopo Bathon’ x m. per libertatem carte Regis. Et Q.E.

Ricardus Luvel [*blank*] iij m. pro quietantia cuiusdam garcionis de cuius manu evaserunt leporarii et ceperunt j damam concelatam ipso Ricardo nesciente ut testatum fuit per Vic. et forestarios per plegium Willelmi de Draiton’.

Jordanus de Alnet’ [*blank*] xx s. pro bosco suo prostrato absque licencia scilicet de Etebere ante perambulationem per plegium Philippi Denebaud’.

Engelramus de Baden’ [*blank*] dim m. pro bosco suo rehabendo qui captus fuit in manu R.

Hubertus de Burgo r.c. de lx li. pro habenda quietantia de CCCC m. sicut continetur ex alia parte rotuli. In thes. nichil. Et in perdona ipsi Huberto lx li. per breve R. quod est in forulo marescalli. Et Q.E.[1]
[*Five lines blank*]

RESIDUUM LOND’ QUIA NON ERAT IBI LOCUS

t Walterus de Essex’ telarius debet dim. m. quia non habuit. *d* Sewalus vinitor debet dim. m. pro vino vendito. *d* Johannes Cisor debet j m. pro eodem. *d* Robinus de Lenn’ debet dim. m. pro eodem. *t* Andreas Bukerell’ et Johannes Travers tunc Vic. debent ij s. de catallis Edmundi barbur. (*t*[i]) Idem Vic. debent xij d. de villata de Kensinton’ de carrucagio. (*d*[i]) Et xvj s. de villatis de Keniton’ et Feltham de eodem. (*d*[i]) Andreas Bukerell’ et Johannes Travers tunc Vic. debent xx li. et x s. de firma ripe Regine de anno ix° de quibus infirmi hospitalis Sancti Egidii Lond’ debent habere xxx s. de elemosinis constitutis.

Willelmus Joynier [*blank*] lxxv[2] li. de firma Camb[er]langarie a festo annunciationis anno viij usque ad Natale domini[3] [*blank*] anni preteriti sicut continetur in rotulis vij° et viij°.

ITEM SUMERSET’

Osbertus G.[4] Giffard’ [*blank*] dim. m. ut scribatur in magno rotulo quod Robertus de Teaumes venit coram baronibus de scaccario et recognovit se dedisse et concessisse et carta sua confirmasse eidem Osberto pro homagio et servicio suo totum manerium suum de Teaumes cum omnibus pertinenciis suis et advocationem (ecclesie[i]) eiusdem manerii habendum et tenendum sibi et heredibus suis de se et heredibus suis libere et quiete integre plene pacifice et honorifice cum omnibus libertatibus in boscis …[5] et plano in viis et semitis in stagnis aquis molendinis in pratis pascuis et pasturis reddendo inde sibi et heredibus suis ipse et heredes sui vj d. ad Pasch’ pro omni exactione et demanda ad ipsum et heredes suos pertinente. Et quod predictus Osbertus et heredes sui faciant inde forinsecum

1 This line is written in fainter ink than the preceding lines.
2 *lxxv* written on an alteration.
3 *Natale domini* written on an alteration.
4 Initial *G.* written, then the whole word *Giffard.*
5 End of line cut away.

servicium capitali domino illius feodi. Et quod predictus Robertus et heredes sui predictum manerium de Teaumes cum omnibus pertinenciis suis et cum advocatione ecclesie predicto Osberto et heredibus suis vel cuicumque illud assignare voluerit contra omnes homines et feminas warantizabunt. Et quod pro hac donatione concessione et carte sue confirmatione dedit predictus Osbertus predicto Roberto l(v^{i}) m. argenti pre manibus.

[*The rest of the membrane is blank.*]

[*Endorsed*]
emend' totum satis
Dorsete Et Sumersete[1]

[*Rot.* 15 *Mem.* 1]

Rotulet 15 is damaged down the left hand side and 15d on the right. There are a number of accounts here and they are treated as though separate counties.
There is strengthening tape down both sides of the rotulet. Down the left hand side of rotulet 15 near the bottom there is some wearing which has taken some of the marginalia from the text.
[*Four lines blank*]

COMPOTUS WALTERI SUBSCRIPTI DE QUARTA PARTE ANNI DECIMI

Walterus Foliot ut custos r.c de xxvij s. de redditu assiso de ij molendinis apud Blockesham de termino Sancti (Michaelis^{c}) Martini anni x^{im}. Et de viij d. de redditu cuiusdam prati ibidem de eodem termino. Et de lxvij s. et j d. de redditu assiso eiusdem manerii de termino Natalis anno eodem. Et de x s. de finibus terrarum in eodem manerio. Et de v s. et ij d. et ob. de padnagio anno eodem. Summa C[2] et ix s. et xj d. et ob.

Idem r.c. de C et iiij s. de xxvj quarteriis frumenti ibidem venditis anno eodem. Et de xxxvij s. de ix quarteriis et dim. alterius[3] frumenti ibidem venditis. Et de xvij s. et iiij d. de viij quarteriis ordei ibidem venditis. Et de xxx s. de xviij quarteriis tremesii ibidem venditis. Et de v s. de iiij quarteriis avene ibidem venditis. Summa ix li. et j m. Summa summarum xv li. iij s. iij d et ob. In thes. nichil.

Et in quadam consuetudine que vocatur metschipe[4] ad blada congreganda xvij s. et iiij d. Et pro blado ad semen et alio suprascripto blado triturando ix s. et vj d. Et pro blado predicto ventilando xij d. Et in minutis expensis

1 There are three vertical dots after *Dorsete* and *Sumersete*.
2 There has been some rubbing out before and after this letter. There is a gap after this letter as though something was rubbed out after the remainder was written.
3 *alterius* written clearly and in full. 'A second batch of wheat'?
4 This is *medsipa* or the customary payment for mowing.

eiusdem manerii iiij d. infra predictum terminum. Et debet xiij li. et xv s. et iij ob. Set respondet infra in magna summa.

Idem r.c. de xxvj s. et viij d. de redditu assiso de Burmeton' membro de Wudestok' de termino Natalis (anni predicti[c]). Et de x s. et ij d. et ob. de teloneo de Wudestok' de eodem termino. Et de xx d. de placitis et perquisitis ibidem infra predictum terminum. Summa xxxviij s. et vj d. et ob. In thes. nichil. Et in expensis (cuiusdam[c]) servientis[1] ibidem infra predictum terminum xv s. ij d. et ob. Et debet xxiij s. et iiij d. Set respondet infra in magna summa.

Idem r.c. de xxxiij s. et[2] iiij d. de redditu assiso de Haneberg' membrus[3] de Wudestok' de predicto termino. Et de iiij s. et vj d. de padnagio ibidem. Et de x s. de placitis et perquisitis ibidem. Et de xxxj s. et iiij d. de viij quarteriis frumenti ibidem venditis. Et de xxix s. et iiij d. de xxij quarteriis avene ibidem venditis. Summa C et viij s. et vj d. In thes. nichil. Et in expensis (servientum[c]) eiusdem manerii infra predictum terminum xix d. Et debet C et vj s. et xj d. Set respondet infra in magna summa.

Idem r.c. de ij s. et ix d. (de ij s. et ix d.[c]) de redditu assiso de Hordlea membro de Wudestok' de eodem termino. Et de iiij s. et iiij d. de padnagio ibidem. Et de xij s. et vj d. de placitis et perquisitis ibidem infra predictum terminum. Et de xvj s. de iiij quarteriis frumenti ibidem venditis. Et de xij s. de ix quarteriis avene ibidem venditis. Summa xlvij s. et vij d. In thes. nichil. Et pro ij bobus emptis ad staurandas carrucas xiij s. Et in minutis expensis infra predictum terminum xj d. et ob. Et debet xxxiij s. et vij d. et ob. Set respondet ibidem.

Idem r.c. de iij s. et viij d. de redditu assiso de Stuntefeld' membro de Wudestok' de eodem termino. Et de xij s. de padnagio ibidem. Et de iiij s. de placitis et perquisitis ibidem infra predictum terminum. Et de v s. et iiij d. de iiij quarteriis avene ibidem venditis. Summa xxv s. In thes. nichil. Et pro j bove empto ad carrucam ibidem staurandam ix s. Et debet xvj s. Set respondet ibidem.

Idem r.c. de xix s. et vij d. et ob. de redditu assiso de Cumb' membro de Wudestok' de predicto termino. Et de vj s. de padnagio ibidem. Et de ix s. de placitis et perquisitis ibidem infra predictum terminum. Et de xiij s. et x d. de iij quarteriis et dim. frumenti ibidem venditis. Et de ix s. et iiij d. de vij quarteriis avene ibidem venditis. Summa lvij s. et ix d. et ob. In thes. nichil. Et in minutis expensis ibidem iij s. et ob. Et debet liiij s. et ix d. Respondet ibidem.

Idem (r.c. de[c]) (debet[i]) xv s. et viij d. de iij bobus de predictis maneriis venditis. Respondet cum (aliis debitis[i]). Summa omnium debitorum supra contentorum xxvj li. et v s. et v d. Set respondet in magno rotulo in Oxon' in compoto suo de quarta parte anni.

[*Two lines blank*]

f' Robertus de Laxinton' r.c. de C et xl li. de firma de alto Pecco de toto anno x°. In thes. quater xx et (vj[c]) (xij[i]) li. Et pro j caretata plumbi empta et

[1] There is a line over the last three letters perhaps as an attempt to alter the word to the plural *servientum*.

[2] *et* written over *d.*

[3] *membrus* written for *membro*.

carriata usque Noting' et liberata Willelmo f. Warini ad gutteras in castro de Noting' et in custo carragii xxviij s. per breve R. Et in defalta pasture de Fairfeld' quam abbas de Miris Vallibus habet usque in iiij annos sequentes x m. Et in defalta pasture de Mainstanesfeld' quam idem abbas[1] habet per eosdem iiij annos v m. sicut continetur in rotulo precedenti in Notingeham. Et in emendatione domorum in castro de Pecco iiij li. et xij s. Et debet xxxij li. Idem r.c. de eodem debito. In thes. lib. Et Q.E.

[*One line blank*]

(*f'*^d^) Idem R. r.c. de vj li. (de Henrico f. Ricardi^i^) de fine suo facto ut sit quietus de instauro sicut continetur in rotulo precedenti post Gloverniam. In thes. iiij li. Et debet xl s. Set respondet in Notingeh'.

f' Idem R. r.c. de xv li. de firma de Bolesor' de dim. anno ante quam traderetur Roberto de Banteshal' ad respondendum inde [*blank*]. In thes. viij li. Et in emendatione domorum in castro xlv s. Et in operatione cuiusdam coquine facte in eodem castro iiij li. et xv s. per breve R. Et Q.E.

[*Two lines blank*]

COMPOTUS DE BAEMBURG' DE ANNO IX ET X R.

Rogerus de Hodesac ut custos r.c. de lxiiij s. et vj d. de redditu assiso manerii[2] de Dominicis maneriis de Baemburg' de anno ix^{o}.

Idem r.c. de xlv s. de annuo redditu xxvij quarteriorum brasii venditorum de anno eodem.

Idem r.c. de vij li. et viij s. et vj d. de placitis et perquisitis et herbagiis et aliis proventibus anno eodem.

Idem r.c. de viij li. et ij s. de vj tonellis veteris vini venditis anno eodem.

Idem r.c. de xxviij li. xvj s. et viij d. de blado vendito de v^{o}[3] anno et vj^{o} et vij^{o} scilicet de quater xx et vij quarteriis et dim. frumenti.

Idem r.c. de xv li. et xij s. de C et iiij quarteriis (ordei^i^) eodem termino ibidem venditis.

Idem r.c. de lvj s. de xxviij quarteriis avene eodem termino ibidem venditis. Et iterum de iiij li. et viij s. de xlviij quarteriis avene eodem termino ibidem venditis.

Idem r.c. de xvij li. de ij decimis emptis anno vij^{o} pro xiiij li.

Idem r.c. de iiij li. et vij s. et viij d. de remanenti compoti precedentis. Summa omnium prescriptarum receptarum quater xx et xiiij li. et iiij d. In thes. nichil.

Et in reparatione turellorum et domorum in castro de Baemburg ix li. et xij s. et x d. et ob. per breve R. et per visum Willelmi f. Johannis et Radulfi Maille.

Et in stipendiis vj bubulcorum et j^{us} carettarii et precariis carrucarum et

1 The word *abbas* is repeated.
2 End of *manerii* altered and squashed in.
3 Altered from *vj*^{o}.

carris et caretis emptis et aliis necessariis expensis per totum annum l s. et iij d. Et debet quater xx[1] li. et xxxvij s. et ij d. et ob. (Set respondet infra.[i]) (Et debet[d])

Idem R. r.c. de lxiiij s. et vj d. de redditu assiso maneriorum de Dominicis de Baemburg' de anno x^{o}.

Idem r.c. de xlix s. et vj d. de annuo redditu xxviij quarteriorum brasii venditis de anno eodem.

Idem r.c. de iiij li. et vj s. et vj d. de placitis et perquisitis et herbagiis et aliis proventibus anno eodem.

Idem r.c. de xvj li. et iiij s. de liiij quarteriis frumenti octavi anni venditis ibidem.

Idem r.c. de x li. et x s. de lxvj quarteriis ordei anni viij ibidem venditis.

Idem r.c. de C et xvj s. de quater xx et vij quarteriis avene anni eiusdem ibidem venditis.

Idem r.c. de ix li. et ix s. de lxiij quarteriis ordei anni noni ibidem venditis.

Idem r.c. de viij li. de quater xx et xvj quarteriis avene anni eiusdem ibidem venditis.

Idem r.c. de lxxv s. de xv veteribus bobus ibidem anno x^{mo} ibidem venditis.

Idem r.c. de v s. et x d. de v coriis boum mortuorum anno eodem venditis.

Idem r.c. de quater xx et j li. et xvij s.[2] et ij d. et ob. de remanenti compoti. sui supra contenti. Summa omnium predictorum C et xlv li. xvij s. vj d. et ob. In thes. xl li. et vij s. et viij d.

Et in turri (de Baemburg'[i]) agistando et planchiando et plumbo cooperiendo cum turella iuxta cameram R. xliiij li. et xiij d. per breve R. et per visum Willelmi f. Johannis et Radulfi Maille.

Et Johanni Wascelin' constabulario de Baemburg xx m.[3] per breve eiusdem ad molendinum R. ibidem faciendum et stagnum vivarii reparandum.

Et iterum eidem Johanni xij m. per breve R. ad proficiendum ei C et xx m. quas percipit per annum pro custodia castri de Baemburg'.[4]

Et pro iiij tonellis vini emptis ad garnisturam castri de Baemburg' C et xij s. de quibus debet respondere.

Et in cartagio et carragio eiusdem vini á Berewic usque Baemburg' vij s.

Et pro duabus decimis emptis xvj li. de quibus debet respondere.

Et pro xx bobus emptis ad instaurandas carrucas viij li. et vj s. et viij d. de quibus debet respondere.

Et in stipendiis vj bubulcorum et j caretarii et precariis carrucarum et carris et caretis et aliis necessariis expensis per totum annum lix s. et vij d.

Et in quietantia terre prepositi per ij^{os} annos scilicet ix^{o} et x^{o} vj s. et

1 Erasure after *xx* and before *li.*
2 *xvij s.* written over an erasure.
3 The *xx m.* has been written over an erasure.
4 There is a symbol after this of an upside down cross.

ij d. Et debet vj li. et x s. et viij d. et ob. *Set*[1] *respondet in Northumbr' in rotulo xlv.*[2]

[*One line blank*]

Idem r.c. de CC et xxxj quarteriis[3] frumenti de exitu horreorum de iiij annis scilicet v, vj, vij et viij. De quibus C et xlj quarterii et dim. fuerunt venditi. De quorum precio idem R[ogerus] respondet supra.

Et xxxviij quarterii (et dim.[i]) seminati per predictum tempus. Et in sustentatione servientum a die assumptionis beate Marie anni vj usque ad diem Sancti Michaelis anni x^{mi} lj quarterii et j bussellus. (xxij^{d}) Et Q.E.

Idem r.c. de xxv quarteriis siliginis de exitu horreorum de predicto tempore quod totum expensum fuit in liberatione servientum per idem tempus. Et Q.E.

Idem r.c. de CCC et j quarteriis et dim. ordei de exitu horreorum de anno v^{o}, vj^{o}, vij^{o}, viij^{o} et ix^{o}. De quibus CC et xxxiij quarterii venditi fuerunt. De quorum precio respondet supra. Et lxviij quarterii et dim. seminati annis vj^{o}, vij^{o}, viij^{o}, ix^{o}, et x^{o}. Et Q.E.

Idem r.c. de M et DC et xxj quarteriis avene de exitu horreorum anno v^{o}, vj^{o}, vij^{o}, viij^{o} et ix^{o}. De quibus CCC et quater xx et xiij quarterii venditi fuerunt. De quorum precio respondet supra in ij^{bus} compotis. Et DCCC et quater xx et viij quarterii seminati anno v^{o}, vj^{o}, vij^{o}, viij^{o} et ix^{o}. Et in prebenda caretariorum et boum per idem tempus C et xlviij quarterii. Et in farrina ad opus servientum per idem tempus C et quater xx et xij quarterii. Et Q.E.

Idem r.c. de CC et lx sperdutis ferri et dim. garba asceri de remanenti compoti precedentis que omnes expense sunt in necessariis expensis domus et carrucarum per predictum tempus. Et Q.E.

Idem debet respondere de frumento anni ix. Et de toto blado anni x^{mi}.

[*Two lines blank*]

COMPOTUS WINDLESOR' Á FESTO SANCTI MICHAELIS ANNI VIIJ USQUE AD FESTUM SANCTI MICHAELIS ANNI X

f' Hubertus de Burgo Ranulfus Britto pro eo (ut custos^{c}) r.c. de xxvj li.[4] de firma de Windlesor'. In thes. nichil.

Et in liberatione constituta Willelmo Barbette lx s. et x d. ad custodiam domorum R. de Windlesor'. Et eidem x s. ad pannos. Et capellano de Windlesor' xxx s. et v d. Et Ricardo de Siffrewast pro escambio terre sue xij s. Et monialibus de Bromhal' xxx s. et v d. per breve R. Et infirmis de Windles'or vij s. et vij d. et quadrans. Et procuratori vineé xxx s. et v d.

Idem r.c. de xxvj li. de eadem firma de anno preterito. In thes. nichil.[5] Et

[1] This sentence is written in a different hand possibly in 1261/2. See n. 2 below.

[2] This is written in a totally different hand. Rotulus *xlv* Henry III is 1261/2.

[3] There is a gap from this word to the next of about 4–5 cms with a line indicating continuity as the next word is in keeping with what would be normal text. See above for a similar text.

[4] This is the same amount owing as in *NS 54*, p. 234, presumably the set annual farm.

[5] There is a large gap between this word and the beginning of the next sentence on

in liberatione et elemosina constituta sicut supra continetur ix li. et xx d. Et in liberatione Radulfi Tirel constabularii de Windles' qui habuit per diem ij s., lxiij li. et x(vij^{i}) s. et vj(d^{i}) de j anno integro ix^{o} et tribus partibus anni x^{mi}. Et in liberatione ij^{orum} militum in eodem castro moram facientium per idem tempus quorum uterque habuit per diem xij d., lxiij li. et x(vij^{i}) s. et vj d. Et in liberatione j servientis equitis qui habuit per diem vj d. et j^{us} alterius servientis equitis qui similiter habuit per diem vj d. per idem tempus xxxj li. et xviij s. et ix

[*Rot.* 15 *Mem.* 2]

d. per breve R. Et in liberatione j portarii cum garcione suo qui habuit per diem iiij^{or} d. per idem tempus, x li. et xij s. et xj d. Et in liberatione vj balistariorum peditum in eodem castro morantium per idem tempus quorum quilibet habet per diem iij d. et ob., lv li. et xvij s. et ix d. et ob. per breve eiusdem. Et in liberatione iiij^{or} vigilum quorum quilibet habet per diem iij ob., xv li. et xix (s.^{i}) et iiij d. et ob. per idem tempus per breve eiusdem. Et in expensis Johannis de Borden' clerici de castro qui habuit per diem xij d., xxxj li. et xviij[1] s. et ix d. per idem tempus per breve eiusdem. Et habet de superplus CC et xl li. et v s. et xj d. quod totum locatur ei infra.

Idem r.c. de C et xlvj li. de warda debita castro de Windlesor' de anno ix^{o} et x^{o} scilicet de lxxiij militibus quorum quilibet debet per annum xx s. In thes. nichil. Et Willelmo Maudoit xviij li. et v s. pro custodia castri de Windlesor' per quartam parte de anni x^{mi} (et xv dies^{i}). Et in defalta eiusdem warde de Roberto de Pinkeinni qui fecit wardam suam in castro per v quarentenas vij li. et xv s. Et Amalrico de parco ad operationem castri C et iiij s. per breve R. de quibus debet respondere. Et in perdona Willelmo de Siffrewast dim. m. de warda sua quia habuit in exercitu de Mungumeri et de Bedef' cum R. per breve R. Et in custo posito in militibus et servientibus apud Windles' tempore obsidionis de Bedef' C s. per breve eiusdem. Et debet C et ix li. et ix s. et iiij d. *Et respondet infra.*

Idem r.c. de C et xx li. de firma de Cokham et Bray de anno ix. Et de C et xx li. de eadem firma de anno x^{mo}. Et de xxv li. et ix s. et iiij d. et ob. de remanenti compoti sui de anno viij. Et iterum de vj li. (et ij s. et ix d.^{i}) de remanenti compoti bladi ibidem de anno eodem. In thes. nichil. Et in superplus quod habet supra CC et xl li. et v s. et xj d. Et debet xxxj li. et vj s. et ij d. et ob. Et respondet infra.

Idem r.c. de xxxv li. et[2] iiij s. bl. de firma de Odiham de anno ix^{o}. Et de xxxv li. et iiij s. bl. de eadem firma de anno x^{mo}. Summa[3] lxx li. et viij s. bl. qui sunt ei extensi ad lxxij li. et ix s. num. In thes. liij li. Et debet xix li.et ix s. *Et*[4] *Cix li. ix s. iiij d. de alio debito supra. Et xxxj li. vj s. ij d. ob. de alio debito ibidem. Summa Clx li. iiij s. vj d. ob. Et respondet infra.*

---

the same line.

[1] Clerk actually wrote *xvijj*.

[2] This is written over an erasure.

[3] Diagonal downstroke in the abbreviation of *Summa*.

[4] From *Et* to the end of this line written in a different hand, probably later.

Idem r.c. de xiiij li. et xvj s. num. de cremento eiusdem ville de anno ix^{o}. Et de xiiij li. et xvj s. num. de eodem cremento de anno x^{mo}. In thes. nichil. Et Philippo de Pery militi constabulario de Odiham per totum annum ix^{num} pro liberatione sua qui habuit per diem xviij d., xxvij li. et vij s. et vj d. Et ij^{bus} servientibus equitibus ibidem commorantibus per idem tempus quorum quilibet habuit per diem vj d., xviij li. et v s. per breve R. Et in liberatione j^{us} vigilis et portarii et parcarii quorum quilibet habuit per diem ij d., ix li. et ij s. et vj d. per breve eiusdem per idem tempus. Et Ade de Bendeng' pro custodia eiusdem castri per totum annum x^{mum} x m. per breve eiusdem. Et in emendatione palicii circa turrim de Odiham et reparatione camini eiusdem turris vij li. et v s. et ob. per breve R. et per visum Roberti Nigri et Roberti f. Rogeri. Et in turri de Odiham discóóperiendo et eodem plumbo et alio plumbo cóóperiendo quod missum fuit ibidem per Vic. de Suhant' iiij li. et iij s. per breve eiusdem et per visum eorundem. Et in emendatione domorum et grangiarum in castro de Odiham ij m. Et habet de superplus xliiij li. et xj s. et ob. *quod*[1] *totum locatur ei infra.*

Hubertus de Burgo r.c. de Clx li. iiij s. vj d. ob. de pluribus debitis contentis supra. In thes. nichil. Et in superplus proximo supra xliiij li. xj s. ob. Et debet Cxv li. xiij s. vj d.

[*Six lines blank*]

[2] Willelmus de Culeworðe Vic. Essex' ut custos r.c. de xxiiij li. et viij s. et ij d. de redditu assiso manerii de Writel' de toto anno. Et de xl d. de novo cremento firme. Et de xj li. et vj s. et v d. de operationibus eiusdem manerii positis ad firmam. Et de lx s. de exitu (fori^{i}) eiusdem manerii. Et de iiij li. et xj s. et x d. de placitis et perquisitis et releviis. Et de vj li. et xvj s. et ix d. et ob. de padnagio et herbagio. Et de C s. et iiij d. de herbagio de Horsfrith. Et de xxv s. et viij d. de Wardiscot. Et de viij s. et (iij^{c}) (vj^{i}) d. et ob. de coriis iij boum et j vacce ibidem venditis. Et de xvij s. et vj d. de tribus veteribus ibidem venditis. (Et^{i}) de corio j affri et j vituli ibidem venditis (xviij d.^{i})[3] Et de xxxiij s. de caseo et butiro venditis. Et[4] de lxiij li. et viij s. et ix d. de CC et liij quarteriis et iij^{bus} estrecis[5] frumenti venditis scilicet v s. pro quarterio. Et de xxiiij li. et xv s. de CC et quater xx et xvij quarteriis avene venditis scilicet [unus] quarterius pro xx d. Summa C et xlvij li. et vj s. et x d. In thes. C et xxvj li. xiiij s. viij d. et ob. Et pro vj affris emptis ad carrucas ibidem instaurandas lj s. et vj d. et ob. Et pro j bove empto ix s. et x d. Et pro ferro et ascero et ferrura affrorum per totum annum xxvj s. et ij d. Et in custo posito ad precarias hyemales iiij s. et v d. Et pro terra hercianda xix s. et ix d. Et in reparatione aule R. ibidem et fossatis faciendis ante aulam v s. et viij d. Et pro sale et aliis minutis rebus ad dayariam necessariis ij s. Et in emendatione et augmentatione j

1 From *quod* to the end of the line and the next line written in a different hand.
2 The left edge of the membrane from here on to the end of the membrane is very worn and torn in places. Any marginalia are impossible to determine.
3 The amount is normally placed after *Et de*... at the beginning of a sentence.
4 A very elaborately written version of '*Et*'. There are others in the membrane of a similar nature.
5 Corrected from *estrecs*.

grangie apud Boyton' xxviij s. et vj d. Et pro ij^bus^ carris [et] ij^bus^ caretis vij s. et vij d. Et in bladis metendis colligendis et carriandis et precariis in autumpno vj li. v s. et viij d. Et in expensis servientis custodis manerii per totum annum iiij li. et xj s. scilicet per diem iij d. Et in stipendiis eiusdem servientis cum homine suo et equo suo per totum annum xx s. Summa expense xix li. et xij s. et iij ob. Et Q.E.

Idem Vic. ut custos r.c. de x li. et v s. et j d. de redditu assiso manerii de Neuport. Et de x li. de mercato posito ad firmam. Et de iij s. et viij d. de wardpani. Et de ix li. de exitu molendinorum. Et de lx s. de placitis et perquisitis. Et de xiij s. de herbagio. Et de vj s. de j veteri bove vendito. Et de v d. de corio j affri. Et de ix li. de xxvj quarteriis frumenti venditis scilicet pro quarterio v s. Et de xvj s. de[1] iiij quarteriis de coraille venditis scilicet pro quarterio iiij s. Et de xix s. et ij d. de[2] v quarteriis ordei venditis scilicet quarterius pro xlvj d. Et de vj li. et x s. de lxxviij quarteriis avene venditis scilicet quarterius pro xx d. Summa l li. et j m. In thes. xlv li. et xx d. [Et][3] pro j bove empto x s. et j d. Et pro ferro et ascero et ferratura affrorum per totum annum ix s. viij d. et ob. Et in emendatione grangie xvj s. ix d. et ob. Et in custo posito in precariis autumpnalibus et hyemalibus xxij s. et vij d. et ob. Et pro terra hercianda xij d. Et in blado sarclando iiij s. et iij d. Et pro ix quarteriis et dim. frumenti triturandis xj d. et ob. Et in consuetudinibus ad prata falcanda et levanda ij s. et ij d. Et in custo posito ad j pilloricum faciendum in foro xij d. Et in blado metendo et carriando et tassando in grangia xxviij s. Et in emendatione stagni molendinorum x s. Summa expense C et vj s. et vij d. Et debet v s. et j d.

[*One line blank*]

Willelmus Briewerr' senior Laurentius de Burton' ut custos pro eo r.c. de xx li. et vj s. et j d. de redditu assiso manerii de Bolesor' de anno ix^o^ (cum redditu molend'^i^). Et de xij li. et xiij d. de xlvj quarteriis et dim. frumenti ibidem venditis. Et de x li. et x s. et vj d. de placitis et perquisitis. Et de xxxj s. et vj d. de padnagio et herbagio hoc anno. Summa xliiij li. et ix s. et ij d. In thes. xxj li. Et pro ferramento carrucarum et affrorum et bladis sarclandis et metendis et in precariis autumpnalibus et stipendiis servientis[4] per totum annum et aliis necessariis (epis^d^) expensis manerii lxxv s. et iiij d. Et pro v quarteriis ordei emptis ad seminandum xvij s. et viij d. et ob. Et pro[5] et[6] xviij quarteriis avene emptis ad seminandam C et xiij s. et j d. Et debet xiij li. et iij s. et ob. Idem r.c. de eodem debito. In thes. nichil. Et in liberatione ipsius Laurencii et ij^orum^ garcionum suorum et j^us^ vigilis (et j^us^ portarii^i^) et j^us^ prepositi et j^us^ servientis custodientis boscum et wainnagium quorum quilibet habet per diem j d. per predictum tempus x li. et xij s. et xj d. per breve R. Et debet l s. et j d. Idem r.c. de eodem debito. In thes. lib. Et Q.E.

1 *de* written over *pro*.
2 *de* written over a *p*.
3 There is something written before *pro*, probably *Et*.
4 A hole in the membrane after this word but the clerk has worked around it.
5 This is at the end of the right hand edge of the membrane and there may be something written at the beginning of the next line which cannot be made out.
6 The *et* might be superfluous.

[Et] sciendum quod Robertus de Laxinton' debet respondere de blado eiusdem anni quod recepit de predicto Laurencio sicut dicit scilicet l quarter' frumenti per estimationem hominum ville. Et xj quarter' ordei. Et CCC quarter' avene. Et de terra seminata de vj quarteriis frumenti et similiter de xxxiiij bobus de instauro. Idem r.c. de eodem debito. In thes. nichil. *Et*[1] *in terra de dominico seminanda a xv diebus post festum Sancti Michaelis anno viij*° *usque in xv dies post Pasch' sequens anno ix*° *xxiij quarter' frumenti. Et in eadem terr*[2] *terra seminanda de dominico vii quarter' et dim. de ordeo. Et in eadem terra seminanda de avena C et lxix quarter'. Et tantam terram (ita*ⁱ*) seminatam reddet Roberto de Tatheshall' quando dimittet castrum. Residuum huius compoti require infra.*[3]

COMPOTUS (OPERATIONISⁱ) CASTRI DOVOR' Á DIE SANCTI PANCRACII[4] ANNO R. X° USQUE IN CRASTINO SANCTI BENEDICTI[5] IN MARTIO ANNO XJ° EIUSDEM *UTRAQUE DIE COMPUTATA*[6]

[7] …s de Nereford' et Joscelinus Doy r.c. de[8] DCC m. quas receperunt de thesauro per plures vices infra predictum terminum. In thes. iij d. et ob. Et in operatione nove turris in fossato iuxta portam -euerell'[9] et emptionibus maremii et plumbi et carriagio sabuli et aque lapidum et calcis empte et plurium aliorum necessariorum ad eandem operationem et stipendiis (js^{d}) custodum dicte operationis et cementariorum et aliorum operatorum in fossato DC et quater xx et xix m. et xiij s. et ob. Et Q.S.

COMPOTUS PETRI F. HERBERTI DE RECEPTIS SUIS DE FIRMIS DE EVERWIKES' CONTENTIS IN ROTULO DE ANNO VIIJ° R. PER PARTES

[Idem] r.c. de C et xlv li. iiij s. et iij d. bl. de predictis firmis bl. extensis ad C et lij li. ix s. et vj d. num. Et de CC et lix li. et vj s. et v d. de receptis suis de firmis numero …[10] comitatus de dim. anno xvj° et dim. anno xvij°

1 From here to the end of the section appears to be written in a different hand.
2 Uncertain reading.
3 There is a mark after this word that looks like a capital E with an elongated centre stroke with two dots on either side of the centre stroke, probably a recognition mark to find where this item should have been or where it continues.
4 Tuesday 12 May 1226.
5 Monday 22 March 1227.
6 The last three words were probably added later.
7 The left hand side now becomes very worn and often the first word is almost impossible to read as in this case.
8 *de* repeated.
9 This might be *Peuerell'* for Peverell.
10 There is something prior to *comitatus* which is at the left hand side of the membrane and is very rubbed.

R. J. Summa CCCC et xj li. xv s. et xj d. In thes. nichil. Et ipsi Petro pro custodia castrorum de Eboraco et Pikering' et Pontis Fracti comitatus Ebor' per predictum tempus et pro bono et fideli servicio suo prestito R. J. et ipsi R. tempore guerre CCCC et xj li. et xv s. et xj d. per breve R.
Et Q.E.

[*One line blank*][1]

[Idem] r.c. de xxvij s. et vj d. de catallis plurium. In thes nichil. Et ipsi P. ut predictum est xxviij s. et vj d. per predictum breve. Et Q.E.

[*One line blank*]

COMPOTUS MANERII DE BLOCKESHAM DE TRIBUS PARTIBUS ANNI DECIMI SCILICET DE MEDIETATE MANERII

[God]efridus de Crawecumb' Robertus de Haya ut custos r.c. de x li. et v s. et v d. de redditu assiso eiusdem manerii de predicto termino preter redditum de ij^{bus} molendinis qui semper redditur in termino Sancti Martini. Et de ij s. et ix [d.] de denariis Sancti Petri hoc anno. Et de xviij s. et viij d. et ob. de ramis spinarum venditis pro emendatione pasture. Et de ij s. et xj d. de herbagio vendito. Et de lxij s. de finibus et perquisitis. Et de dim. m. de fine cuiusdam mes...[2] anno. Et de viij s. et xj d. de iij quarteriis ordei venditis. Et de v s. et vj d. de j bove vendito. Et de ij s. de j veteri affro vendito. Summa (xiiij^{c}) (xv^{i}) li. et xiiij s. et x d. et ob. In thes. nichil.

[Et in] operatione cuiusdam domus de novo facte xxxij s. et iiij d et ob. Et in operatione cuiusdam porte et pro ferruris et aliis minutis et necessariis emptionibus iij s. et v d. et ob. Et pro operatione ij^{arum} carrucarum et ferro et ascero et aliis ...is[3] ad (expensas^{c}) carrucas vij s. et ob. Et pro j quarterio avene empto et ibidem seminato xvj d. Et pro furragio empto ad sustentationem boum et affrorum x s. et iiij d. Et in bladis metendis et colligendis et precariis [autumpn]alibus xv s. et vj d. Et in liberatione et stipendiis j^{us} servientis custodis manerii ix s. et iij d. Et pro j bove empto loco alterius venditi ix s. Summa iiij li. et viij s. et iij d. et ob. Et debent xj li. vj s. et ... Set respondent infra.

[Idem r.c.] de xxxiiij s. et iij d. de redditu assiso burgi de Wudestok' de toto anno. Et de C et viij s. et x d. et ob. de redditu assiso de Haneberg' membro de Wudestok' de iij^{bus} partibus anni. Et de lxx s. et vj d. de redditu assiso de [Cu]mb' membro de Wudestok' de eodem termino. Et de xix s. iij d. et ob. de redditu assiso de Stuntesfeld' membro de Wudestok' de eodem termino. Et de xxxj s. et ij d. de redditu assiso Hordlé membro de Wudestok' de eodem termino. Et de ...[4] et j m. de redditu assiso de

1 There is a PRO stamp which starts on this line and overlaps the next three lines.

2 The word is split over two lines and the right hand margin of the second line is extremely rubbed, perhaps *mesuagii*.

3 The beginning part of this word is illegible, perhaps *necessariis*, or *expensis*, which may be the reason for the crossed out *expensas*.

4 This missing word or number is at the extreme left hand side of the membrane and is considerably rubbed.

Bernintonʼ membro de Wudestokʼ de eodem termino. Et de ij s. de redditu assiso Otuelʼ de Esthalʼ pro j herbario faciendo. Summa redditus assisi xvij li. et xix s. v d. In thes nichil.

[*One line blank*]

...[1] de xliiij s. et v d. de teloneo et finibus et perquisitis de burgo de Wudestokʼ de toto anno. Et de vj li. et ij d. de finibus et perquisitis de Haneberge de tribus partibus anni. Et de ix li. et ix d. de finibus et perquisitis de Cumbʼ de eodem termino. Et de vj li. et xviij d. de finibus et perquisitis de Stuntesfeldʼ de eodem termino. Et de xxiij s. et viij d. de finibus et perquisitis de Hordle de eodem termino. Et de xviij s. de iiij quarteriis et dim. frumenti venditis apud Hanebergʼ. Et [de] ... s. vj d. de iij quarteriis frumenti venditis apud Cumbʼ. Et de ix s. et iij d. de ij^{bus} affris venditis. Et de iij s. de iij^{bus} coriis boum venditis. Et de xxx s. et xj d. et ob. de herbagio vendito per maneria. Summa xxviij li. iij s. et ij [d.] et ob. Summa summarum recepte preter redditum assisum xlvj li. ij s. vij d. et ob. In thes. nichil.

...o empto per maneria predicta xl s. Et pro ferro et ascero ad carrucas et in stipendiis fabrorum fabricantium ferramenta carrucarum infra predictas iij partes anni xix s. et v d. et ob. Et in reparatione domorum per maneria et pro plaustris ... et [a]liis necessariis emptionibus per predicta maneria infra predictum tempus xvij s. et ij d. Et in stipendiss[2] ix bubulcorum per predicta maneria (de toto anno[i]) et j caretarii per dim. annum et iij messorum xxxix s. et viij d. Et in emptione boum ... ad emendationem carrucarum lxiij s. Et pro pratis falcandis per maneria xiiij s. et v d. Et item in pratis falcandis et levandis infra parcum de Wudestokʼ ad sustentationem ferarum xxj s. et xj d. Et pro vj quarteriis ... emptis et seminatis apud Hordlea x s. Et in gurgitibus et[3] vivariorum apud Wudestokʼ et sagenis emendandis vij s. et iij d. Et in expensis servientis custodis manerii de Wudestokʼ xxvij s. et (viij[c]) (xj[i]) d. et ob.

... li. et x d. Et debet xxxiij li. et xxj d. et ob. Et preterea xj li. et vj s. et vij d. sicut supra continetur. Summa summarum debitarum xliiij li. viij s. iiij d. et ob. Set respondet in magno rotulo in Oxonʼ.

... li. et viij s. et iij denarʼ de exitu ville de Littlemorʼ de predictis tribus partibus anni. In thes. nichil. Et debet xj li. et viij s. et iij d. Set respondet in magno rotulo ibidem.

[*One line blank*]

[4]... *in custo posito in viij carrucariis (pascendis*[c]*) et duobus caretariis et tribus herciatoribus et uno serviente et homine suo et portario et homine suo et uno vigili et uno coco et pistore pascendis per predictum tempus xx(iij*[c]*)(viij) quarterʼ [fru]menti et iiij quarteria ordei. Et in equis*

[1] Probably *Idem r.c.* but the membrane is torn and extremely rubbed at this point. This continues down the rest of the left hand side of the membrane until the end of this side.

[2] *stipendiss* written for *stipendiis*.

[3] *et* written in error.

[4] The next three lines are written in a different hand of a later date.

carretariis et (A—is)[1] *Afris et equo servientis et bobus pascendis per predictum tempus C et (xx^d) (xxx^i) quarteria avene per breve R. Et Q.E.*

Robertus[2] *de Catheshall' debet respondere de xxiiij bobus de instauro manerii de Bolesoures quos recepit de Roberto de Lexinton'.*[3]

[*Rot.* 15d *Mem.* 1]

There is strengtening tape down the right hand side of the membrane. As it goes down the membrane it gradually obscures more and more of the text.

COMPOTUS THOME DE CYRECESTR' DE TOTO ANNO X°

Thomas de Cyrecestr' r.c. de xl li. de firma burgi de Berchhamsted'. Et de xxvj li. et viij s. et x d. et ob. de redditu assiso halimoti extra burgum. Et de lxj li. et vij s. et iiij d. et ob. de redditu assiso manerii de Hamelhamsted'. Et de viij li. de firma de Audebir'.[4] Summa C et xxxv li. et xvj s. et iij d.

Idem T. r.c. de xvj li. de relevio Willelmi de Abrincis et Hawis' de Bovill'. Et de xiij s. de placitis et perquisitis de Audebir' dum fuit in manu R. antequam redderetur Willelmo de Abrincis. Et de iiij li. et xvj s. et x (d.^i) de placitis et perquisitis halimoti de Berchamsted' de toto anno. Et de vij li. et xiiij s. et j d. de placitis et perquisitis[5] halimoti de Hamelhamsted'. Et de vij li. vj s. et viij (d.^i) de visu francoplegii manerii de Berchamsted'. Et de xxiiij s. et vj d. de herbagio vendito de Hamelhamsted'. Et de ij s. de ij^bus coriis affrorum venditis apud Hamelhamsted'. Et de x li. de firma de Roking'ham et ballia de Norhantes' pertinente ad Berchamsted'. Et de xiiij li. et xv s. et v d. de veteri bosco vendito apud Berchamsted'. Summa totius recepte C et quater xx li. et viij li. et viij s. et ix d.

Idem r.c. de xlix li. et iij s. et xj d. et ob. de molendino fulerez de Hamelhamsted'. Et de vij li. et viij s. et iij d. de xxx quarteriis bladi venditis de exitu molendini de Berchamsted'. Et de ix li. et viij s. et v d. de xlij quarteriis bladi de exitu molendini de Hamelhamsted' venditis. Summa lxvj li. et vij d. et ob.

Idem r.c. de xx li. de firma de Wintreslawe membro de Berchamsted'. Summa totius recepte CC et quater xx et iiij li. et ix s. et iiij d. et ob. In thes. CC et v li. et iij s. et ob.

Et in ferratura xxiiij affrorum et ferramento iiij carrucarum apud Berchamsted' per totum annum iiij li. Et in ligatura j carete nove ferro ligate et emendatione alterius veteris carette ix s. et ij d. Et pro j equo

1 The crossing out is through the middle of the word and the line is very thick making some of the letters difficult to make out.

2 This is very indistinct but it is just possible to see *Rob'*.

3 There is a pencilled '15' in the middle of the next line.

4 See *Calendar of Fine Rolls*, II, 1224–34, p. 78, no. 125 where Thomas is ordered to take the manor of Aldbury in Hertfordshire into the king's hands.

5 Erasure after *perquisitis*.

caretario et vij affris emptis ibidem lxxiij s. et iiij d. Et pro v molis emptis quarum iiij sunt apud Berchamsted' et j apud Hamelhamsted' lxvj s. et iiij d. Et in emendatione molendinorum ad bladum apud Berchamsted' et Hamelhamsted' et operatione j^us^ novi molendini apud Berchamsted' lxxiiij s. et iij d. Et in operatione magni pontis castri de Berchamsted' et emendatione horrei in castro de Berchamsted' vj li. et iij s. et x d. (et ob.ⁱ) per breve R. et per visum Rogeri f. Walteri et Willelmi de Amiens. Et pro bla(n^c^)do triturando et ventilando xij s. et vj d. Et in emptione et reparatione minutorum utensilium necessariorum in autumpno xxij s. et v d. et ob. Et in pratis falcandis et levandis et bladis sarclandis metendis colligendis et ceteris necessariis ad precarias autumpnales lxx s. Et in emendatione molendini fulerez et carriagio busche et emptione plumbi ad calefaciendam aquam in molendino et reparatione stagni xlij s. et viij d. Et in ferratura ij^orum^ equorum caretariorum portantium pannos et arzill[um] ad molendinum j m. Et pro ferratura ij^arum^ caretarum ad idem faciendum xvj s. Et pro clavis ad emendandas predictas caretas et alio hernasio necessario ad easdem caretas xv s. Et pro xlv quarteriis avene et dim. emptis ad prebendam predictorum caretariorum per totum annum lxxv s. et x d. Et pro vj quarteriis bladi emptis ad liberationem j servientis caretarii xxiij s. et x d. Et in stipendiis eiusdem v s. et viij d. Et[1] in stipendiis viij carrucariorum et j^us^ portarii et j^us^ caretarii et j^us^ ancille in castro predicto xxj s. et vj d. Et in stipendiis j forestarii bedelli et prepositi xj s. et x d. Et in stipendiis ij^orum^ vigilum j m. Et in victualibus et expensis constabularii et clerici et armigeri sui et iiij^or^ garcionum eorum et j capellani et clerici sui ministrantium in[2] castro et ij^orum^ vigilum et j prepositi et j^us^ servientis itinerantis circa wainnagium de Hamelhamsted' et j^us^ clavigeri et j^us^ coci et j^us^ forestarii cum garcione suo et j portarii et j^us^ ancille et j^us^ portarii et j^us^ caretarii xxviij li. et xiiij s. et v d. et ob. Et in vestitura constabularii et clerici sui et subconstabularii et senescalli de Hamelhamsted' et portarii et forestarii C s. Et in ferramento et ferrura ij carrucarum apud Hamelhamsted' et xij affrorum et j^us^ equi caretarii et in emendatione domorum et sepium et aliis minutis expensis contra autumpnum et bladis metendis et colligendis et precariis autumpnalibus et fenis falcandis et colligendis et blado triturando et in stipendiis iiij^or^ carrucariorum prepositi forestarii et bedelli et j^us^ ancille et in expensis eorundem in autumpno vij li et xj d. et ob. Et Q.E.

Idem r.c. de quater xx et viij quarteriis et dim. et ij bussellis frumenti de exitu grangie de Berchamsted' de quibus lxxvj quarterii et dim. (et iij busselliⁱ) fuerunt ibidem seminati. Et in expensis et victualibus predictorum commorantium in castro xij quarterii. Et Q.E.

Idem T. r.c. de CC et lxviij quarteriis et dim. avene de exitu horrei eiusdem manerii de quibus C quarterii et dim. fuerunt ibidem seminati. Et xvij quarterii et dim. et ij busselli positi fuerunt in prebenda j^us^ equi caretarii in castro per totum annum. Et in prebenda xxiiij affrorum de carrucis eiusdem manerii per totum annum quater xx et xj quarterii. Et in

[1] *Et* is repeated at the end of one line of text and at the beginning of the following line.

[2] Looks as though this is written over the Tironian *et* and a *j*.

prebenda equorum constab[ularii] et aliorum equitum commorantium in castro liij quarterii. Et in farrina necessaria ad opus predicte familie per idem tempus vj quarterii et ij busselli. Et Q.E.

Idem r.c. de quater xx et xiiij quarteriis frumenti de exitu grangie de Hamelhamsted' de quibus xlvij quarterii et dim. fuerunt ibidem seminati. Et in victualibus j^us servientis manerii iij quarterii. Et xliij quarterii et dim. missi apud Berchamsted' ad sustentationem familie in castro. Et Q.E.

Idem r.c. de C et xlviij quarteriis et iij bussellis avene de exitu horrei eiusdem manerii de quibus l quarterii fuerunt ibidem seminati. Et in prebenda xij affrorum et j^us equi caretarii ibidem per totum annum lxv quarterii et ij busselli. Et in prebenda equi servientis manerii xviij quarteria. Et xv quarterii et j busselli missi apud Berchamsted' ad sustentationem equorum ibidem. Et Q.E.

Idem r.c. de C et vj quarteriis bladi de exitu molendinorum de Berchamsted' preter decimam de toto anno de quibus lxxvj quarteria expensi fuerunt in victualibus viij carrucariorum et j bedelli et j portarii et j^us curtillarii ibidem per predictum tempus. Et xxx quarteria venditi de quorum precio respondet supra. Et Q.E.

Idem r.c. de lxvj quarteriis bladi et j bussello de exitu molendinorum de Hamelhamsted' de quibus xxiiij quarteria et j bussellus expensi fuerunt in victualibus iiij carrucariorum et j caretarii et j^us herciatoris et j ancille ibidem. Et xlij quarteria venditi de quorum precio respondet supra. Et Q.E.

[*One line blank*]

f' Idem Thomas r.c. de xiij li. et ix s. de redditu assiso civitatis Exon' preter elemosinam constitutam quam prior et canonici Sancte Trinitatis Lond' percipiunt ibidem. In thes. lib. Et Q.E.

f' Idem r.c. de lx li. de firma de Kenton'. Et de xx li. de firma de Maumesbir'. In thes. lib. Et Q.E.

f' Idem r.c. de vij li. de firma de Ailricheston'[1] et de Wica[2] preter terram Alienore contentam in rotulo precedenti. In thes. lib. Et Q.E.

f' Idem r.c. de xl li. de firma de Wilton'. In thes. xxxvj li. Et leprosis extra burgum Wilton' iiij li. Et Q.E.

f' Idem r.c. de xlj li. de firma ripe Regine in Lond'. Et de xx li. et x s. de remanenti eiusdem firme de anno preterito. In thes. xxxviij li. Et in elemosinis constitutis infirmis hospitii Sancti Egidii extra Lond' xxx s. de dim. anno preterito. Et eisdem xxx s. de dim. anno huius anni. Et debet xx li. et x s. de quibus cives Lond' debent respondere de (primo^d) (ultimo^i) dim. anno (I^d) anni preteriti.

[*One line blank*]

f' Idem r.c. de xxx li. bl. de firma ville Ivelcestr'. In thes. xviij li. et xviij s. et vij d. et ob. bl. Et Johanni Daco vj li. et x s. in Haiwarderia et Hechinge. Et eidem Johanni xl s. in molendino de Ivelcestr'. Et in hundredo de

[1] In *NS 54*, p. 254 this place is shown as *Ailrichescot'* and indexed as in South Tawton in Devon.

[2] In *NS 54*, p. 304 it is shown as 'Greatweek [in Chagford], Dev,'. This place cannot be found in or near Chagford but there is a hamlet called Week in Devon midway between Tiverton and Barnstable.

Lestane[1] quod Vic. habet xl s. Et debet xxj s. et x d. et ob. bl. de quibus homines ville respondent.
[*Two lines blank*]

COMPOTUS EIUSDEM DE TERRIS COMITIS DEVON' DE TOTO ANNO

f' Idem T. r.c. de xvj li. et dim. m. de redditu assiso burgi de Plinton'. In thes. nichil. Et in elemosinis constitutis abbati de Bucfestr' dim. m. Et debet xvj li. Set respondet infra in magna summa.

Idem r.c. de x li. et iiij s. et viij d. de exitu molendinorum eiusdem ville. Et de viij li. et ix s. et iiij d. et ob. de redditu assiso de Herdewic'. Et de dim. m. de redditu assiso de terra de Hissekin in Corn...[2] que debet hic reddi. Et de vj d. pro j pari calcarium deauratorum de terra que fuit Galfridi le Véél. Et de xxv s. de hundredo forinseco. Et de xvij s. et ix d. de finibus placitis et perquisitiis de Herdewic' et Botlesford' membro de Herdewic'. Et de xvj s. et vj d. de iij quarteriis et j hop frumenti ibidem venditis. Et de iiij s. et vj d. de j quarterio et dim. et j hop de curaille ibidem venditis. Et de xiiij d. de j quarterio et dim. avene ibidem venditis. Et de xv d. et ob. de coriis j^us^ vacce et j vituli ibidem venditis. Summa xxij li. et vij s. et v d. Set respondet infra ibidem.

f' Idem r.c. de xxv s. (et iij d.^i^) de redditu assiso de Bottesford'. Et de xviij s. et viij d. de aliis minutis receptis ibidem. Summa xliij s. et xj d. Set respondet infra ibidem.

f' Idem r.c. xxiij li. et iiij s. et ix d. et ob. de redditu assiso de Exemenistr' et Toppesham membro eiusdem. Et de lviij s. de placitis et perquisitis ibidem. Et de xvij d. de consuetudine seldarum ibidem hoc anno. Et de viij s. de consuetudine bidentum. Et de v s. de consuetudine batellorum. Et de xiiij s. de consuetudine vinorum hoc anno. Et de lxviij s. et vij d. de blado ibidem vendito. Et de xxviij s. de hundredo de Womford'. Et de lxxvij s. (d^c^) et viij d. et ob. de bosco vendito et aliis minutis receptis. Summa xxxvj li. v s. et vj d. Set respondet infra ibidem.

f' Idem r.c. de lxvj s. et iiij d. de firma burgi de Twiverton'. Et de xxvij s. de finibus et perquisitis[3] eiusdem burgi. Et de xvij li. et viij s. et viij d. de firma manerii de Twiverton'. Et de ij m. de firma molendini fulerez ibidem. Et de lxvij s. et x d. de exitu molendini ad bladum ibidem. Et de xxv s. de finibus et perquisitis manerii de Twiverton'. Et de xxiij s. de forinseco hundredi de Twiver[ton'.] Et de lij s. de xiij quarteriis frumenti ibidem venditis. Et de ij s. et vj d. de j quarterio et j hop de curaille ibidem venditis. Et de v s. de x quarteriis avene ibidem venditis. Et de ix li. et vij s. et v d. de bosco ibidem vendito. Summa xlj li. et xj s. et v d.

f' Idem r.c. de lxvj s. et iij d. et ob. de firma burgi de Huneton'. Et de xxvj

[1] This must be the hundred of Stone in Somerset. However, in *NS 48*, p. 83 and its index it is shown as being in Dorset.

[2] The rest is obscured by the tape at the right hand side of the membrane. It might be *Cornub'* for Cornwall or it could be a place in Devon beginning 'Corn' as in Cornwood or Cornworthy.

[3] The 'p' is written over a capital 'B'.

s. et xj d. de perquisitis et teloneo burgi. Et de C et iij s. et x d. de redditu assiso manerii de Huneton'. Et de viij s. de finibus et perquisitis ibidem. Et de xlv s. de exitu molendini ibidem. Et de v s. et x d. et ob. de ij bobus infirmis et corio j vacce ibidem venditis. Summa xij li. et xv s. et xj d.

Idem r.c. de xv li. de lana et caseo et pellibus ovum[1] et agnorum per maneria predicta venditis. Et de xviij li. et vj s. et viij d. de tercio denario comit' Devon'. Et de xxj s. et ij d. de exitu nundine Exon'. Et de xiij li. et vj s. et viij d. (de^{c}) pro iiij palefridis de fine de Plinton'. Et de lxvj s. (de^{i}) et viij d. de fine heredis Petri de Cháálons pro habenda terra de Leghe. Summa lj li. et xiiij d.

Summa summarum C et quater xx et ij li. et v s. et iiij d. In thes. quater xx et xvij li. et xxj d. et ob.

Et in ferramento et aliis emendationibus necessariis positis in molendino de Plinton' per totum annum xxix s. et iij d. Et in operatione j^{us} novi molendini ibidem lxviij s. et iij d. Et pro iiij^{or} quarteriis et dim. et j hop[a][2] frumenti emptis ad seminandum apud Herdewic xix s. Et pro ij quarteriis et j hop siliginis emptis ad seminandam ibidem vj s. et ix d. Et in custo posito ad bateicium xxxv ac[rarum] terre ibidem xxxiij s. et ij d. Et in operatione j^{us} bovarie et reparatione aliarum domorum ibidem xx s. et iij d. et ob. Et in necessariis expensis autumpnalibus ibidem xlvij s. et vij d. Et in bladis sarclandis et pratis falcandis levandis et bladis metendis et coadunandis xlviij s. et vj d. et ob. Et in liberationibus viij bubulcorum et j pastoris et j^{us} ancille ibidem quorum [quisque][3] habuit singulis septimanis iij d. xlij s. et vj (d.^{i}) á festo Sancti Martini usque ad festum Sancti Gregorii scilicet per xvij septimanas. Et in stipendiis eorundem per totum annum xxxv s. et vj d. Et expensis senescalli in eundo et redeundo ad negotia ibidem expedienda per annum xv s. et ij d. Et in expensis servientis custodis manerii per annum xxvij s. Summa xix li. et xiij s.

Et in custo posito ad bateicium xvij acrarum terre apud Botlesford' xj s. et ix d. Et in ferramento j carruce et pro j plaustro empto et aliis minutis et necessariis expensis domus contra autumpnum x [s.] et j d. Et in liberatione ij servientum ibidem á die Sabbati proximo ante ascensionem usque ad festum Sancti Petri ad vincula scilicet per xvij septimanas quorum uterque habuit iiij d. per septimanam xiiij s. Et [in] pratis falcandis et levandis et bladis (sarclandis^{i}) metendis et coadunandis xxx s. Et in stipendiis ij^{orum} bubulcorum et j^{us} bercarii et j^{us} ancille ibidem per totum annum xiij s. et xj d. Summa iiij li. et …[4]

Et in ferro et ascero et precariis carrucarum et ferratura affrorum et pro blado triturando et aliis minutis et necessariis expensis apud Exemenistr' et Toppesham xxv s. et viij d. et ob. Et pro j […][5] et j bove emptis ad

1 *ovum* written for *ovium*.

2 The clerk has indicated that there should be an ending here whereas in previous uses of the word he has shown no ending just the word *hop*. This word means a measure of a basket for loading grain.

3 There is something written here but the tape at the right hand side of the membrane obscures it, perhaps *quisque*.

4 The rest of this entry is missing under the tape at the right hand side of the membrane.

5 Tape at the right hand side of the membrane again.

staurandam carrucam de Toppesham xij s. et iij d. Et pro bordo empto ad guttarias marisci apud Exemenistr' et carpentaria domus molendini et pro j ...[1]

[*Rot.* 15d *Mem.* 2]

empta viij s. et v d. Et in pratis falcandis et levandis et bladis sarclandis metendis et coadunandis ibidem iiij li. xvj s. et v d. et ob. Et in stipendiis viij bubulcorum et j berc[arii] et j^{us} ancille ibidem per totum annum xxxij s. Et in expensis senescalli in eundo et redeundo ad negotia ibidem expedienda xvij s. Et in expensis servientis custodis maneriorum per annum xxv [s.] Et in operatione j^{us} domus de novo facte apud Exemenistr' lxvij s. et v d. et ob. Et in reparatione cuiusdam piscarie ibidem xx li. et xiiij d. per breve R. per visum Johannis de Chieverton' et Ricardi de V... worðe. Summa xxxiiij li. et vj s. et v d. et ob.

(*t*) Et pro ij molis emptis ad molendina de Twiverton' et emendatione eorundem molendinorum xxiij s. et v d. Et in ferramento et precariis carrucarum et pro blado triturando et compannagio servientum ibidem xxxiij s. [et] vij d. Et in pratis falcandis levandis et bladis sarclandis metendis et coadunandis xvij s. et vij d. Et in stipendiis iiij carrucariorum et j ancille per annum xvj s. et iiij d. Et in expensis servientis custodis manerii per annum xxv s. Et in expensis senescalli ibidem per annum xvij s. Et in emendatione aule et camere ibidem ix li. et vij s. et v d. per breve R. et per visum predictorum ...[2]

Summa xv li. et xix s. et iiij d.

Et pro iij molis emptis ad molendinum de Huneton' et emendatione molendini ibidem xviij s. et ij d. Et in custo posito ad bateicium iij acrarum terre et dim. et ferramento carrucarum et aliis minutis et necessariis expensis ibidem xxxv s. et iij ob. Et in expensis servientis custodis manerii per annum xvij s. Et in stipendiis ij^{or} carrucariorum et j pastoris et j ancille ibidem per annum xiiij s. Et in pratis falcandis et levandis iij s. et ij d. Et in expensis senescalli ibidem per annum xix s. et v d. Summa C et vj s. et x d. et ob.

Et pro robis iij capitalium servientum custodum[3] maneriorum iij m. Et in expensis senescalli itinerantis per maneria ad negotia R. facienda in diversis comitatibus et in eundo ad Sca...[4] et ibidem moram faciendo et inde redeundo lxxviij s. et iij d. Summa C et xviij s. et iij d.

Summa summarum quater xx et v li. iiij s. et viij d. Et Quietus [Est][5]

[*One line blank*]

[1] Tape at right hand side of membrane again. There is the number 29 stamped on the bottom left hand side of this half of the two membranes.

[2] The name is missing.

[3] These last three words are written as though one word.

[4] Tape at right hand of membrane again.

[5] There is only *Et Quietus* written and it is not at the usual right hand side of the membrane. There is a line from *Et* to *Quietus* and another splitting up the word *Quietus* into *Quiet* and *us*.

EXITUS QUINQUE MANERIORUM PRESCRIPTORUM

Idem r.c. de C et iij quarter' (et j hop^{i}) frumenti de exitu horreorum quinque suprascriptorum maneriorum. De quibus lxxiij quarter' et j hop seminati fuerunt per predicta maneria. Et xxx quarter' venditi de quorum precio respondet supra. Et Q.[E.]

Idem r.c. de lxxij quarter' et dim. hop siliginis de exitu eorundem horreorum. De quibus xxj quarter' et dim. et j hop et dim. seminati fuerunt per predicta maneria. Et xxxix quarter' et dim. positi fuerunt in [libera] tione servientum per eadem maneria. Et iij hops venditi de quorum precio respondet supra. Et Q.[E.]

Idem r.c. de DCC et quater xx et x quarter' avene et ij busselli de exitu predictorum horreorum. De quibus CCCC et iij quarter' seminati fuerunt per predicta maneria. Et C et quater xx et xij quarter' et dim. positi fuerunt [in] liberatione servientum per predicta maneria. Et xvij quarter' et dim. expensi in prebenda affrorum per eadem maneria. Et x quarter' venditi de quorum precio respondet supra. Et xij quarter' in prebenda senescalli it...[1] per maneria. Et in excambio frumenti seminati per predicta maneria C et lv quarter' et dim. avene quod excambium fit de consuetudine videlicet pro j summa frumenti vj quarter'i et dim. avene. Et Q.[E.]

Idem r.c. de xv quarter' et j hop et dim. de curaille de exitu predictorum horreorum. De quibus iiij quarter' et dim. (hop^{i}) venditi fuerunt. Et quorum precio respondet supra. Et xj quarter' et j hop positi in libera[tione] servientum cum alio blado per predicta maneria. Et Q.[E.]

[*One line blank*]

DE CATALLIS FUGITIVORUM DE TERRA COMITIS PREDICTI

Idem r.c. de iiij^{or} quarter' et dim. et j hop de catallis Edwi de Herdwic et filiorum suorum fugitivorum quod totum seminatum fuit in dominico de Herdewic. Et Q.[E.]

Idem r.c. de ij quarter' et j hop siliginis de catallis eorundem fugitivorum quod totum seminatum fuit ibidem. Et Q.[E.]

Idem r.c. de xij quarter' ordei de catallis eorundem fugitivorum quod totum expensum fuit in liberationibus servientum per maneria. Et Q.[E.]

Idem r.c. de xxxiij quarter' avene de catallis eorundem fugitivorum quod totum seminatum fuit in predicto manerio. Et Q.[E.]

[*One line blank*]

COMPOTUS MANERIORUM R. IN DEVON'

Idem r.c. de vij li. et xiiij s. et vij d. de redditu assiso de Cassewell' quod fuit Henrici f. comitis Cornub'[2] de termino Sancti Johannis et Sancti

[1] The word is obscured by the tape at the right hand side of the membrane. It might be *itinerantis*. See below p. 280 for a similar sentence construction.

[2] Henry s. of Reginald, earl of Cornwall, had died in 1222.

Michaelis huius anni. Et de xxxij s. de pl[acitis et] perquisitis ibidem infra predictum terminum. Et de xj s. et ij d. de exitu j^{us} molendini ibidem infra predictum terminum. Summa ix li. et xvij s. et ix d.

Idem r.c. de lxj s. de redditu assiso de Depeford' manerio eiusdem Henrici de eisdem terminis. Et de xv s. de placitis et perquisitis ibidem infra predictum terminum. Et de ix s. et v d. de exitu j …[1] ibidem infra predictum terminum. Summa iiij li. et v s. et v d.

Idem r.c. de ix li. et x d. de redditu assiso de Branton' manerio quod fuit Willelmi comitis Sar' de eisdem terminis. Et de lij s. de placitis et perquisitis ibidem de predictis terminis. Summa xj li. et [xij s.] et x d. Summa summarum xxv li. et xvj s. In thes nichil.

Et in emptione cuiusdam preli ad poma premenda et faciendam siceram et ferramento j carruce apud Karsewell'. Et in emendatione j^{us} grangie ibidem xvij s. et xj d. Et pro j mola et ferramento mol[…][2] ibidem v s. et ix d. Et in bladis metendis colligendis et precariis autumpnalibus ibidem xj s. et ij d. Et in stipendiis ij carrucariorum ibidem per predictum terminum v s. et iiij d. Et …tis[3] et necessariis expensis domus ibidem per eundem terminum xxix d. Summa xlij s. et vij d.

Et in bladis metendis colligendis et precariis autumpnalibus apud Depeford' ix s. et x d. et ob. Et pro blado tassando et cooperiendo quia nulla grangia fuit ibi xj s. et ij d. Et in […][4] ij carrucariorum ibidem per predictum tempus vij s. Et pro ij molis et reparatione molendini ibidem j m. Et in stipendiis (ij[i]) servientum ibidem per predictum tempus iiij s. et vj d. Summa xlv s. et x d. et [ob.]

Et in pratis falcandis et levandis et bladis colligendis et metendis et tassandis et (tasso[i]) et cooperiendo (apud Brantone[i]) xxiij s. et ix d. et ob. Et in[5] expensis senescalli itinerantis per predicta maneria ad capi[endam] saisinam xvj s. et j d. Summa xxxix s. et x d. et ob. Summa summarum vj li. et viij s. et iiij d. Et debet xix li. et vij s. et viij d.

Idem r.c. de predicto debito. In thes nichil. Et pro C ovibus matricibus emptis et positis apud Diepeford' C s. (per breve R.[i]) Et pro x bobus emptis et positis ibidem ad instaurandam j carrucam lxx s. per idem breve [et pro] viij vaccis emptis et positis ibidem xlviij s. Et pro j affro empto et posito ibidem vj s. (per idem breve.[i]) Summa xj li. et iiij s.

Et pro CC ovibus matricibus emptis et positis apud Karsewell' x li. (per idem breve.[i]) Et pro x bobus emptis ad instaurandam carrucam ibidem lxx s. per idem breve. Et pro x vaccis emptis et positis ibidem lx s. per idem [breve.] Et pro j affro empto et posito ibidem vj s. per idem breve. Summa xvj li. et xvj s. Et habet de superplus viij li. xij s. et iiij d. *Qui locantur ei in rotulo xv in rotulo compotorum.*[6]

Compotus non redditur hic de manerio de Leghe quia R. reddidit illud Roberto de Chááluns cuius hereditas est et qui respondet supra de

1 Tape at right hand side of membrane obscures the word.
2 Probably *molendini*.
3 Obscured by tape at right hand side of membrane.
4 Obscured by tape at right hand side of membrane.
5 After *in* there is a hole in the membrane which the clerk has worked round.
6 This was obviously written at a later time and in a different hand.

relevio suo per breve R. neque de maneriis de Bocland' [et] de Bickele…[1] Walkinton' neque de Culinton' que quattuor maneria R. reddidit Margarete de Ripariis ut dotem suam unde Willelmus comes Devon' dotavit eam die qua Baldewinus filius eius eam desponsavit sine[2] brevi R. quod est in forulo marescalli in compoto predicti Thome.

[*One line blank*]

W.[3] *episcopus Carleolen' r.c. pro W. archiepiscopo Ebor' et pro se ipso et pro Philippo de Aubineio de C et xxiiij li. et v s. quas recepit de Bartholomeo de Kemes' tunc Vic. Suhantes' de quintadecima*[4] *R. Et de …*[5] *quas recepit de garderoba R. per manum Luce capellani et Walteri de Kirkeham. Summa C et xliiij li. et v s. In thes. nichil. Et in conductu navium prius locatarum per manum H. cancell*[arii] [*Sancti*] *Pauli* Lond' *qui eas pacaverat de xl diebus et ad trasfretationem eorum et que moram fecerunt apud Sanctum Maclovium per alios dies expectantes reditum eorum et in locatione iij navium ad …*[6] *in redeundo et in expensis nunciorum missorum per plures partes pro negotiis R. in partibus transmarinis et in conductu thesauri missi in Wascon' xlviij li. et xj s. et xj d. Et co*[*miti*][7] *Brittan' l m. quas predictus cancellarius et Godefridus de Crawecumb' mutuo acceperant ab eo. Et debet lxij li. et vj s. et v d. de quibus predictus episcopus respondet in Cumberl….*[8]

[*Twenty-six lines blank*]

[*Endorsed*][9]

…[10] *de Wudestok. Et de Blockesham de quarta parte anni. Et compotus de Alto Pecco et Bolesor' de toto anno. Et compotus de Baemburg' de …*[11] *…*[12] *compotus de Windlesor' et Cokham et Bray de anno ix° (et*^{i}*) x°. Et de Writel et Neweport. Et de Bolesour' de anno ix°. Et compotus de … …*[13] *Et Compotus Thome de Cyrecestr' de honore de Bercihamsted' et terris comitis Devon' tunc existentibus in manu R. Et compotus W. Carleol' episcopi.*[14]

1 Obscured by tape at right hand side of membrane, or it might be complete.
2 Obscured by tape at right hand side of membrane.
3 The next five lines in the membrane are written by a different hand. There is no heading for this account of the bishop of Carlisle in the membrane.
4 This was the fifteenth on movables made in 1225. See Carpenter, *Minority of Henry III*, pp. 110, 376, 379.
5 Obscured by tape at right hand side of membrane.
6 Obscured by tape at right hand side of membrane.
7 Obscured by tape at right hand side of membrane.
8 Obscured by tape at right hand side of membrane.
9 This is written upside down at the bottom of the membrane where the writing is very indistinct and rubbed. There may be some writing above what follows given the start of the visible first line.
10 This has been cut off or has worn away completely.
11 Obscured by tape at right hand side of membrane.
12 Obscured by tape at left hand side of membrane.
13 The name is unreadable.
14 There is a printed '30' at the bottom left hand side of the membrane.

INDEX
OF PERSONS AND PLACES

INDEX OF SUBJECTS

THE

PIPE ROLL SOCIETY

ESTABLISHED 1883

FOR THE PUBLICATION OF THE

GREAT ROLLS OF THE EXCHEQUER

COMMONLY CALLED

THE PIPE ROLLS

Annual Subscription due 1 June

Individual Member £10 25 €20 *Institutional Member £15 $40 €30*

Website
www.piperollsociety.co.uk